Also by Andrew Grant Jackson

✳

1965: The Most Revolutionary Year in Music

Still the Greatest:
The Essential Songs of the Beatles' Solo Careers

Where's Elvis?

Where's Ringo?

1973

Rock
at the
Crossroads

**Andrew
Grant Jackson**

THOMAS DUNNE BOOKS
New York

First published in the United States by Thomas Dunne Books, an imprint of St. Martin's Publishing Group

www.thomasdunnebooks.com

Library of Congress Cataloging-in-Publication Data

Names: Jackson, Andrew Grant, 1969– author.
Title: 1973 : rock at the crossroads / Andrew Grant Jackson.
Description: First edition. | New York : Thomas Dunne Books, 2019. |
    Includes bibliographical references and index.
Identifiers: LCCN 2019032701 | ISBN 9781250299987 (hardcover) |
    ISBN 9781250299994 (ebook)
Subjects: LCSH: Popular music—1971–1980—History and criticism. | Rock
    music—1971–1980—History and criticism. | Nineteen seventy-three, A.D.
Classification: LCC ML3470 .J326 2019 | DDC 781.6409/047—dc23
LC record available at https://lccn.loc.gov/2019032701

Our books may be purchased in bulk for promotional, educational, or business use. Please contact your local bookseller or the Macmillan Corporate and Premium Sales Department at 1-800-221-7945, extension 5442, or by email at MacmillanSpecialMarkets@macmillan.com.

First Edition: December 2019

10 9 8 7 6 5 4 3 2 1

For Gerri and Roger, somewhere between Detroit and Shambala that year. For Paul, who lived every year like it was 1973. And for Jeff, even though there are no wizard hats this time.

Contents

✳

III ❋ SUMMER

IV ❋ AUTUMN

Acknowledgments

*

I am incredibly fortunate that editor Stephen S. Power gave me the opportunity to write this book. I will always be grateful for his knowledge and experience, that he's a fan of concerts that stretch to four hours, and that he had the *Superstars of the 70's* four-album set.

I am deeply indebted to assistant editor Samantha Zukergood for her remarkable patience and for making sure nothing fell through the cracks.

Thank you to Paul Hochman, vice president of marketing, and Martin Quinn, marketing director, for giving the green light. Thank you to Rob Grom for another beautiful cover. Thanks to India Cooper for her exemplary copyediting, to publicist Leah Johanson, and to lawyer Henry Kaufman.

Many thanks to S. Ti Muntarbhorn and Topher Hopkins for the photographs. Thank you to publicists Sean Sievers and Lauren Mele of Beachwood Entertainment Collective for helping to get the word out.

Thank you to freelance copyeditor Blake Maddox for going beyond the call of duty, and to proofreaders Angie Bruce and Emer Garry.

I am thankful to Jeff McCarty (for film and Dylan insights), Erick Trickey (for Watergate and Vietnam knowledge), David Jenison, Harold Bronson (stories about the rock press), Louis Hirshorn (insights into AOR radio), Patrick Kelleher (Motown information), Kelly Peach (Elvis), Haley LeRand (Joni Mitchell), Foster Timms (keeping the spirit alive), Jennifer Adams, Jay Burnley, Morgan Hobbs, Sutthiwan Hopkins, Dane Lee, Robert Rodriguez, Jamie Wheatley, Stephanie Van Dyke, Tom Vickers, Victoria Namkung and Tim Koch, Chris Cantergiani and Thom Foley and Ethan Maile (Jobby Nooners), and the Book Doctors Arielle Eckstut and Dave Sterry.

I'm obliged to Top40weekly.com, *Billboard,* Wikipedia, Setlist.fm, and Discogs for the wealth of information they bring to our fingertips.

Infinite thanks to my agent Charlie Viney, as always, for his wisdom and guidance on our fifth book together. Thanks also to Sally Fricker at the Viney Agency and Sam Edenborough at the Intercontinental Literary Agency.

Thanks to Bowie for "Rebel Rebel," the first song I put on my first mix tape. Thanks to Dad for always stopping to point out a great lyric. Thanks to Mom for her love of nonfiction and for finding the balance between counterculture and paying the bills. And thanks especially to Keira for her latest songs.

1973 Selected Time Line

*

Unless otherwise noted, all chart positions reflect the Billboard *US pop chart.*

January

1 Dick Clark reports from Times Square in the first *New Year's Rockin' Eve,* featuring Three Dog Night, Al Green, and Helen Reddy.

1 Guitarist Wayne Kramer of the radical proto-punk band the MC5 quits midperformance at Detroit's Grande Ballroom, and the group breaks up shortly thereafter.

5 Bruce Springsteen releases his first LP, *Greetings from Asbury Park.*

5 Aerosmith releases its self-titled debut album, which includes "Dream On."

6 Carly Simon's "You're So Vain" holds the No. 1 spot for three weeks. Its album, *No Secrets,* tops the *Billboard* chart for five.

8 The trial begins for the five Watergate burglars and their co-conspirators, ex-CIA agent E. Howard Hunt and ex-FBI agent G. Gordon Liddy.

14 Twenty-one countries watch Elvis Presley's live *Aloha from Hawaii via Satellite* concert performance.

14 At Super Bowl VII in the Los Angeles Memorial Coliseum, the Miami Dolphins beat the Washington Redskins, making the Dolphins the only team in NFL history to complete an entire season and a championship game without a loss.

20 Chief Justice Earl Warren swears in Richard Nixon, the only American to date to serve two terms as both president and vice president.

22 "Down goes Frazier!" sportscaster Howard Cosell cries as George Foreman knocks out Joe Frazier in the World Heavyweight Championship in Kingston, Jamaica.

22 The Supreme Court rules in *Roe v. Wade* that the Fourteenth Amendment's "right to privacy" protects a woman's right to an abortion in the first trimester, but states can regulate in the second and third trimesters.

27 The US secretary of state and ambassador to Vietnam sign the Paris Peace Accords with representatives from North Vietnam, South Vietnam, and the Viet Cong, ending the Vietnam War.

February

7 Iggy Pop and the Stooges release *Raw Power,* produced by David Bowie.

8 The reggae film *The Harder They Come,* starring Jimmy Cliff, opens in the US.

17 War's album *The World Is a Ghetto* hits No. 1 on the album chart. *Billboard* later ranks it the bestselling album of 1973.

18 Evel Knievel jumps over fifty cars on his motorcycle at the Los Angeles Memorial Coliseum before a crowd of more than twenty-three thousand.

24 Roberta Flack's "Killing Me Softly with His Song" reaches the No. 1 position and eventually wins the Grammy for Song of the Year, Record of the Year, and Best Pop Vocal Female.

27 The American Indian Movement (AIM) occupies Wounded Knee, South Dakota, protesting the US government's failure to honor treaties.

March

1 Pink Floyd releases *The Dark Side of the Moon,* which becomes the No. 1 US album on April 28 and remains on the chart for over nine hundred weeks. Currently Wikipedia ranks it the fourth-bestselling album of all time.

11 *The New York Times* dubs Thomas Pynchon's novel *Gravity's Rainbow* "a work of paranoid genius." The Pulitzer Prize jury recommends it for the 1974 fiction award, but the fourteen-member Pulitzer advisory board finds it offensive and declines to give it the prize.

11 Approximately twenty people hold the first meeting of PFLAG (Parents, Families, and Friends of Lesbians and Gays) at Metropolitan-Duane Methodist Church in Greenwich Village.

20 Watergate burglar James W. McCord gives Judge John Sirica a letter stating that the White House pressured the burglars to perjure themselves.

April

4 The World Trade Center opens, the tallest building(s) in the world for a month, until Chicago's Sears Tower completes construction in May.

6 New York Yankees Ron Blomberg plays as the first designated hitter in Major League Baseball.

7 Hollywood producer Jennings Lang throws a party to raise $50,000 for Daniel Ellsberg, on trial for leaking the Pentagon Papers to *The New York Times*. Barbra Streisand sings. Guests include John Lennon, George Harrison, Ringo Starr, Yoko Ono, Joni Mitchell, David Geffen, and Hugh Hefner.

13 David Bowie releases *Aladdin Sane*.

13 *The New York Times* reviews *Our Bodies, Ourselves: A Book by and for Women*.

21 Tony Orlando and Dawn's "Tie a Yellow Ribbon Round the Ole Oak Tree" rises to No. 1 en route to becoming the bestselling single of the year in the US.

28 "Walk on the Wild Side," Lou Reed's Bowie-produced homage to Warhol superstars, peaks at No. 16.

30 White House counsel John Dean encourages the Watergate conspirators to confess, so Nixon fires him. Counsel John Ehrlichman, chief of staff H. R. Haldeman, and Attorney General Richard Kleindienst resign.

May

5 Led Zeppelin draws 56,800 fans to Tampa Stadium, breaking the Beatles' 1965 record of 55,600 at Shea Stadium. Zeppelin's new album, *Houses of the Holy,* tops the album chart a week later.

10 The New York Knicks defeat the Los Angeles Lakers in the National Basketball Association finals.

17 The Senate Select Committee on Presidential Campaign Activities begins televised Watergate hearings.

June

1 Waylon Jennings releases *Honky Tonk Heroes* a few weeks after Willie Nelson delivers *Shotgun Willie,* kicking the outlaw country genre into gear.

7 *Rolling Stone* profiles counterculture "Jesus freaks" in a year that also sees the release of *Godspell, Jesus Christ Superstar,* the Doobie Brothers' "Jesus Is Just Alright," and Glen Campbell's "I Knew Jesus (Before He Was a Star)."

19 *The Rocky Horror Picture Show* debuts in London at the Royal Court's Theatre Upstairs.

22 Mark Felt resigns from the FBI after Acting Director William Ruckelshaus accuses him of leaking information. Thirty-two years later Felt unmasks himself as Bob Woodward's source "Deep Throat."

25 John Dean testifies before the Senate Watergate Committee for five days.

29 Republican senator Howard Baker of Tennessee asks John Dean, "What did the president know, and when did he know it?"

July

3 David Bowie performs his last concert as Ziggy Stardust at London's Hammersmith Odeon.

4 Willie Nelson stages the first of his annual Fourth of July Picnics at Dripping Springs, Texas, with performers including Waylon Jennings and Kris Kristofferson.

13 Queen releases their self-titled debut album.

16 In the British Parliament, Jack Ashley uses the term "domestic violence" while commending activist Erin Pizzey for opening the first spousal abuse shelter. In the US, domestic violence and marital rape are legal.

16 Nixon's deputy assistant, Alexander Butterfield, tells the Senate Watergate Committee that Nixon secretly taped conversations in the Oval Office.

20 Bruce Lee dies from possible cerebral edema a month before *Enter the Dragon* premieres.

27 The New York Dolls release their eponymous first album, produced by Todd Rundgren and engineered by future Aerosmith and John Lennon producer Jack Douglas.

28 The Summer Jam at Watkins Glen, New York, with the Grate-

ful Dead, the Allman Brothers, and the Band, attracts 600,000 and makes *The Guinness Book of World Records* for largest concert.

August

3 Stevie Wonder releases *Innervisions,* considered by many to be his finest album. Three days later a car accident outside Durham, North Carolina, puts him in a coma for four days.

11 DJ Kool Herc uses two turntables to extend the instrumental breaks of songs by James Brown and the Incredible Bongo Band at his sister's birthday party in the rec room of their apartment building in the Bronx, later celebrated as the "birthday of hip hop."

13 Lynyrd Skynyrd *(Pronounced 'Lĕh-'nérd 'Skin-'nérd)* arrive with featuring their Southern Rock anthem "Free Bird."

26 Neil Young records 40 percent of *Tonight's the Night* in one drunken evening, though he does not issue the LP for two years. Young calls it "the closest to art that I've come."

28 Marvin Gaye releases Motown's bestselling album to date, *Let's Get It On.*

28 Undercover officers arrest Yippie activist Abbie Hoffman for attempting to sell cocaine.

31 The Rolling Stones release their No. 1 album *Goats Head Soup,* including "Angie," one of the year's top selling singles worldwide.

September

5 Stevie Nicks and Lindsey Buckingham's first album, *Buckingham Nicks,* already demonstrates the sound they will bring to Fleetwood Mac when they join a year later.

13 Vince Aletti writes the first mainstream survey of the burgeoning disco scene in the *Rolling Stone* article "Discotheque Rock '72: Paaaaarty!"

19 Country rocker Gram Parsons dies from an overdose of morphine and alcohol.

20 Jim Croce dies in a plane crash in Louisiana after scoring the second-biggest hit of the year, "Bad, Bad Leroy Brown."

20 Billie Jean King defeats Bobby Riggs in the Houston Astrodome before a crowd of 30,492, the largest audience for a US tennis match, and ninety million television viewers in thirty-six countries.

October

5 Elton John releases *Goodbye Yellow Brick Road,* which holds the US No. 1 position from November 10 until January 4. *Billboard* will rank it the bestselling album of 1974.

6 The Yom Kippur War begins as Egypt and Syria attack Israel on the holiest day of the Jewish calendar.

10 Spiro T. Agnew resigns as vice president of the United States, pleading no contest to tax evasion. His friend Frank Sinatra loans him $200,000 to pay taxes and legal fees.

13 The Allman Brothers' "Ramblin' Man" peaks at No. 2, blocked from the pinnacle by Gregg Allman's future wife Cher's "Half Breed."

15 At A&M Studios in Hollywood, Joni Mitchell records her masterpiece, *Court and Spark,* while John Lennon's *Rock 'n' Roll* sessions with Phil Spector devolve into a train wreck.

15 In the CBS special *Dr. Seuss on the Loose,* the Sneetches learn not to discriminate against those who don't have a star on their belly.

15 The Department of Justice brings suit against Fred Trump and his son Donald for not renting units in their Queens housing development to blacks.

17 The Organization of the Petroleum Exporting Countries (OPEC) launches an embargo against countries that support Israel in the Yom Kippur War, sparking a worldwide energy crisis.

19 Bob Marley and the Wailers release *Burnin',* featuring "I Shot the Sherriff" and "Get Up, Stand Up."

19 *The Way We Were* premieres. Barbra Streisand's theme song will become America's bestselling single of 1974.

20 On *All in the Family,* George Jefferson (Sherman Hemsley) enters Archie Bunker's (Carroll O'Connor) home for the first time, after resisting for a year because he "never stepped into a honky's household and ain't about to start at the bottom of the heap."

20 When Special Prosecutor Archibald Cox demands Nixon hand over the White House tapes, Nixon orders Attorney General Elliot Richardson to fire Cox. Richardson and Deputy Attorney General William Ruckelshaus resign. Robert Bork assumes the position of acting attorney general and fires Cox. The press dubs it "the Saturday Night Massacre."

21 The Oakland A's beat the New York Mets to win the World Series.

26 The Who release their mod-themed rock opera *Quadrophenia.*

November

8 Civil rights hearings officer Sylvia Pressler orders the New Jersey Little League to allow girls to play.

9 Billy Joel releases his autobiographical *Piano Man* album.

11 Bruce Springsteen's *The Wild, the Innocent & the E Street Shuffle* includes "Rosalita (Come Out Tonight)," which becomes his show-closer for the next decade.

17 President Nixon tells the annual conference of Associated Press managing editors at Disney World that "people have got to know whether or not their president is a crook. Well, I'm not a crook. I've earned everything I've got."

20 *A Charlie Brown Thanksgiving* airs for the first time on CBS.

21 Nixon's attorney J. Fred Buzhardt announces that eighteen and a half minutes are missing from the White House tapes subpoenaed by Congress.

24 "The Love I Lost" by Philadelphia's Harold Melvin and the Blue Notes hits No. 1 on the R&B chart, featuring the "disco beat" in-novated by drummer Earl Young.

December

5 Paul McCartney and Wings release *Band on the Run,* which will become the United Kingdom's bestselling album of 1974.

6 Chief Justice Warren Burger swears in Gerald Ford as vice president of the United States.

10 Hilly Kristal renames his dive bar CBGB & OMFUG ("Country, Bluegrass, Blues and Other Music for Uplifting Gormandizers"), and it soon becomes the hotbed of New York punk.

15 The American Psychiatric Association removes homosexuality from the *Diagnostic and Statistical Manual of Mental Disorders*.

25 *The Sting* opens, eventually becoming the highest-grossing film of 1973, followed by *The Exorcist*. Warner Bros. waits until the day after Christmas to release the latter film.

27 Congress enacts the Endangered Species Act.

31 AC/DC and Journey play their first concerts, in Sydney and San Francisco, respectively.

31 The second *New Year's Rockin' Eve* airs, with Dick Clark, George Carlin, Linda Ronstadt, Billy Preston, and the Pointer Sisters.

INTRODUCTION

✳

Raw Power and Innervisions

On February 19, 1973, *Time* magazine printed a story called "The Returned: A New Rip Van Winkle" about prisoners of war arriving back in the US following the end of the conflict in Vietnam. They found themselves profoundly shocked by the changes the country had undergone while they were captured: women's liberation, advances in civil rights, the sexual revolution, proliferation of drugs and divorce. Plenty of people who had never left the country were stunned as well.

If the cultural reformation of 1965–72 was a bomb, 1973 was the aftermath. The debris rained down. The sun streaked through the smoke onto the road ahead. Like everyone else, the musicians tried to process what had just happened and figure out what was next. They did so through a series of albums and singles that represent the zenith of classic rock.

But in rock's triumph lay the seed of its dissolution, for 1973 was the year radio programmers figured out how to commodify "album-oriented rock." The format soon segregated rock from the other genres that once spurred its evolution.

Under the radar, however, new forms flourished that eventually saved rock from its own stagnation, which is why Mick Jagger and Martin Scorsese set their television series *Vinyl* in 1973. Scorsese said, "The early 1970s, and 1973 in particular, was a time of great change in the music industry, and it all started in New York City—punk, disco, hip-hop, they all began that year right here in this city."[1] Beyond New York, country outlaws, reggae prophets, technopop scientists, female rockers, and defiant gender benders emerged to revitalize popular music.

✳

The bestselling artists in history released some of the greatest music of their careers in '73:[2] the former Beatles, Elton John, Led Zeppelin, Pink Floyd, the Rolling Stones, Elvis Presley, the Eagles, Aretha Franklin, Bob Dylan, Willie Nelson, Stevie Wonder, Bob Seger, the Who, Steely Dan, the Allman Brothers—and David Bowie, who recurs the most throughout this book: recording Britain's second-bestselling album of the year, *Aladdin Sane,* retiring Ziggy Stardust at the peak of UK Bowie mania, producing Lou Reed and Iggy Pop, covering Bruce Springsteen, challenging friend and rival Mick Jagger to keep up.

Springsteen, Billy Joel, Queen, Aerosmith, the New York Dolls, and Lynyrd Skynyrd released their debut albums. In fact, Springsteen put out two albums inside the year—as did Elton John, Paul McCartney, Bob Marley, James Brown, Alice Cooper, Roxy Music, Waylon Jennings, Jim Croce, and Bowie.

At Max's Kansas City in Manhattan, in a room that seated approximately 125 people, Billy Joel opened for Jennings. Springsteen and Marley switched off opening for each other throughout their summer residencies. Iggy Pop played midnight shows.

Classic rock stations today play more songs from 1973 than any other year, according to *FiveThirtyEight,* the website that uses statistics to analyze politics and sports.[3] Pink Floyd's *The Dark Side of the Moon* began its 937-week run on the *Billboard* charts on March 17. Many fans consider it one of the most perfect albums of the century.

It was the last year the titans of the British rock establishment pushed themselves to outshine each other, with *Houses of the Holy* (Led Zeppelin), *Quadrophenia* (the Who), *Goats Head Soup* (the Rolling Stones), and *Band on the Run* (Paul McCartney).

All the ex-Beatles scored Top 10 albums, two hitting No. 1 (McCartney's and George Harrison's *Living in the Material World*). Collectively, the foursome had one of their best years ever for singles: McCartney's "Live and Let Die," Ringo Starr's "Photograph," John Lennon's "Mind Games," and Harrison's "Give Me Love (Give Me Peace on Earth)."

Even they didn't match Elton John's dominance on the pop chart: "Crocodile Rock," "Daniel," "Saturday Night's Alright for Fighting," "Goodbye Yellow Brick Road," "Candle in the Wind," "Bennie and the Jets." His albums owned the US No. 1 spot for two and a half months.

Springsteen released exuberant anthems like "Rosalita," in the happy days before he worried about the contracting economy and whether his label was going to let him go. Like the Boss, Acrosmith dealt with poor sales by winning over the heartland in concert, city by city, night by night. Their management team ignored them in favor of their other client, the New York Dolls, but through relentless barnstorming the Boston band eventually turned "Dream On" into the most-played classic rock single of all time, per that *FiveThirtyEight* article.[4]

Dylan recorded the epic "Knockin' on Heaven's Door." Elvis Presley's *Aloha from Hawaii via Satellite* TV special was NBC's highest rated special of the year. In the *Piano Man* album, Billy Joel chronicled his trip to the West Coast to rescue his career from obscurity. The Grateful Dead kept the spirit of Haight-Ashbury alive with the caravan of Dead Heads that followed them across the country. Black Sabbath's guitarist Tony Iommi found the "Sabbath Bloody Sabbath" riff that revived the band in the dungeon of a haunted castle.

Gritty R&B classics crossed over to the pop chart in the golden age of protest soul: Stevie Wonder's "Living for the City," James Brown's "Down and Out in New York City," Bobby Womack's "Across 110th Street." Funkadelic's "Cosmic Slop" was too dark for either chart, though, as the singer lamented his mother's life as a prostitute.

Critic Greil Marcus wrote, "Some months after [Sly and the Family Stone's *There's a Riot Goin' On*] was released—from the middle of 1972 through early 1973—the impulses of its music emerged on other records, and they took over the radio. I don't know if I will be able to convey the impact of punching buttons day after day and night after night to be met by records as clear and strong as Curtis Mayfield's 'Superfly' . . . [War's] 'The World Is a Ghetto,' the Temptations' 'Papa Was a Rolling Stone,' Johnny Nash's 'I Can See Clearly Now,' [or] Stevie Wonder's 'Superstition.' . . . Only a year before such discs would have been curiosities; now, they were all of a piece: one enormous answer record. Each song added something to the others, and as in a pop explosion, the country found itself listening to a new voice."[5]

*

Rockers had enjoyed a similar renaissance, and could now sell albums of long jams without having to release traditional three-minute singles. But then radio programmers synthesized AM Top 40 with "progressive" FM, creating the album-oriented rock (AOR) format, and tamed counterculture rebellion into reliable formula.

"I'm tellin' you, you're coming along at a very dangerous time for rock 'n' roll," warns critic Lester Bangs (played by Philip Seymour Hoffman) in Cameron Crowe's *Almost Famous* (2000).[6] The film was set in 1973, inspired by Crowe's experiences as a *Rolling Stone* journalist covering the Allman Brothers, the Eagles, and Led Zeppelin. Bangs/Hoffman laments to Crowe's alter ego that the music business "will ruin rock 'n' roll, and strangle everything we love about it."

Until now AM had stuck to short pop singles, while FM played whatever it wanted. But program directors like Ron Jacobs began mining demographic data to zero in on the songs that attracted the young white audience that advertisers coveted. *Billboard* gave him the Progressive Contemporary Rock Program Director of the Year Award in August 1973 for his efforts. His rival Mike Harrison began writing the "Album Oriented Rock" section for the *Radio and Records* trade magazine. Program directors started dictating tight playlists to their disc jockeys, and the new format spread nationally.

The Village Voice's Robert Christgau described how the AOR songs on constant rotation eventually settled into the current canon. "Although classic rock draws its inspiration and most of its heroes from the '60s, it is a construction of the '70s. It was invented by pre-punk/pre-disco radio programmers who knew that before they could totally commodify '60s culture they'd have to rework it—that is, selectively distort it till it threatened no one. Three crucial elements got shortchanged in the process: black people, politics, and Pop-with-a-capital-P, Pop in the Andy Warhol sense."[7]

In 1973, AM still garnered more listeners than FM. On many AM Top 40 stations, rock, R&B, pop, easy listening, and country coexisted.[8] Ten of *Billboard*'s twenty-seven No. 1 pop hits of the year were by black artists.[9] But over the course of the decade, FM supplanted AM, arena rock and yacht rock ascended, and by 1980 *Billboard*'s pop chart included only three No. 1 singles by black artists. In 1981, it had two, and 1982 had one by Lionel Richie and a duet by McCartney and Stevie Wonder, "Ebony and Ivory."

In his book *The Heart of Rock and Soul,* critic Dave Marsh covered both genres in the title equally, maintaining they had always informed and intertwined with each other.[10] AOR cleaved that heart in half.

※

For white US males, the crises were over. The war with Vietnam ended on January 27. Nixon would soon be on the ropes with Watergate. Long hair was mostly accepted in the Midwest and on the coasts. With the demons gone, the passion and urgency, the need for catharsis and battle cries, slipped away. But there were others who still had barriers to break and wanted to rock while breaking them: country artists, female musicians, gay liberationists.

In rural areas, long hair and marijuana were still grounds for a beating. Outlaws like Willie Nelson helped make the counterculture acceptable to rednecks who just a few years earlier cheered on the murder of hippies in *Easy Rider.* When Nelson held his first annual Fourth of July picnic at Dripping Springs, *Rolling Stone* writer Chet Flippo noted, "The longhairs weren't beat up. It was the watershed in the progressive country movement. . . . Peaceful coexistence had come to Texas, thanks to Willie's pontifical presence."[11] Kris Kristofferson sang his recent single "Jesus Was a Capricorn," exhorting both hippies and hillbillies to stop looking down on each other.

The outlaws wanted to be free to produce their albums themselves, with their own bands, instead of submitting to the Nashville assembly line—just as Motown artists Marvin Gaye and Stevie Wonder had recently won the right to do. Nineteen seventy-three saw the first fruits of their labors, Nelson's *Shotgun Willie* and Jennings's *Honky Tonk Heroes.*

Two anthems still high in the charts in January reflected the ascendency of the women's liberation movement: Helen Reddy's "I Am Woman" and Carly Simon's "You're So Vain." So did the musicianship of Joni Mitchell, Bonnie Raitt, Suzi Quatro, and the bands Fanny and Birtha. Quatro emerged from the second all-female band to get signed to a major label, the Pleasure Seekers. (Goldie and the Gingerbreads were the first in 1964.) Fanny was the third all-female band to get signed, and the first to release an album.

Mitchell butted heads with guitarist José Feliciano over the guitar chords she invented for "Free Man in Paris," but Jimmy Page idolized her. Bowie raved about Fanny. "They wrote everything, they played like motherfuckers, they were just colossal and wonderful, and nobody's ever mentioned them."[12]

"We were like, 'Yeah, catch up with us,'" said Fanny guitarist June Millington. "Essentially [our message was] fuck you. But fuck you with a smile on our face because we want you to buy our records!"[13]

As they blew the male bands they opened for off the stage, Billie Jean

King beat Bobby Riggs at the Battle of the Sexes tennis match in the Houston Astrodome. The National Organization for Women (NOW) filed a lawsuit to force Little League to allow twelve-year-old Maria Pepe to play. The Equal Employment Opportunities Commission won the most expensive discrimination suit ever—against AT&T for blocking women and minorities from higher-paying promotions—then began its next case, against the Ford Motor Company.[14] The Supreme Court overturned state laws banning abortions in *Roe v. Wade*.

Mitchell and Simon offered lyrics with the groundbreaking frankness of Erica Jong's bestselling novel *Fear of Flying,* recounting their relationships with lovers and husbands like James Taylor, Jackson Browne, and Warren Beatty in songs like "Help Me" and "We Have No Secrets."

As the gay rights movement picked up steam, David Bowie and Lou Reed kissed in publicity photos. Reed celebrated the drag queens from Andy Warhol's films in the Bowie-produced "Walk on the Wild Side," which made it to No. 16 on the pop charts in April.

"I first saw David Bowie as Ziggy Stardust performing at Lewisham Odeon in 1973 just before my twelfth birthday," Boy George wrote. "He validated me and made me realize I was not alone."[15]

The Rocky Horror Picture Show opened in London, celebrating bisexual chic. Freddie Mercury and Elton John dressed and performed with unrestrained flamboyance. Television's first "out" performer, Lance Loud, starred in the reality show *An American Family.* The Gay Activists Alliance "zapped" (interrupted) *The Today Show* and *CBS Evening News with Walter Cronkite* to protest negative portrayals of gay characters by the networks. In December, the American Psychiatric Association voted to remove homosexuality from the *Diagnostic and Statistical Manual of Mental Disorders (DSM)*.

"I belong to a generation that probably has to thank Queer David [Bowie] for the comparative ease with which we came out," author John Gill wrote in *Queer Noises: Lesbian and Gay Music in the 20th Century*.[16]

Music has always served as de facto publicity campaigns for those striving for acceptance by hostile majorities. Martin Luther King's compatriot Andrew Young observed, "I say all of the time, that rock and roll did more for integration than the church and if I was going to choose who I was going to let into the Kingdom . . . I might have to choose Elvis."[17]

✻

In the first episode of *Vinyl,* directed by Scorsese, protagonist Richie Finestra (Bobby Cannavale) plans to sell his record label—but then stumbles into a New York Dolls show at the Mercer Arts Center. Their fren-zied performance reconnects him with the reason he fell in love with rock in the first place. The glam/punk of the Dolls was one of many new genres that rose in 1973 and eventually proved to be antidotes to AOR stasis.

The Dolls showed fans like the future members of the Ramones and Television that they didn't need to be virtuosos to have a blast onstage, inspiring Television to record their first songs in April (under the name the Neon Boys). Todd Rundgren produced the Dolls' self-titled debut, while Bowie produced Iggy and the Stooges' *Raw Power*. Iggy was an ultimate crossroads figure, embodying the transition from garage rock to acid rock to glitter to punk. In July he created the self-immolating archetype imitated by countless punks to follow when he slashed his chest with glass while performing at Max's Kansas City.

Also on the fringes, Big Star perfected the melancholy jangle pop that defined subsequent decades of indie rock with "September Gurls." On *Ralf and Florian,* Kraftwerk began to focus on synthesizers, drum machines, and vocoders, prophesying the rise of electronic dance music.

A later episode of *Vinyl* coveys the rapture a young A&R executive (Jack Quaid) feels when he enters a black and Puerto Rican disco for the first time. Over the course of '73, R&B began turning away from the bleak real-ism of protest soul toward the escapism of disco. Motown Records found a new competitor in Philadelphia International, and both scored proto-disco No. 1s, with Eddie Kendricks's "Keep On Truckin' (Part 1)" and the O'Jays' "Love Train." Philly session drummer Earl Young stumbled upon the "disco beat" while cutting Harold Melvin and the Blue Notes' "The Love I Lost," sung by Teddy Pendergrass. By the end of the year four other disco songs were recorded that would become No. 1 pop hits in '74: Love Unlimited Orchestra's "Love Theme," "TSOP (The Sound of Philadelphia)" (a.k.a. the theme to *Soul Train*), "Rock the Boat," and "Rock Your Baby." Deejay David Mancuso's Loft created the blueprint for the discos that sprang up across Manhattan that spring: the Gallery opened in February, the Hollywood in May, and Le Jardin (the inspiration for Studio 54) in June.

Across town in the Bronx, DJ Kool Herc made his debut on August 11 as a deejay in a party hosted by his sister in the rec room of their apartment at 1520 Sedgwick Avenue. Extending the instrumental breaks of songs through the use of two turntables, he created "break beats" for his friends to break-dance to. Today the date is celebrated as the birthday of hip hop, the form that overtook rock as the bestselling music genre in 2017.

American artists like the Four Tops appealed to the "Keeper of the

Castle" to provide for all people like "the Good Book says," but Jamaican Bob Marley and the Wailers advocated "Burnin' and Lootin'" and shooting the sheriff. The Wailers' "Get Up, Stand Up" and Jimmy Cliff's "The Harder They Come" were two of the most galvanizing anthems of the decade, and reggae started to break through in the West. The Stones, Elton John, and Cat Stevens traveled to the studio where Cliff and Marley recorded, though the environment proved more perilous than they anticipated. McCartney found similar strife waiting for him when he trekked to Nigeria to soak up Afrobeat for *Band on the Run*. It would take the next generation of English rockers like the Clash and the Police to integrate reggae into their sound.

Three new genres emerged that would, decades later, coalesce into modern country: outlaw country, country rock, and Southern Rock. "What's happenin' now is that they're mixin' it, these rock-country groups and they really are bringin' rock and country together," Waylon Jennings told *Rolling Stone* after opening for the Grateful Dead in San Francisco. "That Kezar [Stadium] show showed the influence that rock's had on me and the influence that country's had on the rock groups. It was a complete circle and we didn't sound out of place and they didn't."[18]

On the West Coast, country rock musicians mixed folk rock with the Bakersfield strand of country and western. Gram Parsons recorded two albums that finally captured the "cosmic American music" he'd been reaching for with the Byrds, the Flying Burrito Brothers, and the Stones. Glenn Frey and Don Henley began their songwriting partnership in the Eagles with "Tequila Sunrise" and "Desperado." Both they and Linda Ronstadt fought their producers to get the precise balance of country and rock they wanted.

Southern rockers mixed slide guitar blues, boogie, psychedelic, and jazz. The Allman Brothers survived the deaths of two of their members and released "Ramblin' Man," which they feared was too country but which became their only Top 10 single and turned them into one of the biggest touring bands of the year. In their wake arrived Lynyrd Skynyrd with "Free Bird," the Marshall Tucker Band with "Can't You See," and ZZ Top with "La Grange."

✳

The year marked a turning point beyond music as well. After three decades in which incomes between the middle class and the 1 percent became closer (dubbed "the Great Compression" by historians), the oil crisis of October sparked the moment income inequality began to expand again.

The year 1972 had been a good one economically; the Dow Jones stock market index increased 15 percent. But the Dow peaked at 1,052 points on January 11, 1973, and would not return to that level again until November 1982.[19]

When the US and other Western nations supported Israel in the Yom Kippur War against Egypt and Syria, OPEC (the Organization of the Petroleum Exporting Countries) took advantage of President Nixon's weakness due to the ballooning Watergate scandal. They retaliated by quadrupling the price of oil and cutting off exports, creating a global recession. The Dow went down 45 percent between January 11, 1973, and December 6, 1974.

Middle-class workers had enjoyed a stunning rise in their standard of living since the end of World War II but now witnessed the dawn of the great stagnation. According to the Pew Research Center in 2018, after accounting for inflation, "In real terms average hourly earnings peaked more than 45 years ago: The $4.03-an-hour rate recorded in January 1973 had the same purchasing power that $23.68 would today."[20]

Corporate management sought to contain wages to offset increased energy costs. Other elements hurt the workers' bargaining position as well. One was the rise of automation. In 1969, GM introduced robotic arms to the assembly line in Lordstown, Ohio, and doubled its output of cars to 110 an hour.[21] By 1973, BMW, Fiat, Mercedes-Benz, and Nissan followed suit. Meanwhile, the success of the civil rights movement for minorities and women meant more candidates competing for the same jobs. When corporations eventually returned to profitability, the middle class seemed unable to fight the rise of economic inequality, because it was fighting against itself, split down the middle by the culture war. One of the main fronts in that war was *Roe v. Wade*, decided on January 22.

❋

This book features some overlap with 1972 and 1974. January's biggest hits, such as Stevie Wonder's "Superstition," were recorded the year before. *The Harder They Come* soundtrack had been released in the UK earlier but was not issued in the States until February.

The book also recounts the creation of numerous albums in the second half of the year that did not see release until later, including Joni Mitchell's *Court and Spark,* Neil Young's *Tonight's the Night,* Big Star's *Radio City,* Waylon Jennings's *This Time,* and Gram Parsons's *Grievous Angel,* as well as some singles like Lynyrd Skynyrd's "Sweet Home Alabama."

When I wrote *1965: The Most Revolutionary Year in Music,* I was fascinated by the moment in which the oldies era mutated into the psyche-delic era. Nineteen seventy-three was a year when the '60s legends released their climactic statements while new giants and underground revolutions arrived to save music from decline. In Los Angeles, New York, London, Motown, Philly, Austin, Nashville, the Bronx, and Kingston the music both peaked and was reborn.

Winter

The Dope's That
There's Still Hope

Dylan finds inspiration for one of his greatest songs on a movie set in Mexico. Neil Young kicks off his tour in support of the bestselling album of 1972 on January 4. The following day, Bruce Springsteen releases his debut.

✳

aybe Dylan *had* lost his muse, but he didn't much care. His kids were busy being born, and he stayed home with them. He extricated himself from an unfavorable songwriting royalty deal with his manager. Kept his distance from the militant group that named itself after one of his songs and blew up government buildings and banks. Beat up the nut job who kept ransacking his trash for proof he'd "sold out." Released country and folk-pop albums that radicals didn't like, to ward them off.

But gradually his competitive spirit started flickering again. "The only time it bothered me that someone sounded like me was when I was living in Phoenix, Arizona, in about '72 and the big song at the time was 'Heart of Gold.' I used to hate it when it came on the radio. I always liked Neil Young, but it bothered me every time I listened to 'Heart of Gold.' I think it was up at number one for a long time, and I'd say, 'Shit, that's me. If it sounds like me, it should as well be me.' There I was, stuck on the desert someplace, having to cool out for a while. New York was a heavy place. Woodstock was worse, people living in trees outside my house, fans trying to batter down my door, cars following me up dark mountain roads. I needed to lay back for a while, forget about things, myself included, and I'd get so far away and turn on the radio and there I am, but it's not me. It seemed to me somebody else had taken my thing and had run away with it and, you know, I never got over it. Maybe tomorrow."[1]

Then Elvis's old writers Leiber and Stoller produced a spoof named "Stuck in the Middle with You" by the band Stealers Wheel. *Rolling Stone* called it "the single you thought was the best Dylan record since 1966." Singer Gerry Rafferty was Scottish but did a good impersonation, singing about a bad-trip party right out of "Ballad of a Thin Man," stocked with Dylan-esque clowns and jokers. The title itself was a riff off "Stuck Inside of Mobile with the Memphis Blues Again."

Its line "I don't know why I came here tonight"—that could have come from Dylan's wife, Sara, in January. The couple and their kids were living in Durango, Mexico, filming *Pat Garrett and Billy the Kid*. "My wife got fed up almost immediately. She'd say to me, 'What the hell are we doing here?' It was not an easy question to answer."[2]

Initially it made sense. Screenwriter Rudy Wurlitzer knew Dylan and asked for a song about Sheriff Garrett pursuing cattle rustler Billy the Kid. After all, Dylan's album *John Wesley Harding* romanticized a gunslinger no one could track down. "So I wrote that song real quick and played it for [director] Sam [Peckinpah] and he really liked it and asked me to be in the movie."[3]

As an added bonus, his friend Kris Kristofferson was starring as Billy. He said to Dylan, "Shit, you can get paid for learnin' [how to make movies]. Come on, we'll have a ball."[4]

"I still feel guilty about sayin' that," Kristofferson later admitted. "The first day we shot was also Bob's first day on camera. We had to be ridin' horses after these turkeys and he ropes 'em. Well, Bob hadn't ridden much and it was *hairy* riding, down in gullies and off through a river. . . . And then we had to rope these damn turkeys."[5]

Peckinpah started his mornings off drinking and by afternoon enjoyed firing his revolver into the sky. When they screened the footage and discovered it was unusable due to a damaged lens, Peckinpah stood on his chair and pissed on the screen. Kristofferson said, "I'll never forget Bob Dylan turnin' and lookin' at me like, 'What the hell have you gotten me into?'"[6]

On top of that, Dylan's character, Alias, barely had anything to do on camera except watch the action with an inscrutable half smile. He joins Billy's gang, throws a knife into a bad guy's neck, counts some beans.

There were some good times. Kristofferson recalled that the two "spent a lot of time chatting in our trailers and I told him about my friend Willie Nelson. I asked Bob, 'Why isn't Willie famous? He's a genius.' So, the next day, Bob calls Willie up and gets him to come down to the set, and he made him play his old Martin guitar for ten hours straight. They ended up doing all these old Django Reinhardt tunes. It was fabulous."[7]

But the music was in danger of ending up forgettable. A recording session in Mexico City generated just one cut, "Billy." The soundtrack album featured three variations on it.

Dylan and his session musicians regrouped at Warner Bros.' scoring stage in Burbank that February, to play along live while the film was projected on a screen. Engineer Dan Wallin, veteran of dozens of Hollywood soundtracks, remembered, "[Dylan] kind of slowly walked in, looking up at the ceiling. Then Bob said, 'Wow . . . big room.' I laughed and said, 'Well, don't worry, we'll cut it down a little for you.'"[8]

Dylan's friend Roger McGuinn of the Byrds played guitar, along with top session drummer Jim Keltner, who recalled, "Sam Peckinpah was there, and he was huddled up with Bob, talking to him. I admire Peckinpah as much as anyone, but that day, which was the only day I ever met him, he had a rumpled suit on, a red bandana round his head, and when I got up close to him, I saw his face and I felt so sorry for him, because he had the Hangover of Death. Y'know that one? I mean, his face was *crushed*."[9]

It was early in the morning, not musicians' favorite time to record. They listened to Dylan run through the first song just once, maybe twice. Then the tape started rolling and they stared up at the screen. One of the lawmen, Slim Pickens, was mortally wounded in a gunfight. His beloved wife tried to comfort him as he clutched his stomach and the blood ran out of him. Dylan and the three female backing vocalists hummed like angels mourning beside her. The ominous groan of the harmonium, and the echoey depth of the big room, lent an epic grandeur to Dylan's words about putting guns in the ground. And suddenly, Keltner said, "It was the first time I actually cried when I was playing."[10]

"Knockin' on Heaven's Door" seemingly materialized out of nowhere to become one of Dylan's most covered songs, captured in one or two takes. Keltner said, "The great thing about the really great songwriters, is that the great songs, the really magic ones, they play themselves. There's very little question about what you're supposed to do."[11]

On the other side of the Pacific, some lucky soldiers boarded planes and flew away from the decimated landscape of Vietnam. The United States' involvement had just ended, the peace treaty signed on January 27. That day saw the last US combat casualty. Artillery shells in An Loc hit US Army Colonel William Nolde, forty-three, father of five, eleven hours before the cease-fire.

✳

Dylan was wrong when he said "Heart of Gold" was No. 1 for a long time. Neil Young only enjoyed one week in that spot before his *own* imitator America knocked him out with "Horse with No Name." *Billboard* did rank Young's album *Harvest* the bestselling LP of 1972, however. But that year Young could not tour to support it, first due to health issues, then the arrival of his son Zeke in September. "Neil was so damn happy," mother Carrie Snodgress remembered.[12] Zeke's cerebral palsy from a slight brain aneurysm in utero would not reveal itself until the boy went to school.

But that year Young could not tour to support it, initially due to health issues. Then in September his girlfriend Carrie Snodgress gave birth to their son Zeke. "Neil was so damn happy." Snodgress remembered.[13]

Whitten was a member of Crazy Horse, the band that frequently backed Young, until his heroin addiction grew so debilitating his bandmates fired him, inspiring Young's "The Needle and the Damage Done." When Young heard Whitten was doing his best to get clean, he invited the guitarist to join his 1973 tour.

But during rehearsals Young was dismayed to see that Whitten "couldn't remember anything. He was too out of it. Too far gone. I had to tell him to go back to L.A. 'It's not happening, man. You're not together enough.' He just said, 'I've got nowhere else to go, man. How am I gonna tell my friends?' And he split. That night the coroner called me from L.A. and told me he'd OD'd [on alcohol and valium]."[14] In his memoir Young wrote, "I knew that what I had done may have been a catalyst in Danny's death. I can never really lose that feeling."[15]

Under that grim shadow, Young embarked on his biggest tour to date, sixty-two shows scheduled through early April. He opened with an acoustic set, then brought out his band the Stray Gators for the second half, in the mode established by Dylan and the Band during their 1966 tour. The Gators included Jack Nitzsche, who had produced and played piano for Young intermittently since 1967, alongside the musicians who backed him on *Harvest*.

Young brought a mobile recording truck on tour so he could release a live album afterward. But he threw his label Reprise a curve ball when he informed them the live album would be comprised entirely of original songs—no hits. *Time Fades Away* does not actually sound much different from Young's studio albums that followed, as the audience is seldom heard.

"For years I wouldn't play unless the tape was running. I just recorded everything—all the tours, everything. Make it so there's no difference between playing and recording—it's all one thing. Then you forget you're recording, 'cause ultimately the music gets in your face, you forget what you're doing, and all of a sudden you realize, 'Jesus, we recorded *that.*' That's the ticket, that's the way to get it. So I just tricked myself into not having to worry about whether we were recording or not."[16]

Three of the tracks are lovely piano ballads. Young wrote "Love in Mind" during the first flush of love with Snodgress. He wakes to find it raining outside, but his lover keeps him warm. "Journey Through the Past" came from that period as well, written when he had to leave her for a tour. The rain reminds him of her, and he wonders if she'll return to him when he finishes traveling. The melancholy recalls "After the Gold Rush," but instead of that song's surreal vision of environmental destruction, he offers a straightforward love song.

In the title rocker Young just wants to get through the new tour so he can get back to his family before "time fades away." He borrows the fifteen jugglers of Dylan's "Obviously Fifth Believers" and turns them into fourteen junkies too weak to work, while President Nixon lurks in the window. In "Yonder Stands the Sinner" a different specter yells down to Young through the broken glass of an attic window, "Sinner man!" Young tries to hide in the trees, but the figure follows. Perhaps it's Whitten. "I loved Danny. I felt responsible. And from there, I had to go right out on this huge tour of huge arenas. I was very nervous and . . . insecure."

Or perhaps the phantom represents the other musicians. During the tour, they learned Young was paying the drummer more than anyone else; he was Dylan's frequent session player Kenny Buttrey. Eventually Young raised everyone's salary—and replaced the drummer—but the mutual resentment cast a pall over the proceedings.

In late March, Young developed a throat infection and began to lose his voice, so he called in his CSNY compatriots David Crosby and Graham Nash to sing backup. Crosby also played rhythm guitar on "Don't Be Denied," a litany of the adversity Young had overcome: father leaving the family, bullies in school, struggling for stardom, business strife. Certainly the obstacles he faced would have derailed a less determined soul. He repeated tenth and eleventh grade, then dropped out. In 1966, he joined a group with R&B singer Rick James that got signed to Motown, only to implode when James was arrested for being AWOL from the navy. When Young found a new band, the Buffalo Springfield, he wrote the best songs, but the managers didn't want him to sing because his tenor was too unusual, like an Appalachian mountain man or strangulated Muppet, hunched over from a youth racked by polio, thousand-yard stare under Neanderthal brow. Onstage, psychedelic strobe lights gave him epileptic fits. He quit the Springfield just before *Monterey Pop,* refused to go on Johnny Carson. Later he had to fight to get the name Young added to Crosby, Stills, and Nash. But now here he was touring the biggest album of the previous year. Don't be denied, indeed.

The final song recorded on the journey, in Sacramento on April 1, hints at the new effort that lay before him: reuniting with Snodgress and Zeke after his three-month excursion. "The Bridge" echoed "A Man Needs a Maid," an earlier song he'd written about falling in love with her while watching her Oscar-winning performance in *Diary of a Mad Housewife.* In the new track, the "bridge" of connection he makes in the first verse falls down, but in the final verse she lets him back in to rebuild it.

❋

Like Dylan and Young, Bruce Springsteen grew up playing in rock bands, but at age twenty-two he was stagnating on the Jersey Shore. With his guitar he could emulate anyone from Hendrix to Clapton to Allman, but 1972 was the year of the singer-songwriter. *Billboard*'s top four albums were by Young, Carole King, Don McLean, and Cat Stevens. So Springsteen reinvented himself as an acoustic solo artist—the same choice Dylan made when he switched from Buddy Holly to Woody Guthrie twelve years earlier.

Springsteen won himself a manager named Mike Appel with a new composition called "It's Hard to Be a Saint in the City." It was folk guitar but galloped, danced even, as Springsteen spelled out exactly how he was going to burst like a supernova. Appel quit his job and mortgaged his house to promote Springsteen 24/7. He hustled him into the office of Columbia Records' John Hammond, the man who signed Dylan himself, not to mention Billie Holiday, Aretha Franklin, Pete Seeger, Olatunji, Leonard Cohen. Springsteen played him his new stuff, including "Growin' Up," in which he combed his hair till it was just right, bombed his high school, spent a month-long vacation in the cosmos, then found the secret of the universe to be the blue-collar verity of an old car engine, a year before *Zen and the Art of Motorcycle Maintenance*. Hammond got the green light from label head Clive Davis to record an album. The Dylan parallels continued when Hammond wanted an all-acoustic LP, but Springsteen asked to bring in musicians from his earlier band. Appel had never seen Springsteen play with a group and resisted, but Davis gave his okay.

Of the record's proto–E Street Band, only bassist Garry Tallent remains today. Springsteen's first two albums have a different feel from his later oeuvre because of the drummer and keyboardist. Vini Lopez played in the Keith Moon tradition with wild fills and a looser sense of time than his replacement, solid Max Weinberg. African American David Sancious was jazzier and more ornate than successor Roy Bittan, although on tracks like "Growin' Up" he introduces the tinkling piano keys that would remain one of Springsteen's signatures.

Springsteen fought for a band, but knew what Hammond wanted, and brought the Dylan. The *old* Dylan everyone missed from before his 1966 motorcycle accident, before he jettisoned the phantasmagoric imagery for plainspoken biblical/western verse. Springsteen borrowed liberally from the master: crooked crutches, teenage diplomats, omnipresent jokers, and plenty of multisyllabic words that *sounded* Dylan-esque: masquerades, calliopes, interstellar mongrel nymphs.

"For You" gave his muse a room at the Chelsea, the hotel in which Dylan and his wife lived while he penned hymns like "Sad-Eyed Lady of the Lowlands," and employed the same style of word combinations: barroom eyes, Cheshire smile, pony face. "Lost in the Flood" was Springsteen's "Desolation Row," with borderline blasphemies springing from his childhood abuse by teachers in Catholic school: spastics breaking crosses, bald pregnant nuns drinking unholy blood.

But amid the emulation, Springsteen staked out his own territory. Hot rods and motorcycles race through the night on choked interstates. A Chevy speeds into a hurricane, painted red, white, and blue with Woody Guthrie's words "Bound for Glory" on the side. One protagonist tells his lover he knows a place where they can go to get good jobs and start all over clean. Angels heal Peter Pans and lonely circus acrobats. Characters get sucked into criminal activity inspired by Springsteen's lifelong addiction to B movies on late-night TV. High school friends survive Vietnam only to find their return home to be a new kind of struggle.

At the heart of the Springsteen myth was his turbulent relationship with his father, who was there, too, between the lines. When Springsteen performed "Growin' Up" live, he sometimes added a monologue about how his father cursed his "God-*damned* guitar" and tried to dissuade him from practicing in his childhood bedroom by cranking the heat through the vent. His father's childhood was haunted by his sister's death, run over by a truck at five years old. After serving as an army driver in World War II, he returned home to chronic unemployment and bipolar bouts of depression or anger, frequently directed at his son's long hair. In "Saint," Springsteen sang of being "born blue and weathered"; in "Growin' Up," of surviving a fallout zone.

In later decades Springsteen suffered crippling stretches of depression himself, though in 1973 the rocket ride of his career was medicating him fine. Still, there were undercurrents. *Prozac Nation* author Elizabeth Wurtzel wrote, "I used to listen to 'For You' on a portable Panasonic tape recorder in seventh grade, while I cut my legs up with a razor blade in the girls' gym locker room."[17] The buoyant melody obscures the story of a lover's suicide attempt. Springsteen rams down the door to get her in an ambulance to Bellevue.

Despite the many upbeat tracks, Clive Davis determined the album still needed a hit single that could get on the radio to promote the record. Many recording artists take such dictums with resentment, but Springsteen seized the opportunity to slip another of his favorite musicians onto the LP: a 6'5" black sax player named Clarence "Big Man" Clemons. They had met a year earlier when Springsteen played the Student Prince club on the Jersey Shore. "A rainy, windy night it was," Clemons liked to say, "and when I opened the door the whole thing flew off its hinges and blew away down the street. The band were on-stage, but staring at me framed in the doorway. And maybe that did make Bruce a little nervous because I just said, 'I want to play with your band,' and he said, 'Sure, you do anything you want.'"[18]

Springsteen set about constructing "Blinded by the Light" with rhyming dictionary in tow. That month there was a new Doobie Brothers song released called "Listen to the Music." Perhaps that was kicking around in the back of Springsteen's brain as he started strumming his guitar, singing whatever came into his mind: drummer "Mad Man" Lopez, his Little League team the Indians. Suddenly he locked into his new gimmick: populating scenes with a menagerie of characters with wacky names, Go-Cart Mozart, little Early-Pearly, silicone sisters, while tossing in asides like beating off into your hat and friends none-too-bright catching the clap from hookers, whatever. Though he *did not* sing "cut loose like a douche"' he sang "deuce," as in little deuce coup. Manfred Mann's Earth Band mutated the word when they covered the song later. Springsteen cracked, "One version is about a car, the other is about a feminine hygiene product. Guess which the kids liked to shout more?"[19] (The douche version went to No. 1.) Either way, Clive Davis loved it. He sent out a promo to radio stations featuring himself proudly reading the lyrics of his label's new discovery.

Next, Springsteen finished a song he'd been kicking around with Clemons in jam sessions. "Spirit in the Night" related the evening he fell for the inamorata of "For You" (and most of the songs on his second album), Diane Lozito. He met the sixteen-year-old high school graduate in the fall of 1971, when he was twenty-two, at a concession stand on the Asbury Park boardwalk. "She was Italian, funny, a beatific tomboy, with just the hint of a lazy eye, and wore a pair of glasses that made me think of the wonders of the library."[20]

He knew her boyfriend, a lifeguard/law student Springsteen dubbed "Wild Billy." Lozito recalled, "Billy and his friends were major party boys. But Bruce didn't drink or get high. One night at the beach, when Billy and the others were drinking, Bruce and I tucked around a rock and started kissing. Then I said, 'It's time to go'—because I was so scared of getting busted by Billy. That was a nice night. Light coming off the ocean, nothing like it. . . . The next day he showed me [in his notebook] the line 'She kissed me just right / Like only a lonely angel can.'"[21]

The album now completed, Springsteen dismayed his manager when he insisted he didn't want his face on the cover. He wanted a vintage postcard that read *Greetings from Asbury Park* instead. Appel felt confident there was no way Columbia's art designer would go for it, but when they told John Berg the idea, his face lit up and he showed them his own collection of retro postcards.[22]

From the get-go the critics dug Springsteen. *Crawdaddy* observed, "There is the combined sensibility of the chaser and the chaste, the street punk and the bookworm." Springsteen name-checked *Rolling Stone* in "Blinded," perhaps a ploy to ingratiate himself; either way, the oft-prickly critic Lester Bangs proclaimed him a "bold new talent with more than a mouthful to say . . . reveling in the joy of utter crass showoff talent run amuck and totally out of control."

"Does This Bus Stop at 82nd Street" embodied that assessment. Springsteen composed the track while watching the city fly by as he rode to see his girlfriend in Manhattan. Once he'd practiced endless guitar scales in his bedroom. Now he captured the people and movie posters flashing by outside the bus infusing them with the euphoria of moving out of the hinterlands into the center of the music world. His ebullience stood in marked contrast to the somber leaders of the singer-songwriting movement, James Taylor, Jackson Browne, Joni Mitchell. Even pop stars like the Carpenters sounded morose. True, their depression had been innovative for a few years. Defiant despondency was novel territory to mine in a world previously dominated by bouncy pop or big-band easy listening. But as the media continued to remark on what a downer time it was, what an era of disillusion it was, it was refreshing (for the few who actually heard his first record) to find a non–"torn and frayed" kid carrying on the joie de vivre of Elvis and the British Invasion. Soon enough Springsteen would learn he really *had* been blinded by the light, and signed what he later believed to be an unfair contract with his manager, just like Dylan had with his manager— but at the moment, as he sang, "The dope's that there's still hope."

On February 1, a few weeks after *Greetings* was released, David Bowie dropped by Max's Kansas City nightclub to check out Bif Rose, co-writer of a song Bowie covered named "Fill Your Heart." "I stuck around as there was another act on. So this guy is sitting up there with an acoustic guitar doing a complete Dylan thing. My friend and I were about to leave when he started introducing a band who were joining him onstage. The moment they kicked in, he was another performer. All the Dylan stuff dropped off him and he rocked. I became a major fan that night and picked up *Asbury Park* immediately."[23] Bowie's publicist Cherry Vanilla concurred: "He went bananas over Springsteen."[24] Bowie quickly recorded "Growin' Up" and, a few years later, "Saint in the City." No doubt he recognized someone as adroit at self-mythology as Ziggy Stardust, another brother on vacation in the stratosphere.

Yeah! It Was Time
to Unfreeze

From January 18 to 24, David Bowie records Britain's second bestselling album of the year. Elton John releases the UK's top seller on January 26.

✳

find that I am a person who can take on the guises of different people that I meet. I can switch accents in seconds of meeting somebody," David Bowie told *London Weekend Television* host Russell Harty on January 17. "I've always just seemed to collect personalities. Ideas."

Aladdin Sane stands as homage to the personas who inspired him: Lou Reed, Iggy Pop, Mick Jagger, Andy Warhol, Elvis Presley, the New York Dolls; his wife, Angie; his dance teacher, Lindsay Kemp. It was powered by the amazing run of his last six months: recording *Ziggy Stardust and the Spiders from Mars,* producing Mott the Hoople, Reed, and Iggy and the Stooges, and touring America September through December. "In my mind, [the album] was Ziggy Goes to Washington: Ziggy under the influence of America."[1] The record's sleeve listed the city in which each song was written.

"When I heard someone say something intelligent, I used it later as if it were my own. When I saw a quality in someone that I liked, I took it, I still do that. All the time. It's just like a car, man, replacing parts."[2]

Jagger observed, "If he took one of your moves, he'd say, 'That's one of yours—I just tried it.'"³

Stooges manager Danny Fields summarized, "David was a vampire, but a good vampire, he did something good with the blood. He shared the nutrients."⁴

Aladdin Sane's cover portrayed him with a slit on his neck, offering up unearthly plasma. When labels dumped the Stooges and Mott, Bowie convinced his manager, Tony Defries, to sign them. His work with Reed resulted in Reed's only US Top 20 single, "Walk on the Wild Side."

In return, they fired his imagination and gave him the courage to proclaim he was gay to the British music press, possibly the first rocker to do so. According to Angie, at the time London was so homophobic "even the slightest hint of that kind of scandal could mean the difference between someone getting a recording deal or someone spending their life playing working men's clubs in the North of England . . . so when Lou would talk about the queens in New York and Candy Darling and all of these incredible characters who Andy Warhol was making stars out of . . . for David that was like America must be the most wide open, wonderful place. . . . If he hadn't had all of those experiences, when they ask him in that *Melody Maker* article and he said, 'Actually, I'm gay,' and then he changed it and said 'bisexual' and said what he really meant, he would never have had the balls to do that unless he'd been around Iggy and Lou and realized that fuck it, if the English wanted to behave like that with that kind of hypocrisy, fuck it, but there was this place across the water in the States where things were changing. And you and I both know, of course, it wasn't changing that much at all in the Midwest, but David didn't know that, he just knew New York."⁵

In the album's opener, "Watch That Man," Bowie finds himself in a lame party of old-fashioned married men, bad-looking ladies, and sad music, so he flees to the street, "looking for information," and finds a man who "talks like a jerk" and "could eat you with a fork and spoon"—maybe Reed, renowned for his cruel streak. The song shares the staccato piano of Reed's "I'm Waiting for the Man" and a similar title. One of the dancers at the party is Lorraine, also the heroine of Reed's "Wild Child." Bowie found Reed's (and Pop's) taboo-bursting anthems from the gutter to be the antidote he needed to balance the twee tendencies of his own songwriting. The wall of noise mix and backing vocalists emulate another of Bowie's touchstones, the Rolling Stones in *Exile on Main Street* glory.

The Stones, Reed, and Warhol all featured junkie male prostitutes in their art, so Bowie joined the club with "Cracked Actor." Inspired by his stay at the Beverly Hills Hotel, Bowie sings of a fifty-year-old actor who buys a hooker at Sunset and Vine to abuse and/or be abused by. Bowie had actually ventured closer to the gigolo role than his peers in real life. At age twenty he moved out of his folks' house into the flat of his gay manager, Kenneth Pitt, keeping him wrapped around his finger by walking around nude, per Pitt's autobiography. Pitt even ironed his clothes. Wife Angie wrote in her memoir, "I saw the intensity of Pitt's interest in him, and [Mercury Records A&R executive] Calvin Mark Lee's, and I have no doubt that sex—given, promised, implied, even strategically withheld if that's what got the job done—was a very significant factor in [Bowie's] rise through the gay mafia of the London music business."[6]

"The Jean Genie" celebrated gigolo/thief/Existentialist writer Jean Genet. When Bowie penned the tune, his former dance teacher Lindsay Kemp was in the process of turning Genet's work into a dance production. The skills Bowie learned from Kemp were instrumental to the image he constructed, as evidenced by *Aladdin Sane*'s gatefold, featuring Bowie in proud ballerino stance. Kemp was another older man tormented by the younger Bowie; the singer once carried on simultaneous affairs with him and Kemp's female costume designer.

Musically, the song sprang from a jam session on the tour bus. The "Starman" had resolved to tour America not by air but by Greyhound and Amtrak. His drummer Woody "Gilly" Woodmansey explained the decision came after "we went on holiday to Cyprus and the plane got hit by lightning. He went white and fainted."[7] Bowie invited his childhood friend George Underwood along, and in the excitement following the first American gig in Cleveland, Underwood started playing old favorites by John Lee Hooker and Bo Diddley. Bowie took the guitar and segued into the Yardbirds' cover of "I'm a Man," slowed it down, and changed the lyrics.

The next stop, Nashville, was home to a studio owned by Bowie's label, RCA, where Elvis Presley recorded many of the early classics of rock and roll. "[Elvis] was a major hero of mine. And I was probably stupid enough to believe that having the same birthday as him actually meant something."[8] Bowie cut the "Genie" demo there, and the final version a week later at RCA New York, turning the song into a celebration of the Big Apple. For the video he recruited model Cyrinda Foxe, future paramour of New York Dolls singer David Johansen and Aerosmith's Steve Tyler, and she joined the Bowies on tour.

Two days after recording "Genie" he met the muse for another track,

"Lady Grinning Soul." Claudia Lennear had already served as the inspiration for "Brown Sugar." She got to know the Stones when she sang backup for their opening band, Ike and Tina Turner. Lennear saw Bowie's show in Detroit. "He asked me for some input and we struck up a friendship after that."[9]

Pianist Mike Garson plays in the style of nineteenth-century Hungarian composer Franz Liszt, accompanied by acoustic flamenco guitar.[10] The atmosphere evokes the glittering hotel piano bars Garson and Bowie haunted after gigs, where they performed standards, or a James Bond film, as many online writers have noted. Bowie sings of a woman arriving in a Beetle and beating him at canasta; then clothes are strewn across the room. She "lays belief" on him, comes and goes at her whim. U2's Bono named it one of his favorite Bowie songs.

The doo-wop pastiche "The Prettiest Star" was a tribute to his wife Angie. He'd written it for her a few years ago, when they first entered into one of the most famous open marriages of the '70s. When Bowie's manager refused to allow her to join them at the Ivor Novello Awards (the British equivalent of the Grammys), Angie left Bowie and returned to her home country, Cyprus. To make amends, Bowie wrote the song and played it for her, then proposed, partially so she could legally stay in the UK. A little over a year later their son, Duncan, was born.

He sang that with her help they would "rise up all the way." And her hustling was instrumental to his success. She devised flamboyant costumes for him, added glitter, pushed him to wear a Michael Fish dress on the cover of *The Man Who Sold the World,* to let London stylist Suzy Fussey chop his hippie hair into the rooster mullet and dye it orange red, to go onstage in nothing but a red jockstrap. When Bowie was initially reserved with the Warhol contingent, Angie befriended them.

Angie always had a wild streak; she'd been expelled from high school for a lesbian affair. Actress/singer Dana Gillespie said, "Angie often opened the door to visitors naked. We were wild but it was natural, not forced. There was nothing sordid or nasty at all. It was what one did."[11] After all-night parties at the Bowies' Haddon Hall, Stooges associate Scott Richardson said, "I used to wake under a pile of bodies."[12] Later in '73 the couple moved into a four-story house in Chelsea with a sunken, fur-covered bed in the living room, "the Pit," adorned by fifty cushions. Model Vicki Hodge reminisced, "Angie and David used to have the most amazing orgies at Oakley Street. Everybody fucked everybody in the Pit. Mick Jagger used to come there and be involved with sexual things."[13] Hodge relayed that her boyfriend, actor/gangster John Bindon, "told me that David watched while he had sex with Angie."[14] Sometimes the activities were videotaped.

Tour director Tony Zanetta maintained, "Sex wasn't any big deal for [Bowie]—it was like shaking hands at the end of the evening. To him, it was about being adored."[15]

On the West Coast leg of the American tour, Cyrinda Foxe recalled, Bowie "once called me into the room [from the bathroom] to talk to him while he fucked a girl, and he needed someone to talk to, and that was me. I'd be watching the TV and talking with David, and he'd be screwing the groupie. Very nonchalant. . . . Angela was fucking David's black bodyguard, and David and I used to get down on all fours and peek in their keyhole and watch them fuck."[16]

Richardson also became Angie's lover on the tour. "They had this open relationship that the fans and all the world knew about. They utilized all that to seduce the world—and it was incredibly effective. But what they were trying to do with each other ultimately backfired. . . . David was pulling everybody left and right—and she was doing the same thing. And fantastic as that was for the publicity of the *Ziggy Stardust* era it was also incredibly destructive."[17]

✻

"Panic in Detroit" was inspired by stories Iggy Pop told Bowie about the Motown riot of 1967 and the revolutionaries affiliated with the Stooges' "brother band" the MC5 (Motor City Five). The song opens with a character who "looks a lot like Che Guevara," probably MC5 manager John Sinclair, leader of the militant art collective the White Panthers. Sinclair advocated "a total assault on the culture by any means necessary including rock 'n' roll, dope and fucking in the streets" until he was jailed for three years for possession of marijuana. He was also charged with conspiracy after one of the White Panthers threw a bomb at the CIA recruiting office at the University of Michigan, blowing a hole in the sidewalk in front of the building. Those charges were eventually dropped because the feds had not obtained a warrant before they gathered evidence through electronic surveillance.

In the song, Bowie heads to school, where he finds his teacher crouching in his overalls. Radicals of the era romanticized Chairman Mao, who encouraged Chinese students to rise up in the Cultural Revolution and humiliate their teachers if they acted too bourgeois. From there, Bowie heads into the riots, looting and jumping across cars abandoned at traffic lights.

Bowie's Detroit debut at the Fisher Theatre informed the song's mood as well. Journalist Nick Kent remembered, "Those gigs were like Fellini's *Satyricon*. If you went into the toilet people were openly having sex, everyone was taking Quaaludes or cocaine. . . . People would go to David Bowie concerts in London and they'd turn up as peacocks, it was very much a fashion show, as though you were in Paris. In America it was like, how fucked up can we get? That was Bowie's audience, as somehow it was more radical to be sexually ambiguous in America."[18]

After the gig, sketchy street people carrying drugs crashed Bowie's party in his hotel room, making the singer afraid he'd get busted and lose his visa. Outside, the city loomed like the urban wasteland of Charlton Heston's *The Omega Man*. In the aftermath of the riot and white flight, the city had earned an unwanted title, "murder capital of the world," with five hundred homicides a year.

Bowie employed the Bo Diddley beat the Stooges used on their song "1969" and added percussionist Aynsley Dunbar for "Sympathy for the Devil" flavor. Guitarist Mick Ronson alternated between chugging sludge and searing squall, proving he could hold his own against Detroit skuzz-rockers like Funkadelic, Grand Funk, Ted Nugent, and Bob Seger. *Rolling Stone* called it Ronson's "essential recording" and ranked him No. 64 in their list of the 100 Greatest Guitarists of All Time. Backing vocalists Linda Lewis and Juanita "Honey" Franklin completed the "Gimme Shelter" dread, conjuring an eerie bonfire climax.

Bowie offered an equally apocalyptic vision for the title track, inspired by Evelyn Waugh's novel *Vile Bodies*, which he read onboard the cruise ship RHMS *Ellinis* sailing back home after the tour. The novel concerns the Bright Young Things, English socialites famous in the years between the world wars for their outrageous partying. The song's full title, "Aladdin Sane (1913–1938–197?)," listed the year before each world war broke out, including a third one that Bowie predicted was just around the corner. In the lyrics, decadents consume sake and champagne at sunrise, then dash to the battlefield with a war cry, as millions weep and clutch dead roses.

He'd made a pun with "The Jean Genie," so he mused over a pun for the genie's master Aladdin . . . A Lad In—what? A Lad In Sane. Bowie reflected to *Arena* magazine in 1993, "It scared me that my own sanity was in question at times, but on the other hand I found it fascinating that my family had this streak of insanity—more than a streak. Several of my mother's sisters committed suicide or were manic-depressives or schizophrenics, and my half-brother Terry was both—he was manic-depressive and schizophrenic.

I often wondered at the time how near the line I was going and how far I should push myself. I thought that I would be serving my mental health better if I was always aware that insanity was a real possibility in my life. It was a dangerous game because I was putting myself in an area where insanity is seen as just some kind of personality trait—a characteristic of a person that was to be applauded, almost. The Iggy Pops of the world. And I was drawn to those people, I immediately felt an empathy and an attraction. I was perhaps using these people to create doppelgangers."[19]

Bowie's half-brother Terry Burns, six years older, was the first person Bowie patterned himself after as a teen. Terry introduced him to jazz clubs, Buddhism, authors like the Beats, Nietzsche, and Christopher Isherwood, hookers. But in '66 as the two walked to a Cream concert, Burns suddenly screamed and fell to the pavement in a seizure, hallucinating that flames were rising out of the street. Thereafter, the family intermittently institutionalized Burns, lest he wander for days, homeless, visions of Jesus instructing him to carry out vague missions. In 1984 he laid his head on the train tracks and put himself out of his misery.

Bowie wanted the madness of "Aladdin Sane" to be conveyed by pianist Garson, hired at the beginning of the tour in New York. "I had just met him," Garson recalled, "so I played a blues solo, but then he said: 'No, that's not what I want.' And then I played a Latin solo. Again, Bowie said: 'No no, that's not what I want.' He then continued: 'You told me you play that avant-garde music. Play that stuff!' And I said: 'Are you sure? 'Cause you might not be working anymore!' So I did the solo that everybody knows today, in one take. I always tell people that Bowie is the best producer I ever met, because he lets me do my thing. . . . I don't think there's been a week [since then] without someone, somewhere, asking me about it."[20] Garson performed live with Bowie until Bowie's last tour in 2003.

Co-producer Ken Scott remarked, "The piano is very simple on [the] *Ziggy* [album]. But then you [get] to *Aladdin Sane,* Mike Garson is on board, and it completely changes the whole feel of it."[21]

Bowie wrote "Time" in the cabaret style of Bertolt Brecht and Kurt Weill, who flourished in Germany until the Nazis drove them into exile. It is similar to a Jacques Brel *chanson* he covered on tour, "My Death," in that it portrays Time as a malevolent figure. In Bowie's song, Time/Death "demands Billy Dolls," the drummer for the New York Dolls, Billy Murcia. Little more than a month after the Bowies met him (and Angie had a liaison with him), the twenty-one-year-old overdosed on alcohol and Mandrax (British Quaaludes) at a party in England. Teenagers at the party tried to revive him by lowering him into a bathtub and pouring coffee down his throat but succeeded only in asphyxiating him.

After finishing the songs, Bowie turned his thoughts to the cover. He asked photographer Brian Duffy to sketch ideas with a lightning bolt, perhaps influenced by the insignia Elvis Presley affixed to his rings, belts, sunglasses, and necklaces. The logo was the symbol of Presley's favorite comic hero, Captain Marvel, as well as the logo of his old army battalion, not to mention the West Coast Mafia (the real Mafia, not Presley's Memphis Mafia entourage).

The two icons never met, except from a distance in Presley's Madison Square Garden concert. "I walked in on a Saturday evening in full Ziggy garb to see Elvis and he nearly crucified me. I felt such a fool and I was way down in the front. I sat down there and he looked at me and if looks could kill!"[22]

Makeup artist Pierre Laroche suggested they paint the bolt on Bowie's face. Now it could symbolize the "cracked actor's" conflicted feelings about his rising stardom, "this kind of schizophrenia that I was going through. Wanting to be up on the stage performing my songs, but on the other hand not really wanting to be on those buses with all those strange people. Being basically a quiet person, it was hard to come to terms. So *Aladdin Sane* was split down the middle."[23]

✳

Elton John had been conflicted about his orientation and channeled his energy into his career until finding love with John Reid, a young executive the singer met when he stopped by EMI to cadge free records. Reid found him a "dumpy little guy in a funny jumpsuit"[24]—then saw John in concert and realized he was a "one off." They moved in together, Reid became his manager, and John came out to his folks. "If my mum can accept it and my family can accept it, then I don't give a toss about anybody."[25] His mother said she'd always known anyway.

He wouldn't comment verbally on his sexuality until 1976, when he told *Rolling Stone* he was bisexual, but visually he burst out of his singer-songwriter cocoon of overalls and denim jackets. It was seamstress Maxine Phyllis Feibelman (immortalized in "Tiny Dancer") who got the ball rolling: "Oooh, I've found these mauve tights, I bet you wouldn't wear them onstage."[26] John took the dare. Soon the platforms began rising. The glasses morphed into hearts or squares, goggles sprouting rhinestones, palm trees, sea horses, windshield wipers. One pair flashed the word "Elton" and required him to lug a battery pack across the stage like the Hunchback of Notre Dame.[27] Feathers spilled out of his hats and out of his shoulders. The blouses grew sequins. The jumpsuits glittered pink and purple and tinfoil or Uncle Sam lamé. Cher on an acid trip, he boasted.

"It's been done in a humorous way because I couldn't compete with the Bowies or the Jaggers. I haven't got the figure for it. I'd look like Donald Dumpling from Dover, so I try to make people grin a bit."[28] Donning absurd outfits was John's preshow ritual to get into the mind-set to perform. "I'm a dumpy twenty-six-year-old guy going bald, and I sell millions of records, so I'm going to enjoy myself when I perform, no matter how ridiculous I look."[29]

Despite John's self-effacement, occasional collaborator Gary Osborne revealed, "Elton did feel a sense of rivalry towards Bowie. Most of these rock stars have somebody that they feel more rivalry towards than the others. It's because they're on similar territory. I think Elton slightly resented the fact that Bowie, who is substantially straight, made it partially by pretending to be gay, by courting a gay following, by propagating a gay mystique, whereas Elton, who is substantially gay, had for so long had to conceal his real orientation from the public. From Elton's point of view, here was this guy who had made it as a pretend poof, and here was he, a real poof, having to be a pretend straight. I think that got up his nose a bit."[30]

At the same time, John loved "Space Oddity" and recruited its arranger, Paul Buckmeister, and producer, Gus Dudgeon, to be part of his regular team. When "Rocket Man" performed better than "Oddity" in the States, Angie had to remind her angry husband that "Other people can sing about space travel, too."

Afterward, John made an effort to connect. "I first met David when I took him out to dinner when he was Ziggy Stardust. We had a nice time, y'know? . . . The only other time we met was at Dino Martin's party when I was with John Lennon and David was so stoned that I don't think he remembers. He was out of it completely."[31]

In Bowie's memoir *Moonage Daydream,* the way he remembered it was John invited him over for tea. "I'd met him only once before and although he was cheerful and quite friendly we didn't exactly become pals, not really having that much in common, especially musically. This meeting was even more awkward. His entire living room was barricaded with huge stacks of record albums. He sat, small and bewildered-looking, in the middle, as if in some kind of bunker. . . . We had tea and cakes and we asked each other how we found America and after a polite half-hour I made my apologies, declining a further cuppa, and went for a wander down Sunset."[32]

Musically, of course, Bowie preferred the avant-garde, while John is still tied with the Carpenters for most No. 1 singles on the adult contemporary/easy listening chart.[33] (Ken Scott said Elton walked out of an early Ziggy Stardust show at the Rainbow Theatre remarking, "He's blown it now. He'll never mean anything anymore!") Which is not to say John couldn't rock. He was the fierce successor to Little Richard and Jerry Lee Lewis, pounding the keys, then leaping back to kick away the stool and sprint alongside the audience, slapping hands, strutting and pouting in full-on Jagger impersonation.

He adored performing and had an encyclopedic knowledge of music, owning one of the largest record collections in the world. But when it came time to record his new album for '73, he was burned out, suffering from mono, in dire need of a vacation.[34] Ultimately he decided to get it over with so he could relax and returned to the Honky Chateau, a.k.a. the studio at Château d'Hérouville near Paris. By now his team was such a well-oiled machine that the muscle memory of their formula carried him through the exhaustion, like the Beatles circa *Beatles for Sale*. The unit included guitarist Davey Johnstone, bassist Dee Murray, drummer Nigel Olsson, producer Gus Dudgeon, manager/boyfriend Reid, and lyricist Bernie Taupin (married, incidentally, to seamstress Feibelman).

John's bond with Taupin formed back in the Summer of Love in 1967. Twenty-year-old John had been playing clubs for almost half a decade, backing American R&B groups like the Isley Brothers when they came to town, when Liberty Records suggested he try writing songs with another kid they were working with. Taupin (born 1950) was from a farm town of three hundred people, which was why many of their songs expressed a yearning to return to rustic roots. Taupin left school at fifteen for manual labor, but his mother and grandfather had instilled a love of poetry. He started mailing lyrics to John, who in turn fashioned melodies to accompany them. By the time they actually met in person, they had twenty co-writes under their belt.

John made a pass at Taupin, but Taupin said, "When I started laughing, it sort of broke the ice. He got over it very quickly."[35] Taupin moved in with John and his mother, sleeping in the bunk bed in John's room. John said, "I just adored him, like a brother. I was in love with him, but not in a physical way. He was the soul mate I'd been looking for all my life."[36] When the still-closeted John tried to force himself to marry a woman who wanted him to give up music, Taupin and their friend Long John Baldry convinced John to stick with his career, a conversation immortalized in "Someone Saved My Life Tonight."

Taupin wrote stacks of lyrics alone, then handed them off to John. Guitarist Johnstone said, "Elton has a very short attention span. He always did, always will. When he sits down to write, if something doesn't come to him in fifteen minutes, he's on to something else. He writes very spontaneously, and there's no fat on anything he does. In those early days, demos didn't exist. Elton would come into the studio in the morning with Bernie Taupin's lyrics, sit down at the piano, and he'd write a song with the rest of us right there with him. . . . I think that's why those songs worked so well: You weren't hearing things that were sitting around for years and were labored over and had no energy. What you heard was all energy.[37] . . . I've seen him write songs in the time that it's taken me to make a chicken sandwich. If he wrote a song in roughly 20 minutes, we'd go over there, and by the time we plugged in and got our shit together and played it a couple of times [that would be] another 15 minutes. Then the red light would go on, and usually the second or third take would be the one that we'd end up with. Sometimes it would go to four or five, but that didn't often happen. A lot of times we'd use the first take."[38]

John still plays live with Johnstone and Olsson, though Murray passed in '92. When they weren't recording, they'd play practical jokes, throw someone who was sleeping into the pool. Elton would make the others laugh by crank-calling people at two in the morning and yelling in a German accent, "I want to lick your body!"[39]

The band's secret weapon was background vocals, discovered when producer Dudgeon asked them to sing on "Rocket Man." Johnstone explained, "[Nigel], Dee and I never really discussed what we would do, but we got together and did it. It chilled us when we heard how good it sounded. Dee and I usually changed up on the bottom and the mid part, and Nigel would take the higher harmony. Occasionally, Dee would do a high part, but he'd have to put his head between his legs to do so," Johnstone laughed. "It was a unique technique, but he always managed to pull it off."[40]

One reason John could push through his weariness to create high-quality product was that he knew the power of delegating. Arranger Buckmeister said, "As a matter of policy Elton decided to not be involved in the creative decisions that [producer] Gus and I made. Elton literally said, 'I don't want to be involved in this. I trust you guys.'"[41]

The system bore fruit again when "Crocodile Rock" became his first American No. 1 single in February, ultimately the year's fourth-bestselling single worldwide.[42] Hearing Daddy Cool's "Eagle Rock" in Australia inspired John and Taupin to write their own animal song,[43] harking back to Bill Haley's "See You Later Alligator." They strove to replicate the organ sound of Johnny and the Hurricanes, the guitar from Bobby Darin's "Dream Lover," and the vocals of Del Shannon and the Diamonds.[44] Alas, they emulated the "la-la-la's" of Pat Boone's "Speedy Gonzales" a little too closely, necessitating an out-of-court settlement.

The song was Exhibit A in the nostalgia movement that peaked with *American Graffiti* later in the summer. That yearning for simpler times was satirized by "Texan Love Song," casting John as a redneck who calmly informs a long-haired musician that he's going to kill him for corrupting the values of his small town and fooling around with his woman. The wistful shanty bemoans how kids used to respect the president until rockers came through with their "communistic politics," "negro blues" and "drug-crazy songs." "God*damn*it, you're all gonna die," John sang like one of the good ol' boys who murder Jack Nicholson in *Easy Rider*.

"Daniel" offered a more empathetic portrait of a Texan, written after Taupin read an article about an American soldier returning from Vietnam to the Lone Star State in a wheelchair. The veteran received an outpouring of attention but just wanted to be left alone on his small farm. Taupin combined the tale with an ode to his older brother, whom Taupin missed after he'd moved to Spain in 1968.

The lines mentioning the war were excised in the studio. Johnstone remembered, "[Elton] called me over and said, 'Look at this last verse, I think Taupin's on drugs. He must be taking acid or something.' And we looked at this verse, and I can vaguely remember something about a ship's dog named Paul. And I'm like 'What the fuck is he talking about?' Suddenly out of nowhere he starts talking about this dog. So Elton just kind of took the page and ripped that bottom part off very slowly and very definitely and said, 'Well, that's the end of that.'"[45]

Label head Dick James opposed releasing the track as a single. The standard wisdom in the UK at the time was that releasing two singles from an album hurt the album's sales. When John insisted, James made him agree to reimburse the costs of the promo campaign if the song flopped. It hit No. 4 in England and No. 2 in the US.

"Elderberry Wine" carried a Taupin theme that recurred with increased frequency, the man at rock bottom after his woman leaves over his drinking. John's piano and the horns are so infectious that the song became a concert staple regardless. "High Flying Bird" was another lament for the one who got away, a soaring ballad inspired by Van Morrison, and a precursor to "Don't Let the Sun Go Down on Me." With its gorgeous production sheen, one barely notices the lines about the singer's obsession bleeding on the cold stone floor, under walls stained scarlet.

The album's title sprang from John's friendship with Groucho Marx, who frequently ribbed him for offenses like having his name in the wrong order (should've been John Elton). Once, after a barrage of jibes, John threw up his hands and cracked, "Don't shoot me, I'm only the piano player." *Shoot the Piano Player* had been a 1960 film by Francois Truffaut. Hence the cover featured a theater marquee and a poster for the Marx Brothers' *Go West*. The Crocodile Rocker and his girlfriend in sock-hop dress buy tickets to the show, in the happy days before she leaves him "for some foreign guy." It became the second of Elton's seven consecutive No. 1 LPs in the States, fulfilling the unlikely prophecy of track five, "I'm Going to Be a Teenage Idol."

✳

God Is in the Grooves

In March, Aretha Franklin wins the Grammy for the bestselling live gospel album of all time, while Diana Ross almost wins the Oscar. Marvin
Gaye finds his muse. Stevie Wonder gives Jeff Beck the riff of the century,
then takes it back. The Temptations record the last Motown album made
in Detroit.

In black churches, the word is always musical. God is in the grooves.
—BILLY PRESTON[1]

✳

If you had to pick one song to demonstrate the ecstatic transcendence of twentieth-century gospel, Aretha Franklin's "How I Got Over"
might be it, from her double album *Amazing Grace*. The song was written
by one of her mentors, Clara Ward. In 1951, Ward and her family gospel
group were driving through Georgia when five white men surrounded their
Cadillac and rained down racist abuse for driving a "white man's car."[2] The
men yanked at the door handle until mother Ward decided to act possessed
and shriek curses at them. "Lucifer, oh Lucifer, before they die, make these
vipers writhe and crawl on their bellies like the snakes they are!"[3] The men
scattered, fearing she was putting a hex on them. Ward wrote the song to
thank Jesus for protecting them.

Ward had a long-term romantic relationship with Franklin's father, Re-

verend C. L. Franklin, and sat in the front pew with him when Aretha recorded the set live at Los Angeles's New Temple Missionary Baptist Church.
The performance was preserved in the feature film documentary of the
same name as the album, posthumously released in 2018. James Cleveland
led the Southern California Community Choir. He once served as the minister of music in Franklin's church in Detroit and was one of the men most
responsible for the sound of the modern gospel choir. Producer Jerry Wexler brought in a rhythm section of top session musicians, including a conga
player, to accompany Cleveland on piano. They sped up "How I Got Over"
from its usual tempo and set the congregation dancing in the aisles.

Ward passed away from a stroke two days later. Another of the gospel titans, Mahalia Jackson, died two weeks after Ward. Franklin's double album
became a preservation of the psalms that held the community together
through the epic civil rights era. "Precious Lord, Take My Hand" had been
Martin Luther King Jr.'s favorite song. Her father had been close to MLK, and
she had traveled the country for his voting rights campaign. She sang the
song at his funeral.

Her wailing on "Old Landmark" and "Never Grow Old" could blast Robert Plant or Paul McCartney off the stage. "It makes you feel a bit small
sometimes when you hear these people's voices, so big and powerful," conceded Mick Jagger, who was at the performance.[4] He was in town working
on the overdubs of *Exile on Main Street* with Billy Preston, who started out
playing organ for James Cleveland at age ten. The experience inspired Jagger to add gospel flavor to a number of *Exile*'s tracks.

"I don't think I'm alone in saying that *Amazing Grace* is Aretha's singular
masterpiece," said fellow Detroit native Marvin Gaye, whose "Wholy Holy" she
included in the set. "The musicians I respect the most say the same thing."[5]

The power of her gift came from its double edge. She'd been groomed
by her father's community to take her place among the greats and raised in
affluence. At the same time, she grew up too fast on the paradoxically hard-
partying gospel circuit and had many reasons to know the blues.

Her father had a 4,500-member congregation, a radio show, and seventy
albums as a preacher under his belt. Jackson and Cleveland often stayed at
the house. Franklin watched them jam into the night and blossomed into a
prodigy who could play a song on the piano after hearing it once.

But although she and her father loved each other, he had his dark side.
At age twenty-five, before Aretha was born, he sired a child with a twelve-
year-old congregation member while married to Aretha's mother. Distraught
over Franklin's womanizing and occasional violence, Aretha's mother left

the reverend and moved out of state when Aretha was six. She died of a heart attack when Aretha was ten, the year the future Queen of Soul sang her first solo in church.

Her grandmother and housekeepers raised her until she joined her father's revival show at age twelve. Her father made $4,000 per gig and flew from state to state. Aretha and the gospel caravan, however, drove eight to ten hours a day. Partying one night, she slipped away into Sam Cooke's motel room. Both kept quiet when the reverend banged on the door. Singer Etta James said, "We were out of our homes for the first time, and we wanted to experience it all."[6]

Franklin had her first child at age twelve and another by a different boy at fourteen.[7] When she wanted to break into pop, she didn't think her father knew that genre and found a new manager and husband in a pimp named Ted White. "That was standard operating procedure," James said. "Part of the lure of pimps was that they got us paid. They protected us. They also beat us up. Lots of chicks felt that if her man didn't beat her, he didn't love her. . . . Naturally, women's lib came along and changed all that."[8]

Their tumultuous relationship informed Franklin's incendiary anthems like "Respect" and "Think," as the women's movement rose out of the civil rights and antiwar movements. She finally left White at the end of the decade. Now she had a more stable home with road manager Ken Cunningham and intermittently saw Temptations singer Dennis Edwards.

Amazing Grace went double platinum and won Best Soul Gospel Performance at the 15th Annual Grammy Awards on March 3. She also won Best R&B Vocal Performance (Female) for "Young, Gifted, and Black," the anthem by Nina Simone and Weldon Irvine. How was Franklin going to top that?

She turned back to pop with *Hey Now Hey (The Other Side of the Sky)*, produced by Quincy Jones. "Master of Eyes (The Deepness of Your Eyes)" overflowed with horns, flutes, and funky bass, employing all the tricks Jones had learned from arranging soundtracks. *Rolling Stone* described it as "cramming more ideas into one song than most people can get into five." Next year it won the Grammy for Best R&B Vocal Performance. The yearning ballad "Angel," written by her younger sister, Carolyn, and Sonny Saunders, topped the R&B charts for two weeks and made the pop Top 20.

Easy listening was one song chart she had just begun making serious inroads on. She and Diana Ross both felt competitive with Barbra Streisand, and Franklin's jazzy cover of *West Side Story*'s "Somewhere" pointed in that direction. Jones called the song "his all-time favorite."[9] But *Hey Now Hey* was Franklin's first album for Atlantic Records that failed to make the Top 25, not helped by a strange cover drawn by Cunningham featuring her face superimposed on itself upside down. So Franklin returned to her frequent production team Wexler and Arif Mardin for *Let Me in Your Life,* recorded from April to September.

Franklin was always a producer as well, even if not credited as such. Biographer David Ritz said, "Aretha didn't just walk up to the mic and sing. She came into the studio with her own charts, her own harmonies, her own grooves. . . . It's like Marvin Gaye, Barry White, Isaac Hayes. She has the big vision, the Phil Spector overview. That's a big gift even if you're not a world-class vocalist. That puts her in rarified company."[10]

Her return to traditional soul yielded one of her biggest hits, "Until You Come Back to Me," a song Stevie Wonder recorded in 1967 but never released. When it made No. 3, she became one of the few artists to have a hit at each number of the pop Top 10. (Only Marvin Gaye, Madonna, Taylor Swift, and Drake have done the same.)

Billy Preston summarized, "She can go into her diva act and turn off the world. But on any given night, when that lady sits down at the piano and gets her body and soul all over some righteous song, she'll scare the shit out of you. And you'll know—you'll swear—that she's still the best fucking singer this fucked up country ever produced."[11]

❋

In June, *Black Enterprise* magazine compiled its first Top 100 Black Businesses list, ranking Motown Records as the largest black-owned corporation in America, generating $40 million a year. But although the city of Detroit was embedded in its name, founder Berry Gordy had opened a Los Angeles office as early as '63 and moved his kids there in '68.[12] After the riots, the Detroit office received anonymous calls threatening to burn the place down and endured a shooting in 1969. Gordy's house was vandalized. Rumors of tensions with the Detroit Mafia persisted. Mostly, now that Gordy had conquered pop, he hungered for the new challenge of Hollywood, like another Midwest mogul who moved to LA at the same time, *Playboy*'s Hugh Hefner.

More than a hundred Michigan employees were let go. The label's house band, the Funk Brothers, played their last session in the original Hitsville Building on August 30 for a band called Art and Honey.[13] A few Funk Brothers, like bassist James Jamerson, made the trek to the West Coast, but now some of the Hollywood session musicians known as the Wrecking Crew played on Motown records. Some fans felt the state-of-the-art LA studios made Motown's new records more antiseptic. The Four Tops, and Gladys Knight and the Pips, defected to other labels.

Nevertheless, Motown enjoyed one of its most successful years, racking up five pop No. 1s, almost tying the six it scored in 1965. The five included two from Stevie Wonder and one each from Diana Ross, Marvin Gaye, and Eddie Kendricks. Motown also collected seven R&B No. 1 singles and five R&B No. 1 albums.

The common refrain was that the move was the culmination of Gordy's quest to sell out. But the first Motown film, *Lady Sings the Blues,* opened with Diana Ross as a screaming junkie in a straitjacket. She earned a standing ovation at the Cannes Film Festival for her portrayal of Billie Holiday weathering rape, prostitution, and police harassment. Despite Ross's sequined image, she'd grown up in the projects. "I knew a lot of pimps. It's a possibility if I had've got strung out over one of these guys it could've been me. If I had fallen in love . . ."[14]

What Ross and Gordy wanted more than anything was an Academy Award. Ross was nominated, but she was up against Cicely Tyson for *Sounder,* and Gordy worried that two black women would cancel each other out. He undertook an aggressive ad campaign, flooding Academy voters with gifts. This offended some of the industry, as it was almost two decades before Harvey Weinstein made such tactics commonplace. Liza Minnelli won for *Cabaret.*

Thus when Gordy insisted Ross return to the studio to cut a new ending for her upcoming single, "Touch Me in the Morning," she was not in the mood. The vibe was so poor that lyricist Ron Miller feared the song was on the verge of being scrapped. So he threw a Hail Mary, asking, "Does anybody in this room remember who won the Best Actress Oscar last year?" Everyone froze, fearing Ross's reaction—but Ross smiled, because she realized no one *did* remember, and finished the song.[15]

The producers had to splice together twelve different takes. It almost became a revue of her most famous inflections from "You Keep Me Hanging On," "Someday We'll Be Together," and "Reach Out and Touch (Somebody's Hand)." But there was something haunting about the Burt Bacharach horns, swelling strings, and pulsating bass. The idea of spending one last night together and then walking away in the morning was perfect for a generation facing the rising tide of divorce en masse. Miller recounted, "I analyzed Diane as a person and realized that she was a contemporary woman who was probably liberal about expressing her sexual values, like most *Cosmo* women in a '70s society. Once, it was the man who might give a woman the brush off after a one-nighter telling her 'nothing good's gonna last forever'; now it could be the other way around."[16]

Maybe the song paralleled her relationship with Gordy. When Ross became pregnant with their child at the end of '70, she wanted to get married, but he didn't. He wanted to see other women, and they already fought a lot.[17] Ross felt her mother wouldn't approve of her being an unwed mother, so she married a white publicist named Robert Ellis Silberstein (a.k.a. Bob Ellis) in a quick Vegas wedding.

Her professional partnership with Gordy continued unabated, though old feelings sometimes died hard. When she rehearsed with Billy Dee Williams for *Lady Sings the Blues,* producer Gordy conspicuously interrupted whenever it came time for a kiss, advising them to "save it for the camera."

"Jesus Christ, Berry," she said, "it's only a kiss."[18]

❊

Marvin Gaye felt reluctant to move to LA. His future wife, Jan, wrote, "[His] songs carried the feel of hardcore, urban Detroit. He had great affection for the Motor City."[19] His follow-up to *What's Going On,* "You're the Man," explicitly spelled out what he wanted politicians to focus on ("you know busin', busin' is the issue") and was the grooviest reminder to vote on wax. But when it stiffed at No. 50, Gaye decided he was done with protest music.

The opportunity to create a soundtrack gave him a respite from having to figure out his next major career move. When Isaac Hayes won the Oscar for Best Original Song for "Theme from *Shaft,*" and his score was nominated as well, he started the trend of R&B kings making jazzy scores for blaxploitation films that were typically better than the movies themselves. In February, Gaye's theme song for the movie *Trouble Man* peaked at No. 7. On the album, he sang and played everything: keyboards, piano, synthesizer, and drums (he started out as a drummer at Motown), aided only by three saxophonists.

The title song became a concert favorite, but the LP was mainly instrumental, and Gaye knew he needed a new hit vocal album. Billy Paul and Teddy Pendergrass (of Harold Melvin and the Blue Notes) were rising stars on the R&B chart that winter. His biggest challenger was Al Green, who was originally from Michigan before relocating to Memphis. Two months after *What's Going On* came out, Green had arrived on the pop charts with "Tired of Being Alone." Since then, he'd hit No. 1 with "Let's Stay Together" and accumulated five more Top 10 pop hits along with three chart-topping R&B singles and albums. And the critics all raved. Even *The Village Voice*'s king of snark, Robert Christgau, gave Green's April release *Call Me* an A+.

Another stopgap was a duets album with Diana Ross. Originally Gaye declined, but Gordy appealed to his vanity by saying that she needed him. His passive-aggressive feelings toward the project were apparent when Ross arrived and found the sound booth full of pot smoke. She was pregnant and didn't want to expose her child. "I'm sorry, baby, but I gotta have my dope or I can't sing," he said.[20] She stalked out. When Gordy tried to reason with him, he just blew puffs into the air and grinned. "Sorry B. G., gotta have my stuff."[21] So they recorded separately. Engineer Art Stewart noted, "Adding insult to injury, he sang circles around her."[22]

"I should have done everything in the world to make Diana comfortable," Gaye later conceded. "But I went the other way. It's hard for me to deal with prima donnas. We were like two spoiled kids going after the same cookie."[23] The bittersweet "My Mistake (Was to Love You Girl)" made the effort worth it.

Finally he bit the bullet and headed into Hitsville West to start working on his own album. He had some old tracks in the can: "Come Get to This," "Distant Lover," and "Just to Keep You Satisfied," which he had co-written with his wife, Gordy's sister Anna. He could finish those off with overdubs.

Like Ross, Gaye secured his rise in the Motown empire through a romantic relationship with a Gordy. He and Anna did love each other in the beginning. He called her "Mama," as she was eighteen years older than he. But eventually their mutual infidelities contributed to a suicidal spell for the singer. Gordy's dad, Pops, had to talk Gaye into handing over the gun.[24] Gaye later said the marriage should've ended after a year. Instead, it lingered for fourteen. Growing up with an emotionally and physically abusive father gave him a high tolerance for misery. The ultimate reason they continued, though, was "fear and money," he said.[25]

One day Barbara Hunter, a friend of his co-producer Ed Townsend, came by the studio with her daughter, Janis. Janis's father was jazz singer Slim Gaillard, whose "Yep-Roc-Heresay" had been a favorite of the Beats. In her memoir she pinned the date as her seventeenth birthday, January 5. "His face expressed a gentleness that carried the same promise as [one of his songs]: that life, lifted into melody and framed by harmony, never has to be harsh. . . . His sound erased all pain."[26]

She was eighteen years Gaye's junior, the same age gap he shared with Anna. Hunter's mother encouraged the mutual attraction between daughter and singer. He took her to an Italian restaurant in Hollywood and tipped the server twenty dollars to bring her apricot sours, because the drinking age was twenty-one.[27] Then he took her to an apartment he kept on the side, a one-bedroom with a junkie assistant who lived on the living room couch.

"The explosive power of our sexual union was incredible," she wrote. "We made love at every opportunity, night and day. We knew every inch of each other's bodies."[28]

Co-producer Townsend had conceived the germ of a spiritual song while he was in rehab. Gaye initially commissioned songwriter Kenneth Stover to pen political lyrics for it, but Townsend said no, it was a love and sex song.[29] Now roused by his paramour, Gaye made the track into something even more than that—"something like sanctified." The title split the difference between "What's Going On" and "Let's Stay Together." Gaye sang "Let's Get It On" to Hunter when he recorded it on March 22. They moved in together into a house atop Topanga Canyon with a Great Dane named Piro, and soon she was expecting.[30] "We never used birth control. It was clear that Marvin wanted me pregnant—and I did nothing to prevent that."[31]

✻

Stevie Wonder was looking for a new sound when he heard an album called *Zero Time* by TONTO's Expanding Head Band. TONTO was actually a collection of synthesizers, and the band was Malcolm Cecil and Robert Margouleff. Cecil was a white British jazz bassist who'd been in the original Blues Incorporated with Rolling Stones mentors Cyril Davies and Alexis Korner. Margouleff was a white audiovisual repairman who did commercial jingles with Cecil on synthesizers. Margouleff was friends with Robert Moog, the designer of the first popular synth used by the Doors, Monkees, Byrds, and Beatles.

Cecil and Margouleff built TONTO ("the Original New Timbral Orchestra") out of Moog synths mixed with ARP synths (ARP being Moog's chief rival) and other keyboards and computers. It eventually filled an entire room, looking like the control panel of a science-fiction mastermind. Wonder invited them to collaborate with him. He played almost everything himself, a pioneer of self-sufficiency alongside Paul McCartney, Todd Rundgren, and Sly Stone. He replaced the Motown orchestra with TONTO, electric pianos, or the clavinet. The latter was an electrified version of the clavichord, the European keyboard from the Middle Ages. It became the quintessential funk instrument of the early '70s thanks to the hits of Wonder and Billy Preston.

Wonder decorated TONTO with statues of Eastern religious figures. He would start work after midnight, then plow through till the next afternoon, sometimes working two days straight.[32] Cecil and Margouleff recorded everything he did, then later listened to the tapes, discovered genius fragments Wonder hadn't realized he'd created, and hounded him to turn them into complete songs. Wonder would write the lyrics; then Cecil would speak them into Wonder's headphones, and Wonder would sing them into the mic.[33] He recorded his next four albums, *Music of My Mind, Talking Book, Innervisions,* and *Fulfillingness' First Finale,* all in about a year's time.

He wanted to win over the rock audience, which was larger than the R&B one, as blacks made up only 11 percent of the country's population at the time, despite their outsized contribution to popular music, sports, and politics. So he took a financial hit to open for the Stones on their *Exile on Main Street* tour, doing fifteen minutes, then an encore with Jagger on "Uptight" and "Satisfaction."

Former Yardbird Jeff Beck made his own recordings with the TONTO guys, and they brought him in to add guitar to Wonder's "Lookin' for Another Pure Love." In return, Wonder agreed to write him a song. Beck recalled, "One day I was sitting at the drum kit, which I love to play when nobody's around, doing this beat. Wonder came kinda boogieing into the studio: 'Don't stop.' 'Ah, c'mon, Stevie, I can't play the drums.'" But Beck kept playing, Wonder sat at the clavinet, and the immortal hook of "Superstition" came snaking out.

"I thought, 'He's given me the riff of the century,'" Beck recalled.[34]

Wonder wrote lyrics decrying how "a lot of people, especially black folks, let superstition rule their lives."[35] Beck did a version with his band Beck, Bogert, and Appice. But his record was delayed, which fatally allowed time for Gordy to hear the song. Gordy determined there was no way Motown was giving that song away. Beck's label chief, Clive Davis, freaked, but nothing had been signed on paper. So Wonder's version hit No. 1 on January 27, the third funk single to make the top spot, after Sly & the Family Stone's "Thank You (Falettinme Be Mice Elf Agin)" and "Family Affair." It won Grammys for Best R&B Song and Best R&B Vocal (Male). *Rolling Stone* ranked it the 73rd Greatest Song of All Time. Bootsy Collins, bassist for James Brown and P-Funk, proclaimed it "funk heaven." The kids of *Sesame Street* agreed when Wonder performed it on the show in April. Wonder apologized to Beck and gave him two songs for his next album.

The single helped *Talking Book* hit No. 3 on the pop chart and hold the

R&B top spot through the second part of January. The follow-up single "You Are the Sunshine of My Life" made him the first Motown artist since the Supremes to score back-to-back pop No. 1s. It was also his first easy listening chart-topper and earned him another Grammy (Best Pop Male Vocal). To throw a curve ball he let his backing singers, Jim Gilstrap and Lani Groves, sing the first few lines of the song.

On "Blame It on the Sun" you can hear where Elton John got "Don't Let the Sun Go Down on Me" and where producer Mark Ronson found some of the sound he'd bring to Amy Winehouse's work. On "Big Brother," TONTO transformed Wonder's clavinet into a sparkling acoustic guitar for his take on *1984,* which Cecil had read to him. In the old days Wonder had to fight Gordy to record "Blowin' in the Wind." Now there was no more beating around the bush. An oppressor kills the singer's leaders, then surveills him in a matchbox house overrun with roaches. But Wonder sneered that he didn't need to do nothin' to Big Brother, because "you'll cause your own country to fall." The idea wouldn't seem so farfetched come autumn, when OPEC realized that the president's weakness from the Watergate scandal made it the perfect time to launch the oil embargo.

✳

The Temptations' "Papa Was a Rolling Stone" cleaned up at the Grammys in March: Best R&B Vocal Performance, Instrumental Performance, and Song. Producer Norman Whitfield, convinced of his own genius long before then, decided "Papa's" follow-up should be called "Masterpiece." He set about constructing a song to fit the bill, something worthy to serve as the title track of the last Motown album recorded in Detroit. One last hurrah for the Funk Brothers.

Whitfield stretched the song out to fourteen minutes, the apogee of "CinemaScope soul," as critic Nelson George labeled it, or cinematic funk— epics where the producer fused R&B, pop, and gospel with a little Miles Davis, some Hendrix wah-wah, and a dash of Beatles (hence another popular label for the genre, "psychedelic soul"). Like Phil Spector, Whitfield kept expanding the sonic canvas with strings, synth, trombones, trumpets, tympani, vibes, bells, gourds, and harp.

Marvin Gaye often received the credit for forcing Motown into the topical age, but Whitfield's Temptations chronicled the dark side of the 'hood two years before him with "Cloud Nine," "Runaway Child Running Wild," "Don't Let the Joneses Get You Down," "Ball of Confusion." "Masterpiece" was another bleak mural of the inner city: strung-out kids from broken homes dodge cars for fun, then mug for dope; mothers return home from a grueling day to find their apartments cleaned out.

The Temptations were angry Whitfield only let them sing for three minutes out of fourteen. And he didn't let one person take the lead; he'd break up verses and give different lines to different singers. People called them cogs in Whitfield's grand design. They hadn't even wanted to do "Papa Was a Rolling Stone." Still, "Masterpiece" hit No. 7 on the pop charts, so it was hard to argue with success.

But it was their last single to make the pop Top 20. It might have been the very moment the pop audience hit the saturation point with inner-city protest songs. It had been exhilarating to finally hear the truth about the ghetto over the airwaves for the first time. But how many times could listeners be reminded that poverty was hell before they needed a break?

Nine hours southeast of Motown, Philadelphia International Records' answer to the Funk Brothers zeroed in on a new beat. The MFSB house band (officially "Mother Father Sister Brother," unofficially "Mother-fuckin' son-of-a-bitch") was evolving toward a genre without a name, though *Rolling Stone* writer Vince Aletti soon took a crack at giving it one with an article entitled "Discotheque Rock Paaaaarty!"

The Dark Side of the Moon

Roger Waters's flash of mental illness inspires the fourth-bestselling album in history, released on March 1.

✳

I can remember being in the canteen at Abbey Road, sitting at the table with everybody, and suddenly there was no pain," recalled Pink Floyd bassist Roger Waters. "Everything—the table, all the people at it—receded. The sound became tinny, and the room looked like I was looking at something through the wrong end of a pair of binoculars. I thought to myself, 'Whooah, hold on a minute.' I hadn't been taking any drugs or anything. I thought, 'Wow, this is what it's like to go mad.' I clearly remember thinking that. And I got up from the table and resisted it. I walked up the stairs and went into studio number three and started playing the piano, and slowly things started to come back into a more normal perspective. It didn't happen again, but I was quite clear at the time that this was the beginning of a breakdown. It was a breakdown I resisted and never actually had."[1]

Waters wrote "Brain Damage," originally titled "The Dark Side of the Moon" after a phrase that had been around for hundreds of years, and more recently used in James Taylor's "Carolina in My Mind." Waters sang of a lunatic on the grass, inspired by KEEP OFF THE GRASS signs, which Waters saw as an example of a sick society blocking people from enjoying nature. It was also a pun on the effects of marijuana. The news coming at the lunatic from the morning paper overwhelms him. He's given a lobotomy and locked in a mental institution.

The song was also informed by the breakdown of Waters's childhood friend Syd Barrett, who led Pink Floyd half a decade earlier. Back then they were the house band at London's UFO Club, the space-rock transatlantic counterparts to the Grateful Dead and Ken Kesey's Acid Tests. The band played long improvised jams while Barrett's roommate painted slides, heated them with a blowtorch, and projected the chemical reactions onto the musicians as their manager bathed them in colored lights.

In Barrett's communal living situation, everybody dosed each other incessantly with LSD. He began spacing out and replying with nonsensical non sequiturs. When the band made it onto Dick Clark's *American Bandstand,* Barrett acted catatonic. He refused to move his lips during performances on the Pat Boone and Perry Como shows. At gigs he sometimes detuned his guitar and wandered offstage.

Waters believed it was schizophrenia. Keyboardist Richard Wright assumed the LSD damaged his brain. Drummer Nick Mason thought that although the acid exacerbated his issues, ultimately Barrett just didn't want to be in a band. Either way, Waters recalled, "Syd had been the central creative force in the early days—maybe I provided some of the engine room—and so his having succumbed to schizophrenia was an enormous blow. And also, when you see that happening to someone you've been very close friends with, and known more or less your whole life, it really concentrates the mind on how ephemeral one's sensibilities and mental capacities can be. For me, it was very much 'There but for the grace of God go I.'"[2]

They brought in a friend of Barrett's from Cambridge Tech, guitarist Dave Gilmour, to play his parts. When Barrett resisted their attempts to take him to a psychiatrist, they helped him make two solo albums and set about reinventing Pink Floyd without him. Barrett had written great pop singles, but now the group focused on instrumentals mixing jazz, electronic noise, brass bands, choirs, even a howling dog named Shamus.

But after five experimental albums, it was time to tighten up. "I think we all thought—and Roger definitely thought—that a lot of the lyrics that we had been using were a little too indirect," Gilmour summarized. "There was definitely a feeling that [on the new album] the words were going to be very clear and specific."[3]

Waters took inspiration from the frank simplicity of John Lennon's first solo album, *Plastic Ono Band,* recorded after the ex-Beatle underwent primal scream psychotherapy. "I just think that's one of the truly great moments in the history of rock 'n' roll, or the history of any writing."[4]

When the band discussed potential themes for the new album, they gravitated toward the stress of touring via airplanes (the proto-EDM "On the Run" climaxes with a plane crash), then widened the scope to include all aspects of life that drove people crazy. Usually, Gilmour and Wright generated music and then Waters wrote the lyrics, before handing them over to Gilmour to sing, as he was not confident with his own voice.

They played the songs to audiences for a year as they toured Europe and North America. When they returned to Abbey Road Studios to record them, they produced themselves with the help of engineer Alan Parsons, assistant engineer on the Beatles' last two albums. (Parsons later scored his own Top 5 hit with "Eye in the Sky.") They worked with sixteen tracks, the next step up from the eight tracks the Beatles had at their disposal for *Abbey Road.* The documentary *Pink Floyd: Live at Pompeii* captured some of the sessions.

Wright had written the music for "Us and Them" for Michelangelo Antonioni's *Zabriske Point* (1970), about a university student who goes on the run after shooting a National Guardsman during an antiwar protest. Antonioni found Wright's composition "beautiful, but it is too sad, you know? It makes me think of church."[5] Waters now added lyrics about generals ordering soldiers to die while sitting on the sidelines. Many listeners assumed it was Vietnam commentary, though Waters's father had been killed in World War II. He'd been a teacher, Communist activist, conscientious objector, and ambulance driver before enlisting to fight and dying when Waters was five months old. The title came from a chapter in *The Politics of Experience* by R. D. Laing, the psychiatrist they encouraged Barrett to visit in 1967.

Wright played Hammond organ and grand piano, Parsons ranking it "one of the best things Rick ever did."[6] Gilmour sang lead, and Wright harmonized on the chorus. Waters commented that they worked well together because their voices sounded alike. For this song, "Brain Damage," "Eclipse," and "Time," they enlisted three UK session singers (Lesley Duncan, Liza Strike, Barry St. John) fronted by Doris Troy, a black New York soul singer whose biggest hit was "Just One Look." (She also sang backing on "You Can't Always Get What You Want.") Their vocals were triple-tracked. Gilmour also called on Dick Perry, the saxophonist of his old band Joker's Wild.

Perry played on "Money" as well, which reflected the motivation behind the band's drive for greater accessibility. Said Waters, "I remember thinking, 'Well, this is it and I have to decide whether I'm really a socialist or not.' I'm still keen on a general welfare society, but I became a capitalist. You have to accept it. I remember coveting a Bentley like crazy. The only way to get something like that was through rock or the football pools. I very much wanted all that material stuff."[7]

The blues track recalled Booker T. and the MG's "Green Onions," which Gilmour had played in his earlier band. Waters added a loop of sound effects: coins thrown into a bowl, paper tearing, an adding machine, and a cash register.

Frequently during the sessions, Waters and Gilmour argued about whether to do a "wet" or "dry" mix. For Gilmour's first "Money" solo, he played it twice and superimposed one guitar over the other ("wet"). For the second solo, he played one guitar without any reverb, echo, or effects ("dry"). For the third, he brought back reverb and echo and used automatic double tracking (ADT), looping his guitar over itself on a slight delay, a technique developed by the Beatles' engineers.[8] *GuitarWorld*'s readers ranked it 62 in the "The Greatest 100 Guitar Solos." *Rolling Stone* placed it at 69 for "The 100 Greatest Guitar Songs of All Time." In the latter magazine, Gilmour's peers voted him the 14th greatest guitarist. Originally, Gilmour said, the band couldn't play their instruments but their drugged audiences were happy with an hour of feedback. Now he was in the pantheon with Clapton and the other greats. "You just go out and have a play over it and see what it becomes, and usually it's the first take that's the best one."[9]

Waters wrote "Time" after the realization struck him that his life was no longer a dress rehearsal; this was it. Gilmour's reverbed open low E string became the ominous go-to sound of doom for horror films like *Halloween* and *Phantasm*. Waters plucked two muted bass strings to create a tick-tock effect, while Mason did a two-minute solo on special Rototom drums that had no shells. The immense echo became the template for later classic drum fills in tracks like Phil Collins's "In the Air Tonight."

Having sung the songs for months, Gilmour knew how to milk his inflections for ultimate fury. His vocals shred with contempt, both at himself for wasting his own time and at the uncaring force that dictates human existence. Wright sang the haunting bridges, backed by the female singers and Gilmour, recycling and tightening the melody from an earlier epic of theirs named "Echoes."

Originally "The Great Gig in the Sky" was called "The Mortality Sequence" or "The Religion Song." During live performances, spoken passages from the Bible or right-wing Christian writer Malcolm Muggeridge accompanied Wright's chords. When it came time to record, they decided the track needed a woman's vocals instead.

Engineer Parsons remembered a session singer named Clare Torry who performed covers of pop hits for compilation albums. Initially she passed on their job offer because she had tickets for Chuck Berry. "They weren't my favorite band. If it had been The Kinks, I'd have been over the moon."[10] Eventually she agreed to come in. Gilmour recalled, "We'd been thinking Madeline Bell or Doris Troy and we couldn't believe it when this housewifely white woman walked in."[11]

Torry recounted, "I went in, put the headphones on, and started going 'Ooh-aah, baby, baby, yeah, yeah, yeah.' They said, 'No, no—we don't want that. If we wanted that we'd have got Doris Troy.' And I remember thinking to myself, 'I really, really do not know what to do. And perhaps it would be better if I said "Thank you very much" and gave up.' It wasn't getting anywhere; it was just nothing. That was when I thought, 'Maybe I should just pretend I'm an instrument.' . . . Alan Parsons got a lovely sound on my voice: echoey, but not too echoey. When I closed my eyes—which I always did—it was just all-enveloping; a lovely vocal sound, which for a singer is always inspirational."[12]

She delivered a performance that sounded a bit like Janis Joplin and Aretha Franklin on a high wire between agony and ecstasy. Terror at the onset of death gives way to acceptance, then bliss, gently cooing as if coasting through a sea of clouds.

Gilmour asked for a third take, but she stopped midway, feeling she'd already done the best she could do. "And we all said, 'Wow, that's done. Here's your sixty quid.'"[13] She received the typical studio rate, the equivalent of about £360 today. She figured she'd been too screechy. "I honestly thought it would never see the light of day."[14]

The group pulled the album together by interspersing spoken word interviews. Waters wrote questions on cards, set them on a music stand in Abbey Road's Studio 3, then recorded people's responses and culled the best. Roadie Chris Adamson kicked off the album with "I've been mad for fucking years—absolutely years." Abbey Road doorman Gerry O'Driscoll's snippet began "Gig" with "Why should I be frightened of dying? There's no reason for it. You've got to go sometime." The band didn't use Paul McCartney's responses because he was "trying too hard to be funny."[15]

They began the album with an overture of sound effects from the songs.

The bass drum from "Time" and "On the Run" opened and closed the record, representing the heartbeat. The ticking clock from "Time" followed, then the adding machine from "Money," the whirling helicopter/jackhammer from "On the Run," mad laughter from "Brain Damage" (by road manager Peter Watts, father of actress Naomi Watts, who was there in the studio). Finally, manic screaming from "Great Gig" flew at the listener like a harpy over a backward piano chord. They called the collage "Speak to Me" and credited drummer Mason to give him some publishing royalties.

For the cover they turned to their usual design group, Hipgnosis, whose founder, Storm Thorgerson, had attended high school with Waters and Barrett. Wright pushed for a "simple and bold" design, something "smarter, neater—more classy" than the cow on *Atom Heart Mother* or the underwater ear on *Meddle*.[16] Thorgerson looked through a book of photography and found a photo in which sunlight streamed through a prism and refracted into a rainbow. Thorgerson's associate George Hardie illustrated it, leaving purple out of the rainbow because it was too difficult to see. When Hipgnosis presented different potential covers to the band, they unanimously agreed, "That one." Light shows had been an integral part of their identity since their days in London's psychedelic underground.

In the vein of *Led Zeppelin IV,* the cover featured no words. *IV* captured the imagination of countless stoners with arcane symbols that seemed to spell *Zoso* on the record sleeve. The prism became Floyd's mystic image. VH1 ranked it the fourth-greatest cover in rock history. When the gatefold opened, the rainbow became the line on a heart monitor, echoing the heartbeat that opened and closed the album. The package also included a poster of the Giza pyramids, a poster of the band, and two pyramid stickers.

The band toured the US in March and June, enthralling the audience not with a flamboyant front man but with a spectacle of lasers, giant mirror balls, flaming gongs, and a model plane that flew over the audience and exploded onstage during "On the Run." The LP topped the American chart for one week in April, helped by "Money," which became their first Top 20 single in the country. In the UK it didn't dislodge Alice Cooper's *Billion Dollar Babies,* though it still was the fourth-bestselling album that year. Gilmour attributed the success to stronger compositions. "All the music before had not had any great lyrical point to it. And this one was clear and concise. The cover was also right."[17]

Wright added, "We knew it had a lot more melody than previous Floyd albums, and there was a concept that ran all through it. The music was easier to absorb and having girls singing away added a commercial touch that none of our records had."[18]

In Los Angeles, filmmaker Ivan Dryer helped create an enduring ritual around the album. Dryer had become a "laserist" in 1970 after a California Institute of Technology professor asked him to film her laser demonstration. Now he worked for the film industry and for rock stars like Alice Cooper. He asked the Griffith Observatory if he could stage a show where he shone lasers on the ceiling and walls accompanied by music ranging from Johann Strauss to the Rolling Stones and Pink Floyd. Originally, he used Floyd's "Set the Controls for the Heart of the Sun" and "Echoes,"[19] but *Dark Side* soon became the soundtrack of choice. The following year imitators sprang up across the US, calling "the faithful to hear (and see) the softly spoken magic spell," per the lyrics of "Time." The events became a much-needed source of funding for many planetariums, though directors held misgivings about the drug-taking crowd.

Ironically, the album's climax, "Brain Damage/Eclipse," was a warning that the Acid Test search for transcendence could lead to psychosis. The song borrowed its opening arpeggios and "daisy chains" from "Dear Prudence," the Beatles' song from their Indian idyll with the Maharishi, but played them sadder. Gilmour coupled them with eerie high-pitched tones he'd developed on his slide guitar in "Echoes," sending the signal through a Leslie revolving speaker. For this song, Gilmour pushed Waters to take the lead vocal. "When I say, 'I'll see you on the dark side of the moon,'" Waters said, "what I mean [is] . . . if you feel that you're the only one . . . that you seem crazy, 'cos you think everything is crazy, you're not alone."[20]

Currently it is tied with Whitney Houston's *The Bodyguard* in fourth place for bestselling album in history, with claimed worldwide sales of forty-five million behind *The Eagles' Greatest Hits,* Michael Jackson's *Thriller,* and AC/DC's *Back in Black.*[21] Twenty-one million were sold in the US, where approximately one in fourteen people under fifty owned it.[22] It spent 937 weeks on the *Billboard* Top 200 album chart. The "Eclipse" finale accompanied the fireworks and balloons in the climax of the 2012 Summer Olympics.

Everyone, it seemed, felt like they were shouting but no one heard. "Burnouts" at light shows searching for relief from mental illness in dope. Their friends looking on, powerlessness to help them. Idealists and hedonists jolted from the hippie dream by jarring alarm clocks, blinking in the bright light of real life as the cosmic dust dispersed. Graduates returning home, struck by the terror of realizing that they had no idea what they were going to do with their lives. Parents faced with the need to pay off their debts and save—after "All You Need Is Love" and "Imagine No Possessions," still slaves to the system. "Money" prefigured the punks' and yuppies' cynicism: *Don't give me any more goody-good bullshit; grab that cash and keep your hands off my pie.* It was the credo of rock stars in tax exile and growing numbers of suburban voters drifting from Democrat to Republican as the postwar boom went bust. Middle-aged workers realized they'd "missed the starting gun" as backing vocals swirled like panic attacks around Gilmour's angst-filled solo.

The answer came at the beginning of the album: "Breathe," said the opening song, "and ride the tide."

"When the record was finished I took a reel-to-reel copy home with me and I remember playing it for my wife then," Waters recounted, "and I remember her bursting into tears when it was finished. And I thought, 'This has obviously struck a chord somewhere,' and I was kinda pleased by that."[23]

No Secrets

New laws regarding abortion and no-fault divorce change the relations of the sexes, echoed in hits by Helen Reddy and Carly Simon and the acidic banter of Sonny and Cher. Dolly Parton pens the biggest-selling single by a female artist to say goodbye to Porter Wagoner.

✳

At the Grammy Awards on March 3, Helen Reddy thanked "God because She makes everything possible" when she won Best Female Rock-Pop-Folk Vocal for "I Am Woman." She had been looking for a song "that reflected the feminist consciousness" when "it dawned on me that I would have to write what needed to be said myself. Did I feel up to the task? Not really, but I remember lying in bed with the phrase 'I am strong, I am invincible, I am Woman' going over and over inside my head. I wasn't even too sure what invincible meant, so I decided the phrase must be inspiration from above."[1]

Her record producer fretted it made her seem "butch,"[2] so she sang it on variety shows while she was pregnant to show she could "get a man." It was used in the first women's liberation comedy, *Stand Up and Be Counted,* starring Jacqueline Bisset and Stella Stevens. Deejays started telling Reddy, "I can't stand this record! I hate this song! But you know, it's a funny thing, my wife loves it!"[3]

✳

In the documentary *Gloria:* *In Her Own Words,* feminist Gloria Steinem recounts how in 1969, "I went as a journalist to cover a hearing at which women were standing up and telling their abortion experiences. I had had an abortion when I first graduated from college. I was twenty-two, and there was no women's movement then. There was no companionship. So I never told anybody. And I listened to these women testify about all that they had to go through. The injury, the danger, the infection, the sexual humiliation, you know, to get an illegal abortion, and I suddenly realized, why is it a secret? You know, if one in three women has needed an abortion in her lifetime in this country, why is it a secret? And why is it criminal? And why is it dangerous? And that was the big click. It transformed me, and I began to seek out everything I could find of what was then the burgeoning women's movement."[4]

In 1967, some states decriminalized abortion, including California with the Therapeutic Abortion Act signed into law by Governor Ronald Reagan. The Clergy Consultation Service on Abortion helped women find doctors and lobbied for legalization alongside social workers, doctors, nurses, and NARAL (National Association for the Repeal of Abortion Laws). But in 1971, legalization failed in twenty-five states.

The case that changed everything was, of course, *Roe v. Wade.* Jane Roe was a pseudonym for Norma McCorvey. The daughter of an abusive alcoholic mother, she robbed a gas station at age ten and fled Texas to Oklahoma City with her girlfriend.[5] When the motel maid caught them kissing, McCorvey was arrested and sent to Texas State School for Girls.[6] Upon release, she lived with her mother's cousin, who repeatedly raped her.[7] She married at sixteen, but her husband was abusive. Pregnant, she moved back in with her mother. When she came out as a lesbian, her mother tricked her into signing over custody of her baby, then forced her out of the house.[8] McCorvey put another child up for adoption the following year, then became pregnant a third time at age twenty-one in 1969.

Texas authorized abortion in cases of rape or incest "for the purpose of saving the life of the mother" but required a police report, which McCorvey didn't have. She tried to find an illegal abortion clinic, but the authorities had shuttered them. Finally she was referred to lawyers Linda Coffee and Sarah Weddington.

Coffee was gay and had been working on lawsuits to challenge sodomy laws when she realized a recent California abortion ruling could be applied to Texas.[9] She needed a pregnant woman to build the case around, and an adoption attorney connected her with McCorvey.

Weddington was a minister's daughter who became pregnant during her third year of law school by her future husband and underwent an illegal abortion in Mexico.[10] After graduating she joined a women's group to overturn the state's abortion law and met Coffee.

Coffee gave McCorvey the pseudonym Roe (it rhymed with John Doe), and filed a case in the US District Court for the Northern District of Texas against Dallas district attorney Henry Wade, who was the top law enforcement official in the county where McCorvey lived and thus would have been in charge of enforcing the state's antiabortion law against her. In 1970, the Texas judges agreed the law was unconstitutional, citing the 1965 case *Griswold v. Connecticut,* in which the Supreme Court decided states could not prevent the use of contraceptives by married couples because the Bill of Rights created a "zone of privacy."

But even though the court decided the statute was unconstitutional, it did not grant an injunction to stop enforcement of the law. Coffee and Weddington appealed to the US Supreme Court. Meanwhile, McCorvey gave birth and gave the child up for adoption.

The case was argued in 1971, and reargued in 1972, by the twenty-seven-year-old Weddington. "I couldn't go to sleep the night before. I was very conscious of how the fate of many women for many years would be resting in part on my argument," she said.[11] "There was a sense of majesty, walking up those stairs, my steps echoing on the marble. I went to the lawyers' lounge—to go over my argument. I wanted to make a last stop before I went in—but there was no ladies' room in the lawyers' lounge."[12]

Defense attorney Jay Floyd joked, "Mr. Chief Justice and may it please the Court. It's an old joke, but when a man argues against two beautiful ladies like this, they are going to have the last word." He was met with silence. Civil rights lawyer Margie Hames recalled, "I thought [Chief Justice] Berger was going to come right off the bench at him. He glared him down."[13]

When it was Weddington's turn to speak before the all-male Supreme Court, "I was so nervous until I stood, and once I was up I was totally calm."[14]

On January 22, the court announced that seven out of nine justices voted in favor of Roe. They decreed that in the first trimester, the mother's right to privacy meant the decision to abort was solely the right of patient and doctor. In the second trimester, states could regulate in certain cases. In the third trimester, when the fetus was old enough to survive outside the womb, the "potential life" of the "viable" fetus meant that states could regulate or prohibit abortion unless the mother's health was in danger.

Justices Byron White and William Rehnquist dissented. White wrote, "In a sensitive area such as this, involving as it does issues over which reasonable men may easily and heatedly differ, I cannot accept the Court's exercise of its clear power of choice by interposing a constitutional barrier to state efforts to protect human life and by investing mothers and doctors with the constitutionally protected right to exterminate it. This issue, for the most part, should be left with the people and to the political processes the people have devised to govern their affairs."

The case did not top the headlines of *The New York Times* or *The Washington Post,* which prioritized the death of former president Lyndon Johnson. President Nixon made no public comment, though his private opinions were captured the following day on the Oval Office's secret taping system. NPR's Nina Totenberg summarized his comments: "I know there are times when abortions are necessary, he tells an aide [Chuck Colson], I know that—when you have a black and a white, or a rape. I just say that matter-of-factly, he adds. You know what I mean? There are times. [But] Abortions encourage permissiveness, he says. A girl gets knocked up, she doesn't have to worry about the pill anymore, she goes down to the doctor, wants to get an abortion for five dollars or whatever."[15] Elsewhere in the tapes he opined that "it breaks the family."

The most emphatic criticism came from the American Catholic Church, in a statement calling the decision "a catastrophe for America." Within months it incorporated the National Right to Life Committee (NRLC) to explore "every legal possibility" to challenge the decision. The backlash would play a significant role in the realignment of America's political parties, influencing many Democrats to become Republicans.

But for the moment, the women's movement had the wind at their back. On March 13, *The New York Times* reviewed *Our Bodies, Ourselves: A Book by and for Women*. It was developed during workshops given by feminists from the Students for a Democratic Society at Emmanuel College in Boston in 1969. "We didn't have the information we needed, so we decided to find it on our own," explained contributor Nancy Miriam Hawley.[16] It covered birth control, pregnancy, abortion, postpartum depression, rape, STDs, menopause, sexuality, even how to deal with male doctors and a capitalistic medical system.

Simon & Schuster released the mass-market version of the book just as Carly Simon's *No Secrets* album ended its five-week run in the No. 1 spot, from January 13 to February 10. The title song featured a couple determined to be honest about everything, including affairs, like the spouses in the film *Bob and Carol and Ted and Alice* after they attended a group therapy session at the Esalen Retreat Center. (The movie was adapted to a television sitcom in the fall of '73, with a cast that included Robert Urich, Anne Archer, and Jodie Foster. It didn't touch the movie's spouse-swapping theme but did cover premarital living together and skinny-dipping.) Gradually the singer comes to regret hearing about her man's dalliances.

It's unknown whether her new husband, James Taylor, inspired the song, though he helped her write the opening track, "The Right Thing to Do." In her memoir, she wrote she could tolerate Taylor's distant nature because she grew up ignored by her depressed father, the original Simon of Simon & Schuster.[17] Perhaps the melancholy in her songs like "That's the Way I Always Heard It Should Be" and "Anticipation" sprang partially from that paternal void—and also from the sexual abuse she suffered beginning at age seven from a thirteen-year-old family friend, the same year she developed a debilitating stutter.[18] She told *People* magazine, "It was heinous. It changed my view about sex for a long time. [Yet] I wanted to keep it quiet, because I wanted to keep it going."[19] When her mother said the boy could no longer come over, "I was devastated because I thought I was in a romance, which I think happens to a lot of girls. Your libido overpowers everything. You're so libidinous even at the age of nine and ten. And sometimes there's an outlet there. I bet in many more cases than we know about there is."[20]

"We Have No Secrets" also strangely echoed a day that took place at LA's Chateau Marmont in June 1972, a few months before Simon married Taylor. She was staying there with him when Mick Jagger invited to fly her to San Francisco to see the band perform. Theoretically the trip was to interview Jagger on behalf of *The New York Times,* though she and Taylor knew it was more. As she got ready to leave, Taylor tied a rubber hose around his arm. "This is what I do," he said as he shot up in front of her for the first time, in one of the grimmer passive-aggressive guilt trips in pop history. "Maybe if you see me do it, it will take away the cat-and-mouse game."[21] She hugged him until the front desk called to say her limo was downstairs.

Jagger dueted with her on "You're So Vain," the No. 1 single from January 6 to 26, though Simon maintained it was written before she met him. The second verse was specifically about actor Warren Beatty. Simon's frequent co-writer Jacob Brackman was a screenwriter, and through him she met and had affairs with filmmakers Terrence Malick and Bob Rafelson and actor Jack Nicholson.[22] It was Beatty she fell for, though. He was currently on a two-year hiatus, researching his future epic about American Communists, *Reds,* while living in the decidedly non-working-class Beverly Wilshire Hotel rewriting the script for *Shampoo* with Robert Towne, his self-portrait of a Hollywood sex addict.

The day after one late-night visit from Beatty, Simon spoke rapturously of the experience to her analyst, until the stricken therapist felt compelled to inform her, "You are not the first patient of the day who spent the night with Warren Beatty last night."[23] When Simon confronted Beatty over the phone, he "howled," she wrote in her memoir. "All to his credit that he was up for the hilariousness of the situation."[24]

Initially, Simon's producer Richard Perry enlisted Harry Nilsson to duet with her on "Ballad of a Vain Man." But Jagger got wind of the session and arrived to join them at the mic. Quickly, Nilsson realized, "The two of you have a real blend—you should do it yourselves," and stepped aside.[25]

"Electricity," she wrote. "That's what it was. I wanted to touch [Jagger's] neck and he was looking at my lips. The electricity was raw and hardly disguising its power. Having sex would have actually cooled things off."[26] Jagger no doubt relished celebrating his vanity with a woman who famously resembled him. Many believed that he married his wife Bianca because she looked like him, his own Narcissus pool to gaze upon.

Afterward, she and Jagger improvised on the piano. Jagger biographer Marc Spitz quoted Simon: "We wrote a song together that became a song on the Stones' next album called 'Til the Next Goodbye.' I thought that that was going to be a joint venture, but I'd never heard from Mick about how he'd like me to share the royalties. It's the very least I can do to thank Mick for turning what could of been an ordinary record into an iconic huge song for me over the years."[27]

It was hard to imagine that the worldly mixture of humor, spite, and resignation in "You're So Vain" could have arrived in an earlier decade. It was a fitting anthem for a year that witnessed the toppling of many powerful men, from President Nixon to Marlon Brando's character in *Last Tango in Paris,* branded *"Égoiste!"* by Maria Schneider before she shoots him. On television's first reality show, *An American Family,* Pat Loud inspected her husband's credit card receipts and discovered his philandering, then cornered him when he returned home from a business trip. "I've spoken to a lawyer, and this is his card . . . and I'd like to have you move out."

"Fair deal," he managed with false bravado. "I won't have to pack."

Newsweek's March 12 issue featured the Louds on the cover with the headline THE BROKEN FAMILY. In Sweden, writer-director Ingmar Bergman helmed a six-part miniseries titled *Scenes from a Marriage* that also chronicled a couple's dissolution, starring Liv Ullmann. The Swedish media claimed the country's divorce rate doubled afterward.[28]

In the US, the percentage of marriages that ended in divorce had spiked at 43 percent right after World War II, then dipped to 26 percent in 1950, down to 21 percent by 1958 (per the US Department of Health). But it climbed back to 26 percent in 1967 and increased rapidly thereafter, partially due to the Pill and the success of the women's movement in securing greater employment opportunities.

Many historians also consider the rise of no-fault divorce a primary factor. In previous decades, one partner had to prove that the other broke the marital contract through adultery or cruelty, often necessitating hiring a private investigator to follow the spouse to gather evidence. After a handful of states began allowing couples to claim irreconcilable differences in the 1960s, a slew of states followed suit in the early 1970s. According to the Centers for Disease Control, the divorce rate increased to 35 percent in 1970, then to 43 percent in 1973, on the way to its all-time peak of 53 percent in 1979.

60 Minutes aired a segment on August 17 in which a private detective observed that he used to chase only husbands who vanished, but now investigated the disappearance of an equal number of women. He theorized the women's liberation movement had inspired them to leave their marriages. The episode was based on a *Life* magazine cover story on Wanda Adams called "Dropout Wife (A Striking Current Phenomenon)." On *60 Minutes,* Adams explained how she felt restless in her marriage and missed outside stimulation, so she left to move in with two other women, taking her daughter while her husband kept the two boys, shocking many viewers.

In February, Loretta Lynn's country No. 1 "Rated X" described the fallout from her split with her husband: his friends hit on her, while the women in the community talked behind her back. Even Tammy Wynette, the most vocal advocate for standing by one's man, released "Kids Say the Darndest Things," in which her four-year-old plays dress-up and says, "I want a divorce."

The dissolution of one of the country's most famous couples played out in real time on Wednesday nights at 8 p.m. on *The Sonny and Cher Comedy Hour.* The couple had engineered a remarkable comeback from the previous decade. After their films *Good Times* and *Chastity* failed at the box office, they owed the IRS $270,000 and found themselves playing deserted casino nightclubs.[29] During a gig opening for Pat Boone at the Flamingo in

Vegas, Cher started needling Sonny, and the audience started laughing. She began trying to make the band laugh by calling her husband "dummy" or staring with eyes glazed over in boredom while he spoke. Their onstage shtick synced with the zeitgeist of "putting down the man." CBS gave them a variety show, the writers helped Cher eviscerate Sonny, and the program was one of the top three from 1971 to 1973.

Behind the scenes, they lived in different parts of the house, though he still tried to control when she left and went to bed. The only time he liked her going out was to shop, though he didn't actually want to hang out with her. He went out on his own and cheated. She stayed faithful for a while, then started seeing men in their touring band and, briefly, Elton John's lyricist, Bernie Taupin. Sonny didn't care; he just told her to keep the illusion going. "All we did was work. That was our relationship: work," she said. "For five years before I left him, I wanted to leave, but *The Sonny and Cher Show* was so popular that I was afraid."[30]

"America will hate you," Sonny warned. "You'll never work again."[31]

Then she ran into manager David Geffen at a Neil Young concert. She didn't recognize him, though she'd met him a decade before when he was a gofer for Phil Spector and she sang backup on Spector's records. Now they hit it off. Cher thought she'd found a new gay friend to hang with, but Geffen told his therapist the next day he was in love with her. To her surprise, she found herself embarking on an affair with him that week.[32] The relationship lasted two years.

Even though Bono was seeing other women, he told her not to see Geffen, no doubt recognizing the threat he represented. Geffen reviewed Cher's contract and determined quickly that it was "slave labor."[33] Her solo hit "Gypsys, Tramps & Thieves" was MCA'S bestselling single, yet Bono received half her profits. "Half-Breed" and "Dark Lady" were two more solo No. 1s that he got a piece of.[34] Geffen connected Cher with Lucille Ball and Frank Sinatra's attorney to help her file for divorce, claiming "involuntary servitude."[35]

A similar scenario played out in the realm of country music, though this TV/recording duo was never married. Dolly Parton said, "I was trying to get away on my own because I had promised to stay with Porter [Wagoner's TV] show for five years. I had been there for seven. And we fought a lot. We were very much alike. We were both stubborn."[36] Also, Parton noted, "I don't mean this in a bad way, so don't play it up that way—but he was very much a male chauvinist pig. . . . That's why we fought like crazy, because I wouldn't put up with a bunch of stuff. Out of respect for him, I knew he was the boss, and I would go along to where I felt this was reasonable for me. But once it passed points where it was like, your way or my way, and this is just to control, to prove to you that I can do it, then I would just pitch a damn fit. I wouldn't care if it killed me."[37]

Whenever she broached the subject of leaving, he would grow irate about breach of contract, so she decided the way to best communicate was by writing "I Will Always Love You." "It's saying, 'Just because I'm going, don't mean I won't love you. I appreciate you, and I hope you do great, and I appreciate everything you've done, but I'm out of here.' . . . And I took it in the next morning. I said, 'Sit down, Porter. I've written this song, and I want you to hear it.' So I did sing it. And he was crying. He said, 'That's the prettiest song I ever heard. And you can go, providing I get to produce that record.'"[38]

She cut it on June 13 in Nashville and rode it to the No. 1 country spot twice, in 1974 and again in 1981 when it was featured in her film *The Best Little Whorehouse in Texas*. Elvis Presley wanted to record it, which thrilled Parton—until his manager, Colonel Tom Parker, insisted she had to share half the songwriting royalties with the Presley Organization as part of the deal. She turned them down. People told her she was crazy: it was *Elvis Presley*. "And I cried all night. . . . [But] something in my heart said, 'Don't do that.'"[39]

In 1992, Whitney Houston covered it and topped the pop charts for four-teen weeks—the biggest-selling single ever by a female. And thus, Dolly said, "I made enough money to buy Graceland."[40] Though she didn't. By that point she already had her own theme park, Dollywood.

✳

Houses of the Holy

Led Zeppelin releases their most upbeat album on March 28 and breaks the Beatles' concert attendance record.

✳

Houses of the Holy's opener, "The Song Remains the Same," was the victory lap after "Stairway to Heaven," guitarist Jimmy Page's expression of euphoria as everything he once envisioned had come to pass. Eight years prior, he'd had to delay joining the Yardbirds for over a year due to persistent mononucleosis. He used the time to learn the secrets of the recording studio as one of London's most sought-after session musicians and producers, working on everything from rock to folk to movie soundtracks. When he founded Led Zeppelin, his production wizardry inaugurated a new era of sonic depth, leaving rivals like the Rolling Stones and the Who working overtime to catch up, both on record and as concert draws.

When Page began work on "The Song Remains the Same," he planned to develop the riff from the Yardbirds' "Tinker, Tailor, Soldier, Sailor" into an instrumental overture that could lead into the album's second track, "The Rain Song." But singer Robert Plant wanted to add vocals. Page slightly sped up Plant's voice to complement the twelve-string jangle.[1] Drummer John "Bonzo" Bonham galloped beside them, and the track evolved into a showpiece spotlighting the guitarist as one of the era's greatest virtuosos. Aerosmith's Joe Perry called it his favorite Page track.[2]

After the metal bombast of their first two albums, *Led Zeppelin III* marked a distinct departure with a second side of quieter acoustic numbers. *Untitled* (a.k.a. *Led Zeppelin IV*) synthesized both aspects of the band. Now they wanted to change direction again. Since the songs on the last record were heavy, *Houses of the Holy* focused on "singing about the good things," as "The Ocean" put it. Perhaps the last major rock and roll album to be so consistently cheerful was *A Hard Day's Night*.

"Over the Hills and Far Away" found its origins in another Yardbirds track. "White Summer" was based on British folk guitarist Davy Graham's version of an Irish folk song called "She Moved Through the Fair."[3] Graham played the song in concert during the '60s to demonstrate how both Irish/Scottish songs and Indian songs shared modal tuning.

An Indian song Page and Plant heard in Bombay influenced the humorously warped guitar lines of "Dancing Days." Plant's wife, Maureen Wilson, had been born in Calcutta, though her father moved to Birmingham to run a steel factory when she was young. Plant met her at a Georgie Fame concert in 1964. They shared a passion for dancing, and Plant bucked the prejudice of the era to have a nonwhite girlfriend, absorbing the music and food of her Indian neighborhood. During the lean years before he made it, he poured asphalt and lived off her. The song perhaps references that era, as Plant sings of dating his "flower" without having a car, feeling like he was stuck in a stage somewhere between a lion and a tadpole.

The band recorded the album at Mick Jagger's country estate, Stargroves, using the Rolling Stones Mobile Studio. (They had used the mobile studio on the previous two albums as well.) After the band finished "Dancing Days," they blasted it and danced across Jagger's lawn to their new creation.[4]

"The Rain Song" sprang out of a challenge thrown down by a Beatle. "George [Harrison] was talking to Bonzo one evening and said, 'The problem with you guys is that you never do ballads,'" said Page. (Somehow, Harrison missed "Thank You" and "Tangerine.") "I said, 'I'll give him a ballad.' In fact, you'll notice I even quote 'Something' in the song's first two chords."[5] Bassist John Paul Jones provided an orchestra with his Mellotron, a proto-synthesizer that played tape loops of instruments like strings and flutes at the push of a button. Harrison's reaction to the result is unrecorded, but he did smash a cake into Bonham's face for his birthday. The drummer chased him and threw him and his wife, Pattie, into a pool with their clothes on. Harrison declared the evening the most fun he'd had since the Fab Four.

"The Rain Song" was the only folk song on the album. The last LP had three. *Houses* was also their first LP without blues covers. Instead, they experimented with two other black genres on the rise: funk and reggae, with somewhat mixed results. They had absorbed the blues for a decade before recording Zeppelin albums, but they were novices with the new forms.

"D'yer Mak'r" was initially inspired by Ben E. King's "Poor Little Fool" before the band veered it into reggae.[6] That was the trendy move of the year among English rockers, with the Stones, McCartney, and Elton John all taking a stab on their albums. "It was about 5:00 AM and I had been hoping for a long time to do something like [it]," Plant told *Zig Zag*. "It was born then and there."[7] Bonham resisted because he had trouble with the exotic reggae rhythm and the song's time changes. The others ribbed him for his rare inability to master a beat, resulting in probably the most ham-fisted English reggae tune.[8] Jones didn't like it either, but Plant pushed for its release as a single. His efforts were rewarded by a No. 20 showing in the States. Still a mainstay on classic rock, it showed the band's heretofore hidden light side, which Plant later developed on "Fool in the Rain" and Honeydrippers covers of '50s songs like "Sea of Love." The title itself came from an old joke: "'My wife's gone on holiday.' 'Jamaica?' 'No, she went of her own accord.'"

Page said he kept the funk track ("The Crunge") on the album because you could hear the fun they were having.[9] Bonham's personal jukebox was stocked only with James Brown singles, as Brown's drummers like Clyde Stubblefield and John "Jabo" Starks were some of the few with something to teach him. "The Crunge" evolved when Bonham and Jones started jamming in the vein of Stax soul records. Plant joined in with references to Otis Redding classics like "Mr. Pitiful" and "Respect." James Brown would cry out for his band to take it to the bridge in workouts like "Sex Machine," so Zep jokes that they can't find the bridge. They discussed adding a diagram in the packaging on how to do the Crunge dance.[10] Jones insisted it was "brilliant. [It's] very tight, really, when you think about it. It's one of my favorites."[11] That was true musically, but lyrically Plant didn't make an effort, the main reason *Rolling Stone* critics frequently berated the band. When Plant put his head down and worked, he could emerge with enduring visions like "Stairway to Heaven." Often, however, he was content to focus on his voice as another musical instrument, not bothering to offer words for intellectuals to chew over. Post-Dylan, rock critics were anxious to demonstrate how they were as smart as any other critics, so Zeppelin became their favorite whipping boy, until the grunge era brought a critical reassessment. Zeppelin vacillated between vengeful indignation at the press and apathy as they flew on "the Starship," their rented Boeing 720 with shag carpeting, bar, fur-covered waterbed, and stewardesses scrounging for rolled-up hundred-dollar bills in between the seats after the band deplaned.[12]

Ironically, it was when they weren't consciously attempting a pastiche that they captured their most offhandedly funky track, "The Ocean," thanks mainly to Bonham's slight delay on the beat in the Stax tradition. "The Ocean" was Plant's metaphor for the sea of faces in the stadiums on tour, whom he addressed until the third verse, at which point he switched to singing to his beloved three-year-old daughter Carmen.

The only dark song in the set was Jones's "No Quarter," a phrase meaning "no mercy" that Who drummer Keith Moon used whenever he dressed up as a pirate (which he liked to do when he didn't dress up as a Nazi or a woman). Jones played the electric piano with oscillating effects and a synthesizer bass alongside Page's theremin and wah-wah guitar. They slowed the tape a semitone to create a sludgy, nightmarish mood that recalled their friends and rivals Black Sabbath.[13] Lyrically it was a sequel to "Immigrant Song," which cast the band as pillaging Vikings. Here the singer advises a village to put out the lights because "the winds of Thor" are blowing. Murderous raiders approach through the snow with howling dogs.

One could certainly imagine Bonham in that role. Plant called him "the Beast." He smashed his drums with the largest sticks available ("trees"), occasionally kicking his bass pedal through the bass drum (even as he tuned his instrument with a meticulous care unusual to rock and roll). *Rolling Stone* ranked him the No. 1 rock drummer. Engineer Ron Nevison opined that "the essence to me of the whole Zeppelin thing was John Bonham following the guitar. He would take the riff, and make that his drum part."[14]

Before Bonham's partnership with Page, drummers were typically recorded in small booths. Instead, Page would set Bonham up in a large echoey room, or the stone-walled entrance of the castle they rented to record in. Page and Glyn Johns argued over who created the new rock drum sound. Johns, who also produced the Beatles, the Stones, the Who, and the Eagles, insisted he discovered the technique during their first album. He placed a number of mics in front of Bonham and intended to place all of their signals in the sonic center of the track. However, "half of the drums were coming out of the left, by mistake. And I thought: I wonder what it would sound like if I took the one in the middle, and put it on the other side. And there it was—the beginning of stereo drums."[15]

Page continued to develop spatial dynamics, placing one mic in front of an amp and another twenty feet away. The sensation of depth was created by the time it took the sound to cross from one side of the room to the other, coupled with the ambient noise of the room. Page made the sound even bigger by running it through an echo machine, sometimes laying in reverse echo.[16] By the time he was done, the drums sounded like Bonham was going to beat your brains in. (Which, sadly, was not an inconceivable possibility, as alcoholism transformed him into a vicious brawler as the decade progressed.)

The actual song "Houses of the Holy" was probably the "grooviest" of the new batch, thanks to Page's droll guitar and Bonham's cowbell. But it sounded similar to "Dancing Days," so they decided to hold it for their next album, *Physical Graffiti*. They used the title, though, perhaps because the band Chicago had copped their tradition of numbering their albums.

Another track captured in Jagger's garden was "Black Country Woman," featuring Page and Jones on mandolin and Plant on harmonica. Black Country was the region where Bonham, Plant, and Plant's wife, Maureen, grew up, and the song hinted at the tensions in their marriage. Just before Zeppelin broke through commercially, Maureen got pregnant (frequent story for many a rock band). Plant bought them a home and invited friends to live there in a quasi-commune to keep her company while he toured. But perhaps she'd gotten wind of his "golden god" philandering on tour; in the song she throws beer in his face and "treats him mean."

But it's all right, he shrugs; "I know your sisters, too." According to Pamela Des Barres's memoir *Let's Spend the Night Together*, Plant carried on an affair with Maureen's younger sister Shirley. Reputedly, *Zeppelin II*'s "What Is and What Should Never Be" hinted at their illicit liaison.[17] After he divorced Maureen in 1983, he had a son with Shirley, making his children half-siblings and cousins simultaneously. Plant's only comment was that family celebrations at Christmas were always interesting.[18] "Black Country Woman" did not come out until *Physical Graffiti*, though, because album sides could only hold twenty-two minutes before the sound quality suffered, and they'd run out of space.

The final collection could have rivaled *IV* had they swapped out "The Crunge" for "The Rover," with its Sabbath-like distorted guitar, but it was another held back for the next LP. Page said, "The whole thing about 'The Rover' is the whole swagger of it, the sort of thing that is so apparent when you hear 'Rumble' by Link Wray—it's just total attitude, isn't it? . . . Which is sort of probably in my DNA to be honest with you."[19] A fourth outtake from the sessions, "Walter's Walk," was included in the 1982 rarities LP *Coda*.

The question on fans' minds when they eagerly bought *Houses* was whether Zeppelin could top the anthem of the '70s, "Stairway to Heaven."

In the end, they didn't try, though the folk elements of "Stairway" could be found in "The Rain Song," its guitar fireworks in "The Song Remains the Same," and the doom in "No Quarter." Plant made no effort to channel an epic this time around, content to toss off oblique celebrations of touring life.

This installment wasn't for teens listening on their headphones in the dark trying to divine pagan mysteries, hoping demons didn't materialize. This one was for the kids who'd just got their licenses to plug into their eight-track tape decks. It was the bliss of the six-string acoustic intro of "Over the Hills and Far Away" joined by a twelve-string acoustic over-dubbed in unison. It was the song building as you cranked the speakers and the band blasted in. It was being free with your gang, windows down and wind blowing back your hair. Cruising the strip as the evening starts to glow and looking over to see burnout goddesses stopped at the light beside you. Sneaking into backyards to pool-hop or hanging on bumpers in the parking lot, lighting off M-80s and swigging Mad Dog or whatever the girls scored with their fake IDs.

Road manager Richard Cole pinpointed '73 as Zeppelin's biggest year,[20] touring the UK and Europe in the spring, then on to America, thirty cities from May 4 to July 29. On May 5, they played to 56,800 in Tampa and beat the Beatles' Shea Stadium record for most attendees watching a single artist (by 1,200 people). Miami gave them the key to the city. Every date sold out except San Francisco, and that was their highest-grossing gig. Police on motorcycles escorted them to shows, sirens blaring. No opening act, just Zeppelin for three hours, often improvising. "Fuck me!" George Harrison laughed backstage. "With the Beatles we were on for 25 minutes and could get off in 15!"[21]

Now That It's Over,
What You Gonna Do?

The last American soldier leaves Vietnam on March 29, as new songs reflect both the country's joy and the veterans' struggle to readjust. On March 19, a Watergate burglar confesses perjury and all the president's men begin to fall.

✳

On January 23, Secretary of State Henry Kissinger initialed the Paris Peace Accords with Le Duc Tho, a leader of the Vietnamese resistance since 1929. Tho had fought the French colonial powers, then Japanese occupiers, then the French again, and finally the US and South Vietnamese governments. The following evening, President Nixon told TV cameras in the Oval Office, "We today have concluded an agreement to end the war and bring peace with honor in Vietnam and Southeast Asia."

The organist of Trinity Church in Lower Manhattan hurried to the tower to ring the ten three-thousand-pound bells.[1] At Madison Square Garden, a roadie handed Neil Young a note, and he announced, "The war is over." "The audience of eighteen thousand exploded, cheering, crying, and screaming for the next ten minutes," Linda Ronstadt wrote in her memoir *Simple Dreams*. Young's set that evening included "Lookout Joe," which some fans assumed concerned a vet returning home to an America that had lost its innocence. Twelve blocks northeast, Times Square was quiet,[2] a marked contrast to the day World War II ended, when two million people poured into the area to celebrate.

The US agreed to remove its 23,500 troops and advisers from South Vietnam within sixty days, and North Vietnam agreed to return all prisoners of war. The North was allowed to leave 150,000 soldiers in South Vietnam and hold on to the South Vietnam territory it had won.

The death toll for Vietnamese, Cambodians, and Laotians was estimated to range between 1,326,494 and 4,249,494. The US lost 58,318. Three million Americans had served. Nixon and Kissinger hoped South Vietnam would survive like South Korea, with the help of economic and military aid. That would make the war a stalemate and not a loss.

POWs began returning to the States on February 12 in Project Homecoming. They included future senator John McCain, who had been shot down on a bombing mission and imprisoned at the "Hanoi Hilton" for five and a half years, two of them in solitary confinement. Injuries and torture left him unable to lift his arms above his head for the rest of his life.

Associated Press photographer Slava "Sal" Veder captured the moment on March 17 in his Pulitzer-winning "Burst of Joy" photo. He snapped it at the Travis Air Force Base in California. Fifteen-year-old Lorrie Stirm ran with arms outstretched to greet her father, Air Force Lieutenant Colonel Robert L. Stirm. The rest of the family beamed behind her. Like McCain, Stirm had been shot down in 1967.

"Tie a Yellow Ribbon Round the Ole Oak Tree" ascended to the No. 1 position on April 21, although it would not become overtly affiliated with the military until the 1991 Iraq War. The song had its roots in English folk songs from earlier centuries, such as "Round Her Neck She Wore a Yellow Ribbon," which inspired a 1949 John Wayne movie.[3] There was also a folk tale about a prisoner returning home who wrote to his wife to cover the tree in ribbons if she wanted him back. Some variations changed ribbons to handkerchiefs. Songwriter L. Russell Brown suggested to his partner Irwin Levine that it could make a good song. They had scored a No. 1 a few years earlier with Tony Orlando and Dawn's "Knock Three Times." That song shared a similar scenario; the man asks the girl downstairs to let him know if she wants him by knocking on the ceiling.

They played their new ditty to the A&R man who ran the New York office of the Beatles' Apple Records, Al Steckler, as a possible song for Ringo Starr. Steckler told them the composition was ridiculous.[4] Thus they returned to Tony Orlando and his backing singers, Telma Hopkins and Joyce

Vincent Wilson. Their rendition sold three million copies in three weeks and became the bestselling single of the year in the States. It was No. 2 worldwide behind the Stones' "Angie";[5] eventually it became the No. 37 bestselling song of all time.[6] The following year, CBS gave the trio their own variety show to replace Sonny and Cher when that couple divorced. In 1979, the song was revived when Iranian revolutionary college students took hostages at the US embassy in Tehran. The wife of one of the hostages, Penne Laingen, tied a yellow ribbon to a tree in the front yard until her husband returned.

The O'Jays' "Love Train" did not directly reference the war either, but it was no doubt cranked in many a welcome-home party. Philadelphia International writer-producers Kenneth Gamble and Leon Huff drew upon both the Impressions' "People Get Ready" and Cat Stevens's "Peace Train" in their invitation to "people all over the world"—from Russia, China, Israel, Africa, and England—to join hands and climb on board. It debuted on the pop chart three days before the treaty was announced and peaked at No. 1 the week the last combat soldier, Master Sergeant Max Beilke, left Saigon on March 29.[7]

Beilke's sister Lucille Johnson told the press, "We could see him leaving [Vietnam] on television. We all just beamed, because we knew he'd soon be home safely."[8] (Beilke was also a veteran of the Korean War. He died in the Pentagon on 9/11 when one of the planes hijacked by terrorists crashed into the building.)

Bette Midler's cover of the Andrews Sisters' "Boogie Woogie Bugle Boy," originally from the Abbott and Costello movie *Buck Privates* (1941), also hit the Top 10 that spring. It was intended to be the flip side of Midler's "Delta Dawn," but when Helen Reddy's "Delta Dawn" beat her to the market, the label turned the B side into the A side. Had the war not been over, a song about a bugler who good-naturedly assents to the draft might not have done so well.

The year's tracks that directly addressed the war were considerably darker. "Somebody gotta save my soul," screamed Iggy Pop in the Stooges' "Search and Destroy," about a "forgotten boy with a heart full of napalm" in the middle of a firefight. With typical Stooges timing, it came out two weeks after the war ended. The New York Dolls, meanwhile, roared, "Now that it's over, what ya gonna do?" in "Vietnamese Baby."

In "March to the Witch's Castle," Funkadelic's George Clinton gloomily intoned that for the returning soldier "the real nightmare had just begun; the nightmare of readjustment." To horror-movie organ accompaniment, Clinton's protagonist arrives back home with a "habit he still cannot break" and a wife who'd remarried, assuming he was dead. Curtis Mayfield *sounded* more upbeat in "Back to the World," with his signature "Superfly" groove, but in that song the soldier's wife has also left him. "The doggone war just lasted too long."

The songs echoed the real-life experience of "Burst of Joy" soldier Stirm, who received a Dear John letter from his wife the day he was released from the POW camp. She'd seen other men while he was gone, and though she wanted a divorce, he still had to pay her 43 percent of his retirement pay.[9] Stirm's children kept the "Burst of Joy" photo on their walls, but he didn't. The movie *Coming Home* later dramatized a similar dilemma.

Some of the returning POWs had last seen America when it was still in wholesome *American Graffiti* mode. Many soldiers found their wives no longer content to play the docile, subservient homemaker. Veterans returning to urban areas found masculinity had undergone a sea change as well—cities were "burnin' with wolfman fairies dressed in drag," as Bruce Springsteen's veteran song "Lost in the Flood" put it. The Pentagon offered classes to the veterans on how to reorient themselves.

Many vets felt alienated from their fellow Americans on both sides of the political divide. They believed some viewed them as "good German" baby killers, while older vets looked down on them for not winning. Most people were just indifferent. Relatively few parades were held, in contrast to the massive victory celebrations World War II soldiers enjoyed.

"It was the spookiest thing . . . ," veteran Jamie Bryant told Arnold Isaacs, author of *Vietnam Shadows*. "There has really never been anyone who has asked me: 'What happened to you over there? What was it like?' It's like having a whole year of your life that didn't exist. When you first get back, you don't think about it much. Then you begin to wonder why no one asks the questions. Then you begin to feel like maybe it really isn't something you should talk about."[10]

The Veterans' Readjustment Assistance Act of 1974 offered affirmative action for vets and $200 a month, but it was not comparable to the GI Bill, which gave soldiers living expenses and full college tuition. Veterans hospitals remained notoriously underfunded.

"Father, we pray that we might understand what has happened to his mind," Clinton uttered, echoing the experience of future secretary of state John Kerry, who recalled, "There I was, a week out of the jungle, flying from San Francisco to New York. I fell asleep and woke up yelling, probably a nightmare. The other passengers moved away from me—a reaction

I noticed more and more in the months ahead. The country didn't give a damn about the guys coming back, or what they'd gone through. The feeling toward them was, 'Stay away—don't contaminate us with whatever you've brought back from Vietnam.'"[11]

The VA itself did not acknowledge the existence of post-traumatic stress disorder (PTSD) until 1979.[12] In 1986, *60 Minutes* reported in the segment *Vietnam 101* that more than 100,000 vets had killed themselves, almost double the death toll from combat.

"Lost in the Flood" was Springsteen's dry run for "Born in the USA," about the rage of a discarded vet. Onstage he dedicated "Flood" to "the guys who made it back from 'Nam." A gunner with ankles caked in mud returns only to get stuck in quicksand (perhaps an allusion to heroin). "I had some friends, very close friends of mine . . . guys who came home in wheelchairs, and then, I didn't go. I was a stone-cold draft dodger. . . . I did everything in the draft-dodger's text book. So, perhaps, I felt guilty about that later on. . . . I had friends who went and died."[13]

Springsteen later got the title "Born in the USA" from a script by Paul Schraeder. In 1973, Schrader was living in his car in Los Angeles writing the script for *Taxi Driver,* the ultimate film about a veteran adrift with PTSD.[14] He was inspired to write it when *An Assassin's Diary,* by Arthur Bremer, the man who shot segregationist presidential candidate George Wallace, was published in April.[15]

Taxi Driver wouldn't make it to the screen until 1976. It wouldn't be until 1978 that major directors started dealing with the war, in *The Deer Hunter* and the aforementioned *Coming Home*—a fact that indicates how ambivalent the US had been about the conflict since its inception. A casual count of war movies made during World War II on Wikipedia lists 154 from 1942 to 1945, whereas Wikipedia lists only *four* Vietnam-themed movies released between 1964 and 1973. Even the much shorter Korean War had sixteen US films made about it from 1951 to 1953, again per Wikipedia.

The most resonant representation at the time wasn't even about the Vietnam War per se. The TV adaptation of Robert Altman's hit film *M*A*S*H* was set during the Korean War, though star Alan Alda (Hawkeye Pierce) maintained, "I think [creator] Larry Gelbart saw a connection very clearly."[16] The show's first season ran from September '72 to March '73. Gelbart said, "We all felt very keenly that inasmuch as an actual war was going on, we owed it to the . . . audience to take cognizance of the fact that Americans were really being killed every week."[17]

The episode "Sometimes You Hear the Bullet" aired on January 28, the day after the Paris Peace Accords were signed. In it Hawkeye must operate on a soldier who was a childhood friend—and fails to save him. "The network went nuts," said Alda. "The guy who was in charge of programming said, 'What is this, a situation *tragedy?* What are you doing to me here?' Larry Gelbart thinks it's when we really realized what we could do. Really go all the way with the tragedy of the situation, the horror of the situation and be funny too, both in the same scene."[18]

Another honest portrayal of the war came unexpectedly from the funny pages, in *Doonesbury.* Twenty-four-year-old Garry Trudeau cranked out the strip, with the help of inker Don Carlton, while he got his graphic design degree from Yale. One of the plot lines concerned Doonesbury's college roommate B.D., who goes to fight in 'Nam and is captured by Phred the terrorist, perhaps the first sympathetic portrayal of the Viet Cong in US mass media. Phred tells B.D. about Vietnam history, endures bombing campaigns on his village ("How many tons were dropped in Vietnam? 93,470 tons is absolutely right!"), and brings B.D. to his mother's refugee camp. ("I didn't know commies had mothers," says B.D.) The strip also featured the "Heartless Air Pilots," who absently bomb villages while talking about the Knicks or *Jonathan Livingston Seagull.*

❊

Polls recorded Nixon's approval rating at 67 percent when he was sworn in for his second term on January 20. But under the surface, "the cancer on the presidency"—as White House counsel John Dean called Watergate—was rapidly metastasizing.

Ten months earlier, Attorney General John Mitchell had approved a plan for a covert special investigations unit nicknamed "the Plumbers" to break into the Democratic National Headquarters at the Watergate Hotel to wiretap the phones in order to gather information for the Committee to Reelect the President (CREEP). The bugs they installed malfunctioned, so on June 17 five Plumbers—ex-CIA officer James McCord and four men he had worked with in efforts to overthrow Fidel Castro—returned to fix them and take pictures of documents.

The Plumbers duct-taped the lock on the headquarters door so it appeared closed but remained unlocked. Around midnight, security guard Frank Wills noticed the tape and took it off. An hour later, he saw someone had stuck the tape back on and called the police. At 2:30 a.m. officers arrived and arrested the Plumbers, charging them with breaking and entering, burglary, and attempted interception of telephone and other communications.

Nixon instructed Dean to perform a cover-up by shredding files and paying off the burglars with hush money from the Nixon reelection campaign fund so that they wouldn't talk to FBI investigators. *Washington Post* reporters Bob Woodward and Carl Bernstein doggedly pursued the case and revealed that the Plumbers had been paid by Nixon's reelection campaign. But voters nevertheless reelected Nixon in the third-biggest popular-vote landslide in American history, underscoring how unnecessary the entire break-in had been in the first place.

Still, Woodward said, "What you have to remember is that while maybe everyone wasn't reading about Watergate, we had two subscribers who were reading every word."[19] One was Democratic senator Sam Ervin, who requested a $500,000 budget to fund a Special Senate Committee to investigate. The other was John Sirica, chief judge of the US District Court for the District of Columbia, known as "Maximum John" for his propensity to dole out the harshest sentences possible.

On January 8, the trial opened for the five burglars and two leaders of the Plumbers, ex-CIA agent E. Howard Hunt and ex-FBI agent G. Gordon Liddy. Five of the men pleaded guilty. A jury convicted McCord and Liddy on January 30. The men insisted they acted alone, but Judge Sirica didn't believe them and warned that the length of their prison sentences would depend on whether they cooperated with investigators.

On March 20, McCord gave Judge Sirica a letter admitting, "There was political pressure applied to the defendants to plead guilty and remain silent. Perjury occurred during the trial." Five days later, McCord testified before the Senate, naming Mitchell as the "overall boss" behind the break-in, while also incriminating Dean and others.

On April 28, the acting head of the FBI, Patrick Gray, admitted that he had followed instructions from Dean and counsel John Ehrlichman to burn documents from Hunt's White House safe, then resigned. Nixon pushed Ehrlichman and chief of staff H. R. Haldeman to resign on April 30 so that he could blame the cover-up on them and say he never knew about it until they told him in March. Dean encouraged them all to confess, so Nixon fired him. Attorney General Richard Kleindienst also resigned to avoid a conflict of interest with the Watergate investigations.

On May 17, the networks began broadcasting the Senate Watergate Committee hearings live. Tom Brokaw, NBC's White House correspondent, recalled, "I don't think there's ever been a moment in American nonfiction television history that is as riveting as the Watergate hearings were."[20]

Talk show host Jon Stewart was ten years old that spring. "The Watergate hearings were an absolute unifying television experience for the entire country. I can remember watching and thinking, 'Man, they're interrupting soap operas, wow.' You just figured that this must be something enormously fundamental to our democracy."[21]

People crammed into the congressional hearing room, or rushed home from work and school to catch the afternoon testimony. Others watched in bars and airports. Even *Rolling Stone's* cynical reporter Hunter S. Thompson conceded, "For the first time in memory, the Washington press corps was working very close to the peak of its awesome but normally dormant potential. *The Washington Post* has a half-dozen of the best reporters in America working every tangent of the Watergate story like wild-eyed junkies set adrift, with no warning, to find their next connection."[22]

Until now Trudeau had turned in *Doonesbury* strips six weeks in advance, but things were unraveling so quickly he had to trash a whole week of strips and switch to a new schedule, turning strips in ten days in advance.[23] He eventually won the Pulitzer for his coverage. *Doonesbury's* campus radical Mark Slackmeyer (based on Weather Underground member Mark Rudd) began running "Watergate profiles" on his radio show. "Today's obituary—John Mitchell! It would be a disservice to Mr. Mitchell and his character to prejudge the man, but everything known to date could lead one to conclude he's guilty. That's *GUILTY! GUILTY, GUILTY, GUILTY!!"* *The Washington Post* refused to run that installment, and a number of papers dropped the strip. *The Lincoln Journal* compromised by moving it to the editorial page. Slackmeyer continued unabated: "If you've got a favorite Watergate conspirator, phone in your request. Profile of John Dean going out to Joey with hugs from Donna."

Dean began his four-day testimony on June 25. He told the committee that he had informed Nixon that Hunt was blackmailing them for hush money, and Nixon authorized paying him to keep quiet.

Nixon dismissed Dean's claims. His representatives insisted that Dean was bitter because Nixon had not offered him immunity. So Dean told the committee that he suspected Nixon tape-recorded their meetings. He had noticed the president sometimes moved to different parts of the room before replying softly. "I don't know if a tape exists," Dean said, "but if it does exist, and if it has not been tampered with, and if it is a complete transcript of the conversation that took place in the President's office, I think this Committee should have that tape because it would corroborate many of the things this Committee has asked me."

Author James D. Robenalt observed, "There are few times in American history where the entire country is focused on one television event. One of them was the Kennedy assassination, one of them was the moon landing, one of them was 9/11, and the other one is John Dean's testimony."[24]

Soon the world would learn that Nixon did indeed have voice-activated microphones in his desk and in the lamps on the fireplace mantel. One person particularly delighted with this turn of events was John Lennon. For part of Dean's testimony he sat with Yoko Ono behind Dean's wife, his head shaved, perhaps to draw even more attention to himself than usual. Three months earlier, a frazzled Lennon had called a press conference to request that the Nixon administration cease its effort to deport him over his antiwar activism.

The week after Dean's testimony, Lennon began recording the album *Mind Games* in New York, which included the last of his protest anthems. In the nonchalant "Bring on the Lucie" he cast himself as a sergeant leading his men over the hill to face the paranoid Lucifer of the title.

Your time is up you better know it
You were caught with your hands in the kill

Spring

We'll Help You
Party Down

Aerosmith feels overshadowed by their manager's other client, the New York Dolls. Tensions come to a head between Rod Stewart and the Faces. Deep Purple unleashes the ultimate riff. Grand Funk celebrates the wildest groupie. Hawkwind is just a little too out there for America.

✳

Elvis Presley and Scotty Moore inspired the template for "lead singer alongside guitar slinger" for bands like Led Zeppelin. But in the following decade the Stones became the archetype to imitate, and no one xeroxed it more completely than Aerosmith. When Mick Jagger became famous, suddenly drummer Steven Tallarico's big lips paid off. He'd loiter around hotels where the Stones stayed, lie to the media that he was Jagger's brother, Chris, goad the girls into swarming the car.[1]

His band opened for the Byrds, but six years later he was still playing clubs and knew he should be singing lead.[2] So he found a younger guitarist named Joe Perry, whose black-framed glasses with masking tape couldn't hide his square-jawed good looks or his power with the ax. He got a new drummer, Joey Kramer, and set his own kit in front of Kramer's to coach him. He changed his name from Tallarico to Tyler. They paid to play Max's Kansas City, where Columbia president Clive Davis saw them and decided they could be America's Rolling Stones. On their self-titled first album they covered a song the Stones covered on *their* first album, Rufus Thomas's "Walkin' the Dog," so you could compare how the art of white boys copying black guys had progressed in ten years, post psychedelia and heavy metal.

The enduring rocker on *Aerosmith,* "Mama Kin," was the first of Tyler's many installments about a poor gypsy's battle to find peace of mind in the face of grueling obstacles like groupies and pot, hoping he won't have to go back on the wagon and work for his dad. Like early Stones songs such as "Come On," it has a hyped-up pace that reflected their anxious youth, having not yet relaxed into the sexy, assured groove that turned later ruminations on the same subject matter like "No More No More" into burned-out epics. Still, Tyler was proud enough of "Mama Kin" to have the title tattooed on his arm, though it almost didn't fit because his arm was so thin.[3]

They recorded the album in a Boston studio over the course of a few weeks, the tracks captured live in a couple of takes between trips to the bathroom for coke. Tyler wrote in his memoir, "We were so nervous that when the red recording light came on we froze. We were scared shitless."[4] Finally Tyler unscrewed the red light bulb. Producer Adrian Barber tried to get them pumped, cheering, "Yes! It's got fire; it's got the bloody fire!"[5] But Perry rued, "When I heard the playback, I kept thinking, *We're better than this. We should sound better than this. We're being recorded wrong. We sound fuckin' flat.* But because I lacked the studio chops to prescribe a remedy, I kept quiet."[6] Tyler tried to sing like James Brown and Sly Stone but reckoned the result came closer to Kermit the Frog, except for the one track he sang in his natural voice, "Dream On."

Some of the song's power came from the fact that Tyler had been hauling his dream around for more than a decade. Longer than that, when you considered that he had absorbed the dream from his frustrated father, a common phenomenon among artists. (It had been the case with Paul Mc-Cartney and other Jagger-resembling stars of '73, Carly Simon and David Johansen.) Tyler's dad had studied at the Julliard performing arts school but had to make ends meet running the family's New Hampshire vacation lodge, teaching, and playing weddings. Still, he practiced on his Steinway three to four hours a day. Young Tyler played underneath the piano while he did so. Tyler said that's where the chords for "Dream On" came from.

Tyler played drums in his father's band in the summer and eventually played piano for the guests at the family lodge himself. He stumbled across the "Dream On" melody when he was seventeen or eighteen, around the time Perry Como had a Top 5 easy listening hit called "Dream On Little

Dreamer," and tinkered with it on a pump organ to give it an "Edgar Allan Poe feel."[7]

Tyler revived the melody for the album sessions. He still hadn't written words for it. He'd come up with this melody years ago, but here he was at twenty-four, looking older, and still hadn't made it. What had he been doing all those years? What was taking so long? He poured that vexation into the song. He wanted strings, but they couldn't afford them, so he played the Mellotron. On guitar Perry played what Tyler did with his right hand, and bassist Tom Hamilton played what Tyler did with his left. Tyler snorted some crystal THC (the psychoactive chemical in cannabis) and started singing.[8] When he got to the "past is gone" wail, he went into Yma Sumac mode, as if channeling the Peruvian soprano with a four-octave-plus range who enjoyed hits in the '50s.[9] By the climax he was screaming like his idol Janis Joplin, who had been a "Pentecostal Holy Roller revelation" to him, per his memoir.[10]

Tyler cried after they finished, believing they'd finally captured their breakthrough. But it was buried on an album that appeared to be an afterthought for the label. "Unfortunately the packaging was lame," Perry groused. "We didn't even see the cover until the first printing. It was something that Columbia just threw together."[11]

It was released the same day as Bruce Springsteen's debut, January 5, and the label put its promotional muscle behind the future Boss. Aerosmith's debut single, "Mama Kin," sank without a trace. They didn't get a review in *Rolling Stone*. Other critics harped that they were derivative of the Stones or said they copped their look from the New York Dolls, another band with "a guy with big lips that looks like Mick Jagger" and "a guy who looks like Keith Richards," as Gene Simmons put it.

Aerosmith actually shared the same management team as the Dolls, Leber and Krebs. Johansen aped Jagger even more than Tyler did. Johnny Thunders blew up Richards's black rooster cut into a Dr. Seuss palm-tree explosion that became the archetype for '80s hair metal, perhaps one of the band's most important contributions. ("Who does your hair?" Bowie asked Johansen. He replied that Thunders did.[12])

The critics from *Creem* and *The Village Voice* fell in love with the Dolls. "And we're going, 'Hey! What about us? We can actually *play*,'" lamented Perry.[13] "[The Dolls] came to check us out on their own turf, Max's Kansas City, and they're fucking wild-looking, like *bizarre*. I thought to myself, *What the fuck is this?* They were in drag, the real deal, hair sticking out, high heels, spandex pants."[14]

"I'm thinking, *Why is the singer wearing hot pants?*" remembered Tyler. "The Dolls couldn't tune their instruments or even sing that good, but it didn't matter because they had attitude. I loved them because of the attitude, the clothes, and because they were just so fucking high. They were twice as stoned as we could ever think of being."[15] And that's saying something.

When Clive Davis signed Aerosmith, he told Tyler he was going to be a star. But the album barely shifted thirty thousand copies, and Davis started thinking he shouldn't throw good money after bad. Things didn't look good for the boys from Boston.

✲

Another duo with the Mick-Keith vibe was the Faces' Rod Stewart and Ronnie Wood. Wood had it so much, of course, he eventually became a Stone. In the meantime, the Faces let the Dolls open for them in October '72. Some of the Faces' "laddish" fans screamed the f-word at the Dolls. But also in the audience were all the future Sex Pistols, though they didn't know each other yet. Pistols guitarist Steve Jones hailed the Faces as one of his primary influences, along with Bowie and Roxy Music.

As with the Dolls, half of what the Faces sold was camaraderie, hilariously recounted in drummer Kenny Jones's autobiography.[16] They set up a bar onstage with their roadie in a tux, a white cloth over his arm, and sat there and chilled while Jones took his drum solo onstage. One time when they didn't have the bar, they left Jones to it and went to the pub across the street, leaving Jones to wonder what the fuck was going on after a while, arms getting tired. He was pissed when they finally came back but had to admit it was funny.[17] They were touched by American soldiers their own age being sent off to war, so they'd invite them back to their hotel for the afterparty, though they got banned from Holiday Inns and had to lie that they were Fleetwood Mac to check in.[18] They crammed a hundred people into somebody's motel room and yelled "Surprise!" when he opened the door. On the tour plane, Ron Wood fell asleep and the others streaked his hair with butter. He woke up and found it melting down his face as the others fell over themselves laughing. He flipped out and threatened to open the plane door midflight until they apologized.[19] Food fights, racing their Spyders and Lamborghinis, laughing when they smashed the other's car, the whole fantasy.

"They were kind of a yobs' band, but stylish with it," Sex Pistol Jones wrote. "They had an approachability."[20] Unlike Zep or Floyd. It was the

Faces' tempo Jones and Pistols drummer Paul Cook adopted, not the blitz-krieg of the Ramones. Charlie Hart, a pianist who later played with bass-ist Ronnie Lane, said, "It's a band that you would never see in the States because they took so many elements of blues, country, folk, you name it, and they threw that all together into something that no American band would ever do."[21]

Originally, Rod Stewart signed with a label as a solo artist just before Wood brought him into the band, so Stewart alternated Faces albums with solo re-leases (on which Faces often played). Then "Maggie May" exploded, and it became Rod Stewart and the Faces. On the one hand, Stewart's superstardom benefited everyone. On the other hand, he skipped the first two weeks of recording their fourth album, *Ooh La La*. But the best songs didn't need him anyway. The warm, rustic title track was the ultimate pub sing-along, later fea-tured at the end of Wes Anderson's *Rushmore*. Wood sang it so well you won-der why he never sang a Rolling Stones song in forty-two years. Lane's "Glad and Sorry" was the other standout, carried along by Ian McLagan's hypnotic piano riff and the gentle harmonies of Lane, McLagan, and Wood.

Perhaps because he was outshone, Stewart proceeded to bash the album in the music press, calling it "stinking rotten," "a bloody mess." Lane already had post-traumatic stress from when the Small Faces' *first* lead singer, Steve Marriott, left them in the lurch to form Humble Pie with Peter Frampton. Maybe Lane was paranoid from the refrain in Stewart's track "Cindy In-cidentally" about how it was time to move on. He decided to bail before Stewart did. Partly it was the same problem George Harrison had in the Beatles—Lane wanted more than a couple of slots per album to sing his own stuff. Lane's friend Pete Townshend advised him to stay in and get rich off the publishing. Nevertheless, Lane left after a final gig in London on June 4, which he later conceded was a mistake.

He soon issued "The Poacher," which sounded like the majestic theme of some forgotten Technicolor classic. He recorded the title track of *Anymore for Anymore* live, outside on his hundred-acre sheep farm in Wales. You could hear his kids playing, the livestock, and the breeze.[22] "Roll On Baby" sounded like he was singing with his family around a campfire outside his crumbling barn, hopeful for a future without prima donnas.

✳

Rock historians today often include Deep Purple with Zep-pelin and Sabbath as the founders of heavy metal. This mystifies young metal heads, to whom the old music sounds relatively soft. Purple originally

sounded a bit like Steppenwolf and stood out because instead of two guitars they had a guitarist (Ritchie Blackmore) and organist (Jon Lord) who
merged the blues with classical music like Bach. They wanted to play with
big orchestras and go prog, but when that flopped, Blackmore decided it
was time to prove he could outrock Page and Sabbath's Tony Iommi. "It's
not that I think I'm the greatest guitarist in the world—I am, but that's
got nothing to do with it."[23] His high-speed shredding and skill with the
whammy bar and finger-tapping made him, as the Ultimate Guitar website
put it, the link between Jimi Hendrix and Eddie Van Halen.[24] But his biggest
hit was super simple, which sometimes irritated him later.

The lyrics of "Smoke on the Water" spell out in Hemingway-esque detail
how the band arrived in Montreaux, France, to record their next album.
Frank Zappa was playing a gig at the casino across the lake when an audience member fired a flare gun and set the building on fire. Purple watched
from the distance as Zappa and "Funky Claude" Nobs of the Montreaux Jazz
Festival helped people escape while the building burned to the ground.
The next morning bassist Roger Glover woke up with the words "smoke on
the water" in his head, so lead singer Ian Gillan wrote lyrics to go with it.[25]
Blackmore came up with the riff on his Fender Stratocaster. Jon Lord mirrored the guitar with his organ hooked up to a distorted Marshall amp. Ian
Paice fell in with the hi-hat and snare. Glover strutted in with the ultimate
Spinal Tap "Big Bottom" bass line. Then Gillan recounted the event, elabo-
rating on their moderate anxiety over the deadline to turn in the album,
and how they were worried about securing a new recording facility before
finally booking the "Rolling truck Stones thing" (the Stones' mobile studio).
Which was a rather specific lyrical concern for a tune to which thuggish
heshers would soon whip their hair in slow motion around bonfires in a
haze of turpentine and PCP.

The song was included on 1972's *Machine Head* and the live album *Made
in Japan,* but they figured it was just an album track. Still, the phones lit up
whenever a deejay in Pittsburgh played it. Then Edgar Winter topped the
charts in May with "Frankenstein," with a riff that sounded like a funked-
up version of "Smoke." Winter's song initially appeared on his album *They
Only Come Out at Night* seven months after *Machine Head,* so maybe he'd
been influenced by it. Whatever the case, the label released "Smoke" as a
single in May with the live version on the flip side, which was similar to the
studio version but included hand claps, had a slightly meatier sound, and
was slightly faster.

"Smoke" became the riff all the kids used to test out guitars in guitar shops, after "Stairway to Heaven." They actually played a dumbed-down version, though, not the proper Blackmore version, in which you pluck stacked fourths with fingers in the third position starting on the A and D strings, never with a pick (per his *Guitar Player* interview).[26] The song title also sounded like a bong, which helped.

✳

If someone had asked you before 1971 what band you thought would tie the Beatles for selling out Shea Stadium, Grand Funk Railroad probably would not have been your guess. But they rocked as hard as the other Detroit bands (Stooges, Nugent) while being pretty boys in MC5 afros whose manager had been around and knew how to leverage the system.

They weren't phony, though. It was hard to be phony from Flint, Michigan, an hour north of Detroit, home to autoworkers and Michael Moore. Their bassist was from Question Mark and the Mysterians ("96 Tears"). Rod Stewart called them the "all-time loud white noise" in *Rolling Stone*. Vietnam soldiers embraced "I'm Your Captain," their upgrade of the Who's "Rael."

But after the peak of Shea, their sales were going down, so Capitol Records brought in golden boy producer Todd Rundgren to right the trajectory. "It was almost timed down to the minute. They had already set the release date for the single 'We're an American Band' before we'd ever gone into the studio," Rundgren told *Ultimate Classic Rock*. "We did the track the first day, and the second day we finished the overdubs and mixed it and mastered it. . . . We were still in the studio, I think it was only a week or two later, finishing up the [album] when 'We're An American Band' was already in the Top 10! [It went to No. 1] . . . It was just an amazing and fortunate combination of the music and the promotion. . . . If it hadn't been good music, then all of this promotion would have been for nothing. . . . It was really the heyday of the record labels and the power that they had."[27]

The "sweet, sweet Connie" of the first verse was real-life Connie Hamzy. When the band sang that she had "the whole show," they meant the band *and* the roadies. By that time the eighteen-year-old had become famous for her oral skills among the rockers who passed through Little Rock, like Steppenwolf and Three Dog Night. Per Pamela Des Barres's *Let's Spend the Night Together: Backstage Secrets of Rock Muses and Supergroupies,* after Grand Funk's song came out, she went on to hook up with, Kiss, the Who, Alice Cooper, Black Oak Arkansas, Waylon Jennings, Jimmy Page, the Eagles, Fleetwood Mac, the Stones, ZZ Top, and Doc Severenson, and "all the members of Chicago while everyone watched the proceedings."[28] "One time, with the Allman Brothers, I was with 24 guys," she told Howard Stern.[29] Her hor-rified parents threatened to send her to a "juvenile home" or "the nuthouse," but "it was never a question that I'd graduate high school and go to college because I knew the bands and crews wouldn't respect me if I was just some drop out loser."[30]

✳

Americans loved a lot of British rock, but some bands didn't trans-late. Slade had six No. 1 singles in England, but even "Cum on Feel the Noize" didn't get higher than No. 100 in the States. Americans gradually learned to process it over the ensuing years when Kiss retooled it into "Rock and Roll All Nite" and AC/DC built on Noddy Holder's style of howling. When Quiet Riot brought the song back out again a decade later, they rode it to No. 5.

Americans also couldn't process Hawkwind: Pink Floyd space rockers with a future Motorhead founder on bass alternating between sci-fi epipha-nies and Stooges knock-offs about hippie terrorists, bathed in liquid light shows accompanied by a nude phosphorescent goddess doing interpreta-tive dance.

They formed in Ladbroke Grove, London's version of Haight-Ashbury, where hippies squatted in abandoned houses, later home to the Clash. Fan-tasy author Michael Moorcock often penned their lyrics. Most of the band enjoyed taking acid and visualizing themselves as barbarians who'd hijacked a spaceship,[31] but synth/keyboardist Dik Mik liked speed and wanted an-other guy in the band to do it with. So he gave the bass to roadie Ian Fraser "Lemmy" Kilmister.[32] "I learned to play bass onstage with Hawkwind. . . . It's not like having a bass player; it's like having a deep guitarist."[33]

Nineteen-year-old bookbinder Stacia Blake had an equally easy initia-tion. "I just asked if I could get up and dance and they said yes so I took my clothes off and I danced. At that time most of the audience didn't bother wearing clothes so it wasn't a big deal." Covered in Day-Glo paint, she swayed her hips in time, used the moves she'd learned in ballet, and blew bubbles into the swirling lights. "Remember that song, 'Accept Me for What I Am?' Well, that's me. I don't diet or anything and besides I'm too fond of Guinness."[34]

"She was an impressive woman," Lemmy recounted. "She was six foot two, a fifty-two-inch bust. She was an overwhelming sight for the young-sters in the crowd. And she used to pull them, man. Bring them back to the hotel, you know. I shared a hotel room with her for two tours and it was really fucking funny, you know, to see these kids who thought it was their birthday—and in a way it was."[35]

The band made a brief excursion to the US, and she began dating the New York Dolls' Arthur Kane, also very tall. Her makeup designs took on some Kiss overtones as well, though it's unclear who influenced who.

The Space Ritual Alive in Liverpool and London double album included tracks like "Space Is Deep," which sounded like a mixture of Sabbath, Velvet Underground, and early Floyd, but more uplifting. In "Down Through the Night" and "Born to Go," Lemmy's bass prefigures goth rock like "Bela Lugosi's Dead" mixed with flutes, Moog, tape loops, and audio generator, a contraption that made weird oscillating tones.

"Friends used to hold me down and stick drugs in my mouth," saxophonist Nik Turner recalled. "I did a gig where the audience all turned into skeletons. You just think, *My God, I'll look the other way.* And it goes away, and all the wires turn into snakes. And you just know that it's a hallucination. So it's not something you take seriously. You just carry on playing. And it all sort of works out in the end. You see people with vampire teeth and blood dripping down their face, turning green. But you know they are hallucinations, and you just ignore them, really."[36]

Probably the drugs impacted the decision to follow up their No. 3 UK smash "Silver Machine" with "Urban Guerilla" in July. The song bore a distinct similarity to the Stooges' "Search and Destroy," released in February. Iggy Pop's "street walking cheetah" is replaced by a "two-tone panther" making bombs in his cellar. Hawkwind had done a benefit for members of the Angry Brigade, revolutionaries akin to America's Weather Underground who bombed banks and embassies to protest Vietnam. Defenders of the Brigade argued that their efforts were meant only to draw attention to their issue and resulted in only one injury. But in March the IRA (Provisional Irish Republican Army) began *its* car bomb campaign in London to protest England's involvement in Ireland. "Urban Guerilla" was banned by the BBC and removed from stores. "The best thing we made," Lemmy rued. "Went down like a concrete parachute, that."[37]

We're Coming Out

Artists fight back against gay oppression: Lance Loud becomes the first "out" TV star, "Walk on the Wild Side" reaches No. 16 on April 28, *The Rocky Horror Picture Show* debuts on June 19, and Bowie-mania reaches its peak in the United Kingdom.

✳

On February 17, Lou Reed's tribute to the transvestite stars of Andy Warhol movies, "Walk on the Wild Side," made its first appearance on the *Billboard* Top 100, debuting at 92.[1] At that time, a poll by the National Opinion Research Center at the University of Chicago found that 70 percent of Americans felt same-sex relations were "always wrong." Thirty-five percent opposed allowing gays to speak in public.

For gays, being honest about their sexuality could result in isolation, harassment, being disowned by their family, and losing their job or children. Laws against sodomy were in place in all but a handful of states. In October 1972, the Supreme Court declined to review *Baker v. Nelson,* a case to legalize gay marriage. Relatively liberal publications like *The New York Times* and *Rolling Stone* featured reviewers who threw the f-slur around without a second thought.

In January in New York, three gay men were stabbed to death in their apartment, and two more murder victims were found in the Hudson River. The cases were never solved. On June 24 in New Orleans, an arsonist used a can of accelerant to set a gay club called the Up Stairs Lounge on fire, killing thirty-two. Many churches would not allow funerals for the victims; some families did not claim the bodies.[2]

When a woman wrote to evangelist Billy Graham regarding her love for another woman, he replied in a newspaper column titled "Homosexual Perversion a Sin That's Never Right." "Your affection for another of your own sex is misdirected, and you will be judged by God's holy standards," he wrote. "Reformation is possible. . . . Seize it while there's still a chance." William Masters of the Masters and Johnson sex research team promoted a conversion therapy program from 1968 to 1977.

On the February 20 episode of ABC's *Marcus Welby, M.D.,* Welby (Robert Young) attempts to help a patient who is suicidal because he's gay by telling him he's not really gay—just scared that he *might* be gay, because he was ignored by his father. Welby consoles him that he can win the "fight" and be "normal" if he sees a psychiatrist.

A script was leaked to the Gay Activists Alliance, an organization founded in December 1969 after the Stonewall riots. Inspired by the Yippies' political theater, they staged "zaps" to focus attention on prejudice. First, they wrote a letter to ABC's standards and practices department complaining about the episode; then they met with ABC executives. When the executives told them they still planned to air the episode, thirty to forty GAA members picketed the New York office. Twenty-five picketed the Los Angeles County Medical Association, quacking and waving signs reading MARCUS WELBY, WITCH DOCTOR. When they attempted to take over the ABC president's office, six were arrested, though the charges were dropped.

Before *Welby* aired, however, there were two positive milestones in gay television history. On the January 13 episode of *The Mary Tyler Moore Show,* Phyllis (Cloris Leachman) tries to set Mary up with her brother (Robert Moore) and is frustrated when he takes up with her nemesis Rhoda (Valerie Harper) instead, until Rhoda reveals at the end of the episode that Phyllis's brother is actually gay. During the filming, when Rhoda told Phyllis, the live audience laughed for over four minutes. Show creator James Brooks later explained that the premise was suggested by actor Robert Moore, who was gay, only after the original ending didn't work.

Even more revolutionary was the reality TV program that debuted January 11, *An American Family,* featuring TV's first recurring out star, Lance Loud, age twenty when the episodes were shot. "When I was really at my wildest, I was visiting my dad at his office, I was wearing tons of makeup, bracelets, necklaces, and perfume. I was a total terror."[3] On one segment he dyed his hair purple and wore blue lipstick, startling for the heartland at the time.

Back when he was thirteen, he read a magazine article about Andy Warhol and Edie Sedgwick, became obsessed, dyed his hair silver like his hero, and wrote him a letter. Warhol wrote him back saying to give him a call, and they corresponded until Warhol was shot in 1968. "I was so influenced by [Warhol], in the idea of being outrageous," Loud said. "I felt like I was in *Chelsea Girls II,* the sequel."[4]

He lived in the Chelsea Hotel, in fact. When his mother visited him during an episode, transgender Warhol superstar Holly Woodlawn made a cameo. Mother and son attended a transvestite variety show at La MaMa featuring other Warhol regulars Jackie Curtis and Ondine. Lance met Sedgwick in the last episode, the very night she died in her sleep from alcohol and barbiturate poisoning.

Feminist writer Anne Roiphe (who wrote the book that inspired Streisand's 1972 movie *Up the Sandbox*) wrote a bigoted essay on the show for *The New York Times Magazine* in which she labeled Lance the "evil flower" of the family, with "flamboyant, leechlike, homosexuality . . . camping and queening about like a pathetic court jester, a Goya-esque emotional dwarf." She even speculated that the father cheated on the mother because "the disappointment, puzzlement, haunting shadow such a son as Lance must be . . . may have driven him to prove himself with others."

"I was horrified,"[5] Loud recalled of reading the review. "I got three Bibles from different religious factions. Of course, they just burst into flames the second I opened the pages. And I got a lot of letters from gay guys—gay suburban kids—who thanked me for being a voice of outrage in a bland fucking normal middle-class world."[6]

✳

Originally Lou Reed was commissioned to write a title song for a play based on Nelson Algren's novel *A Walk on the Wild Side,* about a drifter who tracks down his ex to her new job in a New Orleans brothel. The connection made sense, as Algren's earlier novel *The Man with the Golden Arm* concerned heroin addiction, a theme of some of Reed's most notorious songs. But the play fell through, leaving Reed with a melody and title.

When David Bowie began producing Reed's *Transformer,* he was fascinated to hear Reed's stories about Warhol's Factory. Its legendary '60s parties were already receding into nostalgia as the Factory grew quieter in the aftermath of Warhol's attempted assassination. Reed unearthed an old note-book in which he had jotted down quotes from the regulars. Some lines inspired album tracks like "Vicious" and "Andy's Chest." And Reed decided how to flesh out "Wild Side." The Kinks had caused a stir with their ode to one cross-dresser in "Lola"—so why not a song about three?

The song opens with Holly Woodlawn (Haroldo Rodriguez Danhakl) hitchhiking from Florida to the Big Apple, where he refashions himself into a Jean Harlow type named after Holly Golightly. "At the age of 16, when most kids were cramming for trigonometry exams, I was turning tricks, liv-ing off the streets and wondering when my next meal was coming."[7] Wood-lawn attended a Factory screening of the movie *Flesh* and met Jackie Curtis, who began casting Woodlawn in her plays, which led to a role in Warhol's *Trash*. It features one of the most disturbing scenes in Warhol's oeuvre, based on how Woodlawn really met her sixteen-year-old boyfriend Johnny Put-nam, who played himself in the scene.[8] She lures him to her apartment with the promise to sell him marijuana, then offers to shoot him up with heroin instead. When he passes out from the drug, she mauls him.

Reed next turns his attention to the most feminine-looking of the three, Candy Darling, charming the back room of Max's Kansas City, the favored haunt of the Warholians, and "giving head." For the US edition of the single, the label dropped the sound out during the phrase, as it did with "colored girls." The UK censors didn't know what "head" meant and let it fly.

Jackie Curtis "speeds away" thinking she's "James Dean." Curtis wrote plays the three of them acted in, as did actors like Robert De Niro and Patti Smith. She also pioneered the "glitter/lipstick/torn clothes" look the New York Dolls appropriated.

The song's Little Joe (Dellasandro) played a junkie prostitute in the tril-ogy *Flesh, Trash,* and *Heat,* the model for *Midnight Cowboy.* Dellasandro had been a foster kid, a runaway, and a car thief, expelled from school for hitting the principal and sent to juvenile detention.[9] He survived on the streets through nude modeling. By the time he made the films, he was married with kids. Sugar Plum Fairy was dealer Joe Campbell, an actor in Warhol's *My Hustler* and the former boyfriend of gay activist Harvey Milk. Reed said his nickname was too cool not to use.

The song became the theme song for New York after midnight in the era between Stonewall and AIDS. On Pier 48 in the meatpacking district, trucks were loaded with cargo from ships by day, then left empty at night, with the back doors lefts open for orgies that started rolling around ten, peaked at two, and ended at dawn.

One of the trucks' regulars was Patti Smith's former boyfriend Robert Mapplethorpe, who had his first solo gallery show that year, "Polaroids." Often he sported the "clone" look the model wore on the back of *Transformer*: button-fly Levi's, T-shirt, leather cap, aviator jacket, work boots. Another regular was Wayne County, the cross-dressing proto-punk artist who mounted a stage show, *Wayne at the Trucks,* funded by Bowie's manager.

Five dollars got you into the Continental Baths. One floor had a gymnasium with a pool, another had the dance floor. Guys boogied in bathing suits or towels or in the nude, the smell of amyl nitrate thick in the steam. You could rent one of the four hundred private rooms for $15. Nicky Siano, the deejay of the Gallery disco, and later Studio 54, remembered one twenty-four-hour period when he made it with seventeen guys there.[10] Baths frequenter Steve Wallace recalled, "If you went to the Baths and there were twenty guys in the steam room, half an hour later you came out and you'd had some sexual contact with at least half of the guys in that steam room. And then after another half an hour, I'd go in the Jacuzzi, then I'd go in the sauna, then the whirlpool. . . . By the time I'd left, I'd have had some sexual contact with 150 different people."[11] The vending machines carried K-Y jelly, the showers offered anti-lice shampoo, and there was a VD clinic on site.

Founder Steve Ostrow said the place was busted more than two hundred times. "Homosexuality was illegal. Two men dancing together was illegal. Very good-looking policemen would come in, rent a room, get into a towel, go into the steam room and then wait for someone to touch them. And then, from underneath the towel, out would come handcuffs. Then they'd arrest everybody in the place."[12]

Bette Midler (a.k.a. "Bathhouse Betty") rose to fame there, accompanied on piano by her musical director, Barry Manilow. As she grew more popular, other artists signed up to play: Patti LaBelle, Nell Carter (later of the TV series *Gimme a Break*), the Pointer Sisters, Lesley Gore—even older acts like the Andrews Sisters and Cab Calloway, and oddballs like the New York Dolls and comedian Andy Kaufman. Soon it became chic with celebrities like Mick Jagger. Alfred Hitchcock attended, according to Ostrow. "He wouldn't have any sex with anyone; he would just come, watch, look at people, swim in the tub and then leave."[13] Hetero couples could watch the shows, but women had to leave after.

❋

Transformer featured another song, "Make Up," about donning eyeliner, lip gloss, and lacey gowns, with a chorus proclaiming, "We're coming out of our closets." For the cover, he did a goth variation on glam, with pale pancake makeup, black lipstick, and black-rimmed eyes like the somnambulist in *The Cabinet of Dr. Caligari*. Onstage, he added glitter eye shadow and silver high heels, camping it up with Jagger and Bowie moves.

Suddenly it seemed like it was raining transvestites. In February, the drag queen farce *La Cage aux Folles* made its French debut, running for 1,800 performances and inspiring Robin Williams and Nathan Lane's *The Birdcage*. Divine starred in John Waters's *Pink Flamingos*. The two were determined to "out-filth" their heroes Andy Warhol and Paul Morrissey, and succeeded when Divine ate dog poop on-screen. New York's Elgin Theater initially booked it for one night only, but it turned into the theater's next sensation after *El Topo,* running six nights a week for forty-eight weeks. And while Joel Grey was not a transvestite, he won the Oscar in March for *Cabaret*'s high-camp master of ceremonies, rouged, lipsticked, and heavily eyelashed.

The representation wasn't all good-humored. Ralph Bakshi, the filmmaker who brought Robert Crumb's *Fritz the Cat* to the screen, rendered a drag queen named Snowflake who enjoyed being beaten by a hardhat construction worker in *Heavy Traffic,* just one reason why it was possibly the most offensive film of the year.

The most enduring of them all was the Sweet Transvestite from Transsexual, Transylvania, who arrived onstage that June in the London premiere of *The Rocky Horror Picture Show.*

Actor Richard O'Brien wrote the show and played Riff Raff, who sang "The Time Warp." Balding with long blond hair, he looked not unlike Brian Eno. He'd heard Bowie was going to do a Ziggy Stardust stage play, but when it didn't materialize he wrote his own. Drawing on the nostalgia for '50s pop culture that swept both sides of the Atlantic that year, he composed songs like "Science Fiction Double Feature" to advance a convoluted plot about an innocent couple trapped in a gloomy mansion with space aliens, a mad scientist, and a Frankenstein monster inspired by the muscle magazines that predated gay porn. During preproduction, the team studied Russ Meyer's camp classic *Beyond the Valley of the Dolls,* featuring Dr. Frankenfurter's forefather, the transgender Z-Man. Richard O'Brien himself began estrogen therapy in 2003. "Being transgender is a card you're dealt, and you don't know how to deal with it because society doesn't allow it."[14]

Tim Curry came to attention playing an S&M housekeeper in a black corset in *The Maids*, a Jean Genet play directed by Bowie mentor Lindsay Kemp. When Curry was cast in *Rocky Horror,* he added fishnets and heels to the corset and drew on Disney villainesses such as *Snow White*'s Evil Queen and Cruella de Vil to flesh out his look.

It was the fishnets that made his image so disturbing to many straight men, conditioned as they were for Pavlovian arousal whenever they saw stockings and garter belts in magazines. First came the initial sexual response, then the eyes climbed up the body—only to find a man's head with evil eyebrows leering like the Joker, prompting society's homophobic conditioning to come flooding in.

The film metaphorically crystallized the time warp many Norman Rockwell–esque couples found themselves in when confronted by swingers at parties, finding that maybe they did want to embrace their illicit lust. Within a few years, the film adaptation leapfrogged over *El Topo, Pink Flamingos,* and *The Harder They Come* to become the ultimate midnight movie phenomenon, creating a safe haven where misfits could find others like themselves to dance and sing show tunes with, free from aggro meatheads, a tradition captured in the movie *Confessions of a Wallflower.* It survived as a movable glam holiday where people could find their tribe long after the glam movement died out.

The show wouldn't have had legs without some great songs. "The Time Warp" was written as an excuse to give "Little Nell" Campbell a chance to display her tap-dancing skills. "Hot Patootie" was an even better '50s pastiche than "Crocodile Rock." When the play moved to Los Angeles, Meat Loaf's rendition paved the way for his mega success with *Bat Out of Hell.* "Touch-a, Touch-a, Touch-a, Touch Me" summarized the women's movement's emergence from repressed innocence to carnal maturity. Unbound by censors, it was even more direct than Sylvia's "Pillow Talk," radio's orgasm of the year. And, of course, there was Curry's tour de force "Sweet Transvestite."

Brian Connolly of the Sweet called the show "the Spinal Tap of the 1970s. It took everything that was going on in rock—the drag, the fifties, the science fiction—and took them to ridiculous extremes."[15]

Soon Jagger and Bianca, Bowie and Angela, Marianne Faithfull, Keith Moon, Sam Shepard, Vincent Price, Tennessee Williams, and Andrew Lloyd Weber squeezed into the mere sixty-three seats of the Royal Court's Theatre Upstairs. The play quickly moved to King's Road for the next six years. Across the street the future manager of the New York Dolls and Sex Pistols, Malcolm McLaren, and his girlfriend Vivienne Westwood ran a boutique called Too Fast to Live Too Young to Die.

✳

Reed's collaboration with Bowie would be one of his most memorable works even if you stripped away the defiant gender politics and Factory nostalgia. "*Transformer* is easily my best-produced album," he told journalist Nick Kent. "That has a lot to do with Mick Ronson. No, his influence was stronger than David's—but together, as a team, they're terrific."[16]

Ronson arranged the subtle violins for "Wild Side." The instrumental track is a master class in how to sustain repeated listening through minimalism. Bowie played acoustic guitar in the right channel, Ronson an electric in the left. John Halsey displayed impressive dexterity with drum bass pedal and hi-hat brushes. Bowie enlisted his sax teacher Ronnie Ross. Although Reed sang they were "colored," backup singers Karen Friedman, Dari Lalou, and Casey Synge were white; they recorded their own singles as Thunderthighs.

The track was a glimpse into an alternate rock reality where bands had two bassists. Session musician Herbie Flowers played the large acoustic stand-up bass for the verses. For the intro and choruses he overdubbed an electric bass guitar an octave higher in tone. He made the suggestion because session musicians received double the £12 pay for overdubs. Soon afterward, the producer for David Essex's "Rock On" sought Flowers out to re-create the vibe for that Top 5 hit.

Ronson made Reed as accessible as he ever got with the string arrangements on "Satellite of Love" and "Perfect Day" (a gentle account of an early date with future wife Bettye Kronstad). "Boy, Ronson's good," Reed commented as he listened back to the tracks during a *Classic Albums* television documentary.

Reed originally recorded "Satellite" with the Velvets for the *Loaded* album in 1970 but left it off. It was the perfect song to revive with Mr. "Space Oddity" and was released as the album's second single in February. "[Bowie] has a melodic sense that's just well above anyone else in rock and roll. Most people could not sing some of his melodies. He can really go for a high note," Reed said. "There's a part at the very end where his voice goes all the way up. It's fabulous."[17]

The album peaked at No. 29 the week of April 28, the highest he ever made it on the US charts, except for 1974's *Sally Can't Dance*.

Bowie's *Aladdin Sane* debuted in the UK's No. 1 spot when it was released on April 13. He was England's bestselling artist that year, with a No. 2 hit, "The Jean Genie," and three No. 3s: "Drive-in Saturday," "Sorrow," and "Life on Mars?" (the latter from 1971's *Hunky Dory*). Even a bizarre novelty single of his from 1967 was reissued and made No. 6—"The Laughing Gnome," which sounded like Alvin and the Chipmunks visiting Middle Earth. Like Elvis and the Beatles before him, Bowie amassed a large back catalog before he made it, so when he broke through there was a tidal wave of product to unleash on new fans.

"He validated me and made me realize I was not alone," recalled Boy George, who saw him live in '73.[18] Boy George looked even more androgynous nine years later but generated only a fraction of the shock value. In January 1973, it was considered edgy when Bowie wore chandelier earrings on Russell Harty's weekend talk show. Onstage he cavorted in miniskirts, lingerie, boa, and knee boots, when not wearing Speedos or sumo loincloths.

Ultimately, Bowie's assault on homophobia added up to about six judo chops: wearing a dress on *The Man Who Sold the World*'s cover; posing like Lauren Bacall on *Hunky Dory*; telling *Melody Maker*, "I'm gay and always have been"; putting his arm around Mick Ronson during "Starman" on *Top of the Pops* in July 1972; kneeling before Ronson and biting his guitar string while grabbing his hips in a photo; and kissing Lou Reed in another.

"I belong to a generation that probably has to thank Queer David for the comparative ease with which we came out," John Gill wrote in *Queer Noises,* "at a time when appearances in the media tended to be in the form of arrests and police statistics. Queer David's clever (if ultimately meaningless) packaging of sexual outrage created a safe space where many of us, gay, bi, and straight, could play out games and experiment with difference, finding ourselves and going through the motions of teenage rebellion, in a way that not even punk could imitate."[19]

"As a young trans person, long before 'trans' had any real cultural currency, that is, before I could name myself, listening to [Bowie] changed everything," writer Alex Sharpe wrote. "It was simultaneously: recognition, connection and hope, that moment when we sense something more, something different, something richer."[20]

In Todd Haynes's film about the glam movement, *Velvet Goldmine,* the young protagonist sees the Bowie character on the tube and cries excitedly, "That's me! That's me!"

"No matter what or who you've been, I'll help you with the pain / Just turn on with me, and you're not alone," Bowie sang in "Rock and Roll Suicide" at the end of each show that year. "Gimme your hands, 'cause you're wonderful."

＊

AOR, Prog, and Yacht Rock

The heyday of progressive radio winds down as programmers figure out how to cash in on album-oriented rock. Prog rock peaks, Genesis just misses the UK Top 20, and Queen makes their album debut. Yacht rock begins to take shape as the Doobie Brothers, Steely Dan, and Hall & Oates hit their stride.

＊

Originally, AM radio had sister FM stations that played mostly identical content. But in 1965, the FCC decreed there weren't enough FM channels around to waste, so they had to broadcast at least 50 percent different programming than their AM siblings. FM pioneers like San Francisco's Tom Donahue bought struggling stations and began focusing on deep cuts from albums. AM didn't like to play songs that were over three and a half minutes or had lyrics about drugs or (overt) sex. But FM deejays could play what they wanted, mix genres, talk about the war—and they didn't have to run commercials. Some bands began selling huge amounts of albums through FM exposure without even releasing singles.

In September 1971, New York's WPLJ decided to apply the tight format of Top 40 to FM.[1] The station told its deejays to cut down on the rapping and focus on the most popular cuts from top-selling albums by big bands like

Led Zeppelin, the Beatles, and Cream. Its ratings skyrocketed, allowing it to charge the advertisers more. ABC owned WPLJ and introduced the format to some of its other stations, KLOS in Los Angeles and WRIF in Detroit.[2]

Meanwhile, Ron Jacobs of San Diego's KGB-AM/FM began using hardcore data to improve ratings. He dispatched researchers to interview almost four thousand San Diego residents.[3] The researchers noted the interviewees' demographic information and asked them about the records they bought, the stations they listened to, and what times they listened.[4] The info was plugged into a computer and it printed out graphs that indicated when listening peaked and waned for specific groups of people who liked specific records.[5] Jacobs thought it might have been one of the first times such graphs were created. They broke the audiences down by race and by age (10–13-year-olds, 14–15-year-olds, 16-year-olds) and showed what stations each group listened to and what times they listened.[6] Osmonds listeners were 12–14 years old, Sabbath listeners 15–17, Grateful Dead listeners 18–20, Elvis 25+, etc. etc.[7]

"I'm sitting here until 4 a.m. with (promo man) Rick Williams and we're like two mad freaks going over this information last March [1972], and no one had seen this before," Jacobs recalled. "Then we put [the new format] on the radio and we have to wait ten months for a rating to come out and tell us we're doing the right thing. I mean, that was like a long, dark tunnel . . . with not too many people saying, 'You guys are right on.'"[8]

But in August 1973 *Billboard* named Jacobs the Progressive Contemporary Rock Program Director of the Year at its Radio Programming Forum. Jacobs's statistical analysis soon upended FM radio, not unlike the way sabermetrics changed pro baseball, as recounted in the book and film *Moneyball.* "This data allowed us to move, for the first time, out on a scientific premise," Jacobs said.[9]

New York deejay Mike Harrison wanted "the opportunity to go head-to-head [against] Jacobs," so he took a job at San Diego's KPRI, a "weak-signal station" that was "getting its clock cleaned" by Jacobs's KGB.[10] Harrison also brought the AM Top 40 approach to FM. "You have to give [listeners] what they want. It was apparent when I played the best progressive rock music I had better ratings than when I showed hippie friends how much esoteric music I knew. It sounds quaint today, but those were major issues in FM music radio's [early] days."[11]

Additionally, he joined the staff of the trade magazine *Radio and Records,* founded in 1973 as a competitor to *Billboard.* "I had a beef with *Billboard* because they only wrote about Ron Jacobs. They didn't show any interest whatsoever in what I was doing. I told [founder] Bob [Wilson] I'd be his FM Rock Editor and began [*Radio and Records*'s] AOR section."[12] Harrison believed advertisers dismissed FM rock radio because they thought the audience was too young and too fringe. "MOR [Middle of the Road] was a very popular term and I thought AOR would work. 'Progressive' was more descriptive about subjective determination [while] 'Album Oriented Rock' was objective. Radio didn't know how to research albums—they just researched singles."[13]

From Detroit's WRIF, program director Lee Abrams brought the new format to WQRD in Raleigh, North Carolina.[14] The goal was to make the station "as commercial as possible without losing progressive identity" through "familiarity" (playing the same songs and artists frequently) and "jock discipline."[15] Program directors began telling deejays they could only pick from a handful of "focus tracks" on new albums or just gave them playlists.

The new wave of program directors increasingly "narrowcasted" their playlists to lure the young white listeners advertisers paid the most to reach. The catholic or "unformatted" approach of many AM stations—where pop, rock, R&B, and easy listening intermingled[16]—began to recede. In 1973, ten of the twenty-seven No. 1 hits were by black artists (if you included Dawn, a mixed group).[17] In 1980, there were three No. 1s by black artists; 1981 had one by Kool and the Gang and a duet by Diana Ross and Lionel Richie; 1982 had one black No. 1, while arena rock and yacht rock flourished.

✳

The Beatles' concert at Shea Stadium on August 15, 1965, was the first time a rock band played a stadium. The problem was that the 100-volt amps run through the stadium's PA system were no match for 55,600 people screaming, even for Ringo. "I could not hear anything. I'd be watching John's arse, Paul's arse, his foot tapping his head nodding, to see where we were in the song."[18]

Flash forward to February 9, 1973, when the Grateful Dead played the Stanford University pavilion: sound man Stanley Owsley combined six sound systems of amps, speakers, tweeters, and subwoofers to assemble the Wall of Sound, more than three stories tall and nearly a hundred feet wide. Each instrument had its own speaker. Bassist Phil Lesh had a different speaker for each string. The bass drum had a speaker, as did the snare, the tom-toms, and the cymbals. Since each speaker handled only one element, distortion was almost eliminated. The band kicked in with their opening number, Chuck Berry's "Promised Land."[19]

And the speakers shorted out. It was back to the drawing board for Owsley for the next year. After the Wall's Sound Test at San Francisco's Cow Palace on March 23, 1974, it blasted sound for a quarter to half a mile on tour.[20] But it weighed seventy-five tons, requiring twenty-one roadies to transport it in four semis during the height of the oil crisis, so the band abandoned it after seven months.[21]

Even less ambitious sound systems made the Beatles' problem a thing of the past, opening the arenas to the bands, which in turn made them focus on composing grandiose anthems with guitar pyrotechnics that could inspire crowds to pump their fists and lift their lighters. Some historians theorize the lighter tradition started with the Doors' "Light My Fire." By the time of Woodstock, it was prevalent enough that Melanie wrote "(Lay Down) Candles in the Rain" about all the lighters she saw ignited by the crowd.[22]

For the outsized egos of progressive rock, enormous audiences were their due. It *was* perhaps the most ambitious scene happening, determined to fuse rock with classical, jazz, and experimental. Bands like Yes, Jethro Tull, King Crimson, and Emerson, Lake & Palmer, believed they were developing the most advanced music *of all fucking time.* Suites took up entire sides of triple albums, with multiple time changes and double bass drums that most hacks with their measly three chords could never dream of playing. Teenaged and twentysomething males loved to watch the prodigies show off on their instruments like athletes, and if there weren't that many women in the audience[23]—well, maybe that was a relief to the chess club stoners. They could trance out and imagine worlds of Greek mythology or Tolkien or the dreamscapes William Roger Dean illustrated for Yes covers.

Prog was one of the bestselling genres that year, with No. 1 albums on the US charts by Jethro Tull, the Moody Blues, and Pink Floyd. The only problem, for some, was that the big prog three (Tull, Yes, and ELP) no longer believed they needed songs with hooks. They'd all released some great singles to establish themselves. Now, Keith Emerson twirled his keyboard around and stabbed it with a knife before heaving it across the stage to make feedback, while Carl Palmer's stainless steel drum kit with Chinese gongs and church bell spun around 360 degrees with him inside, and Greg Lake stood on a $5,000 Persian rug.[24] Paintings by their cover artist H. R. Giger (designer of *Alien*) were projected behind them 150 feet high. So who needed catchy singles?

Some elements of arena rock were still in their infancy: Cameron Crowe toured with the Who and noted, "This was the dawn of T-shirt merchandising: one stoned guy with a box of T-shirts."[25]

Two bands transcended their prog roots by incorporating other genres, including glam and metal: Genesis and Queen.

The founding members of Genesis attended one of the most expensive boarding schools in England, Charterhouse, which opened in 1611. The school banned guitars, so they slipped away into the countryside to write odes to British poets and fairies.[26] Their 1969 debut sounded as if it picked up from where the Zombies' baroque classic *Odessey and Oracle* left off. But lead singer Peter Gabriel and the others were all high-strung and got on each others' nerves like brothers, having gone to school together for so long. Keyboardist Tony Banks rankled at any suggestion that they were Gabriel's backing band. So Phil Collins was the emollient the band needed when he became their fifth drummer, bringing jazz fusion chops. He was working class, a former child actor, and had no baggage with any of them, so he could joke around with each member and keep it light.[27]

Gabriel came up with a gimmick that he put into action one night without telling the others, because he knew Banks would say no. During the instrumental section of "The Musical Box," Gabriel slipped backstage then returned transformed. "My wife, Jill, had a red Ossie Clark dress which I could just about get into, and we had a fox head made. The first time we tried it was in a former boxing ring in Dublin, and there was just a shocked silence."[28] The others didn't like it, but it won them magazine covers, which enabled them to double their fee. *New Musical Express* labeled them "Top Stage Band." So the masks kept coming. For "Watcher of the Skies," Gabriel painted his face fluorescent and donned headgear sprouting bat wings. The cover of July's *Genesis Live* showed Gabriel in costume as Magog with a head of triangles, which presumably related to Pythagoras, referenced in the Revelation-inspired "Supper's Ready." Flower heads, florid Britannia helmets, and mushroom monsters followed.

With *Selling England by the Pound*, they began to streamline toward a more radio-friendly sound. When Gabriel and Collins harmonized on "I Know What I Like (in Your Wardrobe)," you could hear the beginning of the prog pop with which the band conquered the '80s, and of Gabriel's solo work as well.

Probably the most prog aspect of Queen was the fantasy world named Rhye that recurred in songs throughout their first three albums, influenced by Freddie Bulsara's exotic roots as a Persian growing up in Zanzibar and

Bombay. In "My Fairy King" Freddie sang of horses with eagle wings, dragons, Cyclops, gnomes, ogres, and Mother Mercury—from whom he took his new surname. Like ELP, the band based a song on a famous painting, in Queen's case *The Fairy Feller's Master-Stroke* by Richard Dadd.

Their first British Top 10 was "Seven Seas of Rhye" from *Queen II,* recorded in August. Brian May achieved his unique guitar tone by running his instrument through a customized amp built by bassist John Deacon and mixing it with a homemade treble booster effects pedal.[29] "Doing All Right" included many of the elements that soon coalesced into "Bohemian Rhapsody": bittersweet piano, guitar eruptions, Beatle-esque harmonies by May and drummer Roger Taylor, and Mercury's yearning vulnerability and resolve to persevere. They found the look for the "Bohemian Rhapsody" video when they commissioned Mick Rock for the *Queen II* cover. Rock was the photographer for Bowie, Reed's *Transformer,* and the Stooges' *Raw Power.* He suggested Queen emulate Marlene Dietrich in *Shanghai Express.*[30]

✳

While prog combined classical and rock, horn bands like Chicago and Blood, Sweat & Tears mixed jazz with rock. Fusion artists like Herbie Hancock, Chick Corea, and Weather Report mixed rock into their jazz. Joni Mitchell teamed with fusion band L.A. Express. The Grateful Dead's recent addition, keyboardist Keith Godchaux, directed the band away from folk and country toward bebop and modal jazz. Steely Dan covered Duke Ellington's "East St. Louis Toodle-oo," a song referenced in William S. Burroughs's novel *Naked Lunch,* from which they got their name.

Chicago and Steely Dan embodied the gradual shift from jazz-rock into the smooth soft rock style affectionately labeled yacht rock. By the end of the decade, their voices would dominate the soundscapes of banks and supermarkets along with Michael McDonald's of the Doobie Brothers. (McDonald would get his start in Steely Dan's touring band.) But in 1973, the Doobies were still a biker band fronted by singer-guitarist Tom Johnston.

Johnston's post–Bo Diddley style, a mixture of passionate strumming and hammering on the fingerboard, made for a nice juxtaposition with the plucking "fingerstyle" of Patrick Simmons, a folk and bluegrass player.[31] They could both sing lead or harmonize. Johnston recalled, "We had a guy in the house who said, 'Why don't you call yourself the Doobie Brothers because you're always smoking.' Everybody looked at each other and said, 'Well that's really a stupid name.'"[32] They figured they'd use it for a few shows until they thought of something better, but they never did.

They got their start in Santa Cruz, about two hours south of San Francisco, at a bar called Chateau Liberté where the Hells Angels hung out among the mountain people. "Which was a little funky," Johnston said. "A lot of stabbings, shootings and kicking butts in general."[33] But the label thought it would be a good angle to hype them as the house band for bikers and their mamas, and it dressed them in sullen black leather on covers like the one for their single "Jesus Is Just Alright," which peaked at No. 35 in February. "After a while, I started to chafe at [the image] a little bit, because it wasn't really what the band was all about."[34]

They went jam band like the Dead and the Allmans by adding a second drummer and black bassist-singer Tiran Porter, with whom Simmons had played before in an acoustic trio, and found their voice with hippie anthems like "Listen to the Music." Their soaring three-part harmonies and banjo were perfect for summer festivals where dogs jumped in the air to catch Frisbees as everybody danced, their hair swaying down to their cutoffs.

Johnston came up with "China Grove" after seeing a sign for the city outside San Antonio.[35] Little Feat's Billy Payne sat in, and they stumbled across the ultimate fat riff for cruising with your speakers blasting all the way. Johnston said he owed Payne "for the words because he played this wacky bridge that started the thinking process with this wacky sheriff, samurai swords, and all that."[36] "Grove" and "Long Train Runnin'" pushed *The Captain and Me* to No. 7 that summer, their best showing yet.

While recording the album, Simmons started picking the lick for "Black Water." Producer Ted Templeman told Simmons to write a song to go with it, but Simmons didn't finish it at the time.[37] Later in the year the band was in New Orleans and he was riding a streetcar to do his laundry, daydreaming about the Mark Twain books he'd read as a kid. "The sun was shining while it was pouring rain, the way it does down there sometimes. And the lyrics just came to me there."[38] The song's image of a raft floating down the Mississippi recalled the friendship of Huck Finn and Jim, reinforcing the band's aura of interracial brotherhood, the kind Springsteen liked to highlight with Clarence Clemons. But bassist Porter thought that "Black Water" was just a throwaway,[39] and the band relegated it to a B side. Nevertheless, its feel-good sentiment of "no worries/no hurry" took off on Virginia radio, and up north in Minnesota as well—Minnesotans in the winter probably needed to hear it more than anyone else. After the song finished its unhurried ascent to No. 1, Simmons would not have to take a streetcar to do his laundry again.

✳

Chevy Chase drummed briefly in a band with Donald Fagen at Bard College in upstate New York. "Don sort of looked like a crow most of the time. He'd walk around with this beak of a nose and he always wore black clothing and looked down with his hands in his pockets. People thought he was kind of weird and quiet. They didn't realize that he was really intelligent, a very funny, bright guy."[40]

Steely Dan was college rock a decade before R.E.M., though they facetiously dubbed their music "smart rock." Instead of reviving the folk-rock jangle like R.E.M., they took their cues from the Beats, jazz, Dylan, and the Velvet Underground. Fagen sang and played keyboards, while Walter Becker—he of the long stringy hair and Fu Manchu mustache—played bass and sang backing vocals. They took their moniker from the brand of strap-on dildo preferred by transvestites and lesbians in *Naked Lunch*. The duo got their first break playing keyboards and bass for the most unhip band of the '60s, Jay and the Americans. The Americans' Kenny Vance helped them make demos and sold one to Barbra Streisand. The completely unironic "I Mean to Shine" betrayed their resolve to attain stardom themselves, even if Vance thought "they looked like insects, with no vibe coming from them. Like librarians on acid."[41] Lead singer Jay Black called them "the Manson and Starkweather of rock n' roll."[42]

But Steely Dan made it to No. 6 in February with their second single, "Do It Again." Fagen matched a Santana-like mambo with a hipster wail and a Doors-like solo busted out on his plastic Yamaha organ. His predominant theme was already in place: he was brought to his knees by two-timing women but kept going back to do it again.

In the follow-up single, "Reelin' in the Years," the conceited object of Fagen's desire worries that she's growing old and losing her opportunity to snag the good life, so she goes with the rich guy, not appreciating what she could have had with the singer. "I was always in love with someone [who] ignored me completely. That was my Bard experience. There was a *Sorrows of Young Werther* vibe about it,"[43] Fagen said, referencing Goethe's novel in which the young protagonist shoots himself over unrequited love.

The duo revealed their perfectionism when they decided the band's two guitarists (Denny Dias and Jeff "Skunk" Baxter) didn't have the "flavor" they wanted for the instrumental. Instead, they reached out to Elliott Randall, who'd played with Jay and the Americans and worked on some of their early demos. "Most of ["Reelin'"] was already complete, so I had the good fortune of having a very clear picture of what the solo was laying on top of. They played it for me without much dialog about what I should play. It just wasn't necessary because we did it in one take and nothing was written. Jeff Baxter played the harmony parts, but my entire lead—intro/answers/solo/end solo—was one continuous take. . . . The whole solo just came to me."[44] Jimmy Page later claimed it to be his all-time favorite solo.[45] *Guitar World* ranked it the thirtieth-best solo of all time. Becker and Fagen invited Randall to join the band (which would have given them three guitarists like Lynyrd Skynyrd), but he demurred. His best-known later song was Irene Cara's "Fame."

"Reelin' in the Years" peaked at No. 11 in May, an uneasy anthem for the baby boomers now plunged full-on into adulthood, with postcollege life not shaping up as planned, a companion to "American Pie" and "Running on Empty."

They recorded their biggest hit that fall, a gentler take on the unrequited scenario. In college, Fagen had been infatuated with a professor's wife, Rikki Ducornet. She would recall that "we had a great conversation and he did suggest I call him, which never happened. But I know he thought I was cute. And I was cute. [Laughing.] I was very tempted to call him, but I thought it might be a bit risky. I was very enchanted with him and with the music. It was so evident from the get-go that he was wildly talented. Being a young faculty wife and, I believe, pregnant at the time, I behaved myself, let's say. Years later, I walked into a record store and heard his voice and thought, 'That's Fagen. And that's my name!'"[46] The song hit No. 4, and she went on to become a writer herself. "I notice it walking into a sushi bar, going into a drugstore. Take an airplane, there it is. It's become a constant, something to hold onto."[47]

Initially Fagen didn't like his voice and didn't want to front the group onstage. He had the opposite of LVS, "lead vocalist syndrome," as Keith Richards termed front-man egomania. "I had a very small [vocal] range and really hardly any experience, and the [label] sort of looked at it two ways—on the one hand they wanted somebody with a bigger voice, a kind of thrilling rock 'n' roll vocalist, but I think we knew we weren't gonna find anybody who could convey the attitude, which was really the most important thing, so they wanted me to do it."[48]

They enlisted David Palmer, formerly of the Myddle Class, to sing the majority of songs in concert, and gave him two tracks on the debut album, including "Dirty Work," graced by Fagen's sublime keyboard and organ work. But gradually Fagen found his sea legs. He'd steel himself with brandy and a Valium and warm up backstage with oldies like "Ruby Baby."[49] By September, Palmer had moved on to write lyrics with Carole King ("Jazzman"), and Steely Dan was no longer an opener but a headliner.

In the style of the day, they hired a second drummer, Jeff Porcaro (later of Toto), who told a twenty-one-year-old session musician named Michael McDonald that the group was looking for a backing vocalist and keyboardist. "Steely Dan were my favorite band so I got there as fast as I could and miraculously got the job."[50]

Soon Fagen and Becker would decide to give up live performance to focus solely on making albums with a revolving cast of session players. Guitarist Baxter knew the Doobies after opening for them and playing on *The Captain and Me*. They invited him to join, and he brought McDonald with him. Gradually McDonald's voice mutated the Doobies from biker band to yacht rock, a genre that received its name from a web series that debuted on June 26, 2005, *Yacht Rock*. As director JD Ryznar put it, "You know, like Michael McDonald is singing background vocals and like there's guys on boats on the covers; it feels like you're on a yacht listening to it."[51] The show spoofed artists like Steely Dan, McDonald, and their '73 touring mate Kenny Loggins, along with Daryl Hall and John Oates.

The duo grew up in Philadelphia, the original home of *American Bandstand,* countless street corner doo-wop singers, and Motown's rival Philadelphia International Records. "The early 70s was an amazing time to be in Philadelphia," Oates recalled. "We were living in this hippy ghetto with a lot of crazy freaks and cool people. All we did was walk around the city and play music in art galleries and coffee shops."[52]

Their first album, in the folk vein, did not sell, so they went Philly soul for *Abandoned Luncheonette,* though "Had I Known You Better" hinted at the Simon and Garfunkel aspect of their earlier incarnation. It made clear why producer Arif Mardin wanted to squeeze them into his calendar between sessions with Aretha Franklin, Willie Nelson, Bette Midler, and Dr. John. Together they created one of the lushest opening tracks of the year, revamping a desolate Chi-Lites lick into the strangely cheery "When the Morning Comes."

When Oates's girlfriend blew him off for New Year's, he took solace in strumming the blues and came up with the chorus for "She's Gone," then showed it to Hall, who was going through his first divorce and finished the song off.[53] Soul group Tavares quickly covered the song and sent it to No. 1 on the R&B charts. With its epic build and cathartic howl, it contained all the ingredients that eventually made Hall & Oates the world's bestselling music duo.

The Harder They Come

February 8 sees the American release of the film *The Harder They Come* and its accompanying soundtrack, a milestone in the popularization of reggae in the West.

*

The Village Voice's Robert Christgau spoke for many when he wrote, "The soundtrack to the greatest rock and roll movie this side of *The TAMI Show* is the greatest rock and roll compilation this side of *18 King Size Rhythm and Blues Hits*."[1] *Rolling Stone* later rated *The Harder They Come* the 3rd Greatest Soundtrack of All Time, one of the 40 Most Groundbreaking Albums of All Time, and the 119th Greatest Album of All Time.

The movie's star, Jimmy Cliff, had been making records for over a decade. Back in 1962, when he was fourteen, the other kids made fun of him because he only had shorts to wear. To raise the cash to get some long pants, he hustled himself into a Kingston record store/restaurant/ice cream parlor named Beverly's and convinced the Chinese Jamaican owner Leslie Kong to cut a single with him. After Cliff scored some hits, he brought his friend Desmond Dekker to Beverly's, and Kong started recording records with him, too. Dekker worked at a welding plant with Bob Marley and hooked Marley up.

By the end of the decade, a director of TV commercials had begun to think the island's music scene would make a good milieu for a movie. Perry

Henzell, born in 1936, grew up on a sugar plantation managed by his father, who was of French descent. He was friendly with the Rastafarians, a spiritual counterculture that arose in Jamaica in the '30s. They believed the Bible prophesied their eventual return to Africa; they dreadlocked their hair and considered cannabis the central sacrament of their religion honoring Jah, their name for God. Henzell recalled, "They talked to me about the Bible, because in those days I loved Bible stories. They looked ferocious, but in fact [they] were very friendly to [this] little white boy on a horse."[2]

Henzell wanted to make Jamaica's first full-length feature film and decided it should center around "the original rude boy," Vincent "Ivanhoe" Martin (a.k.a. Rhyging for "raging"). He was both Robin Hood and bogeyman to the locals. After escaping from prison in 1948, he went on a robbery spree and shot three policemen and several other people before the authorities gunned him down.

With African Jamaican playwright Trevor Rhone, Henzell crafted a script about a young man who travels from the countryside to Kingston to pursue his dream of being a singer. After a record producer rips him off, he turns to the illegal cannabis trade, shoots a cop, and goes on the run, which ironically turns his record into a hit.

Originally Henzell considered Johnny Nash for the role, until the *Jimmy Cliff* album sleeve intrigued him. Henzell felt the singer looked tough on the front cover but vulnerable on the back. He tracked Cliff down to Kingston's Dynamic Sound Studios, where the artist was recording "You Can Get It If You Really Want It," and asked him, "Do you think that you can write some music for a movie I am making?"

"What do you mean 'do I think'? I can do it."

Cliff later said with a laugh, "So, that answer made [Henzell] say, 'This is the man that I want to do my movie.'"[3]

Cliff had been scared of Ivanhoe as a child and was excited by the script, tentatively named after Cliff's song "Hard Road to Travel," but was wary of Henzell. "To be straight with you, I treated him how I treated most white Jamaicans; with mistrust. But he was very intelligent so by talking with him I found this out. He was very spiritual and very well read. I came to have much respect for him."[4]

Henzell raised $200,000 from his relatives and shot the film in one- and two-week increments, or on weekends, with a mostly novice cast. Production dragged on for over eighteen months. Actors dropped out or died, necessitating reshoots. Sometimes Cliff was gone and Henzell had to use a double for him.[5]

Influenced by the cinema verité realism of directors John Cassavetes and Ken Loach, Henzell ventured into gritty neighborhoods with his camera. Cliff said, "Perry was criticized for showing poverty, but he wanted to depict Jamaica's hardship, not the tourist areas. He asked everyone to speak their natural patois rather than English. And he wouldn't instruct me how to act; he'd tell me to really dig into myself."[6]

Cliff projected a charismatic naturalism, cool in gold shades and hat. His James Dean moment came when his girlfriend chided him for being a dreamer instead of getting a job. "Me? Dreamer? Who's a bigger dreamer than you? Always talking about milk and honey in the sky. Well, no milk and honey in the sky—not for you, not for me. It's right down here, and I want mine now! Tonight!"

Cliff came up with the movie's final title while shooting the scene where he defends himself against a bicycle-shop owner with a knife. "In real life, if you come on hard like [the owner], you're going to die hard. When I told Perry my line, he loved it. He thought it was a stronger film title and asked me to write a theme song to go with it. He didn't give me much time— just two days—because he wanted to film me singing it in the studio with the band for the movie. The first development of my song is actually in the movie—when the guitarist and I are rehearsing a song in the church. What you see in the movie—in the recording studio—is the song being recorded."[7]

The band on-screen is the same one that transfixed Paul Simon when he heard Cliff's "Vietnam," which compelled Simon to travel to Jamaica in spring 1971 to record "Mother and Child Reunion" with them: Hux Brown on lead guitar, Jackie Jackson on bass, Winston Grennan on drums.

The indefatigable optimism of "The Harder They Come" theme fit any occasion, from government oppression to Henzell's campaign to get his movie to the screen, far more grueling than the filmmaker initially anticipated. *Rolling Stone* ranked it the 350th Greatest Song of All Time.

The soundtrack included three other self-help classics by Cliff. "You Can Get It If You Really Want It" was a rocksteady song perhaps inspired by the Stones' "You Can't Always Get What You Want" (rocksteady being the evolutionary link between earlier ska and later reggae).

Cliff wrote "Sitting in Limbo" after his producer-mentor Kong died of a heart attack at the young age of thirty-eight. The head of Island Records, Chris Blackwell, suggested Cliff travel to Muscles Shoals Sound Studio in Alabama to find a sound that could cross over to the soul market. The house band, called the Swampers, backed the likes of Wilson Pickett,

Aretha Franklin, and the Staple Singers (though, ironically, the Swampers were white). The lyrics reflect Cliff's confusion, but the chorus provides a catharsis almost as strong as "The Harder They Come," echoing the Afro-Caribbean limbo dance. "My influences have been calypso and rock and roll. When I was a boy we would sing those Harry Belafonte songs in the fields as folk songs."[8]

The gospel lament of "Many Rivers to Cross" was considered by many to be his finest hour. "When I came to the UK, I was still in my teens. I came full of vigor. I'm going to make it, I'm going to be up there with the Beatles and the Stones. And it wasn't really going like that. I was touring clubs, not breaking through. I was struggling, with work, life, my identity, I couldn't find my place; frustration fueled the song."[9] He originally wrote it for his album *Jimmy Cliff,* then decided there wasn't room on the record for such a ballad. But as the session musicians prepared to leave for the day, Cliff decided to give it a shot. "I started singing, the band came in, and that was it. Once. That was it. And then Chris [Blackwell] said, 'OK, let's put this one in to fill out the album.'"[10] The song inspired many covers. When Harry Nilsson and John Lennon covered it for *Pussycats* (1974), Nilsson blew out his vocal cords and suffered a hemorrhage in his throat.

Working with Cliff wasn't easy for Henzell. "Jimmy was always supposed to choose the music for the soundtrack, and we were coming up to the deadline."[11] But after production dragged on for years, Cliff said he wouldn't do it. Devastated, Henzell retreated to his bed for the weekend. With a pad of paper, he ran through the movie in his mind, thinking of songs that might fit. "It's the best weekend's work I've ever done."[12]

The other songs on the album encapsulate the evolution of ska to rocksteady to reggae. Ska was high-energy dance music for rude boys (gangsta thugs) to skank to. When the summer of 1966 grew too hot for skanking, prominent ska guitarists like Lynn Taitt slowed the tempo into rocksteady. Dekker wrote "007 (Shanty Town)" in 1967 after a student protest against beachfront development turned into a riot. Rude boys dressing like James Bond and the Rat Pack in *Ocean's 11* loot and shoot up their town for bail money. The song made it to No. 14 in the UK and inspired Paul McCartney to write "Ob-la-di, Ob-la-da" about a character named Desmond.

Dekker didn't actually appear in the movie, but fellow reggae titans Toots and the Maytals provide the film's most euphoric scene. Cliff wanders into a recording studio for the first time and finds the three singers harmonizing under the microphones on the wedding song "Sweet and Dandy." Frederick "Toots" Hibbert (oft compared to Otis Redding) sang in the church choir as a youth and formed a vocal trio with Henry "Raleigh" Gordon and Nathaniel "Jerry" Mathias in Kingston in 1962. In 1968, the Maytals' "Do the Reggay" gave the next era its name. Toots: "There's a word we used to use in Jamaica called 'streggae.' If a girl is walking and the guys look at her and say 'Man, she's streggae,' it means she don't dress well, she look raggedy. The girls would say that about the men, too. This one morning me and my two friends were playing and I said, 'OK man, let's do the reggay.' It was just something that came out of my mouth. So we just start singing 'Do the reggay, do the reggay' and created a beat."[13]

"Pressure Drop" secured their spot in the firmament alongside Cliff and Marley. The song referenced how barometers measure pressure to warn when storms are approaching. Toots: "It's a song about revenge, but in the form of karma: if you do bad things to innocent people, then bad things will happen to you. The title was a phrase I used to say. If someone done me wrong, rather than fight them like a warrior, I'd say: 'The pressure's going to drop on you.'"[14] In years to come, English venues would erupt with crowds skanking in circles and howling "Pressure! Pressure! Pressure!" as artists like the Clash and the Specials covered the song.

When rocksteady evolved into reggae, the pulsating bass came to the fore as a lead instrument, while the scratchy guitar often functioned as percussion. The scratch guitar evolved when producers added tape echo, transforming a "cha cha cha" sound on the guitar strings into "chakachakachaka." When musicians tried to re-create the tape delay while playing live, they strummed down on the strings, then "chucked" up. Meanwhile, the drums diverged from the Western style. Most US/UK songs accented the second and fourth beats, a.k.a. the backbeat: one TWO three FOUR. Rocksteady switched to the third beat: one two THREE four, continued by reggae drummers like the Wailers' Carlton Barrett with "one-drop rhythm" (dropping/not playing the first beat[15]—the inverse of James Brown's funk, which stressed "the one"). Electric organ often supplanted piano, while horns, which had dominated ska, receded.

The epitome of the throbbing bass groove can be found in "Johnny Too Bad." The archetypal rude boy lopes down the road, pistol and ratchet in his belt, preternaturally mellow even as he robs and loots, somehow keeping the encroaching sense of doom at bay. It encapsulated the plot of the movie in two verses,[16] and perfectly expressed reggae's twin poles: finding "Be Here Now" peace through the help of ganja in the face of street danger, with the beat that hypnotized English rockers hungry for the next phase after R&B.

Increasingly, reggae's lyrics moved away from romance and partying toward politics and spirituality. "Rivers of Babylon" by the Melodians was a biblical lamentation, in the doo-wop style of Kingston street corner singers, with the beat of Rasta drum circles. The nyabinghi style had been passed down from the Bantu of the Eastern Congo, mirroring the heartbeat: "boom-boom, pause, boom-boom, pause."[17] In the drum circles, twenty or more drummers played hand drums while chanting everything from hymns to R&B songs by Marvin Gaye.[18] One of the hymns was Psalm 137, which Melodians singer Brent Dowe echoes here. After being carried away from Zion into Babylonian captivity, he sits by the river and weeps, remembering his old home. Some Rasta sects believed they were descendants of the Twelve Tribes of Israel. The government banned the song until producer Leslie Kong pointed out the lyrics were from the Bible; when the ban was lifted, "Rivers" shot to the top of the Jamaican charts.[19]

✳

Chris Blackwell put up $5,000 to finish the film and locked in a music distribution deal. On June 5, 1972, it premiered in Kingston. The Carib Theatre only had 1,500 seats, but half the city swarmed to check out the first Jamaican full-length movie. Neither Jimmy Cliff nor Jamaican prime minister Michael Manley could get through the mob.

The film went on to Ireland's Cork Film Festival in June. In July, Henzell booked it in London's Brixton neighborhood, home to the majority of the city's Jamaican immigrants. The first night the Classic Theatre was practically empty, so the director printed up five thousand flyers and handed them out at the Brixton subway—another of the many times his hustler's stamina turned the fate of the film around.[20] It continued on to the Venice Film Festival in August, then the Los Angeles Film Expo in November. There Henzell secured a distribution deal with Roger Corman's New World Pictures.

When New World released it in February 1973, they hyped it as "Super Fly Goes to Jamaica" to capitalize on the blaxploitation movie craze. (*Live and Let Die* was promoted as "James Bond Goes to Jamaica" four months later.) The poster proclaimed, "With a piece in his hand he takes on the man! He makes women and the charts and is on top with both."

The campaign rubbed Henzell the wrong way, and it didn't work with black audiences. On the surface, the movie seemed to have the same theme as *Sweet Sweetback's Baadasssss Song*: black man on the run after killing a white cop. That film had been a smash, particularly with the Black Panthers under siege by the FBI and police, and had kicked off the blaxploitation movement, so *Harder* seemed a natural.

But unlike *Sweetback,* the cops killed Cliff at the end. Cliff observed that his character "connected with the college students in the US and UK [but] didn't connect too much with black America at the time because they very much had their own thing going on. Black America normally doesn't really understand what is going on in the rest of the black world. And it's still very much like that today. America as a whole doesn't really know what is going on in the rest of the world. America sees America and thinks, 'There is the world!' Maybe you could say middle class black America liked it."[21]

Strong reviews in *The New York Times, The Washington Post,* and *Time* proved irrelevant. Probably the biggest impediment was that the Jamaican accents were so thick the film required subtitles for English audiences. Henzell determined that college audiences, already fans of foreign films, were a better target. He pulled out of the deal with New World and decided to handle the marketing and PR himself.

In April his approach was validated at the Orson Welles Cinema outside Boston. The film drew seventy-five thousand over the next six months. After that, the theater began screening the film as its midnight movie and drew a full house for the next six years. Cliff visited once. During his character's confrontation with the cops, "I jumped up in front of the screen like I had the six shooters. The people went wild! Really, really wild!"[22] Similar runs followed in New York, DC, and San Francisco. Hippies toked whenever a character on-screen did. Henzell went to forty-three countries over the next half decade, renting a theater for a week or two per engagement. After six years he paid back his investors with a profit and broke even.

Cliff theorized that the film had legs for two reasons: "First it expressed the spirit that was going on in the world at the time. The rebelliousness against the system. It was at the same time as the end of the hippy movement who were also rebelling against society. And then you had this character which connected with people. . . . And the other reason was it was fresh, showing you another culture. New music. The music was, 'Wow!' The music was already familiar in England and parts of Europe but to see where that music came from; to see the culture that it came from; to see the cause of that music."[23]

Ballerina Wolfmen

Alice Cooper tops the album chart, and the Sweet release the year's third-bestselling single, but T. Rex can't break through in America. Todd Rundgren and David Bowie produce the year's seminal proto-punk albums, the New York Dolls' debut and the Stooges' *Raw Power*.

✳

In the beginning, a lot of the New York Dolls' audience was gay, but, of course, we were all straight," said bassist Arthur Kane. "We were all girl crazy. And let me tell you something: it turns out women knew immediately. It was the men who were confused. The women knew, I don't care what we wore. And they loved us for it, that we had the balls to look and act the way we did."[1]

Bowie remarked, "Girls are always presuming that I've kept my heterosexual virginity for some reason. So I've had all these girls try to get me over to the other side again: 'C'mon, David, it isn't all that bad. I'll show you.' Or, better yet, '*We'll* show you.' I always play dumb."[2]

In retrospect, few of the major figures of glam seem to have been even bi, except Reed and Bowie. Vincent Fournier and his band took the moniker Alice Cooper "simply as a spit in the face of society."[3] In interviews, Fournier often felt compelled to clarify his sexuality: "I'm straight. But if I could have chosen I might have chosen bi."[4] "I've never made it with a guy but that doesn't mean I won't."[5]

He wasn't a dreamboat like Robert Plant, so he had to come up with a shtick to hold the audience. In 1968, he got the idea of a man who killed women in women's clothes—maybe after watching *Psycho*—and picked a name that sounded deceptively innocuous like Lizzie Bordon. He mixed Bette Davis's look from *Whatever Happened to Baby Jane?*, Anita Pallenberg's from *Barbarella,* and Emma Peel's from *The Avengers.* Leopard thigh boots with high heels, the de rigueur feather boa, leather gloves, negligee with paper cone breasts. "People are both male and female, biologically. The typical American thinks he is all male but he has to realize he has his feminine side, too."[6]

Mark Feld also scuffled for years before stumbling on androgyny. Back in '65, he was a folkie and became Marc Bolan, a contraction of "Bob" and "Dylan." He joined a mod band, John's Children, that stage-fought each other with blood capsules,[7] then switched to Donovan-styled psychedelic folk with a bongo player, under the name Tyrannosaurus Rex.

He met Bowie when the manager they shared enlisted them both to paint his office. They'd both been mods, then hippies with high elf voices. Bolan played on an early version of Bowie's "The Prettiest Star" and was at the London Roundhouse in 1970 when Bowie appeared as Rainbow Man, backed by Ronson dressed as a gangster and the drummer as a cowboy. Bassist/producer Tony Visconti said, "I think that is the night that the germ of glam rock was born."[8]

The following year, Bolan dabbed his wife's glitter under his eyes and wore satin to perform "Hot Love" on *Top of the Pops* and kick-started the movement. The Sweet's bassist Steve Priest summarized, "Glam rock started with something as stupid as Marc Bolan wearing a pink boa. The gates opened and we all poured through."[9] (At the time, articles in *The New York Times, People, Variety,* and *NME* called it glitter rock as opposed to glam.)

For many Brits, the six-year-old hippie scene with its earth tones, denim, no makeup, and straight hair had grown stale.[10] Roxy Music's lead guitarist, Phil Manzanera, commented, "A lot of musicians were getting strung out on heavy drugs. They were out of it, so they weren't even bothering to wear kaftans or other hippie stuff, which had been stylish in their own way."[11]

"There was a gap in the market," observed Nina Myskow, editor of British teen mag *Jackie.* Female tweens wanted "non-threatening, not overtly sexual boys."[12] Bolan threw his locks back like Maria Schneider and flung his arm up like John Travolta. His rockabilly guitar and bubblegum vocals were more appetizing to girls than hard rock, and his backlog of songs about unicorns and doves didn't hurt either. Though his new stuff was getting harder. "Twentieth Century Boy" took the chewy distorted guitar from "Suffragette City," slowed it down into Bolan's most sinuous groove yet, and added soaring backing vocals by sister duo Sue and Sunny.

Mott the Hoople's lead singer, Ian Hunter, had been a street brawler in a gang and fathered two kids by age twenty. He was still struggling at thirty-three when Bowie offered his band "All the Young Dudes," which Lou Reed trumpeted as a "gay anthem."[13] Bowie told *NME*, "If they were doing okay at the time, I don't think they would have wanted to link up with me, because they were quite macho, one of the early laddish bands. But things weren't good, and I literally wrote that within an hour or so of reading an article in one of the music rags that said their breakup was imminent. I thought they were a fair little band and I thought, 'This will be an interesting thing to do, let's see if I can write this song and keep them together.' . . . So I wrote this thing and thought, 'There, that should sort them out.'"[14]

"The song made us instant gays," said Hunter. "We were tranny magnets when we played the US. Touring with Bette Midler probably helped add to that reputation. At first, I was scared to go into gay bars, but it was fabulous, people loved us there, we had some great hilarious times."[15] Guitarist Mick Ralphs was uncomfortable, however, and quit the band in August to form Bad Company with Free vocalist Paul Rodgers.

Bryan Ferry embraced the gay sensibility of his friends from art school and employed them to design Roxy Music's covers while camping onstage in leopard skin. "The line about us was that the other bands wanted to wreck their hotel rooms, we wanted to redecorate ours," Ferry told the *Financial Review*.[16]

Roxy's synth player, Brian Eno, summed it up: "I was not gay, but I wanted to look great, and looking great meant dressing like a woman."[17] Indeed, the story was he suffered a collapsed lung after sleeping with six girls in thirty hours. Perhaps to balance out his receding hairline, he came on even more outrageous than the rest of the band in costumes made by girlfriend Carol McNicoll. Ferry meanwhile dated the models on their album covers, including 1973's Playmate of the Year, Marilyn Cole, who appeared on November's *Stranded*.

The Sweet's Steve Priest looked so much like a woman in their promotional appearances that it freaked out straight guys, but "if it breathed and was female, it was fair game. The '70s were magical. They were like the '60s, only crazier. God knows how we got away with it."[18] Despite the perks, it required bravery to appear so over the top. In Kilmarnock, Scotland, the assholes in the audience progressed from spitting on the Sweet to attacking them with hurled bottles. In their song recounting the evening, "Ballroom Blitz," vocalist Brian Connolly upped the ante with the most brazenly camp vocal to hit the airwaves yet. It became the bestselling single of the year worldwide, after "Angie" and "Tie a Yellow Ribbon." It took two years to hit No. 5 in the US, though, where it was the only English glam single to make the Top 10 except for T. Rex's "Get It On" (perhaps inspiring the Ramones' "Blitzkrieg Bop").

Then there were glam rockers who just liked fashion. Guitarist Sylvain Sylvain (born Sylvain Mizrahi in Cairo) grew up poor, so he had to learn how to sew his own clothes. He turned his skill into a clothing business called Truth and Soul with drummer Billy Murcia. They sold their wares at Betsey Johnson's store. Sylvain also worked at a boutique across the street from a toy repair shop called the New York Doll Hospital.

"Of course, we were crazy about T. Rex and Marc Bolan. One day we saw [Bolan] wearing these gray suede Mary Janes, and the next day I see Johnny [Genzale, later Thunders] and he's got a pair almost like them!"[19]

"When the Dolls got together," lead singer David Johansen recalled, "that was a time when everybody, at least in the East Village, had taken a lot of acid and was real into this utopian idea of androgyny. This was when real radical feminism started."[20]

Johansen's girlfriend Cyrinda Foxe said he "very much wanted to be in with the whole Charles Ludlam gang," who were known for the drag shows of the Ridiculous Theatrical Company. "But I think he was as close as he could get to that world, because David was a little more heterosexual than they wanted him to be. They were a little set back by this babe on David's arm. I think that hurt him. David wanted out of Staten Island and Warhol wasn't interested in him, Ludlam wasn't."[21]

Initially Sylvain said the Warhol scene at Max's Kansas City didn't like the Dolls because they weren't real drag queens. When they toured London at the end of '72, they were supposed to open for Lou Reed, but he canceled them. They had their own scene bubbling at the Mercer Arts Center, though.

Thomas Erdelyi (later Tommy Ramone) said the Mercer and Max's were the only places in New York where bands could play original songs and not covers at the time, along with Coventry in Queens. Mercer became the hub for people who wanted to dress up and find the other freaks like themselves. The players who would soon create New York punk rock were all there. Patti Smith read poetry to open for the Dolls. Singer Alan Vega and keyboardist Martin Rev named themselves Suicide after an issue of the Ghost Rider comic and played some nights with the Dolls, hyping their shows as "Punk Music Mass" on flyers. Richard Hell and Tom Verlaine were inspired by the Dolls to start the Neon Boys, later renamed Television. Kiss was galvanized to invent their own makeup.

The ultimate misfit who trekked to see them, Jeffrey Hyman, was the lead singer of a band named Sniper. He'd been born with an incomplete Siamese twin growing out of his back, which was removed.[22] Suffering from OCD, he'd recently stayed at St. Vincent's Hospital for a month and was diagnosed as a paranoid schizophrenic. For his Sniper gigs, he had a black jumpsuit custom-made out of stretchy material with rhinestones and augmented it with jewelry, scarves, and makeup stolen from his mother. Black leather gloves reached to his elbows, a bullet chain dangled from his belt, and pink lavender boots rose to his knees. His outfit was the opposite of the back-to-basics look he later adopted after rechristening himself Joey Ramone.

To get to Mercer, Hyman had to hitchhike. As his brother, Mickey Leigh, observed, "It was really dangerous to hitchhike down Queens Boulevard looking the way Joey did. Joey's so unusual looking to begin with, so tall— he's about 6'6" naturally, but in platform shoes he stood over seven feet tall. And he wore a jumpsuit. At that time, you really couldn't be doing that safely."[23]

When he did manage to score a lift, Ramone recalled, "All of a sudden you'd be halfway there and they'd say, 'What do you think about going under the bridge?' Usually, if I was close enough, I'd just jump out of the car."[24]

✳

Max's Kansas City was a restaurant and nightclub at 213 Park Avenue South opened by Mickey Ruskin in December 1965. It was originally dominated by abstract expressionist painters but was one of the few spots that allowed drag queens, so Warhol's contingent took over the back room. One of the actresses from Warhol's *Heat,* Andrea Feldman, regularly stood on the table, announced, "It's showtime!" and flashed her breasts. The Velvet Underground played. Ruskin let the crowd get rowdy and throw the free chickpeas at each other or have sex in the phone booth. He also let them run up a tab, which Warhol sometimes paid off with paintings. When a scenester named Taylor Mead slipped and fell, he cracked, "I'm going to sue Mickey for everything I owe him."[25]

Ruskin turned the upstairs into a place where the models, photographers, actors, musicians, hippies, and bikers could dance to favorites like "The Letter" by the Box Tops or "Monkey Man" by the Stones.[26] Even though the upstairs only had a capacity of 125, Ruskin started letting musicians gig there, and Max's entered a second phase as the cutting-edge East Coast equivalent of the Troubadour (less denim, more deviant). A January poster trumpeted the Dolls and Waylon Jennings in his first New York show, with Jennings supported by Billy Joel. (Jennings's band started playing without him because he was on the street getting high. When he heard them he bolted inside to the mic.) Another poster featured Bruce Springsteen, Bob Marley, Iggy and the Stooges, and Tim Buckley. For a month in the summer of '73, Springsteen and Marley alternated top billing week to week. Singer-songwriters like Tom Waits, Bonnie Raitt, Odetta, and Dave Van Ronk mixed with yacht rock progenitors Steely Dan, the Doobie Brothers, and Hall & Oates. Graham Parsons and Emmylou Harris one night, Charlie Mingus or Andy Kaufman another. In the audience might be John Lennon and May Pang, Malcolm McLaren, Prince Charles, or Don Johnson.

Alice Cooper reminisced, "I was like a social vampire. I'd get up around seven p.m., watch TV, leave around midnight, and stay at Max's until the sun came up. I probably lived on chick peas and Black Russians. . . . I liked it there because all of my friends were there. Iggy was there, Bowie was there, and the Dolls."[27]

Johansen called it the high school soda pop shop. If so, the freshman girls were Debbie Harry and Patti Smith. Harry was a waitress at Max's (and the Playboy Club) while doing off-off-Broadway shows with Jackie Curtis. Smith just sat outside on the curb with Robert Mapplethorpe at first, then worked up the nerve to go in, sometimes dancing alone by the jukebox.

The two queens of the scene were Cyrinda Foxe and Bebe Buell. Foxe acted in Warhol's *Pork,* inspired some lyrics of "The Jean Genie," and appeared in the video prancing as an updated Marilyn Monroe. She lived with the Stooges' guitarist James Williamson, then married the Dolls' David Johansen, before leaving him for the richer Steven Tyler.

Eighteen-year-old Buell wanted to be a singer, supported herself as an Eileen Ford model, and dated Todd Rundgren. His song "Hello It's Me" peaked at No. 5 in December '73. It was the anthem for sensitive guys who assured their women they didn't want them to change, or not be free. (Translation: don't give the guy grief when he sleeps around.) Buell sparked perhaps the most legendary showdown at Max's, between Rundgren and Bowie. Each had produced one of the year's two seminal glam/proto-punk albums, the Dolls' self-titled debut (Rundgren) and the Stooges' *Raw Power* (Bowie).

Buell remembered, "I was there the night [Bowie] walked into Max's for the first time, in the baby blue suit and the bright orange hair. It was striking. Everybody else in there was dressed in black and this colorful alien came in and just enchanted and charmed us all."[28]

The look was preserved in the video Bowie made on June 13 for the single "Life on Mars," shot by top glam photographer Mick Rock. The video opened on Bowie's unearthly pupils under turquoise eye shadow. The pupils were different sizes because in high school Bowie's best friend, George Underwood, punched him when he tried to steal Underwood's girl, leaving one eye permanently dilated. Typically, Bowie turned something that would make other people insecure into an asset, writing songs like "Wild Eyed Boy from Freecloud." His mime-white face and vampiric incisors contrasted boldly with his red shag and blue satin suit. New Wave started here.

Bowie entered Max's with his wife and beelined over to Buell, telling her she was very beautiful. Perhaps that rubbed Rundgren the wrong way. When Buell introduced them, Bowie told Rundgren, "I've heard of you. You're supposed to be pretty fucking smart."

"Yes I am," Rundgren replied, "and I hear you're supposed to be ripping me off."[29]

Actually, Buell claimed it was Rundgren who copped Bowie's space suits, dyed hair, and androgyny. (Rundgren also employed a backup band of mimes called the Hello People.) Either way, Bowie was miffed. The next day he tracked down Buell and took her to the Rockettes. She took him to the Dolls, then Bette Midler at the Continental Baths, and they did each other's makeup. "We made one feeble attempt at having sex and we ended up in a heap of laughter."[30]

Later, she was sitting at Max's with Bowie and Alice Cooper when Rundgren arrived. "He walked into the back room so glammed out, he had feathers on his eyes and glitter," she recalled, "and he just came walking in and over to the table and said, 'Hi,' and sat down next to me. So here I am in the middle of Todd and David, and David burst into tears. And Todd said, 'David, it's okay, I'm leaving to go on the road tomorrow, she's all yours.' And then I went, 'What do you mean, I'm all his? You're my boyfriend, he's my friend.' Todd said, 'You mean you're not having sex with him?' I said, 'David, would you please tell him we're not having sex?' And David just sat there crying. And Alice was sitting there—he was very macho for a guy who carried a woman's name—and said, 'What the hell's going on here with you guys? Smarten up!' Todd just turned around and walked out. So I chased him, of course. And the feathers were falling off of him as he was walking off and I was picking the feathers up behind him going, 'Todd, Todd.'"[31] Maybe Bowie was worried Rundgren was going to sock him in the other eye.

The first of their albums to debut was *Raw Power* on February 7. In a sense, it was born at Max's one night in September 1971, after Bowie and Lou Reed had dinner with their wives. Journalist Lisa Robinson said, "We called Danny Fields [manager of the Stooges and MC5] mid-meal to tell him to send Iggy up. We met Iggy later at Max's, and while no one remembers much about the evening, I do remember that Iggy was not stoned (that night), as the fiction in the movie *Velvet Goldmine* had it, and that he and David instantly hit it off. The next day Iggy moved into the Warwick Hotel, where [Bowie's management] camp was in residence."[32]

Pop broke up the Stooges before *Raw Power* because he thought they weren't motivated enough. When Pop told guitarist Ron Asheton that he was going to replace him with James Williamson and go to London to make the new album, Asheton was devastated. But they couldn't find a good rhythm section, so in the end Pop asked Asheton to return as the bassist, with his brother Scott back on drums. Asheton was irked but agreed. When he arrived, Bowie grabbed him by the ass and kissed him. Asheton almost punched him, but remembered the big picture and had an affair with Angela Bowie instead.

Bowie's manager, Tony Defries, hassled them to write better songs, but then Bowie-mania distracted him, and the Stooges were left to record undisturbed the last great album of Detroit proto-punk/metal. The MC5's Dennis Thompson summed up the sound: "One of the things about being from Detroit was we were all into the drag strip—more power, high energy. And that was symbolic of Detroit, the Motor City—it was loud, it was crushing, it's banging and it's noisy and it's gritty and it's tough, it's rough."[33]

Alice Cooper recalled, "Detroit audiences would only respond to bands that had attitude, offered no excuses and played it loud. Every week, we would play bills like Stooges, MC5, Alice Cooper and The Who at the Grande [Ballroom], and even at that time we realized that these were some of the greatest rock 'n' roll shows that would ever happen."[34] The Michigan scene "was good old-fashioned, gloves-off, bare-knuckled, fist-in-your-face competition. The locals would show up in droves to see what was going to happen between Alice and Iggy. Last week, Iggy Stooge smeared peanut butter all over his body or rolled around on broken glass? How are we going to one-up them? Let's do something like blow a bunch of feathers around the stage. . . . Iggy was the total street-punk sex god—no shirt, his private parts sticking out of his pants. . . . I hated going on after Iggy!"[35]

For his review of *Raw Power* in Detroit's *Creem* magazine, Lester Bangs wrote, "Iggy Pop would fling his scabbed body to the floor of the stage in a truly convincing display of the self-destructive impulse at its purest, whereupon he would proceed to perform fellatio on the microphone while his lead guitarist jabbed him brutally from behind with the neck of his in- strument. It was crude, even disgusting, but the Stooges were innovators of a sort, and both Bowie and Cooper have freely looted Iggy's stage act for gimmicks to beef up their own highly controlled but rather cold shows."[36]

Five of the album's eight tracks were basically variations on the "Raw Power"/"Search and Destroy" motif. "Shake Appeal" was the clearest exam- ple of how the Stooges linked the mid-'60s garage rock of the Sonics, Stan- dells, and Wailers to the next-generation Ramones. The Stooges also taught the Ramones how to write lyrics that seemed moronic and brilliant at the same time. "Death Trip" prophesied hardcore. There *were* slight variations: in "Your Pretty Face Is Going to Hell," Pop sounded like a demon, whereas in "Shake Appeal," he alternated between rabid dog and shrieking monkey.

In "Gimme Danger," they figured out how to harness the goth elements of earlier slow tracks like "We Will Fall" into propulsive drama. It was Pop's Narcissus death dance of seduction. Like a will-o'-the-wisp he sang to naïve groupies that he needed them to be his master and kiss him in the ocean breeze. Or, more accurately, give him money for heroin, have sex with him, then leave, as Williamson's guitar descended to the bowels of fiery apoca- lypse.

On the subtly named "Penetration," Pop played an eerie celesta key- board while hissing like the depraved incubus he appeared to be on the cover. With his vampire eye shadow, he came off preposterous and creepy all at once. The label apparently thought so, choosing a font for the title that dripped with low-budget horror movie blood, which Pop hated.

Bowie's contribution was remixing the songs in one day in Hollywood and fucking it up. He made "Search and Destroy" sound like a tinny, trebly one-hit wonder by a Midwest garage band who couldn't afford a studio. Pop eventually remixed it in 1997, bringing up the bass, making it much easier to enjoy—though Williamson defended Bowie's mix: "Jack White made an entire career around that sound of guitar and drums."[37] Like the White Stripes, the Strokes, the Ramones, Lou Reed, and most artsy garage bands,

the Stooges did better in the UK, where the album crawled to No. 44. It was
below subterranean in the US, peaking at No. 182.

✻

It took a true artist like Rundgren to know *not* to touch the ragged
Dolls sound—aside from flourishes like adding Velvet Underground "Sunday Morning" echo to the backing vocals on "Trash," and keeping Sylvain's
guitar on the left channel and Thunders' on the right throughout. That is,
it took a virtuoso Picasso to appreciate primitive art. Or really, again like
Bowie, Rundgren was too busy promoting the crazy prog experimental excess of his own album *A Wizard, a True Star* to worry about it. The same
spring he produced the Dolls, he toured, produced *Mother's Pride* by the
all-female rock band Fanny, then helped Grand Funk Railroad bang out
We're an American Band.

Alice Cooper engineer Jack Douglas and his assistant Jimmy Iovine were
the ones in the trenches daily with the Dolls at the Record Plant that April.
Douglas hung out at Max's Kansas City and appreciated Johansen's lyrics
and how the band "was about playing with complete abandon and being
as shocking as you possibly can. That was part of the Alice thing, but with
a New York twist."[38]

They recorded live except for a few lead guitar parts overdubbed by
Thunders, at full blast in a small room with the different instruments leaking into each other. Douglas said, "They had no patience for getting a [good]
sound on anything. 'Is there sound going through the microphone into the
board?' 'Yes.' 'Well, that's good.'" Some members occasionally nodded out,
or they'd make a mistake and stop, then start again from where they'd left
off, and Douglas would splice it all together. He'd play cowbell to help them
stay on tempo. "You know, every time we would complete a song it was
like 'Wow, maybe we can do another one.'"[39]

Thus emerged half-beautiful and half-incompetent tracks like the ballad
"Lonely Planet Boy": clear, warm, but defiantly shambolic. When the Rolling
Stones' Mick Taylor and Atlantic mogul Ahmet Ertegun came to see them
perform, Ertegun was unimpressed and Taylor advised them to polish it
up, but they didn't care. That was the attitude that heartened the future Ramones when they watched the Dolls at Mercer. Thunders was painfully out
of tune when he hollered into the mic alongside Johansen—but he looked
great posing, and you could tell he was having the time of his life. Who
cares if they couldn't play like Emerson, Lake & Palmer? It made Johnny want

to get onstage, too. Thus, the New York Dolls begat the Ramones, who begat the Sex Pistols and the Clash and the third act of rock and roll.

The album boasted two enduring anthems, "Personality Crisis" and "Trash." The latter had been the title of a Warhol film. As Warhol actor Perry King noted, "Trashy, to the Andy Warhol universe, was what they liked. Trash was big art to them."[40] *The Village Voice*'s Robert Christgau named it the fifteenth-greatest album of the decade. Young John Mellencamp formed a glitter band called Trash in Indiana. But the album stiffed at No. 116, hindered by the band in full drag on the cover. Most customers in a small-town record store couldn't handle waiting in line with a tranny album under their arm. The track "Private World" pretty much summed up the glam scene in America.

Summer

✳

Honky Tonk Heroes

Inspired by Kris Kristofferson, Willie Nelson and Waylon Jennings release the first outlaw country albums and thwart the repressive Nashville music industry. Nelson moves to Austin and brings hippies and rednecks together in his first annual Fourth of July Picnic.

✳

If you went by *Billboard's Hot Country Chart,* Nashville's royalty in 1973 included Merle Haggard, Charley Pride, and Tammy Wynette, who each scored three No. 1s that year. Loretta Lynn, Tanya Tucker, Conway Twitty, and Charlie Rich had two; Marie Osmond, one. Valhalla was crossing over to the pop chart, since that meant selling a lot more records. Charlie Rich pulled it off with "The Most Beautiful Girl." The bluegrass instrumental "Dueling Banjos" from *Deliverance* peaked at No. 2 pop on February 24. Buck Owens and Roy Clark brought down-home humor to the rest of the nation through their syndicated show *Hee Haw.*

The "countrypolitan" singles issued by Nashville moguls like Chet Atkins were generally easy listening with a vocal twang and conservative lyrical bent. If you were a singer you stuck to moon-and-June lyrics and didn't necessarily pick your songs. Producers laid orchestra strings and a choir behind you. You wore golf clothes, a tie, a plaid jacket, maybe rhinestones or a Nudie suit if you were getting wild. No jeans, leather, long hair, or hippie devil weed.

Bob Dylan recalled how Tom T. Hall "and a few other writers had the whole Nashville scene sewed up in a box. If you wanted to record a song and get it in the Top 10 you had to go to them."[1] Hall's "I Love" was one of the year's No. 1s, about baby ducks, pickup trucks, and country streams. "Tom T. Hall, he was bitching about some kind of new song, and he couldn't understand what these new kinds of songs that were coming in were about. . . . Everything was all right until Kristofferson came to town. Oh, they ain't seen anybody like him. He came into town like [the] wildcat that he was, flew a helicopter into Johnny Cash's backyard, not your typical songwriter. And he went for the throat. 'Sunday Morning Coming Down.' You can look at Nashville pre-Kris and post-Kris, because he changed everything. That one song blew ol' Tom T. Hall's world apart."[2]

Kris Kristofferson was the son of an air force major general and studied poets like William Blake at Oxford as a Rhodes Scholar. Later, he got a job as a janitor at Nashville's Columbia Studio; he was there when Dylan arrived to cut *Blonde on Blonde.* "I saw Dylan sitting out in the studio at the piano, writing all night long by himself. Dark glasses on."[3] Within a few years Kristofferson started writing classics like "Me and Bobby McGee" and "Help Me Make It Through the Night."

Waylon Jennings wrote that Kristofferson "brought a new maturity and sophistication to country lyrics, an explicitness to . . . the standard country fare. Spelled X-plicit, meaning Sex. One time we counted up and Kris had used the word 'body' a hundred and forty-four times in his various songs. Nasty nasty nasty. For a while Nashville was a little afraid of him; but his songs were undeniably poetry, and he taught us how to write great poems."[4]

Kristofferson was equally at home in Nashville and LA, where he opened for Linda Ronstadt at the Troubadour and starred in *Cisco Pike.* "Why Me" was his biggest pop hit, making it to No. 16 pop and No. 1 country in July. It was from his album *Jesus Was a Capricorn,* which epitomized how he walked the line. The title had that long-haired astrology, but it also had Jesus, so nobody could get mad.

Kristofferson was inspired to write "Why Me" after going to a church service where they played Larry Gatlin's song "Help Me (Lord)," which annihilated him. "I'm kneeling there, and I carry a big load of guilt around, and I was just out of control, crying. It was a release. It really shook me up."[5]

"Why Me" also asked Jesus for help after a lifetime of waste. Gatlin sang backup along with Rita Coolidge. She and Kristofferson married on August 17, one of the era's most illustrious couples. Leon Russell had already written "Delta Lady" for her. Stills and Nash's fight over her contributed to the first CSN breakup. Jim Gordon reputedly ripped off the piano section of "Layla" from her. She had a brief part in *Pat Garrett and Billy the Kid,* in bed with Kristofferson. The first of their three duet albums, *Full Moon,* included the Grammy-winning "From the Bottle to the Bottom" and the ballad "Loving Arms."

Kristofferson somehow managed to rebel yet rise in Nashville at the same time. The opposite was true for Willie Nelson. For years his songs flopped. He had to sell Bibles, encyclopedias, and vacuum cleaners. His wife tied him up with jump ropes while he was sleeping and beat him with a broom handle.[6] Then in '60–'61, he wrote "Crazy" for Patsy Cline and "Hello Walls" for Faron Young and scored two Top 10 hits of his own. Things were looking good, but that was as high as he could get. He tried to fit in, kept his hair short, accepted it when RCA said his own band couldn't play on his records. His true sound, when he was playing with his band, was stripped down with offbeat phrasing. His "guitar playing was a startling mixture of Charlie Christian and Mexican blues picking,"[7] as *Rolling Stone*'s country expert, Chet Flippo, described it. Nelson let RCA pour on the sugar strings, but it still wouldn't do any good. So he'd get frustrated, get in fights. He went outside Tootsie's bar and lay down in the middle of the road and waited for a car to run over him. His wives threw ashtrays and beer bottles at him. Then the house where he was living with two wives burned down. He rushed in to salvage his guitar case, stuffed with a pound of weed. "I was trying to keep the firemen from finding it and turning me over to the police."[8]

Nelson much preferred Austin, twelve hours southwest of Nashville. Most of Texas shared the conservative values of Music City, but Austin was its own weird little oasis. Threadgill's bar staged hootenannies where beatniks like the young Janis Joplin once played. The psychedelic garage band 13th Floor Elevators ("You're Gonna Miss Me") were locals. The city had a rock club called the Vulcan Gas Company that hosted everyone from Muddy Waters to the Velvet Underground. Shortly after it closed, the manager of the Texas psychedelic rock group Shiva's Headband, Eddie Wilson, noticed an abandoned National Guard armory and drove his car inside to check it out. "My heart still beats fast when I talk about that moment. It was like I had found a cave, Carlsbad Caverns or something."[9]

It held about 1,500 people. He placed a carpet in front of the stage for people to sit on and sold beer and christened it the Armadillo World Headquarters. Country-tinged artists like the Flying Burrito Brothers, Riders of the Purple Sage, and Ry Cooder played, as did Bette Midler, Frank Zappa, and Captain Beefheart. Mystic Ram Dass held lectures and would "pack the place like he was a rock star," Nelson wrote.[10]

The cultural mix was reflected on the radio in 1972 when local station KOKE-FM switched to "progressive country," interspersing country artists with rockers like the Stones, sometimes calling it country rock, sometimes redneck rock.

Nelson realized he had both hippie and hillbilly in him. His mother was three parts Cherokee; one of his ancestors died on the Trail of Tears. He meditated, read poet Kahlil Gibran and proto–New Age clairvoyant Edgar Cayce, and was sick of having to hide his pot. So Nelson moved to Austin in the summer of '72.

Although a counterculture did exist there, the rednecks and truck drivers disdained the freaks' hallucinogens, preferring booze and pills, and cherished "just kickin' hippies' asses and raisin' hell," as Jerry Jeff Walker ("Mr. Bojangles") sang on "Up Against the Wall, Redneck Mother." "You have to realize," journalist Michael Corcoran wrote, "that 1972 was still the Sixties in Austin, with the thick air of conflict whenever crew cutted rednecks and longhaired peaceniks were in the same establishment. It was jocks vs. nerds, bullies against the passive, with the war in Vietnam drawing a line that felt like a moat. But the debut of Willie and his band [at the Armadillo on August 12] . . . brought both sides together without incident. As conducted by Willie, who had just started growing out his hair, two quite divergent groups of people realized, through the shared experience of music, that they had more in common than they had thought."[11]

Just as Nelson found his audience, he finally found a sympathetic producer. One night at the after party following the Country Music Awards, Nelson played his latest batch of songs for some attendees. When he was through, Atlantic Records producer Jerry Wexler told him, "I've been looking for you a long time."

"You're not worried that it's not commercial?"

"Fuck commerce. You're going for art. You're going for truth. When the art is truthful, sales will follow."

Nelson recounted in his autobiography, "I'd never heard a record man talk that way. On the spot, I decided that Wexler was my man."[12]

Wexler, a German Polish Jew from the Bronx, had already been an important figure in R&B. In 1949, he was an editor for *Billboard* and didn't like the label "race records," so he came up with a new title for the chart, coining the term "rhythm and blues." He joined Atlantic Records and produced Ray Charles and the Drifters. He discovered down-home studios like

Stax in Memphis and FAME in Muscle Shoals and took his artists there to revitalize their careers. Now Atlantic was opening a country division, but Wexler and his partner, Ahmet Ertegun, didn't know the genre. Nelson could be their first artist and their guide to the country world.

Nelson arrived in New York in February '73 to record with Wexler and producer Arif Mardin, the same team handling Aretha Franklin's album that year, with some help from Neil Young's producer David Briggs. At last, Nelson was allowed to use his own touring band, which included his pianist sister, Bobbie. For two days they recorded a collection of gospel songs in honky-tonk mode, released a few years later as the album *The Troublemaker.* "Uncloudy Day" crystallizes his ebullience at his improved change of fortune. Next, they did *Shotgun Willie,* "possibly his finest album ever," per Stephen Thomas Erlewine at AllMusic. Waylon Jennings contributed.

The improved record sales allowed Nelson to buy a forty-acre ranch near Austin. He grew out his facial hair and got an earring. He wanted to do a concept album about divorce next, *Phases and Stages.* One album side would present the wife's perspective, the other the husband's. He played the songs to Wexler over the phone, and they reduced the producer to tears. Wexler surprised Nelson by suggesting they record it in Muscle Shoals. "You've written a blues story, Willie, and Muscle Shoals has the funkiest rhythm section in all creation."

By playing with them, Nelson said, "I was able to sharpen the edges. Wexler was right. That studio brought out the blues in me, big time."[13]

✳

Waylon Jennings was a quarter million dollars in debt. RCA agreed to front him $5,000 if he signed up for another five years.

Label head Chet Atkins was a control freak like Berry Gordy at Motown, but even more uptight. Just like Nelson, Jennings couldn't use his own damn band. Had to record at RCA. Had to use their engineers. The engineers told on Waylon if he got high. Maybe it was time to go back to Phoenix and get a job in radio.

But Jennings's drummer, Richie Albright, said, "Before you pack it in, I think we can give it one more shot. Just try it. There's another way of doing things, and that is rock and roll."[14]

Albright hooked Jennings up with Neil Reshen, the lawyer for Miles Davis and Frank Zappa. In the negotiations, Reshen and Jennings stared down Atkins and his assistant, until Jennings had to get up to take a leak.

Afterward, Reshen found him in the hall. "You're a friggin' genius, walk-ing out like that! That sewed it up. Where'd you go?"

"I had to take a piss."

"Well, that was a $25,000 piss."[15]

RCA had just lost Nelson and didn't want to lose Jennings. He got a bet-ter advance, a better royalty, and the ability to produce his own records and use his band, the Waylors. "I always wanted a live sound in the studio. . . . I liked things that weren't perfect. It was okay for microphones to leak into each other like they do on a stage performance, and I wanted to hear Richie's foot drum loud and clear. I wanted to feel some excitement."[16] The result was *Lonesome, On'ry and Mean,* technically the first outlaw country album since it was released in March, three months before *Shotgun Willie.* It was the first cover on which Jennings wore a leather vest and a beard, which he grew when he got hepatitis.

Meantime, a songwriter named Billy Joe Shaver was stalking Jennings. Shaver had a hard life: dad ran off before he was born, and mom had to leave him with grandma to go to work at the honky-tonk. Shaver left school to pick cotton, lost two fingers on his right hand in a lumber mill, but still taught himself guitar. He got backstage at the first Dripping Springs Festival in Texas and hung out in a trailer with the other country singer-songwriters trading songs. When he played his composition "Willy the Wandering Gypsy and Me," Jennings said, "Hey man, I've got to have that song."[17]

Shaver was excited, but then Jennings blew him off for six months. Dur-ing that time, Kristofferson produced Shaver's first album, *Old Five and Dimers Like Me.* Emboldened, Shaver kept after Jennings. "Finally, I caught him in Studio A of RCA. He came out of the control booth and he had a couple of bikers—bikers hung around with him a lot, some pretty tough-looking customers—and I'd had enough. I just said, 'Hey Waylon!' And he turned. I said, 'I got these songs that you claimed you was gonna listen to, and if you don't listen to 'em I'm gonna whip your ass right here in front of everybody.' And boy, whew. Man! Everything got quiet and them old boys started formin' and Waylon stopped 'em. He said, 'Hoss, you don't know how close you come to gettin' killed.' I said, 'Well, I've had enough. You done told me you was gonna do this. Now I'm full of songs and I want you to listen to 'em.' "[18]

Jennings led Shaver to a room where they could be alone. "Hoss, you don't do things like that. I'm going to listen to one song, and if it ain't no good, I'm telling you goodbye. We ain't never gonna talk again."[19]

So he played one, and Jennings told him to play another one. Then another one. Soon Jennings "was practically jumping up and down he was so fired up."[20] Jennings decided to record an entire album of Shaver tracks as a symbolic return to his roots. As Jennings wrote in his memoir, "In a bid to become respectable, country music had been shying away from its rural past, its birthright in the honky-tonks and skull orchards."[21] Skull orchards being the dangerous dive bars where a good ol' boy might kill you.

Not that Shaver was any easier to take once they started cutting *Honky Tonk Heroes*. He hovered and complained when Jennings altered his songs so much that an exasperated Jennings had to tell him to leave him alone. But after the album came out in July, Jennings offered to get Shaver a doctor to fix his fingers. Shaver laughed and said not to worry about it.[22]

Shaver wrote that the album "really did change Nashville. You used to have to wear a tie everywhere, and all of the sudden clubs were letting people in with their Levi's and long hair."[23]

Still, when Jennings played the Armadillo at Nelson's request, he was alarmed by the mass of hippies and pot smoke. "Somebody find that red-headed bastard and get him in here," Jennings snarled. When Nelson arrived backstage, Jennings snapped, "What the hell have you got me into?"

"Just trust me."[24]

The gig went so well Jennings decided to play Max's Kansas City, the Palomino in Los Angeles, and—opening for the Grateful Dead—Kezar Stadium in San Francisco in May, his biggest concert to date.

In July, Nelson staged his first annual Fourth of July Picnic, which has remained a tradition to this day. It was a sequel to the Dripping Springs Festival held in March 1972, which was supposed to be a country Woodstock but flopped due to poor promotion. Nelson figured the infrastructure was there, so he tried it again. Both years were headlined by Nelson, Jennings, and Kristofferson. Other artists in '73 included Doug Sahm, John Prine, and Tom T. Hall, scourge of Bob Dylan.

Rolling Stone's Flippo noted the difference between the two years. In 1972, "the crowd was a hostile mix of young longhairs looking for their own Woodstock and traditional country fans who just wanted to get drunk. The truce was an uneasy one, broken by beatings of the longhairs by both the drunks and the security goons." But in 1973, "the longhairs weren't beat up. It was the watershed in the progressive country movement. Prominent state politicians mingled with longhaired kids. University of Texas football coach Darrell Royal had his arm around Leon Russell. Peaceful coexistence had come to Texas, thanks to Willie's pontifical presence."[25]

Jennings wrote of the '73 gig, "Everything we did was wrong, and it didn't matter. Nobody paid to get in; the fences were torn down. I'm singing 'Bob Willis Is Still the King' and women are throwing brassieres on stage. My band just went to pieces. Girls with no tops, no bottoms, up on boys' shoulders and taunting you. If you didn't look, people were going to wonder about you; if you did look, they were going to know about you. They caught you either way. . . . One ol' gal took her clothes off and got up on a tall camera platform. She was just lying there squirming and some cowboy jumped up and mounted and went to work. It started a whole orgy over in that area. Debbie couldn't do Dallas like she did. I never quite got used to that. . . . Billy Joe [Shaver] put it best. 'We were all melted into the same comet.' All we could do was grab it by the tail and hang on for dear life."[26]

Jennings had invited his best friend, Tompall Glaser, to co-produce *Honky Tonk Heroes*. Glaser's song "Streets of Baltimore" was on Gram Parson's first album, *GP*. When Jennings recorded his follow-up, *This Time,* in October, he moved production to Glaser's studio at 916 Nineteenth Avenue South, nicknamed "Hillbilly Central."

In his book *Outlaw,* Michael Streissguth evocatively described the scene. "Its doors propped open to let in the young breezes sweeping through the West End, the so-called Hillbilly Central offices became an outlaw safe haven. Former employees recalled Willie Nelson lazing on the front lawn, and Waylon haunting the offices at three in the morning. The studio hosted a fraternity of singers, songwriters and Nashville dropouts living the verse of a strumming and bumming honkytonk song. Sessions burned into the small hours until Tompall and his entourage peeled out into the streets in search of pinball machines, drinks, and greasy food."[27]

"There was a freedom there that I didn't have any place else," Jennings said. "It was a fraternity, and Nashville was our college town."[28] Glaser made membership certificates. They worked on Jack Daniel's and diet pills. There were no windows, so they didn't know if they'd been up for two days, maybe three, maybe five, not unlike Keith Richards. Shel Silverstein helped out with lyrics if Jennings got stuck. They blew $35,000 a year playing pinball machines two days straight at a time.

Hazel Smith handled publicity for Jennings, Nelson, Glaser, and other alternative country acts like Kinky Friedman and the Texas Jewboys. (Friedman's haunting "Sold America" was well covered by Glen Campbell on his album *I Knew Jesus (Before He Was a Star),* released in May.) Smith wrote the "Hillbilly Central" column for *Country Music* magazine. When a North Carolina deejay asked her what the new style of country music was called, she realized she didn't really like the term "progressive country." She flipped through the dictionary and found "outlaw."[29] *Ladies Love Outlaws* had been one of Jennings's 1972 releases.

Nelson co-produced *This Time* with Jennings, played lead guitar, and wrote four of the ten tracks. "You just can't believe how different everything sounded when [Jennings] moved from RCA," Glaser said. "The bottom was fat and big again. You could hear the drum, it wasn't a little tick in the back. It was marvelous."[30]

RCA had a rule that all records had to be produced at an RCA studio if the artist was within a two-hundred-mile radius. But Jennings didn't budge. RCA reluctantly released the album. The title track became Jennings's first No. 1 country single, at age thirty-six. He'd score fifteen more over the next fourteen years, three of them duets with Nelson and one with the High-waymen, the supergroup they formed with Kristofferson and Johnny Cash. When other RCA artists learned Jennings didn't record at RCA, they insisted they be free to record where they wanted as well. RCA lost its monopoly and had to sell its studios.[31] On "This Time," the guitars jangled and har-monica wailed like outlaws riding off into the sunset, mission accomplished.

The Once and Current Kings

Elvis Presley, Paul McCartney, and George Harrison own the No. 1 album spot from May through July, alongside the Beatles' own greatest hits collection *1967–1970*. John Lennon writes a comeback anthem for Ringo Starr. The father of the rock and roll image, Marlon Brando, receives an X rating and upsets the Oscars.

✳

Much of 1973 could be traced back to the Big Bang when Elvis Presley shook like a cross between a Pentecostal Holy Roller and R&B shouter on television and birthed the industry of rock and roll. To date he's the only person to have five singles reach the No. 1 spot on the pop, R&B, and country charts at the same time. He was the father of both country rock and glam. Roy Orbison remembered the first time he saw him, back when Presley wore pink suits and had royal blue eyeshadow streaming down from his eyes mixed with sweat. "I can't overemphasize how shocking he looked and seemed to me that night. Actually, it affected me exactly the same way as when I first saw that David Lynch film [*Blue Velvet*]. I just didn't know what to make of it. There was just no reference point in the culture to compare it."[1] And then Presley would sing his family's favorite hymns, saying without having to say anything that the walls between passion, spirituality, and the raccs were false.

He was still on top in the spring of '73. *Elvis on Tour* won the Golden Globe in January. *He Touched Me* won the gospel Grammy in March; the album featured some of his most joyous rockers. He played more shows (167) than in any other year.

His manager, Colonel Tom Parker, wanted to beat the Beatles' performance of "All You Need Is Love" on the One World TV special, reputedly viewed by more than three hundred million worldwide in 1967. *Aloha from Hawaii via Satellite* was broadcast to over twenty countries on January 14. In the US, NBC held it until April 4 so as not to compete with the Super Bowl.[2] At $2.5 million, it was the costliest television program to date,[3] and with 51 percent of TV viewers tuning in, it would be NBC's most-watched show of the year.

Presley lost twenty-five pounds to look good in the gem-studded American Eagle jumpsuit created for the event, Presley's favorite of the many costumer Bill Belew designed for him. With the set list he summed up his career from "Hound Dog" through "Suspicious Minds." "Burning Love," which had peaked at No. 2 three months earlier, was a worthy addition to his canon. The *Aloha* concert generated its own No. 17 pop hit with his rendition of James Taylor's "Steamroller Blues."

He was more sedate now than he had been in 1970's *That's the Way It Is,* where he danced Mick Jagger under the table, flailing and pounding wildly. This was partly because he was now as big an opioid addict as Keith Richards, if not bigger (as Taylor's lyrics about "injecting your soul" and "shooting you with rhythm and blues" implied). And it was probably partly because he had just filed for divorce four days before the *Aloha* concert. Thus one of the program's most impassioned performances was "You Gave Me a Mountain," about a man struggling to cope after his wife leaves and takes their child.

"American Trilogy" sought to reflect all sides of the Civil War by combining "Dixie," a blackface minstrel song from the Confederacy, with "The Battle Hymn of the Republic," a Union Army song based on an ode to abolitionist John Brown, and "All My Trials," a lullaby from the Bahamas that became an anthem of the civil rights movement. Perhaps the best track was left off until the reissue of *Aloha,* a wistful interpretation of Gordon Lightfoot's "Early Morning Rain."

Aloha became the first quadrophonic album to top the charts and is still the bestselling quadrophonic LP. It was Presley's first pop No. 1 since 1965's *Roustabout,* and his last.

Two weeks after the show he canceled some dates in Vegas for the first time, blaming the flu. He obsessed on how Priscilla had left him for her karate instructor, Mike Stone, even though he precipitated it with his own womanizing. Then when he was back in concert on February 18, four men, possibly drunk, climbed onto the stage, the reason unclear. Presley's bodyguards intercepted them, and Presley himself used karate on one to propel him back into an audience table, roaring, "Come on, you motherfuckers!" Afterward, he apologized to the audience: "I'm sorry, ladies and gentlemen. I'm sorry I didn't break his goddamn neck is what I'm sorry about."[4] In the aftermath, an amped-up Presley decided that Mike Stone must have sent them, and he told his bodyguard Red West to arrange a hit on Stone. "There is too much pain in me. . . . He has no right to live." When Presley kept talking about it for two days, West reluctantly made inquiries and told Presley it would cost $10,000.

"Aw hell. Let's just leave it for now. Maybe it's a bit heavy."[5]

When he played Lake Tahoe in May, he was thirty pounds overweight and canceled thirteen gigs. His divorce was finalized on October 9, and six days later he was hospitalized in Memphis for pneumonia, hepatitis, and an enlarged colon. It was there his doctor, George Nichopoulos, learned that Presley had been receiving daily acupuncture treatments from someone who put Demerol, a synthetic opioid like morphine, in the needles. He was also addicted to another synthetic opioid, Dilaudid, which was five times stronger than Demerol and two and a half times as powerful as heroin.[6] Presley told himself he was different from regular junkies because he had employees inject him in the hip rather than shooting up himself. But he made sure to collect as many badges as he could from various police departments and the Bureau of Narcotics, even scoring one from Nixon himself, to help ward off the authorities should he ever be busted. He also had a California dentist who gave him cotton swabs dipped with liquid cocaine to put in his nostrils. He overdosed twice that year. His mother had struggled with similar addiction to pills and alcohol, which killed her at forty-six.

Despite the drug problem, he recorded enough great songs in 1973 to form an album that could have been his own *Blood on the Tracks,* Bob Dylan's 1975 masterpiece about his dying marriage. Presley captured twenty-eight in two sessions at Stax Records in July and December. (He picked the soul studio because it was five minutes from his house and his daughter was due to visit.) However, instead of selecting the best twelve songs to create one devastating LP, his management dispersed the tracks into five singles and three albums over the next two years.

After Presley's '68 comeback, he released critically acclaimed albums for three years, then started falling back into bad habits, putting out tons of filler in slapdash albums that seemed like they all had the same damn cover. Only hardcore fans could tell the difference between the spangled outfits he wore, whether it was the Sun King jumpsuit cover, or the Peacock cover, or the Aztec bling superhero cover, or maybe the Greg Brady Johnny Bravo matador jacket cover (that *Brady Bunch* episode aired September 14). The '60s covers at least had vibrant primary colors, but now they were all burned out. To compound the absurdity, they had indistinguishable titles like *Elvis* or *Elvis Now* or *Elvis Today*. The original title for *Elvis* was going to be *FOOL,* named after the opening track, but at least someone woke up for a minute to stop that.

Members of the Beatles, Stones, and other British bands with cool covers had all gone to art school. But the Colonel was an ex-carny who sneered, "Those guys at RCA want to do fancy artist stuff, but they don't know who the audience is."[7] Meanwhile, the Colonel blew a million a year in the casinos gambling (per the Memphis Mafia), and sold Presley's back catalog for $5 million, ensuring that Presley would never receive royalties for songs he recorded before 1973. He sabotaged it when Barbra Streisand tried to get Presley to star opposite her in *A Star Is Born,* just like he convinced Presley to pass on *West Side Story.*

Hardcore Elvis fanatic Bruce Springsteen saw the Colonel as a cautionary tale. A few years later he found the anti-Colonel manager in Jon Landau, who had edited *Rolling Stone,* mentored Lester Bangs, produced the MC5, and taught Springsteen about great films and literature. Like Presley, Springsteen recorded dozens of songs a year, but in the middle of the decade he started to wait two or three years before putting an album out, picking only the best songs. Then twenty years later he would put out a box set of outtakes for fans who appreciated them in that context, something Dylan did, too.

Yet for all the career missteps, Presley's canon equaled Sinatra's for songs of failed relationships to be played on jukeboxes in the wee small hours—only in country bars instead of New York saloons—and they didn't get really dark until the '70s. In the '60s when Presley sang sad songs he interpreted them beautifully, but he wasn't critically depressed, so they were safe. When he sang that he had no reason to live, you knew he didn't mean it. But a hint of doom crept into the tearful lion voice around '70–'71. He told his friend Larry Geller that 1972 was his worst year since 1958, when he lost his mother and went into the army. As U2's Bono said, "The big opera voice of the later years—that's the one that really hurts me."[8]

A well-sequenced Presley '73 album could start out deceptively happy with "I've Got a Thing about You Baby," his last sunny single. Like "All Shook Up," it had no snare drum, no big beat, just took it light and laid-back and made it to No. 4 country. His cover of Chuck Berry's "Promised Land" was his last song to make the pop Top 20, celebrating the touring lifestyle, a barreling successor to "Guitar Man." The writer of "Guitar Man," Jerry Reed (Burt Reynolds's sidekick in *Smokey and the Bandit*), provided "Talk About the Good Times," commemorating the church socials where Presley first learned to love the music.

The record could take a turn toward the pensive with "Where Do I Go from Here," the Paul Williams song that closed the Clint Eastwood–Jeff Bridges starrer *Thunderbolt and Lightfoot,* then start heading toward the broken dreams with "Mr. Songman," arriving at "Good Time Charlie's Got the Blues." You could compare how mournful Presley's version sounded next to the original, by Danny O'Keefe, or even Waylon Jennings's cover. The song could be Presley's epitaph: "Play around, you lose your wife / play too long, you lose your life."

"Thinking About You" clothed Presley in an unusual (for him) singer-songwriter/soft rock acoustic sound, and his voice betrayed a touching fragility, trying to stay upbeat even though his woman's left. Then the final suite of post-Priscilla despair: "Separate Ways," co-written by Memphis Mafia member Red West, which peaked on February 3 at No. 20. The *Elvis on Tour* documentary showed Presley recording it and "Always on My Mind," which made No. 9 in the UK. "Man, you're killing me with these songs," Presley said in the movie, before finding solace singing gospel with his friends, the way he'd always done.

"Loving Arms" was perhaps the best of them, a bleak contrast to the warm duet version Kris Kristofferson and Rita Coolidge offered on their *Full Moon* album that year. Presley almost goes over the top on "Fool," with a Morrissey-like vibrato baritone, walking the tightrope between camp and something that could depress the hell out of you if you heard it at the wrong time. That song rose to No. 12 on easy listening. Finally, in "My Boy," a father watches over his sleeping son. His marriage is dead, but he resolves to stay in it because he doesn't want to be separated from his child. It was the kind of song you didn't hear in rock and roll, only easy listening and country, where it made No. 1 and No. 14, respectively (and No. 20 in pop).

❋

A week after Presley filmed *Aloha from Hawaii,* Time magazine put Marlon Brando on the cover to celebrate his return to form, after
a decade of mediocre films, with *The Godfather* (1972) and *Last Tango in
Paris.* The latter movie was released in the US in February after a four-
month delay due to a struggle with the Motion Picture Association of America, which ended up giving the film an X rating.

Almost as much as Presley, Brando created the *image* of rock and roll.
Rebelling against a cold father who stuck him in a military academy, he
popularized ripped T-shirts and jeans in *A Streetcar Named Desire* (1951)
and made it cool to be a sweaty, sullen, mumbling slob, flouting the dress
code of the Sunset Strip nightclubs. When he starred in *The Wild One*
(1953), based on fabricated news reports about biker gangs running amok
in Hollister, California, the leather-jacketed Brando defined the rock and roll
attitude seven months before Presley's first single. "What are you rebelling
against?" they asked his character in the film. "Whaddaya got?" he dead-
panned.

Presley copped Brando's surly attitude in *Jailhouse Rock* but seemed
lightweight in comparison. Both he and Gene Vincent borrowed the actor's
leather look. Lennon howled, wounded, like Brando yelling, "Stella." Pete
Townshend and Keith Moon smashed their instruments like Brando smashing windows in *Streetcar.* Keith Richards named his son after him. Kurt
Cobain slouched like him.

His X-ray presence exposed the mainstream's inherent phoniness. Before cinema, actors onstage needed to overact to project to the back row.
They no longer needed to after the invention of the close-up, but continued
performing in a mannered style, which no one noticed until Brando's naturalistic method acting revealed how unrealistic the others were.

Jack Nicholson had recently established himself as heir apparent in *Five
Easy Pieces,* both exploding in rage—punching cars, smashing dishes off
restaurant tables—and crying tears of regret in front of his father rendered
immobile by a stroke. Brando took back the crown in *Last Tango* with his
own tour de force. Confronting the corpse of his wife, who had cheated
on him before killing herself, he excoriates her with a string of foul abuse
before breaking down, apologizing, and sobbing. He later wrote, "When
it was finished, I decided that I wasn't ever again going to destroy myself
emotionally to make a movie."[9] Perhaps he was drawing on his confused
feelings for the two women he said influenced his relationships with all

other females: his mother, who abandoned him in his youth for alcoholic benders, and his nanny, who co-slept nude with him until he was seven, before abandoning him to get married.

When he was awarded Best Actor for *The Godfather* at the Academy Awards that March (after having been nominated for both films), he showed again that he was ahead of the curve, in this case on the issue of diversity. He stayed away from the venue and asked Apache/Yaqui actress Sacheen Littlefeather to take his place at the podium, where she announced, "He very regretfully cannot accept this very generous award. And the reasons for this being are the treatment of American Indians today by the film industry and on television in movie reruns, and also with recent happenings at Wounded Knee." At that moment the American Indian Movement (AIM) was in a stand-off with FBI agents and federal marshals in South Dakota, protesting failures to honor treaties, which resulted in shootouts that killed two Native Americans and left one marshal paralyzed. Littlefeather later recalled, "John Wayne was in the wings, ready to have me taken off stage. He had to be restrained by six security guards."[10]

Along with Brando, *Last Tango*'s director, Bernardo Bertolucci, was nominated for an Oscar. "This must be the most powerfully erotic movie ever made, and it may turn out to be the most liberating movie ever made," *The New Yorker*'s Pauline Kael raved. "Bertolucci and Brando have altered the face of an art form. This is a movie people will be arguing about, I think, for as long as there are movies."

She proved more prescient than even she suspected. Forty-three years later, a Spanish nonprofit condemned the film on the International Day for the Elimination of Violence Against Women and ignited a Twitter storm. The controversy concerned nineteen-year-old actress Maria Schneider's lack of consent in a scene in which Brando's character raped hers. The scene had been written in the script, but on the day of the shoot Brando and Bertolucci decided to add the detail that he uses butter to anally rape her—and didn't discuss it with Schneider beforehand.

"Maria knew everything because she had read the script, where it was all described. The only novelty was the idea of the butter," Bertolucci maintained. "We wanted her spontaneous reaction to that improper use [of the butter]."[11]

"When they told me, I had a burst of anger. Woo! I threw everything,"[12] Schneider recounted. In another interview she remembered, "Marlon said to me: 'Maria, don't worry, it's just a movie,' but during the scene, even though what Marlon was doing wasn't real, I was crying real tears. I felt humiliated and to be honest, I felt a little raped, both by Marlon and by Bertolucci."[13]

Ironically, Brando felt exploited by Bertolucci's process as well. "Marlon said he felt raped and manipulated by it and he was 48. And he was Marlon Brando!"[14] Schneider said.

The director wanted Brando to actually have sex with Schneider on camera, as the actors had in Andy Warhol's *Blue Movie*. "But I told him that was impossible," Brando said. "If that happens, our sex organs become the centerpiece of the film. He didn't agree with me."[15]

Still, he did try to do a scene nude, but, as he wrote in his 1994 autobiography, "it was such a cold day that my penis shrank to the size of a peanut. . . . It simply withered. . . . I was humiliated, but not ready to surrender yet. . . . One of the more embarrassing experiences of my professional career."[16]

Brando's secretary advised him to quit, but Brando believed he would be sued if he did so. Robert Hofler wrote in *Sexplosion,* "[Schneider] often rolled her eyes at his habit of disrobing behind drawn curtains."[17] The actress said, "Marlon was shy about his body, but nudity wasn't a problem for me in those days as I thought it was beautiful."[18]

In the end Bertolucci cut Brando's nudity. "I had so identified myself with Marlon that I cut it out of shame for myself. To show him naked would have been like showing me naked."[19]

Brando didn't speak to him for fifteen years.

✳

Red Rose Speedway had the makings for a strong album, but McCartney fumbled the assembly, like Presley. The sessions included "Live and Let Die," "Hi, Hi, Hi," "C Moon," "Country Dreamer," and "Mama's Little Girl," but he decided to use them for singles and not include them on the LP. He did perform three of them in the album's promotional TV special, *James Paul McCartney,* which aired on April 16. The program was memorable primarily for the glam androgyny sequence where he sang a Busby Berkeley number surrounded by dancers who wore tuxes on one side of their body and sequined bathing suits on the other.

"Hi, Hi, Hi" was cut from the broadcast because it advocated meeting up with your woman, buying a bootleg record, smoking marijuana, and doing it with your "sweet banana." After it peaked at No. 10 in February, the police fined him £240 for growing cannabis on his Scottish farm. He maintained that a fan had sent him some seeds and he didn't know what they were, so he just planted them to find out. He would rack up an impressive list of pot busts (Sweden '72, Los Angeles '75, Tokyo '80, Barbados '84).

The best moment of the special was the opening sequence, which featured McCartney and Wings jamming "Big Barn Bed" in front of a wall made up of dozens of TV sets. The song carried some of his finest post-Beatle harmonies, though it was a pity he wasted the cool groove on lyrics like "sleeping on a pillow / leaping armadillo." But after years of pushing himself to write significant anthems like "Hey Jude," "Let It Be," and "Maybe I'm Amazed," he was giving his brain a rest. Or maybe it was the pot.

The best of his new songs celebrated his bucolic life in Scotland. Wading in a stream in "Country Dreamer," playing with his daughter on a mountainside in "Mama's Little Girl," commiserating with a bird after a fight with his woman in "Single Pigeon," or with a sheep in "Little Lamb Dragonfly," before drifting into an orchestral reverie with the New York Philharmonic.

Only two songs, perhaps, drew on the bad blood from the Beatles' breakup, the first being his theme to the James Bond film *Live and Let Die*. Maybe the subtext of lyrics about how "you got to give the other fella hell" was "All right, Lennon, you wanted to leave the group? Well, I'll crush you"—which he did on the charts, if not with the critics.

"C Moon" was McCartney's answer to Lennon's line in "How Do You Sleep," which sneered that McCartney lived "with straights." "So what if I live with straights?" McCartney shrugged in an interview. "I like straights. I have straight babies."[20] The title was inspired by "L7" from "Wooly Bully," meaning "square," the shape that the symbols L and 7 make when combined. The opposite of a square is a circle, which a C and a half-moon form. He gave the song a Jamaican feel, to further underscore that he was hip.

Harrison addressed the animosity more directly in "Sue Me Sue You Blues." But fans actually had cause to hope for a thaw in ex-Beatle relations when Lennon, Harrison, and Starr announced they were not renewing their contract with Allen Klein in March. Klein was one of the main reasons the group split three years earlier; McCartney didn't trust him and didn't want to be managed by him. "Let's say possibly Paul's suspicions were right," Lennon conceded in an interview.[21] Indeed, Klein conned the Rolling Stones out of the publishing rights to their songs before 1970.

"Well you know they were wrong . . . and you knew it all along, you did the right thing," McCartney sang in "Get on the Right Thing," an exuberant example of why he was the guru of the power pop genre featuring the Raspberries, Big Star, and Apple's own Badfinger.

Even after their split, the Beatles were bigger than ever on the pop chart. Their greatest hits compilation *The Beatles 1967–1970* (known as *The Blue Album*) was No. 1 the week of May 26, while its companion *1962–1966*

(*The Red Album*) was No. 3. Then *Red Rose Speedway* took over the peak for three weeks, before being knocked out by Harrison's *Living in the Material World* for *five* weeks. In the UK, neither album made the summit, because they were blocked by the soundtrack to Starr's movie *That'll Be the Day*. On the singles chart, McCartney's "My Love" ruled for a month starting June 2, before Harrison's "Give Me Love (Give Me Peace on Earth)" replaced it, followed by Beatles compatriot Billy Preston's "Will It Go Round in Circles."

Harrison produced *Material World* himself. He regretted the excess echo Phil Spector glazed *All Things Must Pass* with, though he brought back classical musician John Barham to orchestrate a few epics like "The Day the World Gets Round," which Harrison wrote the day after he staged the Concert for Bangladesh.[22] (The album for that charity benefit won the Grammy for Album of the Year in March '73.)

"Give Me Love" managed to be a remake and sequel to "My Sweet Lord" while transcending it, standing alongside "Imagine" as the purest expression of the Beatles' Aquarian Age idealism. The fact that Harrison's voice did not have the raw power of Lennon's or McCartney's actually made the song more moving, as his strain to hit the high notes mirrored his effort to connect with God. It might be a standard hymn today were it not for the line "keep me free from birth." It reflected his Hindu goal of attaining enlightenment so he would not have to reincarnate again—and maybe a desire not to have kids at that time, though he certainly loved his son, Dhani, when he had him years later. But most listeners didn't analyze the lyrics, and everyone from Presbyterians to Jesus freaks to Hare Krishnas bought the record in droves.

"Don't Let Me Wait Too Long" should have been the follow-up single, as it delivered that exuberant Beatles sound so many craved. But maybe Harrison wanted people to have to buy the album to get it, since LPs cost four and a half times as much as singles. The album was otherwise a more minor-key, somber effort, but its warm sound grew on you with sustained listens.

❊

April saw the release of two Ringo Starr films. He directed the documentary *Born to Boogie* about his friend Marc Bolan. He acted in *That'll Be the Day* alongside David Essex ("Rock On"); they played young men in the early days of British rock and roll. Starr brought the same naturalistic, low-key charm that he had to the Beatles' films. But just as he got his film career rolling, an old mate dragged him back into music.

Lennon wrote "I'm the Greatest" after catching a rerun of *A Hard Day's Night* on TV. "It's the Muhammad Ali line, you know. I couldn't sing it, but it was perfect for Ringo. He could say 'I'm the greatest' and people wouldn't get upset. Whereas if I said 'I'm the greatest,' they'd all take it *so* seriously."[23]

Lennon, Starr, and Harrison were all in Los Angeles that spring, attending a fundraiser for Daniel Ellsberg together on March 7. Six days later Starr and Lennon entered Sunset Sound Recorders with the backing group that regularly played on Lennon and Harrison albums: keyboardist Billy Preston, drummer Jim Keltner, and bassist Klaus Voormann (a friend since the Beatles' early days in Hamburg).

When Harrison called the studio, Lennon told him to come down to help. Harrison added the guitar hook, as he often did on Lennon-McCartney songs like "And I Love Her" and "Help!" They tweaked the lyrics so Starr could revisit his Billy Shears persona from *Sgt. Pepper.* Lennon harmonized. Starr climaxed with a rant that he was the greatest in any world, and in eighteen minutes it was done. Harrison said they should form a new group called the Ladders. Within four days *Melody Maker* was reporting that Voormann was "the bassist rumored to replace Paul McCartney after his departure from the group."

McCartney was stuck in the UK, his visa blocked due to his pot conviction. When Starr returned to London the following month, McCartney gave him another song for his rapidly evolving *Ringo* album, "Six O'Clock," a dawnbreak vow from a husband to treat his wife better after a night spent fighting.

Back in New York, Lennon filled his new album, *Mind Games,* with many such appeals to his wife to save their marriage. He'd shattered it the previous November when he and Ono watched the presidential election results with Abbie Hoffman and Jerry Rubin. The landslide for Nixon shocked Lennon, and he quickly grew bitter over how "stupid" he'd been to believe in the possibility of Revolution. Now Nixon would be able to eject him from the country for sure, he assumed. He got hammered on tequila and cocaine and turned on the other three, just as he did with everyone who at one time or another served as a guru in his life. He'd put them on a pedestal, then decide they betrayed him, from the Maharishi to Allen Klein—replaying the pattern with his parents, who had both abandoned him as a child.

Per Jerry Rubin's roommate Carol Realini, Lennon told Ono in front of the party, "I don't want to be John and Yoko anymore." Later that evening he had sex with Realini in the basement. "He told me that before he and Yoko married, they made a pact and were totally monogamous for all the time up until that moment. It's true, she told me. And he told me he wanted to break the pact. He wanted her to know that he was through with her and he had been trying to tell her this for some time and he couldn't get through to her. He felt the one way that he could get through to her would be to break the pact in a way that she would know he broke the pact."[24]

Almost immediately he was consumed with regret, as photographer Bob Gruen captured in a picture the next day. He, Ono, and Lennon "took a walk down to the river and as we were walking along the jetty [Lennon] suddenly prostrated himself at Yoko's feet. It was very spur of the moment, totally unposed."[25] Many songs on *Mind Games* were likewise apologies or tribute songs, "Aisumasen" (Japanese for "I'm sorry"), "You Are Here" (the name of a joint art exhibition they staged in happier times), "I Know (I Know)," and the best of them, "Out the Blue," which could be a wedding standard. He strove to get Ono pumped back up for more political activism with "Only People": "We can't be denied with woman and man side by side!" He whooped like a cheerleader while the gospel chorus clapped.

But Ono was done with Lennon—though she wasn't ready to say goodbye permanently. She noticed Lennon was attracted to their Chinese assistant, May Pang, and decided to set them up together, so she could still call him multiple times a day and take him back later, if she felt like it. Pang (born 1950) was shocked when Ono suggested the arrangement; she resisted for two weeks but eventually found herself falling for Lennon. When the time came for Lennon to actually sing "Out the Blue" in the studio, it was Pang he sang it to. On "Meat City" he yelled, "I'm going to China!" He departed for Los Angeles with Pang in tow.

Goodbye to Glitter

Ziggy Stardust announces his retirement on July 3. Marc Bolan proclaims that glam is dead. Brian Eno departs Roxy Music. Lou Reed breaks with Bowie. Iggy creates the template for the self-immolating punk. Kiss dons makeup.

✱

None of the glam rockers had much success in the US except for Alice Cooper, the Sweet (who had three Top 5 hits), and Bowie, whose touring began to pay off when "Space Oddity" reached No. 15 in April. But even in San Francisco, Bowie filled only 400 seats in the 5,400-seat Winterland Ballroom. In the UK, he packed 19,000-seat venues like Earl's Court. Aside from New York and LA, he and Roxy Music only drew big crowds in, ironically, the industrial cities of Detroit and Cleveland.

The fans in those working-class towns shared lead singer Bryan Ferry's desire to transcend gritty reality. Ferry was the son of a coal miner and grew up without indoor plumbing.[1] Thus he camped it up as a smarmy film star in dinner jacket and bow tie and named his band after the Roxy movie theater. The scantily clad beauties on Roxy album covers harked back to lounge music LPs of yore, even as the songs critiqued the sensibility: in "In Every Dream Home a Heartache" Ferry orders a blow-up beauty doll to keep him company in his penthouse.

Ferry sounded like he was stuffed up as he sneered like Bob Dylan, but he was a handsome 6'1" with thick black hair, and the women flipped over him. It was an intriguing combination. Simon Reynolds wrote in his history of the glam movement, "In purely musical terms, Ferry's greatest invention is his voice on the first two albums, the reptilian vibrato that paved the way for neurotic new wave mandroids like Gary Numan and Devo."[2] (Not to mention the Talking Heads' David Byrne.)

Brian Eno started out as Roxy's soundman, but he made such a show out of mixing their music with his equipment that they put him onstage alongside the sax player. Soon Eno began playing the VCS3 synth. But Ferry dug soul and the Beatles, while Eno wanted to experiment like the Velvet Underground. The contrast made for a groundbreaking two albums, but Ferry felt his vision was being hijacked both in the studio and onstage. After a tour to support the March release of *For Your Pleasure*, Eno left in May. Ferry managed to squeeze in a solo album of covers (including a song by Bob Dylan) before Roxy cranked out a third album, *Stranded*, in time for the holidays. Eno praised it as their best, even though he wasn't on it.

He recorded his solo debut, *Here Come the Warm Jets*, with the help of musicians from Roxy, Hawkwind, the Pink Fairies, and King Crimson. "I wanted to see what happens when you combine different identities like that . . . with the knowledge that there might be accidents, accidents which will be more interesting than what I had intended."[3] Todd Haynes used "Needle in a Camel's Eye" to open his 1998 glam epic *Velvet Goldmine*, featuring glitter fans running through the city just as Beatlemaniacs had in the beginning of *A Hard Day's Night*.

❊

While Ferry's and Eno's fortunes rose, the original glitter king was getting worried, though he would never admit it. Marc Bolan's best single, "20th Century Boy," went unnoticed by Yanks. (Even when the Replacements covered it for their album *Let It Be* ten years later, they changed their mind and shelved it in favor of a cover of Kiss's "Black Diamond.") "Glam rock is dead," he proclaimed on the cover of *Melody Maker*.

"Essentially what they tried to do with Bowie was create another Marc Bolan, but the interest with the kids was not there," he railed preposterously to Cameron Crowe in *Creem* that July. "I don't think that David has anywhere near the charisma or balls that I have. Or Alice (Cooper) has. Or Donny Osmond has got. He's not gonna make it, in any sort of way. . . . I mean, I don't consider David to be even remotely near big enough to give me any competition."[4]

Maybe he and Bowie laughed about the smack talk behind the scenes. The same month, he visited Bowie backstage during his "farewell" concert. But he seemed preoccupied with his rival, naming one album *Zinc Alloy and The Hidden Riders of Tomorrow*.

It was actually Bowie who followed Bolan's lead when T. Rex went soul on *Tanx,* with beguiling songs like "Electric Slim and the Factory Hen," drenched in proto-disco strings by Tony Visconti. Bolan brought black backup singers onstage, including Gloria Jones, who sang the original "Tainted Love" in 1965. On NBC's *Midnight Special* they smashed their tambourines and screamed like Tina Turner while he howled on his guitar like Hendrix and Prince, which even Bowie couldn't do, though Bowie got his own black backup singer in 1974, Ava Cherry. Bolan left his wife for Jones, and Bowie moved Cherry into the house with Angie, sending his wife over the edge with rage.

✳

By July, Bowie's entourage had lived so extravagantly off the record label (limos, four-star hotels) that there was no money left for another leg of the tour. His manager suggested he announce his retirement to milk some publicity out of the last scheduled date.

"I think he stopped Ziggy when he did because the reality of fame was more than he could handle," said music journalist Tony Parsons. "He had wanted it all his life, and had tried to get it for over a decade, but when it finally came it frightened the living daylights out of him. I remember the Earls Court gig [May 12, London] when he came out in the Japanese robe as the music from *A Clockwork Orange* came blasting out, there were all these Australians taking their clothes off and getting in fights and vomiting on girls in the front row."[5]

His last show as Ziggy was at the Hammersmith Odeon on July 3, filmed by D. A. Pennebaker (*Don't Look Back, Monterey Pop*). An hour-long special aired in 1974, later released theatrically as *Ziggy Stardust and the Spiders from Mars*. The film captures an audience full of Ziggy mullets. Schoolgirls freak like bygone Beatlemaniacs and future Durannies. Angie arrives in a limo and struts through the fans, reveling in the attention. Ringo and Bolan hang backstage. The future Sid Vicious, John Ritchie, is glimpsed in a Bowie shirt. Off-camera, future Sex Pistols guitarist Steve Jones managed to steal some unattended equipment.

It seems surprising today to see the audience presented primarily as crying teenyboppers, especially juxtaposed against Bowie's proto-goth cabaret songs like "My Death." Frequently, though, the singer beamed. He got down on all fours and Ronson climbed on his back, then kneeled over him and played his guitar into Bowie's ear. Former Yardbirds guitarist Jeff Beck joined them for a few numbers, including "The Jean Genie," making the song's connection to the Yardbirds' "I'm a Man" explicit.

Then Bowie announced, "This show will stay the longest in our memories, not just because it is the end of the tour but because it is the last show we'll ever do."[6] He launched into "Rock and Roll Suicide," to his audience's confused dismay.

Journalist Charles Shaar Murray said the Bowie camp had alerted him in advance, "enabling *NME* to have its 'Bowie: That's It, I Quit' cover story rolling off the presses before Bowie had made the onstage announcement."[7] Murray wrote in the piece, "Glitter fans all over the world went into mourning."

Bowie returned to touring nine months later, but it *was* the end of his live performing with Ronson and other Spiders from Mars. Their camaraderie helped ignite Bowie mania when Bowie threw his arm around Ronson while singing "Starman" on *Top of the Pops*. Ronson did occasionally pull some slight *Spinal Tap* poses when blasting the guitar, but his gorgeous string arrangements were one of Bowie's secret weapons. Alas, intraband money tensions sank the group, as it did Neil Young's touring band. When Bowie hired pianist Mike Garson, bassist Trevor Bolder and drummer Mick Woodmansey got wind that Bowie was paying the new guy more than them and demanded a raise. Five days after the concert, the Spiders reunited to play on Bowie's *Pin Ups* cover album, but when he recorded *Diamond Dogs* the following January none of the Spiders were involved.

For director Todd Haynes, the last Ziggy show took on significance as the moment Bowie left his gay identity behind, as if he had appropriated queerness for a gimmick, then discarded it, the way some white artists did with the blues. In *Velvet Goldmine* the ambitious Bowie figure transforms into a cold, whitewashed mainstream performer who doesn't even appear to be played by the same actor.

Bowie did concede that queerness "seemed to be the one taboo that everyone was too afraid to break. I thought—well, if there's one thing that's going to put me on the edge, this is it. Long hair didn't mean much anymore."[8] Twenty years later he explained his fascination with gay culture to *Rolling Stone,* "There might have been free love, but it was heterosexual love. I like this twilight world. I like the idea of these clubs and these people and everything about it being something that nobody knew anything about."[9]

In some ways his trajectory paralleled that of Bob Dylan, who wrote some of the greatest civil rights anthems in the space of two years, then moved on. Of his period as a gay lightning rod, Bowie commented, "I'm quite proud that I did that. On the other hand I didn't want to carry a banner for any group of people, I didn't like that aspect of it: this is going to start overshadowing my writing and everything else that I do."[10]

Some fans felt betrayed and branded them poseurs, but Dylan was a Jew born while the Holocaust unfolded overseas, and Bowie was bisexual. "When I was 14, sex suddenly became all-important to me. It didn't really matter who or what it was with, as long as it was a sexual experience. So it was some very pretty boy in class in some school or other that I took home and neatly fucked on my bed upstairs."[11] In the late '60s he read *City of Night* by John Rechy, "and that led me a merry dance in the early Seventies, when gay clubs really became my lifestyle and all my friends were gay."[12]

But "as the years went on it became a thing where, sexually, I was pretty much with women the majority of the time. . . . Although I no longer consider myself gay or even bisexual it shouldn't be assumed that therefore I have decided that heterosexual is correct and gay is wrong. . . . It is just that psychologically it was a decision that was made for me, in my head somewhere. There was never the thought, oh well, I'll be straight now."[13]

✳

After the success of *Transformer*, it seemed natural Reed should ask Bowie to return as producer. But Bowie was touring the US, Asia, and England when Reed wanted to record. Also, journalist Murray theorized, Reed did not want to look dependent on Bowie. Instead, he reached out to Alice Cooper's producer Bob Ezrin. Reed felt that Ezrin produced the best version of his song "Rock and Roll," in a cover version by Mitch Ryder and his band Detroit.

He was tired of the rock press attacking him for going glitter, saying his white phantom makeup made him look like "an effeminate Frankenstein monster" (*Rolling Stone*) "giving rim jobs to the Fugs" (*Creem*).

"I just think that everyone's into this scene because it's supposedly the thing to do right now," Reed said. "You can't fake being gay. If they claim they're gay, they're going to have to make love in a gay style, and most people aren't capable of making that commitment. . . . That line everyone's bisexual—that's a very popular thing to say right now. I think it's meaningless."[14] He told Lester Bangs, "I may come out with a hardhat album. Come out with an anti-gay song, saying 'Get back in your closets, you fuckin' queers!' That'll really do it!"[15]

Reed enlisted Steve Winwood and Cream's Jack Bruce to play on *Berlin,* which was actually recorded in London, not Germany. The recently released *Cabaret* had revived a fascination with the city; perhaps that influenced the titling. Also, in "Caroline Says I" he sings to his "Germanic Queen." The record focused on the disintegration of his marriage to Bettye Kronstad, his own *Blood on the Tracks.* They married in '73 and divorced less than a year later.

"We dated for a couple of years before we moved in together," Kronstad said. "Lewis was quiet, reflective—a writer—and a teddy bear. I admired his writing very much. A simplistic explanation for why I married him could be that he wrote 'Sweet Jane.'"[16]

She met him in 1968 when she was a nineteen-year-old Columbia student. Drunk, he slapped her behind at the end of their first meeting. She ignored his requests for dates afterward until she read a newspaper article praising the Velvet Underground. He liked that she seemed square, innocent, and his parents loved her. In "Sweet Jane" the prince of decadence envisions a life of conventional domestic bliss.

But in "Caroline Says I," the female tells the singer he's not a man and she'll "get it" somewhere else. In "Oh Jim," he "beats her black and blue," reviving the domestic violence theme from the early Velvet track "There She Goes Again."

"One night, Lou had been drinking and snorting cocaine in a veritable marathon," Kronstad recalled. "Suddenly, he turned around and hit me in the face—hard, [then] started laughing hysterically and fell down onto the bed."[17] In "Caroline Says II" (a remake of an unreleased Velvets classic, "Stephanie Says," with new lyrics), the woman picks herself off the floor and tells him, "You can hit me all you want to, but I don't love you anymore," then takes speed and punches a windowpane.

"The Kids" recounts the true story of how Kronstad's eighteen-year-old mother left her abusive father before social services took Kronstad away. Producer Ezrin asked his seven-year-old to act out the child being separated from the parent, crying for mommy. In the process, Ezrin's two-year-old began screaming, which Ezrin used for the end of the track.

In "The Bed," the female protagonist cuts her wrists to ghostly horror-film music. Finally, "Sad Song" recasts "Satellite of Love" as a guitar-and-strings epic in which Reed resolves not to obsess over the lost relationship anymore, though he keeps circling back to the idea that "someone else would have broken both her arms."

Today, after Chris Brown, Rhianna, and the #MeToo movement, few artists hoping for success would release songs with those lyrics. And even then, *Berlin* didn't do well in the States upon its July release, stalling at No. 98, particularly dismal after *Transformer* had reached No. 29. In the UK, it made it to No. 9. *The New York Times* liked it; *Rolling Stone* didn't at the time but includes it today among the 500 Greatest Albums.

The album became a self-fulfilling prophecy when the twenty-four-year-old Kronstad left him in Paris on September 17. Five days later, he collapsed onstage in Brussels. He asked the doctor who gave them amphetamine shots to implore her to return on his behalf, to no avail.

When Kronstad went to purchase the album, the record store clerk informed her that people were returning it because it was "the most depressing album in the world."[18] It was the lyrics that made it so. The orchestration on tracks like "Caroline Says I" sounds deceptively upbeat. "How Do You Think It Feels" and "Oh, Jim" boast juicy horn sections.

"[Reed] didn't even want to listen to the album," Ezrin said. "Every time he listens to the album it gets to him. I mean, I can see tears coming into his eyes and everything."[19]

✳

Glam forked into proto-punk and glam metal, though some bands like the New York Dolls straddled both camps. Really, "metal" and "punk" were names marketing executives selected to organize the record store bins. The Stooges rocked as hard as any metal band, but Iggy Pop created the punk archetype by simultaneously antagonizing and entertaining his audience, often while destroying himself onstage.

He designed his glam look to piss guys off as much as to attract the females. "I would take a little glass bottle of Johnson & Johnson baby oil, pour it all over my body and face, then cover myself in gold and silver glitter."[20] In eyeliner, dog collar, silver-lame evening gloves from Kmart, thigh-high boots, cheetah jacket, leopard print pants or skirt or tutu or black bikini underwear with pubes (and more) poking out, he'd pant, "I stick it deep inside," then flip his head over and contort like a snake charmer on a bad acid trip.

According to the Jim Jarmusch documentary *Gimme Danger*, Pop (né Jim Osterberg) was getting back at society for insulting his family. His parents were loving, well-read schoolteachers who lived in a trailer. Some well-to-do boys from school came by, shook the trailer, and laughed at the Osterbergs. Jim Morrison became Pop's favorite singer when Pop saw him in concert making fun of University of Michigan students, mocking them as "the Mighty Men of Michigan," then grunting like a gorilla, which sparked the crowd into throwing beer at him.[21]

The songs the Stooges tested live in '73 were as obnoxious as any by later Michigan trailer-trash idol Eminem: "Wet My Bed," "Head on the Curb," "Open Up and Bleed," "Fresh Rag" ("I can smell you walkin' down the street with your fresh rag on"). In a radio station on March 27, he took off his pants, danced around, and told the audience that he was naked and playing with his balls, all the while slapping his member against his stomach. The station almost lost its FCC license, and Bowie's manager dropped the band. Helen Reddy's husband took the reins briefly but dropped them after Pop said gay and Jewish slurs onstage.

Sometimes it seemed Pop might hurt the audience. In June he threw a piece of watermelon into the crowd and gave a woman a concussion. Journalist Nick Kent said, "Once, he grabbed a chick and stared blankly into her face, almost beating up some poor wretch who dared to laugh at him."[22] When Warhol superstar Geri Miller taunted him to throw up on her, he obliged.

Or he might hurt himself, like a rock and roll Evel Knievel. He was one of the originators of stage diving, but on at least one occasion nobody caught him and he chipped his tooth. The live album *Metallic K.O.,* recorded in October 1973 and February 1974, "is the only rock album I know where you can actually hear hurled beer bottles breaking against guitar strings," Lester Bangs maintained.[23] The title came from the war that erupted between Pop and a pack of bikers at the Michigan Palace. When a biker ignored Pop's warning to stop heckling him, Pop charged into the audience at him—and was promptly beaten up.

He didn't feel the pain because of the smack, which infested the band in late 1970. Guitarist Scott Asheton said he was hanging out backstage with Parliament-Funkadelic when one of them offered him "horse."[24] Asheton didn't know what it was but liked it. When he told Pop, Pop wanted to try some, too.

By July 1973, Pop was ravenous for any fix. Lynn Edelson, who painted Robert Plant's pants, recalls the night he showed up at Plant's room in New York's Drake Hotel. At the time, Zeppelin was playing onstage at Madison Square Garden. "There's this banging and banging at the door and I looked through the peep hole and it's *Iggy Pop* . . . so I figure what the hell. I let him in and he's beet red. He's as red as that paint that you have in kinder-garten. I hadn't met Iggy before. I could see him shaking all over and he was perspiring, and I feel his head and he must have a 103 fever. And I get really nervous. I said, 'What did you do?' He said, 'Well I ran out of coke so I shot up niacin.' So I'm like, 'Oh shit, we've got to get your body tempera-ture down. Take your clothes off.' So he takes off his clothes and he lies down on Percy's [Robert Plant's] bed. Now this is getting really bad, here he is lying naked on the bed. I wrapped him up in towels and could feel his temperature going down, and he fell asleep. A couple hours later Percy comes back and he says, 'Who the bloody hell is in my bed.' And he's freak-ing out. And I just laughed and I said, 'Go and look.' And there's Iggy totally fucked up with towels all over him. They really thanked me."[25]

She led the Zeppelin road crew to one of the midnight shows the Stooges played at Max's Kansas City from July 30 to August 6. Warhol superstar Jackie Curtis told Pop she wanted "to see blood tonight."[26] Legend has it that Alice Cooper, Lou Reed, Todd Rundgren, and Bebe Buell were there. Pop said it was like "trying to do a rock and roll show in front of your first-grade class with the teacher present, except all the students had morphed into your critics." He started walking on the tables and stepped on a chair that slipped, knocking him onto a table filled with glasses that smashed on the floor. He fell on them and his chest was cut up, but he kept performing, after inquiring, "Is there a professional photographer in the house?"[27] There was, and the images inspired Sid Vicious to carve up his own chest onstage five years later. Alice Cooper took Pop to the emergency room. "Everybody thought the stitches were really sexy," Buell said.[28] (It wasn't the first time he'd cut himself onstage. He did it with a drumstick in May 1969 at Ohio Wesleyan University.)

The following night, Pop saw Rundgren and Buell at a New York Dolls show, then popped up unannounced at Rundgren's apartment just before Rundgren was leaving on tour. Rundgren warned Buell not to leave Pop in the apartment unattended or he'd steal everything to fund his habit. He didn't steal, but he did give downers to the dog, who survived apparently unscathed.

Karmic justice, perhaps, was enacted a few weeks later when Buell's friend gave Pop powder he assumed was coke but was something very dif-ferent. The Stooges had traveled to the Kennedy Center in Washington, DC, to open for Mott the Hoople on August 19. The powder was angel dust/PCP, a dissociative anaesthetic that had been outlawed for humans (replaced by ketamine) and was now supposed to be used only as an animal tranquil-izer. Halfway through a set featuring new songs like "I've Got a Cock in My

Pocket" and "Buttfuckers Trying to Run My World," he collapsed onstage, mumbling, "My doctor told me not to play tonight."[29] Keith Moon and Waylon Jennings were also waylaid onstage by the suddenly trendy drug.[30] Sly Stone and James Brown became addicts.

Pop managed to stagger into the crowd, where he reached out to shake an audience member's hand, then pulled away. A fan splattered him with Hostess cherry pies, and another doused him with wine, an Iggy tradition since he'd rubbed peanut butter on himself onstage three years ago. He rubbed these condiments in as well. "Dance to the beat of the living dead," the lyrics to "Raw Power" went.

✳

Like Lou Reed, the members of Mott the Hoople were determined to prove they could make it without David Bowie (who had written and produced their biggest hit, "All the Young Dudes"). When Bowie offered them the quasi-retro "Drive-in Saturday" they turned it down. (Bowie said, "I was so annoyed that one night in Florida, I got very drunk and shaved my eyebrows off."[31]) The joke was on Mott, because Bowie's song rose to No. 3 in the UK. But *Mott,* self-produced and released in July, had its own classics like "Honaloochie Boogie" and "I Wish I Was Your Mother," both with the band's uniquely haunting, bittersweet edge. The latter featured the requisite gender bending but sported a Faces-like mandolin and lyrics in which Ian Hunter acknowledged that his mean behavior toward his lover was dooming their relationship. At the same time, he felt bad about it and yearned for a family—a theme that seemed more country than glitter rock.

On their next single, "Roll Away the Stone," he implored his partner to keep their love alive, enticing her with a rockabilly party on Saturday night. Hunter sang in Bowie mode, accompanied by Thunderthighs, the "Walk on the Wild Side" backing vocalists. The song was so catchy the Hollies tried to rush out a cover before Mott released the original, but Mott made it to No. 8 UK. Then, Hunter said, "I made a fatal error. Tony Brainsby was our publicist at the time and I remember walking into his office and saying: 'I've got the formula. I've cracked it.' And that was the minute I stopped having the formula."[32] It was their last British Top 10.

✳

In the end, the group to rise out of the glam rock scene with the biggest record sales after David Bowie (seventy-five million to Bowie's hundred million) was about as far on the other end of the spectrum as possible.[33]

Gene Simmons's arrogance initially annoyed Paul Stanley,[34] but they both shared an unrelenting drive to conquer Manhattan, and they could both sing lead or harmony, like their beloved Beatles. They broke up their original band, Wicked Lester, because it sounded too much like Three Dog Night, then found drummer Peter Criss through the *Rolling Stone* classifieds. Criss had been in a band called Lips, so Stanley suggested the name Kiss for the new band. They painted their faces kabuki white at their first gig together in November 1972 because, according to New York Doll Sylvain Sylvain, "Kiss quickly found out that if you're a guy wearing makeup you get a lot of chicks."[35]

They found lead guitarist Ace Frehley after auditioning over fifty candidates, then played their first gig as a foursome on January 30 in front of six people at Coventry in Queens, the frequent haunt of the Dolls. Initially the accouterments were standard glam: eyeliner, eyebrow pencil, rouge, high heels, and shoulder pads. Their mothers embroidered their shirts and glued glitter onto the Kiss logo, designed by Frehley and Stanley. They bought skintight Lurex pants with metallic threads, black knee socks, leather belts, and, from the pet store, studded collars. Finally, they found an S&M shop in the Village that specialized in gay biker outfits and paid them to make black leather costumes with studs.

They vowed to be different from the Dolls by only using black and white makeup, then made an exception for silver. But Simmons noted, "We weren't convincing as androgynous guys."[36] After seeing Alice Cooper at Madison Square Garden in June they asked themselves, what if we were four Alice Coopers? They decided they each needed a different facial gimmick. Frehley continued the Ziggy spaceman tradition. Criss considered himself moody like a cat, so he made himself a feline. Stanley painted stars on each eye but gradually got lazy and reduced it to one.

Simmons was the one who put them over with all the kids who, like him, grew up reading *Famous Monsters of Filmland*. Photographer Bob Gruen said, "Kiss decided that they couldn't compete with the Dolls in the sense of being better looking. So they did something completely opposite, which was to be monsters instead of trying to be attractive."[37] Simmons mixed Lon Chaney's Phantom of the Opera leer with Batman studded leather wings under his arms. He pulled his hair into a ball to keep it out of his face and took to sticking out his unusually long tongue.

They recorded a demo at Electric Ladyland that included "Strutter" and

"Black Diamond." Onstage they brought in dry ice, plugged in red revolving lights, and threw buckets of water (actually mere confetti) at the audience. Future Ramones Jeffrey Hyman and Tommy Erdelyi attended early gigs. Erdelyi likened the band to Slade. Kiss asked the Dolls if they could do a gig with them, but their progenitors declined. "You'll kill us."

Counterculture '73

The Summer Jam at Watkins Glen, New York, on July 28 makes the *Guinness Book of World Records* for largest concert with the Grateful Dead, Allman Brothers, and the Band. Esalen fuels the Human Potential Movement. *Time* puts Carlos Castaneda on the cover while the authorities put Timothy Leary in a cell next to Charles Manson. George Harrison and Steve Jobs pay heed to Ram Dass. The Sexual Revolution reaches a peak with New York Yankee wife swappers, key parties, streakers, and *Deep Throat* court cases. The New Hollywood filmmakers bring visionary realism to the big screen.

✳

oodstock, Isle of Wight, and Watkins Glen—those were the big three for us," said the Band's Rick Danko.[1] They played Watkins Glen's Grand Prix Racecourse after two long sets by the Grateful Dead, interrupted by a thunderstorm. The Allmans played last, as they were the biggest draw, a few days away from releasing *Brothers and Sisters,* which sold 760,000 in less than a month. All three jammed for the encore on "Not Fade Away," "Mountain Jam," and "Johnny B. Goode."

The Dead had inspired the Allmans to incorporate jazz into their extended blues rock improvisations, while the Band had inspired the Dead to explore their Americana roots on *Workingman's Dead* and *American Beauty.* The Dead was moving away from Americana now toward a smooth jazz sound with the arrival of keyboardist Keith Gordchaux. The cover of their new album, *Wake of the Flood,* featured a benign reaper, re-flecting the loss of their original organist, the blues-oriented Pigpen (Ron McKernan), who died on March 8 from gastrointestinal hemorrhage due to alcohol abuse. It also reflected how the band was beginning to reap the rewards of their endless trip.[2] They were now able to fill stadiums, and they'd done it all their way: through touring, regardless of record sales, establishing the economic model for jam bands like the Dave Matthews Band and Phish.

For a time, Watkins Glen was listed in the *Guinness Book of World Records* as "largest audience for a pop festival," with a crowd estimated at 600,000. It beat Woodstock by approximately 200,000 but carried none of the cultural resonance. No movie was released, and only a couple songs made it onto record: "Come and Go Blues" on the Allmans' *Wipe the Windows, Check the Oil, Dollar Gas* and an eighteen-minute sound check on the Dead's *So Many Roads* box set.

It had already been done: the hordes getting in for free, dancing in the nude, breastfeeding. There was no longer any war they needed to bond together against. But its very meaninglessness revealed the extent to which the counterculture had been absorbed into the culture. Documentarian Michael Moore wrote in his memoir that by 1971 the longhairs outnumbered the jocks in his high school, though hippies still had to travel in packs or get jumped.[3] Even the hair of conservative kids jutted out from behind their neck in yearbook photos. Richard Carpenter visited Nixon in the White House with hair over his ears. Merle "If you don't love it, leave it" Haggard's thick muttonchops puffed down to his neck.

The original hippie mecca Haight-Ashbury had fallen on hard times. *The New York Times* reported that a third of its shops were boarded up.[4] But the Dead transformed the neighborhood's spirit into a movable holiday through its tours. Believers could check in once every few years, or follow them around in a raggedy caravan of Volkswagen buses for months at a time. As Robert Christgau noted, "Regulars greeted other regulars, remembered from previous boogies, and compared this event with a downer in Boston or a fabulous night in Arizona."[5] Dead Heads sold items in the parking lots to fi-nance their treks: jewelry, fanzines, burritos, dope, tie-dye shirts (a tradition carried over from Ken Kesey's Merry Pranksters, who made tie-dye shirts on their own 1964 cross-country road trip).

One thing they didn't sell but traded was tapes of Dead shows. The tradi-tion started when fans hungered to replay the music the Dead performed in concert but realized they couldn't find it in their studio albums. The band seldom played a song the same way twice and made a point of playing at least one different song a show. Fans started taping shows off radio broadcasts or sneaking recording equipment into gigs.[6] The Dead had been close to the Haight-Ashbury activists the Diggers, who promoted the radical policy that "everything should be for free," so they did not complain when mic stands rose above the crowds, reaching for better sound. One of the central figures in the Dead tape exchange was Dick Latvala; decades later, his favorite shows were officially released through the Dead under the name *Dick's Picks*. The first concert he chose to release was their December 19, 1973, concert in Tampa, Florida, because it included "Nobody's Fault but Mine," a track prized for its rarity.

The Dead officially released one live album in 1973, and it introduced two of their most enduring logos. *Bear's Choice* was named for their soundman Owsley "Bear" Stanley, originally one of the biggest acid manufacturers, and featured marching bears on the back cover. The front showed a skull with a lightning bolt in the brain cavity, representing the effect of his lysergic product. Stanley originally designed the image to print on stickers that he slapped on band equipment, to identify it as theirs when they played gigs with other bands.

The Dead community propagated another hallucinogen-related tradition that spread far beyond their own scene. Bassist Phil Lesh had a personal manager who was brother to a San Rafael high school student who ran with a clique that called themselves the Waldos, after the wall they sat on between classes.[7] One day in '71 the Waldos gave each other the code "420 Louis"—meaning meet at the school's statue of Louis Pasteur at 4:20 p.m. in order to get high and search for a marijuana patch they heard had been planted in the area.[8] "420" became the teens' go-to term for pot, so parents or teachers wouldn't know what they were referring to, and spread into the Dead's orbit. Years later, the *Oxford English Dictionary* credited the Waldos with originating the term, after studying a 1974 issue of their school paper in which they used it.[9]

The main Dead Head tradition, of course, was going to a show, ingesting hallucinogens to block the serotonin receptors, and "somehow hitting that chord of realization of the unity of God in you all," as comparative religion scholar Joseph Campbell put it in his symposium with Dead drummer Mickey Hart called *Ritual and Rapture: From Dionysus to the Grateful Dead*.[10] As Tom Wolfe noted in *The Electric Kool-Aid Acid Test*, hallucinogens created a chemical reaction in the brain analogous to religious awe.

Or a plunge into the abyss, depending on how your trip was going. But *Wake of the Flood* included "Eyes of the World," which became the new happy anthem to bring audience members back from staring at their shoes on the edge of freaking out. "Wake now, discover that you are the song the morning brings," and look around at the concert and realize holy shit how beautiful everything is and we're all made of atoms and we're all just one field of energy endlessly permutating on the surface and everything is one, and WHOOOOOOOO!

The fates of the original Dynamic Duo of Acid, Timothy Leary and Richard Alpert, illustrated with jarring clarity just how well—or how bad—the great mental/spiritual experiment could go. They had been professors at Harvard investigating the benefits of psychedelics until the university fired them because the program had grown too controversial, and because Alpert gave a hallucinogen to an undergraduate. ("He was an attractive kid," said Alpert.[11]) With the help of theorist Marshall McLuhan Leary concocted the slogan "Turn on, tune in, drop out" and proclaimed it at the San Francisco Human Be-In, which might have been fine, but he followed the line with "I mean drop out of high school, drop out of college, drop out of graduate school." They gave him twenty years in prison for two roaches of marijuana. The acid cartel the Brotherhood of Eternal Love paid the Weather Underground militants to help him escape from prison. But officials nabbed him again in Kabul International Airport on January 17. As the authorities dragged him past the news cameras, it was terrifying to look at him. He'd always been handsome, known for his smile. McLuhan advised him always to smile to the press, so he did so now, to show that they couldn't crush him. But he looked crazy, like the Joker or Dracula, or a scary beaten dog. They took him to Folsom two days before Nixon's second inauguration and stashed him in the cell next to Charles Manson.

Alpert embodied a preferable trajectory: Western academic psychiatry to psychedelics to Eastern mysticism. He traveled to India and met fellow seeker Kermit Riggs, who had renamed himself Bhagavan Dass. "When my mind would go off into Jewish neuroticism, Bhagavan Dass would say, 'Come back here and be here now.'"[12] Alpert renamed himself Ram Dass ("servant of God") and published *Be Here Now* in 1971. He hit the lecture circuit in a white robe, sponsored retreats, and sold tapes. *Be Here Now* sold two million copies and was followed by *Doing Your Own Being* in 1973.

George Harrison included a song called "Be Here Now" on *Living in the Material World*. On the title track Harrison proselytized for the Hare Krishnas. The Krishna teacher Srila Prabhupada had arrived in the States in

1965, the year the US ended its policy of severely restricting non-European immigrants. Prabhupada started chanting in Tompkins Square Park with Allen Ginsberg. Not long after, Harrison and Lennon heard his first album, *Krishna Consciousness.*

After the passage of the Immigration and Nationality Act of 1965, many swamis and yogis arrived in the States, often teaching yoga, an Indian tradition since 1500 BC. By 1975, *Time* estimated that 600,000 Americans—including Mike Love, Shirley MacLaine, and Joe Namath—practiced it. On January 13, Cat Stevens's song about meditation, "Sitting," peaked at No. 16.

March saw the release of *Lost Horizon,* about survivors of a plane crash in the Himalayas who stumble upon the utopia of Shangri-La. The author of the original novel, James Hilton, probably named his city after Shambhala, a Sanskrit word that means "peace/serenity/joy." Ancient Tibetan Buddhist scripture referred to it as a fabled city in the Himalayas. The movie didn't perform well, despite a Burt Bacharach/Hal David soundtrack, clanging the death knell for the big Hollywood musical. The songwriters stopped working together. Not very Zen. But perhaps it inspired LA-based songwriter Daniel Moore's euphoric "Shambala," which Three Dog Night took to No. 3 in July. Its yodeling groove was so uplifting that Moore rewrote it as the secular "My Maria" and got another hit out of it when it was released a month later by "progressive" country artist B. W. Stevenson.

Many were still "on the road to Shambala" in real life, on the hippie trail to India. Tony and Maureen Wheeler traveled from London through the Middle East to India to Australia, arriving down under with $0.27 to their name. They shared what they learned in *Across Asia on the Cheap,* the first of their Lonely Planet Travel Guide books.

John Lennon celebrated all the journeys he'd been on—"in space and in time," from meditation to primal scream therapy—in "Mind Games," recorded that summer. He was inspired by a book called *Mind Games: The Guide to Inner Space* by Robert Masters and Jean Houston, consisting primarily of exercises to increase visionary thinking and intuition (hence another song on the *Mind Games* album, "Intuition").

Houston was a figure in the Human Potential Movement, which had its own Shambala in Esalen, off the winding Pacific Coast Highway in Big Sur. Nude sulphur baths built into the mountains looked out over the ocean as the surf crashed and shimmered in the moonlight. Founders Michael Murphy and Dick Price brought in speakers and held workshops covering the latest advances in Western psychiatry along with Eastern philosophy and psychedelics. That was the Great Synthesis: Western psychiatry + Eastern mysticism + psychotropic shamanism. Buddhist scholar Alan Watts gave the first lecture at Esalen. Aldous Huxley provided the movement with its name when he gave talks on Human Potential before his death in 1963. Leary and Alpert spoke there alongside others promoting self-actualization techniques ranging from Gestalt to Rolfing to biofeedback.

The Esalen encounter group was re-created in *Bob & Carol & Ted & Alice* (1969) and in the 2015 series finale of *Mad Men*. It rose out of the "Sensitivity Training Group" pioneered by social psychologist Kurt Lewin. In 1946, the Connecticut State Interracial Commission asked him to create a program that could help fight racial and religious discrimination.[13] He gathered forty-one people together, half of them Jewish or black, so psychologists could analyze their interactions and give them feedback in a group setting, helping them become more "sensitive" to the other attendees' feelings.[14]

Now Marvin Gaye sang, "We're all sensitive people," in "Let's Get It On." "It's all right to cry," Rosie Grier sang on the *Free to Be You and Me* album, in development for a TV special. In 1970, approximately one million Americans went to therapy. In five years the number was six times as great. Celebrities like Hugh Hefner, John Denver, and Peter Fonda spoke of their sadness at their parents' inability to demonstrate affection. *I'm OK— You're OK* and *How to Be Your Own Best Friend* were on the bestseller list throughout the year.

The No. 1 bestseller from January 1 through March 18 was *Jonathan Livingston Seagull,* a fable about an outcast yearning to fly on a higher plane. Many readers wondered what religion author Richard Bach himself belonged to (if any). His son said, "Dad regards flying as his religion, and he's very serious about that."[15] Bach had been a pilot in the US Air Force Reserve in France, a member of the New Jersey Air National Guard, then a technical writer for Douglas Aircraft and contributor to *Flying* magazine.

In 1959, Bach heard a "voice" behind him say "Jonathan Livingston Seagull."[16] John Livingston had been a race pilot. Bach asked the "voice" what it meant, and the story poured out of him onto the page, unfolding like a movie in his mind. Eight years later he published part of it in *Private Pilot* magazine.

He'd been a Christian Scientist, then decided that "organizations can ruin anything" and started searching through occult bookstores. "It took nerve, just to go in one of those places," he told *Time* in their cover story on him.[17] *Time* reported that his interest led him to a medium named Jane Roberts, who claimed to channel a spiritual being with an Indian accent named Seth.[18]

The movie version of *Seagull* was poorly received by critics, like *Lost Horizon,* but the Neil Diamond soundtrack went to No. 2 and won the Grammy for Best Original Score, along with a Golden Globe.

Another bestselling writer made the cover of *Time* in March. Carlos Castaneda was an ethnobotany student whose anthropology professor instructed him to interview a shaman about psychotropic plants. Castaneda supposedly found one named Don Juan on the Arizona/Mexico border. His thesis was eventually published as *The Teachings of Don Juan: A Yaqui Way of Knowledge* (1968), which made Castaneda a millionaire and inspired three sequels. Castaneda had more surreal visions than Aldous Huxley or Ram Dass; on Don Juan's medicine he witnessed giant gnats and talking coyotes and turned into a bird. But his message of enlightenment was the same: stop the world to see, a.k.a. be here now. The Eagles' name was partially inspired by his books; Marvin Gaye dug them. But *Time* and other journalists couldn't find a real Don Juan. The tribe Castaneda said Don Juan belonged to didn't use the same kind of peyote Castaneda said he used.[19] Critics noted that Don Juan's personality seemed to change from book to book. After the *Time* piece, Castaneda claimed Don Juan died in 1973, then retreated from view for the next twenty years, after which he returned to teach seminars about Mexican shamanism.

A third author who combined ancient mysticism with psychedelics was about to join Castaneda on the chart, though he was painfully up-front about his tortured past. Robert Pirsig's *Zen and the Art of Motorcycle Maintenance* recounted his attempt to reconnect with his son on a motorcycle trip following a nervous breakdown and electroshock therapy, precipitated by his quixotic attempt to create his own system of metaphysics. After serving in Korea, Pirsig had become intrigued by Buddhism and studied in India, then did peyote on a Cheyenne reservation. The next year he was institutionalized on Christmas. When he got out, he grew violent toward his wife and received shock therapy.[20] After recovering, he worked on *Zen* for four years, the last few months working in a camper in Minnesota. He sold the book in January 1973, and it eventually sold five million copies.

Alongside those authors, the "Occult and Astrology" bookshelf in bookstores now offered up much of the entire Western mystery tradition, a catalog that once had to be studied in secret, lest the reader incur the wrath of the Church. Samuel Weiser's Inc., Specialist in the Occult, Orientalia, and Metaphysics, was one of New York's oldest occult bookstores. Weiser started selling Aleister Crowley's papers in the '50s but was not able to expand his operation until the '60s, when he began selling to the new occult bookstores bourgeoning in California.[21] A watershed in occult publishing occurred in 1973 when two competing versions of a book called *Pyramid Power* sold a million, abetted by chain bookstores in malls rapidly spreading across the country, Waldenbooks and its competitor B. Dalton. Eventually the Trade Association of Independent Bookstores gave the "Occult" category a new name, "New Age," replacing a horror-movie term with one used by theosophists and the Fifth Dimension in their hit from *Hair,* "Aquarius/Let the Sunshine In."

✳

A few rows over in the bookstore, the sexual revolution had arrived with an explicitness unimaginable to earlier authors crushed by obscenity court cases. Alex Comfort's *More Joy of Sex,* his sequel to last year's smash *The Joy of Sex: A Gourmet Guide to Lovemaking,* featured positions illustrated by Chris Foss and Charles Raymond. *The New York Times* later ranked the author on par with Dr. Spock in terms of impact,[22] while Planned Parenthood's executive Joan Malin said, "The groundbreaking publication of this book took us from an era of silence and shame about sexuality to one of greater openness and discussion."[23] It started out as a textbook for medical students by Comfort, who admitted he was hardly an expert on the topic at the outset. "That's the way to find about anything, to write a book about it."[24] He advised that female armpits "should on no account be shaved" and deodorant should be "banned absolutely," and he cautioned, "Never fool around sexually with vacuum cleaners."

Next to it on the shelf was George and Nena O'Neill's *Open Marriage: A New Life Style for Couples,* which spent over forty weeks on the bestseller chart. "We are not recommending outside sex, but we are not saying that it should be avoided, either. The choice is entirely up to you."

By the early '70s there were over 650 swinging publications. Typical was the scene at the Swing Bar in LA's Studio City, with a marquee that read LUV THY NEIGHBOR.[25] The bartender determined whether you got the invite to the mansion party, where men had to arrive with a date. The Swing's owner, Greg McClure, told *Newsweek,* "In my first marriage I cheated and never felt comfortable about it. Swinging is way ahead of the infidelity scene. I swing so I won't break up my marriage."[26]

The Club 101 mansion boasted waterbeds and a chamber of mirrors. In a Detroit swingers gathering, guests mingled as at any cocktail party until the appointed time, when the host announced that "anything went" as long as all partners consented. Some couples waited in line for private rooms;

others made do with the rows of cots in the basement. The "key party" was re-created in the 1997 film *The Ice Storm*. Attendees threw their car keys in a bowl, then plucked them out at random to see who would go with whom. The National Key Club (NKC) staged hotel events.

Key parties reputedly began on air force military bases during World War II, according to historian Terry Gould, "as a kind of tribal bonding ritual, with a tacit understanding that the two-thirds of husbands who survived [the war] would look after the widows."[27] Gould maintained that military bases across the country had swing clubs, which spread into the suburbs in the early '50s, along with swinger magazines.

On March 4, 1973, wife swapping reared its head in the great American pastime when New York Yankees pitchers Mike Kekich and Fritz Peterson figured they'd better get ahead of the story and held separate press conferences to announce they had switched wives.

Peterson later explained, "During (a) party, we all had a couple of beers and were having a great time. When we were deciding to leave, we had driven two different cars and happened to park behind each other out in the street. I said to my wife, Marilyn, 'Why don't you ride with Mike to the diner in Fort Lee, N.J., and I'll take Susanne with me and we'll meet there and then we'll go home from there.' We did that and we had so much fun together, Susanne and I and Mike and Marilyn, that we decided, 'Hey, this is fun, let's do it again.'"[28]

Peterson and Susanne Kekich remained together over the ensuing decades, but Marilyn Peterson soon wished she was back with her former husband and split with Kekich. Marilyn's mother lamented to the press, "Fritz is not the same person he used to be. We can't understand any of his ideas or his problems anymore."[29] The crowd booed Peterson, both players' games suffered, and both were traded within the year. Dr. Joyce Brothers opined, "It's very rare that a four-way swap ever works."[30]

Still, curious couples ventured to the Shambala of swinging, Sandstone Retreat, in the mountains of Santa Monica. The fifteen acres in Topanga Canyon looked out at Malibu and the Pacific Ocean. If you were over eighteen, the nude woman at the front desk interviewed you to decide whether you could come in. Sometimes people had sex in the reception room, but more typically downstairs by the fireplace on pillows and mats. Gay Talese wrote that in 1973, "often the nude biologist Dr. Alex Comfort, brandishing a cigar, traipsed through the room between the prone bodies with the professional air of a lepidopterist strolling through the fields with a butterfly net. With the least encouragement—after he had deposited the cigar in a safe place—he would join a friendly clutch of bodies, and contribute to the merriment."[31] Its five hundred members included Bobby Darin and Daniel Ellsberg. Sammy Davis Jr. and Peter Lawford visited.

Alas, the owners had to sell the resort in '73, though it stayed open for another three years. Barbara Peterson, founder with husband John, observed, "Sandstone had been a great source of fulfillment, learning, and pleasure. It had been everything, in fact, except financially viable."[32]

Even in the mainstream, Puritan/Victorian conventions were rapidly melting away, such as the need to be a virgin until marriage, the need to be in love to have sex, the need to marry early, the traditions of female subservience. More unmarried couples lived together, as did the protagonists in McCartney's "C Moon," though they "never told her daddy." There did not seem to be any permanent STDs. If you got the clap, you got a shot. "We had a soft spot in our hearts for the free clinics," said Jackson Browne.[33] Steven Tyler wrote about lighting his pubic hair on fire to get the crabs to run out, but that seemed as bad as it got.

In March, a reporter covered a nude run at the University of Maryland with 553 participants and popularized the name for the new trend when he cried, "They are streaking past me right now. It's an incredible sight!"[34] *Time* declared streaking a Los Angeles fad, reporting on a female streaker in tennis shoes who led the police on a chase across the ice during a hockey game at the Inglewood Forum.[35]

The braless look graced Carly Simon's *No Secrets* cover and Linda Ronstadt's publicity photos, though Ronstadt lamented, "In all of the world, outside of California, if you don't wear a bra it supposedly means you want to fuck everybody."[36] When a man at the airport asked her, "Hey, chick, you wanna get laid?" "I just hauled off and slugged him right in the mouth."[37]

Advertisements even hawked bras with nipples built into them. "Imagine having that sensual cold weather look all the time. It's so sexy, it'll give your shape a whole new eye-opening dimension."[38]

Responding to competition from *Penthouse,* Playboy showed a few wisps of pubic hair in 1971. Marilyn Cole (later on Roxy Music's *Stranded* cover) went full frontal a year later, but with a shadow across her. It wasn't until March 1973 that Hugh Hefner presented the first unobstructed view, with Playmate Bonnie Large.

That was the same month Judge Joel Tyler decreed *Deep Throat* obscene and fined Manhattan's New Mature World Theatre $100,000 for screening it. His decision came down after a ten-day trial during which experts argued over whether oral sex was "within the bounds of normal behavior." The prosecutor against *Deep Throat,* William Purcell, argued, "A woman seeing this film may think that it is perfectly healthy, perfectly moral to have a clitoral orgasm. . . . She is wrong. She is wrong. And this film will strengthen her in her ignorance."[39] Defense experts countered that educating couples in sexual practices helped prevent divorce.

For a brief moment, before stories of Linda Lovelace's abuse leaked out, seeing porn became an idealistic cause célèbre. It was exercising the First Amendment, embracing personal liberation against outmoded Victorian repression, asserting that nudity and sex were beautiful, not sinful. *Deep Throat*'s attorney, Herbert Kassner, argued, "It indicates that women have the right to a sex life."[40]

The New York Times's Vincent Canby opined, "You can argue that Linda in her way is a kind of liberated woman, using men as sex objects the way men in most porno films are supposed to use women."[41]

Even Bob Hope joked about it now. "I went to see *Deep Throat* because I'm fond of animal pictures. I thought it was about giraffes."[42] On *Maude,* Bea Arthur fought to stage a burlesque show for a library benefit.

The groundbreaking sex scenes between *Last Tango* stars Brando and Schneider emboldened director Nicolas Roeg to attempt to top them in *Don't Look Now* with Julie Christie and Donald Sutherland. The latter film was shot in Italy just as police were seizing all of the countries' copies of *Last Tango* on grounds on obscenity.

✳

Filmmakers with counterculture sensibilities had, for the moment, the run of Hollywood. After a string of box office bombs, the studios realized they were out of touch with modern sensibilities and (briefly) gave young filmmakers carte blanche to experiment in films like *Badlands, American Graffiti, The Long Goodbye,* and *Paper Moon.* Though the studios sometimes drew the line: Hal Ashby's *The Last Detail* was delayed for six months because the film included the word "fuck" sixty-five times, until praise for Jack Nicholson's performance as a navy lifer forced Columbia to release it.[43]

Many of the New Hollywood directors gathered in Nichols Beach Canyon along the Pacific Ocean (a few minutes from where Neil Young lived at Zuma), at the homes of Julia and Michael Phillips (producers of *The Sting*) or actresses Margot Kidder and Jessica Salt, who lived down the block, where they flew a tie-dye flag and sunbathed topless.[44] Hitchcock disciple Brian De Palma wrote *Sisters* as a vehicle for them. Steven Spielberg worked on *Watch the Skies,* his concept based on a great wave of UFO sightings that spiked in the fall of 1973, with the Phillipses and screenwriter Paul Schrader. In the end he didn't like the script Schrader wrote. Spielberg wanted the film to be about how average Americans yearned to transcend their mundane lives of quiet desperation through contact with mystical higher beings. Schrader nevertheless interested the Phillipses and Martin Scorsese in his script for *Taxi Driver.* Scorsese meanwhile was inspired to use the tracking-shot technique he saw in the Pink Floyd concert film *Live at Pompeii* for his new film *Mean Streets.* His use of classic songs by artists like the Stones and Ronettes changed the way the movies used rock in soundtracks, as did George Lucas's *American Graffiti.* Lucas was already working on the script for his follow-up, a science-fiction epic loosely based on Akira Kurosawa's *The Hidden Fortress* by way of *Flash Gordon.* "It was really about the Vietnam War, and that was the period where Nixon was trying to run for a [second] term, which got me to thinking historically about how do democracies get turned into dictatorships?"[45] John Milius surfed and shot off his guns. He was the token conservative in the clique, a script doctor for *Dirty Harry* and writer of *Apocalypse Now* and *Big Wednesday.*

Even big-budget studio soap operas that year had radical heroines. *The Way We Were* starred Barbra Streisand as a Communist idealist who pushes her screenwriter husband (Robert Redford) to stand up to the blacklist and write art instead of easy entertainment. He doesn't want to work that hard, however, and they split—a conflict that resonated with activists who had to decide if they wanted to keep on pushing or become proto-yuppies. Arthur Laurents wrote the screenplay; he'd been blacklisted for years before bouncing back with *West Side Story.*

Along with daring to play a sympathetic Commie, Streisand led the vogue for actors who broke the WASP mold of beauty that dominated the industry. Her own mother had warned her she wasn't pretty enough to make it, and others had advised her to change her nose and accent, but she ignored them. Movie historian Lester Friedman wrote, "Streisand's name and nose in their unaltered state represents a turning point in the cinematic portrayal of Jews, one that shows Jewishness as something to be proud of, to exploit, and to celebrate."[46] Cher, too, turned her unconventional, half-Armenian beauty into an asset, making it the theme of her hits "Gypsys, Tramps & Thieves," "Half-Breed" (which made No. 1 in October), and "Dark Lady."

Dustin Hoffman's success in *The Graduate* also helped open the doors to performers who never would have been offered leads before: Al Pacino, Elliot Gould (Streisand's husband), Richard Dreyfuss, Donald Sutherland,

Gene Wilder, Robert De Niro, Jill Clayburgh. The vogue for cinematic authenticity paralleled the ascendance of offbeat musicians like Bob Dylan, Mick Jagger, Janis Joplin, and Neil Young, whose appeal was partly based on the fact that they looked and sounded real, not like airbrushed product.

For Redford, *The Way We Were* was a cautionary tale he spent the second half of his career refuting. His character mused uneasily that "everything came too easily to him . . . he was a fraud." Redford turned that into the theme of the movies he directed, which centered on the guilt of golden boys who have everything handed to them while their brothers struggle. He became the patron saint of the Sundance Film Festival, which became the haven for artistically ambitious films after the studios lost their brief interest in funding experimental directors.

✳

The bête noir of the counterculture was, of course, the military-industrial complex. But in a mind-boggling twist, the antagonists merged toward a great synthesis that determined the next phase of human evolution.

Significant milestones in computer technology that year included the first TV typewriter and the first computer monitor. Motorola's Martin Cooper made the first call with his invention, the handheld cell phone, inspired by Dick Tracy's wrist radio. Xerox Palo Alto Research Center employees created the Ethernet when they linked all the computers and printers in their network with a coaxial cable. The forty-three high-powered US computers linked in the Advanced Research Projects Agency (ARPA) network made their first connection to computers outside the US in England and Norway.

Author Dean Koontz riffed off the *Rosemary's Baby* premise with his bestselling novel *Demon Seed,* about a computer that takes a woman hostage and impregnates her, creating a cyborg. But the Dead Heads who worked in Silicon Valley found benign uses for the technology, employing proto-messaging boards to arrange rides to concerts and compile lyrics to Grateful Dead songs, a resource the band itself eventually used.[47] Merry Prankster Stewart Brand, creator of the commune-oriented *Whole Earth Catalogue,* wrote in *Rolling Stone,* "Ready or not, computers are coming to the people. That's good news, maybe the best since psychedelics. . . . Half or more of computer science is heads. . . . The rest of the counterculture is laid low and back these days, showing none of this kind of zeal."[48]

In the article, Brand asked Alan Kay of the Xerox Research Center to describe the "standard Computer Bum." "About as straight as you'd expect hotrodders to look. It's that kind of fanaticism. A true hacker is not a group person. . . . They're kids who tended to be brilliant but not very interested in conventional goals. And computing is just a fabulous place for that, because it's a place where you don't have to be a Ph.D. or anything else. It's a place where you can still be an artisan. People are willing to pay you if you're any good at all, and you have plenty of time for screwing around."

The man who most famously epitomized the archetype walked around barefoot, dropped out of college, read *Be Here Now,* ate at the Hare Krishna Temple, saved up to go to India, lived at his friend's commune, and pruned the commune's apple orchard, which inspired the name of the computer he eventually created with compadre Steve Wozniak.[49] "I came of age at a magical time. Our consciousness was raised by Zen, and also by LSD," Steve Jobs said. "LSD shows you that there's another side to the coin, and you can't remember it when it wears off, but you know it. It reinforced my sense of what was important—creating great things instead of making money, putting things back into the stream of history and of human consciousness as much as I could."[50]

U2's Bono said of the techies, "The people who invented the twenty-first century were pot-smoking, sandal-wearing hippies from the West Coast like Steve, because they saw differently. The hierarchical systems of the East Coast, England, Germany, and Japan did not encourage this different think-ing. The sixties produced an anarchic mind-set that is great for imagining a world not yet in existence."[51]

*

Southern Rock

The Allman Brothers survive two crushing deaths to release a No. 1 album in August and become the biggest touring act of the year, with the help of the euphoric "Ramblin' Man," which the band initially feared was too country. Lynyrd Skynyrd unleashes their classic debut album, which includes "Free Bird," and records an answer to Neil Young's anti-South diatribe.

*

You could say the Allman brothers, Duane (born 1946) and Gregg (born 1947), came to know the blues when their father was shot to death by a hitchhiker in 1949. Afterward, their mother sent them to military boarding school so she could become an accountant.

They attended high school in Daytona, Florida, but spent their summers with their grandmother in Nashville. Gregg started playing guitar first, but Duane became so obsessed with the instrument that he dropped out to play all the time. They started gigging on the chitlin' (African American) circuit, six sets a night every night of the week, then tried their hand in Los Angeles.

One day Gregg bugged Duane to go horseback riding with him. Duane's horse fell over and caused a hairline fracture in his elbow. Duane stopped talking to Gregg after that. Gregg left a peace offering on Duane's doorstep for his birthday: a Taj Mahal album and some pills for his brother's cold.

Duane called him two hours later and asked him to come over so he could show him something. He'd emptied the pill bottle, put it on his finger, and taught himself slide guitar while listening to Mahal's guitarist Jesse Ed Davis.[1]

Despite Duane's progress, their record label thought Gregg should be a solo artist, with his looks and instantly recognizable, soulful voice. So Duane left for Muscle Shoals, Alabama, to work as a session musician at FAME Studios, playing for singers like Aretha Franklin.[2] The guitar he played for Wilson Pickett's cover of "Hey Jude" "changed music to the point that Southern Rock was born," said producer Jimmy Johnson.[3]

Eric Clapton: "I remember hearing Wilson Pickett's 'Hey Jude' and just being astounded by the lead break at the end. I had to know who that was immediately—right now."[4] He invited Duane to join the sessions for *Layla and Other Assorted Love Songs* and called him the "musical brother I'd never had but wished I did."[5]

Otis Redding's manager, Phil Walden, decided to build a band around Duane. Duane brought in fellow FAME session musician Jai Johanny "Jaimoe" Johanson, who'd drummed for Redding and for Sam and Dave, then found the rest in Florida: guitarist Dickey Betts, bassist Berry Oakley, and a second drummer, Butch Trucks. Duane liked how the Grateful Dead had two drummers. Trucks said, "We don't get in each other's way. I think it has a lot to do with me playing hard, powerful, driving rock 'n' roll, and [Johanson]'s a jazz drummer. So jazz rhythms tend to be very syncopated. So when I'm driving on the downbeat, then he's playing on the offbeat."[6]

Duane told Gregg to get his ass back to Jacksonville and join his new band. When Gregg finally showed up, the band sounded so good Gregg didn't think he was good enough to sing for them. Duane said, "You little punk, I told these people all about you and you don't come in here and let me down." Gregg sang "[his] guts out."[7] The group skyrocketed for three albums. But during the recording of *Eat a Peach* in Macon, Georgia, a truck stopped suddenly and Duane crashed into it on his motorcycle at 90 mph.

After the funeral, the band was unsure whether to continue. They unearthed an older song of Gregg's that Duane loved, "Melissa." Betts took over the slide guitar. Desolation permeated the track. They decided to keep going.

When it came time to start the new album, Betts went back to toying with a rewrite he'd thought about doing of Hank Williams's "Ramblin' Man." He had the music for years, then finally wrote the words in twenty minutes, about the son of a gambler who, like Mr. Allman, wound up on the wrong end of a gun.

"We knew it was a good song but it didn't sound like us," Trucks said.[8] They decided to just cut a demo and give it to a friend. But the jam ignited. When they played it back, no one said anything until roadie Red Dog ventured, "That's the best I heard since Duane."[9]

✖

During rehearsals for *Brothers and Sisters,* Gregg arrived with a song he'd been working on for a year, "Queen of Hearts." The others ignored him because he was so drunk, which didn't sit well with him. He and Betts were both hovering uneasily around the leadership vacuum left by Duane. Gregg was the only Allman left in a band named the Allman Brothers, but he was weighed down by grief and addiction. Betts made time to write songs every day. Indeed, Gregg had encouraged him. Betts hadn't wanted to sing "Blue Sky," an ode to his future wife and eventual theme song of countless summer-day festival beauties, but Gregg told him, "Man, this is your song and it sounds like you and you need to sing it."[10]

After they blew Gregg off, the singer stalked away by himself and worked on his own stuff for forty-four hours straight, slept for six, then worked another twenty-eight. Afterward, he threw the tapes away, but producer Johnny Sandlin encouraged him to keep working on a solo project.[11] He resumed with a cover of Jackson Browne's "These Days."

Gregg had roomed with Browne back when he and Duane made their first run at LA as the band Hour Glass, when they made two albums that went nowhere. For their 1967 debut, Hour Glass cut Browne's "Cast Off All My Fears." "These Days" was one of the saddest compositions by the singer-songwriter: Browne was already struggling with depression when he wrote it as a teen; then his lover Nico covered it in her indelible goth baroque style and made it even bleaker. It reminded Gregg of when he was alone in LA after Duane left. It was a period when "I had been building up nerve to put a pistol to my head," Gregg later wrote.[12] Maybe he was sometimes feeling that way again.

Browne said of Gregg's cover, "I thought that he really unlocked a power in that song that I sort of then emulated in my version."[13]

From that point on, Gregg split his time between the Allmans' *Brothers and Sisters* (contributing "Wasted Words," in which he brushed off requests to get clean) and his "mistress," the solo album, which annoyed the others.

For his album, Gregg hired session pianist Chuck Leavell after seeing him play for New Orleans funkster Dr. John. Leavell started jamming with the Allmans, and his new spirit seemed to rejuvenate them. They decided to make keyboards the second lead instrument instead of hiring a new guitarist. (In 1982, Leavell clicked with the Stones, and he has remained with them since.)

Then, a year and thirteen days after Duane's death, bassist Oakley crashed his motorcycle into a bus three blocks from where Duane perished. (Drummer Butch Trucks survived a car crash in the same area nine months later.) "It was so hard to get into anything after that second loss," Gregg said. "I even caught myself thinking that it's narrowing down, that maybe I'm next."[14] But they knew Oakley would not want them to give up. They asked Jaimoe's friend Lamar Williams to take over bass.

Betts's baby, Jessica, inspired the album's second single after "Ramblin' Man." He was trying to write something that mixed Western swing with the gypsy jazz of Django Reinhardt but wasn't getting anywhere until Jessica crawled in. "I started playing along, trying to capture musically the way she looked bouncing around the room."[15]

They put Trucks's blond three-year-old, Vaylor, on the cover, celebrating new life in the face of crippling loss. The producer didn't think it made sense to release "Ramblin' Man" as a single because it didn't sound rock. But they did anyway, and it shot up the charts, crossing over from country to easy listening to pop, where it climbed to No. 2, blocked only by Gregg's future wife Cher's "Half-Breed." Critic Dave Marsh wrote that it was the closest that true blues slide guitar ever came to hitting No. 1.[16]

The album spent five weeks at the top, eventually selling seven million, helping to lift the record industry out of a slump. By year's close, they were clearing $100,000 a gig and flying to stadiums in Zeppelin's Boeing, the Starship.

Rolling Stone assigned sixteen-year-old Cameron Crowe to do a cover story on them (he'd graduated high school early the year before). The experience was integral to the plot of his autobiographical film, *Almost Famous* (2000). "I finally got [Gregg] to talk to me because I knew that he thought Jackson Browne was a great songwriter, and that Jackson thought Gregg did the best version of his song 'These Days.' So one night in his room, I ask Gregg to play it."[17] Gregg proceeded to play many songs. Crowe finally gathered the nerve to ask about Duane.

Gregg told him, "I've had guys come up to me and say, 'Man, it just doesn't seem like losing those two fine cats affected you people at all.' Why? Because I still have my wits about me? Because I can still play? Well, that's the key right there. We'd all have turned into fucking vegetables if we hadn't been able to get out there and play. *That*'s when the success was, Jack.

Success was being able to keep your brain inside your head. . . . I played for peace of mind."[18]

But after opening up, Gregg got weird. Crowe remembered, "After the show in San Francisco [September 26], Gregg called me up to his room and told me to bring all of the tapes. I did, except the one with him singing on it. He answered the door, looking like he was just in another place— 'fucked up' doesn't do it justice. He looked like he had seen a vision."[19]

Allman demanded to see Crowe's ID. "Gregg says, 'Who are you? You're 16! How do we know you're not a cop? We could be arrested for having you out here with us. How dare you not tell us your age! You see that empty chair? My brother is sitting there right now, laughing at you!' I had never been more scared in my entire life."[20]

Crowe gave him the tapes and, without them for reference, could only turn in a diluted version of his story without the soul-searching quotes. Luckily, photographer Neal Preston managed to retrieve them from Allman, who didn't remember why he had them. Crowe revised the article and the magazine used it for the issue that named the Allmans Band of the Year.

Twenty-six years later, Preston did another photo shoot with Gregg, who asked him what happened to Crowe. "We really put that kid through the wringer."[21]

When Preston told Crowe, the journalist/director recalled, "It really got me, because I had just finished the movie about the kid who gets put through the wringer."[22]

Other elements from the Allmans made it into the movie. Gregg maintained, "Duane jumped into a swimming pool off a two-story Travelodge in San Francisco."[23] Even the *Almost* in the title sounds like "Allmans."

Gregg's solo album, *Laid Back,* was released in October and reached No. 13. After the Allmans tour ended, he did a solo tour with sixteen members of the New York Philharmonic, a five-piece horn section, and three background singers.

✳

The four core members of Lynyrd Skynyrd started playing together in Jacksonville back in 1964: Ronnie Van Zant on vocals, Gary Rossington on lead guitar, Allen Collins on rhythm guitar, and Bob Burns on drums. They played high school dances, like thousands of other garage bands across the country, and fended off attackers angered by their long hair. Their gym teacher, Leonard Skinner, persecuted them so intensely that Rossington dropped out. Naturally they named themselves after him, eventually Byrds-izing the spelling. (They later buried the hatchet with Skinner, and he introduced them in concert in Jacksonville.)

They'd rehearse for sixteen hours, bickering with each other, barely scraping by. Van Zant's girlfriend Judy (later wife) supported him and loaned them her car.[24] They saw the Allman Brothers in their earlier incarnations, the Allman Joys and Hour Glass, and played some gigs with them. Ricky Medlocke, Skynyrd's occasional second drummer, said, "I would go over to the [Allmans'] Big House in Riverside and sit on their porch and listen to them rehearse and I just used to love listening to those guys get together and jam and play at those things."[25]

Alan Waldman, the younger brother of the Allmans' manager, Phil, wanted to bring Skynyrd onto the brothers' label, Capricorn. But Phil thought the bands were too similar and refused. Thus, Skynyrd was snagged by Al Kooper, the keyboardist-producer famous for providing the organ on Dylan's "Like a Rolling Stone." (Kooper also played on the Taj Mahal album that inspired Duane Allman, *The Natch'l Blues*.)

The group composed "Free Bird" back in high school. "Allen had the chords for the pretty part in the beginning for two full years, but Ronnie kept saying that because there were too many chords he couldn't find a melody for it," guitarist Gary Rossington remembered. "Then one day we were at rehearsal and Allen started playing those chords, and Ronnie said, 'Those are pretty. Play them again.' Allen played it again, and Ronnie said, 'Okay, I got it.' And he wrote the lyrics in three or four minutes—the whole damned thing!"[26] Van Zant built off a question Collins's wife had asked: "If I leave here tomorrow, would you still remember me?"[27]

"[Van Zant] came up with a lot of stuff that way, and he never wrote anything down," Rossington said. "His motto was, 'If you can't remember it, it's not worth remembering.'"[28]

They played three or four sets a night, so Van Zant asked the band to add a second half to the song so he could have a few minutes to take a break. Rossington came up with the final three chords, and he and Collins traded solos. Van Zant kept encouraging them to stretch it out. "Then one of our roadies told us we should check out this piano part that another roadie, Billy Powell, had come up with as an intro for the song," Rossington remembered. "We did—and he went from being a roadie to a member right then."[29]

When they recorded the album version, Rossington said, "the whole long jam was Allen Collins, himself. He was bad. He was super bad! He was bad-to-the-bone bad. . . . I could've gone out and played it with him. But the way he was doin' it, he was just so hot! He just did it once and did it again and it was done."[30]

Onstage, Van Zant dedicated the mournful slide guitar epic to Duane Allman and Berry Oakley with the words, "They were free birds, people,"[31] not suspecting he would join them in a plane crash in 1977.

Their debut, *(Pronounced 'Lĕh-'nérd 'Skin-'nérd)*, featured another woozy stinging blues in "Tuesday's Gone." Van Zant turns it into a quin-tessential southern epic by singing "Gone with the Wind" as his train rides away from his woman against the backdrop of a sweeping orchestra (actu-ally Kooper's Mellotron). "Simple Man" achieved a similar majesty, inspired by the wisdom Van Zant's grandmother imparted before her death. "Three Steps" recounted the time a man at a biker bar pointed his .44 at him for dancing with his woman.

When bassist Leon Wilkeson left, the group reached out to Ed King of the Strawberry Alarm Clock ("Incense and Peppermints") to replace him. The two bands wouldn't seem to have much in common, but the south-erners had opened for the psychedelic pop stars in '68. Then Van Zant got Wilkeson to come back anyway, so they could have three guitarists to re-create the album's mammoth guitar onslaughts made in the studio via overdubbing. Both men ended up on the cover, along with keyboardist Billy Powell, a sprawling seven-man contingent in the vein of the San Francisco acid rock bands.

They started the album on March 27 and finished on May 1, with a re-lease date set for August 13. In June they were back rehearsing at their cabin in the Jacksonville woods, where they could be as loud as they wanted without the cops hassling them, though it had no air conditioning (hence the name Hell House) and lots of rattlesnakes. Van Zant was fishing at the creek, below the moss draping from the oaks, when he heard the boys come up with a new jam.[32] He thought it would be the perfect vehicle to reply to some Neil Young songs that had gotten under his skin: "Southern Man" and "Alabama," both critiques of the Jim Crow South.

Even though none of the band was from the specific state targeted by Young, Van Zant told *Rolling Stone,* "We thought Neil was shooting all the ducks in order to kill one or two." So he wrote a defense of Alabama in which he hoped Neil Young would remember that a "Southern Man" didn't need him around anyhow. "I showed the verse to Ed King and asked him what Neil might think. Ed said he'd dig it; he'd be laughing at it."[33]

"Like the Beatles, Neil Young was another guy who helped us get started writing real songs," Rossington said. "It was because of his unique style, his chord changes and what his songs expressed, all the shit he did back then. As much as we loved his songs, when he wrote about 'Alabama and bull-whips crackin'' we had to answer with 'Sweet Home Alabama.' We toured all through Alabama for years, and it's pretty country, with plenty of great people. . . . So, we were just kidding him when we wrote that we didn't need him cuttin' down Alabama. We loved him so it was meant kind of tongue-in-cheek. He immediately sent a telegram to our manager saying he liked the song, which we thought was pretty cool. Then he came on-stage in California and actually played the song with us. That was *very* cool."[34]

Young loved writing instant topical songs like "Ohio," so he no doubt relished having a dialogue over the airwaves. "My own song richly deserved the shot Lynyrd Skynyrd gave me with their great record. I don't like my words when I listen to it. They are accusatory and condescending, not fully thought out, and too easy to misconstrue."[35]

Van Zant wore a T-shirt featuring the cover of Young's *Tonight's the Night* on the final album he appeared on, *Street Survivors*; reputedly he was wearing it the night his plane went down.

In the second verse Van Zant sang how Alabamans loved their segrega-tionist governor George Wallace, but he insisted that "the lyrics about the governor of Alabama were misunderstood. The general public didn't notice the words 'Boo! Boo! Boo!' after that particular line. . . . Wallace and I have very little in common. I don't like what he says about colored people."[36]

Kooper: "The [next] line 'We all did what we could do' is sort of ambigu-ous. 'We tried to get Wallace out of there' is how I always thought of it."[37]

Van Zant sang that Watergate didn't bother him and asked if the lis-tener's conscience bothered them—i.e., you're criticizing us for Wallace, but did you vote for Nixon in the 1972 landslide?

But the waters get muddier at the end of the song when he sings, "The skies are so blue and the governor's true." There's also the fact that they performed with the Confederate flag hung behind them.

At the time, many southerners saw the flag as a symbol of pride in their regional identity, an agrarian society invaded by northern industrial-ists 108 years earlier. Even Tom Petty used it in the marketing for his 1985 *Southern Accents* album. But after Petty toured with Bob Dylan he came to regret it. "I wish I had given it more thought. It was a downright stupid thing to do. . . . People just need to think about how it looks to a black per-son. It's just awful. It's like how a swastika looks to a Jewish person. It just shouldn't be on flagpoles."[38]

Politics aside, Ed King's count-off into his lead riff, and the song's incandescent bridge, made for two of the most uplifting moments on the radio that decade. Producer Kooper knew just whom to enlist for the backing vocals: African American singers Merry Clayton and Clydie King. Clayton was best known for her scarifying duet with Mick Jagger in "Gimme Shelter." King sang on *Exile on Main Street* and Steely Dan's *Can't Buy a Thrill*; she later had two children with Kooper's compatriot Bob Dylan. When King first invited Clayton to join her, Clayton cried, "I'm not singing about Alabama! I remember those poor little girls killed by racists!" But King corralled her. After the session, she told her, "We did our part and this song will live in infamy, Merry. And we'll continually get paid."[39]

Skynyrd signed on as the opening act for the Who's *Quadrophenia* tour that November, learning the fine art of throwing TVs out the window, which they matched by blowing up TVs with finely aimed beer cars.[40] They proved they could be as nightmarish when drunk as English rockers, punching teeth out in street fights and getting DUIs on Quaaludes. When "Sweet Home Alabama" came out the following year and made it to No. 8, "Free Bird" got a retroactive boost and flew to No. 19.

Critic Chet Flippo declared that the founding fathers of Southern Rock were "total opposites. Skynyrd's music has always been more heavy and ponderous. If the band were an animal, it would be a bull elephant. The Allmans' music has always been jazz and blues-based and is more feline and sinuous. Like a graceful leopard."[41] But their success heralded the first bona fide movement in Southern Rock since rockabilly.

South Carolina's Marshall Tucker Band arrived that year with "Can't You See," like "Midnight Rider" with a flute. The band wanted the Jethro Tull vibe, so Jerry Eubanks lied that he was a flautist in order to be allowed to join. ZZ Top had their first major hit that summer with "La Grange," about the Chicken Ranch brothel that inspired *The Best Little Whorehouse in Texas*. Back in 1969 they had played in Laurel Canyon with Hour Glass.

Charlie Daniels had been kicking around for years, co-writing Presley's classic "It Hurts Me" back in '64. But it wasn't until August that he had his first Top 10 hit, "Uneasy Rider." Black Oak Arkansas had likewise been striving for a decade before getting onto the pop chart in December with "Jim Dandy." Wet Willie, Molly Hatchet, and the Ozark Mountain Daredevils were out there looking for their break. And in Florida Tom Petty led a band called Mudcrutch, which included guitarist Tom Leadon, brother of the Eagles' Bernie.

"I never liked the term 'Southern Rock,'" said Gregg Allman, "except for the fact that it made a new slot in the record shops to put our records. The way I see it, there are four kings of rock and roll, two white, and two black: Jerry Lee Lewis, Elvis Aaron Presley, Richard Penniman (Little Richard)—they're all from the South—and then we got Chuck Berry, who's from St. Louis . . . so saying 'Southern Rock' is like saying 'rock rock.'"[42]

✳

Keep Gettin' It On

On August 3, Stevie Wonder releases his greatest album, *Innervisions*, three days before a car crash puts him in a coma. Marvin Gaye's *Let's Get It On* becomes the biggest-selling R&B LP of the year. And a strange Jackson Browne cover by the Jackson Five hints at the dysfunction beneath their idealized surface.

✳

They put a whole batch of us on a bus in Times Square and blindfolded us," rock critic Dave Marsh recalled. "Each of us had a guide. (Mine turned out to be Patti Smith, a good friend of Stevie's, as it turns out.) Then they played us the record. It was an amazing thing. Totally disorienting. The music had a clarity, a lucidity, and a flat-out *power* that was greatly increased by the limitation of the visual sense; no distraction, or complete distraction, but in the end, it really focused the whole experience, and *not* only because the music was unforgettable, although of course it was. It was one hell of a way to experience 'Living for the City' for the first time."[1]

Marsh later judged *Innervisions* Wonder's best album. *Rolling Stone* ranked it the 24th Greatest Album of All Time. Critic Jon Landau opined that the twenty-three-year-old surpassed Sly Stone as the most innovative R&B artist of the era.[2] The album made it to No. 4 on the pop charts, No. 1 R&B, buoyed by three hit singles: the aforementioned "Living for the City,"

"Higher Ground," and "Don't You Worry 'bout a Thing." And it was the first of three Grammy Album of the Year wins for him over the next four years. "Living for the City" won Best Rhythm and Blues Song.

Again, Wonder played the majority of instruments himself. Topical concerns dominated much of *Innervisions*. In "Living for the City" a family struggles to hold itself together through love as the parents work fourteen-hour days scrubbing floors, grossly underpaid. The son can't find a job due to discrimination. When another family member rides a bus to join them, he's wrongly arrested and sentenced to ten years. "Too High" laments a woman's overdose. "He's Misstra Know-It-All" was believed to be Wonder's critique of the president. In this interpretation, the counterfeit dollar in the character's hand refers to Nixon's choice to take the country off the gold standard. Yet the song remains as devastating today, equally relevant for later generations of loudmouth con men.

The melancholy "All in Love Is Fair" reflected the end of his marriage to Syreeta Wright. She started out as a Motown receptionist, moved up to background vocalist, then cut her own singles. She and Wonder began dating and co-wrote hits like "Signed, Sealed, Delivered" and "If You Really Love Me," marrying in September 1970. But Wonder stayed wrapped up in his music, didn't spend enough time with her, and cheated. They divorced after eighteen months but remained friends, and he produced her solo albums.

Relief could be found in the Latin-inflected "Don't You Worry 'bout a Thing," in which Wonder showed his humorous side as he tried to woo a woman in Spanish. "Jesus Children of America" extolled transcendental meditation.

With "Higher Ground" he gave radio a new installment of percolating funk perfection, but instead of the disturbing lyrics of "Superstition," he offered words of relentless determination and optimism, praising God for allowing him another chance to rise beyond past sins.

Three days after the album was released, on August 6, Wonder was riding in a car driven by his cousin John Harris in Durham, North Carolina. Harris attempted to pass a logging truck but sideswiped one of the logs. "The log flew off the truck and crashed through the windshield," wrote biographer Mark Ribowsky. "[It] plowed into [Wonder's] forehead, shattering his glasses and knocking him unconscious."[3]

Wonder remained in a coma for four days. Some horrified fans couldn't help but notice the grim irony of the album cover. Efram Wolff had illustrated a beam of inspiration shooting out from Wonder's forehead; it now recalled the accident.

"I lost my sense of smell a little bit; my sense of taste for a minute," Wonder told *Today*. "I suffered a brain contusion and some lacerations on the right side of my forehead." He had to take anticonvulsive medication.[4] But on September 25, Elton John flew him to Boston Garden to join him onstage for an encore of "Superstition" and "Honky Tonk Women." He received a fifteen-minute ovation from the audience.

"I wrote 'Higher Ground' even before the accident. But something must have been telling me that something was going to happen to make me aware of a lot of things and to get myself together. This is like my second chance for life, to do something or to do more, and to value the fact that I am alive."[5]

❋

Marvin Gaye had a breakthrough realization while recording *Let's Get It On*. He didn't need to get worked up and belt out the songs, he could just sit down and sing. He didn't need to write down lyrics in advance, he just needed to relax and croon whatever came into his head, then overdub duets and harmonies with himself.[6] Just "Keep Gettin' It On."

As his passion for Janis Hunter grew more intense, and as Sylvia Robinson groaned across the airwaves in "Pillow Talk," Gaye added moaning to tracks like "You Sure Love to Ball," kicking off the Quiet Storm genre alongside competitors like Al Green, Barry White, and Bill Withers: soft R&B to play in the background while making love all night long.

Janis wrote in her memoir that Gaye tried to talk her into dropping out of high school so he didn't have to share her with "all those strapping young high-school football players looking to love on you. . . . I can teach you everything you need to know. I'll be a far more loving and patient teacher than whomever the school provides."[7] She was pregnant by the end of the year with their first daughter, Nona.

The album's final track broke the reverie lyrically, if not sonically. "Just to Keep You Satisfied" was a song he wrote with wife Anna Gordy four years earlier,[8] when they were penning hits for the Originals together. Now Gaye saved the backing track but added new lyrics that bade Anna farewell, though they didn't technically divorce for another four years. He assured her that he never loved anyone as much as her but was unable to resist a few twists of the knife, laying their demise as a couple on her "jealousy" and "bitchin'," singing from the vantage of the one leaving and not being left, secure in his new love.

One day when Gaye and Jan drove to Anna's house to pick up Gaye's son, Anna emerged from the house to glare at Jan through the car window. Jan wrote, "Anna was scary. Her eyes burned with anger."

"I just want to see what someone like you looks like," Anna said. "Now that I've seen it, don't ever bring it back here again."[9]

Upon its release at the end of August, *Let's Get It On* became Motown's bestseller to date, shipping over three million in the next couple of years.[10] The title track became his second No. 1 single.

❋

Like Gaye, Jermaine Jackson married into the Gordy empire, tying the knot with Gordy's daughter Hazel. Smokey Robinson wrote a song for their wedding ("Starting Here and Now"), during which 175 doves were released.[11]

Jackie (born 1951), Tito (1953), Jermaine (1954), Michael (1958), and Marlon (1957) were into their ninth year as the Jackson Five. It had been three and a half years since Gordy promised to make them the biggest group in the world. Critic Nelson George called the Five Middle America's safe antidote to black militancy.[12] They performed on *Ed Sullivan, Bob Hope, Andy Williams, Mike Douglas, Carol Burnett, Flip Wilson,* and *The Midnight Special.* They played the Royal Variety Performance alongside Liberace and Carol Channing and met the Queen Mother. They toured Japan in the spring.

If the Beatles were a boy band that played their own instruments, in the "band" tradition that continued on through Duran Duran, the Five was one in the New Kids/Backstreet Boys sense, singer-dancers with choreographed dance moves like the Temptations, though in concert Jermaine played the bass and Tito the guitar. In the boy band tradition, an explosion of merch was unleashed in their image: View-Master reels, board games, coloring books, dolls, lunchboxes, posters, stickers, cereals, toy instruments, trading cards, Christmas albums.[13] They had the first black cartoon series, beating *Fat Albert* by a year.

And they had their inverse/mirror-image rivals, the Osmonds, who also had a Rankin/Bass cartoon. The Osmonds were also fronted by the younger one who sounded like a girl, with a middle one who sometimes took the lead, and younger ones and sisters looming on the horizon for the spin-off operations. They both claimed allegiance to slightly nonmainstream yet determinedly wholesome religions: Jehovah's Witnesses and the Church of Jesus Christ of Latter-day Saints.

The Osmonds came first, singing barbershop-quartet-style songs at Disneyland, then on *The Andy Williams Show* for the bulk of the '60s. Patriarch

Joe Jackson made his boys study the Osmonds. But the Osmonds didn't make it big in the charts until they recorded a song that Gordy rejected for the Jacksons, "One Bad Apple," at FAME Studios, where Aretha Franklin and Otis Redding cut soul classics.

The rivals were wary of each other, then became friends and played sports together.[14] The Osmonds had one No. 1 hit versus the Jacksons' four. Donny and Michael also both had solo chart-toppers. In the UK, Donny and his brother Jimmy had even more No. 1s. Their sister topped the country chart in November with "Paper Roses," which was why the theme song for *The Donny and Marie Show* later became "I'm a Little Bit Country/I'm a Little Bit Rock and Roll."

Like the Osmonds, David Cassidy of *The Partridge Family* also did better in the UK with "Daydreamer," hitting No. 1 there in October. *The Brady Bunch* tried to get in on the bubblegum action as well, performing "It's a Sunshine Day" on their January 26 episode. Meanwhile, the Bay City Rollers released "Saturday Night," though it wouldn't be a hit in the US for another three years.

In February, the Jacksons released a UK-only single that sounded sprightly but contained the most un-bubblegum lyrics possible: a cover of Jackson Browne's "Doctor, My Eyes." Why the label decided to pair them with this song is a mystery. Maybe the producers stumbled across it because of the shared Jackson name. But in retrospect, the lyrics, about a man appealing to his psychiatrist after a lifetime spent learning not to cry, were weirdly apropos for fifteen-year-old superstar Michael. One could imagine a cinematic montage unfolding to Michael and Jermaine's vocals: Joe Jackson looms over his sons, forcing them to endlessly rehearse, belt in hand. Father flagrantly cheats while mother in denial tells her sons that Jehovah's Witnesses have no sex outside of marriage. She cleans them with rubbing alcohol. The young group plays Joe Tex's "Skinny Legs and All" at Mr. Lucky's club in Gary, Indiana. Michael recounted, "We'd start and somewhere in the middle I'd go into the audience, crawl under the tables, and pull up the ladies' skirts to look under."[15] The audience throws money; Michael picks it up as he dances. Father books them to play strip clubs.[16] They make it when Michael turns ten. Amazon women lunge to tear him apart as he bumps and grinds onstage, snatch at him at airports. Father calls Michael "Big Nose,"[17] hounds him about his acne. Both father and the label stress out when the boy's voice cracks and changes from soprano to tenor. There's no time off. He's always recording (ten Jackson Five albums from 1970 to 1975, four solo albums) or shooting photo sessions for *Tiger Beat* or *Ebony* or *Jet*. *Jet* puts

Michael on its cover forty times, more than any other celebrity. After shows, father organizes groupies for his sons and takes some for himself. One, Yolanda Lewis, recalls having sex with Jermaine in the hotel while fourteen-year-old Michael and Marlon "were sleeping three feet away in the next bed. Or at least I thought they were sleeping. As I was slipping out of the room, I heard Michael say to Jermaine, 'Nice job. Now, can we please get some sleep?'"[18] In 1973, Michael's brothers decide it's time for the fifteen-year-old to lose his virginity. Laughing, they lock him in the room with two hookers. He reads the Bible to the women, and they leave crying.[19]

"Michael Jackson: Too much . . . too fast . . . too soon?" asked the cover of *Black Stars* magazine.

Star-Crossed in Pleasure

The Stones record their most underrated album in Jamaica, featuring the lushest ballads of their career. Mick Jagger begins his bromance with Bowie, and they create "It's Only Rock 'n' Roll" with future Stone Ron Wood.

✻

The accepted wisdom is that the quartet of albums the Rolling Stones released from 1968 to 1972 (*Beggar's Banquet, Let It Bleed, Sticky Fingers,* and *Exile on Main Street*) represent their pinnacle. Still, a smaller subset of fans prefers *Goats Head Soup* (1973) and *It's Only Rock 'n' Roll* (1974), which have a sound distinct from any other era in the band's history.

After the lo-fi, sludgy production of *Exile* was criticized in the press, they strove for a cleaner mix with *Goats*. In contrast to the previous rootsy vibe, they colored their guitars with wah-wah pedals, phaser pedals, and a Leslie speaker cabinet. The cabinet housed multiple speakers that spun around in different directions to give the instruments a swirling, undersea sound. Billy Preston often played along on clavinet for blistering funk workouts like "Doo Doo Doo Doo Doo (Heartbreaker)" and "Fingerprint File," which could have fit in the year's blaxploitation movies.

On songs like "Winter" and "Time Waits for No One," Mick Jagger and guitarist Mick Taylor returned to the style they explored on *Sticky Fingers* tracks "Moonlight Mile" and "Sway," with Taylor unleashing endlessly ascending solos accompanied by majestic strings. It was the richest Stones era for melancholy ballads with opulent landscapes you could get lost in, like "Coming Down Again," a way for the average listener to vicariously experience the effects of Richards's opioid and Quaalude addictions without actually taking the drugs.

The band didn't want to record in the UK because the government would tax them at 97 percent. They couldn't record in France anymore because Richards and longtime partner Anita Pallenberg had been found guilty of possessing enough heroin to traffic. So they decamped to Dynamic Sound Studios in Kingston, Jamaica, to work in the same room where Jimmy Cliff recorded *The Harder They Come,* with the same Chinese Jamaican engineer, Mikey Chung. Bob Marley and the Wailers recorded *Catch a Fire* there a month before the Stones arrived.

Richards wrote in his memoir, "Two large, double gates guarded by the man with the shotgun would open and let us in and then close behind us."[1] Bassist Bill Wyman recalled, "Studio A was a low building, little bigger than an outhouse. Inside was an eight-track recorder and the room where we recorded. Someone described it as just this side of claustrophobic; they were right."[2] The drum stool was nailed to the floor.

Ironically, there's no reggae on *Goats Head Soup*. "We just didn't want to do it at that juncture," Jagger later explained.

"More important, we didn't think we were capable of doing it," Richards chimed in.[3] Jagger, Richards, and drummer Charlie Watts were avid fans, but they didn't feel competent enough to tackle a reggae cover until 1976 ("Cherry Oh Baby"). The only song to carry a hint of Jamaica on *Goats Head* Soup (named after a local food dish) was "Can You Hear the Music," with a flute that vaguely recalls Johnny Nash's version of Marley's "Stir It Up." The song harks more to Brian Jones's world music album *Brian Jones Presents the Pipes of Pan at Joujouka.*

Richards did, however, bond with a pack of Rastafarians for life and thereafter returned to the island almost yearly. "After *Goats Head Soup* I've lived there whenever I can. I have family there—villages welcome me with open arms."[4] After the Rastas grew accustomed to him, they invited him to smoke the covenant in the Rasta village Steer Town, where he joined in playing drums and singing hymns from a hundred years ago.

Richards came up with the title and music for the album's most famous track, "Angie," during a stay at a clinic to get (temporarily) clean while Pallenberg gave birth to their second child, Dandelion (later renamed Angela).

Richards wrote in his memoir that as soon as he could move without feeling he had to shit the bed, he grabbed his guitar and started singing "Angie," which he claimed was an arbitrary name but shares the first syllable with Anita.[5]

The band recorded a rough version called a guide track, then over-dubbed more polished performances. On the final version of the song, you can hear Jagger's original vocals in the background, sometimes out of sync with his final overdubs.[6] Being the Stones, it was probably a sloppy accident that couldn't be fixed, but it wound up sounding cooler than if the track had been antiseptically polished.

Rumor had it that the song was about an affair Jagger had with Bowie's wife, Angela. However, it was recorded at the end of 1972, and he became close with Bowie the following spring.

Label exec Ahmet Ertegun did not want to release it as a single, but it became the biggest hit single of the year worldwide, per Wikipedia. Today it stands as the band's sixth-bestselling song across all platforms ("Paint It Black" and "Satisfaction" being first and second).[7] It resonated with activists frustrated by the lack of obvious progress since the '60s, with its lyrics of dreams, love, and money all gone up in smoke. Eight days after the single was released, Abbie Hoffman was busted for selling coke. Black Panthers fled the organization in the wake of Huey Newton's cocaine-fueled inter-necine violence. Commune members confronted the fact that living off the land with a crowd of people could actually be more stressful than getting a conventional job.

The song was a tragic bookend to "As Tears Go By," one of Jagger-Richards's earliest songwriting jobs, commissioned by their manager for folk pop artist Marianne Faithfull nine years earlier. She and Jagger became one of the era's most glamorous couples. But by decade's end, her escalating addiction to cocaine and heroin contributed to a miscarriage and derailed her career. She lost custody of her son and attempted suicide twice. Jagger fought to hold the relationship together, but, per her memoir, she preferred squatting in Piccadilly Circus for a year and a half as an anorexic junkie.[8] Her stunning beauty gone, she blended into the demimonde of drug deal-ers, prostitutes, and street people, finding strange relief in anonymity. Jagger tried to scare her straight with *Exile*'s "Shine a Light," painting a picture of her dead in the alley. On "Angie" he implores her, "Ain't it good to be alive?"

In "Winter," Jagger wishes he could wrap a coat around his former love to keep her warm. He sings that he's burning his bell, book, and candle, a tradition from the ninth century in which clerics burned candles to excommunicate someone. "We judge him damned," bishops would intone, "to eternal fire until he shall recover himself from the toils of the devil and return to amendment and to penitence."[9] Faithfull eventually recovered and launched a second act as a singer-songwriter. She credited a brief affair with Bowie at the end of the year with inspiring her to think about lyric writing in a new way.[10] (She and the Troggs were guests on the TV special he taped that fall, *The 1980 Floor Show*.)

The other women in the Stones' entourage endured even more horrific calamities during the Jamaica sessions. A local man pushed his way into Bill Wyman's room with a knife demanding money, then forced him to go under the bed while he raped his common-law wife, Astrid.[11]

Richards returned to London without Pallenberg after the two had a fight. When she attempted to enter their hotel with six Rastas, the manager would not let them in, and Pallenberg blew up at him. In return, the hotel helped the police bust her for pot. According to the memoir of Richards's assistant and dealer "Spanish Tony" Sanchez, she was raped in jail by guards and inmates before being released to return to England.[12] The experience no doubt accelerated her spiraling need to self-medicate.

"She was dying to survive," Richards sang in "Coming Down Again," his strongest ballad, with gentle accompaniment by Mick. Richards said that musically the song was in the vein of both "As Tears Go By" and the country style taught to him by his friend Gram Parsons,[13] who died nineteen days after *Goats Head Soup* was released from a morphine and alcohol overdose.

The song was followed on the album by "Doo Doo Doo Doo Doo (Heartbreaker)." The band first attempted the track in Jamaica but re-recorded it later that spring. The new lyrics focused on an April 28 police killing in South Jamaica—the one in Queens, New York. While investigating a robbery, two undercover policemen stopped ten-year-old Clifford Glover and his stepfather to question them. Glover and his stepfather thought the officers were muggers, as they were not in uniform, and ran. Officer Thomas Shea shot Glover in the back; the bullet went through his heart, as in the song. Shea was subsequently acquitted, igniting protests and riots in Queens, not unlike more recent events with Black Lives Matter. Jagger denounces the cop as a heartbreaker "with your .44," the same gun Clint Eastwood celebrated that year in *Magnum Force,* the latest installment of his Dirty Harry series about an undercover cop.

The album would have a better reputation today if it opened with the incendiary "Heartbreaker" instead of the somewhat corny "Dancing with

Mr. D."—and if they had replaced "Hide Your Love" with "Through the Lonely Nights," a haunting Gram Parsons–influenced song with Eagles-like country rock harmonies that they consigned to a B side.

✳

Todd Haynes's glam epic *Velvet Goldmine* focuses on the friend-ship/love affair the Bowie-esque lead has with a figure who appears to be Iggy Pop on the surface, but the story includes elements from Bowie's rela-tionship with Jagger, such as Angie finding them in bed together.

Bowie had been a fan for years, stage-naming himself after the Jim Bowie knife because Jagger meant "knife" in Old English. Their friendship began in earnest after Jagger and his wife, Bianca, visited Bowie backstage at his May 12 show at Earl's Court.[14] Soon the two singers were observed at the London club Tramp, at a Diana Ross show, at the Muhammad Ali/ Ken Norton fight. The Bowies moved close to the Jaggers on Cheyne Walk in October. When Angie returned home one morning to find the two men sleeping naked together in the bedroom, she "felt absolutely dead certain that they'd been screwing. It was so obvious, in fact, that I never even con-sidered the possibility that they hadn't been screwing."[15]

Bebe Buell recalled, "I used to get some pretty strange phone calls from Mick and David at three in the morning, inviting me to join them in bed with four gorgeous black women. Or four gorgeous black men."[16]

Bowie's backup-singer/girlfriend Ava Cherry reportedly told biographer Christopher Anderson that the two "were really sexually obsessed with each other. Even though I was in bed with them many times, I ended up just watching them have sex."[17] She told the *New York Post,* "It's called a cookie. I was the tasty filling. It was wonderful, just like it should have been—everybody on their respective side doing whatever they do. We were friends."[18]

Years later, though, Cherry backpedaled. "Nah, honey. I told them I didn't say that, but it didn't stop them from writing it."[19]

LA club owner and disc jockey Rodney Bingenheimer maintained, how-ever, "Mick and David were lovers, of course. They didn't exactly make a secret of it."[20]

Whatever they were, they were also rivals. Once Jagger had been the twenty-one-year-old enfant terrible singing "Time Is on My Side," but Bowie had supplanted him as the outrage du jour. Perhaps that was why "Time Waits for No One" was the first song the band tackled when they regrouped for *It's Only Rock 'n' Roll* sessions in November.

"I went to Brazil, which is possibly why there is a little Latin influence there," Taylor said. "It was done in one or two takes."[21]

Richards kicks things off with a riff that plays throughout the song. Elton John's percussionist Ray Cooper provides the tambourine, maracas, and the sound of a ticking clock. But the key to the track's eerie grandeur is Bill Wyman's mysterious synth riff, always hanging back a beat before entering each verse.

Richards had been playing Dobie Gray's recent hit "Drift Away" constantly; maybe its lyric about wasting time had gotten to Jagger. Echoing Shakespeare, the singer acknowledges the band is star-crossed and sated by leisure. Filler songs have started to gather on their albums for the first time in six years. Quoting Deuteronomy 11:14 ("gather thy corn") and Confucius ("The years do not wait for us"), he goads himself, "Hours are like diamonds, don't let them waste."

The Stones pushed themselves for another ambitious track, "Fingerprint File," a protest song about "some little jerk in the FBI keepin' papers on me six feet high" who wiretaps Jagger while the SIS (the Los Angeles Police Department's Special Investigation Section) takes ultraviolet/infrared photos of him. There *was* a "fat FBI file" on Jagger. According to biographer Philip Norman, in 1967 the FBI conspired with Britain's MI5 and the *News of the World* tabloid to bust Jagger and Richards. The band also wrote a song sympathetic to black dissident Angela Davis, "Sweet Black Angel." Perhaps Jagger felt safe releasing "Fingerprint File" because the Supreme Court had recently decreed the FBI couldn't conduct electronic surveillance without a court order. The decision forced the FBI to drop charges against the Weather Underground and the White Panthers. "Fingerprint File" sounds as relevant today, only as of this writing it's the president claiming he's the victim of FBI surveillance (in a government program labeled "Crossfire Hurricane," after a lyric from "Jumpin' Jack Flash," no less). "What a price to pay," Jagger laments.

Just as the Stones were working hard on those tracks, Lester Bangs published an article in *Creem* magazine entitled "1973 Nervous Breakdown: The Ol' Fey Outlaws Ain't What They Used to Be—Are You?" "There is a sadness about the Stones now, because they amount to such an enormous 'So what?'" he wrote in one of the gentler lines. "Somehow it blows all the Jagger charms to see him and Bowie dancing and lolling on each other's laps at David's 'retirement' party while their wives made out with quiet dignity in the glare of the paparazzi." *Rolling Stone* critic Gordon Fletcher, meanwhile, dismissed the group as "a senior, 'safe' bizarro-perversion band." Critics like

Bangs wanted the Stones to remain the embodiment of everything parents feared (black bisexual long-haired junkie devils leading the street-fighting revolution) and hated to see Jagger jetting about in the gossip column with Bianca, the era's equivalent of Kim Kardashian.

Jagger grumbled, "I was getting a bit tired of people having a go, all that, 'oh, it's not as good as their last one' business."[22] In "It's Only Rock 'n' Roll (but I Like It)," he wondered if it would appease the critics if he committed suicide onstage, echoing Bowie's set closer "Rock and Roll Suicide." The cover of the single showed him committing hari-kari with a pen, like a vampire staking himself.

The song marked the band's transition from the ambitious Mick Taylor era to the Ron Wood era, in which they maintained the same template for the next four decades. Taylor had known Wood since he was fifteen in the mid-'60s London R&B scene, but Jagger and Richards didn't start hanging with Wood until spring '73. Wood had recently purchased a house called the Wick that overlooked the River Thames, and it had become one of the most popular haunts for the inner circle of British blues rockers. When Wood's wife, model Krissy Findlay, ran into Richards at a club, she told him Jagger was over at the house jamming with Wood. Per biographer Victor Bockris, it was awkward when Richards showed up, because Jagger had been discreetly checking out Wood as a possible candidate to fill in for Richards if the US blocked Richards from entering due to his drug convictions.[23] But Richards and Wood got on like doppelgänger brothers. Richards moved into the coach house for months because he was fighting with Pallenberg and was paranoid the authorities were plotting to bust him again.

Wood starting working on a solo record, *I've Got My Own Album to Do,* and asked Jagger to sing on "I Can Feel the Fire," which had a hook more reggae than anything the Stones had tried to date. Wood recalled, "After we'd done that, he said, 'Help me with this song, 'It's Only Rock 'n' Roll,' 'cause I wanna see how it turns out.' So, say on a Tuesday evening: two guitars—Mick and I—and Mick singing lead vocal and David Bowie and myself on backup vocals."[24] They called in the Faces' Kenny Jones for drums, as he lived nearby. Wood utilized the same Chuck Berry "Little Queenie" hook T. Rex had for "Bang a Gong." Jagger worked himself into a lion's roar for the song's climax, voice still shredding at full power.

"Steal that motherfucker back," Richards insisted when he heard it.[25] "That song is a classic. The title alone is a classic and that's the whole thing about it."[26]

Jagger did a trade with Wood: "I Can Feel the Fire" would be credited solely to him in return for "It's Only Rock 'n' Roll" being Jagger-Richards. A bad trade, but perhaps it was the entry fee to joining the Stones (which wouldn't technically happen for another year and a half). The Stones tried to cut their own version, but, per Richards, "it just didn't have that one-off feel."[27] So they put out the original with Jones drumming on the record, though they dubbed out Bowie.

When the band named their next album after the song, the critics charged that the title set up an interesting premise that the rest of the album failed to develop. Perhaps the album would have garnered more respect if they had opened with the title track, then followed with a song they recorded but left off, "Drift Away."

When Richards lived with Wood, he continued to play the single daily. It was written by Mentor Williams, brother of singer-songwriter Paul Williams. R&B singer Dobie Gray's cover debuted on the chart February 24 and made it all the way up to No. 5 in May. Gray had been struggling to get back in the Top 20 for the last eight years, since "The In Crowd." In the song, he thanks his fellow musicians for being the "light through the pouring rain," something Richards no doubt needed that summer. On June 26 he was arrested for heroin, Mandrax (Quaaludes), cannabis, and unregistered guns. The following month, his house Redlands burned, possibly after he nodded off with cig in hand. The night after he was convicted for the bust, he accidentally set his hotel room on fire. He *looked* like the Mr. D of *Goats Head Soup*, front tooth broken and gray. The busts and fire surely only worsened Pallenberg's own post-traumatic stress from the Jamaica sojourn. The lyrics of "Drift Away" celebrated the joy of guitars and harmony, how they soothed the blues and kept one strong. The song would have answered why it *wasn't* just rock and roll. If they had swapped that in and taken out "Dance Little Sister," it would have kept the classic album streak going. (The outtake can be found on YouTube.)

❊

By then Mick Taylor was drifting away. Unknown to them at the time, an October 19 performance in West Berlin would be his last live gig with the band for the next thirty-nine years.

Jagger later reflected, "I think he found it difficult to get on with Keith."[28] As Richards's heroin dependency continued apace, Richards found himself in the eerie position of being the new Brian Jones of the group, the weak link losing it to drugs, merely strumming the rhythm while the other guitarist outshone him with virtuoso leads he could never play himself. He and Jones used to switch it up, sometimes one would play lead, sometimes the other, but Taylor always took the lead unless the song sounded like Chuck Berry, "which completely destroyed the whole concept of the Stones," Richards later complained.

Richards grew sharp to Taylor in the studio. "Oi! Taylor! You're playing too fuckin' loud. I mean, you're really good live, man, but you're fucking useless in the studio. Lay out, play later, whatever."[29] Taylor would come in early and record something; Richards would arrive and erase it.

Taylor was angry that songs he and Jagger wrote were credited to Jagger-Richards. Jagger was no doubt loath to rock the boat in the most lucrative songwriting partnership since Lennon-McCartney. When Taylor picked up a copy of *It's Only Rock 'n' Roll* and saw he was not credited for "Time Waits for No One" and "Till the Next Time We Say Goodbye," he quit.

"The Mick Taylor period was a creative peak for us," Watts acknowledged. "A tremendous jump in musical credibility. Now Keith won't say that; Keith, I think, would prefer to play with Ronnie as a partner. But Mick Taylor was an incredible virtuoso. Brian wasn't, he was a good all-round player, and Ronnie's the same. He'll play wonderful bottleneck guitar and pedal steel—any instrument, like Brian—but Mick gave our music terrific lyricism. Ronnie is a very likeable person, a great sense of humor."[30]

Jagger said Taylor "would play very fluid lines against my vocals. He was exciting, and he was very pretty, and it gave me something to follow, to bang off. Some people think that's the best version of the band that existed."[31]

Still, it's unlikely the band would have endured if Wood hadn't made it fun for Richards again. But their adventurous era came to an end, both musically and lyrically. Marianne Faithfull had been a folkie pursued by Dylan, and she stoked Jagger's ambitions as a wordsmith, inspiring him to write songs based on Russian novels. Bianca and, later, Jerry Hall couldn't have cared less. Jagger would push himself on a handful of compositions over the ensuing decades: "Memory Motel," "Undercover of the Night," "High Wire," "Saint of Me." But none had the eloquence of "Time Waits for No One," or Taylor's guitar climbing into the stratosphere.

The dreams of the night time will vanish by dawn.

more intense than what Kanye West received for supporting President Trump. Nixon's administration had supported the FBI'S COINTELPRO's efforts to sabotage the Black Panthers and other dissidents, and his "Southern strategy" appealed to racist voters through dog-whistle codes of "state's rights" and "law and order."

"I'm not selling out, I'm selling in," Brown insisted.[2] But protesters picketed his shows with signs like JAMES BROWN, NIXON'S CLOWN.[3] His concert attendance significantly dropped, and 1973 became the first year since 1964 he did not score a No. 1 single on the R&B chart. Davis, meanwhile, received death threats. He and Brown were scheduled to sing at January's inauguration, but neither turned up.

Nixon made some calls to the FCC on Brown's behalf and had his IRS case changed from criminal to civil, but otherwise didn't deliver. In the spring Nixon also cut over a hundred social programs overseen by the War on Poverty's Office of Economic Opportunity. Brown didn't comment much, except for a song on his band the JBs' album *Doing It to Death*: "You Can Have Watergate Just Gimme Some Bucks and I'll Be Straight," whatever that meant.

It was a catastrophic year for Brown for an infinitely more important reason. His son Teddy was killed on June 14. In the aftermath, he got to know a friend of Teddy's who, though young, had already toured as a preacher with Mahalia Jackson and served as activist Jesse Jackson's youth director—Al Sharpton. "I first knew James because his son, Teddy, and I were close when we were teenagers. When Teddy was killed in a car accident in 1973, James took me in like a son. I was 19, the same age as Teddy."[4]

Sharpton served as Brown's tour director while continuing his leadership of the National Youth Movement, which fought to alleviate poverty in the inner city. Brown told him, "If you listen to me I'll make you the biggest [civil rights leader] out there."[5]

Brown told Jesse Jackson how he saw the difference between Jackson and Sharpton. "You're a Motown act. You are black but you are accepted. He's (Sharpton's) a James Brown act. He's raw and authentic, and he's going to outrun you in the end."[6]

In the *Wattstax* concert film released in February, Jackson led the stadium in raising fists and shouting the "I Am—Somebody" poem by Reverend William Holmes Borders, which Jackson fused with Amiri Baraka's poem "What Time Is It? Nation Time!" Jackson had an angrier edge to his voice than his mentor MLK, but then he had seen MLK shot to death right in front of him. He also led the children of *Sesame Street* in a gentler version.

20.

✳

The World Is a Ghetto

Rejected by fans after his embrace of Nixon, James Brown records his final string of classic albums and No. 1 R&B singles. George Clinton fuses Motown and Detroit hard rock on acid and creates the P-Funk empire. The Black Panthers attempt to go mainstream. And DJ Kool Herc births hip hop when he deejays his sister's party on August 11.

✳

James Brown had been unassailable in the Black Power movement. Poet Amiri Baraka wrote, "If Elvis Presley is King / Who is James Brown, God?"

Then Brown threw his support behind Nixon in the 1972 campaign, as did Sammy Davis Jr., Jim Brown, and Wilt Chamberlain. Theoretically, this was so Brown could get into the White House and push Nixon to make Martin Luther King Jr.'s birthday a national holiday. Nixon took the meeting, though he initially complained to his staff (captured on the White House taping system), "I've done the blacks! . . . I don't want any more blacks, and I don't want any more Jews, between now and the election."[1]

Many biographers now assume Brown also hoped Nixon would protect him from the IRS in return for his support. The agency said he owed $4.5 million in back taxes. Brown also wanted FCC approval for radio stations he owned.

The backlash from the black community blindsided Brown; it was far

His organization PUSH (People United to Serve Humanity) secured government grants for black businesses and arranged for companies like Schlitz, Coke, and General Foods to hire more blacks.[7] When Dick Clark attempted to start his own version of *Soul Train,* Jackson said Clark was attempting to destroy the only black-run show on television and threatened ABC with a boycott, so the network canceled Clark's show.[8]

It was a banner year for blacks securing mayorships of huge cities: Tom Bradley in Los Angeles, Coleman Young in Detroit, Maynard Jackson in Atlanta. They diversified bank boards and integrated police departments, reducing police brutality.[9] Following the Voting Rights Act of 1965, federal registrars monitored the South to make sure blacks could vote, and the number of African Americans holding elective office rose from 1,185 in 1969 to 2,991 in 1974.[10]

In the wake of such progress, even the Black Panthers believed they could go mainstream. Their membership had fallen from its peak of five thousand in five states,[11] due to sabotage by the FBI and infighting between the faction led by co-founder Huey Newton, who wanted to work with the US government, and the faction led by Eldridge Cleaver, who advocated revolution through guerilla warfare. (Cleaver advocated revolution from the safety of France, where he lived in exile.) Newton closed all Panther branches except the original in Oakland, California, and called in the remaining members to focus on a five-year plan to win power in the city's political establishment.[12]

Newton himself did not run for office, even though 1973 saw the publication of his memoir *Revolutionary Suicide,* featuring him on the cover with a rifle in his right hand and a spear in his left, wearing his black beret. Co-founder Bobby Seale ran for mayor, and Minister of Information Elaine Brown ran for city council. (Brown also released two albums as a singer that year with gospel-inflected songs like "Until We're Free.") They gave speeches on buses, organized black gangs and white radicals to stick thousands of chickens into bags with voter registration forms and handed them out.[13] They registered somewhere between twenty thousand and fifty thousand people, but Seale ultimately lost the runoff to the incumbent in May. Brown garnered 30 percent of the vote but lost as well.

Numerous disheartened members resigned after the losses, and Newton purged many of those who remained. Perhaps if they had won the election Newton might not have gone mad. But now he prioritized a plan to become kingpin of the Oakland underworld. He sent a team of former prisoners to rob dealers and pimps, or force them to join his protection racket. They resold the drugs they stole and pulled stickups.[14]

Newton and Seale had started the group together to monitor police harassment, inspired by the death of Malcom X. They had written the manifesto while playing Dylan's "Ballad of a Thin Man" in the background. Now they argued over a movie Newton wanted made about them, to be produced by his patron, Hollywood mogul Bert Schneider (*Easy Rider, Five Easy Pieces,* the Monkees' *Head*). Newton lashed Seale with a bullwhip, and Seale left the party.[15] Newton pistol-whipped his tailor and fractured his skull, murdered a hooker, fled to Cuba. The Panthers' accountant was killed.[16]

✳

For all the past decade's progress in civil rights, many cities witnessed an alarming decline in quality of life. In the aftermath of MLK's assassination, President Johnson pushed through the passage of the Fair Housing Act of 1968, prohibiting discrimination in housing, which enabled many to leave the inner city for the suburbs. The black exodus was accompanied by white flight after the riots of 1965–68. Detroit lost up to 27 percent of its white population. As the inner city's tax base for police and schools plummeted, the murder rate surged. The MC5's Wayne Kramer observed in his memoir that before the riots, Detroit had been safe to walk anytime, and people solved conflicts with their fists. After the riots, gun purchases skyrocketed, and people increasingly settled beefs with bullets.[17]

Billboard identified War's *The World Is a Ghetto* as the bestselling album of the year, hitting No. 1 on both the pop and R&B album charts.[18] The title track made it to No. 7 on the pop singles chart and "The Cisco Kid" hit No. 2.[19] In Bobby Womack's "Across 110th Street," the pensive opening instrumental coupled with Womack's indelible howl created the template for future songs about treacherous landscapes like Guns N' Roses' "Welcome to the Jungle." Rapper 50 Cent told *NME* it was the first song he fell in love with. "Because of how the situation was for black people in America at that time, there were a lot of struggle songs around. It seemed to be something that really moved the people around me. I felt the power of music to raise people up; to make them angry or proud."[20]

Willie Hutch provided the soundtrack to the pimp drama *The Mack* ("Brothers Gonna Work It Out"). After Curtis Mayfield agreed to score *Super Fly* (directed by the son of *Shaft*'s director, both named Gordon Parks), he grew dismayed when he saw that the film amounted to a "cocaine infomercial,"[21] especially since he had been the premiere songwriter of civil rights anthems like "People Get Ready." He turned one of the film's instrumentals

David Bowie and Stevie Wonder, 1973.
(Courtesy of Echoes/Getty Images)

Pink Floyd from left: Rick Wright (keyboards, vocals), David Gilmour (guitar, vocals, synthesizer), Nick Mason (drums), Roger Waters (bass, vocals, synthesizer). *(Courtesy of Photofest)*

Linda Ronstadt at Boston Music Hall in February 1973. *(Courtesy of S. Ti Muntarbhorn)*

Merle Haggard (left) performs for Pat (center) and Richard Nixon at the White House on March 17.
(Courtesy of Photofest)

Parliament-Funkadelic. From left: Ray Davis (vocals), Calvin Simon (vocals), "Shady" Grady Thomas (vocals), George Clinton (vocals), Bernie Worrell (keyboards), unidentified member, Billy "Bass" Nelson, Garry Shider (guitar), Clarence "Fuzzy" Haskins (vocals).
(Courtesy of Michael Ochs Archives/Getty Images)

Lynyrd Skynyrd from left: Billy Powell (keyboards), Allen Collins (guitar), Leon Wilkinson (bass), Bob Burns (drums), Ronnie Van Zant (vocals), Gary Rossington (guitar), Ed King (guitar).
(Courtesy of Photofest)

Suzi Quatro reached number one on the U.K. singles chart with "Can the Can" on June 10.
(Courtesy of Photofest)

Bob Marley in Trenchtown, Jamaica, photographed by Arthur Gorson on assignment for the July *Rolling Stone* article "The Wild Side of Paradise."

(Courtesy of Photofest)

The New York Dolls from left: David Johansen (vocals), Sylvain Sylvain (rhythm guitar, piano), Arthur "Killer" Kane (bass), Johnny Thunders (lead guitar), Jerry Nolan (drums).
(Courtesy of Photofest)

The Rolling Stones' Mick Jagger (left, vocals) and Keith Richards (guitar) with Richards's son Marlon backstage at Wembley Empire Pool in London on September 7.
(Courtesy of Michael Putland/Getty Images)

Joni Mitchell with *Court and Spark* drummer John Guerin (far right).

(Courtesy of Photofest)

Billy Joel performs at the Troubadour nightclub in West Hollywood on November 6.
(Courtesy of CBS Photo Archive/Getty Images)

into the single "Freddie's Dead," warning that dealing could get you killed. In the "Superfly" single, which made it to No. 8 on January 13, Mayfield sang there was "no happiness" in "mov[ing] a lot of blow."

The movie spurred the NAACP's Junius Griffin to invent the term "blaxploitation" ("black" plus "exploitation film," a term for B movies). "We must insist that our children are not exposed to a steady diet of so-called black movies that glorify black males as pimps, dope pushers, gangsters, and superfly males."[22] CORE's Roy Innis said the movie promoted "Black genocide in the Black community."[23]

The big three civil rights groups—NAACP, CORE, and SCLC—teamed to form the Coalition Against Blaxploitation (CAB) and boycotted theaters to try to stop the film's distribution. Star Ron O'Neal countered, "The heroin pusher is indeed the scourge of the black community, but we're talking about cocaine, which is basically a white drug. Very few black people can afford cocaine at $800 an ounce. And since cocaine is not physically addictive, people do not steal and rob to get it. There are no coke junkies."[24]

O'Neal directed the sequel, *Super Fly T.N.T.*, and tried to redeem the character by having him leave the dealer's life behind to help African revolutionaries. Alex Haley wrote the script, presumably needing money between his dual landmarks *The Autobiography of Malcolm X* (1965) and *Roots* (1976). In the end, CAB's fears were realized as Superfly and the Mack ignited the imaginations of future gangsta rappers like Tupac and Biggie and drug dealers like "Freeway Rick" Ross.

James Brown released soundtracks to two blaxploitation films that year: *Black Caesar* and *Slaughter's Big Rip-Off* (one of Jim Brown's action films as the titular ex–Green Beret). The poster of *Black Caesar* trumpeted the "Godfather of Harlem," and Brown quickly turned the phrase into a new nickname, "Godfather of Soul."[25] Originally the producers sought Stevie Wonder, but Wonder decided the film was too violent.[26] It included a scene in which an informant's ear is cut off, later echoed in blaxploitation fanatic Quentin Tarantino's *Reservoir Dogs*.

Though James Brown was credited for the instrumentals, he delegated them to his trombonist Fred Wesley. The single for *Black Caesar*, "Down and Out in New York City," was written by outside songwriters and gave him something more to chew on than his usual dance-song catchphrases, allowing him to channel the feeling of being abandoned by some of his audience. For the B side, "Mama's Dead," he insisted on being alone to record and cried when he did,[27] even though its lyrics of a loving parent conflicted with the fact that his own mother abandoned him to an abusive father when he was four, leaving him to live in his aunt's brothel. In press releases Brown claimed his mother died when he was that age.

Brown recorded "The Payback," the song that eventually returned him to the top of the R&B charts, for a third blaxploitation film in August, *Hell Up in Harlem*. Wesley believed Brown was angry when he recorded the revenge mantra after hearing that one of his female employees had dated Harold Melvin of the Blue Notes. He hollered so many "damns" that the engineer had to work overtime editing them out.[28] When they submitted the soundtrack, however, the film producers called it "the same old James Brown stuff" and replaced him with Edwin Starr.[29]

The joke was on the producers, though. Brown released the material as the nonsoundtrack album *The Payback* in December. AllMusic's Mark Deming ranked it "one of James Brown's last inarguably great albums." Another song recorded that August for the movie, "Papa Don't Take No Mess," became Brown's final R&B No. 1 when released the following summer.

✳

James Brown's direct impact on the R&B charts waned in the immediate years ahead, but a second life awaited him as the most sampled man in hip hop. Another figure whose samples provided the foundation for rap was about to lead his Parliament-Funkadelic empire to a new plateau.

George Clinton co-founded the doo-wop group the Parliaments in 1956 in New Jersey with Grady Thomas, Stingray Davis, Fuzzy Haskins, and Calvin Simon and soon emerged as the leader. "I couldn't play an instrument. I couldn't sing as well as some and I couldn't arrange as well as some others. But I could see the whole picture from altitude, and that let me land the planes."[30] After Clinton briefly scored a gig as a Motown songwriter-producer, they moved to Detroit in 1967. Clinton pulled together a permanent band to play with the vocalists onstage, including guitarist Eddie Hazel, who proved a contender for Hendrix's throne.

That year Clinton did acid for the first time in Harvard Square as the band and a crowd of students and teachers got naked in the rain.[31] Clinton decided to tear down the wall between R&B and the psychedelic British rock he loved by the Beatles, Pink Floyd, Cream, and the Who. When a label dispute prevented them from using the name "the Parliaments," they renamed the outfit Funkadelic. Clinton claimed Motown producer Norman Whitfield secretly taped their shows and copped ideas for the more polished version of psychedelic soul he was creating with the Temptations.[32]

Clinton received mail from his R&B base imploring him not to rock, but the band signed with the management team that handled the Stooges, the MC5, Ted Nugent, and Mitch Ryder. "We saw that Detroit had its own version of rock 'n' roll coming out. [The MC5 and the Stooges] influenced us a lot. We was changing from Parliament to Funkadelic, and it would've been Iggy Pop (who) had a lot to do with that. That craziness. I saw how far you could go and still entertain people."[33] Their publicist encouraged Clinton and Iggy Pop to get married onstage for coverage in *Creem* magazine. Clinton said Pop's rudeness inspired him and guitarist Garry Shider to start wearing diapers made of hotel towels (or sometimes the flag) onstage. Clinton progressed to face paint, penises painted on his shaved head, and plastic duck feet. The only time the group experienced tension was when they opened for Black Oak Arkansas. The redneck crowd sang "Dixie" at them, but keyboardist Bernie Worrell played a monumental version of the song back at them and won the audience over.[34]

For the time being, Clinton avoided the hard drugs and booze engulfing the rest of the band, sticking to hallucinogens and *Star Trek*. Bootsy and Catfish Collins, who joined after defecting from James Brown's band, called him "Prez," the president of the no-pussy-getting club.[35] But no one else in the heyday of protest soul released a song as darkly empathetic as the title track of *Cosmic Slop*. Instead of "Papa Was a Rolling Stone," here was "Mama Was a Prostitute." She tries to hide what she does to feed her family from her kids, asking God for forgiveness as she hears the Devil call to her, "Would you like to dance with me? We're doing the cosmic slop." On the other side of the album, "Trash A-Go-Go" features the singer receiving ten to twenty years for pimping a woman "to support my high and keep me fly," to the foreboding strains of a Hendrix–meets–Chambers Brothers jam. Clinton was writing what he knew. "We called [our] shows 'Pimps, hos, and hippies,' because that's what they were, and the groups converged in these wild after-show parties, orgies up the yin yang."[36] You could see it in the cover art by Pedro Bell, the first of many albums he illustrated for the group. Originally Bell introduced himself to Clinton by sending in his artwork as fan mail.

"This Broken Heart" reached back to simpler days for relief. Sung by Parliament Ben Edwards, with strings arranged by Worrell, it was a cover of a '50s doo-wop song by the Sonics (not the garage rock band)—though the spoken-word interlude sounded not unlike Tupac's spoken word break in "Life Goes On" twenty-three years later.

But the album missed the R&B Top 20, and Clinton feared the band had been too "far out" for too long. "The view was breathtaking, but the air was thin."[37]

He decided it was time to come back down to earth with a return to horn-and-vocal-based tracks that could get on mainstream R&B radio. He pitched his new vision—"Jazzy James Brown" or "pop Pink Floyd"[38]—to label executive Neil Bogart. Bogart had enjoyed success with bubblegum groups like the Ohio Express and 1910 Fruitgum Company and was starting his own label, Casablanca, the title riffing off his last name. He had just signed Kiss to bring in the hard rock fans.

Warner Bros. funded Casablanca, which enabled Clinton to regain control of the original group's name. He modernized "the Parliaments" to "Parliament" to resemble contemporary British groups. Clinton played the songs he was developing for Bogart, and if Bogart liked them they became Parliament songs. The hard rock/funk jams went on the next Funkadelic album. "Up for the Down Stroke" returned Parliament to the Top 10 for the first time since 1967's "Testify." Funkadelic's "Alice in My Fantasies" went toe-to-toe with Sabbath or any other metal band for roller-coaster anarchy. Both sides toured together under the moniker Parliament-Funkadelic or P-Funk and planted the soil for West Coast G-funk by artists like Dr. Dre and Snoop Dogg.

❊

The genre that eventually overtook rock and roll as the most popular American genre germinated in records by proto-rappers the Last Poets, the Watts Prophets, and Gil Scott-Heron. But hip hop DJ Kool Herc maintained, "Hip hop came out of Trenchtown," a ghetto of Kingston, Jamaica.[39] An example could be found on the *The Harder They Come* soundtrack.

"Draw Your Brakes" by Scotty featured the Jamaican tradition called toasting. Back in the 1950s, most people in the Kingston ghettos could not afford to pay for live music. Instead, deejays orchestrated street parties by loading up trucks with generators, turntables, and huge speakers the size of wardrobes to blast American rhythm and blues. They charged admission and sold food and drinks, drawing thousands. They called their setups Sound Systems.

Count Machuki became famous for his ability to imitate the frantic jive of American deejays, whom the islanders heard through radio broadcasts emanating from New Orleans. He proto-rapped or chanted over the music, bragged, shrieked, commented on social issues—i.e., toasted, something the musicians of West Africa (griots) had been doing for centuries over percussion.[40]

Deejays often paid studios to make vinyl copies of records for their

Sound System. Around '67 or '68, a Sound System operator named Ruddy Redwood requested a copy of the Paragons' "On the Beach."[41] The studio inadvertently left off the vocals, turning it into an instrumental. The operator gave it to his deejay to toast over anyway, and the crowd went wild. Other deejays began asking for copies without vocals. Producers like Duke Reid issued singles with the song on one side and the instrumental on the other. Instrumentals were named "dubs." Engineers like Lee "Scratch" Perry turned up the drum and bass, moved parts of the song around, added echo and sound effects. The Jamaicans called these "versions."[42] When the technique became popular in the US in the '80s, the States called them "remixes." In 1973, Perry released the first pure dub album, *Upsetters 14 Dub*.

On "Draw Your Brakes," DJ Scotty took a rocksteady single called "Stop That Train" by Keith and Tex and dropped out their vocals on the verses so he could toast and shriek. Six months after it was released in the States on *The Harder They Come,* a deejay from the Bronx pioneered an American variation of the process.

❊

Clive Campbell was born in Jamaica in 1955 and moved with his family to the South Bronx in 1967, the neighborhood with the largest Jamaican community in the US. He was tall and lifted weights, so the kids called him Hercules, a.k.a. Kool Herc. He decided to become a deejay after seeing how James Brown's "Sex Machine" drove dancers to ecstasy. His father was a technician for a band and helped Herc score two turntables and a mixer.

His little sister Cindy needed money to buy clothes for the upcoming school year, so she decided to hold a "Back to School Jam" in the first-floor recreation room of their hundred-unit apartment building at 1520 Sedgwick Avenue. She enlisted her brother to provide the music. Her mother rounded up snacks. Her father handled soda and beer. She wrote out invites on index cards: twenty-five cents for girls, fifty cents for guys, 9 p.m. to 4 a.m.

Kool Herc asked his friend Coke La Rock to be MC (master of ceremonies) so he could concentrate on spinning records. Coke recalled, "The first time I got on the mic, it was just me goofing with my friends. Dudes like Pretty Tony, Easy Al and Nookie Nook, I'd be messing with them, telling them to move their cars."[43] Even though none of them actually had cars. "We were trying to impress the girls."[44]

Just as the Jamaican dub producers switched song sections around, Kool Herc extended the intros, instrumental breaks, and drum solos, because that's when the dancers cut loose. With a copy of the record on each turntable, he could jump back and forth between the discs and stretch out "the break" as long as the crowd seemed to dig it.

He tried the technique (which he later dubbed "the Merry Go Round") with James Brown's "Give It Up or Turn It Loose," then the Incredible Bongo Band's "Bongo Rock '73" and "Apache." The Incredible Bongo Band was a group of studio musicians hired to create the soundtrack for the camp horror film *The Thing with Two Heads*.[45] They went on to release two albums. Hip hop artists later dubbed "Apache" the "National Anthem of Hip Hop." (Ironically, the drummer and bassist were white, though the percussionist was black.)

Kool Herc: "I was sittin' back, observin', watching the crowd who were all waiting for this particular part of the record. And after I did it for the first time, there was no turnin' back—everybody was comin' to the party for that particular part of my set. . . . They always wanted to hear breaks after breaks after breaks."[46]

The kids bugged Herc's family for more parties, and they obliged, staging dance contests with a $25 prize. Herc christened the kids dancing to his breaks "b-boys" and "b-girls."

Future deejay Grandmixer DXT recalled, "Everybody would form a circle and the B-boys would go into the center. At first the dance was simple: touch your toes, hop, kick out your leg. Then some guy went down, spun around on all fours. Everybody said wow and went home to try to come up with something better."[47]

Soon the parties grew too big for the rec room, then too big for their high school. When Herc saw a construction crew plug into the base of a lamp post, he realized he could hotwire lamps for his equipment, and saw how they could expand to block parties, not unlike the street fairs of Jamaica, when summer came round again.

Country Rock

Linda Ronstadt endures a baptism of fire on tour with Neil Young. The Eagles fight for their right to rock. Gram Parsons finally makes the album he always wanted to with the help of Emmylou Harris, before his overdose on September 19.

✳

Los Angeles was only 112 miles from Bakersfield, the major country outpost outside Nashville, home to Buck Owens and Merle Haggard. Byrds bassist Chris Hillman grew up playing in honky-tonks in the Southern California area, and in the mid-'60s he began fusing Owens's sparkling chimes with driving folk rock in songs like "Time Between" and "The Girl with No Name." Mike Nesmith made sure that each Monkees album had at least one bona fide country rock classic, exposing millions of kids to the embryonic genre.

"At that point country music was still considered hopelessly unhip," Linda Ronstadt said. "When I met Gram Parsons and Bernie Leadon, they were like closet country music lovers."[1]

Gradually the genre began to gather steam. Bob Dylan's road manager, Bobby Neuwirth, cracked, "Country music's the last authentic goddamned shit left for us to rip off."[2] Rockers needed to reground themselves after years spent in the lysergic stratosphere. *Easy Rider* featured Jack Nicholson getting murdered by rednecks, but his next film, *Five Easy Pieces,* by the same production team placed him in Bakersfield.

Linda Ronstadt (born 1946) grew up in Tuscon, Arizona, near the Mexican border. Her father was German/English/Mexican, her mother German/English/Dutch. The family was friends with Lalo Guerrero, the father of Chicano music. Ronstadt drew on ranchera music (Mexican bluegrass) for the sound of "crying tears" in her singing voice. She started playing folk clubs at fourteen.

"The Byrds were what brought me to California," she said. "I thought, 'Gee, 12-string guitar amplified, and Chris Hillman,' who we knew as a bluegrass player."[3] Nesmith gave her band their big break with "Different Drum," which she transformed into an early anthem for liberated women refusing to be tied down.

She went solo and wanted to cut country songs, but her label resisted. Then her single "Long Long Time" was big with country fans, so the label pushed her to go 100 percent Bakersfield.[4] But she wanted a rhythm section, too. She wanted to mix country and ranchera into rock and pop. "I can remember my manager at the time saying, 'Ecchh. It's too country for rock, and too rock for country. It's too corny.' My feelings were hurt, but it was too much a part of who I was."[5]

She kept plugging away: she assembled the Eagles to be her backing band; then, when they wanted to fly off on their own, she wished them well. She sang backup on Neil Young's "Heart of Gold" and "Old Man" with James Taylor, then joined Young's *Time Fades Away* tour, opening for him for seventy-eight gigs.

She was used to clubs, but now she had to win over fifteen thousand people at a time. She'd never had to sing that loud before. To steel herself she indulged in one of Young's favorite vices, coke. "I had to have my nose cauterized twice—I think they shot sodium nitrate up there—I'm okay now. I don't put anything up my nose anymore, except occasionally my finger."[6]

In her memoir she wrote that watching Young helped her find her own voice. His pianist Jack Nitzsche tried to undermine her, though. Nitzsche had been Phil Spector's arranger and conductor and had contributed to brilliant recordings by Young, the Monkees, and the Stones. But he was an ugly drunk, snarling Ronstadt wasn't good enough. He'd wanted Jackie DeShannon or Claudia Lennear (Bowie's "Lady Grinning Soul") to open.[7] He cursed into his mic onstage so often the soundmen finally turned it off.

One night at the afterparty, he put his arm around Ronstadt and complimented her for a while before turning dark again. When she tried to slip away, he wouldn't let her go.[8] "Because he was a keyboard player, he had powerful arms and had me locked in a tight grip. He continued to slur the cruelest and most insulting things he could muster in his inebriated state. I asked him to let me go. He said that he was going to make me fight my way out. . . . Though I tried hard not to, I began to cry."[9]

Her band members saw them and approached, so Nitzsche retreated, popping up later in the evening to spew negativity at singer-guitarist Gram Parsons, who was hanging out that night. "You're a junkie, Gram. You're going to die. Danny Whitten [from Crazy Horse]'s dead, and you're next."[10] When the others held a jam session, Nitzsche pissed in the middle of the room. Parsons threw Nitzsche's hat into the urine.

Parsons's wife cried at Nitzsche's prophecy, and Ronstadt returned to her room crying as well. Parsons's duet partner, Emmylou Harris, knocked on Ronstadt's door and offered her a yellow rose to help her feel better. Ronstadt wrote in her memoir that she still has it, pressed.[11]

"Jack Nitzsche was a musician who I admired," she wrote, "but I didn't want to be cowed by anybody. I didn't need to have Jack Nitzsche's approval to have a good opinion of myself. I knew what I was trying to do, and I knew I wasn't there yet. I was working on it, and I didn't need him to get in my way. That was an experience that made me stronger. . . . I ultimately felt sorry for him. He missed out on an opportunity to have a good friend. We had a lot of similar musical interests, and we could have shared some good listening together."[12]

Maybe she was venting at Nitzsche when she started to perform "You're No Good" onstage that tour. Her guitarist Kenny Edwards suggested she cover it.[13] It was originally a 1963 R&B hit by Betty Everett. Ronstadt played it on the *Midnight Special* TV show later that year, and it eventually became her first No. 1.

✳

Gram Parsons grew up in Georgia, the son of a World War II pilot who survived Pearl Harbor, then became an alcoholic and killed himself two days before Christmas when Parsons was twelve. His mother's drinking killed her via cirrhosis when he graduated high school. When he went to Harvard to study theology, his stepfather married the babysitter and sent his younger sister off to boarding school.

He found solace in country. "The musicians [at Harvard] had their ears open and they actually reintroduced me to country music after I had forgotten about it for ten years. And the country singers like George Jones, Ray

Price and Merle Haggard—they're great performers, but I had to learn to dig them."[14]

He joined the Byrds as David Crosby's replacement and unveiled his vision of hybrid country/R&B "cosmic American music" on *Sweetheart of the Rodeo*. He and Hillman splintered off to form the Flying Burrito Brothers. But then Keith Richards befriended Parsons and he started arriving to gigs wasted, then not arriving at all, so Hillman had to fire him.

Parsons's style bled into the Stones. Before him they played country for laughs on "Dear Doctor" and "Country Honk." But he taught both Richards and Jagger how to play and sing it deeper, and their country rock turned elegiac in "Wild Horses," "Dead Flowers," "Torn and Frayed." He and Richards tried to kick heroin in the same bed. But Jagger grew resentful of their bond, or Parsons's distracting effect, and he was eventually given the hint to move on.

So it was time for Parsons to do his own album; he'd burned all his other bridges. He enlisted a number of Elvis Presley's band members to help him make *GP*. He also wanted a female duet partner, like Cash and Carter, Jennings and Colter, Kristofferson and Coolidge. Hillman saw a singer named Emmylou Harris at a Georgetown, DC, club called the Cellar Door and recommended her.

In her Alabama high school Harris had been in the marching band, a model, and valedictorian. She won a scholarship to drama college but dropped out to be a folk singer in Greenwich Village like Baez and Mitchell. Her first album flopped. She had a kid, and the father split.[15] On food stamps, she and her baby moved back in with her folks.[16]

Parsons tested her out by singing "Streets of Baltimore" with her, which had been written by Tompall Glaser, Jennings's producer. Parsons was convinced, though Harris admitted that privately she "didn't get his music; I didn't quite get his singing either. I had always sung folk music and I saw country music as kind of hokey. So at first I just saw what we were doing as an opportunity to make some money singing on a record."[17]

She herself embodied "the audience he wanted to reach. I hadn't really heard [country]. I couldn't get past the layers and country music being politically incorrect."[18] But as she sang with him, or just watched him record while crocheting[19] in the corner, it started sinking in. "Just by singing with him, I learned that you plow it under and let the melody and the words carry you. Rather than this emoting thing, it will happen on its own."[20]

He asked her to come on tour with him in a retrofitted Greyhound bus. Parsons admitted, "We were fired from our first gig in Boulder because it was just a train wreck. So we got on the bus and went down to Austin early and we rehearsed. And that night we rocked the Armadillo World Headquarters—we got so many encores we had to go out and start the show over again since we didn't know any more songs. After that it was great."[21]

Jimmy Page and Robert Plant checked them out in Houston. Ronstadt sat in one night, Young the next. They played Max's Kansas City. The only problem was that Parsons's wife, Gretchen Burrell, had to watch him and Harris sing "Love Hurts" to each other every night. Parsons had told Hillman he wanted someone whose eyes he could fall in love with, and Hillman had delivered.[22] Understandably, Burrell would sometimes freak out, as recounted in Ben Fong-Torres's biography *Hickory Wind*: crying and asking other band members to comfort her, rushing down motel hallways booting doors, getting into shouting matches with Parsons that one time actually drew the cops. Parsons pulled a karate move; the cops Maced him and took him to jail. She'd interrupt rehearsals, banging past Parsons and Harris to hitchhike in front of the house, jumping in a stranger's car before Parsons could stop her, leaving him to say with a smile, "God damn! She's so sexy!"[23]

Harris's boyfriend stayed with them that summer as they recorded Parsons's second album, *Grievous Angel,* though the chemistry between Parsons and Harris remained palpable. Years later she reflected, "We were probably heading in that direction but the timing was just terrible. We had elements of being a couple through a musical relationship that became very intense. I think I kept a little bit of a distance, though. I mean, Gram was married and, though I wasn't that much of a prude, I probably didn't want to mess with that. Toward the end, I couldn't really deny it any more. I knew what I felt for him, and I just assumed that that was something that was going to happen, never thinking that we would never have the chance."[24]

Parsons wrote or co-wrote half the album, proud to finally create the record he'd always hoped to. When it was released the following year, *The Village Voice* proclaimed it one of the year's best.

In the midst of the sessions, a drunk driver killed Byrds guitarist Clarence White. At the graveside, Parsons and Bernie Leadon, a Burrito Brother who was now an Eagle, sang the southern gospel standard "Farther Along," and it inspired *Grievous Angel*'s closing track, "In My Hour of Darkness."

At the funeral, Parsons told his friend Phil Kaufman that if he died he didn't want his body to be taken back to New Orleans for a funeral. Instead he asked Kaufman to take him to the Joshua Tree desert and burn him.

Parsons loved the desert, and it was there, only two months later, on

September 19, that he expired in a Joshua Tree motel room, overdosing on morphine and alcohol. Harris said, "What I think happened was that he paid the price for being straight for a while and then going back to it one last time."[25] His level of tolerance had reset.

Kaufman later told *The Guardian* what he believed to be the reason for Parsons's request. "His stepfather was trying to get the body moved to New Orleans, trying to establish residency by death, and get hold of the family estate. When I decided to do it, I called the funeral parlor and they said, 'The body's on its way to LA, to be transferred to New Orleans.' It was, 'Ding!' The dime dropped. I knew, right away, what was going on. I found out that the body was being shipped to LAX on Continental Airlines, and it just so happened that a friend of mine owned a hearse. I called her and she said, 'I know what you want—you want my car.' I said, 'Yeah, and I want your boyfriend to come too.' The two of us just pulled up at the airport and told them that the family had changed their plans, and they wanted to fly the body out of a private airport. They went, 'Oh—OK.'"[26]

They drove Parsons to the desert, poured kerosene on him, and set him aflame. Kaufman was arrested but got off with a fine because there was no specific law against stealing bodies. Parsons's ashes were flown to New Orleans. Burrell forbade Harris from attending the memorial service.

Five days before Parsons's death, fellow country rockers Poco released an album called *Crazy Eyes*. Richie Furay had written the title track about Parsons.[27] He also covered "Brass Buttons," a song Parsons had written for his lost mother. "[Parsons] taught me that one when we lived across the street from each other in Greenwich Village in 1964."[28]

✳

The first time Ronstadt heard Harris sing, in a Texas club while on tour with Young, "it was really a crisis for me." Until that moment she'd felt like the undisputed queen of country rock. "Then came a split-second decision I made that affected the way I listened to and enjoyed music for the rest of my life. I thought that if I allowed myself to become envious of Emmy, it would be painful to listen to her, and I would deny myself the pleasure of it. If I simply surrendered to loving what she did, I could take my rightful place among the other drooling Emmylou fans, and then maybe, just maybe, I might be able to sing with her."[29]

After Parsons's death, Harris felt like she had been "amputated." Ronstadt invited her to stay with her and join her onstage for a week of shows at the

Roxy. Harris bought Nudie suits for them to wear, and they harmonized on Hank Williams. At Ronstadt's house, Harris played her a song she'd written about Parsons called "Boulder to Birmingham."

> *I would walk all the way from Boulder to Birmingham*
> *If I thought I could see, I could see your face.*

Ronstadt said she almost fell over when Harris played it for her. She helped Harris get a record deal.

"[Harris] gave girl country singers elegance, taste, class and dignity. I don't mean to demean the girl singers that had been in country music before, but they never appealed to me," Ronstadt said. "They seemed like girls who'd gone into the city, hung around the bars and become very jaded. They seemed hard; their makeup was on too thick. I didn't like it as a role model, and their singing was too twangy, too hard and too nasal, because of the hardness of their lives and their attitudes. Emmy brought more country fresh air, a real rural style. More like the Carter Family and Jean Ritchie."[30]

"I tried to carry on as best I could as [Parsons's] student, and follow some kind of inner barometer that he instilled in me. Gram really bequeathed me an extraordinary life,"[31] Harris said. Decades later, she recalled, "It was like he left me this gift, this stage, and said, 'Here you are. Now get out there and do it.'"[32]

✳

Glenn Frey originally came to LA from Detroit, forming the duo Longbranch Pennywhistle with another Michigan boy, J. D. Souther. (The Long Branch was the saloon in *Gunsmoke*.) They found a manager in Doug Weston, who owned the Troubadour, which enabled them to eat there for free and get to know everyone on the scene.

They made friends with Jackson Browne, who introduced them to David Geffen, who gave Souther a solo deal. Geffen told Frey he wasn't strong enough to be a solo artist and advised him to form a band. Ronstadt had moved in with Souther and needed a touring band, so she asked Frey to put one together for her. Longbranch had been on the same label as a group from Texas called Shiloh, with Don Henley on drums, so Frey enlisted him. They toured with Ronstadt and played on her next album, then told her they wanted to form their own group. Ronstadt recommended two session guys from her album: Bernie Leadon (from the Burritos), and bassist Randy

Meisner, who had played in Poco and Rick Nelson's Stone Canyon Band. Ronstadt and Souther let the group rehearse in their apartment while they went to the movies.

"We'd watched bands like Poco and the Burrito Brothers lose their initial momentum. We were determined not to make the same mistakes," Frey recalled. "Everybody had to look good, sing good, play good and write good. We wanted it all. Peer respect. AM and FM success. Number one singles and albums, great music and a lot of money. . . . I was driven, a man possessed."[33]

His unrelenting focus was in opposition to the band's early hit singles, "Take It Easy" and "Peaceful Easy Feeling," the latter of which peaked at No. 22 on March 10. It was penned by Jack Tempchin, a songwriter Frey and Browne met in San Diego.

The song epitomized the laid-back ethos of the SoCal soft rock scene. The singer resolves to stay happy and keep his feet on the ground regardless of whether the woman stays with him or not, which could be self-protective Zen wisdom or could be narcissism. Frey loved the song the moment he heard Tempchin play it. "Well, it reminded me so much of Poco. Back then, Poco was the band that impressed me most. Their vocals were pristine and perfect. They were the band I wanted to model us after . . . and I wanted to go beyond them, too."[34]

Tempchin gave the Eagles permission to cover it, and a day later Frey returned with a demo featuring himself on lead vocal, Leadon on harmony in the second verse, then Meisner joining in. "It was so good I couldn't believe it," Tempchin said.[35]

As they began work on their second album, Frey and Henley decided to aim for becoming the next Lennon-McCartney or Jagger-Richards. "Being in close proximity to Jackson Browne, Joni Mitchell, and Crosby, Stills and Nash, this unspoken thing was created between Henley and me, which said, 'If we want to be up here with the big boys, we'd better write some fucking good songs.'"[36]

For their first co-write Frey suggested a concept based on the popular drink Tequila Sunrise, then worried it was too cliché. But Henley dug it. "You've been drinking straight tequila all night, and the sun is coming up!"[37]

They called tequila "instant courage." "We very much wanted to talk to the ladies," Frey said, "but we often didn't have the nerve, so we'd drink a couple of shots and suddenly it was, 'Howdy, ma'am.'"[38]

The same week they knocked out "Desperado," at Henley's place in Laurel Canyon, previously inhabited by the Byrds' Roger McGuinn. "It was one of those houses on stilts, and when the winds were high, the house would rock gently. It was sort of unsettling, but I got used to it after a while. Anyway, Glenn came over to write one day, and I showed him this unfinished tune that I had been holding for so many years. I said, 'When I play it and sing it, I think of Ray Charles—Ray Charles and Stephen Foster. It's really a Southern gothic thing, but we can easily make it more Western.' Glenn leapt right on it—filled in the blanks and brought structure. And that was the beginning of our songwriting partnership. . . . That's when we became a team."[39]

They subsequently co-authored "One of These Nights," "Lying Eyes," and "The Long Run." Unlike Lennon-McCartney and Jagger-Richards, they also freely co-wrote with other members in the band, Souther, and even Frey's friend from Detroit, Bob Seger.

For the *Desperado* album released in April, most songs tied into an Old West theme, long a preoccupation with Frey, Souther, and Browne. Henley said, "Apparently, it began with a book on gunfighters that somebody— Ned Doheny, I believe—had given them when they were living in Echo Park. . . . Glenn sat everybody down and mapped out which characters in the gang could have songs written about them, or encouraged us to write songs about this concept. . . . You know, mythical, majestic images of the great American Southwest . . . or as [Steely Dan's] Donald Fagen later called it, 'cowboy dream crap.'"[40]

Browne's debut album cover had been fashioned to resemble the wanted posters in the Time-Life *The Old West* books. For *Desperado,* the Eagles dressed up as cowboys with bandoliers over their chests. On the back cover they acted out the capture of the Dalton gang. Released in April, the album predated Willie and Waylon's *Wanted! The Outlaws* by two years. By now, three streams were heading toward the point at which they would one day coalesce into modern country: country rock, outlaw country, and Southern Rock. Southern Rock had the country accent but was white southerners playing blues, rock, psychedelic, and jazz. Country rock was mainly West Coast musicians mixing the "western" strand of country and western with folk rock (or singer-songwriter soft rock, as it had been rebranded). The outlaws were country artists demanding the creative freedom singer-songwriters enjoyed, and the freedom to rock. And the Eagles found themselves having to fight for the right to rock themselves.

When they finished their *Desperado* album, the band was so happy with producer Glyn Johns that they carried him around on their shoulders. Johns had worked with the Beatles, the Stones, the Who, and Led Zeppelin. The Eagles' harmonies had convinced Johns to take them on.

When their new sessions began at Olympic Sound Studios in November, it seemed like things would run as smoothly as before. They cut "Best of My Love," inspired by a guitar tuning Joni Mitchell had shown Frey. The lyrics had been written by him and Henley in Dan Tana's, the restaurant next to the Troubadour, in the wake of Henley's breakup with his girlfriend.

But the band was determined to record some rockers as well. Frey said, "We're taking a beating opening for Jethro Tull, and our feeling was 'We gotta have kick-ass songs.'"[41]

Johns told them brusquely, "You are not a rock-and-roll band, The Who is a rock-and-roll band, and you're not that."[42] He said that Henley couldn't slam the drums as hard as John Bonham. But then, who could?

On top of that insult, Frey chafed at Johns's "no pot in the studio" rule. (Johns was weary of the Stones' dope shenanigans.) So after recording just two songs, the band cut ties with Johns. They returned to California and brought in guitarist Don Felder to turn songwriter Tempchin's "Already Gone" into their hardest rocker yet.

"[Johns] was so intimidating, I was always afraid to be forthright and tell him what I thought," Frey said. "He was a taskmaster, and that was probably good for a young band, but the great thing for me about ["Already Gone"] is that I left England behind and had a much more positive energy in the recording studio. The 'all right, nighty-night' at the end of the song was sort of typical of the spontaneous feeling we wanted on our records. It was at this time that we changed producers and started working with Bill Szymczyk. I was much more comfortable in the studio with Bill, and he was more than willing to let everyone stretch a bit. 'Already Gone'—that's me being happier; that's me being free."[43]

Ironically, the song they cut with Johns in November, "Best of My Love," became their first No. 1 on both pop and easy listening. Frey resisted its release, but when it was finally issued, it climbed to the top in March 1975, two weeks after Ronstadt hit the summit with "You're No Good."

Papa, Don't Lay That S**t on Me

Suzi Quatro inspires Joan Jett. Birtha challenges Fanny. Billie Jean King beats Bobby Riggs on September 20. Maria Pepe opens the door for female Little Leaguers.

✳

There had always been women who jammed on guitar: Mother of Rock 'n' Roll Rosetta Tharpe, Maybelle Carter, Mary Ford, Wanda Jackson. Carol Kaye of the Wrecking Crew played bass on more hits than almost anyone else. Female drummers included Maureen Tucker in the Velvet Underground, Helen "Peaches" Price in Merle Haggard's band, and Ann "Honey" Lantree of the British Honeycombs.

However, the first female musician to become famous for donning a leather suit and *looking* like a rock 'n' roller was bassist Susan Kay Quatro, born in Detroit in 1950. "When I saw Elvis for the first time when I was five, I decided I wanted to be him, and it didn't occur to me that he was a guy. That's why it had to fall to somebody like me."[1]

Her father played bass in a jazz band and eventually gave her his instrument. After the Beatles appeared on *Ed Sullivan,* she and her sisters Patti and Arlene formed the Pleasure Seekers, the second all-female band to sign to a major label (after Goldie and the Gingerbreads). Mickie Most, manager of the Animals, Donovan, and Herman's Hermits, offered Suzi a solo deal. He hooked her up with the Sweet's writer-producers Mike Chapman and Nicky Chinn, who gave her "Can the Can," which topped the UK and Australian charts in June. For the first time, female teens had their own larynx-shredding rocker fronting an all-male band, with aforementioned black jumpsuit, in the mold of Gene Vincent, Presley, and Marianne Faithfull in *Girl on a Motorcycle* (1968), the first film to be rated X in the US.

Her disciple Joan Marie Larkin (a.k.a. Joan Jett, born 1958 in Pennsylvania) saw the New York Dolls live when she was barely in her teens. She asked her folks for a guitar, specifying an electric, not an acoustic, and found a guitar teacher. "I said, 'teach me how to play rock n' roll.' He said, 'Girls don't play rock n' roll.'"[2]

Quatro proved the teacher wrong. "Suzi Quatro was a huge thing to me, 'cause I never had seen a woman play rock n' roll," Jett said. "And to see her with her bass, screaming, really inspired me. I thought, well, if she can do it, I can do it, and if I can do it, then there's got to be other girls out there that are thinking about doing this."[3]

Jett resolved to find herself "an all-girl band, serious about playing. I read about this place in Hollywood that catered to teenagers, playing British music that never made its way over here. A defining moment for any teen misfit is finding others like yourself, even if the only thing you share is the feeling of not belonging anywhere else."[4]

The place was Rodney Bingenheimer's English Disco, which opened in December 1972 after Bowie suggested the publicist open a glitter club. The venue was small but contained lots of mirrors for people to dance in front of while the strobe washed over them and the speakers blasted T. Rex, Silverhead, and Slade (whom Quatro opened for).

Quatro hung out in the section roped off for the pop stars when she played Los Angeles. Jett would stake out Quatro's hotel lobby, or a spot in front of the stage, but was always too nervous to say anything to her idol. Quatro recalled later, "Sometimes it was a little too much though, I must admit. She was obsessed with me for a while, which I am sure she would be the first to admit. But again, always cute."[5]

Eventually Jett started her own band the Runaways with fellow English Disco regular Cherie Currie, who cut her hair like Bowie and painted her face to look like Aladdin Sane when she went to the club, and Lita Ford, who took up the guitar at eleven to emulate Deep Purple's Ritchie Blackmore.

There were other role models for them in Los Angeles. Sisters June and Jean Millington moved from the Philippines to California in their early teens and formed the first of many bands that eventually became Fanny. The unit became the third all-female rock band to sign to a major label, and the first to release a full album in 1970, produced by Richard Perry, who also got them session work on his client Barbra Streisand's album. In 1973, Todd Rundgren produced their fourth LP between his work with the New York Dolls and Grand Funk Railroad. *Mother's Pride* took its title from a line in "I'm Satisfied," their answer to the Stones anthem. "All Mine" was one of the warmest love songs of the year.

"We knew how to play, we knew how to please an audience, we knew how to get people to dance, we knew how to set up a PA," said Jean. "I knew how to back up a trailer full of equipment. You have those skills— they're very practical, they're aside from the music—and so we were confident when we got down."[6]

They opened for rockers ranging from Jethro Tull to Humble Pie and Slade. "We played before The James Gang in Denver [featuring Joe Walsh] and their heads were hanging when they came on stage. They didn't want to play because at that time apparently we were better than they were."[7]

They turned down an offer to pose for *Playboy*. Jean cracked, "We'll pose nude when Hugh Hefner poses for the centerfold with a hard-on. Let them show Mick Jagger's cock first or somebody cute."[8] *Penthouse* actually ran a centerfold of Quatro in October, but she was fully clothed. Quatro's sister Patti joined Fanny after *Mother's Pride*.

Bowie later told *Rolling Stone* that Fanny "were one of the finest rock bands of their time, in about 1973. . . . They're as important as anybody else who's ever been, ever; it just wasn't their time."[9] His future guitarist Earl Slick later married Jean.

Fanny's success helped another local all-female band to get signed. Instead of promotional stickers reading GET BEHIND FANNY and FANNY: END OF AN ERA, their rival's trumpeted BIRTHA HAS BALLS. Birtha also formed in high school; they opened for the Stones way back in '64 and continued to do so for everyone from B. B. King to the Dolls. "We want male groupies," they proclaimed on the cover of British magazine *Titbits*. But "Rock Me" featured the opposite perspective from most male bands: the ladies sang they wanted the man, but "you gotta mean more to me than just one night."

Each member contributed lead vocals and harmonies. On their second album, *Can't Stop the Madness,* tracks like "Sun" sounded like a cross between Heart, Funkadelic, and the all-female band in *Beyond the Valley of the Dolls.* Or rather, Heart sounded a little like Birtha; the group fronted by sisters Ann and Nancy Wilson was just forming in Canada. Sherry Hagler's organ solos on songs like "All This Love" recalled Steppenwolf, whose producer worked on Birtha's first album. They shared the label Dunhill with Steely Dan, so they also released a strong cover of "Dirty Work." After their breakup two years later, bassist Rosemary Butler became one of the most sought-after backup singers on the Los Angeles scene, working with Bonnie Raitt, Linda Ronstadt, Warren Zevon, Taylor, Browne, and Young.

Raitt's father had starred in Broadway musicals and she started playing bottleneck guitar in summer camp. She progressed so quickly that she dropped out of her African studies program at Radcliffe to open for country blues legend Mississippi Fred McDowell (whom the Stones covered in "You Gotta Move" on *Sticky Fingers*), hitting the Jim Beam to add a "patina of age" to her vocals.[10] In October, she released her well-received third album, *Takin' My Time,* initially produced by Little Feat's Lowell George, though she had to replace him. "It's hard to have a strong woman telling the man her ideas when, in fact, the man wants to take over the situation. So that album had a lot of heartache in it. At the time it was a difficult one to make, but now I like it."[11] Linda Ronstadt had the same problem that year on *Don't Cry Now,* going through two producer-boyfriends until finding a platonic partnership in Peter Asher.

Raitt insisted on creative control as a condition for joining Warner Bros., though it meant no chart hits for her first two decades, as the label declined to put promo muscle behind her. "I paid the price by being independent. If I had let them produce me more, perhaps they would have liked what I was doing better."[12]

Karen Carpenter had the opposite problem. In the early days in the band with her brother, Richard, she didn't even want to sing, just wanted to drum. She didn't cut loose when she drummed on that year's Carpenters hits "Sing" and "Yesterday Once More," but TV specials allowed her to demonstrate her impressive percussion skills.

✳

"I want to prove that women are lousy, they stink, and they don't belong on the same court as a man," taunted fifty-five-year-old tennis pro Bobby Riggs.[13] Sometimes he contradicted himself and switched to "I'm not saying women don't belong on the court—who would pick up the balls otherwise?"[14]

He'd been World No. 1 in the late '30s and '40s, and wanted to revive his career to finance his gambling. He challenged twenty-nine-year-old tennis star Billie Jean King, but she declined. So he faced off against the current female champion, Margaret Court, on May 13. He defeated her in a rout dubbed the "Mother's Day Massacre" and scored the covers of *Time* and *Sports Illustrated*.

"Male is supreme!" Riggs gloated. "I am a male chauvinist!"[15]

King changed her mind and agreed to a prime-time match, cash prize $100,000. To prepare, she closely studied his style of drop shots and lobs. On Thursday, September 20, a crowd of 30,472 gathered in the Houston Astrodome. Approximately ninety million people around the globe tuned in. Riggs entered on a cart drawn by women. Four bare-chested men carried King in on a litter like Cleopatra. She presented Riggs with a small pig.

In the first set, King fell behind but forced herself to rally. "I thought it would set us back fifty years if I didn't win that match. It would ruin the women's tour and affect all women's self-esteem."[16] She won all three sets: 6–4, 6–3, 6–3.

Riggs wanted a rematch, but she never granted one, though they appeared on an *Odd Couple* episode that November playing Ping-Pong. They remained friends until his death in 1995. The pig lived out the rest of its life on a farm.

Just as King faced down Riggs, a hearings examiner in New Jersey's Division on Civil Rights oversaw a case to determine whether young females had the right to participate in America's great national pastime, Little League baseball.

In June 1972, Congress passed Title IX of the Education Amendments Act, which stipulated that there could be no discrimination by sex in any educational program that received federal funds. Almost immediately, twelve-year-old Maria Pepe put Title IX to the test in Hoboken. "My friends all went in and signed their name [to play on the baseball team] and I stood at the door but my coach came out—his name was Jimmy Farina—and he asked why I wasn't signing up. . . . He said, 'Can you play?' And I was like, 'Yeah.' There was no question I could play."[17]

She pitched three games and batted .300, but when Little League officials at headquarters in Pennsylvania found out, they were not happy. The organization's regulations read, "Girls are not eligible under any conditions."

"My coach came to me and told me that Little League said they had to take me off the team or the league would lose its charter," Pepe said. "I didn't want to make a hundred kids mad at me, so I had to step down."[18] She was given the role of scorekeeper, but "being out of the uniform and just keeping score was so extremely frustrating that I knew I couldn't do that anymore."[19]

The National Organization for Women (NOW) filed a lawsuit on behalf

of Pepe and "girls 8–12." Starting August 9, 1973, civil rights hearings officer Sylvia Pressler listened to six days of testimony from "experts" on both
sides of the argument. One warned that girls could get breast cancer "being
tagged out on the boobs."[20] A Little League VP who was also a psychologist
argued that girls were unable to react as quickly as boys, and their bones
were weaker. Another child psychologist countered that girls reacted faster.
A pediatric orthopedic surgeon who consulted for the Philadelphia 76ers
argued that girls' bones were actually more resistant to breaking than boys'.

One doctor stated that girls and boys preferred to be with their own
gender, and that forcing them to do otherwise could endanger their mental
health. It was this testimony that Pressler directly responded to. "I have no
doubt that there are many reputable psychologists who would agree with
the birds-of-a-feather theory. However, the extension of that is that whites
like to be with whites, and blacks with blacks, and that whole theory is in
contradiction to the law of this state."[21]

Pepe ran home every day to ask her mother if the decision had been announced. On November 8, a *New York Times* headline ran "Little League in
Jersey Ordered to Allow Girls to Play on Teams."

Little League officials condemned the decision as "prejudicial fashion of
the worst kind" and organized eight hundred people to protest at the New
Jersey state capitol. They appealed to the New Jersey Supreme Court, lost,
and the following year allowed girls to play. They also instituted a female
softball league; thirty thousand girls signed up. By then Pepe was too old
to play, but her story perhaps inspired screenwriter Bill Lancaster's creation
of the ace pitcher portrayed by Tatum O'Neal in 1976's *The Bad News Bears*.

✳

On January 18, AT&T settled with the Equal Employment Opportunity Commission in the EEOC's most expensive discrimination suit to date.
The federal agency charged the telephone behemoth with blocking women
and minorities from higher-paying promotions. The corporation was forced
to give thirty-six thousand employees raises collectively worth $26 million
and pay fifteen thousand employees $15 million in back pay. EEOC's David
Copus said, "Employers won't have any trouble reading between the lines
of this settlement."[22]

Next the EEOC investigated Ford Motor Company for discriminating
against women and minorities. Ford eventually paid $23 million in damages
to rejected applicants—the fourth-largest EEOC settlement of its kind, after

AT&T, and later suits against General Electric and a group of steel companies.

The EEOC enjoyed another victory on June 21 when the Supreme Court upheld its ruling that forbid newspapers from running separate want ads for men and women.

On May 18, Gloria Steinem gave a speech entitled "What Do Women Expect?" "Suppose you were the same person with all the hopes and dreams and ambitions that you have now, but you had been born a woman. What would you want?"[23]

She denounced the fact that women were the "cheap labor on which a variety of economic systems have run. . . . And black women are on the bottom of the economic ladder when it comes to median incomes: they make $4,674 a year; white women make $5,490 a year; minority men, contrary to myth, make more than white women, or $6,598 a year; and guess who—white men, of course are on top with $9,373 a year."

On TV, Mary Tyler Moore confronted Lou Grant about the fact that he paid her less than the men in the same position. Maude fought her husband over her decision to take a job as a real estate agent. In real life, the vice president of the United Farm Workers, Dolores Huerta, led a consumer grape boycott that eventually led to the California Agricultural Labor Relations Act, which allowed farm workers to unionize. In a North Carolina textile mill, Crystal Lee Sutton stood on her worktable with the sign UNION to galvanize her fellow workers to fight for more than $2.65 an hour—a moment immortalized in the Sally Fields drama *Norma Rae* (1979).

That spring, Yale's first class of female undergraduates received their diplomas. At Harvard Business School, 4 percent of the Class of 1973 was female, 34 out of 776, a significant enough change that *Forbes* magazine reckoned it the first class with a "critical mass of women." As if 4 percent were a critical mass. (Women made up approximately 2.8 percent of the House of Representatives at the time.) The US Navy accepted Judith Neuffer for flight training. The US Army promoted its first woman to two-star general, Mary E. Clarke. Julia Phillips's work on the year's highest grossing film, *The Sting,* made her the first female producer to win the Best Picture Oscar.

Equality in language saw gains that year as well. On February 7, Congress added "Ms." to the list of acceptable government prefixes. Female activists asserted they should not have to disclose their marital status with "Miss" or "Mrs." since men did not have to with "Mr." On October 13, pediatrician Dr. Benjamin Spock announced he would no longer use the pronoun "he" in *The Common Sense Book of Baby and Child Care* and would switch to "they."

Equality in lust arrived with November's publication of Erica Jong's *Fear of Flying,* in which her married alter ego fantasizes about the "zipless fuck": "For the true ultimate zipless A-1 fuck, it was necessary that you never got to know the man very well. . . . The man is not 'taking' and the woman is not 'giving.' No one is attempting to cuckold a husband or humiliate a wife. No one is trying to prove anything or get anything out of anyone. The zipless fuck is the purest thing there is. And it is rarer than the unicorn. And I have never had one." John Updike wrote in *The New Yorker* that the novel had a "sexual frankness that belongs to, and hilariously extends the tradition of, *The Catcher in the Rye* and *Portnoy's Complaint*."[24] The book sold twenty million copies. Bette Midler also asserted her right to be as raunchy as a man during her between-song banter at the Continental Baths, accompanied on piano by Barry Manilow.

Nightclub owner Douglas Lambert published the test issue of *Playgirl* in January. He originally planned to create his own version of *Playboy,* but his wife encouraged him to print a magazine aimed at women, perhaps noting the attention *Cosmopolitan* garnered the previous year when it featured a centerfold of Burt Reynolds. *Playgirl* sold 600,000 copies in four days.

Editor Zina Klapper later said, "I was told our typical readers were college girls in the Midwest who had never seen a naked man."[25] The magazine avoided full frontals until July's centerfold, George Maharis, who recalled, "The photographer kept saying, 'Well, you can't show that.' I said, 'For Christ's sake, man, if it's gonna be a nude centerfold, that's what I was born with,' . . . I don't know how many [copies] they printed, but they got a call for so many more that they turned everybody face-forward after that."[26]

Troubadour Underdogs

Tom Waits bites the hand that feeds him. Bob Seger strives to catch up to his onetime protégé Glenn Frey. Billy Joel recounts his westward odyssey on the *Piano Man* album. Jim Croce scores the second-biggest hit of the year before a fatal plane crash on September 20.

✳

In San Diego, Tom Waits and Jack Tempchin knew they needed to get up north to West Hollywood's Troubadour. The Byrds met there. The Buffalo Springfield did their first gig there. Elton John, Gordon Lightfoot, Joni Mitchell, Kris Kristofferson made their US or LA debuts there. Lenny Bruce was arrested for obscenity there. Richard Pryor recorded his first live album there. Carole King played piano for James Taylor's first solo gig there. King and Taylor worked on each other's albums and defined the singer-songwriter sound with session musicians known as the Section, a.k.a. the Mellow Mafia, including guitarist Danny Kortchmar and drummer Russ Kunkel, who also played on records by Jackson Browne, Linda Ronstadt, Joni Mitchell, Warren Zevon, Crosby and Nash. Kingmaker David Geffen checked out Monday open mic night, still called a hootenanny, to see who he could add to his stable.

America's third-bestselling single of 1973, "Killing Me Softly with His Song," was co-written by singer-songwriter Lori Lieberman about the time she was blown away by Don McLean's performance of "Empty Chairs" at the Troub. Roberta Flack heard Lieberman's version, which came in handy one night when she opened for Marvin Gaye and he asked her to do a second encore. "I said, 'Well, I got this song I've been working on called 'Killing Me Softly' and he said, 'Do it, baby.' And I did it and the audience went crazy, and he walked over to me and put his arm around me and said, 'Baby, don't ever do that song again live until you record it.'"[1]

So Waits said goodbye to San Diego and did in fact score a manager at a Monday hootenanny. "For a while there anyone who wrote and performed their own songs could get a deal. Anybody."[2] Jackson Browne recommended him to Geffen, who brought him to Asylum Records. "Jackson was Prince Charming to Tom's Shrek," said Ron Stone, who worked in the management firm that handled them both.[3]

Waits's *Closing Time,* released in March, featured the ultimate "new Dylan" acoustic anthem, "Old Shoes and Picture Postcards"—bidding farewell to the girl crying in the rain as the road called him. "I Hope That I Don't Fall in Love with You" could be a sketch of the Troubadour itself. The bar's crowded, but the singer and the lady he's watching from afar are both alone. He doesn't have the guts to approach her, until he gets drunk, but in the third verse when he goes to make his move she's already left.

When Waits recorded his hymn to his Buick Roadmaster, "Ol' 55," the session drummer got so swept up that he started singing along on the chorus.[4] Geffen played it for Glenn Frey, who convinced the Eagles to cover it. Frey explained, "Your first car is like your first apartment. You had a mobile studio apartment! 'Ol' 55' was so Southern California, and yet there was some Detroit in it as well. It was that car thing, and I loved the idea of driving home at sunrise, thinking about what had happened the night before."[5]

Waits dug Tin Pan Alley as much as folk, like LA singer-pianists Randy Newman and Harry Nilsson, and used a stand-up double bass player and trumpeter. *Rolling Stone* called his album "all-purpose lounge music." He was only twenty-three but wrote "Martha" as an older man calling up a long-lost girlfriend forty years later, both of them married to other people. The echoey piano has the same 1930s Depression feel as *Ironweed,* the 1987 film Waits later acted in. It was a sepia-toned sequel to Jim Croce's "Operator" after the singer wasted his life. At the chorus, Waits seems to be veering toward "Ol' Man River," but the string quartet swells and the song goes widescreen Technicolor. The ghostly chorale lifts the final chorus to an even more bittersweet plane.

As he prepared for his second album, he began to explore the down-and-out milieu more deeply. "He had all these cameras and he would go downtown and photograph the bums," Tempchin said.[6] New songs like "Depot, Depot" focused on the denizens of skid row to the accompaniment of woozy dive bar jazz.

He worked on new lyrics in the Venice Poetry Workshop, envisioning a concept album called *The Heart of Saturday Night* about the rituals of nightlife. It would open with a song about getting ready in the early evening and finish up "after hours at Napoleone's Pizza House," where he worked as a teenager.

The title track was an homage to Beat writer Jack Kerouac. Waits was inspired by a spoken word LP Kerouac cut, backed by Steve Allen's jazzy piano. Waits visited Kerouac's hometown in Massachusetts and hung out with Beat poet Gregory Corso. "Diamonds on my Windshield" was Waits's *On the Road* pastiche, appearing both on *Saturday Night* and in the poetry magazine *Sunset Palms Hotel*. The same issue bore a cover painted by another major influence on Waits, Charles Bukowski, chronicler of Los Angeles barflies.

Just as Bowie had constructed a bisexual spaceman persona, Waits created a retro beatnik bum pose to set him apart from his coke snorting, bedenimed peers at the Troub. "I'm getting pretty sick of the country music thing. I went through it, wrote a lot of country songs and thought it was the answer to everything. Anyway, so much of it is really Los Angeles country music, which isn't country, it's Laurel Canyon."[7]

He even bashed the band that gave him his first big royalty check, calling the Eagles' version of "Ol' 55" "a little antiseptic." Soon he was sneering, "I don't like the Eagles. They're about as exciting as watching paint dry. Their albums are good for keeping the dust off your turntable and that's about all."[8]

Years later, he conceded in Barney Hoskyns's *Lowside of the Road,* "I was a young kid. I was just corking off and being a prick."[9]

He received his own brickbats when another Los Angeles iconoclast, Frank Zappa, asked him to open for him in November and December. Waits faced down Zappa's notoriously belligerent crowd with just his guitar, piano, and stand-up bassist, forced to dodge more than his share of hurled fruit.

✳

Another raspy-voiced singer-songwriter had a warmer relationship with Glenn Frey. Frey never hesitated to acknowledge, "The most important thing that happened to me in Detroit was meeting Bob [Seger] and getting to know him. He took me under his wing."[10]

Seger went to Ann Arbor High School two years ahead of Iggy and the Stooges and started cutting records at age fourteen in Del Shannon's studio. By the mid-'60s he was scoring local hits. He and Frey enjoyed cruising the metro area while cranking the radio and analyzing the tunes. Seger told Frey he needed to start writing his own songs. Frey planned to join Seger's band, but his mother forbid him to do so after learning the guys smoked pot together. Frey did play acoustic guitar and sing backing vocals on Seger's 1968 classic "Ramblin' Gambling Man" but then lit out for LA.

A few years later, Seger heard "Take It Easy," the Eagles' exhilarating paean to the open road, coming over the airwaves, and thought, "What a great-sounding record! He did it!"[11]

But hearing it sparked mixed emotions. Seger played 265 gigs a year but pulled in maybe $6,600. He'd drive six hours to a gig, then drive home because he couldn't afford a room. His 1973 album *Back in '72* was "one of the great lost hard rock albums of its era,"[12] AllMusic's Stephen Thomas Erlewine wrote in his review, but quickly fell out of print, where it remains today with his other early records.

Some years earlier he'd seen a psychiatrist twice a week for suicidal thoughts. He didn't have them anymore, but you wouldn't necessarily know it from the somber weariness of "Turn the Page," which captured the unrelenting slog of tour life, and how it was still dangerous to be a longhair in Omaha, Nebraska. "Is that a woman or a man?" the locals taunt Seger in a restaurant, ominous like the rednecks in *Easy Rider*. "And you always seem outnumbered," Seger sings, so "you don't dare make a stand."

He wrote *Back in 72*'s "Rosalie" to butter up Rosalie Trombley, a deejay at CKLW-AM, one of the most powerful Top 40 stations of the period. He flipped the Stones' dark "Soul Survivor" riff into a sunny horns-and-gospel tribute to the woman who "knows music" and has "got the power." But even that didn't lift the album higher than 188 on the charts.

Around that time he noticed a Leonard Cohen book of poetry called *Beautiful Losers* and thought that would be a good title for a song. "It took over a year to put it together. I wrote five different 'Beautiful Loser's' before I settled on one for the record. There was a ballad, a blues. . . . I couldn't find the right tone. So I played it for Glenn Frey, an old friend, to get some advice. He was the first person to ever hear it."[13]

Frey said, "Oh, that's good, that's good, keep at it, keep at it!"

Seger remembered, "He was a cheerleader for me. He was always a positive influence for me, throughout my career."[14]

A track from the *Beautiful Loser* album, "Katmandu," just missed the Top

40 and held him over till his breakthrough "Night Moves." Eventually the Eagles sang backup on some of Seger's own hits. He vowed, "I'm gonna catch you fuckers!" And sometimes he did on the pop chart.[15]

By that point, said Prince biographer Alan Light, Prince "was following Bob Seger into a lot of arenas, and was really interested in why was Bob Seger such a big star, especially in the Midwest. And Matt Fink, the keyboard player, remembers that he was talking to Prince and said, 'Well, it's these big ballads that Bob Seger writes. It's these songs like "We've Got Tonight" and "Turn the Page." And that's what people love.' And Prince went out to try to write that kind of arena-rock power ballad that resulted in 'Purple Rain.'"[16]

❊

Much of Billy Joel's November album *Piano Man* recounts his road trip from the East Coast out to Los Angeles, where he made his debut at the Troubadour opening for a Chicago-like band called Ballin' Jack. The hook-master of later megasmashes like *The Stranger* and *Glass Houses* is already peeking out in the infectious "Worse Comes to Worst," "Ain't No Crime," and "Somewhere Along the Line."

It was a dramatic odyssey that brought him to LA. His piano prodigy father abandoned the family in Levittown, on New York's Long Island, when Joel was four to return to Vienna. Joel had a brief career as a Golden Gloves boxer in high school before switching to music. He formed a duo named Attila with drummer Jon Small that imploded when Joel had an affair with Small's wife, Elizabeth. Though Small forgave Joel, the singer still decided to take all the Nembutals he had at once, before calling Small to apologize again. Concerned, Small checked in on him, found him overdosed, and got him to the hospital in time. When Joel came to after they pumped his stomach he thought, "Oh, great, I couldn't even do this right." Upon returning from the hospital, he decided to try again by drinking furniture polish. After surviving that attempt, he checked himself into an observation ward for three weeks. "All things considered, it was probably one of the best things I've ever done, because I learned not to get so hung up on self-pity that I couldn't think straight."[17]

He released a debut solo album, but it was mastered at the wrong speed, so his voice sounded sped up. "He ripped it off the turntable, ran out of the house, and threw it down the street," recounted AllMusic's Stephen Thomas Erlewine. To add insult to injury, Joel said, "I signed away everything—the copyrights, publishing, record royalties, my first child—I gave it all away. And I said, 'I've got to get out of this deal.'"[18]

He decided to hide out in Los Angeles and find someone in the industry there to help him. By now he was back with Elizabeth, and she accompanied him, taking along Sean, her two-year-old son with Small—without Small's consent, something Joel was not aware of.[19]

Piano Man's "Traveling Prayer," "Stop in Nevada," "You're My Home," "Worse Come to Worst," and even "Billy the Kid" all describe their cross-country trip. But not Small's reaction. When the drummer learned Elizabeth had taken their kid, he flew out after them, though he didn't know where they were staying. Joel had mentioned he was going to play the Troubadour. Small happned to see them emerge from the nearby Tropicana Hotel and climb into their car. "I got you," he boomed as he slammed their hood.[20]

But, Small said, "within twenty minutes we were all laughing because we all realized how much we missed each other."[21] Ultimately, Sean split his time between both parents on different coasts.

To support himself while he tried to figure out his next step, Joel got a gig at a piano bar called the Executive Room on Wilshire Boulevard a few blocks from Western Avenue (demolished in the '80s). Under the name Bill Martin, he played there for six months while Elizabeth worked as a cocktail waitress. They married on September 5.

"Somebody would ask for a song, and I didn't know the song from a hole in the wall, but if you play enough in major sevenths, you can make a lot of songs sound like other songs,"[22] Joel reminisced. "What you're doing in a piano bar basically is playing for tips, so you try to pick out what will get bread out of the audience. Is this guy Italian? You play the 'Godfather Theme' or something like that. Is this guy Irish? You play 'Danny Boy.' You try to get those five dollar bills in the brandy glass. . . . The characters that Bill Murray and Steve Martin do, I was doing too, only people didn't know I was kidding. . . . If somebody asked for a Sinatra song, I would get into doing a whole put-on Sinatra thing. I'd be having a blast and they would think I was really into it."[23]

He started building a song out of the gig, perhaps inspired by a line in "Tiny Dancer" by one of his big influences, Elton John: "Piano Man he makes his stand."

"All the characters in that song were real people. John at the bar was this guy named John—and he was at the bar." There was a real estate novelist, but the old man "wasn't really making love to his tonic and gin, because that could be pretty gross, actually."[24]

And as in the song, customers did tell him he was too good for the Executive Room. But when he played the composition for Atlantic's Jerry Wexler, the producer chided him for copping the chord progression of "Mr. Bo-jangles." "If 'Bojangles' wasn't written, you probably wouldn't have written that, right?"[25]

By then Columbia's Clive Davis was trying to track Joel down. Davis got wind of a live concert Joel recorded in Philadelphia's Sigma Sound Studios for a local radio station. One of the numbers, "Captain Jack," had become so frequently requested that other stations made dubs of it to play themselves, even though a studio version had not yet been cut.[26] Joel said he was inspired to write "Captain Jack" back in Long Island after watching kids score smack at a housing project across the street from his apartment. Maybe he drew on the despair of that Nembutal OD night as well.

Davis bought out Joel's old manager, with a deal giving him twenty-eight cents an album for Joel's next ten albums.[27] The final album in that sequence would be *Greatest Hits Volume I and II,* which included "You're Only Human" ("Don't forget your second wind"). Joel donated all that song's royalties to the National Committee for Youth Suicide Prevention.

✻

Jim Croce said he based "Bad, Bad Leroy Brown" on a guy he knew from the army. "He was strong, so nobody'd ever told him what to do, and after about a week down there he said, 'Later for this,' and decided to go home. So he went AWOL—which means to take your own vacation—and he did. But he made the mistake of coming back at the end of the month to get his paycheck. . . . They put handcuffs on him and took him away."[28]

All that may have been true. But in the grand pop tradition, "Brown" was also a remake of his last Top 10 hit, "You Don't Mess Around with Jim." Jim was powerful like Superman and the Lone Ranger, but he stole another man's money and got his comeuppance when the guy stabbed and shot him. Leroy was like King Kong and a junkyard dog but in the end got pounded for hitting on another man's woman. "Brown" was even more euphoric than its predecessor, thanks to the gospel-style backing chorus. It was post–Lovin' Spoonful good-time music, and everyone clapped along, from old folks to little kids singing around the day care record player.

But even with a couple of hits, Croce's wife, Ingrid, had to still buy clothes for their two-year-old Adrian in the resale shops. Long before Springsteen sang about dead-end jobs, Croce wrote "Workin' at the Car Wash Blues." Between songs he bantered about past gigs as a painter, trucker, special education teacher, cement pourer. He wrote songs about Roller Derby queens and stock car racers, about getting mugged in New

York City and sleeping in doorways because he had no money for hotels, about playing barrooms where they hung chicken wire in front of the stage to protect performers from thrown bottles, about broken dreams and learning the hard way every time.

He opened for comedians like Woody Allen and George Carlin, and told his share of jokes onstage as well, like one about Allegheny Airlines. "They give you an apple and a glass of water served inside an air sickness bag. It's more of an omen than a meal. They are the originators of what we call the white-knuckle flights, the ones that make you feel like you're strapped in a dentist's chair with duct tape."[29]

His skills as a raconteur and his rugged offbeat character looks made him popular on Johnny Carson and Dick Cavett. He played the Troubadour June 19–24, then received a standing ovation at Madison Square Garden a week later. Now his hangdog face graced a billboard in Hollywood, and "Leroy" hit No. 1 for two weeks on July 21. *Billboard* later ranked it the second-bestselling song of the year in America. "I guess you could say he's a man of the people," Helen Reddy said when she introduced him on her show that week. "Maybe that's why he writes about them so well."

Of course, it was more complicated on the home front. He'd met Ingrid a decade earlier at a hootenanny, and for a while they performed as a folk duo à la Richard Fariña and Mimi Baez, until they had their son, at which point she stayed home while he went solo. Now he didn't really want her and Adrian joining him on the road, because he was having a blast living at the Sunset Marquis and chilling with Jimmy Buffett, Cheech and Chong, Harry Nilsson, and Leon Russell.[30] But he liked her at home for the security when he needed it. When he'd come home they'd fight and then he'd write some more great songs, righteous bitter ones like "One Less Set of Footsteps on Your Floor," or wistful regretful ones, "Photographs and Memories," "Dreaming Again," "It Doesn't Have to Be That Way," "Alabama Rain."

A prime example, as recounted in Ingrid's memoir of their life together, was when he arrived home and played her "Five Short Minutes," a song about his experience with Cynthia Plaster Caster, one of the groupies renowned for making molds of rock star penises. "It's their thing, and if they dig it, they should do it,"[31] he told Ingrid. She cried and told him she was pregnant again. They yelled at each other, and then he let her know oh yeah, a fifteen-person crew was due to arrive to shoot a promotional film. He'd been afraid to tell her because he knew she'd be mad. But she cooked for everyone, and, remorseful, he promised he'd go to counseling.

"After the film crew left, I asked Jim about our finances," she wrote. "We were barely making ends meet, but Jim wouldn't talk about it. He hated questions as much as he hated confrontation. He just stormed out of our bedroom and went down to the kitchen table to brood. The next morning he woke me gently to sing his new song. 'Every time I tried to tell you the words just came out wrong. So I'll have to say "I love you" in a song.'"[32]

The song was on his fifth album, *I Got a Name,* which he finished recording in mid-September. He also included a new version of "Age," a haunting song they co-wrote on their 1969 album as a duo, lamenting the wasted years but resolving to avoid repeating the same mistakes as he "headed toward the top."

Charles Fox and Norman Gimbel wrote the album's title track; they also penned "Killing Me Softly" with Lori Lieberman. Gimbel said, "Jim liked ["Name"] because his father had a dream for him but had died before his son's first success."[33] It served as the theme song to *The Last American Hero,* a movie starring Jeff Bridges as a NASCAR driver based on a Tom Wolfe story. "Movin' ahead so life won't pass me by," Croce sang in his most optimistic performance yet.

The day before the single was released, the thirty-year-old boarded a small twin-engine plane to fly from Louisiana to his next show in Texas. The pilot had heart trouble and ran to make the flight. Debilitated, he failed to lift off high enough to clear a thirty-foot tree. The plane hit the tree, flipped over, and crashed, killing the six people on board.

A week later, Ingrid received a letter Croce mailed just before the crash. Among the paragraphs he wrote was "I know that you see me for who I am, or should I say, as who I are. 'Cause I've been lots of people. If Medusa had personalities or attitudes instead of snakes for her features, her name would have been Jim Croce. . . .

"This is a birth note, Baby. And when I get back everything will be different. We're gonna have a life together, Ing, I promise. . . .

"Give a kiss to my little man and tell him Daddy loves him."[34]

IV.

Autumn

24

*

Quadrophenia

The Who's rock opera, released October 26, lays the groundwork for the Mod revival as the band struggles to survive a tour wracked by intra-band fistfights, angel dust ODs, malfunctioning equipment, and arrests for hotel trashing.

*

For the next Who album, guitarist-songwriter Pete Townshend initially envisioned a rock opera called *Rock Is Dead, Long Live Rock,* about a band struggling not to lose its ideals to decadence. Townshend decided to tie it in with a movie and enlisted rock critic Nik Cohn to write the script. In spring 1972 the band recorded "Long Live Rock," "Love Reign o'er Me," and "Is It in My Head?" but then Townshend abandoned the concept.

He gave "Long Live Rock" to Billy Fury to sing in *That'll be The Day,* the film with Ringo Starr, in which Who drummer Keith Moon also had a role. But the other two tracks eventually found a home in the rock opera the Who actually did do next, *Quadrophenia.* The melody of "Long Live Rock" became a recurring motif in some of its songs.

The key inspiration for Townshend arrived when he agreed to organize Eric Clapton's Rainbow Concert on January 13, to help Clapton get back on his feet after a long struggle with heroin. To complete the band they recruited the Faces' Ron Wood, Steve Winwood, Traffic drummer Jim

Capaldi, and bassist Ric Grech of Family. During the rehearsals, Grech introduced Townshend to liquid amyl nitrate, a.k.a. poppers. After the show, crashing from all the amyl nitrate, Townshend felt depressed. He had given up drugs after some bad trips six years ago (though he still drank), so the comedown was particularly acute, reminding him of a night in 1964 when he was nineteen.[1]

It was right when the Who had been taken over by a manager who decided to turn the band into *the* Mod band, changing their name and their wardrobe and encouraging them to write with Mod lingo to cash in on the burgeoning English subculture. Mods drove scooters, listened to R&B and jazz, tended to work in offices in the southern cities, and were obsessed with fashion. Cohn said, "It was the Mods who first made Carnaby Street happen, 1962–3."[2]

On Easter weekend 1964, the Mods made national headlines with their first major rumble with the Rockers, who wore leather, rode motorcycles, still listened to '50s rock, and often worked in factories in the country. The next weekend the Who played gigs at the seaside resort town of Brighton, during the famous two-day "Battle of Brighton" in which over a thousand youths skirmished in various resorts along the coast.

That Saturday night Townshend and an art school friend named Liz Reid missed their train home, so they took a walk on the beach where some Mods and Rockers were still fighting. When it started to rain, Townshend and Reid took refuge under the pier and found Mods in parkas wading barefoot in the water. Townshend had taken Purple Heart speed pills that were wearing off, so he felt bleak, but he also felt a spirit of camaraderie, a part of the Mod movement. And he fell in love with Liz as they rode the train back home together that morning.[3]

He never went out with her again (his memoir doesn't say why). But his sudden flashback to the fleeting idyll, on the morning after the Clapton show, inspired him to write a short piece that became the basis for *Quadrophenia*'s plot, eventually included in the album's liner notes. *The Village Voice*'s Robert Christgau called the prose "as brilliant a piece of writing as Townshend's ever done."[4]

The story centers on Jimmy, a teen in 1965 London in love with a girl who is "a perfect dresser / wears every fashion / gets it to the tee." But he works as a trash man, and neither she nor the rest of their crowd notice him. The one thing Jimmy feels he has going for him is being a Mod ("I'm One"), wearing a zoot suit or Italian clothes or Levi's (just come into fashion in England that year). His one great memory is when the Mods beat the

Rockers at the pier. "When I was [in Brighton] last time there were about two thousand Mods driving up and down the promenade on scooters," reads the liner-notes story. "I felt really anonymous then, sort of like I was in an army."

But the lifestyle goes hand in hand with amphetamine addiction. When his mom finds a box of pills in his room, his folks kick him out. He goes to the dance hall and hopes the girl will join him on the beach, but she doesn't. He takes the train to Brighton, the scene of his one triumph. There he discovers that the head Mod, Ace Face, is a bellboy at a hotel. All the Mods copped Ace's style; he took on two Rockers at once and beat them. But Jimmy realizes Ace is still going to be "licking boots" for the next fifty years. In the end Mod means nothing. The song covers the same working-class desperation Springsteen made his own at the end of the decade.

No illusions left, Jimmy goes on a bender and gets beaten up. He decides to steal a boat and row out to a rock in the sea to drown himself. "Something else happens to him though," Townshend wrote in the press release, "something inside clicks, and his original drive to suicide becomes sidetracked as he starts to feel, on the boat at sea, his first genuine high."

The sound of crashing waves has recurred throughout the album, as if the sea has been calling him from the beginning. Townshend later elaborated, "God's love being the ocean and our 'selves' being the drops of water that make it up. [His guru] Meher Baba said, 'I am the Ocean of Love.' I want to drown in that ocean, the 'drop' will then be an ocean itself." In "Drowned" and "Love Reign o'er Me" the water heals Jimmy, giving him an epiphany of a life beyond pills, fashion, and street fights.

The songwriter summarized, "When it's over and he goes back to town he'll be going through the same shit, being in the same terrible family situation and so on, but he's moved up a level. He's weak still, but there's a strength in that weakness. He's in danger of maturing."[5]

Townshend made demos in his home studio, then began recording with Moon and bassist John Entwistle on June 1. They arrived daily around two, joked around for a few hours at the bar built in the studio, then got down to work. The rhythm section followed the demos fairly closely, though Townshend encouraged embellishments.

For the opening rocker "The Real Me," Entwistle sat on the bass cabinet and turned himself into the star of the song without trying, in one take, via his deliriously over-the-top playing. "I was joking when I did that bass part. The band said, 'Wow, that's great, that's great!'"[6] Moon avalanches across the toms at the end of every line, Townshend slams away at power chords, and Roger Daltrey roars, announcing the band had returned to rock even harder than "Won't Get Fooled Again." The customized studio speakers were so loud they ruptured one of the secretaries' ears.[7] The musicians usurp Daltrey, but he fights back howling, all slamming for attention, a prime example of why *Rolling Stone* readers voted Entwistle the No. 1 bassist of all time and Moon the No. 2 drummer (after his protégé Bonham). Despite Jimmy's *Catcher in the Rye*–esque dark night of the soul, Townshend wrote in his memoir that "recording *Quadrophenia* with The Who was a joyful experience."

On the gentler end of the spectrum is the folkish opening of "I'm One," not far from Simon and Garfunkel, its slightly eerie echo perfectly invoking the mood of falling leaves. Jimmy (Townshend) sings of facing another year as a loser before erupting into a defiant vow that everyone will notice him now that he's a Mod.

"5:15" was one of the few songs not demoed. Townshend made up the riff in the studio during a sound check, a variation on "Long Live Rock." As Jimmy wanders the streets on booze and pills, Entwistle plays along on brass like the band of a strip show, appropriate for a guy who met his demise doing coke with a stripper twenty-nine years later. Jimmy walks into a Beatles concert; Townshend explained in the *Quadrophenia* documentary that the lines about "girls of 15, sexually knowing," with ushers "sniffing eau de cologne," were inspired by the time he saw the Fab Four live in Blackpool. After the female fans wet themselves in excitement, the ushers sprinkled cologne on the seats in a futile attempt to mask the smell.

One of their most ferocious jams, "5:15" was also one of their most poignant. The aching refrain "Why should I care? Nowhere is home" resonated with young Who fans with troubled home lives, runaways, or kids kicked out by their parents, self-medicating on the boulevard.

The plot is mostly conveyed through the trio of "Cut My Hair," "I've Had Enough," and "Sea and Sand." In the former, Townshend sings the quiet verses like a mixed-up vulnerable kid, until aggressive Daltrey joins in on the choruses to boast he's "dressed right for a beach fight," defiantly strutting down the street with his gang on "leapers" (speed). "I've Had Enough" fiercely catalogs the clothes Jimmy believes make him cool enough for the girl as he rides through the sleet on his scooter. But halfway through, his reverie is interrupted by the glimmering synthesizer of "Love Reign o'er Me," the first hint of the epiphany that will later save him.

For the climactic "Love Reign o'er Me," Moon's toms and cymbals echo the "Psalm" of Coltrane's *A Love Supreme* before Daltrey enters and progresses from crooning to belting. During the sessions he came in after the others were gone to add his voice to their instrumentation. He didn't party like them; on tour he went to bed early. He also bristled at being directed too much by Townshend. Daltrey told *Billboard* that Townshend saw "Love Reign o'er Me" "as a kind of a gentle love song, whereas I saw it as a scream, a heart-wrenching, internal scream of frustration. The first time I played my (performance) of it to him, he didn't like it at all!"[8] But Daltrey wanted to top, or at least try to match, his career-defining howl at the end of "Won't Get Fooled Again."

✳

The recording industry believed quadraphonic sound to be the new cash cow that would convince consumers to buy new hardware and repurchase music they already had in a new format. Stereo had taken over from mono in the mid-'60s, and now the industry hoped people would want four channels instead of just two. Quadraphonic eight-track debuted in 1970, quadraphonic vinyl the following year, and by '73, artists like Jeff Beck, Blue Oyster Cult, Bachman Turner Overdrive, Black Oak Arkansas, and the Doobie Brothers had released albums with a quad version.[9] Townshend was most impressed by Pink Floyd, who issued a quad mix for *Dark Side of the Moon* and achieved amazing sound in their live shows by positioning speakers in four corners of the concert halls.

Always hungry for a gimmick, Townshend decided Jimmy would not only be schizophrenic (at the time generally misconstrued as "split personality" syndrome) but quadrophenic with four distinct personalities. Each band member would sing one of the personalities, and each voice would come from one of the four speaker channels.

But after they wrapped recording in early August, the label pressured him to mix the double LP in less than a month so they could release it on October 13, two weeks before the Who's new tour, and capitalize on the Christmas-present-buying season. Scheduling a quad mix would mean postponing the tour until spring. Thus the album called *Quadrophenia* was issued only in stereo, continuing the long Who tradition of grand ambitions compromised by time crunch. (The radio station concept of *The Who Sell Out* was carried through only for part of the record; the *Lifehouse* rock opera was truncated into *Who's Next*.) Not that it made any difference to the brilliance of the individual songs. In the end, consumers were happy with stereo, and quad petered out by the second half of the decade.

Townshend realized listeners would not be able to discern his plot through the song lyrics, so he commissioned a photo book to be included with the double album, photographed by Ethan Russell, who shot the covers for *Who's Next* and the Beatles' *Let It Be*. Townshend's synthesizers sounded nothing like 1965, but the black-and-white photos grittily evoked the British New Wave films of the era, with smokestacks, housing developments, boiling kettles, and greasy British breakfast food, along with the Mod fashion of parkas and bull's-eye T-shirts. The shot of Jimmy on the train featured him with a dead ringer for the old man on the train in *A Hard Day's Night* (and the film later played up the connection with schoolgirls dressed like Pattie Boyd).

Still unsure he'd gotten his message across, he sent the album to journalists with a multipage explanation of the songs' meanings, "specifically intended to be used for reviewer purposes as a guide to your appreciation of *Quadrophenia*."

By that point Townshend was on the edge of quadrophenia himself from the pressure. He stayed up for two days putting together backing tracks of synthesizers and sound effects that would play along with the band onstage, then headed over for a tour rehearsal with the others, which was set to be captured by a film crew. Townshend arrived late, soused from brandies imbibed en route in the limo. Daltrey was mad at waiting around for the imperious Townshend. He had his own solo Top 5 hit that year with "Giving It All Away" (written by his discovery Leo Sayer); he didn't need this shit. After some film crew snafus, he said he was going home.

Townshend thrust his finger into his chest. "You do as you're fucking told." The roadies rushed to hold Daltrey back as he yelled that Townshend had mixed his vocals too low on the record. Townshend sneered, "Let the little c—t go, I'll fucking kill him."[10]

"Pete was very drunk and has come at me with a guitar, then he's tried to punch me so I ducked the punch and hit him. It was a very clean uppercut and it knocked him spark out. He still reckons that's what caused his bald spot." Daltrey had been a sheet metal worker in his youth. "I had a pair of shoulders on me and my hands were like rocks."[11]

"I probably deserved to get knocked out," Townshend conceded, ". . . but it was the only one—there was too much respect there for it to happen again."[12]

The album, their sixth, debuted on October 26, and climbed to the second spot on both sides of the Atlantic, blocked by Bowie's *Pin Ups* in the

UK and Elton John's *Goodbye Yellow Brick Road* in the US. Still, it was their best album performance in America.

They introduced "5:15" on *Top of the Pops,* Daltrey in the bare-chested, curly gold mane mode he popularized with Robert Plant. He pumped his arms, stomped in place, threw his mic like a lasso, and spun around. Moon leered amid a ridiculous amount of tom-toms and a giant unused gong. Townshend did his split-leg leap, kicked in Moon's drum set, and then smashed his guitar perfunctorily, pissed off at having to go through the motion of being pissed off, not even waiting till the prerecorded music was finished. Moon joined in, stabbing his tom-toms, while Townshend flipped off the show's producer, which got them banned from the BBC. As opposed to the Stones' perversion, this was untrammeled aggression, which was why all the nerdy young Hulk and Godzilla fans loved them.

On the first night of their US tour at San Francisco's Cow Palace on November 20, someone slipped Moon some animal tranquilizer, a.k.a. PCP, a.k.a. angel dust. Just like Iggy Pop a few months earlier, Moon started slowing down, then collapsed behind his kit. "We're just gonna revive our drummer by punching him in the stomach," Townshend told the audience.[13] Backstage Moon briefly rallied; he tried to return for "Magic Bus" but passed out again, the first time any of them had blown a gig. The woman Moon was with, who also took the stuff, was taken to the hospital.[14] Townshend asked if anyone in the audience could play the drums. A nineteen-year-old from Iowa named Scot Halpin climbed onstage and sat in. *Rolling Stone* gave him the Pick-Up Player of the Year Award.

Even on a good night, the band had trouble playing in sync with the prerecorded synthesizer tapes, which frequently malfunctioned. In Newcastle when the tapes came in late on "5:15," Townshend grabbed soundman Bob Pridden by the neck and yanked him over the soundboard, then smashed his guitar, tore the wires from the board, destroyed the tapes, and stalked offstage. The other three gaped, then followed in silence. (Pridden continued to work with the band for the next four decades.) A little while later they returned to play oldies.

Townshend was also angry because the audience kept yelling for him to leap and slam his guitar strings like a windmill. His right hand was already damaged from the tradition. It hurt when he was sober, and he was trying not to drink as much. Decades later he would say, "This wrist is only connected to the hand by cartilage."[15]

Back in their hotel after a gig in Montreal, someone hit a ketchup bottle too hard and the condiment splattered on the wall. Townshend suggested framing it, so Moon punched a picture frame and took the picture out so they could use that. Townshend cut his hand with a steak knife to add some more red. Some accounts claimed he and Moon smashed a marble table through the wall between rooms. Townshend wrote in his memoir, "What had started as a joke ended with a sofa being thrown out of a window into the beautiful courtyard gardens. As it exploded through the tempered glass . . . we all stood quiet for a moment. Directly opposite us was the hotel reception area behind a glass wall. The hotel staff looked at us in shock; we stared back, equally horrified as we slowly came to our senses."[16] They were escorted to jail, even Daltrey, who had gone to bed early and wasn't present for the carnage. Moon kept the cops waiting as he donned his smoking jacket and found his cigarette holder. At the station he told the officer behind the desk, "I believe I booked a suite."[17]

✳

Nik Cohn, who was originally tapped to write the script for the aborted *Long Live Rock* project, was hired by *New York Magazine* a few years later to write about the disco scene popular among Brooklyn Italians. Instead of researching, he drew on his experiences in the Mod scene and just recast it in the current setting. "Tony and [his gang] The Faces are actually Mods in everything—except the dances," he later told *Melody Maker*.[18] The article was adapted into the John Travolta vehicle *Saturday Night Fever*. After it became the fourth-highest-grossing film of the year, a movie adaptation for *Quadrophenia* received the green light.

The album's photo book served as a storyboard. Phil Daniels scored the role of Jimmy, because he looked like a cross between Pete Townshend and the model in the photo book, and gave a critically acclaimed performance. Sting played Ace Face, the bellboy. The film gained added significance when Moon fatally overdosed during development. The movie did well in England, and *The New York Times* gave it a strong review, though it languished on the American midnight-movie circuit.

The film, along with revival band the Jam, helped the Mod movement endure as a small but surprisingly durable subculture. Over the ensuing decades, Mod revival clubs intermittently sprang up on both sides of the Atlantic, given a further boost by '90s Britpop. The cast still reunites at comic cons and *Quadrophenia* conventions in Brighton.

"The reason why the album is so important to me is that I think it was The Who's *last* great album, really," Townshend told *Billboard*. "[The Who] never recorded anything that was so ambitious or audacious again. And it was kind of the last album where Keith Moon was in a fit state to be a working member of a band. He kind of went off into space after that, so it's a poignant album for me."[19]

Standing on the Sound of Some Open-Hearted People

Neil Young mourns lost friends in the lo-fi masterpiece *Tonight's the Night*. Springsteen stretches out in his most musically ambitious song suite, *The Wild, the Innocent and the E Street Shuffle*, released November 11. Dylan reunites with the Band to record *Planet Waves*.

✳

In June, Young rejoined Crosby, Stills, and Nash to record their next album, but Stills's coke- and booze-fueled megalomania prompted him to unceremoniously split the following month.

"If we are not giving 100 percent he's gone like that," Nash observed.[1]

"Once the muse is gone, I'm out," Young conceded. "And that's hell. I try to be mature but . . ."[2] In another interview he said, "I've left some charred paths behind me."[3]

But more than Stills's abrasive behavior, what Young loathed most was dragging the recording process out. In contrast, the following month he captured 40 percent of his next album in one drunken session on August 26.

"*Tonight's the Night* was the closest to art that I've come," Young said.[4]

AllMusic's William Ruhlmann claims, "It has continued to be ranked as one of the greatest rock & roll albums ever made."

Its genesis was grief. Six and a half months after he lost Crazy Horse guitarist Danny Whitten to heroin, another friend overdosed on June 4: twenty-two-year-old roadie Bruce Berry. Berry's older brother Jan was half of the surf rock duo Jan and Dean, and their brother Ken owned the site of the recording sessions, Hollywood's Studio Instrument Rentals. "It is a wake of sorts," Young wrote in his memoir.[5]

Crazy Horse rhythm section Billy Talbot and Ralph Molina returned to the fold. Pedal steel guitarist Ben Keith was the only holdover from the acrimonious tour Young undertook in the first half of the year. Musician Tim Drummond compared Keith's style with "how when you're in San Francisco and the fingertips of fog crawl in from the ocean and cover the city."[6]

Joining Young on guitar was twenty-two-year-old Nils Lofgren, whom Young had mentored since he was seventeen. "I'd sneak backstage and ask advice anywhere and everywhere I could, more out of fear than courage. I was nervous because I knew nothing about the business. But Neil Young, at the Cellar Door in D.C., was kind enough to spend two days and nights with me, let me watch four shows. . . . He said, 'Look me up when you get [to LA]' and we did, and true to his word, he took us under his wing."[7] In the '80s, Lofgren would join Springsteen's E Street Band.

Every night the musicians arrived at the space, played pool, ate burgers, got high, and slammed Jose Cuervo, which, Young said, "Does something else to me than alcohol usually does," before moving to the small stage in the basement rehearsal room after midnight.[8]

Molina recalled, "We'd just get to a point where you get a glow, just a glow. When you do blow and drink, that's when you get that glow. No one said 'Let's go play,' we all just knew it was time. We never talked about what anyone was playing, who's playing what part or any of that kinda shit. It was so fucking emotional."[9]

"It was a very freeform, just 'trust your instincts and go' kind of thing. It was just a great, rough record to make, and still one of the great live records in the studio ever because in addition to it being live, we were playing songs we barely knew,"[10] Lofgren said. "Just as we were learning a new song and tying to sing at the same time, [Neil]'d be rollin' tape, lookin' for a final take. It freaked us all out. We were like, 'Hey c'mon, man, let's rehearse a little. Let's learn the song.' But Neil's attitude was, 'I know the song and that's all that matters.'"[11]

The title track celebrates the sparkle in Berry's eye and his shaky singing voice and laments his death "on the mainline." "We played Bruce and
Danny on their way all through the night. I'm not a junkie and I won't even
try it out to check out what it's like," Young told *Rolling Stone,* "but we all
got high enough, right out there on the edge where we felt wide-open to
the whole mood. It was spooky."[12]

The second song spotlighting what Young called the dope epidemic was
"Tired Eyes," inspired by an event that happened the previous year near
his home in Topanga Canyon: a coke dealer to the rock community got
into a gunfight outside an orgy, resulting in multiple homicides.[13] As Keith's
mournful steel guitar wavers, Young deadpans, "Well, it wasn't supposed to
go down that way"—a desolate counterpart to Hunter Thompson's *Fear and
Loathing in Las Vegas,* epitomizing the counterculture's slide from idealism
to degradation.

Young's biographer James McDonough wrote, "For me, the seventies can
be summed up by just three things: those grotesque early shopping malls,
Texas Chainsaw Massacre and *Tonight's the Night.* Decay, but with a gleam
in its eye."[14] (Incidentally, *Massacre* filmed the same summer that Young
recorded *Tonight's,* though the film was released the following year.)

Still, *Tonight's* reputation for being unrelentingly bleak is unwarranted.
There are no other dark songs on the record. "Albuquerque" sounds road-
weary, "Roll Another Number (for the Road)" and "Speaking Out" sound
woozy, but all are ultimately positive. "Lookout Joe" sings of "rolling to the
bottom" but "havin' a ball" en route. "Come on Baby Let's Go Downtown"
is tragic in the sense that it's an older track from the vaults with Whitten
singing lead, but the euphoria he and Young share on the harmonies is palpable. A wake is about remembering "old times were good times," as Young
sang in "Lookout Joe."

On "Roll Another Number," Young sings he's not going back to
Woodstock—i.e., back to Crosby, Stills, and Nash, whom he played the legendary festival with, because now he's "standing on the sound of some
open-hearted people." After all the stress with CSNY and his touring band
before it, he'd found the right home at last. Now he was "able to get under
any load." Forty-five years later he was still playing with the same musicians, except for Keith, who had passed away. In that sense, the album
was about grieving with like minded souls, being healed by the camaraderie, and moving ahead together. "New Mama," meanwhile, was a gorgeous
hymn to his partner, Carrie Snodgress, and their baby, Zeke (with harmonies, ironically, not unlike CSNY).

The group premiered the new collection live on September 20 and 22 for the opening nights of the Roxy, a new club on the Sunset Strip next to the Rainbow, opened by partners including Young's managers, Elliot Roberts and David Geffen. Eerily, the occasion marked another loss to opioids, Gram Parsons, who died from combining morphine and alcohol on September 19.

Still, the mood at the shows was upbeat. They covered the stage with fake palm trees, women's shoes, and a statue heisted from an arts and crafts store, leaving a note, "We stole your wooden Indian. If you want your money, come to the Roxy."[15] Billie Jean King beat Bobby Riggs on ABC in the Battle of the Sexes from 8 to 10 p.m. Cher came in by herself, asked if she could sit down with Dylan, Robbie Robertson, and their wives, and instantly hit it off with Geffen.[16]

Young walked onstage, playing the part of the slimy MC featured on the album's cover. "Welcome to Miami Beach. Everything is cheaper than it looks."[17] He announced that the first woman to go topless would receive a pair of shoes. Snodgress surprised him by running onstage without a shirt and hugged him from behind. "Oh my God," he laughed, and launched into "Tonight's the Night."

Along with the album tracks, the band played "Walk On," which built on a line from "Come On Baby Let's Go Downtown." As captured on the *Roxy* live album, it almost sounded like a remake of the Allman Brothers' sunny "Blue Skies," thanks to Keith's slide guitar. The lyrics featured Young shrugging off people talking behind his back—perhaps his ex-tour band, perhaps CSN.

The new group played a few gigs in Canada the following month, then crossed the Atlantic to England. They brought the Eagles as their opening act, continuing Young's support of up-and-coming country rockers. Young delighted in antagonizing the audience by thwarting their desire to hear the hits they paid good money to listen to. After making them sit through his new songs, he would at last offer relief with "Now I'd like to play something you're familiar with," then lurch back into another rendition of "Tonight's the Night."

The tour "was a lot more fun [than *Time Fades Away*] 'cause I was with my friends. I was havin' a fantastic time," Young said. "I think there was more drama in *Tonight's the Night* because I knew what I was doing to the audience, but the audience didn't know if I knew what I was doing. . . . I was fucking with the audience. From what I understand, the way rock & roll unfolded with Johnny Rotten and the punk movement—that kind of audience abuse—kinda started with that tour. I have no idea where the concept came from. Somebody else musta done it first, we all know that. Whether it was Jerry Lee Lewis or Little Richard, somebody shit on the audience first."[18]

Still, Young was unhappy with the mix of the album, so the following February he recorded a whole new batch of songs (including "Walk On") that he released as *On the Beach,* while *Tonight's the Night* languished in the vault. Another year passed, and he was set to release *Homegrown,* a return to the mellow acoustic feel of *Harvest.* One night he hung out with the Band's Rick Danko at the Chateau Marmont and played him both *Homegrown* and *Tonight's* (in the bungalow John Belushi later died in from a "speedball" injection of heroin and cocaine). Danko encouraged him to "go with the raw one."[19] *Homegrown* chronicled Young's crumbling relationship with Snodgress, and he now found it too painful to listen to, so he decided to put *Tonight's* out as it was, even with off-key and out-of-tune moments.

Young explained to Lofgren, "Hey, I've made records where you analyze everything and you do it three thousand times and it's perfect. I'm sick of it. I want to make a record that's totally stark naked. Raw. I don't wanna fix any of it."[20]

When he told record executive Mo Ostin, Ostin warned him it might not go over well but put it out anyway. "Which makes him one of the greatest record men of all time, along with Ahmet Ertegun and Clive Davis," Young wrote.[21] It made it to No. 25 in the US but No. 12 in the UK charts in the summer of 1975—the same summer Johnny Rotten joined the Sex Pistols and spearheaded the punk back-to-basics movement.

✳

The mother of Bruce Springsteen's keyboardist David Sancious lived on 1105 E Street in Belmar, New Jersey, a block from Tenth Avenue, and the band practiced there. Before gigs, they always picked up Sancious last, because he was always late. They waited in organist Danny Federici's van, killing time by boasting of their latest sexcapades, singing to the radio. Guitarist "Little Steven" Van Zandt would analyze the songs. Sax player Clarence Clemons would debate their merits. Bassist Garry Tallent would throw out trivia questions. Springsteen made up stories about passersby and cracked them up. Finally he said, "This band has spent so much time parked on this fucking street we should call it the E Street Band."[22]

When they toured, if they played a city for more than one night, the first evening would be sparse, but by the end of the run the house would be packed. Springsteen played solo acoustic for an hour; then the band joined him to blow the roof off. Springsteen listened when Clive Davis advised him to make use of the entire stage, instead of just standing in one place.[23] He put into action all the hours he spent studying the moves of James Brown and Mick Jagger.[24] Unlike them, he could suddenly whirl around and shred on the guitar.

He was becoming the white version of Brown's "hardest-working man in show business," his concerts turning into marathons, as if he didn't want to go home. "My issues weren't as obvious as drugs. Mine were different, they were quieter—just as problematic, but quieter. With all artists, because of the undertow of history and self-loathing, there is a tremendous push toward self-obliteration that occurs onstage. It's both things: there's a tremendous finding of the self while also an abandonment of the self at the same time. You are free of yourself for those hours; all the voices in your head are *gone*. Just *gone*. There's no room for them. There's one voice, the voice you're speaking in."[25]

Then the first big hiccup since he signed his record deal arrived, though it initially seemed like a terrific opportunity. Chicago asked him to open for them for thirteen gigs in sports venues starting May 30, climaxing at Madison Square Garden on June 15. *Chicago IV* was zooming along to No. 1. The E Streeters enjoyed hanging with Chicago, but soon the video screens were turned off for their opening sets, their sound turned down. In Philly the crowd booed Springsteen and whipped toilet paper rolls at him. A basketball hit the piano. Springsteen didn't get a sound check at Madison Square Garden and flopped. He later declared the period "the worst state of mind I've ever been in." He told his manager angrily, "From now on, we're a club act, and we'll work our way up from there."[26]

Not that he had given up ambitions of superstardom on his own terms. When the band regrouped two days later to record the next album,[27] Springsteen sang of wanting "to try the big top" in the first track they captured, "Wild Billy's Circus Story." Tallent's tuba sounded a bit worse for wear, as the human cannonball misses his fall and the fire-eater lies in a pool of sweat.

They got their groove back with "The E Street Shuffle," speeding up the chords from Major Lance's 1963 soul hit "The Monkey Time,"[28] written by Curtis Mayfield, updating them with Sancious's funky clavinet. Springsteen used the Van Morrison "Wild Night" template to paint a typical evening for the band at a club where "teenage tramps" hang on the corner in the "sweet summer night" and the "band of boy prophets" walk in "handsome and hot," making the ladies' "souls grow weak." Mad Dog Lopez gets in a fight; Phantom Federici hides from the cops. The jam, and the whole album, was infused by the excitement of a rocker who had been forced to be an acoustic balladeer on his last album but was now given free rein to cut loose with his band and show all sides of his identity.

The same day, June 28, they cut the basic track for a "twisted swing tune,"[29] "Kitty's Back," where Springsteen showed off the guitar fireworks he wowed audiences with. The song was inspired by a sign he saw while driving in the equipment van on tour, the neon marquee of a strip club trumpeting the return of one of their dancers.[30] The blogosphere still argues whether Thin Lizzy copped the song's vibe for "The Boys Are Back."

That day they also laid down "New York City Serenade."[31] Tallent's bass coos, and Sancious fuses Tchaikovsky classical with Charlie Mingus jazz on his piano (per biographer Peter Ames Carlin) as Springsteen pans across Manhattan from lucky couples making love in the backseat to lonely boys rejected because they got no money, left to sing the blues with the junkman. (Springsteen covered Patti LaBelle's 1962 "I Sold My Heart to the Junkman" in his act at the time, a song "so sad that sometimes I have to leave the stage and cry backstage a little bit while I'm singing this song."[32]) But in the end, singing in the city after midnight is all the medication they need. Springsteen travels from a whisper to a rhapsodic duet with Clemons's sax, capturing the sound the *Saturday Night Live* house band would embrace in a year and half upon their inception.

Springsteen took his first stab at Norman Rockwell Americana with "4th of July, Asbury Park (Sandy)," the apotheosis of his Jersey Shore mythos, complete with fireworks and the archetypal name for a girl on the beach. He and his girlfriend Diane Lozito lived five minutes from the boardwalk. Springsteen faithfully painted the pier with its "cheap little seaside bars," greasers, and real-life denizens like fortune-teller Madam Marie. Factory girls promise they'll unsnap their jeans under the boardwalk (though in real life, drummer Lopez maintained, there were only rats down there). When Lozito heard the song, she blew her top, believing he was unfaithful.

"Incident on 57th Street" opens with Springsteen trying to hook up with the ladies on the scene but getting shot down because everyone knows he's a cheater. Then Puerto Rican Jane (maybe Crazy Janey from "Spirit in the Night," a.k.a. Lozito?) takes pity on him, and they sleep together until his friends call up to the window. He slips out down the fire escape to join them, heading either to a fight or a gig. He sings with such extravagant *West*

Side Story–esque passion that Jane doesn't really mind (supposedly) that he's a hound dog.

The Springsteen fan site Bruce Base says he cut that song and probably "Rosalita" on his birthday, September 23. If true, cutting one of the most enduring anthems of the year was a hell of a way to commemorate turning twenty-four. The song kicks off with a sped-up snatch of the Byrds' "My Back Pages," their cover of Dylan's original. Tallent and Lopez make their introductory thumps, Sancious leans in on the organ, Clemens's sax suffuses the air, and the band is off on an ode to gathering up your friends to celebrate all night as Springsteen cuts cinematically between his cast of characters.

In his memoir he said "Rosalita" was partially inspired by the ex-girlfriend he lost his virginity to and her mother, who told him she was going to get a court order to keep him away. But Rose Lozito was the name of Diane's grandmother.

After the summer night he and Lozito first hooked up, recounted in the first album's "Spirit in the Night," her boyfriend returned to law school; Springsteen asked her out for a proper dinner and soon asked her to move in with him. Lozito said he charmed her mother, but nevertheless her mother still wanted her to stick with the law student. Her father liked Springsteen, too, but he had been a musician, so he said no because he knew musicians slept around. In the song, Springsteen exhorts her to defy them and ecstatically breaks the news that he's received a big advance from the record label (in real life for $65,000).

Springsteen was also yelling it to his own father, who had long disparaged his dream. Springsteen's sister said after his record deal, "That was when [their father] began to say, 'From now on, I'm never going to tell anyone what they should or shouldn't do with their lives.'"[33]

Springsteen wrote in his memoir that songs like "Rosalita," "Kitty's Back," and "Thundercrack" (held off the album) "were the soul children of the lengthy prog pieces I'd written for Steel Mill and were arranged to leave the band and the audience exhausted and gasping for breath. Just when you thought the song was over, you'd be surprised by another section, taking the music higher. It was, in spirit, what I'd taken from the finales of the great soul revues."

"Rosalita" might have been the most jubilant single since "I Want to Hold Your Hand," had it actually been released as a single, though it wasn't for another six years. But it quickly became his show-closer and remained so for a decade thanks to its audience shout-alongs, like rowdy football games with Springsteen as ultimate cheerleader. In *Springsteen on Broadway* he recounted how his mother and aunts loved to dance, and how his mother's buoyancy countered the melancholy he inherited from his father. Here the joie de vivre of the Zerilli sisters shines through.

He named the LP after a CinemaScope Western he caught on late-night TV, and it stands today as the most light-hearted in his canon—the moment before record-business woes, depression, and marriage issues started weighing him down.

But trouble was already brewing: his champion at Columbia, Clive Davis, was fired. The powers that be put their juice behind a new guy, Billy Joel, and ignored him—as Davis had ignored Aerosmith in favor of Springsteen just eleven months ago. There was even a campaign in some quarters to get Springsteen dropped. And that big advance? It was history, after the managers' fees and taxes and band overhead. He had to write his mother for money at the end of the year.[34]

On the next album he howled in desperation at dreams slipping away in songs like "Backstreets." By then, in the wake of October's oil crisis, factories in the Northeast and Midwest were shutting down with increased frequency, as corporations moved south to nonunion states or to Asia to save on labor costs. Springsteen's loss of optimism mirrored that of the country's blue-collar workers. Their struggle became his most enduring theme as he evolved into his generation's John Steinbeck, protesting through records instead of novels.

✳

Springsteen and Young's musical father, Dylan, flashed his twitchy, enigmatic, sweet almost-smile in *Pat Garrett and Billy the Kid* and released two albums within six months of each other, the soundtrack and *Planet Waves*. On their own, they were lightweight entries in his canon. But if you mixed the best tracks together you had a good year, with two of his biggest standards: one about death ("Knockin' on Heaven's Door") and one about birth (his lullaby to his oldest son, Jesse, "Forever Young" on *Planet Waves,* though the best version is the demo on *Biograph*).

After Columbia fired Clive Davis, David Geffen lured the singer to his own label, Asylum, with a master plan to reunite Dylan with the Band, release an album, go on a massive tour, and cash in. In retaliation, Columbia released *Dylan,* a collection of outtakes from the album considered the one bomb of his career, *Self Portrait*—sort of a double insult.

In November Dylan and the Band regrouped at the Village Recorders

Studio in West LA, their first sessions since *The Basement Tapes* six years ago. Guitarist Robbie Robertson said, "We went in and made [*Planet Waves*] in three or four days, just hammered it out. It was like making a blues record for us."[35] Only a few of the songs needed second takes.

Dylan created his masterpieces in the mid-'60s in an equally short time. Back then the mutant prince detonated hypocrisies with surrealistic grandeur. Now he offered pleasant odes to his wife: "You Angel You," "Something There Is About You," "Never Say Goodbye," "Tough Mama," like a funkier, murkier *Nashville Skyline*. No dark haughty sneer, not even the gypsies and quasi-biblical locusts of *New Morning*. The painting Dylan made for the cover seemed to show him with an anchor on his head. "It's never been my duty to remake the world at large," he sang in "Wedding Song."

Still, the return to greatness was only weeks away. His tour with the Band kicked off on January 3 and produced *Before the Flood*, "one of the best live albums of its time. Ever, maybe," said AllMusic's Stephen Thomas Erlewine. Promoter Bill Graham claimed 12 million mail-order requests came in for tickets at a time when the US population was 214 million.[36]

As the temptations of the road led to the erosion of his marriage, chronicled in the anguished *Blood on the Tracks*, *Planet Waves* gained poignancy as a lost idyll. "I'm closin' the book on the pages and the text and I don't really care what happens next, I'm just going," he sang in "Going Going Gone." Maybe the song wasn't a throwaway after all; maybe it was the theme to the Never Ending Tour that became his life.

26

*

Time to Get Down

Eddie Kendricks hits No. 1 with "Keep On Truckin'" on November 8. Producers Gamble and Huff and Thomas Bell challenge Motown with the Sound of Philadelphia. Their drummer Earl Young stumbles upon the disco beat in "The Love I Lost" by Harold Melvin and the Blue Notes. The success of David Mancuso's underground Loft inspires discos to open across Manhattan.

*

The Jackson Five was grasping for a new direction when songwriter-producer Hal Davis and his team came up with "Dancing Machine," the perfect track for Michael to do the Robot to, a dance popularized by *Soul Train* dancer Charles Washington. The song made it to No. 2 as a single, and its album *G.I.T. Get It Together* sold two million copies. They named their next album *Dancing Machine* and put a shorter version of the track on that one. Critic Robert Christgau observed, "My friend who goes to discos tells me The Jacksons are the first major artists to put out a real disco album."[1]

But Eddie Kendricks could lay the strongest claim to being Motown's disco pioneer. He was the Temptation with the Smokey-like falsetto. After his shining moment in "Just My Imagination" he went solo, causing his disgruntled ex-bandmates to release "Superstar (Remember How You Got

Where You Are)." Initially his singles barely made the Top 40, and it appeared that maybe he'd made a mistake.

But "Girl You Need a Change of Mind" gradually became so popular in the (as-yet unnamed) discos that they eventually carried it all the way to No. 13 on the R&B chart in early '73. In the song he tries to appease a protester burning her bra: "Now I'm for women's rights, I just want equal nights." Historian Alice Echols wrote that it was the missing link between soul and disco because "two qualities distinguished the cut from the label's usual sound: [producer Frank] Wilson's inversion of Motown's four on the top beat and his deployment of the gospel break, which emptied the track of most instrumentation and then gradually built it back up . . . [and] came to be called the 'disco break.'"[2]

Its songwriting team (Poree/Caston) returned with "Keep On Truckin' (Part 1)," which became either the first or second disco song to top the pop charts, depending on how you classify the O'Jays' "Love Train." The song's title came from a cartoon of a hitchhiker drawn by underground comic artist Robert Crumb in 1968, an image bootlegged onto so much merchandise that in 1973 Crumb went to court to claim copyright, although he was unsuccessful.

While Kendricks's star ascended, his childhood friend and co-founder of the Temptations, Paul Williams, succumbed to alcoholism. The Temptations started paying him to stay home after he appeared onstage too drunk to perform too many times. He threatened to kill himself if they didn't let him back onstage. Kendricks tried to help get him back on track, producing the haunting "I Feel like Giving Up." But shortly after the recording, on August 17 in Detroit, Williams had a fight with his girlfriend, then drove his car to an alley and killed himself with a shotgun, a few blocks from the old Motown studios, now closed.

✣

Philadelphia was one of the centers of the pop world in the late '50s and early '60s because *American Bandstand* was made there. Future R&B producers Kenneth Gamble and Thomas Bell lived a few blocks away from the studio, but the show's policy was to let only a few black kids in and to avoid photographing them on the dance floor.[3]

The two met in 1959. Gamble came over to Bell's house one day looking to woo his sister but was quickly distracted by Bell's piano playing. Bell, originally from Jamaica, was classically trained and could play eighteen other instruments. Gamble needed a pianist for his doo-wop group the Romeos. They started writing together.

Bell dreamed of a career on Broadway and did well on the conductor's exam. But he was made to understand that blacks weren't wanted on the Great White Way.[4] So he signed on as Chubby Checker's touring conductor. Gamble found a new pianist in Leon Huff and started a label with him.

They did well enough that Columbia's president, Clive Davis, offered to distribute their music. R&B was the one genre Columbia didn't dominate, and his research indicated it was poised to explode.[5] Gamble and Huff named their new label Philadelphia International Records.

Bell had also made a name for himself as a producer by now, so they asked him to join them. He wanted to stay independent but joined them in publishing and real estate companies. They all recorded at Sigma Sound Studios and had offices in the Philadelphia International building. Bell covered his floor and wall with blue shag carpet and installed a pale blue piano. Huff put his name in three-foot letters in front of his desk. Gamble gave himself a throne. They were all obsessed, working twenty-hour days, seven days a week, according to the definitive history of Philly soul, *A House on Fire* by John Jackson.[6] Gamble juggled up to five LPs concurrently. Philadelphia International scored its first R&B No. 1 in 1972 with "Back Stabbers" by the O'Jays. Four of Columbia's nine gold singles that year were from Philly, and they were just getting started.

The R&B Gamble and Huff produced was harder than Bell's, often with political overtones in the Norman Whitfield mode. Along with the O'Jays they handled Harold Melvin and the Blue Notes ("If You Don't Know Me by Now") and Billy Paul ("Me and Mrs. Jones"). Unlike Bell, Gamble didn't play an instrument or read music, and Huff only wrote basic charts, so they often relied on the house band MFSB to improvise a riff or beat to get a song started. They'd arrive at the studios while the musicians were jamming and start rolling tape. Drummer Earl Young says that the O'Jays' smash "For the Love of Money" (later the theme to Donald Trump's TV show *The Apprentice*) sprang from a bass line improvised by Anthony Jackson. The producers ran it through a phaser sound processor and coated it with echo.[7]

MFSB noticed that they received minimum scale pay and no songwriting credit while Gamble and Huff banked $30 million a year. Young, bassist Ronnie Baker, and guitarist Norman Harris told the producers they would no longer originate anything, only play as instructed. To placate them Gamble gave them their own sublabel and publishing company. Young also was in the Trammps, who released the classic "Hold Back the Night" (which didn't chart for a few years), and later *Saturday Night Fever's* "Disco Inferno."

Not only did most Philadelphia International songs share the same instrumentalists; they usually featured the same background vocalists— frequently only the groups' lead singers actually appeared on record. The backing vocalists of the Spinners, the Stylistics, Blue Magic, and the Blue Notes sang onstage but not on disc, either because the producers didn't feel they were up to snuff or because they thought it would take too long to teach them their parts.[8] (Bell said the O'Jays could all sing.) On most Philly tracks, Gamble, Huff, Bell, and a few other regulars like the female Sweethearts of Sigma sang backup.

In contrast to Gamble and Huff, Bell planned out his songs in advance, and MFSB followed what he wrote down on paper. Bell was the leader of the post-doo-wop Sweet Soul movement, the missing link between Burt Bacharach and the Bee Gees. He strove to create orchestration even more elegant than Motown's, with flutes, oboes, French horns, tympani, orchestra bells, chimes, and vibraphones.

Linda Creed often served as his lyricist, writing words to fit the melodies he constructed. "She was just one of the guys," Bell said. "As rough as any of us. No one ever called her 'Linda.'" Neither her sex nor race (white) was an issue. "You didn't know whether she was white, pink or green! That was just Creed."[9] (Later she wrote "The Greatest Love of All," recorded by Whitney Houston.)

The songwriting duo enjoyed a string of six gold singles and four gold albums with the Stylistics, mainly duets between high tenor Russell Thompkins Jr. and Bell's orchestra. Their hits in 1973 included "Break Up to Make Up" and "I'm Stone in Love with You."

Everybody wanted to work with Bell, so naturally he pursued a group that didn't want him: the Spinners. They had been around since 1955 without major success, had recently left Motown, and thought they needed a white producer to make it to the next level. Bell promised he would give them each ten grand if he didn't generate a chart-topper for them. If he delivered, they'd have to get him a Cadillac.[10] "I'll Be Around" made No. 1 R&B and No. 3 on pop. "Could It Be I'm Falling in Love," "One of a Kind (Love Affair)," and "Mighty Love" kept the streak going. They alternated between two lead singers, smooth Bobby Smith and slightly raw Philippe Wynne. On "Mighty Love" they traded lines until Smith stepped aside to let Wynne cut loose and improv for the last minute.

Bell's Spinners template was so distinctive that when a friend asked him to help out another band named New York City, many people assumed their No. 17 hit "I'm Doing Fine Now" *was* the Spinners.

❊

Dave Marsh called the O'Jays' "Love Train" disco gospel, but many musicologists believe the birth of the disco drumbeat came during the recording of Harold Melvin and the Blue Notes' "The Love I Lost (Part 1)." They were another group that kicked around for a decade and a half until they hired a twenty-year-old drummer named Teddy Pendergrass. After he started piping up from the back with his powerful gravelly voice, they quickly decided to stick him up front. "If You Don't Know Me by Now" topped the R&B chart and made it to No. 3 pop, but when they tried to perform the follow-up "The Love I Lost (Part 1)" in the same slow vein, it didn't click. Huff suggested speeding things up. Guitarist Bobby Eli said, "Right there on the spot, [drummer Earl Young] came up with that hi-hat pattern that everybody started using, like for the disco records and everything."[11]

The Motown Beat was often 4/4 time, hitting the snare on every beat in a bar. Young's "disco beat" was "four on the floor," hitting the bass drum on every beat, the snare on beats two and four. What was different was the variations he'd play on his hi-hat cymbal, as well as his metronomelike timing.[12] "Some drummers play a little behind the beat, some drummers are a little ahead of the beat," said guitarist T. J. Tindall. "Earl was right up the middle, almost like a machine."[13] In that sense, he was the John Henry precursor to the drum machines that rose at the end of the disco era to supplant studio musicians.

The requisite sweeping strings were added, and the single was released in September, around the time MFSB issued its second instrumental album, *Love Is the Message.* The title track became a standard at underground discos like the Loft, as well as on the set list of DJ Kool Herc. The percussion solo at the end of the eleven-minute version also became an ingredient of hip hop evolution. A New York after-hours club deejay named DJ Hollywood made a ritual out of rapping the lyrics of Isaac Hayes's "Good Times" over it.[14]

Another seminal cut on the album was "TSOP (the Sound of Philadelphia)." Originally *Soul Train* host Don Cornelius commissioned Gamble and Huff to write it as a theme for his TV show. When G&H wanted to release it as a single, Cornelius insisted they remove any reference to the show, so they pulled out the ladies singing "Soul Train" and changed the title. When the song hit No. 1 on the pop charts the following year, Cornelius realized he'd lost a massive branding opportunity. It was the first TV theme to go to No. 1. It set MFSB apart from Motown's Funk Brothers, who never had chart hits themselves.

The female vocalists on "TSOP" were the Three Degrees, struggling since 1963. Their 1973 self-titled album contained the classic "When Will I See You Again." Originally the label passed over the song as a single in favor of the ill-advised "Dirty Ol' Man." But after the success of "TSOP," they gave "When Will I See You Again" a chance, and it made it to No. 2. For one moment the Three Degrees rivaled the Supremes as the melodramatic strings and sexy South American rhythm encapsulated the yearnings of a million morning-afters. For the fade-out Sheila Ferguson did her best Diana Ross, riffing with the jaunty horns.

Within a year, Philadelphia International was the second-largest black-owned US company behind Motown. The Grammys named Bell Producer of the Year. Gamble, Huff, and Bell topped the R&B charts twenty-one times between 1972 and 1976. Gamble and Huff scored more gold singles than any other producers in the '70s.

※

The Whisky à Go-Go opened in 1947 in Paris, perhaps the first discotheque. In the mid-'50s its manager, Regine, began using two turntables so there would be no pause between records. In 1969, a New York club named Sanctuary in Hell's Kitchen became the first nightclub where men could dance together freely, often to the Bump, a "frank pantomime of buggery," per journalist Albert Goldman,[15] though the dance was later water downed to hip-bumping by the masses. It closed in 1972 amid complaints of public sex and Mafia-supplied drugs. But David Mancuso's Loft in New York is considered the birthplace of '70s disco as a genre and lifestyle.

Mancuso (born 1944) was a member of Timothy Leary's meditation center in New York, called, naturally, the League for Spiritual Discovery (LSD). Leary intended to create a religion with acid as the sacrament so it could be taken legally. Eventually Leary moved to California, but Mancuso kept the flame going in New York. On Valentine's Day 1970 he deejayed his first party in a loft at 647 Broadway (about five minutes from the Mercer Arts Center). The flyers called the party Love Saves the Day, which shared an acronym with what was in the punch. In front of his Buddhist shrine he played sets organized around the Three Bardos (states of existence) described in the *Tibetan Book of the Dead,* which had been translated by

Leary, Ram Dass, and Ralph Metzner in their *Psychedelic Experience* book. Mancuso described the first state as "calm," the second "a circus," "and the third Bardo was about reentry, so people would go back into the outside world relatively smoothly."[16] Like hip hop deejays, he used two copies of the same record on two turntables to extend the most popular parts of songs.

His parties provided an alternative to gay bars, where police harassment was so frequent that men had to factor bail money into their nightly budget. Mancuso's Loft was invitation only and sold no liquor, food, or beverages, though amyl nitrate, Quaaludes, and coke were usually easy to find. "It was probably about sixty percent black and seventy percent gay," the Loft's soundman Alex Rosner recalled. "There was a mix of sexual orientation, there was a mix of races, a mix of economic groups. A real mix, where the common denominator was music."[17]

"If you can mix the economical groups together, that's where you have social progress," Mancuso said. He accepted IOUs at the door. "People didn't abuse that system."[18] It was the antithesis of the exclusionary door policy of the club it led to: Studio 54.

By summer '73, Mancuso helped make hits. In a Jamaican record store in Brooklyn, he unearthed an import called "Soul Makossa" by Manu Dibango, a saxophonist from the French-speaking African country Cameroon. It featured the hook "ma-mako, ma-masa, mako-makossa" that Michael Jackson later used in "Wanna Be Starting Something."

After Mancuso played it at the Loft, "people went wild trying to find that record," said deejay Nicky Siano,[19] who soon became Mancuso's biggest rival, spinning at a club called the Gallery. A band named Afrique covered "Soul Makossa" and leapt onto the pop charts in June without any radio airplay. Atlantic quickly licensed Dibango's original, and the two versions duked it out through July: Afrique at 47, Dibango at 50, then both at 49, then Dibango passed Afrique at 37 and they dropped out. Dibango's ultimately peaked at 35.[20]

By then discos were sprouting up across Manhattan. The Gallery opened in Chelsea in February, the Hollywood opened at the site of the old Peppermint Lounge in May, and Le Jardin opened in the basement of the Diplomat Hotel in June, enlisting the deejay from the Continental Baths, Bobby Guttadaro.

Vince Aletti helped point the scene toward a name in his *Rolling Stone* article "Discotheque Rock '72: Paaaaarty!," which came out in September '73 despite the '72 in its title. "The best discotheque DJs are underground stars discovering previously ignored albums, foreign imports, album cuts and obscure singles with the power to make the crowd scream and playing them overlapped, non-stop so you dance until you drop."

The Gallery's Siano described how he added drama to the records he spun. "I would turn everything off except the tweeter arrays and have them dancing tss,tss,tss for a while. Then I would turn on the bass, and then I'd turn on the main speakers. When I did that the room would just explode."[21]

Many of the famous disco deejays were Italian, per Tim Lawrence's history *Love Saves the Day*, "thanks to the fact that Italian Americans ran a high proportion of New York discotheques, and many of them were linked to the Mafia."[22] Thus it made sense the protagonists were Italian in *Saturday Night Fever*, the film that later codified the movement for the masses.

In the movie, John Travolta faces off in a dance contest against a black couple and a Latin couple. The latter reflected the third major cultural influence on the budding genre. Puerto Rican teens in the South Bronx originated the Hustle dance at house parties when adults wouldn't allow them to grind.[23]

A New York record label named Fania Records housed Latin artists like Celia Cruz, Rubén Blades, Willie Colón, and Larry Harlow. They mixed Puerto Rican songs, Cuban mambo, cha-cha-cha, Dominican merengue, and boogaloo into a new genre named for the Spanish word for "sauce." The term was popularized in 1973 when Izzy Sanabria began hosting a Latin version of *Soul Train* on New York's channel 141 called *Salsa*.[24] Soon after, Fania artist Joe Bataan released an album called *Salsoul*, reflecting how New York Latinos mixed soul music with salsa.[25] He co-founded a new label, also called Salsoul, that poached Philadelphia International's arranger Vincent Montana Jr. to lead the Salsoul Orchestra, a.k.a. the disco orchestra, stocked with disgruntled MSFB veterans.

On August 24, Dibango, the Fania All-Stars house band, and Celia Cruz played to forty thousand people at Yankee Stadium. Music historian Will Hermes wrote, "It could have been called the '1st Latin Soulrock Jazz Fusion African Proto-Disco Fiesta!' in its spectacular attempt to fuse nearly all the blooming local music scenes of the moment."[26] During the conga showdown "Congo Bongo" between Ray Barretto and Mongo Santamaria (included on the album *Latin Soul Rock*), "the audience went wild and stormed the field," said Harlow. "A girl started dancing on top of my piano, and I got scared. We had placed fireworks inside the piano to set them off later, during the show. I saw that crazy crowd taking the stage, and I told [music director Johnny] Pacheco, 'Let's get out of here before this thing blows up.'"[27] The musicians fled, and the audience stripped the stage, even stealing the piano.

Coming at the dawn of disco, it made for an interesting bookend with Disco Demolition Night in 1979, when the backlash peaked. That evening at Chicago's Comiskey Field baseball park, the crowd chanted "Disco sucks," disc jockey Steve Dahl blew up a huge box of disco records between four and six feet tall, and the audience streamed onto the field around the bonfire. But that was six years away.

✳

Born in 1944, Barry White grew up in South Central Los Angeles in a gang, a lifestyle that killed his brother. In jail, White heard Elvis sing "It's Now or Never" and decided to get out of crime and pursue music.[28] Upon release he wrote and arranged songs for groups ranging from the Bobby Fuller Four to TV's Banana Splits. He finally hit the Top 20 as the writer-producer of "Walkin' in the Rain with the One I Love" by the female trio Love Unlimited. He featured in a cameo at the end of the song, talking sexy with future wife Glodean James. He had an even more mellifluous bass-baritone than Isaac Hayes, and his business partner prodded him to sing himself. After some resistance, he did so on "I'm Gonna Love You Just a Little More Baby," the most intimate proto–Quiet Storm love music to hit the Top 5 yet.

In December he released an instrumental by his forty-piece Barry White Orchestra called "Love's Theme," replete with wah-wah and French horn. The New York clubs pushed it onto the charts—another disco song that sold a ton of copies before receiving substantial radio airplay. "Love's Theme" became the third-bestselling song of 1974. After *ABC Sports* used it for its golf show, it set the template for TV theme songs for the rest of the decade.

The Hues Corporation also lived in LA. Until now they were best known for performing in *Blacula*. But their fortunes changed when they included "Rock the Boat" on their *Freedom for the Stallion* album, released December 7. The LP featured lush pop in the Fifth Dimension vein, but for "Rock the Boat" session drummer Bobby Perez switched the rhythm to a cumbia beat: a Columbian style that mixed African rhythms with indigenous music.[29]

In Miami, Harry Wayne Casey, a.k.a. KC of KC and the Sunshine Band, did all right with his first single, "Blow Your Whistle," in September, so he entered the studio to record a follow-up called "Rock Your Baby." He and his co-writer, bassist Richard Finch, recorded the music in forty-five minutes, with drum machine set to bossa nova, 4/4 beat with the open hi-hat sound. But KC couldn't hit the high notes.[30] So they contacted singer Gwen McCrae to sing it, but she was late for the session. Her husband and manager, George, was there, however, so they asked him to take a crack. And thus George McCrae sang on one of the fewer than forty singles in history to sell over ten million copies, soon imitated by Abba's "Dancing Queen" and Lennon's "Whatever Gets You Through the Night."

In the year ahead, "Love's Theme," "TSOP," "Rock the Boat," and "Rock Your Baby" all topped the pop charts, and Kendricks's December release "Boogie Down" made No. 2, fomenting the most unifying (and polarizing) music craze since the British Invasion.

✳

Underground Vibrations

Rock critics popularize the concept of "punk," Richard Hell originates the look, Hilly Kristal opens CBGB—and Lou Reed goes arena rock. Big Star's melancholy jangle sets the template for indie, while Kraftwerk heralds the dawn of synth pop.

And they will ruin rock 'n' roll, and strangle everything we love about it, right? You know, because they're trying to buy respectability for a form that is gloriously and righteously dumb. Now, you're smart enough to know that. And the day it ceases to be dumb is the day that it ceases to be real, right? And then it just becomes an industry of cool.

—LESTER BANGS (PLAYED BY PHILIP SEYMOUR HOFFMAN)
IN *ALMOST FAMOUS*[1]

✳

In 1968, twenty-two-year-old critic Nik Cohn thought rock was spent as a creative force, and banged out a book in seven weeks to summarize its rise and fall. "There was no more good fierce and straight-ahead rock 'n roll, no more honest trash,"[2] he wrote in *Awopbopaloobop Alopbamboom*. "Groups like Family and the Nice in England, or Iron Butterfly or the Doors in America, were crambos by their nature and that was fine—they could have knocked out three-chord rock and everyone would have been content. But, after the Beatles and Bob Dylan, they've turned towards culture and wallowed in third-form poetries, fifth-hand philosophies, ninth-rate perceptions."[3]

The antidote arrived the following year in a group named after self-abusive comedians, singing deliberately cretinous songs like "No Fun" and "Real Cool Time." Their antics transfixed Alan Vega of the New York musical duo Suicide. "Suddenly Iggy's flying into the audience. Then he's back onstage and cutting himself up with drumsticks and bleeding."[4]

Vega was also struck by Lester Bangs's review of the Stooges' 1970 album *Fun House*. Bangs wrote how people loved to hate "that Stooge punk. . . . Someday, somebody's gonna just bust that fucked-up punk right in the chops!"[5]

Vega decided to promote Suicide's second gig at Manhattan's OK Harris Gallery on November 20, 1970, as "Punk Music by Suicide." Afterward, he began advertising gigs in *The Village Voice* as "A Punk Music Mass by Suicide." Onstage the leather-jacketed Vega hit himself with his own motorcycle chain. "If the violence got really bad, what I'd do was smash a bottle and start cutting my face up. That seemed to have a calming effect on the crowd. I guess they reasoned that I was so fucking nuts that nothing they could do would bother me. I figured out a way of doing it so that I drew a lot of blood but I wouldn't be scarred for life. I had it down to a fine art."[6]

In 1971, Bangs moved with his fellow *Creem* writers into a communal house on a farm in Michigan, a living situation that did not last long. Dave Marsh took issue with the fact that Bangs's dog relieved himself inside and put some dogshit on Bangs's typewriter, which resulted in a brawl.[7] But they were on the same page with the concept of "punk," which they applied to mid-'60s garage bands. Bangs originally used the term in the title of an unpublished, William Burroughs–influenced novel he wrote in 1968, *Drug Punk*. Marsh raved about a May 1971 gig by ? and the Mysterians ("96 Tears") as "a landmark exposition of punk rock." The following month, Bangs extolled Count Five in "Psychotic Reactions and Carburetor Dung," then used the term "punk" again in an article ostensibly about the Troggs, "James Taylor Marked for Death" which advocated stabbing the singer-songwriter with a broken bottle of Ripple. The latter article ran in the fanzine *Who Put the Bomp*, edited by Greg Shaw, which celebrated "punk rock bands as white teenage hard rock of 64–66."[8]

Around then, Stooges handler Danny Fields contributed to an *Esquire* article about "movers and shakers" in the industry and included a friend named Lenny Kaye, who wrote for *Rolling Stone*, *Creem*, and *Crawdaddy* (and would later serve as Patti Smith's guitarist). Elektra Records founder Jac Holzman saw the article and asked Kaye to talent-scout for him.

"I used to visit Lenny at the Village record store at which he worked. I was fascinated by the garage bands of the early '60s who would have a single that was memorable over a short lifespan and no meaningful albums to speak of."[9] Holzman enlisted Kaye to compile a double album of such tracks and write the liner notes, which became *Nuggets: Original Artyfacts from the First Psychedelic Era.*

On January 4, 1973, Greg Shaw reviewed the collection in *Rolling Stone* in an article entitled "Punk Rock: The Arrogant Underbelly of Sixties Pop." It claimed "the real vitality of American rock" was the "ephemeral local band." "Punk rock at its best is the closest we came in the Sixties to the original rockabilly spirit of rock and roll."

Kaye acknowledged, "[*Nuggets*] was critically very well-received, [which] wouldn't surprise me because it was the product of a kind of critical group-think that was in the air at the time. It was commercially received indifferently, and marketed fairly perfunctorily, all of which leads to your usual cult item. I would doubt—I mean, I don't know how many copies it sold—I would doubt that there's more than 10,000 in circulation. Saleswise, I can't imagine that it topped 5,000."[10]

Kaye later observed, "What punk came to be known as—which is a very Ramonesish-based chant, and quick songs and black leather jackets, you know, that very specific kind of punk—you can really draw an analogy from one to the other in the sense that, you know, here [in *Nuggets*] you had short, very catchy songs played with a kind of iconic sneer."[11]

University of Buffalo student Billy Altman started the fanzine *Punk,* in May 1973, with the Seeds ("Pushin' Too Hard") on the cover. He invited Bangs to write for it (and later became executor of Bangs's estate).[12] This was a precursor to *Punk Magazine,* started in 1975 by Legs McNeil and John Holmstrom, which centered on the CBGB scene.

"Punk" was now the trendiest word in rock criticism, even applied to newer bands ranging from the New York Dolls to Aerosmith, Black Sabbath, and the Guess Who. Kiss played with a New York band called Street Punk at the Hotel Diplomat in August. Townshend shoehorned a song named "The Punk Meets the Godfather" into *Quadrophenia.* "The punk" of the title chastises "the godfather" (Townshend) for being arrogant and lost in self-pity while people in the real world starve. Apparently none of the cognoscenti knew that in prison culture "punk" meant someone forced to sexually submit. It meant prostitute back when Shakespeare used it in *All's Well That Ends Well*.

That spring, a new band called the Neon Boys recorded a demo of six songs that combined *Nuggets* garage rock with ragged avant-garde guitar à la the Velvet Underground. Some of the songs were released years later in compilations, including "Love Comes in Spurts" and "That's All I Know (Right Now)." Bassist Richard Hell (Richard Lester Meyers) and guitarist Tom Verlaine (Thomas Miller) had relocated from Kentucky and been inspired by the Dolls at Mercer. They renamed themselves after poet Arthur Rimbaud's book *A Season in Hell* and Rimbaud's compatriot Paul Verlaine and formed the group with drummer Billy Ficca.

In search of a second guitarist, they auditioned Doug Colvin (later Dee Dee Ramone) and Chris Stein (later of Blondie) before settling on Richard Lloyd and renaming themselves Television (after briefly considering the moniker the Libertines). Along with the demo songs, Hell worked on an early version of "The Blank Generation." "It was based on this 'Beat Generation' single by Rod McKuen that Tom had. He collected obscure, kitschy singles. . . . No-one figured that out for 10 years."[13] The song became one of punk's anthems, but Hell's biggest contribution to the genre was fashion.

While Iggy Pop created the prototype for the self-injuring front man, and Johnny Thunders created the hairstyle adopted by '80s glam metal rockers, Hell introduced the spiky haircut. Since all the musicians sported long hair, whether they were hippies or glam rockers, Hell chopped his locks short and uneven to rebel. And he took to wearing ripped T-shirts like Brando in the "Stella!" scene of *A Streetcar Named Desire*. Later he used safety pins to hold pieces of the shirts together and scrawled phrases like "Please Kill Me" on them.

Hell told Lester Bangs, "One thing I wanted to bring back to rock and roll was the knowledge that you invent yourself. That's why I changed my name, why I did all the clothing style things, haircut, everything."[14]

A few years later, boutique owner (and Dolls manager) Malcolm McLaren asked Hell if he could manage him. Hell politely declined, and McLaren went on to mastermind the Sex Pistols in London. Hell observed, "Everyone in the band had short, hacked-up hair and torn clothes and there were safety pins and shredded suit jackets and wacked-out T-shirts and contorted facial expressions. The lead singer had changed his name to something ugly. It gave me kind of a giddy feeling. It was flattering."[15] The style soon boomeranged back across the Atlantic. "I was amazed, walking by Macy's in Herald Square, to see ripped-up T-shirts in the windows. That was just three years after I was in my first band, when I was the only person in the world wearing ripped T-shirts."[16]

By that time the emerging punk scene had relocated from the Mercer Arts Center in the Broadway Central Hotel. The building was destabilized when a wall in the basement was removed. On August 3, air-conditioning engineer Seymour Kaback noted, "I heard the walls groaning. By 2:30 p.m. on Friday it was Panicsville in there."[17] At 5:10 p.m., just before performances were due to begin, the eight-story building imploded, killing at least three.

Around that time, a club owner named Hilly Kristal was forced to close his East Village niterie Hilly's due to noise complaints. So he turned his attention to a dive bar he owned on skid row called Hilly's on the Bowery. On December 10, he rechristened it CBGB & OMFUG, an acronym for "Country, Bluegrass, Blues and Other Music for Uplifting Gormandizers" (gormandizers defined as "ravenous eaters"). He intended to focus on the genres listed in the name but relented when bands like Television and the newly formed Ramones asked him to let them play there in the spring of '74. Since he was lucky to get twenty people a night, the stakes were not high.

Punk founding father Lou Reed, meanwhile, attempted to repackage his Velvet Underground catalog for mass consumption on December 21, when he recorded *Rock and Roll Animal* live at New York's Academy of Music. "I heard Mitch Ryder's Detroit Wheels, produced by Bob 'Wonderboy' Ezrin, doing [the Velvets song] "Rock And Roll" and I said, 'Aha, that's fun.' So Ezrin got Alice Cooper's band for me. I can't play that way, I don't wanna play that way, but they were as good at 'that way' as anybody else around. So I said, 'Okay, here's the material.' They didn't know it from the Velvet Underground, they'd never heard it, so I just taught them the whole thing. Now we'll try it again, see what happens five years later. Duh. Let's see if they [the record-buying public] get it this time around. Change the presentation. I mean, it is not something that I would want to keep doing, but it was probably one of the greatest live records ever made."[18]

Paul Nelson wrote in *Rolling Stone* that "when his new band came out and began to play spectacular, even majestic, rock & roll, management's strategy for the evening became clear: Elevate the erratic and unstable punkiness of the centerpiece into punchy, swaggering grandeur by using the best arrangements, sound and musicians that money could buy."[19]

After squandering his "Walk on the Wild Side" momentum with the alienating *Berlin,* Reed "played ball" and earned his first gold record. Still, had any parent actually listened, the polished "Heroin" was more terrifying than a hundred faux-satanist heavy metal songs.

❊

Alex Chilton scored a No. 1 single at age sixteen with "The Letter," his first shot out of the gate as lead singer for the Box Tops. After leaving that group, he turned down an offer to sing for Blood, Sweat & Tears, deeming them "too commercial,"[20] and joined forces instead with fellow Memphis native Chris Bell. They named their new group after the Big Star grocery store near the studio they recorded at, Ardent. On their debut, *#1 Record,* they alternated lead vocals like Lennon and McCartney on Beatles albums, while carrying on the chiming guitar sound of the Byrds.

But Bell resented that Chilton was receiving more attention and struggled with depression and substance abuse issues. He attempted suicide, fought with bassist Andy Hummel, smashed Hummel's instrument, attacked the studio owner's car, and was briefly institutionalized.[21] By early '73 the band seemed dead in the water.

Ardent's promo man John King revived the group when he staged the First Annual National Association of Rock Writers Convention on Memorial Day weekend in May. King flew in 140 critics (including Bangs, Lenny Kaye, Cameron Crowe, Nick Tosches, and future Rhino Records co-founder Harold Bronson) into Memphis to watch a slate of bands and convinced Chilton, Hummel, and drummer Jody Stephens to reunite for the occasion. They played Big Star originals along with covers of the Kinks, T. Rex, and Loudon Wainwright. The positive response convinced Chilton to turn the solo album he was working on into the second Big Star album, *Radio City.*

The trio captured many of the tracks live in the studio and mastered the completed disc on December 3.[22] Included was Big Star's most beloved ballad, "September Gurls." *Popdose*'s Dave Lifton summarized, "We often describe jangly melodic rock songs as 'Beatle-esque,' but the brilliance of 'September Gurls' is how Chilton, at his prime, showed he could be three members of The Beatles at once and yet sound entirely original. Its effortlessly catchy melody and sing-able chorus is straight out of Paul McCartney's Big Bag O'Hooks; the bitterly introspective lyric, notably the couplet, 'I loved you, well, never mind / I've been crying all the time' would have made John Lennon take notice. And that bright and shiny guitar tone is straight out of George Harrison's Sonic Blue Stratocaster on 'Nowhere Man.'"[23] In 2011, *Time* magazine listed the track among its All-Time 100 Songs.[24]

The band played Max's Kansas City in late December, "mainly to music writers on the first night" per the club's website. *Billboard*'s Sam Sutherland called their December 22 performance a "triumph," with an "aura of fragility [that] shifted into electric overdrive with full force." Unfortunately, he noted, "with virtually no publicity outside the industry itself, the second night crowd was lean."[25]

The Village Voice's Christgau gave the album an A when it was released in February. But the label Stax was embroiled in a fight with its distributor Columbia that led to its bankruptcy. With almost no promotion, *Radio City* sold approximately twenty thousand copies. Hummel returned to college. Chilton and drummer Jody Stephens recorded a third album, then shelved it and parted ways.

Singer-songwriter Robyn Hitchcock said in the documentary *Big Star: Nothing Can Hurt Me,* "To me, Big Star was like some letter that was posted in 1971 that arrived in 1985—like something that got lost in the mail."[26] That was around the time R.E.M. began trumpeting the band in interviews. Paisley Underground veterans the Bangles covered "September Gurls" on their 1986 album *A Different Light,* which hit No. 2. The following year, the Replacements released their anthem "Alex Chilton," recorded in Ardent Studios. The Gin Blossoms pilgrimaged there to capture their 1992 breakthrough *New Miserable Experience.* Cheap Trick covered "In the Street" for the theme to *That '70s Show.* Katy Perry spelled "California Gurls" in honor of the earlier classic.

✳

Fellow power-pop progenitors the Raspberries offered the inverse to Big Star's "oddness and darkness," as *The Guardian*'s Michael Hann put it. "Unlike Big Star, the chord changes in their songs go to the places you expect—they always sound comfortable, as a result."[27]

The Ohio band formed in 1970 when lead singer Eric Carmen joined forces with the Choir, the garage band behind the winsome 1966 nugget "It's Cold Outside." Carmen did a shameless McCartney imitation, earnest big-eyed peeking, twitchy head nods, and all.

Carmen remarked, "Progressive rock had taken over the pot-addled airwaves of FM radio, and to me, long, boring flute solos and endless jamming had replaced the great songs I grew up listening to. Instead of the Beatles, we got Jethro Tull and Traffic and the like. I hated prog rock; to me, it was the ultimate expression of a bloated sense of self-importance and mindless self-indulgence. I wanted to have a band that could rock as hard as the Who and sing like the Beatles and the Beach Boys; a band that could play concise, three-and-a-half minute songs with power and elegance. Apparently, there were a few other guys that had similar ideas. Alex Chilton comes to mind, although we went after things in different ways. It wasn't until after Raspberries, Big Star and Badfinger came to exist that power pop became a genre. In each case, I suspect Pete Ham, Alex Chilton and I all felt the same void after the Beatles broke up, and somehow we were all trying to fill it."[28]

Chilton: "I remember when I first heard the Raspberries. Big Star were in a van travelling around doing some dates and we heard 'Go All the Way' on the radio, and we said, 'Wow, those guys are really doing it!' I thought that was a great song."[29]

While Chilton quoted Lou Reed's desire to "nullify my life" in "Daisy Glaze," the Raspberries released relentlessly up-tempo singles like "I Wanna Be with You" (peaking at No. 16 in January) and August's "Tonight." Springsteen was a vocal fan and later incorporated power pop into his own work. But for the moment, the jangle was both too old and too recent to be popular, caught out of time in the twenty-year nostalgia cycle. After another year swimming upstream, Carmen went solo with "All by Myself."

✳

In Germany, two men pioneered the use of synths and drum machines, the vanguard of a movement that would eventually remake pop as radically as Dylan's lyrics and the Beatles' sonic experimentation once had.

Classical music students Ralf Hütter and Florian Schneider formed Kraftwerk ("Power Station") in Düsseldorf in 1970, part of the "Krautrock" scene that included Tangerine Dream, Can, and Neu. They each played multiple instruments, but in their promotional films Schneider played the flute while Hütter took keyboards. Originally they enlisted conventional drummers to supplement their sound. But in early '73 the band Kingdom Come (featuring Arthur Brown, famous for dancing with a headpiece of fire) built their album *Journey* around a drum machine, one of the first rock albums so constructed.[30] (Sly Stone's *There's a Riot Goin' On* used one intermittently.) So Kraftwerk used the rhythm box presets built into an electric organ for their October album *Ralf und Florian*. (Organs with proto-drum machines were popular with keyboardists, who could use them to play events like weddings by themselves without hiring a band.[31])

Kraftwerk began running their voices through the synthesizer called the vocoder, which later pervaded funk, hip hop, and electronic dance music. *Ralf und Florian* still featured Farfisa electric pianos, guitar, and flute, but songs like "Tongebirge" ("Mountain of Sound") sounded like jazzy computerized

New Age ambient music and, in some places, the background music of early video games.

After the album they patented their own version of electronic drum pads and added percussionist Wolfgang Flür to their lineup to play the pads, without a bass drum, hi hat, or cymbals. The trio released their first single in December, named "Kohoutek Comet Melody" ("Kohoutek-Kometenmelodie") after the comet that could be seen passing Earth for the first time in 150,000 years.[32]

Schneider already sported short hair parted in old-fashioned style. Now Hütter shaved his mustache, cut his hair, and began wearing suits as well, shedding the last of his hippie vestiges. Next year, they created the "robot pop" of "Autobahn," ground zero for New Wave, house, techno, trance, and electro pop.

28

✳

Court and Spark

Joni Mitchell channels her angst over Jackson Browne and Warren Beatty into her bestselling album, after finding a band that can keep up with her.

✳

oni Mitchell was the quintessential free spirit—writing the anthem "Woodstock," living in a cave with hippies in Greece, posing nude on the inside gatefold of *For the Roses*. She challenged herself to be completely transparent in her lyrics, inspired by Brando's method acting.[1] She turned down Graham Nash's marriage proposal because "I just started thinking, 'My grandmother was a frustrated poet and musician. She kicked the kitchen door off the hinges.' And I thought maybe I'm the one that got the gene who has to make it happen. . . . As much as I cared for Graham, I thought, 'I'll end up like my grandmother, kicking the door off the hinges.'"[2] In *Court and Spark*'s biggest hit, "Help Me," she sang of loving her freedom.

But in the same song she worries that she's falling for a "sweet talking ladies' man" who loves freedom even more than she does.

In 1972, Jackson Browne opened for her as she toured the US, the UK, Canada, and Europe. In *Court and Spark*'s title track, she describes a singer busking on the sidewalk until the "glory train" passes through him—perhaps a reference to how Browne's "Doctor, My Eyes" broke into the Top 10 during the middle of the tour. The busker takes the coins he makes and buries them in People's Park, perhaps a reference to Browne's long-standing political activism. The park was the Berkeley cause célèbre in which hippies usurped 2.8 acres owned by the University of California and transformed them into a public park, reversing the trajectory in Mitchell's protest song "Big Yellow Taxi," in which nature was paved to put up a parking lot.

Along with political idealism, she and Browne shared a close friend in David Geffen and an early champion in David Crosby (who sang backup on "Doctor, My Eyes"). Here was someone who could help her forget the singer-songwriter who inspired much of her last album, *For the Roses,* and had left her for Carly Simon. Drummer Russ Kunkel commented, "Jackson was a West Coast version of James [Taylor]; James was an East Coast version of Jackson."[3] In the spring she told former flame Roy Blumenthal that "Jackson and I are in love."[4]

Mitchell biographer Sheila Weller said Jackson "was the one guy who really seriously got to her in a very painful way. They met and she fell in love with him at her near-nadir, depression-wise. He was just becoming famous, he was younger than she (about five years), and he was very good looking."

But Weller also noted, "They fought quite a bit."[5] His friend singer Pamela Polland observed, "It became too heavy for Jackson to be with someone who was so much more prolific than he. She was creative in so many ways, and it came out of her so easily, that to face his own struggle with his craft, his own slowness with his craft—to have those two mirrored against each other—I think was very painful for him."[6] (One example was "Take It Easy." Browne wrote the first verse, and Eagle Glenn Frey was eager to record it. Frey waited for weeks for Browne to write the second verse, then finally asked if he could finish it himself.)

Mitchell played electric piano on "Sing My Songs to Me" on Browne's second album, *For Everyman,* but during the sessions he met model Phyllis Major at the Troubadour. He describes the evolution of their relationship in "Ready or Not." At the Troubadour he gets into a fight with an "unemployed actor" while "defending her dignity." He tells Major that he wants his freedom (echoing "Help Me"), but she does his laundry and cooks (which, presumably, Mitchell did not), and before he knows it she's moved in with him, pregnant with their son, Ethan (born November 1973).

Thus most of *Court and Spark* deals with Mitchell processing rejection. "Raised on Robbery" looks at it from a humorous angle. A lady takes a seat at the bar and tries to encourage the man sitting next to her to come home with her, but he walks off. In a way, the song is a jovial celebration of liberated women's freedom to get shot down without shame at singles bars just like men. Robbie Robertson adds the Band's funky humor with his guitar. Mitchell overdubs her own voice to add a hint of Andrews Sisters, recently revived by Bette Midler. (Both Midler and Mitchell covered Lambert, Hendricks and Ross's "Twisted" that year as well.)

"Car on a Hill" also *sounds* upbeat—you could almost dance to it in parts—with guitar by Wayne Perkins (who worked with Bob Marley and later the Stones) and smooth jazz reed by Tom Scott. But the track recounts a night she waited for three hours for Browne to show and he never did. Though the lyrics do not reflect it, Weller writes in *Girls like Us* that "one confidante says she 'took pills. She cut herself up and threw herself against a wall and got completely bloodied—glass broke. She vomited up the pills.'" Weller later told journalist Lois Alter Mark, "David Geffen rescued her and, having hit bottom, her healing then began."[7]

A third of the way into the song, a ghostly heavenly choir (comprised of overdubbed Mitchell voices) interrupts the groove, perhaps the release of death calling to her, or perhaps an epiphany that the relationship is over.

In the 2017 biography *Reckless Daughter,* Mitchell denied the account in Weller's book. "It said, when Jackson Browne dumped me, I attempted suicide and I became a cutter. A cutter! A self-mutilator! . . . I'm crazy but not that crazy."[8]

When Browne played the Roxy club in October, they had a confrontation on the stairs, and she ran onto Sunset Boulevard without her shoes. Some retellings say he hit her. Years later Browne countered that she attacked him twice.[9]

The Daily Telegraph assumed Browne's haunting "Fountain of Sorrow" was his take on their relationship.[10] The song ended with the hopeful extension of an olive branch. But Mitchell was not so forgiving. After Daryl Hannah accused Browne of assaulting her in 1992 (a charge he denied), Mitchell released "Not to Blame," which excoriated Browne for domestic abuse and for supposedly driving Major to suicide in 1976. (Though she had reportedly attempted suicide before Browne, once after a breakup with Keith Richards.[11])

✳

Movie star Warren Beatty inspired at least two songs on the album. Geffen met the actor when he considered buying Geffen's house and soon introduced him to Mitchell.[12] "People's Parties" describes the Hollywood soirees they attended with Beatty's friend Jack Nicholson ("Jack behind his joker"). The song was recorded at the same time Beatty began preproduction on *Shampoo,* his film about a sex addict adrift in Los Angeles. Mitchell had been the doyenne of the Laurel Canyon musician community, but Hollywood struck her as a colder scene. "Stars are hardly ever fun. They're neurotic, they're self-centered, they're nervous, they're insecure, especially movie stars. I'm more comfortable with farm people."[13]

One night, Mitchell went to Hugh Hefner's mansion with Nicholson and Beatty. "The three of us had been out to dinner together. All these girls came up to me, and if their ass was their best feature they stuck it forward. 'Hi!' they said and they stuck their bum out. 'Hi!' they said and they stuck their tits out. I felt so bad for these girls. At a certain point I just decided to sneak away. And I ran out of gas in the driveway! They were running with jerry cans to get me out of there—I couldn't get out fast enough—and I burst into tears. The next time I went there I had adapted, but the first time I felt so sorry for who would live the brief part of their life—'cause old age is going to come on them all too soon and then what are they going to live their life for—for this one aspect of their physical contours. For many, the culture grooms this as all there is. A woman's power is her beauty, or the illusion of it. And that's tragic."[14]

She sings of "Photo Beauty," one minute "crying on someone's knee," the next "laughing it all away." Mitchell overdubs herself singing the latter phrase like a shimmering chorus of sedated Stepford Wives in a record skipping on the run-out groove.

A later relationship of Mitchell's, Dave Naylor, believed "The Same Situation" was about Beatty, "weighing beauty and imperfection to see if I'm worthy . . . tethered to a ringing telephone in a room full of mirrors." When the character in the song says that he loves her, she asks, "Do you think this can be real?" She assumed he and Nicholson had a wager over who would seduce her first, so she always drove to parties separately from them in her own car.

"I knew the game [Beatty] was playing. He told [the psychiatrist they shared, Dr. Martin Gotjahn] that I was the only woman that beat him at his own game, and I said at that point, 'I don't know what the game is, but I don't feel like a victor. If I won something, what did I win?'"[15]

In the song, she sends a prayer up to "the Lord on death row" to send her "somebody who's strong, and somewhat sincere." The violins arranged by Tom Scott swell like wind sweeping back her hair on a Hollywood balcony as the bass pulses and rim shots click like lost time ticking by.

"My problem was that I was sad. I wasn't mentally ill. I was sad, trying to get something going in impossible situations. When someone's undermining your self-worth, it's not a healthy situation. Well, it's not James (Taylor)'s fault he's fucked up. And Jackson's just a nasty bit of business. So to go from one to the other kind of scared me against going into another relationship."[16]

On "Just like This Train," she stares out a locomotive window at a desert as the slide guitar groans with melancholy. She's given up trying to find "a strong cat without claws" and instead dreams of the pleasure she'll have watching her vain man lose his hair. Mitchell recorded the song that fall just as Erica Jong released *Fear of Flying*. Jong's protagonist yearns for a "zipless fuck" with a "stranger on a train," but when she actually lives it out, Jong wrote that "instead of turning me on, it had revolted me! Puzzling, wasn't it? A tribute to the mysteriousness of the psyche. Or maybe my psyche had begun to change in a way I hadn't anticipated."

In "Down to You," Mitchell goes to the "pick up station craving warmth and beauty," waking in the morning to a stranger who leaves. But the sad horn leads into a healing orchestral arrangement, accepting the emptiness and gathering the strength to persevere. "Everything comes and goes," but how you deal with it is "down to you. You can crawl, you can fly, too." She and Scott won the Grammy for Best Arrangement Accompanying Vocalist for the song.

✳

Had Court and Spark wrapped with "Down to You," the climax would feel epic, bittersweet but empowering. Instead she closed with two songs inspired by her visit to a treatment center partially run by Dr. Grotjahn, the psychiatrist who treated her, Beatty, and Geffen.[17] "Trouble Child" opens on her in a "sterilized room" in Malibu feeling spacey, recalling novels where the protagonist winds up institutionalized, like Sylvia Plath's *The Bell Jar* or Joan Didion's *Play It as It Lays*. The bass moves slowly with a touch of funk, mirroring both her sedated mind and the chip on her shoulder about dealing with psychiatrists she doesn't want to believe in. She knows she has to change her attitude in the aftermath of her confrontation with Browne ("some'll try to clock you") and purported suicide attempt ("you can't live life and you can't leave it"), but she sees the doctor as both friend and foe. Mainly she tries to figure out how she wound up in such a lonely place. "Why does it come as such a shock to know you really have no one?"

When Mitchell was nine, she was hospitalized for polio. Unable to go home for Christmas, she consoled herself with singing. In art school, when she lost her virginity to her boyfriend, she got pregnant. Both the Pill and abortion were unavailable in Saskatchewan at that time. "He left me three months pregnant in an attic room with no money and winter coming on and only a fireplace for heat."[18]

Within a month of placing her daughter in a foster home, she began performing her own compositions for the first time. She married another folk singer who said he'd help get her child back. "Then, the moment we were married, he intimated strongly, he had no interest in raising another man's child. . . . I started writing to develop my own private world and also because I was disturbed."[19]

She referred to her daughter obliquely in the melancholy "The Circle Game" and "Little Green." "Depression can be the sand that makes the pearl. Most of my best work came out of it. If you get rid of the demons and the disturbing things, then the angels fly off, too."[20]

For the final track, Mitchell again sang of disagreeing with her analyst, but this time from a humorous angle by covering the satirical "Twisted," from Lambert, Hendricks, and Ross's 1952 album *The Hottest New Group in Jazz*. "I considered that album to be my Beatles. I learned every song off of it, and I don't think there is another album anywhere—including my own—on which I know every note and word of every song."[21] She sings that her psychiatrist can't understand her because she's really a genius—and gets Cheech and Chong to guest star, bouncing back through comedy.

✳

Initially she intended to work with the session musicians who played for Browne, Taylor, Linda Ronstadt, and CSNY, but "they couldn't play my music, because it's so eccentric. They would try, but the straight-ahead 2/4 rock & roll running through would steamroller right over it. . . . They couldn't grasp the subtlety of the form. I've never studied music, so I'd always be talking in abstractions. And they'd laugh, 'Aww, isn't that cute? She's trying to tell us how to play.' Never negatively, but *appeasingly,* you know. And finally it was [drummer] Russ Kunkel who said, 'Joni, you'd better get yourself a jazz drummer.'"[22]

Saxophonist Tom Scott had worked on her previous LP *For the Roses,* so she attended a show by his fusion band L.A. Express, then invited them to a session. "When they got in the studio, it was the same problem. They didn't really know how heavy to play, and I was used to being the whole orchestra. Many nights I would be very discouraged. But one night we suddenly overcame the obstacles. The next thing we knew, we were all aware we were making something quite unique."[23]

They practiced at Studio Equipment Rentals in August and September, while her old friend from the Canadian folk scene, Neil Young, was there recording *Tonight's the Night.* The actual tracks were recorded at A&M Studios in Hollywood in October, where John Lennon and Phil Spector drunkenly floundered through *Rock and Roll.*

Puerto Rican flamenco guitarist José Feliciano ("Feliz Navidad") was playing on Lennon's sessions when he heard Mitchell working on her portrait of David Geffen, "Free Man in Paris." "I already knew Joni from when we both worked in Canada, so I walked in and said I thought I could play some good electric guitar for it. The great guitarist Larry Carlton of the L.A. Express was already on the track, but I knew I could hold my own with him. Joni didn't try to direct me at all, just let me do what I do, and it turned out really good."[24]

Afterward, however, he rubbed her the wrong way with some unsolicited advice. "She was playing with her guitar in an open tuning, so I pointed out that although open tunings are nice, they can be restrictive. I said that she'd be better off just to tune her guitar in the normal way. She didn't like that. I think it put her off me a little."[25]

She had taught herself guitar in art school listening to a Pete Seeger instruction record. The struggle with polio left her unable to press the strings with her left hand in the standard way, so she developed her own unique tunings, just as Jimi Hendrix, Keith Richards, and Black Sabbath's Tony Iommi had. Regardless of Feliciano's opinion, Jimmy Page revered her, as he revealed to *Rolling Stone* a few years later when the magazine asked if he could top "Stairway to Heaven." "I have to do a lot of hard work before I can get anywhere near those stages of consistent, total brilliance. I don't think there are too many people who are capable of it. Maybe one. Joni Mitchell. That's the music that I play at home all the time, Joni Mitchell. *Court and Spark* I love because I'd always hoped that she'd work with a band. . . . She brings tears to my eyes, what more can I say? It's bloody eerie. I can relate so much to what she says."[26]

Zeppelin's "Going to California" was partially inspired by her "I Had a King." When they performed it in concert, Robert Plant murmured "Joni" after the line "to find a queen." Still, he was too shy to talk with Mitchell at parties, he revealed in the Zeppelin bio *Hammer of the Gods.*[27]

✳

Graham Nash and David Crosby sang backup on "Free Man" as she pole-vaulted through her three-octave range, thrilled to sync her acoustic groove with the power of L.A. Express—drummer John Guerin in particular.

Guerin had worked sessions for artists ranging from Sinatra to Zappa, briefly served in the Byrds in the early '70s, and most famously beat out the rhythm in the *Hawaii Five-0* theme. He was initially unimpressed at the idea of working for the "folksinger," until he realized, "She was the whole orchestra in one guitar! . . . You didn't go whistling Joni's tunes. They were much more complicated; not A-A-B-A form, not Gershwin. Joni's songs didn't have the usual hook; she would form the music to her lyrical thought and sometimes go across bars and in different time signatures—she didn't care."[28]

The way his drums dramatically fell into the intros of "Help Me" and "Free Man" gave her signature propulsive strumming an added kick. With thick black hair like Beatty's and rugged good looks, he soon shared her bed, listening to artists they both loved like Davis and Coltrane. Maybe he inspired "Help Me" and not Browne. In a future song, "Refuge of the Road," she paid tribute to Guerin as "a friend of the spirit" whose sanity "mirrored me back simplified" and got her to laugh again.[29]

"Joan's a very complicated person and I'm a pretty straightahead guy," he said. "I think she lightened up a lot with me."[30] She later married bassist Larry Klein. The rhythm section, it seemed, was more conducive to her happiness than tortured, competitive singer-songwriting heartthrobs.

Geffen's Asylum label held back the album's release till just after the holiday season in a strange coordinated assault on the pop charts by three of his acts: *Court and Spark* was released January 1, 1974, Carly Simon's *Hot Cakes* January 11, and Dylan's *Planet Waves* January 17. Mitchell's went double platinum and peaked at No. 2, blocked by Dylan. Simon made No. 3. A year earlier Simon dominated the charts, but now "Help Me" went to No. 7 and topped easy listening, bringing a new level of wit, sensuality, and vulnerability to the radio and the dance floor. Mitchell had always loved to dance. "Free Man" went to No. 2 on easy listening.

Los Angeles Times critic Robert Hilburn dubbed the LP "virtually flawless." *The Village Voice* named it the best album of the year. *Rolling Stone* later ranked it the 111th Greatest Album of All Time (*Blue* was No. 30).

The only one who didn't seem wowed was Dylan. One night he, Mitchell, Geffen, and some friends listened to both new records. "There was all this fussing over Bobby's project, 'cause he was new to [Geffen's] label, and *Court and Spark,* which was a big breakthrough for me, was being entirely and almost rudely dismissed. Geffen's excuse was, since I was living in a room in his house at the time, that he had heard it through all of its stages, and it was no longer any surprise to him. Dylan played his album, and everybody went, 'Oh *wow*.' I played mine, and everybody talked and Bobby fell asleep. I knew [*Court*] was good. I think Bobby was just being cute," she told an interviewer with a laugh.[31] She painted her own cover, as Dylan had.

Guerin cheated on Mitchell and they broke up, during which time she briefly dated Wayne Perkins. But she missed him, and when the L.A. Express joined her on tour mid-January, the couple reunited.

"It took me six records to find a band that could play my music,"[32] she told Robert Hilburn, but now that she had found the right band, her joy was self-evident in film footage from the tour and in the live album, *Miles of Aisles* (which hit No. 2). After the tour Guerin moved into her new house in Bel Air.

Headbangers Apotheosis

Aerosmith bounces back through relentless touring with the help of the New York Dolls' engineer. The sorcerers of madness descend into a haunted dungeon for "Sabbath Bloody Sabbath." Led Zeppelin travels time and space to top "Stairway to Heaven."

✳

Columbia debated whether to drop Aerosmith from the label as their debut album languished, selling around thirty thousand copies. Guitarist Joe Perry recalled, "There was nothing at all: no press, no radio, no airplay, no reviews, no interviews, no party. Instead the album got ignored and there was a lot of anger and flipping out."[1] Steven Tyler yelled that Perry cranked his amp too loud and was going to blow out his ears. Tyler rode Joey Kramer so hard about his drumming that Kramer developed a facial tic.

But Jack Douglas was intrigued. He was the engineer who served as de facto producer on the first album by the Dolls, the band that shared the same management team as Aerosmith. "I'd seen the Jimmy Page Yardbirds, and [in Aerosmith] I thought I saw the American Yardbirds—not a copy, not an imitation, but the real thing. A hard-rocking blues, R&B rock group. I'm thinking to myself, 'this is a great American rock band!' . . . My attitude was: 'What can I do to make them sound like themselves?'"[2]

They went into the studio mid-December for *Get Your Wings*. The title was a nod to the insignias of the bikers who populated the club the band frequently played in Massachusetts, Scarborough Fair. They offered up their own take on the R&B standard the Yardbirds performed in the movie *Blow-Up*, "Train Kept A-Rollin'." Perry came up with the riff for "Same Old Song and Dance," and Tyler scatted along till he found words that fit—"automatic writing" he called it.[3] The pimps of Times Square outside the Record Plant studio inspired "Lord of the Thighs."[4]

Perry judged, "Of all the ballads Aerosmith has done, '[Seasons of] Wither' was the one I liked best."[5] Tyler wrote it on barbiturates and incense with a guitar salvaged from a Dumpster, depressed by winter and taxes. The "oooo" bridge presaged the monster ballad hooks that set high school gyms slow-dancing when glam metal conquered MTV a decade later.

But it was during the opening of "Woman of the World"—with its ringing arpeggios, pulsating bass, and Kramer hanging back half a beat—that Aerosmith relaxed into their swagger and forgot their fear of the red recording light for good. For those first twenty seconds, the best-sounding record of the decade ("Sweet Emotion") flickered on the horizon.

Touring was paying off. After the first album they still rode to high school dances, university gymnasiums, and ski lodges in their station wagon. But more kids started trying to jump onstage. The audiences grew from two hundred to two thousand. In September fans at Boston College smashed the bathroom windows to get into the hall. That month the band left Massachusetts to play the rest of the New England states, then headed down south, then back up to the Midwest, farther up to Canada, over to the northwest coast, then down to LA. By 1974, Tyler said, they'd played every state in the country three times.

Even though they were from Boston, Tyler wrote in his memoir, "our core audience was always the Blue Army—the hard-core kids from the Midwest. They were the Blue Army because they all wore denim jackets; the place was a sea of blue."[6]

"Detroit, Cincinnati, Cleveland. We felt like if we could win the heart of America, the rest of the country would follow," Perry said. "And through constant touring we learned what kinds of songs and grooves went over best. As a songwriter you start thinking in terms of: 'If I was sitting in the audience, what would I want to hear?'"[7]

Tyler wrote, "Judy Carne—the English comic who starred in the iconic TV show *Laugh-In* and dated Joe for a stint in the early seventies—thought we were the voice of the mills and the malls. And those working-class towns were the places that embraced us early on."[8]

Rolling Stone called the band's music Wrench Rock, labeled them greasers. Their fans were the same auto-shop kids that would have dug "Train Kept A-Rollin'" back in 1956 when Elvis's neighbors Johnny Burnette and the Rock and Roll Trio recorded it. The only differences were denim instead of leather, bad acid and Quaaludes, more distortion—and long hair down the back instead of greased-up ducktails, perfect for whipping while you lost yourself in the new sonic cataclysms. An early sighting of the new tradition was the DVD for the 1970 Zeppelin gig at the Royal Albert Hall where fans headbanged in the front row.[9] Black Sabbath's Ozzy Osbourne and Deep Purple's Ian Gillan did the move onstage.[10]

Lester Bangs had promulgated his concept of "punk" by cramming the term into many of his reviews throughout the first half of the '70s. Presumably his fellow critic Mike Saunders (later of the punk band Angry Samoans) took notice, because he began using the term "heavy metal" with equal vigor, perhaps derived from a lyric in Steppenwolf's "Born to Be Wild," or from Beat writer William Burroughs's character The Heavy Metal Kid from his early '60s *Nova Trilogy*. A blogger named A. S. Van Dorston chronicled all the times Saunders used the term in his reviews in the early '70s.[11] In a 1970 Humble Pie review for *Rolling Stone,* he brandished the term as an insult, but by 1971 in *Creem* he was using it positively for Sir Lord Baltimore. The following year he used it in multiple reviews in *Rolling Stone* and *Phonograph Record* magazine for bands like Deep Purple and Uriah Heep (and even Fanny), dubbing Sabbath the "Dark Princes of Heavy Metal." That year other writers like Dave Marsh in *Creem* started picking it up as well. By 1973 *NME* followed suit, as did *Melody Maker* in 1974.

In Saunders's April '73 article "A Brief Survey of the State of Metal Music Today" for *Phonograph Record,* he declared, "When you get right down to it, the story of heavy metal rock has been the tale of Led Zeppelin. As indicated by its name, heavy metal has been an evolution of heavy rock—you know, the stuff that emerged back in 1967."[12] Bands he included in the genre were Sabbath, Alice Cooper, Deep Purple, Grand Funk, Uriah Heep, and even the Stooges and Blue Oyster Cult.

Sabbath's guitarist Tony Iommi said, "The term heavy metal came about from a journalist when I came back from America (in the '70s). He said, 'You're playing heavy metal,' and I said 'No, it's heavy rock—what's that?'"[13]

Bassist Geezer Butler said, "At first we didn't like being called heavy metal. But everyone likes to put you into certain pigeon holes, so we sort of got used to it. And then instead of it being derogatory, it became a whole lifestyle."[14]

❊

Black Sabbath knew exactly what the burnouts, heshers, stoners, and dirt bags wanted because they *were* their audience. Osbourne dropped out at fifteen to work in construction, in plumbing, and at the slaughterhouse, serving ninety days in prison for robbing a clothes store, briefly becoming a skinhead.[15] Iommi worked in a sheet metal factory where the tips of two fingers were sliced off. He believed his dreams of being a musician were destroyed until the factory manager played him a record by guitarist Django Reinhardt, who also lost the use of some fingers. Iommi began using banjo strings because they were lighter and tuned the guitar low to compensate, creating his unique sound.[16] Early on the band called itself Earth. (Also one of Springsteen's early band names. His group Steel Mill later opened for Sabbath.)

Their ominous odes to marauding iron golems, paranoia, "hands of doom," and "burned out confusion" were perfect for the average day of a zitty delinquent: sulking through high school, getting suspended, scoring weed at the arcade, fighting at the Brownsville Station concert, screaming at parents, finally retreating to the bedroom to write poetry about nuclear apocalypse under black light posters of sword and sorcery.

The surprising thing for those put off by the group's Boris Karloff vampire-movie name was how Osbourne clowned like a Keith Moon sheepdog onstage. Cute but schlubby, though he could care less, he tripped onstage bare-chested, clapping and yelling, "Are you high? Let's have a party!" He mostly left the lyric writing to Butler, as he was too busy destroying bathrooms with sledgehammers, setting money or drummer Bill Ward's beard on fire, or almost killing Ward by spraying him with gold paint, blocking his pores and causing a seizure. Osbourne boasted of sleeping with seven women a night on tour, without concern for being politically correct. "Other bands' roadies got better looking groupies than we did. They would be so bad you'd have to put a bag over their head. The really bad ones we called Two-Baggers. One bag for her head, to stop you seeing what you were doing, and one bag for your head—in case anyone came in, so they wouldn't know it was you."[17]

But Iommi brooded that the band got no respect from the music press. The critics resented that Sabbath's LPs flew off the shelf from the moment of their debut, without radio airplay or media coverage, due to both the satanic imagery and their sound, which, even more than Zeppelin, split rock into the era before the band and the era after. Younger metal fans no longer consider Zeppelin metal, but Sabbath's minor-chord sludge still sounds heavy. Yet their music was surprisingly nimble and jazzy, even prog, their signature "Devil's tritone" tuning derived from classical music. For their fifth album, Iommi was determined to make a record the critics could no longer dismiss.

But the band was worn down by incessant touring, booze, and the coke they'd been introduced to by American roadies. Fisticuffs between members were not unusual. To Iommi's dismay, Stevie Wonder had filled up their favorite room at the Record Plant with TONTO, the giant synthesizer. Iommi stayed up for days at a time trying to come up with riffs but got nothing. He cut his hair short and shaved his mustache off. Still nothing. "We almost thought that we were finished as a band," said Butler.[18]

Finally, they decided Los Angeles's tony Bel Air neighborhood was not a conducive atmosphere, and searched for a crumbling castle to record in like Zeppelin. They found one in Gloucestershire's Forest of Dean: Clearwell Castle, built in 1728.

"We rehearsed in the armoury there and one night I was walking down the corridor with Ozzy and we saw this figure in a black cloak," recalled Iommi. The year before, at the Hollywood Bowl, there had been a man who hid backstage to stab Iommi before security apprehended him ("one of these like Satanists or religious freaks or whatever he was," Iommi said). So Iommi was particularly unsettled by the idea of nefarious strangers lurking about. "We followed this figure back into the armoury and there was absolutely no one there. Whoever it was had disappeared into thin air! The people that owned the castle knew all about this ghost and they said, 'Oh yes, that's the ghost of so and so. We were like 'What!?'"[19]

Sabbath biographer Mick Wall recounted that the female ghost's "modus operandi was apparently to enter locked rooms and leave them a mess, as though a strong wind had blown though the room."[20] (That was probably Osbourne's MO, too.) She would also reputedly "sing lullabies to her ghost child on the landing at night while playing a tinkling musical box."[21]

"We had to leave in the end, everybody terrified of each other because we were playing jokes on each other and nobody knew who was doing it," Iommi said. "We used to leave and drive all the way home and drive back the next day. It was really silly."[22]

"We weren't so much the Lords of Darkness as the Lords of Chicken-shit when it came to that kind of thing," Osbourne wrote. "We wound each other up so much none of us got any sleep. You'd just lie there with your eyes wide open, expecting an empty suit of armour to walk into your bedroom at any second to shove a dagger up your arsc."[23]

Ward actually slept with a dagger. Osbourne, meanwhile, fell asleep with his boots in the fireplace and almost set the castle ablaze.

But the exercise proved fruitful. "We rehearsed in the dungeons and it was really creepy but it had some atmosphere, it conjured up things, and stuff started coming out again," Butler said. "Once Tony came out with the initial riff for 'Sabbath Bloody Sabbath,' we went, 'We're baaaack!'"[24]

The album's title track boasted the most menacing chainsaw riff of the year. Guns N' Roses' Slash maintained, "The outro to 'Sabbath Bloody Sabbath' is the heaviest shit I have ever heard in my life." But what took the song to the next level was the dynamic shift between snarling verse and lush, mellow chorus. Their LPs often had a soft track you wouldn't expect from them, and here they captured both musical sides in one song. When Osbourne railed against bastards who lied "but you don't want to know," perhaps he was alluding to the manager they began to suspect was ripping them off (driving in a Rolls while they tooled around in VWs), though for the time being it was easier to get wasted than to confront him.

"Looking for Today" remade the song into an upbeat track you could dance to—if you ignored the lyrics about a band "rotting in decay" and doomed to fall because they just lived for the moment and didn't think ahead. It was a galloping dry run for Osbourne's later solo hit "Crazy Train," with groovy acoustic chorus featuring flute and organ. There was an acoustic instrumental with harpsichord named "Fluff" in honor of Alan "Fluff" Freeman, a deejay who played them when others wouldn't. Off duty, Iommi listened to softies like Peter, Paul and Mary or the Carpenters.[25] Rick Wakeman, their friend from Yes, came by to play keyboards on "Sabbra Cadabra." "Spiral Architect" closed the album with orchestra and bagpipes, the album's second meditation on the cosmic implications of sperm ("National Acrobat" being the first).

The album sleeve, by future *Star Wars* and *Indiana Jones* poster painter Drew Struzan, recalled the covers Frank Frazetta created for horror comics like *Eerie* and *Creepy*. Both the front and the back featured men at the moment of their death. On the cover, an evil man is mauled by demons in a bed with the number of the beast on the headboard. On the back, a good man is tended to by his brokenhearted loved ones.[26]

Osbourne considered it their last real album as a functioning group. Iommi called it their pinnacle. It earned their first rave from *Rolling Stone*.

✳

Zeppelin visited Sabbath at the castle and jammed, though
Ward hated it when Bonham played his drums because he'd wreck them.
Plant and Bonham grew up in Birmingham, England, as all the members
of Sabbath had. Zeppelin was Sabbath's favorite group; they were originally
afraid to release their hit "Paranoid" because it was a reconfiguration of
"Communication Breakdown."[27] Bonham served as Iommi's best man in
November.

Around that time Zeppelin reviewed the footage from their Madison
Square Garden dates the previous July, the basis for their concert film *The
Song Remains the Same*. Much of the footage was unusable, so they re-
shot some of the songs lip-syncing on an English soundstage (by which
time Bonham was twenty pounds heavier) and also added some fantasy
sequences. For a band that privately hoped to improve its standing with
snobby outlets like *Rolling Stone* and *The Village Voice*, these Dungeons and
Dragons–like interludes were surprisingly cheesy. On the plus side, they
helped viewers stay awake when they watched the 137-minute film in midnight movie screenings, a grueling rite of passage for Zeppelin fans. (Even
label head Ahmet Ertegun fell asleep when he had to watch the movie.[28])

In the "Rain Song" segment, Plant sails a Viking boat, eats mushrooms,
rides his horse to a misty ruined castle with a raven, and swordfights to
save a maiden. Page climbs a mountain where he finds the Hermit from the
Tarot deck (and *Zoso*'s album cover). The guru ages backward into Jimmy,
then a child, then an embryo, then his wand casts a rainbow—*2001: A
Space Odyssey* meets *Spinal Tap*. John Paul Jones menaces his wife in a
Mr. Hyde mask to "No Quarter." The band's manager, Peter Grant, and tour
manager, Richard Cole, play gangsters mowing down their enemies with
machine guns. In real life, Grant drew on his past as a wrestler to force pro-
moters to reduce their cut from 40 percent to 10 percent, changing the way
the concert industry worked.[29]

Page proved himself to be a master of the art of guitar posing in the
same league as Townshend and Richards with his double-necked ax, which
gave him the ability to switch between six-string and twelve-string. He
brandished his violin bow like a magus casting a spell over the audience.
Plant threw his hair back, trusty bulge in jeans, and asked, "Does anybody
remember laughter?" during "Stairway to Heaven."

Plant composed the lyrics for that song after reading Lewis Spence's
The Magic Arts in Celtic Britain, partially improvising the lines one night

beside the fire as Page strummed the guitar.[30] Plant had the vision for their next epic as he was driving through the Sahara Desert while vacationing in southern Morocco after the 1973 North American tour. "It was a single-track road which neatly cut through the desert. Two miles to the East and West were ridges of sand rock. It basically looked like you were driving down a channel, this dilapidated road, and there was seemingly no end to it."[31]

At the end of the year, Page and Bonham recorded a demo Page called "Kashmir,"[32] inspired by his trips to India, so Plant incorporated the name into his lyrics about a wasteland of sun and sand. But when it came time for Plant to record his vocals, he found "it was quite a task, 'cause I couldn't sing it."[33]

After a bout with the flu in January, his voice had changed, and he'd undergone vocal surgery, not speaking for three weeks. Onstage he could no longer hit some of the high notes and had to sing a number of songs in lower octaves than before.

"It was like the song was bigger than me. It's true: I was petrified, it's true. It was painful; I was virtually in tears."[34]

But ultimately, as the lyrics had it, "the father of the four winds filled his sails," and he found himself wailing like a muezzin. Bonham's drums led the Bollywood brass and strings like a stately march of prehistoric behemoths, their heads swaying far above in the distance.

And then, "across the sea of years," almost four decades later, President Obama lowered medals around the necks of the three surviving band members for their lifetime contribution to American culture at the Kennedy Center Honors in 2012.

"It's been said that a generation of people survived teenage angst with a pair of headphones and a Zeppelin album," Obama said. "Of course, these guys also redefined the rock 'n' roll lifestyle. We do not have video of this, but there were some hotel rooms trashed and mayhem all around, so it's fitting that we're doing this in a room with windows that are about three inches thick and Secret Service all around. So guys, settle down—these paintings are valuable."

*

If We Make It Through December

Amid the oil crisis, Watergate disillusion, militants, cults, and faux-satanic rockers, the one thing both sides of the cultural divide share is nostalgia for '50s rock. *American Graffiti*'s director George Lucas (and its triple-platinum soundtrack) preserve the rituals of an earlier, more wholesome adolescence in danger of expiring.

Jerusalem remembers in the days of her affliction and bitterness all the precious things that were hers from days of old.
—LAMENTATIONS

Well, it wasn't supposed to go down that way.
NEIL YOUNG, "TIRED EYES"

*

When Merle Haggard asked his guitarist Roy Nichols how things were going with his wife, Nichols replied, "It'll be fine if we make it through December."[1] The line inspired Haggard to write a song about a man struggling to keep a brave equanimity as he gets laid off at the factory while trying to save enough to buy his little girl presents for the holiday.

Released on October 27, it was the No. 1 country song for the last two weeks of the year. It was the kind of song you never heard in the wall-to-wall Christmas programming, a song for weary parents skidding through the sludge reminding themselves to love this time of year as they made their way to the stores after work.

This year the ordeal was compounded by OPEC's oil embargo. The song kept you philosophical while sitting in your car for half an hour waiting to get to the pump, windshield wipers slapping the snow, watching your gas gauge go down while you waited to buy gas. Then you realized the price had increased more than once in the last twenty-four hours and got pissed off all over again. Or maybe it was playing as you sped toward the station, running on empty, only to find a sign waiting for you: SORRY, NO GAS TODAY.

It was Haggard's sixteenth country No. 1, though none of his songs had broken the pop Top 50 before. This one, however, went to No. 28, his best showing ever on that chart. Critic Dave Marsh called it "the first record—perhaps the first meaningful piece of pop culture—to come to grips with the fears, frustrations, and hopes-against-hope of the workers thrown into disarray by the initial round of deprivation as the world economy cooled after three decades of post–World War II expansion."[2]

*

Merle Haggard was more of an outlaw than the Outlaws Waylon and Willie. He lived out the Bakersfield version of *The 400 Blows*, breaking out of juvenile detention centers seventeen times by his own count, hopping trains, escaping to Oregon with a girl from juvie,[3] acting out his future hit "I Am a Lonesome Fugitive." When he tried to rob a roadhouse he landed in San Quentin. Johnny Cash performed for the prisoners and inspired Haggard to turn his life around. Years later when Haggard appeared on Cash's show, Cash suggested they talk about it, but Haggard was worried about advertising his criminal past. "If you let me tell them in my way," Cash assured him, "they'll love you like we do. And no one will ever be able to harm you with it."[4] So on the air they reminisced about Cash's San Quentin performance.

"That's funny, Merle. I don't remember you being on that show."

"I wasn't, John. I was in the audience."[5]

Haggard knew the Nashville/Austin Outlaws but wasn't in their scene, partly because he was from Bakersfield on the West Coast, which had already been rebelling against Nashville for a decade. Also, his gambling addiction alienated Jennings, who felt Haggard took advantage of him one night in 1969. Jennings's bassist Chuck Conway had been killed in an auto accident en route to a gig in Peoria. Jennings had been traveling separately and soldiered through his live performance on booze and pills. Afterward, even though he was "wobbling," he played poker with Haggard and his manager, and they won all the $5,000 in cash Jennings had on him. "We've never been close since that night," Jennings wrote. "I can still remember their faces. When I was broke, they said their goodbyes and left. I never forgot that."[6] Haggard later owned up to his gambling addiction in his autobiography.

Also, Haggard stayed away from Willie Nelson's Dripping Springs hippie-redneck festivals because he was the anti-hippie spokesman for Nixon's Silent Majority. "Okie from Muskogee" praised the city's residents for not burning their draft cards or smoking marijuana (even though band members were smoking it on the bus when the song was created[7]). "Fightin' Side of Me" snarled, "If you don't love it, leave it."

Nixon's wife, Pat, invited Haggard to play the White House for her birthday on March 17. Nixon had been shoring up his country music base since 1970 when he created Country Music Month. But Haggard wrote in his memoir that he was dismayed to find the president's crowd as unresponsive as "a bunch of department store mannequins."[8] Chief of staff H. R. Haldeman wrote in his diary, "The 'Evening' was pretty much a flop because the audience had no appreciation for country/western music . . . except when Haggard did his 'Okie from Muskogee.'"[9]

Later Haggard realized the White House had been trying to hide its anxiety. It was the same day that James McCord gave his letter to Judge Sirica stating that the Watergate burglars had been pressured to perjure themselves.

✻

Eighty-five percent of the population watched the Watergate hearings in May and June, but then people started to tune out, bored . . . until John Dean testified that he believed Nixon could have been taping their conversations.

On Friday, July 13, the Senate Watergate Committee staff conducted a nonpublic background interview with deputy assistant to the president Alexander Butterfield. When they asked him if Dean was correct about being recorded, Butterfield replied, "I was wondering if someone would ask that. There is tape in the Oval Office."[10] Aaron Latham recounted in *New York Magazine*, "He paused to confess that he had hoped no one would ask him that question . . . [but] had decided he would have to respond truthfully and candidly if asked."[11]

On July 23, Special Prosecutor Archibald Cox and the Senate committee demanded the tapes from Nixon. Nixon refused, so they subpoenaed them. On August 29, Nixon addressed the nation on television, saying he was not going to turn over the tapes because they contained national security secrets. He asserted that he had the right to do so through executive privilege.

"This is kind of a strange country, isn't it?" Johnny Carson asked. "Judges can see *Deep Throat* but they can't listen to those tapes."

Viewing the chaotic state of the US government, the Organization of the Petroleum Exporting Countries realized that the opportunity they had been hoping for had arrived.

✳

After World War II the US mutated into a nation dependent on the car. Per *The Prize: The Epic Quest for Oil, Money, and Power* by Daniel Yergin, that period saw the population in cities rise by ten million while the population of suburbs rose by eighty-five million, enabled by the newly built freeways.[12] Fast food chains and drive-in restaurants exploded. In 1946 there were eight shopping centers; by the early '80s there were twenty thousand.[13] The landscape transformed to one of strip malls, motels, and brutalist office buildings.

The Arab world wanted Israel out of the Middle East, and had long wanted to use its oil as leverage against the US to make it happen, but for decades the US had a surplus of its own oil. Then in the late '60s the American surplus ran out (a state of affairs that would last until the fracking boom of the mid-2000s). By 1971, the country was forced to increase its imports and began rush-ordering nuclear power plants to try to offset its dependence on fossil fuels. The clock was ticking, as in the opening act of the disaster film *The Poseidon Adventure,* one of the year's highest-grossing movies.

In the old days, the Western oil companies (Standard, Texaco, Gulf) told the Arab nations the price they were going to buy the oil for. Then OPEC managed to secure a veto. Gradually, they began to negotiate. Now OPEC wanted to dictate what they charged for their own oil.

Concurrently, Egypt's Anwar Sadat planned an attack to regain the land his country lost to Israel in 1967's Six-Day War. In Saudi Arabia, the people sympathized with Egypt, and King Faisal did not want to look too accommodating to the US. He issued a statement on August 30: "We are deeply concerned that if the United States does not change its policy in the Middle East and continues to side with Zionism, then, I am afraid, such course of action will affect our relations with our American friends because it will place us in an untenable position in the Arab world and vis-a-vis the countries which Zionism seeks to destroy."[14]

Faisal gave half a billion to Sadat for war against Israel and told him to keep the war going long enough so that OPEC could use it as justification for an oil embargo. Egypt and Syria attacked Israel on October 6, Yom Kippur, the holiest day on the Jewish calendar, when the country was quiet. It was their own Pearl Harbor. Within three days, Israel lost five hundred tanks and forty-nine planes.

The Soviet Union resupplied Egypt and Syria, so the US began resupplying Israel with strategic airlifts. On October 16, the Arab nations of OPEC announced that in retaliation for US support of Israel, they would raise their prices from $3 a barrel to $3.65, a 21 percent increase. By the end of the year they would raise it up to $4.75–5.11 a barrel.[15] They also embargoed Great Britain, the Netherlands, Canada, and Japan, the countries that—alongside the US—consumed half the world's energy. In May gas had been 31 cents a gallon in the US. Now it jumped from 39 cents to 50 cents, to 70 cents by December. Cars averaged eight miles a gallon.

Saudi minister of petroleum Ahmed Zaki Yamani proclaimed, "This is a moment for which I have been waiting a long time. The moment has come. We are masters of our own commodity."[16]

✳

On October 10, Vice President Spiro Agnew resigned after being indicted for taking bribes and pleading guilty to tax evasion. Nixon, meanwhile, responded to subpoenas for the tapes by sending in written summaries of their contents. Special Prosecutor Cox insisted they needed the actual tapes. Nixon countered that he would allow Senator John C. Stennis (a Democrat from Mississippi) to listen to the tapes and summarize them, leaving out parts that were important to keep secret for national security. The joke in town was that Stennis was hard of hearing. Again, Cox said no. So on October 20 Nixon ordered Attorney General Elliot Richardson to fire Cox. Richardson refused, as did Deputy Attorney General William Ruckelshaus; both resigned. Robert Bork became the acting attorney general and fired Cox. Anchorman John Chancellor led off the *NBC Nightly News* with "Good evening. The country tonight is in the midst of what may be the most serious constitutional crisis in its history." Two days later journalist David Broder wrote in *The Washington Post* that the event "is being called the 'Saturday night massacre.'"

On October 23, Nixon handed over some of the tapes. Nevertheless, the Democrats in Congress introduced many new impeachment resolutions. The next day, Nixon got drunk, ranted (per Secretary of State Henry Kissinger), probably took some of his prescribed Valium, and went to sleep. It was then a telegram arrived from USSR general secretary Leonid Brezhnev. The tide of the war had turned, and it looked like Israel was on the verge of defeating Egypt and Syria. The US and USSR had helped broker a cease-fire, but both sides were ignoring it. Brezhnev was concerned Israel might end up with more land than it started with before the war. In the telegram he said both the US and USSR should send military to the region to make sure both sides maintained the cease-fire. "It is necessary to adhere without delay. I'll say it straight. If you find it impossible to act jointly with us in this matter we should be faced with the necessity urgently to consider the question of taking appropriate steps unilaterally."[17]

Kissinger tried to call Nixon to discuss it at 9:50 p.m. but chief of staff Alexander Haig insisted Nixon was asleep for the night and could not be awakened. So the two of them, along with three other military officials, held their own National Security Council meeting without the president (or vice president, as Gerald Ford would not be sworn in until December). They assumed Brezhnev was trying to bully them because he knew Nixon was falling apart, so they set the global nuclear alert level to DEFCON III, one step under nuclear war, the highest since the Cuban Missile Crisis. They sent three warships to the Mediterranean, called in sixty to seventy-five B-52 nuclear bombers from Guam, and put the 82nd Airborne on alert, mobilizing thousands of soldiers.[18]

The Soviets were shocked at the intensity of the US response, assuming it had been Nixon's call. (He later took credit for it.) Neither the Soviets nor the US wanted to risk having their own war in the region, and the Soviets dropped the issue. The Yom Kippur War ended on October 25.

Israel would eventually return Sinai to Egypt, but that was years away. In the short term, Israel had won, so OPEC cut production by 25 percent on November 5. The embargo continued into the following year.

❊

On November 17, Nixon appeared at the annual conference for Associated Press managing editors in Disney World. During a question-and-answer session he gave what became his most infamous sound bite: "I made my mistakes, but in all of my years of public life, I have never profited, never profited from public service—I earned every cent. And in all of my years of public life, I have never obstructed justice. And I think, too, that

I could say that in my years of public life, that I welcome this kind of examination, because people have got to know whether or not their president is a crook. Well, I am not a crook. I have earned everything I have got."

Four days later, on November 21, Nixon's lawyer admitted to US District Judge John Sirica that one of the relevant tapes had eighteen and a half minutes missing from it. Nixon's chief of staff H. R. Haldeman's notes indicated that at that time on June 20, 1972, they were discussing arrests at the Watergate hotel and how to manage public perception of the event.

On November 26, Nixon's personal secretary, Rose Mary Woods, testified that she was partially responsible. She had been transcribing the tapes when the phone rang. When she leaned over to answer it, she accidentally pushed down on the pedal of the transcription machine and hit the record button and taped over part of the tape. She agreed to pose for photos demonstrating how she stretched to reach the phone while keeping her foot on the pedal. The press dubbed it "the Rose Mary Stretch."[19] But she insisted she only accidentally taped over five minutes; she didn't know how the other thirteen minutes got erased.

Carson cracked that Nixon's favorite ice cream was "im*peach*ment." Outside the White House, demonstrators carried HONK TO IMPEACH signs. Dickie Goodman's comedy record "Watergrate" made No. 42 on the charts. David Allan Coe released "How High's the Watergate, Martha," backed by "Tricky Dickey, the Only Son of Kung Fu." Tom T. Hall released "Watergate Blues."

Paul Simon's "American Tune" debuted on the Hot 100 on December 1, eventually making it up to 35. To the melody of Bach's *St. Matthew Passion*,[20] Simon sang about dreaming that he was dying, with the Statue of Liberty sailing away to sea. "You can't be forever blessed."

✳

"Are the good times really over for good?" Haggard asked years later in his song of the same name, in which he looked back to "when the country was strong . . . back before Nixon lied to us all on T.V."

If you went to the movies you thought so. *Serpico*'s police force was racked with corruption. The James Dean–like protagonist of *Badlands* was a charismatic young psychopath. So was Harvey Keitel's best friend Robert De Niro in *Mean Streets*; when Keitel tried to help him he got shot for his trouble. When *Deliverance*'s "Dueling Banjos" came across the airwaves (it made No. 2 in February), it was hard not to think about what happened to Ned Beatty in the movie. In *Soylent Green,* overpopulation reduced the poor in the slums to cannibalism. When Roman Polanski filmed

Chinatown in the fall, he changed Robert Towne's ending so the evil father wins, a truer resolution for someone whose wife had been murdered by Charles Manson.

The movies even looked different. They used to be shot in Technicolor on sound stages with bright floodlights, richly colorful. Now technology allowed them to be shot on location in low available light, making them look grainier and grittier.[21]

Comic books had unhappy endings now, too. In the June issue of *The Amazing Spider-Man*, the Green Goblin threw Spider Man's girlfriend, Gwen Stacy, off the George Washington Bridge. When Spider-Man shot out his web to catch her, he inadvertently caused her death. The editors felt compelled to clarify on the letters page four issues later, "It saddens us to say that the whiplash effect she underwent when Spidey's webbing stopped her so suddenly was, in fact, what killed her."

On the news, former John Birch Society member Phyllis Schlafly argued that the Equal Rights Amendment threatened the very foundation of American womanhood. If the amendment was ratified, she insisted, housewives, widows, and divorcées would lose child support, alimony, and "dependent wife" Social Security benefits. Men would be able to leave their wives and not have to support them. Women would no longer be the preferred parent in divorce custody cases. Women would be eligible for the draft, bathrooms would become unisex, and all college dormitories would become coed.

On the other side of the spectrum, *Village Voice* writer Jill Johnston advocated separatism in *Lesbian Nation*. "Feminists who still sleep with men are delivering their most vital energies to the oppressor. . . . Until all women are lesbians there will be no true political revolution."[22] The only thing the conservatives and radical feminists agreed on was that porn was a plague that was getting worse. Upon its release in December 1972, *Behind the Green Door* with Marilyn Chambers became the fourth highest grossing film worldwide for the year. *Deep Throat* director Gerard Damiano returned with *The Devil in Miss Jones*.

Militants were still out there, too, fighting for "the destruction of US imperialism and the achievement of a classless world: world communism," per the Weather Underground manifesto, though it was difficult to interest people in revolution now that the draft was over, amid a twenty-year rise in income with low unemployment. Where the Guess Who once sang "Share the Land," their spin-off band Bachman-Turner Overdrive now sang "Takin' Care of Business." Nevertheless, on May 18 the Weather Underground protested the police shooting of ten-year-old, black Clifford Glover by setting off a bomb that hit three cruisers of the 103rd Police Precinct in Queens. An off-duty Transit Authority patrolman was injured. On September 28, they bombed an International Telephone and Telegraph Corporation building in New York because the company helped fund a coup in Chile.

In Berkeley a new twenty-one-person militant group, the Symbionese Liberation Army, formed, partially inspired by the movie *The Spook Who Sat by the Door,* about a black CIA agent who leads the black revolution.[23] On November 6, they assassinated the first black superintendent of the Oakland Unified School District because they believed he planned to institute Orwellian student ID cards and station police officers in schools, though they were actually mistaken as to his position on those issues. In three months they would kidnap Patty Hearst.

Lyndon LaRouche plotted to take over trade unions to launch a Trotskyite revolution. After being expelled from the Socialist Workers Party, he became a teacher at the Free School in New York and built an organization (National Caucus of Labor Committees) of six hundred members in twenty-five cities. From April to September they carried out Operation Mop Up, rumbling with other communist organizations like the Socialist Workers Party and Communist Party to gain control of American Communism, fighting with chains, pipes, bats, and nunchucks.[24] Inside his organization LaRouche used brainwashing and deprogramming techniques to "ego strip" members.[25]

By now there were so many cults that Esalen held a conference in December in San Francisco called "Spiritual and Therapeutic Tyranny: The Willingness to Submit." Esalen's founders were concerned about groups they had originally promoted, such as Oscar Ichazo's Arica and Werner Erhard's EST, and had stopped holding encounter sessions because they felt some group leaders abused their power. Across the country, kids who'd gotten deep into acid yearned for gurus to tell them what to do so they could be here now and not have to sweat the future; "Acid Fascism," *Rolling Stone* dubbed it. The cults ran the gamut from the benign to the unspeakable, from evangelicals inspired by Hare Krishnas to rediscover speaking in tongues while utilizing guitar and drums, to Father Yod and the Source Family, Bhagwan Shree Rajneesh, Reverend Moon, Scientology, Synanon, Jim Jones. Parents fretted over children who cut family ties and gave away their assets. In August the *CBS Evening News* followed deprogrammer Ted Patrick on a "rescue mission" as he abducted Kathy Crampton from the Love Israel Cult, a.k.a. Church of Jesus Christ at Armageddon, isolated her in a motel, and tried to get her to disavow the group's teachings. She submitted for a few days, then went back shortly afterward.[26]

Patrick got his start as a deprogrammer attempting to rescue someone from the Children of God, the most infamous of the cults.[27] In 1973, the organization began the practice of "flirty fishing," wherein women slept with men outside the organization in order to convert them to the group, in reality funding their communes through prostitution. Most heinously, the cult encouraged the sexual abuse of its children. Actor River Phoenix, who grew up in the cult, stated he was abused at age four.[28]

⁂

"Are we rolling downhill like a snowball headed for hell?" Haggard asked in the song that lamented Nixon's lies. If you listened to the kids' favorite bands, it seemed so.

The Stones started the fashion for devil rock with *Their Satanic Majesties Request* and "Sympathy for the Devil." Now *Goats Head Soup* featured Jagger in some Luciferian veil, like a head of flame à la Dr. Strange's nemesis the dread Dormammu. Inside the gatefold the band all wore weird veils, like muggers trying to autoerotically asphyxiate themselves in plastic bags. On the back cover, Richards's head seemed to be going up in black flame. The opening track sang of "Dancing with Mr. D."

In 1969, an American band named Coven with a bassist named Oz Osbourne released a song called "Black Sabbath." Shortly thereafter the English band Earth with the singer Ozzy Osbourne recorded a different song with the same name and received such a powerful response they renamed themselves Black Sabbath. Their song was inspired by the time bassist Geezer got into satanism, painted his room black with upside-down crosses, then one night woke up and thought he saw a black shape at the foot of the bed and got so freaked out he repainted the room and started wearing crosses. For the music Iommi employed the diminished triad or diminished fifth, called the "Devil's tritone," a sound used in medieval music to symbolize the devil or crucifixion, often heard in horror movies, *The Twilight Zone* and *The Munsters*.[29] They cashed in with the morbid kids who bought scary comic books even though they knew the images would torment them at bedtime. Their audiences filled up with Hells Angels, witches, devil worshippers, and Jesus freaks. A famous tour story concerned the night the hallway of their hotel filled with weird hooded types chanting and holding black candles. The band called each other in their various hotel rooms to synchronize, then opened their doors at the same time and blew out the candles and sang "Happy Birthday" to the weirdos.[30] All the members took to wearing crosses that Geezer's father made.

When it came time for Jimmy Page to pick a guru, as Harrison had picked the Maharishi or Townshend had picked Meher Baba, Page picked Aleister Crowley, a bisexual junkie who said a spirit dictated a new religion to him that boiled down to *do whatever you want and freak out conservatives*. Page inscribed Crowley's phrases "Do what thou wilt" and "So mote it be" into the runout grooves of *Led Zeppelin III* and bought Crowley's five-bedroom mansion on Loch Ness. Page appeared there in the opening segment of the film *The Song Remains the Same,* eyes glowing demonically red thanks to special effects. For their record label, Swan Song, Page picked an image of a winged man falling, maybe Icarus, probably Lucifer being cast out of Heaven. The most unsettling thing, though, was the cover of *Houses of the Holy* by the Hipgnosis design team. Young naked children climb ancient volcanic rocks in Northern Ireland (actually just two kids, brother and sister Stefan and Samantha Gates, superimposed a number of times).[31] *The Song Remains the Same* featured Robert Plant's kids frolicking nude in a stream, in "back to the garden" hippie freedom mode, with Plant and his wife, so maybe the cover was in that vein. But the inside gatefold showed a man holding a child up to the heavens in a Stonehenge-like setting, which was jarring in context of Page's promotion of Crowley, who wrote about human sacrifice—though some writers maintain Crowley used the term as a tongue-in-cheek reference to masturbation.[32]

Alice Cooper developed his 1971 "Dead Babies" song (in which a drunken mother fails to notice when her kid overdoses on aspirin) into the *Billion Dollar Babies* album and stage show. He decapitated hundreds of baby dolls and mannequins with an ax, trying to top his shticks with electric chairs, guillotines, and boa constrictors. The album was a transatlantic No. 1, and the tour made more money than the Stones' and Zeppelin's.[33] In the single "No More Mr. Nice Guy" he goes to church and the reverend punches him in the nose. In real life his father was a pastor. He appeared on *Hollywood Squares* in March with Sammy Davis Jr., Milton Berle, Bill Bixby, Janet Leigh, and Paul Lynde.

Meanwhile, Kiss's Gene Simmons amped up his Demon performances: slavering DuPont fake blood like Christopher Lee in *Horror of Dracula,* stalking the stage like the Ymir from *20 Million Miles to Earth,* learning from a magician how to spit fire.[34] George Clinton used Luciferian imagery inspired by the Process Church of the Final Judgement in a number of his

Funkadelic songs until he realized it was scaring off too many fans, particularly female ones.[35]

Even Sammy Davis Jr. got in on the act, following up "The Candy Man," the fifth-bestselling pop song of 1972, with *Poor Devil,* a made-for-TV movie NBC aired on Valentine's Day with an eye toward turning it into a TV series. *It's a Wonderful Life* told the story of an angel helping to save a suicidal man, and this movie featured Davis as a demon charged with convincing Jack Klugman to sell his soul. Christopher Lee played Davis's boss, Satan, giving the devil's horn salute with an inverse pentagram in his office.[36] In real life Davis had attended orgies at the Church of Satan, where he bumped into his hairstylist Jay Sebring in a hood, a year or two before Sebring was killed in the Manson murders. "It was a short lived interest, but I still have many friends in the Church of Satan," Davis wrote in his memoir. Anton LaVey made him a Warlock II.

Infinitely more terrifying was *The Exorcist,* released the day after Christmas. Author William Peter Blatty had been inspired to write the novel after growing irate that *Rosemary's Baby* did not confirm the existence of God. Director William Friedkin did not share Blatty's fear of higher forces. To get the facial expression he wanted, he slapped real-life priest Father William O'Malley, who played Father Dyer. To make it look realistic when the possessed girl (Linda Blair) flings her mother (Ellen Burstyn) across the room, Friedkin told the stunt coordinator to yank the wire tied around Burstyn hard, and, unfortunately, permanently injured her spine.

People stood in the snow before dawn to line up for the movie. *Variety* quoted one attendee, "I wanted to see what everyone was throwing up about."[37] The film inspired a slate of demonic-children films like *The Omen.* It seemed particularly resonant to those parents tempted to call deprogrammers like Ted Patrick, the ones whose children had joined new religions, chanting words in foreign tongues.

Bowie sang of being "immersed in Crowley's uniform of imagery" in the haunting "Quicksand," then added the other favorite trope of would-be evil rock stars, Nazism, into the mix, singing that he lived "in a silent film portraying Himmler's sacred realm of dream reality." Himmler was the Nazi who brought occult rituals into the SS; Hitler put him in charge of the concentration camps.

In the *Ziggy Stardust* concert film from his final performance in July, Bowie hangs the lightning bolt from the cover of *Aladdin Sane* over the stage. The shape has mutated, a little closer to the SS symbol, not unlike Kiss's logo, which resembled the SS symbol so much it was banned in

Germany. Ace Frehley was a collector of Nazi memorabilia—even though Gene Simmons's mother had survived the concentration camps. The '73 Bowie film climaxes with lights flashing on and off over him and the symbol, as if to hypnotize the audience. For a moment it almost seems as if he's *heil*-ing the audience as he impels them to give him their hands, which could be dismissed if a few years later Bowie hadn't ranted to *Rolling Stone* that "Adolf Hitler was one of the first rock stars. . . . I think he was quite as good as Jagger. . . . Music and lights would come on at strategic moments. . . . I think I might have been a bloody good Hitler. I'd be an excellent dictator. Very eccentric and quite mad."[38] Years later he disavowed his fascination with Nazis as naïve and married a Somali woman.

❊

"It's 10 p.m., do you know where your children are?" the television intoned as the Valley girls sneaked out of the house and clattered up the Strip in too-high heels and tube tops and hot pants, from the Rainbow to the Roxy to the Whisky to the Continental Hyatt House (Riot House), where bands like Zeppelin stayed, as immortalized in *Almost Famous*. And to glam's western outpost, Rodney Bingenheimer's English Disco.

Bingenheimer's mother abandoned him when he was sixteen, and he scuffled homeless on the Sunset Strip until Sonny and Cher took him in to be their live-in publicist. He got a gig playing Davy Jones's double on a *Monkees* episode (both were 5'3"), did publicity for Linda Ronstadt and Rod Stewart, wrote a music column.[39] When Bowie first came to LA, Bingenheimer borrowed a Cadillac to chauffeur him to promo events. Bowie suggested he open a glitter club, so in October '72 he opened the E Club, then two months later moved a mile east and renamed it the English Disco, with a door policy that had no age limit.[40]

There had always been a dark side to the Strip. Even before the Summer of Love, the Mamas and the Papas sang of "strange young girls" "offering their youth on the altar of acid" (written by John Phillips, one of Hollywood's most twisted parents). But there had been the belief, delusion or not, that psychedelics led to enlightenment. Now the coins of the realm were Quaaludes, leading to oblivion or date rape, or the increasingly popular coke, or PCP, or amyl nitrate (poppers).

"The groupies were usually girls who did not have fathers, lived in disenfranchised homes, and had mothers who worked," said record producer Kim Fowley,[41] who preyed on them at the disco.

Iggy Pop, however, wrote in "Look Away" that the most well-known groupie of the era, Sable Starr (Sabel Hay Shields), had parents who were "too rich to do anything" in the same line he sang of sleeping with her when she was thirteen. He dated both her and her sister, Coral, while living at the Laurel Canyon home of the manager he shared with David Bowie.

Even if Starr wasn't disenfranchised, she did have the requisite esteem issues, feeling she "didn't get pretty" till getting her nose fixed at fifteen, a process chronicled in the local magazine *Star,* which arrived in February to cover the exploits of self-proclaimed teenage groupies like her and Lori Maddox. After five months, the wife of the publisher convinced him to stop printing the magazine.[42] By then the groupies were were well-known enough that when NBC premiered a new program called *The Tomorrow Show Starring Tom Snyder* on October 15 Snyder's first guests were Starr and her compatriot Queenie (along with double-amputee private eye Jay J. Armes). *Newsweek* ran a story on Rodney's in January discussing its fourteen-year-old clientele, but the club continued for another year, unhindered.

Bowie originally met Starr and Maddox at Bingenheimer's E Club, in late '72. Bowie wanted Maddox to leave with him, but she was a virgin and scared, so she told him she was with Rodney. Five months later, Bowie's huge black bodyguard Stuey called to invite Maddox to dinner on behalf of his boss. She agreed if she could bring Starr. They went to the Rainbow and got high. John and Yoko came by and said hello. A crazed man attacked Bowie, raving homophobic slurs and vowing to kill him, before Stuey dispatched him.

Bowie took the girls back to the Beverly Hilton, where he had a separate room from wife Angie. He changed to his kimono, asked Maddox to bathe him alone without Starr, and took her virginity.[43] Afterward, she mentioned Starr wanted to join them, so he suggested, "Well, do you think we should go and get her?" At the concert a few days later he gave them seats with his publicist and shone a spotlight on them.[44]

"That's when he thanked me for being there," Maddox said in an interview in 2015, responding to the outrage on the blogosphere over her age, which was fourteen, as she was born on November 11, 1958, and his concert in Long Beach was on March 10, 1973. "Who cares what people said about me? I feel like I was very present. I saw the greatest music ever. I got to hang out with some of the most amazing, most beautiful, most charismatic men in the world. I went to concerts in limos with police escorts. Am I going to regret this? No."[45]

Four years later, however, after the #MeToo movement, she told *The Guardian,* "I don't think underage girls should sleep with guys. I wouldn't want this for anybody's daughter. My perspective is changing as I get older and more cynical."[46]

Two months after the Bowie concert, Led Zeppelin arrived in Southern California for three shows. Michael Des Barres, the lead singer of English glam band Silverhead, showed pictures of Starr and Maddox to Jimmy Page.

Starr warned Maddox, "You keep your hands off Jimmy. If you touch him, I will shoot you. He's mine."[47]

But again it was Maddox Zeppelin's manager, Peter Grant, sought at the Rainbow. "You're coming with me, young lady."[48] He hustled her into a limo and transported her to the Hyatt/Riot House, where Page waited in his candlelit room clutching a cane, hat over his eye like the gangsters in *The Song Remains the Same*.[49]

Soon Page asked her mother for permission to date her. "He had to be afraid of getting sued for being with such a young girl, so maybe he thought it would be better if he cleared it with my mother and told her he was in love with me. And I do think he was in love with me. He bought me beautiful maxi dresses to wear and wouldn't let me do drugs or anything. At that point, I was 15 and totally in love with this man. I put him on a pedestal."[50]

The idyll ended during one of Page's stays at a Los Angeles hotel when Maddox "told my friend Bebe Buell that she could have the room next door. I didn't know she would steal my man. I had a key to Jimmy's suite, walked in, and saw them in bed together. I looked at him and said, 'What did you do to me?' I never trusted him again. He was like a god to me and instantly destroyed this whole image I had of him. I remember going to a party they had at Bel-Air Hotel that night. I probably took a Quaalude or something and wound up with a bloody nose. I wore a white dress and got blood all over it. That was an awful night."[51]

Starr cut her wrists at Bowie's manager's house, where the Stooges stayed, floating facedown in the pool till someone pulled her out. Silverhead's album that year was called *Sixteen and Savaged* ("blood on your arms, blood on your lip"). Starr ran off with Johnny Thunders and got pregnant, and he wanted to marry her, but he beat her, so she had an abortion and moved back home.[52] Impresario Kim Fowley assembled the teenage female rock band the Runaways with English Disco regulars Joan Jett, Cherie Currie, and Lita Ford, and allegedly raped sixteen-year-old bassist Jackie Fox in front of other guests at a New Year's party while she was incapacitated on Quaaludes.[53] Originally, Currie had sought refuge in the glam scene to escape sexual violence. She told *Spin*, "My twin sister's boyfriend had raped me and took my virginity. That's why I was angry, that's why I cut my hair to look like David Bowie's."

✳

"I became really aware of the fact that the kids were really lost, the sort of heritage we built up since the war [World War II] had been wiped out by the '60s, and it wasn't groovy to act that way anymore, now you just sort of sat there and got stoned," George Lucas said. "I wanted to preserve what a certain generation of Americans thought being a teenager was really about—from about 1945 to 1962."[54]

Partially inspired by Federico Fellini's *I Vitelloni* (Laybouts), which focused on five friends in a small town, Lucas wrote about four friends on the last night of summer vacation who cruised around Modesto, California. Each was based on different stages of his life (nerdy youth, years spent racing hot rods, etc.).[55] Set in September 1962, *American Graffiti* captured the era before the Kennedy assassination and the sex and drug revolutions. He came up with the scenes while listening to his old rock and roll singles, and the songs formed the "spine" of the movie.[56] Throughout the film, deejay Wolfman Jack spins them and they echo out of car windows in the background as the kids pursue their adventures.

Lucas directed, and his mentor Francis Ford Coppola produced it for $777,000. At the test screening the audience loved it, but Universal executive Ned Tanen deemed it "un-releasable." Coppola blew up at him. "You should go down on your knees and thank George for saving your job!"[57] He offered to buy it off the studio, but Universal declined, figuring it could be edited into a TV movie. Then Coppola won the Oscar for Best Picture for *The Godfather* in March, so Universal eventually released *Graffiti* in August. Initially a "sleeper," it slowly gained steam and became the year's third-highest-grossing film behind *The Sting* and *The Exorcist*.

Lucas said, "We all know, as every movie in the last ten years has pointed out, how terrible we are, how wrong we were in Vietnam, how we have ruined the world, what schmucks we are and how rotten everything is. It had become depressing to go to the movies. I decided it was time to make a movie where people felt better coming out of the theatre than when they went in."[58]

Before Lucas made *American Graffiti*, star Ron Howard acted in a '50s-themed pilot for ABC called *New Family in Town* by creator Garry Marshall, alongside future *Happy Days* stars Marion Ross and Anson "Potsie" Williams.

It didn't sell and was instead included on the anthology show *Love, American Style* under the title "Love and the Happy Day." Lucas had decided to cast Howard after viewing it. Now that *Graffiti* was a hit, ABC decided to rush the show into a series, complete with diner and classic cars, starting production in November for a January '74 premiere.

For the role of the local rebel, they cast a supporting actor named Henry Winkler from *The Lords of Flatbush,* which had just wrapped that summer, about a gang of leather-jacket-wearing toughs; it also starred the unknowns Sylvester Stallone and Perry King. Winkler only had a few lines in the audition, but he used them to intimidate his scene partner into sitting down, then threw his script in the air and sauntered out of the room, scoring the part. "The Fonz was everybody I wasn't. He was everybody I wanted to be."[59] Initially the network decreed that he could not wear a leather jacket because hoods weren't appropriate for 8 p.m., but eventually relented, and Springsteen soon adopted the image himself. Suzi Quatro joined the cast as rocker Leather Tuscadero in 1977. In a few years, Howard's girlfriend in *Graffiti,* Cindy Williams, would get her own *Happy Days* spin-off, *Laverne and Shirley* (with Marshall's sister, Penny).

Graffiti opened with the first rock and roll hit to top the pop charts, Bill Haley's "Rock Around the Clock," and *Happy Days* used it as its theme song for the first two seasons. Haley's song climbed back up to No. 39. The movie soundtrack itself made it to No. 10 and went triple platinum. Its forty-one hits encapsulated its era, and it stands alongside *The Harder They Fall, Nuggets,* and *The Anthology of American Folk Music* in the canon of classic compilations. In the wake of its success, oldies radio stations proliferated across the country.

Many of the '50s greatest artists enjoyed a second life on tour: Jerry Lee Lewis, Little Richard, Dion, Chuck Berry, Bo Diddley. Presley's "Raised on Rock" made it to No. 41, though it was strange to hear Elvis singing about growing up listening to rock and roll. (Actually, *Billboard* used the term as early as 1942 for artists like Sister Rosetta Tharpe.)

Lennon, Bowie, Bryan Ferry, the Band, and the Carpenters released cover albums. Mott the Hoople sang of "a rockabilly party on Saturday night" in "Roll Away the Stone." David Essex celebrated James Dean in "Rock On." Elton John, Bette Midler, Diana Ross, and Barbra Streisand all had nostalgic hits. The Statler Brothers won the Best Country Group Performance Grammy for "The Class of '57."

Ringo Starr scored a No. 1 with one of *Graffiti's* oldies, "You're Sixteen," and acted in *That'll Be the Day,* the soundtrack of which became a bestselling UK album, the British version of *Graffiti*. Some of the movie's costumes came from the retro boutique Too Fast to Live Too Young to Die, run by Malcolm McLaren and Vivienne Westwood.

On September 23, the Wigan Casino nightclub, northeast of Liverpool, held its first Northern Soul all-nighter. In a sense it revived the tradition Townshend celebrated in *Quadrophenia,* English kids dancing till dawn to black music from the States.

The twist was that Northern Soul deejays like Richard Searling traveled to Detroit and Philadelphia to hunt for soul singles that had never made it. Like DJ Kool Herc and the disco deejays, they wanted to find things no one had heard before. So they mined dusty warehouses for 45s that had languished for up to a decade, songs that Berry Gordy had deemed second tier and released without the full Motown treatment of strings and lush background vocals.[60] Searing's most famous discovery was Gloria Jones's "Tainted Love," later turned into technopop by Soft Cell.[61]

That was emblematic of the '70s nostalgia for the '50s, which created a new hybrid somewhere between both decades. The parents on *Happy Days* discussed "getting frisky" more frankly than their real-life '50s counterparts ever would; the good girl in the Broadway show *Grease* met her greaser boyfriend halfway by donning tight black leather. It was about finding the healthy balance between repressed and decadent.

❋

Gladys Knight once had the bestselling single at Motown, the original version of "I Heard It Through the Grapevine," but she always felt like a second-class citizen. So she left the label for Buddha Records; maybe that was one reason she related to "Midnight Train to Georgia," about leaving a place where things hadn't worked out.

The song was written by Jim Weatherly, who played football with up-and-coming actor Lee Majors (whose TV movie pilot for *The Six Million Dollar Man* aired in March). One day when Weatherly called Majors, his girlfriend Farrah Fawcett answered and said Majors had taken "a midnight plane to Houston," and she was packing to go there as well.[62]

Weatherly wrote the song around her phrase as soon as he got off the phone. When Whitney Houston's mother Cissy covered it, she changed the state and the mode of transport. "My people are originally from Georgia, and they didn't take planes to Houston or anywhere else."[63] Knight and the Pips followed her template and knocked the Stones' "Angie" out of the No. 1 spot on October 27.

Critic Dave Marsh projected an epic backdrop onto the song, as he did with Haggard's "If We Make It Through December." "The most dramatic change in the United States between the end of World War II and 1965 was not a generational shift but the massive migration off the land into the cities. In the weeks and months that 'Midnight Train to Georgia' lasted on the charts, the thoughts of a million transplanted Southerners, black and white, turned to the places they—or their parents—had come from. You can feel the weariness and the inability to fathom new customs and regulations that might drive a man back to his homeland . . . just as the bubble of economic prosperity on which the migration had been built was deflating."[64]

"Goin' back to find a simpler place in time," the Pips sang. Americans could do that without leaving their couch with *The Waltons,* the new-ish show about a Norman Rockwell–esque household in the Blue Ridge Mountains of Virginia. Watching the Waltons make it through the Great Depression helped put the present in perspective. Maybe things weren't *that* bad now, even with the oil crisis.

After the show's premiere in September 1972, CBS assumed it was only a matter of time before it died, but then it won five Emmys. Competitor NBC quickly shot a pilot for its own rural drama, *Little House on the Prairie,* more balm for families who needed some relief from the day's grim headlines. They could always put on the *Graffiti* soundtrack as well, to be briefly transported by the uncomplicated positivity of songs like Bobby Freeman's "Do You Wanna Dance."

*

I Hope You're Having Fun

Chaos in Lagos inspires McCartney's best album. Chaos with Phil Spector
fuels Lennon's lost weekend. Starr and Harrison form their own songwriting duo until Harrison plays musical chairs with one wife too many.

*

The Rolling Stones' and Elton John's trips to Jamaica had not
gone well, but Paul McCartney thought Lagos, Nigeria, might be a
good place to reboot his career. His last album had done well commercially,
but the critics derided him for not living up to his potential. When he discovered that his label, EMI, had a record studio on the Atlantic coast in Central Africa, he figured he could hire local musicians to give his project exotic
flavor, plus relax on the beach with Linda when not working.

The first hiccup came when Wings guitarist Henry McCullough quit,
because McCartney didn't allow him creative input and paid low. Drummer Denny Seiwell resigned the night before they were scheduled to fly,
irked at his salary of $175 a week. McCartney wasn't unduly alarmed; he
played drums on his first solo album. So he set out with Linda and guitarist-
vocalist Denny Laine on August 9. EMI sent a letter warning him to avoid
the country because of cholera, but McCartney did not receive it before his
departure.[1]

He was disappointed to find the studio had just one eight-track recorder.
The power often went out. Fela Kuti, leader of the local Afrobeat music

scene, warned McCartney not to steal their music, so McCartney gave up the idea of employing Nigerian musicians.

The city was under the control of a military junta, and the McCartneys were told it was too dangerous to go out at night. Still, he and Linda attempted to walk twenty minutes to Laine's house. Five or six muggers, one brandishing a knife, jumped out of a car.[2] "Don't kill him, he's a musician!" Linda screamed. They stole McCartney's money and a bag containing demos and lyrics.

When they returned to work, he was forced to reconstruct the songs from memory. "It seemed stuffy in the studio, so I went outside for a breath of fresh air. If anything, the air was more foul outside than in. It was then that I began to feel really terrible and had a pain across the right side of my chest and I collapsed. I could not breathe and so I collapsed and fainted. Linda thought I had died. The doctor seemed to treat it pretty lightly and said it could be bronchial because I had been smoking too much. But this was me in hell. I stayed in bed for a few days, thinking I was dying. It was one of the most frightening periods in my life. The climate, the tensions of making a record, which had just got to succeed, and being in this totally uncivilized part of the world finally got to me."[3]

Perhaps he started refining "Picasso's Last Words" in bed. The song had its genesis the previous spring when Dustin Hoffman invited McCartney and Linda to dinner. "He was asking me how I write songs; I explained that I just make them up. He said, 'Can you make up a song about anything?' I wasn't sure, but he pulled out a copy of *Time* [April 23 issue], pointed to an article and said, 'Could you write a song about this?' It was a quote from Picasso, from the last night of his life, April 8. Apparently, he had said to his friends, 'Drink to me, drink to my health, you know I can't drink anymore,' and then gone to bed and died in his sleep. So I picked up a guitar, started to strum and sing 'Drink to me, drink to my health . . .' and Dustin was shouting to his wife, 'He's doing it! He's doing it! Come and listen!' It's something that comes naturally to me but he was blown away by it."[4]

Hoffman later said of the evening, "It's right under childbirth in terms of great events in my life."[5]

McCartney also toyed with a phrase from the pub sing-along segment of his *James Paul McCartney* special, where the patrons belted out "Pack Up Your Troubles in Your Old Kit-Bag." "What's the use of worrying?" they all sang, and he turned it into the chorus of "Mrs. Vanderbilt." "When your light is on the blink . . . you don't complain of robbery." If this album was going to be his own last words, what would they be?

✤

John Lennon also endured a tumultuous session that fall, for his album of '50s covers called *Rock 'n' Roll*. The threat to him was his producer, Phil Spector, later given a life sentence for shooting actress-waitress Lana Clarkson. Spector would arrive at A&M Studios in Hollywood late, perhaps dressed as a surgeon, then keep Lennon waiting for hours as he tinkered with the thirty-piece band, leaving the singer with too much time on his hands to get bombed. Once Lennon grew so irate he smashed his headset on the console. The studio owner left the damage unfixed to stand as a Beatle memento. After one endless session when a wasted Lennon threatened to get violent, Spector's bodyguard spirited him back to the house he was staying at, against his wishes. When Lennon attempted to strangle Spector, the bodyguard tied Lennon facedown on his bed to allow for their escape.[6] Another night, Spector, without provocation, hit Lennon's assistant Mal Evans in the nose. When Evans warned him, "Watch that!" Spector yelled back "You watch it!" and fired his pistol into the ceiling.[7] Lennon retorted, "Phil, if you're going to kill me, kill me. But don't fuck with my ears. I need 'em."[8]

The best performance was "Bony Moronie." The first track recorded, it reflected the initial excitement before the project devolved into sodden debauchery. But the most compelling Spector-produced track was the ridiculous train wreck "Be My Baby." It was not released until 1998 on the *John Lennon Anthology,* because Lennon slurs and yelps, as if on the verge of passing out. He seems to stagger all the way back to 1960, to the famous night in Beatles history when he took the stage of a dive club in the Hamburg red light district wearing only his underwear and a toilet seat around his neck. (The album's eventual cover featured a shot of him from this period.)

The studio finally ejected Lennon and Spector over "a matter of pee," as Lennon titled a note he wrote to Spector. (The note was sold in 2014 for more than $88,000 by Cooper Owen Auction House.[9]) "Should you not yet know, it was Harry [Nilsson] and Keith [Moon] who pissed on the console!" he wrote. "Anyway tell [the studio owner] to bill Capitol for the damage if any. I can't be expected to mind adult rock stars. Nor can May [Pang, his girlfriend and assistant]."

Spector disappeared with the master tapes. While Lennon debated whether to abandon the project all together, he marked time producing a solo track for Mick Jagger, "Too Many Cooks." He watched his *Mind Games* album, released at the end of October, make it to No. 9 in the US. McCartney and Harrison had made it to No. 1; Starr would make it to No. 2 with his album. The cover depicted a tiny John walking away from a mountain that was Yoko Ono's profile, facing up as if she lies in a sarcophagus. For the "Mind Games" single sleeve, he superimposed her profile so it came out of the top of his head, much like the face of Harry Potter's villain Voldemort coming out of the head of Quirinus Quirrell. Ono, meanwhile, pursued an affair with her guitarist David Spinozza. With no Ono, no politics, no new self-help tool like acid or meditation or primal therapy to believe in, Lennon went off the rails with his clique of fellow rock stars, who dubbed themselves the Hollywood Vampires: Starr, Nilsson, Moon, Alice Cooper, Marc Bolan, Bernie Taupin, Joe Walsh, Mickey Dolenz, Keith Emerson, and Keith Allison (of Paul Revere and the Raiders).

"In L.A. you either have to be down at the beach or you become part of that never-ending show business party circuit. That scene makes me nervous, and when I get nervous I have to have a drink and when I drink I get aggressive," Lennon explained.[10] He told *Playboy*, "For me, it was because of being apart (from Ono). I couldn't stand it. They had their own reasons, and it was, 'Let's all drown ourselves together.' From where I was sitting, it looked like that. 'Let's kill ourselves but do it like Errol Flynn, you know, the macho, male way.'"[11]

Or maybe the *Curse of the Werewolf* way. One night fans spied Lennon in the window of On the Rox, the lounge atop the Roxy nightclub on the Strip. When they hollered up at him, per biographer Albert Goldman, "he kicked out the window overlooking the lot. Then he started screaming at the fans, 'You want me, ya fucks! You want me!'"[12] He ran down and started brawling with them until producer Jack Douglas and session drummer Jim Keltner pulled him into a car. Lennon kicked out the back windows as it drove away.

That autumn Lennon received an uneasy visit from his ex-wife and son Julian. The day after, he got wasted at the Troubadour and slapped a Kotex maxipad on his head. The waitress avoided his table, so he demanded, "Do you know who am I?"

"Yeah, you're some asshole with a Kotex on his head."[13]

When Annie Peebles began her set, which included her recent hit "I Can't Stand the Rain," Lennon called out, "Annie, I wanna suck your pussy!" and was promptly ejected by the bouncers.[14] (They kicked him out again a couple of months later for heckling the Smothers Brothers.) Returning home with session guitarist Jesse Ed Davis and their girlfriends, the two musicians smashed the furniture, then began wrestling. Lennon got Davis in a full nelson and began kissing him, trying to stick his tongue in. Davis bit his tongue, prompting Lennon to hit him on the head with a marble ashtray, knocking him out. As the women screamed, Lennon doused Davis with orange juice to revive him, then "bandaged" his head by wrapping a roll of film around it.

It was then the cops arrived with shotguns, perplexed to find the sheepish icon amid the destruction.

One of the police ventured, "Do you think the Beatles will ever get together again?"

"You never know. You never know."[15]

✳

After George Harrison co-wrote and produced two hits for Ringo Starr, "It Don't Come Easy" and "Back Off Boogaloo," it appeared a new partnership was emerging from the Beatles' demise. After Starr and his wife, Maureen, attended Jagger's wedding to Bianca in the South of France in 1971, he rented a yacht to live on during the Cannes Film Festival, and Harrison and his wife, Pattie, joined them. There the two began working on a song called "Photograph."[16] They took a stab at it during Harrison's *Material World* sessions; then Starr redid it for his *Ringo* album, produced by Richard Perry. Stones regulars Nicky Hopkins and Bobby Keys contributed piano and sax. Spector's former arranger Jack Nitzsche created his own version of the Wall of Sound orchestra, complete with bells and chorale— perfect for the holiday season, as were the bittersweet lyrics yearning to "have and hold . . . as we grow old and gray." It hit No. 1 in the US two days after Thanksgiving, the finest of the year's many odes to nostalgia. Starr sang the best he ever would, eager to prove himself, undergirded by Harrison's harmonies and twelve-string acoustic. Lennon and McCartney also contributed to *Ringo* ("I'm the Greatest" and "Six O'Clock," respectively), but nothing came close to the Harrison-Starr production.

McCartney also joined Harry Nilsson in backing up Starr on a cover of the 1960 Johnny Burnette hit "You're Sixteen," recorded a month after *American Graffiti* featured the song. McCartney imitated a kazoo in the instrumental, and the song, surprisingly, followed "Photograph" all the way to No. 1. Another track from *Ringo* made No. 3, the proto-disco "Oh My My," written by Starr with his songwriting partner Vini Poncia, featuring Martha

Reeves and Mary Clayton on backing vocals. For a few years, Starr was second only to McCartney for ex-Beatle with Most Consecutive Top 10 US Singles, with seven to McCartney's eight.

Ringo shot to No. 2 in the US, abetted by its *Sgt. Pepper*–esque cover and the public's craving for the Fab Four spirit. Lennon telegrammed him, "Congratulations. How dare you? And please write me a hit song."[17]

✳

"George was happy to talk to me about Indian mysticism and music, even his use of cocaine," Pete Townshend wrote in his memoir. "I found it hard to follow his reasoning that in a world of illusion nothing mattered, not wealth or fame, drug abuse or heavy drinking, nothing but love for God. . . . Yellow-robed young Hare Krishna followers living in [Harrison's] house wandered in and out as we chatted."[18]

Pattie's occasional affair with Eric Clapton mattered little to Harrison. Their liaison began after Harrison slept with Charlotte Martin, Clapton's ex. Eric confessed one night to Harrison in front of a mortified Pattie, "I have to tell you man, that I'm in love with your wife."[19] Despite Harrison's initial anger, the marriage, the men's friendship, and the affair continued.

Ron Wood married another ex-girlfriend of Clapton's, model Krissie Findlay. In Wood's autobiography he wrote, "One night at George's house, Friar Park, in Henley, I took George aside and told him quite seriously that when it was time for bed I would be going to Pattie's room. Seemingly unflustered he pointed to the room Krissie and I were staying in and added, 'I shall be sleeping there.' When the time came, the two of us were left on the landing, hands on knobs (doorknobs) of the respective rooms. 'Are we going to do this?' I asked. 'I'll see you in court,' George replied and in we went. Pattie was a little surprised to see me. I told her I thought she was seriously neglected, was going to waste and unleashed that I felt so strongly for her. The following morning we were woken by George, who informed me that he had called his lawyers. He never actually did. Pattie and I headed off to the Bahamas and Krissie and George left for Portugal."[20]

In Pattie's own memoir, she wrote, "Krissie often came to stay at Friar Park. I was desperately hurt: another one of my friends was sleeping with George. When I challenged him, he denied it and tried once again to make me feel as though I was paranoid."[21]

In Pattie's telling, she and Harrison were scheduled to go to Portugal in the spring of '73, but at the last minute he told her he didn't feel well, so she went to the Bahamas instead with her friends. As soon as Pattie was gone, Harrison contacted Krissie. Per *Krissie*'s memoir, "George said he had rented a holiday villa in Portugal, and since Pattie was too busy to go, he asked me. I was a bit run down at the time and needed a break so Ronnie was happy for me to go."[22]

As soon as Krissie was gone, Wood contacted Pattie in the Bahamas. "He was on tour and said he might come to see us for a few days. It was such a relief to have someone else to party with, someone who is light and fun. . . . He didn't seem upset that his wife was with George—just thought it was funny that they'd gone to see Salvador Dali. . . . A pair of comforting arms were what I needed."[23]

Krissie wrote of Harrison, "He was gentle, kind and considerate, just what I needed at that moment. Our affair was on a very serious and spiritual level. On our return from Portugal, George and I returned to Friar Park, but Pattie and Ronnie were not in England. They had flown off to the Bahamas for a holiday, which upset George because Pattie had said she didn't want to go to Portugal. Rather than sit around and wait for her, George and I then flew to Switzerland for another holiday. We returned to England and I stayed with George until his wife returned. But [Pattie] was not at all jealous. If anyone was jealous, it was me. I felt [Pattie] was very pretty and I wasn't really happy that she was together with Ronnie."[24]

Pattie began to suspect that something was going on with Harrison and Starr's wife, Maureen, when she found some photos that showed Maureen had been at their estate one weekend when Pattie was away. She noticed Maureen had begun to visit more frequently to watch Harrison and his fellow musicians record in his home studio. Pattie would go to sleep and find Maureen still there in the morning. Maureen began wearing a necklace Harrison gave her. One day Pattie heard them in Harrison's room and found the door locked. When she banged on the door, Harrison laughed that Maureen was just tired and lying down. When Pattie told Starr, he grew enraged, but Harrison initially denied any affair.[25]

But finally, one night when the Harrisons and Starrs dined with Harrison's assistant Chris O'Dell, a wine-drunk Harrison confessed, "You know, Ringo, I'm in love with your wife," a phrase not unlike the one Clapton had uttered to him.[26]

According to O'Dell's memoir, Starr responded, "Better you than someone we don't know."[27] Pattie's memoir depicts Starr stalking off quoting Lennon's "Strawberry Fields Forever": "Nothing is real." Maureen went red and just shook her head, looking down.

Maureen did not want to split from Starr, but he left her and England for his friends in Los Angeles and divorced her. Harrison eventually settled down with a secretary from his record label, Olivia Trinidad Arias. Pattie married Eric Clapton; Harrison attended their wedding. Maureen tried to kill herself by driving her motorcycle into a brick wall, necessitating facial reconstruction.[28] She married a co-founder of the Hard Rock Café, Isaac Burton Tigrett.

To the world outside, it appeared that the obstacles blocking a Beatles reunion were melting away. Harrison, Starr, and Lennon had jettisoned the manager who McCartney objected to. Lennon separated from Yoko Ono, who famously clashed with McCartney and Harrison. The three had played together on "I'm the Greatest." McCartney and Lennon tentatively jammed when McCartney was allowed back into the States the following spring.

But there was no Harrison track on *Goodnight Vienna,* Starr's follow-up to *Ringo.* The Beatles' former assistant Peter Brown wrote in his biography of the group, "When George was later asked why of all the women in the world he had to choose his buddy's wife, George shrugged his shoulders and said, 'Incest.'"[29]

❋

"We just would rather do [marijuana] than hit the booze—which had been a traditional way to do it," McCartney observed. "There were a lot of musicians at the time who'd come out of ordinary suburbs in the '60s and '70s and were getting busted. Bands like the Byrds, the Eagles—the mood amongst them was one of desperados. We were being outlawed for pot."[30] Some of the pot busts in '73 included Marvin Gaye, the Grateful Dead's Phil Lesh, *The Last Detail* director Hal Ashby, and McCartney, for growing cannabis on his farm in Scotland.

So he wrote a mini rock opera about a gang who make a prison break and escape into the sunset. The line "If I ever get out of here" was actually something Harrison said during one of the interminable business meetings that consumed the Beatles during their breakup. The first two segments of "Band on the Run" were recorded in Lagos, but the last section was captured in London. McCartney could sing "I hope you're having fun" like Butch Cassidy to the Sundance Kid with jubilation now that the Nigerian odyssey with his wife and Laine was a crazy memory. For cinematic flourish he enlisted T. Rex's producer Tony Visconti to arrange a sixty-piece orchestra, fresh off Bolan's *Tanx.*

The Fab Four had always released albums for the Christmas market, and on December 5 McCartney issued his most Beatle-esque album. "Jet," named after his black Labrador puppy, was the sound of McCartney recapturing his swagger after two LPs in the wilderness. "Helen Wheels," the name of McCartney's Land Rover, blazed with the euphoria he felt to be touring again. (Lennon and Harrison hadn't wanted to play live anymore.) "Mamunia" was a hotel the couple stayed in in Marrakesh, the word for "safe haven" in Arabic.[31] Written in the desert, it reminded listeners to appreciate the rain. "No Words," a co-write with Laine, offered warped Harrison-esque guitar coupled with Visconti strings. McCartney chopped "Picasso's Last Words" into pieces and reassembled them to make the song cubist like the master's paintings; then Visconti added Philly proto-disco strings. "Nineteen Hundred and Eighty-Five" built to a frenzied climax featuring McCartney's good-natured imitation of Lennon circa "Cold Turkey," a song McCartney initially didn't want to record with the Beatles because of its heroin references. Only "Bluebird" seemed saccharine.

Like *Ringo,* the cover recalled the whimsy of *Sgt. Pepper,* featuring Wings and celebrities including Christopher Lee and James Coburn as convicts escaping. In the US, "Helen Wheels" went to No. 10, followed by "Jet" at seven; then "Band on the Run" hit No. 1 on June 8 in 1974. The album itself made the top spot on April 13 and returned there June 8 for three more weeks. It was the bestselling album of 1974 in the UK and Australia.

Harrison contributed indirectly to another song on the album. "Let Me Roll It" was a line from "I'll Have You Anytime," the opening track of *All Things Must Pass*—though the vocals and primitive guitar echoed a different bandmate's. "I hadn't realized I'd sung it like John," McCartney later conceded.[32] The record's title track, meanwhile, carried more than a whiff of nostalgia for the old days when the four of them shared the eye of the hurricane together.

"*Band on the Run* is a great album," Lennon told *Rolling Stone.*[33] It challenged him to pull himself together and record *Walls and Bridges,* one of his best, and enlist Elton John to help nab the No. 1 single that had so far eluded him with "Whatever Gets You thru the Night."

The record capped the final year in which each Beatle released classics that fired on all cylinders: "Band on the Run," "Mind Games," "Give Me Love," "Photograph," "Live and Let Die." On the radio it was almost as if the group still existed.

Bob Marley

The Wailers break through beyond Jamaica with *Catch a Fire* and *Burnin'*, the latter featuring "I Shot the Sheriff" and "Get Up, Stand Up."

�֍

With *The Harder They Come,* Jimmy Cliff seemed poised for stardom on both sides of the Atlantic, but it didn't happen, perhaps due to his falling-out with Island Records founder Chris Blackwell on the eve of the film's release in London.

Blackwell, white, was born in London in 1937, but his family moved to Jamaica when he was young. His mother was descended from one of the twenty-one families who controlled the country through rum and sugar. Blackwell himself sold liquor and cigarettes in school, but it got him kicked out. At age twenty, he began selling US records to Jamaican Sound System operators, then started producing his own artists. Realizing the Jamaican market was too crowded, he moved to London to sell ska records to the Jamaican immigrants. He named his company Island Records after the Harry Belafonte movie *Island in the Sun,* driving to record shops with his Afro-Jamaican girlfriend Esther Anderson to hawk records out of their Mini Cooper.

Island released Cliff's records throughout the sixties, but Blackwell's bread and butter gradually became white acts like the Spencer Davis Group, Traffic, Cat Stevens, Mott the Hoople, and King Crimson (and later U2), and

Cliff felt underappreciated. When the difficult *Harder They Come* production dragged on for multiple years, he ran out of money, and thus was tempted when EMI Records offered him $50,000 to switch labels. Blackwell promised Cliff that he would be able to give him a better deal as soon as the movie and soundtrack came out. When the film premiered in London, Cliff wanted the better deal from Island. But from Blackwell's perspective, the American release had not yet been determined. "I can't hang around no more," Cliff sang in the brooding "Sooner or Later" on his 1973 *Struggling Man* album. He took the EMI deal.

Blackwell admitted, "It was a lot of money at the time. But I'd been putting a lot of energy into him. I was bitter."[1] Cliff was bitter, too, denouncing Blackwell in "No. 1 Rip-Off Man."[2] (Which itself ripped off the chorus of Elvis's "Burning Love.")

According to legend, it was a week after Cliff departed the label that Bob Marley walked through Blackwell's door. "I transferred the whole plan I had for Jimmy over to Bob," Blackwell said, "and was motivated to make it work."[3]

✳

Robert Nesta, Marley's father, was a Syrian Jew from England who supervised plantation workers. He married Cedella Booker, an eighteen-year-old black Jamaican, then left the next day. He never saw his son much after his birth on April 6, 1945, and died when Marley was ten. Marley grew up sometimes ostracized for looking whiter than the others; he found solace in American radio.[4]

His mother took up with Thaddeus Livingston, and Marley befriended his son, Neville (nicknamed Bunny). They all moved in together, and the parents had a daughter. The two young men met Winston "Peter Tosh" Macintosh, a self-taught guitarist and keyboardist, and the three began singing together on Trenchtown street corners, like doo-woppers in America. (In photos Tosh is the one always wearing shades.)

Marley got a job as a welder, but when metal flew into his eye he vowed to make it as a singer.[5] Fellow welder Desmond Dekker brought him to his label, run by Leslie Kong, and Marley released his first single, "Judge Not," in 1962. Marley, Bunny, and Tosh formed the Teenagers, renamed the Wailing Rudeboys, then Wailing Wailers, finally Wailers circa 1966. Their first ska single, "Simmer Down," was released in 1964.

Tosh taught the others how to play guitar. He alternated between guitar, piano, and organ, harmonizing with Bunny, who played bongos or conga, while Marley sang lead and played guitar. In 1970 they found their permanent rhythm section, Aston "Family Man" Barrett on bass and Carlton "Carlie" Barrett on drums.

Marley wrote songs for Johnny Nash's breakthrough album, *I Can See Clearly Now*. In August 1972, while backing Nash on a tour of the UK, they decided to pop in on Blackwell's Island Records. The Wailers' Jamaican singles had been licensed by Island for release in England.

When the Wailers walked into his office, Blackwell said, "I must say they were an overwhelming presence. Incredibly charismatic. It was all three of them, Bunny Livingston, Peter Tosh and Bob Marley, that collectively and individually exuded this sense of power. I signed them on the spot."[6]

All three had converted to Rastafarianism, and a Rasta once saved Blackwell's life in his early twenties. He'd been caught by a storm in his small sailboat and "thrown up against some rocks along a barren stretch of isolated coast. I had been knocked unconscious, and when I woke up I had no idea how long I had been there and no idea where I was. The storm had passed and the sun was blaring and I was scarred and parched and felt like I would be overcome by thirst and dehydration. Then—and it seemed a miracle to me—out of nowhere, there was a Rastaman standing above me, with long thick dreadlocks. He led me to some shade and climbed a tree. He chopped down some coconuts and split them, and I felt like I was being brought back to life. . . . From that time I have always felt close to Rasta culture."[7]

Blackwell gave them £4,000 to cut *Catch a Fire*, which alternated between Marley's twin poles of politics and sex. The title came from "Slave Driver," which advocating setting those who kept Jamaica "chained in poverty" aflame. "Concrete Jungle" lamented being trapped in the housing projects. "No More Trouble" exhorted his compatriots to stop warring among themselves. "Stir It Up," on the other hand, languidly celebrated "pushing the wood" in his lover's pot.

Blackwell suspected Marley could be as big as Hendrix, but in his last eight years working in London, Blackwell hadn't been able to score consistent hits with Jamaican artists, so he wanted to sell the Wailers like Sly and the Family Stone, War, and Earth Wind & Fire. "There were radio stations that would only play music by white artists, and then there were the R&B stations that would only play black music. The problem was that reggae didn't fit either format."[8]

Johnny Nash's cover of Marley's "Stir It Up" actually peaked at No. 12 on the US pop chart in April, but the Wailers' laid-back shuffle was far less glossy. Both Nash and Jimmy Cliff frequently utilized flutes, strings, and horns. Nash started out as an R&B artist, and Cliff lived in the UK for half a decade and mixed his style with pop and R&B, recording in Muscle Shoals, with tracks like "Trapped," produced by Cat Stevens. Marley made little attempt to dilute his accent, and whereas the others had haircuts that looked familiar to the West, Rasta dreadlocks were alien to most.

Blackwell strategized, "I felt initially that the Wailers would have a better chance to expand their audience beyond Jamaica by adding elements that would have some sense of familiarity to foreign listeners."[9]

He remixed the album they delivered, sometimes repeating instrumental passages to make the songs longer. He enlisted John "Rabbit" Bundrick of Texas to add organ, clavinet, or synthesizer to all of the tracks. Bundrick had played on Nash's *I Can See Clearly Now* album (and would later work on *The Rocky Horror Picture Show*). His clavinet work on songs like "Concrete Jungle" influenced the Wailers' own keyboardist, Tyrone Downie.[10]

Also at the Island studio at the time was a twenty-year-old half-Cherokee guitarist from Muscle Shoals named Wayne Perkins, cutting a record with his group, Smith Perkins Smith. Blackwell grabbed him on the studio's spiral staircase and told him he needed Southern Rock guitar. He hustled him into the basement, where, amid a fog of pot smoke, Perkins saw Rastas and heard reggae for the first time.

"Blackwell explained that the bass drum, sock cymbal, and the snare [drum] are on the one and three [beats]," Perkins recalled. "He told me to ignore the bass guitar because it was more of a lead instrument. It's great music, but it's kinda weird in that everything feels like it's being played backwards. 'Concrete Jungle' was the very first thing that I was handed. That was the most out-of-character bass part I'd ever heard. But because the keyboards and the guitars stay locked together doing what they're doing all through the song, that was sorta my saving grace."[11]

He began to process the music as a combination of Appalachian, bluegrass, and the Twist and tried to figure out a countermelody.[12] "I nailed that guitar solo down on the second or third take, I think. It was a gift from God, because I really didn't know what the hell I was doing. And then Marley came into the recording room. He was cartwheeling, man, he couldn't get over what had just happened to his song, he was so excited. I couldn't understand a damn thing he was saying. And he was cramming this huge joint down my throat and wouldn't take 'no' for an answer. He got me real, real high."[13]

Marley dubbed him "the White Wailer." Perkins also added guitar to "Stir

It Up" and "Baby We Got a Date." When the Stones later needed to replace Mick Taylor, they almost gave the job to Perkins before deciding to go with fellow Brit Ron Wood.

On later deluxe editions of the album, both Blackwell's version and the original "naked" version are included so the listener can compare the two.

Along with the sonic makeover, Blackwell marketed Marley's image as a lifestyle. "I was dealing with rock music, which was really rebel music. I felt that would really be the way to break Jamaican music. But you needed someone who could be that image. When Bob walked in he really was that image, the real one that Jimmy had created in [*The Harder They Come*]."[14]

Anderson became the band's photographer and Marley's new girlfriend. She recalled, "I was teaching Bob how to be a rebel, based on what I learned from living with Marlon Brando for seven years. In fact, I bought him a jacket just like the one Marlon wore in 'On the Waterfront' when he said he coulda been a contender."[15] (Though technically Brando did not wear leather in that scene.)

The Wailers' Rastafarianism was in many ways identical to the hippie outlook, with wild hair representing an insistence on personal freedom. Both hippies and Rastas felt persecuted by conservatives who judged them on their appearance; both got pushed around by cops. They wanted to reject the rat race, stop sweating the small stuff, and take it slow, using music and cannabis to attain the mind-set. Thus Blackwell fashioned the album cover as a giant Zippo lighter that flipped open, a gimmick cover not unlike the Stones' *Sticky Fingers,* which unzipped. When the Zippo cover failed to make its money back, Blackwell replaced it with Anderson's shot of Marley toking on a gigantic spliff, guaranteed to freak out pot-fearing parents.

The album was released in April in the US and only sold about fourteen thousand copies, struggling to No. 171 on the *Billboard* chart. Today *Rolling Stone* ranks it as the 126th Greatest Album.

✳

The Wailers returned to the studio in Kingston that month to record the follow-up, then overdubbed and mixed it in London between tours, though this time around Blackwell brought in no outside musicians.

Marley composed "Get Up, Stand Up" while flying over Haiti, musing on the nation's history of slavery and poverty, similar to his own country's. Like Cliff in "The Harder They Come," Marley admonishes a preacher for encouraging his congregation to accept their lot and exhorts the listeners to fight for their rights.

In Trenchtown, the police/military enforced a strict curfew and constantly drove their jeeps through the ghetto. Marley wrote "Burnin' and Lootin'" after Joe Higgs, who had given the Wailers free vocal lessons in their youth, suffered a police raid. Marley sings of rioting in the face of police brutality and lack of food. The song gave another shout-out to Cliff, asking how many rivers they had to cross before they could talk to the boss, which Bunny said was a reference to how the music business executives in Jamaica ripped them off, then tried to avoid them.

The Wailers' call to arms was even more direct in the album's most famous track, though they softened it slightly by couching it in the guise of a Marty Robbins cowboy ballad.[16] "I want to say 'I shot the police' but the government would have made a fuss so I said 'I shot the sheriff' instead," Marley explained. "But it's the same idea: justice."[17]

Their manager, Lee Jaffe, a New York photographer who worked for Island, recalled, "The song came out of me playing harmonica on a beach in Jamaica. Bob was playing guitar and he said, 'I shot the sheriff,' and I said, 'But you didn't get the deputy.' It was a joke, because they don't have sheriffs in Jamaica. Bob was funny, he was witty, so it was about him hanging out with this white guy, me, it was a comment about that. And yes, it came out of Western movies, which Jamaicans really love. *The Good, The Bad and the Ugly* was always playing somewhere in Kingston. So they're into that whole attitude, and here Bob was hanging out with this white guy, so it was like being in some Western movie with me. I remember there was these two really, really fat girls dancing on the beach when Bob came out with that line. And then, it was like such a funny song, the beach wasn't that crowded, but we had a whole bunch of people just dancing to that song."[18]

The most paradoxical element of the Wailers' music was that it sounded so mellow while advocating revolution, rioting, and cop killing. In the States, Marvin Gaye and Stevie Wonder had to go to war with Berry Gordy, and James Brown had been "blacklisted" from white radio, over far less radical songs.

The album's title, *Burnin'*, like its predecessor, punned on uprising through fire, smoking the sacrament, and jamming on their instruments. "Small Axe" referred to how the Wailers took on the Jamaican music establishment with their own label, Tuff Gong, in the days before they signed with Island. The "Big Three" labels controlled the country's industry, so the band called them "the big tree" and sang they were the tool to cut it down.[19] According to legend, they used to make the rounds to radio stations with baseball bats to ensure the stations would play their records. Since they had not been paid for many of their early songs, Blackwell encouraged them to rerecord a number of them for the album, like "Duppy Conqueror"— duppies were evil spirits in Caribbean folklore.

The cover photo, taken by Anderson, was printed on orange wood for the album jacket. (The image was re-created years later on *The Miseducation of Lauryn Hill*; that singer had five children with Marley's son Rohan.) The album was released on October 9 and has been included in the National Recording Registry by the Library of Congress for cultural significance.

✳

The band toured the UK in April and May, appearing on the BBC and *The Old Grey Whistle Test*. They felt England finally starting to crack when they played the Speakeasy, a favorite of the rock elite from the Beatles' era to Elvis Costello's. Family Man recounted, "We opened the show with 'Rastaman Chant.' The first track cast a spell on them."[20]

"Chant" was the climax of *Burnin'*, a traditional song performed in Rasta Nyabinghi drum gatherings. Bunny said, "We were coming to England on a mission. We were going to establish Rastafarian culture and reggae music. So I knew that we had to have the Nyabinghi drums so as to make the chant so that the people would understand that we had some foundation, that this music did not come out of nowhere."[21]

They went on to Boston, then New York, where they stayed at the Chelsea and shared the bill with Springsteen at Max's Kansas City in July. Pop artist Ronnie Cutrone remembered they "blew my mind. I went every night. Nobody knew who they were so I could watch them with ten people and they were raw and vital then. By the last few nights everybody was saying this music is insane, what is it? They were trying to disco and rock dance to it."[22]

Writer Glenn O'Brien noted, "Ronnie just kept saying, 'They are so noble.'"[23]

The band opened for Sly and the Family Stone for a couple of gigs until Sly determined they were upstaging him and dropped them from the tour. Nevertheless they kept touring the US, then returned to England in November.

By that point the original trio was falling apart, as the others chafed over the attention Blackwell lavished on Marley. Marley stepped aside to let Tosh sing his own compositions on both albums ("400 Years" and "Stop That Train" on the first, "Foundation Time" on the second), and his deeper, raspy voice made a nice contrast to Marley's. He took the lead on the angriest verse in "Get Up, Stand Up" ("You can fool some people some time"). On

Burnin' Bunny got his chance to shine with his compositions "Pass It On" and "Hallelujah Time," the influence of Curtis Mayfield's falsetto evident.

But while Marley stayed in his girlfriend Anderson's flat in England, Bunny said, "We were taken to a dump in a commercial district owned by Chris Blackwell, King Street, above an Indian restaurant. There was a basement where we rehearsed, which was also a dump. . . . There was not a bed in the place, there was just mattresses. . . . And when there were break times, days off, we were in the studios doing the *Burnin'* album. No days off."[24]

Perhaps since Bunny and Marley had shared a house as young teens, the sudden schism in their status was particularly annoying. Also, Blackwell booked them on back-to-back tours throughout the year, and Bunny resented that they were not going to be paid for touring. He refused to go to the US in the summer, believing the others would back him up, but they wanted to press on, so he quit, taking some comfort that his replacement was their old vocal teacher, Joe Higgs. Bunny went on to have his own storied career, releasing twenty-eight albums, picking up three Grammys.

By November, back in the UK, Tosh had the flu, hated the snow and low pay, and had dubbed Blackwell "Whiteworst."[25] When he wanted to release a solo album on Island, Blackwell declined because it would compete with the Wailers, so Tosh quit. "It was belittling my integrity. I taught Bob Marley. How can you compare the teacher with the taught? I and I and the devil are at war. The devil make Marley leader of the band."[26]

One of the last songs Tosh and Marley worked on before the split was "No Woman No Cry," captured on a London demo featured in the documentary *Marley*. Tosh provided gospel piano.[27] It was a fitting farewell, with lyrics about sitting in a Jamaican housing project, sharing food, burning wood, remembering good friends lost along the way, but pushing on through the tears. Marley assigned the publishing rights to Vincent "Tata" Ford, a man in a wheelchair who ran a soup kitchen in Trenchtown, where Marley received food as a child.[28]

Tosh went on to release seven albums, many on the Rolling Stones' record label, before a motorcycle gang murdered him in 1987.

✳

Jerry Garcia saw the Wailers play San Francisco's New Matrix in October, and reggae began to permeate the Dead's stew of influences. When Eric Clapton's cover of "Sheriff" climbed to No. 1 the following summer, Jamaica became an increasingly popular vacation destination for white hippies. Reggae-inflected drum circles became a regular fixture of hippie gatherings and, later, jam band festivals.

Punks like Johnny Rotten and the Clash also embraced the genre, which was natural, Lester Bangs wrote, since its songs consisted mainly of two or three chords, no solos, and a guy hollering things no white person could understand about class oppression and street war.[29] England enjoyed a ska/reggae movement spearheaded by the Specials, English Beat, Madness, UB40, which climaxed with the Police's mega-stardom. Australia's adherents included Men at Work; America's featured Fishbone and the Mighty Mighty Bosstones. Twenty years later, No Doubt, Sublime, and Rancid revived the revival. By then, Snoop Dogg and Dr. Dre had taken up Marley's cop-challenging, riot-celebrating torch/spliff.

Blackwell told *Rolling Stone*'s David Fricke in 2005 that Marley was disappointed black Americans did not embrace him during his lifetime. "But there was no market in black music then for a rebel. Black music in America has a different sensibility now—it's all rebel."[30] In 2018, *Forbes* ranked Marley the fifth highest-paid dead celebrity, right after Charles Schulz and right before Dr. Seuss; his estate earned $23 million that year.[31]

Jimmy Cliff went on to play stadiums in Africa and South America, though he never matched Marley's level of sales. The two remained friends until Marley's death in 1981 from melanoma. Cliff reflected, "Even though we had similar revolutionary aspirations, spirits and thoughts, I'm a bit of a loner, and he loved all the people. And so he attracted the good, the bad and the ugly."[32] Perhaps Cliff was referring to the unknown gunman who shot Marley in 1976. "We had always talked together, what I was going to do, what he was going to do. The same thing with Desmond Dekker, especially when we were in London at the same time. So we stayed really close like artist brothers. With that love and respect for each other. All along the way."[33]

Goodbye Yellow Brick Road

Elton John's double album controls the No. 1 spot for the last two months of the year. "Saturday Night's Alright for Fighting" reflects the tension of recording in Jamaica. "Candle in the Wind" becomes the second-bestselling single of all time. Black radio turns "Bennie and the Jets" into John's second American pop chart-topper.

✳

Elton John and his team arrived at the Pink Flamingo Hotel in Kingston, Jamaica, just a few weeks after the Stones vacated following their *Goats Head Soup* sessions. John was disturbed to learn he was staying in the same room Bill Wyman's wife, Astrid, had been assaulted in three weeks before.[1] The streets outside felt tumultuous as the city hosted the world heavyweight boxing championship between George Foreman and Joe Frazier. John stayed in his room and composed the music to twenty-one sets of lyrics by Bernie Taupin.[2]

John was equally unnerved by Dynamic Sound Studios, where the Stones, Marley, and Jimmy Cliff had recorded (and Cat Stevens would later in the year). Guards with machine guns and barbed wire protected the facility from record plant workers on strike, who pounded on the cars when John's entourage drove in. The protesters even spit fiberglass at them through pipes.³ Attempting to channel the hostility, the band took a stab at Taupin's tongue-in-cheek anthem for pub brawlers, "Saturday Night's Alright for Fighting."

"In those days, whenever a song came up, I'd immediately start working on what I should do," guitarist Davey Johnstone recalled. "Elton would write so fast, and I had to be just as quick to keep up. As soon as I heard him writing ['Saturday'] I knew it was a total guitar-rocking track. So I wrote the intro and all the guitar parts. It was so much fun."⁴

But John felt the studio's sound quality was poor and decided to cut out early, sparking real-life confrontations with the studio and hotel managers over bills. They returned to the Honky Château (Château d'Hérouville), where they'd recorded their previous two albums, and cut a snide pastiche called "Jamaica Jerk-Off," probably musing that there was no place like home.

On a typical day they recorded up to four songs. John would polish off the music to one of Taupin's compositions, then, while the band learned that one, he'd write the music for another. "Funnily enough, you do fall into a groove with success," Johnstone said. "It must be like gambling, when you hit a lucky streak and you just can't lose. Or that feeling of invincibility you get when you've had a few drinks. We were racking up the hits—'Daniel,' 'Rocket Man,' 'Crocodile Rock' and so on—and it was amazing. What happened was, our musical inhibitions went away. Success became our drug, and I don't just mean the financial rewards, I mean how great we felt when we played, and how we were received. The more successful we got, the better we played, and the easier it became to know what to play. It almost felt effortless."⁵

Returning to "Saturday Night's," the absurdity of John stomping ass at the local bar was erased by Johnstone's blistering riff, a hook so fierce even the Who eventually covered it. Initially John thought the rhythm section wasn't rocking enough, so he stood up from the piano and roared, "Come on you bastards!"⁶ As they captured the music and vocal in one take, he jumped around, then lay on the floor and whipped himself into a vocal-shredding frenzy. Producer Gus Dudgeon stacked the guitar track onto itself multiple times, and John overdubbed pounding piano.

Despite John's goofy camp image (belligerently swigging wine in a Slade-like get-up on the single's cover), some radio stations banned the song, as it was the year that *A Clockwork Orange* was blamed for copycat violence. (The film was recut in the US and withdrawn from release in the UK.) It was the only single John released between 1972 and 1975 that did not go Top

10 in the States (stalling at 12), too aggressive to cross over to easy listening. In concert the song gave John a chance to preen like Jagger, clapping his hands and exhorting the audience to chant "Saturday!" before making his way back to maniacally slam the piano keys.

✻

Inspired by the movie-theater cover of their last record, Taupin initially envisioned a concept album called *Silent Movies, Talking Pictures*. "Roy Rogers" depicted a man escaping his mundane life by watching the old cowboy films that excited his imagination as a kid. "The Ballad of Danny Bailey" romanticized celluloid gangsters; "Candle in the Wind," doomed starlets. The track that ultimately became the title song paid homage to the first movie Taupin saw as a child, *The Wizard of Oz*. "I've Seen That Movie Too" expanded the metaphor as the singer rues that he can see through his lover's play-acting.

The new collection was also a reaction to the last. John considered *Don't Shoot Me* "a disposable album. I think it's a very happy album, very ultra-pop."[7] So Taupin provided a darker set of songs for the follow-up, maybe borrowing a page from the Beatles' playbook: they'd followed the high spirits of *A Hard Day's Night* with the downcast *Beatles for Sale*.

Perhaps feeling overworked, John imagined his own death and composed music that he wanted played at his memorial service. Producer Dudgeon combined this with a piece he commissioned from engineer David Hentschel, an overture that drew on melodies from "Candle in the Wind," "Danny Bailey," and other tracks, played on the ARP synthesizer.[8] "Funeral for a Friend" segued directly into the second-best riff on the album, "Love Lies Bleeding," its chewy twang a precursor to the Police's "Synchronicity II."

"I'll tell you something incredible: The whole song, including 'Funeral for a Friend,' was one take," Johnstone said. "We rehearsed it a couple of times, but that was it. Again, Elton's attention span—he's very impatient. So as soon as we knew what the song was going to be, we went in and nailed it, played it straight through. I knew I would do some layering and overdubs, but still, the idea was to do as much as possible all at once."[9]

Two years earlier, John had given Taupin one of Marilyn Monroe's dresses for his birthday, and she became the heroine of the album's third track. "What I was enamored with was the idea of fame or youth and somebody being cut short in the prime of their life," said Taupin of "Candle in the Wind." "How we glamorise death, how we immortalise people."[10]

He'd heard Clive Davis refer to Janis Joplin as a "candle in the wind," a term that had already served as the title of two plays and a novel in T. H. White's series about Camelot, *The Once and Future King.* Taupin said the song "could have been about James Dean, it could have been about Montgomery Clift, it could have been about Jim Morrison."[11]

But the song became permanently associated with another icon in 1997. John had grown close to Princess Diana, and she comforted him after the loss of his friend Gianni Versace in July—a month before she herself was killed in a car crash while being chased by paparazzi, a dark echo to the song's lyrics mourning a heroine hounded by the press. John requested Taupin revise the lyrics and played this version only once, at her funeral. It became the fastest- and bestselling song in UK history, eventually the second-biggest-selling single of all time after Bing Crosby's "White Christmas."

Death also haunts "All the Girls Love Alice," about a sixteen-year-old rejected by her mother who becomes the go-to girl for middle-aged women to call when their husbands are out of town, until she's found dead on the subway, her demise unexplained. It covered some of the same ground of that year's debut novel by Rita Mae Brown, *Rubyfruit Jungle,* in which young lesbian Molly Bolt gets kicked out of the house by her mother and tries to survive on the streets of New York. Her lover encourages her to become a kept woman to older lesbians, though Molly rejects that option, unlike Alice. After being published by a small feminist press, *Rubyfruit Jungle* became one of the first successful novels featuring a lesbian heroine.

The other gender-nonconforming female on the album does not share the same grim fate. Taupin said, "I saw Bennie and the Jets as a sort of proto-sci-fi punk band, fronted by an androgynous woman, who looks like something out of a Helmut Newton photograph."[12]

In mohair suit and electric boots, Bennie sounds like a precursor to Annie Lennox, a female Ziggy Stardust with a "spaced out" band leading children to fight parents in the street. John and the band figured the song was so weird it would probably not make it onto the album. Perhaps that freed John to give one of his most idiosyncratically assured performances, using the Benzedrine double entendre of the name to stutter like the Who's amphetamine anthem "My Generation," masterfully employing vocal fry, unhurriedly drawing out syllables, then endlessly repeating the title in beautifully absurd falsetto.

Even though John wrote the track off, Dudgeon decided to mess around with it. À la *Sgt. Pepper* he faded in crowd sounds from a show John gave at Royal Festival Hall. At the end he used applause from Jimi Hendrix's Isle of

Wight performance. Then, to be perverse, he added the sound of an audience clapping on "the wrong beat, because English audiences always clap on the 'on' instead of the 'off' beat, which drives me crazy."[13] He threw in some whistles, then coated it with glossy reverb.

Afterward, Johnstone said, "we just sat back and said, 'This is really odd.'"[14] There was no intention to make it a single.

But a black station in Detroit, WJLB, started playing it. It became one of their most requested songs, and the album started selling in black record stores. The music director of Detroit's Top 40 station CKLW, Rosalie Trombley (the one immortalized in Bob Seger's "Rosalie"), added it to their playlist. Listeners bombarded the station with requests to hear it again. She let John's label know. The singer called her a few days later.

"If you want to reach a black audience, you really should consider making this your next single," she told him.[15]

John resisted. "I had an argument with MCA and the only reason I caved was because the song was the No. 1 black record in Detroit. And I went, 'Oh my God.' I mean, I'm a white boy from England. And I said, 'Okay, you've got it.' I'm such a black record fanatic that to think I'm actually in the R&B chart means that even if it doesn't get higher than 34 I'm gonna stick it up and frame it."[16] Though he fretted, "What am I going to do on my next American tour? Play the Apollo for a week, open with 'Bennie and the Jets' then say, 'Thanks, you can all go home now.'"[17] It actually made it to No. 15 on the R&B charts, and No. 1 US pop.

He was even more shocked when *Soul Train* invited him to perform it on the show, making him one of only a handful of white artists so honored. Thus a song the producer used to spoof how white people couldn't clap on the beat became one of the few white performances in the program's history.

"It just shows you that you can't see the wood through the trees," John said. "To this day, I cannot see that song as a single."[18]

Other highlights in the collection included "Grey Seal," a remake of an older Elton John B side. Taupin denied knowing what the lyrics meant, but John's glistening piano triplets suggested the animal swimming free in Arctic Ocean purity. "Harmony," another exemplary mix of Taupin sardonicism obscured by warm John melodicism, would eventually be considered for the album's fifth single. But by that point the prolific team already had a new album, *Caribou,* on the conveyor belt.[19]

Amid the riches, the finest moment was the title track itself. If "Honky Cat" was split down the middle between the appeal of country life and city life, Taupin was now ready to return to the small village of his childhood. In his youth he'd romanticized the London music industry, but after years spent drinking backstage with the "dogs of society" and partying in their penthouses, he saw through the glamour. And as he confessed on an ABC TV special, since his gig only necessitated working two weeks a year, he had too much time on his hand and was, as recounted in "Social Disease," "getting bombed for breakfast."

"The lyrics to the title track do say that I want to leave Oz and get back to the farm. I think that's still my M.O. these days. I don't mind getting out there and doing what everybody else was doing, but I always had to have an escape hatch."[20]

John said that during the making of the album he was very happy. His own substance abuse issues didn't start until the following year, when he discovered cocaine. But there was something ineffable about the way John's falsetto high-jumped through the Leslie speakers with Dudgeon's echoey orchestra. It carried both the sadness and freedom of letting go of dreams, catharsis for a year that saw the death of many illusions: that the country would always win its wars, that its presidents were always noble, that its families would always stay together, that its economy would always grow.

✳

John liked a *Creem* magazine cover that Ian Beck illustrated of Bowie in front of a poster on a brick wall. So he hired Beck to render John stepping through a poster on a city wall into Oz. His platform boots updated Judy Garland's ruby slippers. The cover's burned-out yellow color scheme became synonymous with the early '70s.

A month before the double album's release, for his triumphant Hollywood Bowl performance on September 7, John asked *Deep Throat*'s Linda Lovelace to open the show. She introduced a panoply of characters who would have been at home on the Hollywood-themed record: the Queen of England, Elvis, Frankenstein's monster, the Pope, the Beatles, Batman and Robin, Groucho, and Mae West. As she called their names, performers dressed as the figures took the stage and lifted the lids of five rainbow-colored pianos. The open lids spelled ELTON, and doves hidden in the pianos flew out above the crowd as the singer arrived. "Here he is: the biggest, the largest, the most gigantic and fantastic man, the costar of my next movie, Elton John!" Lovelace raved as Elton pounded out "Elderberry Wine" (and Taupin threw out birds who tried to remain in the pianos).

For the press conference promoting the album, John's image was transmitted by satellite from, apparently, a midwestern Holiday Inn and he took questions from journalists until the signal abruptly cut out. The journalists waited for it to return, but finally gave up and approached the buffet arranged for them. John nonchalantly walked in and stepped into line beside them. He'd been broadcasting from a nearby room the whole time.[22]

Goodbye Yellow Brick Road held the No. 1 spot for two weeks in the UK and for two months in the US starting November 10, making him the only artist to have two chart-topping records in the States that year (unless you count McCartney with *Red Rose Speedway* and *Beatles 1967–1970*). It ended up becoming the bestselling album of 1974, eventually selling thirty million worldwide and going eight times platinum, the highest-selling album of John's career. *Rolling Stone* placed it as No. 91 in its list of the 500 Greatest Albums. Had it been boiled down to a single disc, it would have given *The Dark Side of the Moon* a run for best record of the year.

John flew to arenas, coliseums, and stadiums in the Starship, the plane Zeppelin and the Allman Brothers used, with its multiple rooms and waterbeds. Fans mobbed his limos and stormed the security guards to get onstage, held lighters aloft for "Your Song." To capitalize on Elton mania he rushed into the studio to cut "Step into Christmas" backed with "Ho, Ho, Ho (Who'd Be a Turkey at Christmas)." For a moment, his pop domination recalled the heyday of Presley and the Beatles.

"The preeminent rock star of the '70s seems out of time, untouched by the decade's confusion," wrote Robert Christgau. "The best way to explain him is to steal an idea from Greil Marcus: Elton is the superfan, the ultimate music consumer. This is literally true—his collection of popular records is almost certainly one of the largest in the world, and he seems to listen to all of them. . . . And finally, the superfan's reward is the fans' reward. Elton is our tabula rasa—the very sureness of his instinct for sales makes him a kind of one-man Zeitgeist."[23]

"I think in those days, because we were a unit, because of my relationship with Bernie and the band and the management team and everything that went with it, it was just like a little family and it was great," John said. "It was magic. That time in my life, that creative period will never, ever come back again. You search for it and you try to say, 'Oh, it would be great to do,' but it'll never happen like that again. It was a special time."[24]

Epilogue

※

Keep On Truckin'

Due to the ongoing fuel crisis, Nixon appealed to citizens to cut back on holiday lights. The White House did not bring in the typical giant Christmas tree and illuminate it with 74,500 watts. They decorated one on the grounds with 9,640 watts. Inside the White House, the Nixons used just tinsel on their tree, no bulbs.[1] Many towns reduced the number of days they lit their trees. Cities from Houston to Detroit decorated trees but did not light them. St. Paul abstained from decorating altogether.

The No. 1 song as 1973 became 1974 was Jim Croce's "Time in a Bottle." He had written the song three years ago in December, when his wife told him she was pregnant. His producer Tommy West added a harpsichord, having heard the instrument in a horror movie the night before the recording session. The song was originally just an album track. But in the wake of Croce's death, his lament that "there never seems to be enough time" inspired deejays across the country to start playing it, so ABC released it as a single, a fitting reminder at the end of the year to make the most of the life you have left.

Other artists in the Top 20 included the Steve Miller Band with "The Joker," Elton John, Todd Rundgren, the Carpenters, Stevie Wonder, Chicago, and two Beatles, McCartney with "Helen Wheels" and Lennon with "Mind Games." Starr wasn't far below with both "You're Sixteen" and "Photograph."

Thus passed the crowning year for the rock and roll monoculture, a year that witnessed milestones from five of the eight artists who have sold over 250 million units: the Beatles, Elvis, Elton John, Led Zeppelin, and Pink Floyd.[2] Fifteen of the year's nineteen No. 1 albums were rock albums. By contrast, in 2018, only eight out of the forty-one No. 1 albums were rock.[3] The genre is almost gone from the singles chart, comprised now mostly of hip hop and pop, with some electronic dance music and some country.[4] Blues rock, the strain that dominated the genre after the Rolling Stones and Yardbirds rose out of the British club scene is now gone except for occasional albums by Jack White, the Black Keys, and John Mayer, faded like Tin Pan Alley before it.

In 2017, Nielsen announced that hip hop and R&B had surpassed rock as the top genre in overall sales in all formats, accounting for 25.1 percent of music purchased as opposed to rock's 23 percent. Rock was still responsible for 40 percent of all album sales.[5] However, album sales now only made up 4.3 percent of the Recording Industry Association of America's (RIAA) revenue.[6] In 1973, they made up 61.8 percent. Streaming now generates more money than the sale of CDs, downloads, and vinyl put together, accounting for 75 percent of music industry revenue. The music business is now once again all about the singles, as it was in the era before 1967's *Sgt. Pepper's Lonely Hearts Club Band*.

Most of today's singles sound closer to Kraftwerk than to the earthy rock that dominated '73. You'd be hard-pressed to find a real drum in pop music today, and even rock drums are airbrushed by "drum replacement"—with each hit of the snare swapped out for a clip of the perfect drum beat, to make the track sound flawless.[7]

There's also the "loudness war." Producers once allowed dynamic contrast between the quiet moments of a song and its loud sections. But starting in the late '80s many producers strove to be louder than the other songs on the radio by mixing their quiet parts to be almost as loud as their peaks, while pushing the loud parts into the red zone so that the guitars distorted or "clipped."[8] Dylan complained in 2006, "You listen to these modern records, they're atrocious, they have sound all over them. There's no definition of nothing, no vocal, no nothing, just like—static."[9] Which is one reason vinyl endures (currently making up 2.17 percent of all music sales, including streaming and downloads). Analog allows for more depth between quiet and loud, and vinyl holds more information than the MP3 digital format, so it is closer in quality to the original master tape recorded in the studio.

Another reason 1973 sounds distinct from today is the omnipresence of

Garageband, the music software available for free in Apple computers. Its beats and mixing features have been used on everything from Rhianna's smash "Umbrella" to songs by Radiohead, Duran Duran, Kendrick Lamar, and Usher.[10]

On today's radio, 1970s rock is closer to country than to the hits played on the pop stations. "Nashville is America's new rock capital," *Rolling Stone* wrote in January 2019. Today's country sounds like the Eagles or Lynyrd Skynyrd with a more pronounced twang and updated production sheen. Ronnie Dunn of Brooks and Dunn noted that the Eagles would be "hard-core country by today's standards."[11] Vince Gill observed, "Those guys [the Eagles] and those songs affected this music more than all of our heroes. If you look at today's incarnation of what country music is, the Eagles had more to do with it than Hank, George Jones and Merle. There's nothing that you hear out of our music today that harkens to that."[12]

But there is one area of the business where rock still leads. "Hip-hop is huge, but on the concert circuit, rock is king," *The Wall Street Journal* wrote in late 2018. Four of that year's top twenty-five touring acts were 1973 stars: the Stones, the Eagles, Billy Joel, and Elton John. In 2019, Kiss, Paul McCartney, and Queen were scheduled to join them on the road. And the *Journal* noted hope for the future. "Older rockers like the Rolling Stones get most of the credit for driving North America's $8 billion concert-touring industry, but an underappreciated reason for live music's boom is the strength of smaller acts."[13]

✳

In Hollywood, Capitol Records took down the seventy-five-foot Christmas tree it traditionally lit atop its headquarters. The oil crisis also affected the records themselves. LPs usually weighed up to 120 grams (about 4 ounces), but a vinyl shortage reduced them to as light as 80 grams. On both sides of the Atlantic, people returned records for being warped and too thin.

The New York Times's January 1 editorial "Resolution for a New Era" proclaimed, "With 1973, an era died, an era of profligacy unprecedented in human experience when most Americans embarked on an orgy of consumption, following the lean years of the Depression and World War II."[14]

Many American consumers wondered why they should keep buying Detroit cars that only managed ten miles to the gallon and frequently broke down, and began buying more Japanese and German cars. When Toyota,

Honda, and Volkswagen opened American factories, they did so in "right to work" (nonunion) southern states. General Motors followed suit, building eleven new southern factories by 1978.[15] The United Auto Workers' efforts to unionize these regions were largely thwarted.

Between the 1940s and 1970s, the American worker enjoyed a 90 percent increase in compensation. But from the early 1970s to 2018, the increase in average worker compensation (when adjusted for inflation) was 12 percent.[16] According to *Forbes,* in 1950 the average CEO made 20 times the salary of the average worker. In 1980, the CEO made 42 times as much as a worker. In 2000, 120 times.[17] In 2013, *Bloomberg* reported the average CEO compensation was 204 times as great. In 2018, 361 times.[18]

As mentioned in the introduction, the average worker's wage peaked in 1973 when adjusted for inflation. The year also saw the opening of the World Trade Center twin towers and the completion of the Sears (now Willis) Tower. Nearly half a century later, the rebuilt One World Trade Center and the Willis Tower remain the largest buildings in the western hemisphere.[19]

✳

On New Year's Eve, a Monday, Kiss opened for the Stooges and Blue Oyster Cult at New York's Academy of Music. The band could not afford top-of-the-line Marshall speakers but loaded huge (empty) speaker cabinets onto the stage to make it look like they used the same high-powered equipment as the major groups. They also brought a sign that flashed their name on and off like a marquee, four feet high by ten feet wide, a foot deep.

"Dude, it's etched in my mind," Iggy Pop recalled. "Kiss were third on the bill that night, probably getting fifty bucks, but they had a giant Kiss sign made of lights that must have weighed five hundred pounds."[20]

Smoke machines hissed fog while Peter Criss's drum platform rose. His drumsticks exploded, made of flash paper (a flammable compound used by magicians). During the song "Firehouse," Gene Simmons filled his mouth with kerosene and spit it onto a torch for the first time. The torch set his hair spray on fire. "The left side of my head was in flames. I didn't know what was going on except all of a sudden, the *entire* audience was on its feet."[21] A man ran onstage from the wings and put a leather jacket on his head to put the flames out.[22]

Simmons threw flash paper above the audience, as if shooting fireballs to explode above them. "That night my aim wasn't so good and some guy was standing on his chair and that flash went off in his face. I saw it explode in his face, and he fell over like a pin in a bowling alley."[23]

The band's manager, Bill Aucoin, rushed to call his lawyer to get language for a release, which he asked the poor kid to sign. Criss recalled, "Bill ushered the kid backstage after the show and we had him pose with us for a photo and then Bill gave him a lifetime pass to the Academy of Music."[24]

The young man had singed eyebrows and blisters on his face. Simmons said it looked like "Velveeta cheese had melted over the left side of his face. He looked like someone from a Hammer horror movie."[25]

But the kid said, "You guys are awesome! Wow, that was the coolest show I've ever seen!"[26] En route into the ambulance he told reporters that Kiss was his favorite band.[27]

✳

Over the holidays, twenty-seven-year-old Donald Trump wondered if the strategy he and his father, Fred, had adopted to fight the Department of Justice would work. They were scheduled to face off against the agency in January at the US courthouse in Brooklyn.

The DOJ had brought suit against the Trump Management Corporation on October 15 for discriminating against blacks, claiming the family blocked them from renting units in their Queens housing development. Folk singer Woody Guthrie had noticed this after he signed a two-year lease in 1950, prompting him to write the angry song "Old Man Trump."

> *I suppose*
> *Old Man Trump knows*
> *Just how much*
> *Racial Hate*
> *he stirred up*
> *In the bloodpot of human hearts*

In 1927, multiple newspapers—including *The New York Times,* the *Daily Star,* the *Queens County Evening News,* and the *Richmond Hill Record*—had reported that Fred Trump was arrested at a Ku Klux Klan march in Queens "on a charge of refusing to disperse from a parade when ordered to do so."[28]

The morning the DOJ brought suit against the Trumps, Donald read an editorial by Roy Cohn, former right-hand man of Senator Joseph McCarthy, the anti-Communist witch hunter. In the editorial, Cohn criticized Spiro Agnew for resigning as vice president, arguing that he should have fought to hold his position. Trump found Cohn that day in Manhattan's Le Club and asked his advice.[29] Cohn encouraged him to never admit guilt, to double down, to fight back. With Cohn as his lawyer, Trump filed a $100 million countersuit against the Justice Department on December 12 for false claims.

That year in Queens, white kids still dressing like the Lords of Flatbush in leather jackets and ducktails rioted against busing, forcing classes to be canceled and schools to be closed.[30] Another Queens native on *All in the Family* was watched each week by up to a third of all Americans. Some feared the show made racism more palatable. Others found Archie Bunker lovable despite his flaws. "You think it, but ole Archie says it, by damn," praised a fan.[31]

❊

The day before Trump filed his countersuit, the Gay Raiders zapped the Most Trusted Man in America. A twenty-three-year-old activist named Mark Segal told CBS that he was a college student and requested permission to watch the taping of the evening news. At 6:44 p.m., Segal said, "I sat on [Walter] Cronkite's desk directly in front of him and held up the sign [GAYS PROTEST CBS PREJUDICE] while the technicians furiously ran after me and wrestled me to the floor and wrapped me in wire [cables]—on camera. The network went black while they took us out of the studio."[32]

Cronkite said to his audience, "Well, a rather interesting development in the studio here—a protest demonstration right in the middle of the CBS News studio. . . . The young man was identified as a member of something called Gay Raiders, an organization protesting alleged defamation of homosexuals on entertainment programs."

Segal was charged with trespassing. After testifying in the court case, Cronkite asked him, "Why did you do that?"

Segal told him that CBS had neglected to do stories on the twenty-three cities that enacted gay rights legislation, doing only one story on how New York failed to pass it. CBS also did not cover Gay Pride Day.

Cronkite introduced Segal to CBS management and began regularly covering the gay rights movement on his program, closing his next installment on the local New York struggle with "Part of the new morality of the 60's and 70's is a new attitude toward homosexuality. The homosexual men and women have organized to fight for acceptance and respectability. They've succeeded in winning equal rights under the law in many communities. But in the nation's biggest city, the fight goes on."[33]

Segal said Cronkite became "his friend and mentor."[34] The $450 fine he paid for trespassing was "the happiest check I ever wrote."[35]

✳

"I've got this riff and it's a bit Rolling Stonesy—I just want to piss Mick off a bit,"[36] Bowie said to guitarist Alan Parker, whom Bowie enlisted to back him now that he no longer employed the Spiders from Mars.

Parker said, "I spent about three-quarters of an hour to an hour with him working on the guitar riff—he had it almost there, but not quite. We got it there, and he said, 'Oh, we'd better do a middle. . . .' So he wrote something for the middle, put that in."[37]

Bowie wrote "Rebel Rebel" that autumn for his musical based on *1984*. When George Orwell's widow refused to grant him the rights, he turned it into the album *Diamond Dogs*. "Rebel" was for the female glam rock fans, the ones who danced at Rodney's English Disco like Cherie Currie and Joan Jett, the ones whose mothers were "not sure if you're a boy or a girl."

That could be Patti Smith, who fit into the androgynous Max's/Warhol milieu (doing plays with Wayne County, opening for Jackie Curtis). But she arrived from the other direction; instead of a guy dressing like a girl, she was a woman who looked like a man. "I was in my beyond-gender mode," Smith said.[38] When Allen Ginsberg hit on her, she had to tell him, "Look at the tits, Allen! Notice the tits!"[39] She cut her hair like Keith Richards, wore torn T-shirts, spit, swore, the ultimate beatnik angry-looking chick, something the pop machine would never manufacture.

Last New Year's, when 1972 became 1973, she'd felt adrift. "Once again I found myself contemplating what I should be doing to do something of worth. Everything I came up with seemed irreverent or irrelevant."[40]

But she started opening for the New York Dolls at Mercer, reading poetry, maybe performing an occasional song. It was rough going at first, but she learned how to face off against the drunken hecklers, and during the summer she began to win the crowd over.

She saw *The Harder They Come* and loved how the Rastas connected themselves to the ancient tribes of Israel and the Bible. "Somewhere along the line I decided to try their sacred herb."[41] Smoking pot helped her improvise when she jammed with Lenny Kaye, the critic-guitarist who curated the *Nuggets* garage-rock/punk compilation. She was a rock critic, too, writing for *Rolling Stone, Creem, Circus, Crawdaddy*. She sought him out after appreciating an article he wrote for *Creem* about doo-wop. He recognized her from Max's. "She would come into Village Oldies, the record store I worked in on Bleecker Street, and we'd drink a little beer on Saturday nights and pull records from the stacks and dance to them and hang out."[42]

Gradually she started thinking more about rocking. She went out with the bassist for Blue Oyster Cult, wrote a song for them called "Baby Ice Dog." She and Bebe Buell would put on *Raw Power* and sing "Gimme Danger" into the mirror, practicing their moves.[43]

Finally, she went on a pilgrimage to Paris to visit the haunts of her favorite poet, Rimbaud.[44] When she returned she started doing "Rock and Rimbaud" shows with Kaye accompanying her on guitar at Le Jardin, one of the city's discos. Mickey Ruskin gave them six nights at Max's opening for folk singer Phil Ochs, including New Year's Eve.

On New Year's Day, the duo performed at the Poetry Project at St. Mark's Church. As she took the stage, she passed a writer she knew from Warhol's *Interview* magazine, Victor Bockris. "She spat on the ground right in front of me, and said, 'You owe me money, motherfucker!' And I was like, 'Fuck you!' I mean, I thought, she's an asshole, but she's really good."[45]

She and Kaye climaxed, as had become tradition, with "Piss Factory," her autobiographical account of working in a New Jersey factory when she was sixteen, enduring the harassment of her fellow employees. "I'm gonna be somebody, I'm gonna get on that train, go to New York City," she chanted. "Never return, no, never return, to burn out in this piss factory."

And with that she strode past the cheering crowd and out the door, into the new year. Elsewhere, Nixon futilely stonewalled the release of tapes that exposed his obstruction of justice. Stevie Wonder prepped for his return to the stage later that month. Mid-level bands like Golden Earring drove all night with "Radar Love" coming in from above. Neil Young sat at his piano at Broken Arrow Ranch, drawing on the Stones' "Lady Jane" to write "Borrowed Tune," singing, "I'm climbin' this ladder, my head in the clouds. I hope that it matters." The next underground movements gathered steam, to bloom and wash away like those before, leaving behind an endless beach of jewels to be rediscovered in the decades to come, new ones rising from the algorithms of YouTube and Spotify every day.

Notes

✳

Citations without page numbers are from the e-book version of the book.

INTRODUCTION: RAW POWER AND INNERVISIONS

1. Clark Collis, "Vinyl: Martin Scorsese Talks New HBO Show, Chooses Favorite Records for EW," *Entertainment Weekly,* January 15, 2015, https://ew.com/article/2015/01/15/vinyl-martin-scorsese-hbo/.
2. Walt Hickey, "Why Classic Rock Isn't What It Used to Be," *FiveThirtyEight,* July 7, 2014, https://fivethirtyeight.com/features/why-classic-rock-isnt-what-it-used-to-be/.
3. "List of Best-Selling Music Artists," https://en.wikipedia.org/wiki/List_of_best-selling_music_artists.
4. Hickey, "Why Classic Rock Isn't What It Used to Be."
5. Marcus, *Mystery Train: Images of America in Rock 'n' Roll Music.*
6. *Almost Famous,* directed by Cameron Crowe (2000), DVD.
7. Christgau, *Is It Still Good to Ya? Fifty Years of Rock Criticism, 1967–2017.*
8. Breithaupt and Breithaupt, *Precious and Few: Pop Music of the Early '70s.*
9. "List of *Billboard* Hot 100 Number-One Singles of 1973," https://en.wikipedia.org/wiki/List_of_Billboard_Hot_100_number-one_singles_of_1973.
10. Marsh, *The Heart of Rock and Soul: The 1001 Greatest Singles Ever Made.*
11. Chet Flippo, "Willie Nelson: Holy Man of the Honky Tonks," *Rolling Stone,* July 13, 1978, https://www.rollingstone.com/music/music-country/willie-nelson-holy-man-of-the-honky-tonks-118425/.
12. Eric R. Danton, "Fanny Lives: Inside the Return of the Pioneering All-Female Rock Band," *Rolling Stone,* March 16, 2018, https://www.rollingstone.com/music/music-features/fanny-lives-inside-the-return-of-the-pioneering-all-female-rock-band-125635/.
13. Ibid.
14. Eileen Shanahan, "A.T&T. to Grant 15,000 Back Pay in Job Inequities," *New York Times,* January 19, 1973, https://www.nytimes.com/1973/01/19/archives/att-to-grant-15000-back-pay-in-job-inequities-36000-expected-to.html.
15. Bullock, *David Bowie Made Me Gay: 100 Years of LGBT Music.*
16. Gill, *Queer Noises: Lesbian and Gay Music in the 20th Century.*

17. Andrew Young, "SCOPE Orientation, June 18, 1965. Discussion of Problems of Understanding," KZSU Project South Interviews (SC0066), Department of Special Collections and University Archives, Stanford University Libraries, Stanford, CA, www.oac.cdlib.org/findaid/ark:/13030/tf7489n969/entire_text/.

18. Chet Flippo, "Waylon Jennings Gets Off the Grind-'Em-Out Circuit," *Rolling Stone,* December 6, 1973, https://www.rollingstone.com/music/music-news /waylon-jennings-gets-off-the-grind-em-out-circuit-249.

19. Bob Frick, "Diary of a Bear Market," *Kiplinger,* October 1, 2008, https://www .kiplinger.com/article/investing/T031-C000-S001-diary-of-a-bear-market.html.

20. Drew DeSilver, "For Most U.S. Workers, Real Wages Have Barely Budged in Decades," Pew Research Center, August 7, 2018, https://www.pewresearch.org /fact-tank/2018/08/07/for-most-us-workers-real-wages-have-barely-budged-for -decades/.

21. Megan Ray Nichols, "Why Was the Robotic Arm Invented?" *Interesting Engineering,* February 9, 2019, https://interestingengineering.com/why-was-the-robotic -arm-invented.

1. THE DOPE'S THAT THERE'S STILL HOPE

1. Scott Cohen, "Bob Dylan: Not like a Rolling Stone Interview," *Spin,* December 1985, https://www.interferenza.net/bcs/interw/85-dec.htm.

2. Cameron Crowe, Biograph Liner Notes, 1985, *All Dylan,* http://alldylan.com /november-7-did-bob-dylan-invent-the-modern-box-set-with-biograph/.

3. Chet Flippo, "Dylan Meets the Durango Kid," *Rolling Stone,* March 15, 1973, https://www.rollingstone.com/music/music-news/dylan-meets-the-durango-kid -kristofferson-and-dylan-in-mexico-242768/.

4. Ibid.

5. Ibid.

6. Lee Siegel, "Pat Garrett and Billy the Kid: The Wildest Western Ever Made," *Men's Journal,* October 1, 2013, https://www.mensjournal.com/features/pat-garrett-and -billy-the-kid-the-wildest-western-ever-made-20131001/.

7. Max Bell, "Q&A: Kris Kristofferson," *Classic Rock,* August 2010, 34.

8. Kevin Pergantis, "Danny Wallin: Six Decades of Classic Film Tracks," *Mix Online,* October 26, 2018, https://www.mixonline.com/sfp/danny-wallin-six-decades-of -classic-film-tracks.

9. "Bob Dylan Special: The Complete Tell Tale Signs," *Uncut,* October 17, 2008, https://www.uncut.co.uk/features/bob-dylan-tell-tale-signs-special-part-nine -37893.

10. Don Zulaica, "SoundSpike Interview: Drummer Jim Keltner," *SoundSpike,* August 4, 2000, http://jimkeltnerdiscography.blogspot.com/2012/04/.

11. "Bob Dylan Special: The Complete Tell Tale Signs."

12. William Plummer, "'Mad Housewife' Carrie Snodgress Sues Rocker Neil Young for Support of Their Handicapped Son," *People,* September 26, 1983, https:// people.com/archive/mad-housewife-carrie-snodgress-sues-rocker-neil-young-for -support-of-their-handicapped-son-vol-20-no-13/.

13. "Remembering Danny Whitten & The Memories," *Neil Young News,* January 16, 2013,

http://neilyoungnews.thrasherswheat.org/2013/01/remembering-danny-whitten
-memories.html.

14. Cameron Crowe, "The Rebellious Neil Young," *Rolling Stone,* August 14, 1975,
https://www.rollingstone.com/music/music-news/the-rebellious-neil-young
-117887/.

15. Young, *Waging Heavy Peace: A Hippie Dream.*

16. McDonough, *Shakey,* 415.

17. Wurtzel, *More, Now, Again: A Memoir of Addiction,* 110.

18. Luerssen, *Bruce Springsteen FAQ: All That's Left to Know About the Boss.*

19. Hugh Fielder, "Story Behind the Song: Blinded by the Light," *Classic Rock,* February 12, 2018, https://www.loudersound.com/features/story-behind-song-blinded
-by-the-light-by-manfred-mann-s-earth-band.

20. Springsteen, *Born to Run.*

21. "Rosalita," *Springsteen Lyrics,* https://www.springsteenlyrics.com/lyrics.php?song
=rosalita.

22. Carlin, *Bruce.*

23. Sewall-Ruskin, *High on Rebellion: Inside the Underground at Max's Kansas City.*

24. Ibid.

2. YEAH! IT WAS TIME TO UNFREEZE

1. Rob Sheffield, "How America Inspired David Bowie to Kill Ziggy Stardust with
'Aladdin Sane,'" *Rolling Stone,* April 13, 2016, https://www.rollingstone.com
/music/music-news/how-america-inspired-david-bowie-to-kill-ziggy-stardust
-with-aladdin-sane-230827/.

2. Cameron Crowe, "David Bowie: Ground Control to Davy Jones," *Rolling Stone,*
February 12, 1976, https://www.rollingstone.com/music/music-news/david-bowie
-ground-control-to-davy-jones-77059/.

3. Mick Jagger, "Mick Jagger Remembers David Bowie: 'He Would Share So Much
with Me,'" *Rolling Stone,* January 26, 2016, https://www.rollingstone.com/music
/music-news/mick-jagger-remembers-david-bowie-he-would-share-so-much-with
-me-231370/.

4. Jones, *David Bowie: The Oral History.*

5. Gillian McCain, "Angela Bowie: The PKM Interview 3," *Please Kill Me,* December 30, 2015, https://pleasekillme.com/angela-bowie-pkm-interview-3/.

6. Bowie and Carr, *Backstage Passes: Life on the Wild Side with David Bowie.*

7. Leigh, *Bowie: The Biography.*

8. Alice Vincent, "Does a 1960s Elvis Song Hold the Key to Bowie's Blackstar, and
5 Other Theories Behind His Mysterious Farewell," *The Telegraph,* January 13,
2016, https://www.telegraph.co.uk/music/news/does-a-1960s-elvis-song-hold-the
-key-to-bowies-blackstar-and-5-o/.

9. Pauline McCloud, "My Favorite Photograph by Mick Jagger's Ex Girlfriend, Singer
Claudia Lennear," *Express,* March 30, 2014, https://www.express.co.uk/life-style
/life/467453/Mick-Jagger-ex-Claudia-Lennear-interview.

10. Chris O'Leary, "Lady Grinning Soul," *Pushing Ahead of the Dame,* https://
bowiesongs.wordpress.com/2010/06/30/lady-grinning-soul/.

11. Ben Griffiths, "Ziggy's Sex Van," *Sun,* January 8, 2017, https://www.thesun.co.uk /tvandshowbiz/2561057/david-bowies-first-girlfriend-reveals-how-the-superstar -would-prowl-the-streets-in-an-old-ambulance-and-pick-up-infatuated-fans-for -sex-sessions/.

12. Maureen Callahan, "A Life on Mars," July 10, 2011, https://nypost.com/2011/07/10 /a-life-on-mars/.

13. Leigh, *Bowie: The Biography.*

14. Ibid.

15. Ibid.

16. Foxe-Tyler, *Dream On.*

17. Trynka, *David Bowie: Starman.*

18. Jones, *David Bowie: The Oral History.*

19. Tony Parsons, "David Bowie Interview," *Arena,* Spring/Summer 1993, https:// welcomebackbowie.wordpress.com/articles/david-bowie-interview-in-arena -springsummer-1993/.

20. Maarten de Haan, "Mike Garson: History and True Abandon," *Artist Interviews,* 2008, http://www.artistinterviews.eu/home/mike-garson/?parent_id=22.

21. Harvey Kubernik, "David Bowie's Aladdin Sane," *Record Collector,* August 31, 2013, http://recordcollectornews.com/2013/08/david-bowies-aladdin-sane/.

22. Buckley, *Strange Fascination: David Bowie: The Definitive Story.*

23. Pegg, *The Complete David Bowie.*

24. Buckley, *Elton: The Biography,* 118.

25. Doyle, *Captain Fantastic: Elton John's Stellar Trip Through the '70s,* 73.

26. Paul Gambaccini, "Elton John: The *Rolling Stone* Interview," *Rolling Stone,* August 16, 1973, https://www.rollingstone.com/music/music-news/elton-john-the-rolling -stone-interview-76059/.

27. Doyle, *Captain Fantastic: Elton John's Stellar Trip Through the '70s.*

28. Ibid.

29. Buckley, *Elton: The Biography.*

30. Ibid.

31. Cliff Jahr, "Elton John, Lonely at the Top," *Rolling Stone,* 1976, https://www .rollingstone.com/music/music-news/elton-john-lonely-at-the-top-rolling-stones -1976-cover-story-238734/.

32. Buckley, *Elton: The Biography,* 148.

33. Gary Trust, "Elton John Charts Record-Extending 72nd Adult Contemporary Hit," *Billboard,* July 13, 2016, https://www.billboard.com/articles/columns/chart-beat /7401402/elton-john-charts-record-extending-adult-contemporary-hit.

34. Buckley, *Elton: The Biography,* 144.

35. Doyle, *Captain Fantastic: Elton John's Stellar Trip Through the '70s,* 73.

36. Buckley, *Elton: The Biography.*

37. Joe Bosso, "Davey Johnstone: My Career with Elton John," *Music Radar,* April 4, 2011, https://www.musicradar.com/news/guitars/exclusive-interview-davey-johnstone -my-career-with-elton-john-413589.

38. Jeff Giles, "Weekend Songs: Elton John, 'Saturday Night's Alright for Fighting,'"

Ultimate Classic Rock, July 12, 2013, https://ultimateclassicrock.com/elton-john -saturday-nights-alright-for-fighting-weekend-songs/.

39. Buckley, *Elton: The Biography.*
40. Bosso, "Davey Johnstone: My Career with Elton John."
41. "Paul Buckmaster: In His Own Words," *Elton John,* January 19, 2018, https://www .eltonjohn.com/stories/paul-buckmaster:-in-his-own-words.
42. "1973 in Music, Biggest Hit Singles," Wikipedia, https://en.wikipedia.org/wiki /1973_in_music#Biggest_hit_singles.
43. "Crocodile Rock," Wikipedia, https://en.wikipedia.org/wiki/Crocodile_Rock.
44. Ibid.
45. Jon Kutner, "Single of the Week: Daniel," *Jon Kutner,* January 8, 2017, https:// www.jonkutner.com/?s=Daniel.

3. GOD IS IN THE GROOVES

1. Ritz, *Respect: The Life of Aretha Franklin.*
2. Ward-Royster and Rose, *How I Got Over: Clara Ward and the World-Famous Ward Singers.*
3. Ibid.
4. Flanagan, *Written in My Soul: Conversations with Rock's Great Songwriters.*
5. Patrick Boyle, "Aretha's Greatest Albums: Amazing Grace," *Rolling Stone,* August 22, 2018, https://www.rollingstone.com/music/music-features/aretha-franklin-amazing -grace-gospel-album-714487/.
6. Ritz, *Respect: The Life of Aretha Franklin.*
7. Ibid.
8. Ibid.
9. Gerrick D. Kennedy, "Quincy Jones on Aretha Franklin: She Turned This Country Upside Down," *Los Angeles Times,* August 22, 2018, https://www.latimes.com /entertainment/music/la-et-ms-quincy-jones-aretha-franklin-20180822-story.html.
10. Roy Trakin, "Aretha's Biographer on the Complicated Woman Behind the Diva: 'She Tried to Paint a Picture of a Happy Life,'" *Variety,* August 16, 2018, https:// variety.com/2018/music/news/arethas-biographer-on-the-complicated-woman -behind-the-diva-she-tried-to-paint-a-picture-of-a-happy-life-1202907825/.
11. Ritz, *Respect: The Life of Aretha Franklin.*
12. Douglas Wolk, "What It Is, What It Is: When Motown Left Detroit," *Red Bull Music Academy Daily,* May 23, 2016, https://daily.redbullmusicacademy.com/2016 /05/when-motown-left-detroit-feature.
13. Ibid.
14. Michael Thomas, "Diana Ross Goes from Riches to Rags," *Rolling Stone,* February 1, 1973, https://www.rollingstone.com/music/music-news/diana-ross-goes -from-riches-to-rags-165274/.
15. Taraborrelli, *Call Her Miss Ross: The Unauthorized Biography of Diana Ross.*
16. Ibid.
17. Gordy, *To Be Loved: The Music, the Magic, the Memories of Motown: An Autobiography.*

18. Taraborrelli, *Call Her Miss Ross: The Unauthorized Biography of Diana Ross.*

19. Gaye and Ritz, *After the Dance: My Life with Marvin Gaye.*

20. Taraborrelli, *Call Her Miss Ross: The Unauthorized Biography of Diana Ross.*

21. Ibid.

22. Ibid.

23. Ritz, *Divided Soul: The Life of Marvin Gaye.*

24. Ibid.

25. Taraborrelli, *Call Her Miss Ross: The Unauthorized Biography of Diana Ross.*

26. Gaye and Ritz, *After the Dance: My Life with Marvin Gaye.*

27. Ibid.

28. Ibid.

29. "Let's Get It On," Wikipedia, https://en.wikipedia.org/wiki/Let%27s_Get_It_On _(song)#cite_ref-edm7_1-0.

30. Ritz, *Divided Soul: The Life of Marvin Gaye.*

31. Gaye and Ritz, *After the Dance: My Life with Marvin Gaye.*

32. Ribowsky, *Signed, Sealed, and Delivered: The Soulful Journey of Stevie Wonder.*

33. Ibid.

34. Jeff Giles, "Stevie Wonder Stole a No. 1 Hit from Jeff Beck," *Ultimate Classic Rock,* https://ultimateclassicrock.com/stevie-wonder-jeff-beck-superstition/.

35. "Song on Song: Superstition," BBC, http://www.bbc.co.uk/radio2/soldonsong /songlibrary/superstition.shtml.

4. THE DARK SIDE OF THE MOON

1. Harris, *The Dark Side of the Moon: The Making of the Pink Floyd Masterpiece.*

 2. Ibid.

 3. John Harris, "'Dark Side' at 30: David Gilmour," *Rolling Stone,* March 12, 2003.

 4. Harris, *The Dark Side of the Moon: The Making of the Pink Floyd Masterpiece.*

 5. Alex Wexelman, "Pink Floyd's Rick Wright: 12 Essential Songs," *Rolling Stone,* September 15, 2018, https://www.rollingstone.com/music/music-news/pink-floyds -rick-wright-12-essential-songs-722901/.

 6. "Us and Them," *Songfacts,* https://www.songfacts.com/facts/pink-floyd/us-and -them.

 7. Matthew Gwyther, "The Dark Side of Success," *Observer,* March 7, 1993.

 8. "Pink Floyd: The Making of 'The Dark Side of the Moon,'" *Classic Albums,* directed by Matthew Longfellow (BBC, 2003).

 9. Ibid.

10. John Harris, "Clare Torry: *Brain Damage* Exclusive," *Brain Damage,* October 2005, http://www.brain-damage.co.uk/other-related-interviews/clare-torry-october -2005-brain-damage-excl-2.html.

11. Phil Sutcliffe and Peter Henderson, "The True Story of Darkside of the Moon," *Mojo,* March 1998.

12. Harris, "Clare Torry: *Brain Damage* Exclusive."

13. John Harris, "Dark Side at 30: Roger Waters," *Rolling Stone,* March 12, 2003.

14. Harris, "Clare Torry: *Brain Damage* Exclusive."

15. Mark Blake, "10 Things You Probably Didn't Know About Pink Floyd," *Times Online,* October 28, 2008.
16. Harris, *The Dark Side of the Moon: The Making of the Pink Floyd Masterpiece.*
17. Gwyther, "The Dark Side of Success."
18. Dallas, *Pink Floyd: Bricks in the Wall.*
19. Jason George, "A 70's Duo Rocks On: Pink Floyd and Lasers," *New York Times,* February 5, 2005.
20. Blake, *Comfortably Numb,* 195.
21. "List of Best-Selling Albums," Wikipedia, https://en.wikipedia.org/wiki/List_of _best-selling_albums.
22. Povey, *Echoes: The Complete History of Pink Floyd.*
23. "Roger Waters Revisits the 'Dark Side,'" *Billboard,* May 5, 2006, https://www .billboard.com/articles/news/58519/roger-waters-revisits-the-dark-side5.

5. NO SECRETS

1. Reddy, *The Woman I Am,* 139.
2. Ellen Cohn, "She Is Woman, She Is Helen Reddy," *New York Times,* June 24, 1973.
3. Bronson, *The Billboard Book of Number One Hits.*
4. *Gloria: In Her Own Words,* directed by Peter Kunhardt (HBO, 2011), DVD.
5. Alex Witchel, "Norma McCorvey: Of Roe, Dreams and Choices," *New York Times,* July 28, 1994.
6. Michael Carlson, "Norma McCorvey Obituary," *Guardian,* February 19, 2017.
7. McCorvey and Meisler, *I Am Roe.*
8. Ibid.
9. Joshua Prager, "Roe v. Wade's Secret Heroine Tells Her Story," *Vanity Fair,* January 19, 2017, https://www.vanityfair.com/news/2017/01/roe-v-wades-secret-heroine -tells-her-story.
10. "Sarah Weddington," Wikipedia, https://en.wikipedia.org/wiki/Sarah_Weddington.
11. "Makers: Women Who Make America: Sarah Weddington," *PBS,* February 26, 2013, https://www.pbs.org/video/makers-women-who-make-america-sarah-weddington/.
12. "Famous Speech Friday: Sarah Weddington's Roe v. Wade Arguments," *The Eloquent Woman,* November 14, 2014, http://eloquentwoman.blogspot.com/2014/11 /famous-speech-friday-sarah-weddingtons.html.
13. Clare Cushman, "Women Advocates Before the Supreme Court," http://clarecushman .com/about/Cushman-2001-Journal_of_Supreme_Court_History.pdf.
14. "Makers: Women Who Make America: Sarah Weddington."
15. Nina Totenberg, "Tape Reveals Nixon's Views on Abortion," NPR, June 23, 2009, https://www.npr.org/templates/story/story.php?storyId=105832640.
16. Molly Ginty, "Our Bodies, Ourselves Turns 35 Today," *Women's eNews,* May 4, 2004, https://womensenews.org/2004/05/our-bodies-ourselves-turns-35-today/.
17. Simon, *Boys in the Trees: A Memoir.*
18. Ibid.
19. Kathy Ehrich Dowd, "Carly Simon Reveals She Had Sexual Encounters with an Older Boy When She Was 7: 'It Was Heinous,'" *People,* November 18, 2015,

https://people.com/celebrity/carly-simon-reveals-she-had-sexual-encounters-with
-an-older-boy-when-she-was-7/.

20. Julia Brucculieri, "Carly Simon Reveals She Had 'Heinous' Sexual Encounters at Age 7," *Huffington Post,* November 11, 2015, https://www.huffpost.com/entry/carly-simon-sexual-encounters-age-7_n_564dcdc4e4b031745cefe28d.

21. Simon, *Boys in the Trees: A Memoir.*

22. Ibid.

23. Ibid.

24. Ibid.

25. "You're So Vain," *Harry Hillson Web Pages,* http://www.nilssonschmilsson.com/misc-3647-21374.html.

26. Simon, *Boys in the Trees: A Memoir.*

27. Spitz, *Jagger: Rebel, Rock Star, Rambler, Rogue,* 191.

28. Ben Brantley, "A Marriage in Trouble, in Triplicate," *New York Times,* September 22, 2014.

29. Bego, *Cher: If You Believe.*

30. Hirshey, *We Gotta Get Out of This Place: The True, Tough Story of Women in Rock,* 93.

31. Ibid.

32. King, *The Operator: David Geffen Builds, Buys, and Sells the New Hollywood.*

33. Ibid.

34. Ibid.

35. Ibid.

36. Craig Shelburne, "Dolly Parton Shares Inspiration of 'I Will Always Love You,'" CMT, February 14, 2011, http://www.cmt.com/news/1657965/dolly-parton-shares-inspiration-of-i-will-always-love-you/.

37. Schmidt, *Dolly on Dolly: Interviews and Encounters with Dolly Parton.*

38. Shelburne, "Dolly Parton Shares Inspiration of 'I Will Always Love You.'"

39. Ibid.

40. Ibid.

6. HOUSES OF THE HOLY

1. Bream, *Whole Lotta Led Zeppelin: The Illustrated History of the Heaviest Band of All Time.*

2. Somach, *Get the Led Out: How Led Zeppelin Became the Biggest Band in the World.*

3. Shadwick, *Led Zeppelin: The Story of a Band and Their Music, 1968–1980.*

4. Davis, *Hammer of the Gods.*

5. Jordan Runtagh, "Led Zeppelin's 'Houses of the Holy': 10 Things You Didn't Know," *Rolling Stone,* March 28, 2018, https://www.rollingstone.com/music/music-features/led-zeppelins-houses-of-the-holy-10-things-you-didnt-know-204694/.

6. Dave Schulps, "Interview with Jimmy Page," *Trouser Press,* October 1977.

7. Shadwick, *Led Zeppelin: The Story of a Band and Their Music, 1968–1980.*

8. Davis, *Hammer of the Gods.*

9. Walker, *What You Want Is in the Limo: On the Road with Led Zeppelin, Alice Cooper, and the Who in 1973, the Year the Sixties Died and the Modern Rock Star Was Born.*

10. Williamson, *The Rough Guide to Led Zeppelin.*

11. Editors of *Guitar World, The Complete History of Guitar World: 30 Years of Music, Magic and Six-String Mayhem.*

12. Bream, *Whole Lotta Led Zeppelin: The Illustrated History of the Heaviest Band of All Time.*

13. Tolinski, *Light and Shade: Conversations with Jimmy Page.*

14. Hoskyns, *Trampled Under Foot.*

15. "I Found It by Mistake: How Glyn Johns Helped Showcase Led Zeppelin's Huge Drum Sound," *Something Else,* July 30, 2013, http://somethingelsereviews.com /2013/07/30/i-found-it--mistake-how-glyn-johns-helped-showcase-led-zeppelins -huge-drum-sound/.

16. Tolinski, *Light and Shade: Conversations with Jimmy Page.*

17. Des Barres, *Let's Spend the Night Together: Backstage Secrets of Rock Muses and Supergroupies.*

18. Rees, *Robert Plant: A Life.*

19. Kory Grow, "Jimmy Page on the 'Swagger' of Led Zeppelin's 'Physical Graffiti,'" *Rolling Stone,* February 23, 2015, https://www.rollingstone.com/music/music -news/jimmy-page-on-the-swagger-of-led-zeppelins-physical-graffiti-192270/.

20. Rees, *Robert Plant: A Life.*

21. Runtagh, "Led Zeppelin's 'Houses of the Holy': 10 Things You Didn't Know."

7. NOW THAT IT'S OVER, WHAT YOU GONNA DO?

1. "Trinity's Bells Ring Out News of Accord," *New York Times,* January 24, 1973, https://www.nytimes.com/1973/01/24/archives/trinitys-bells-ring-out-news-of -accord-bells-at-trinity-ring-out.html.

2. Ibid.

3. "Tie a Yellow Ribbon Round the Ole Oak Tree," Wikipedia, https://en.wikipedia .org/wiki/Tie_a_Yellow_Ribbon_Round_the_Ole_Oak_Tree.

4. Gary James, "Gary James' Interview with Songwriter L. Russell Brown," *Classic Bands,* http://www.classicbands.com/LRussellBrownInterview.html.

5. "1973 in Music, Biggest Hit Singles," Wikipedia, https://en.wikipedia.org/wiki /1973_in_music#Biggest_hit_singles.

6. "Tie a Yellow Ribbon Round the Ole Oak Tree," Wikipedia.

7. "1973," *Top 40 Weekly,* https://top40weekly.com/1973-all-charts/.

8. Associated Press, "Some Terrorist Attacks Victims," *AP News,* October 18, 2001, https://www.apnews.com/2f470d22a066fceec67b72b9d82b67f9.

9. Nancy Faber, "A POW's Marriage Ends Bitterly," *People,* April 1, 1974.

10. Isaacs, *Vietnam Shadows: The War, Its Ghosts, and Its Legacy.*

11. "Coming Home: Vietnam Veterans in American Society," *Encyclopedia.com,* 2001, https://www.encyclopedia.com/history/encyclopedias-almanacs-transcripts-and -maps/coming-home-vietnam-veterans-american-society.

12. Richard D. Lyons, "Vietnam Veterans Turn to Therapy," *New York Times,* November 13, 1984.

13. "Springsteen: 'I Was a Stone-Cold Draft Dodger,'" *Fox News Radio,* May 1, 2017, https://radio.foxnews.com/2017/05/01/springsteen-i-was-a-stone-cold-draft-dodger/.

14. Geoffrey Macnab, "I Was in a Bad Place," *Guardian,* July 6, 2006, https://www.theguardian.com/film/2006/jul/06/features.geoffreymacnab.

15. Killen, *1973 Nervous Breakdown: Watergate, Warhol, and the Birth of Post-Sixties America.*

16. Michael Rosen, "Alan Alda on His M*A*S*H Character, 'Hawkeye' Pierce," *Television Academy Foundation,* November 17, 2000, https://interviews.televisionacademy.com/interviews/alan-alda.

17. Stempel, *Storytellers to the Nation: A History of American Television Writing.*

18. Rosen, "Alan Alda on His M*A*S*H Character, 'Hawkeye' Pierce."

19. Rosenstiel and Mitchell, *Thinking Clearly: Cases in Journalistic Decision-Making.*

20. *All the President's Men Revisited,* directed by Peter Schnall (Discovery, 2013), DVD.

21. Ibid.

22. Hunter S. Thompson, "Fear and Loathing at the Watergate," *Rolling Stone,* September 27, 1973, https://www.rollingstone.com/politics/politics-news/fear-and-loathing-at-the-watergate-37739/.

23. Walker, *Doonesbury and the Art of G. B. Trudeau.*

24. Becky Little, "Watergate: How John Dean Helped Bring Down Nixon," *History,* October 16, 2018, https://www.history.com/news/watergate-nixon-john-dean-tapes.

8. WE'LL HELP YOU PARTY DOWN

1. Tyler and Dalton, *Does the Noise in My Head Bother You? A Rock 'n' Roll Memoir.*

2. Ibid.

3. Aerosmith and Davis, *Walk This Way: The Autobiography of Aerosmith.*

4. Tyler and Dalton, *Does the Noise in My Head Bother You? A Rock 'n' Roll Memoir.*

5. Ibid.

6. Perry, *Rocks: My Life in and out of Aerosmith.*

7. Tyler and Dalton, *Does the Noise in My Head Bother You? A Rock 'n' Roll Memoir.*

8. Aerosmith and Davis, *Walk This Way: The Autobiography of Aerosmith.*

9. Tyler and Dalton, *Does the Noise in My Head Bother You? A Rock 'n' Roll Memoir.*

10. Ibid.

11. Perry, *Rocks: My Life in and out of Aerosmith.*

12. McNeil and McCain, *Please Kill Me: The Uncensored Oral History of Punk.*

13. Aerosmith and Davis, *Walk This Way: The Autobiography of Aerosmith,* 169.

14. Ibid.

15. Ibid.

16. Jones, *Let the Good Times Roll: My Life in Small Faces, Faces, and the Who.*

17. Ibid.

18. Ibid.

19. Ibid.

20. Jones, *Lonely Boy: Tales from a Sex Pistol,* 69.

21. *The Passing Show: The Life and Music of Ronnie Lane,* directed by Rupert Williams, (BBC, 2006), DVD.

22. Ibid.

23. Harrington, *Sonic Cool: The Life and Death of Rock 'n' Roll,* 266.

24. "Ritchie Blackmore: The Link Between Hendrix and Van Halen," *Ultimate Guitar,* June 12, 2017, https://www.ultimate-guitar.com/articles/features/ritchie_blackmore _the_link_between_hendrix_and_van_halen-62045.

25. "Deep Purple: Machine Head," *Classic Albums,* directed by Matthew Longfellow (ITV, 2002), DVD.

26. GP Editors, "Ritchie Blackmore: This Is How I Play 'Smoke on the Water,'" *Guitar Player,* December 4, 2017, https://www.guitarplayer.com/players/ritchie-blackmore -this-is-how-i-play-smoke-on-the-water.

27. Matt Wardlaw, "Grand Funk Railroad, 'We're An American Band,'" *Ultimate Classic Rock,* June 6, 2011, https://ultimateclassicrock.com/grand-funk-railroad-were -an-american-band-lyrics-uncovered/85.

28. Des Barres, *Let's Spend the Night Together: Backstage Secrets of Rock Muses and Supergroupies.*

29. "'Sweet' Connie Hamzy Has Been Around," *Howard Stern Show,* December 8, 2010, https://www.howardstern.com/show/2010/12/8/sweet-connie-hamzy-has -been-around-RundownGalleryModel-2911/.

30. Des Barres, *Let's Spend the Night Together.*

31. Heller, *Strange Stars: David Bowie, Pop Music, and the Decade Sci-Fi Exploded.*

32. Michael Molenda, "Lemmy Kilmister Explains How He Stole His First Bass Gig and How Jimi Hendrix Helped," *Bass Player,* February 20, 2018, https://www .bassplayer.com/artists/lemmy-kilmister-explains-how-he-stole-his-first-bass-gig -and-how-jimi-hendrix-helped.

33. *Hawkwind: Do Not Panic,* directed by Simon Chu (BBC, 2007), DVD.

34. "Stacia, Hawkwind's Buxom Cosmic Dancer Discusses Her Wild Sex Life in Vintage Interviews," *Dangerous Minds,* https://dangerousminds.net/comments/stacia _hawkwinds_buxom_cosmic_dancer.

35. *Hawkwind: Do Not Panic,* directed by Simon Chu (BBC, 2007), DVD.

36. David Weigel, "Prog Spring: The Brief Rise and Inevitable Fall of the World's Most Hated Pop Music," *Slate,* August 15, 2012, http://www.slate.com/articles/arts/prog _spring/features/2012/prog_rock/prog_comes_alive_emerson_lake_palmer_at _madison_square_garden_1973_promo_ill_cast_comedy_for_fools_the_birth_of _prog.html.

37. "Urban Guerilla," Wikipedia, https://en.wikipedia.org/wiki/Urban_Guerrilla.

9. WE'RE COMING OUT

1. "US Top 40 Singles Week Ending 17th February, 1973," *Top 40 Weekly,* https:// top40weekly.com/1973-all-charts/.

2. Fieseler, *Tinderbox: The Untold Story of the Up Stairs Lounge Fire and the Rise of Gay Liberation.*

3. PT Staff, "How Loud Were We?" *Psychology Today,* January 1, 1992, https://www
.psychologytoday.com/us/articles/199201/how-loud-were-we.

4. "Lance Loud! A Death in 'An American Family,'" *PBS SoCal,* https://www.pbs.org
/lanceloud/lance/warhol.html.

5. PT Staff, "How Loud Were We?"

6. Ruoff, *An American Family: A Televised Life.*

7. Paris Lees, "Holly Woodlawn Was a Transgender Inspiration," *Guardian,* December 8, 2015, https://www.theguardian.com/commentisfree/2015/dec/08/holly
-woodlawn-transgender-icon-struggle.

8. Eric Henderson, "Review: Trash," *Slant,* July 31, 2005, https://www.slantmagazine
.com/film/trash/.

9. "Joe Dallesandro," Wikipedia, https://en.wikipedia.org/wiki/Joe_Dallesandro.

10. Dan Gentile, "Electric Relaxation: The Continental Baths Birthed NYC Disco and
the Careers of Frankie Knuckles and Larry Levan," *Wax Poetics,* May 4, 2016,
http://www.waxpoetics.com/blog/features/continental_baths_nyc_disco_frankie
_knuckles_larry_levan/.

11. Sam Davies, "Sex, Disco and Fish on Acid: How Continental Baths Became
the World's Most Influential Gay Club," *Guardian,* April 27, 2018, https://www
.theguardian.com/music/2018/apr/27/sex-disco-and-fish-on-acid-how-continental
-baths-became-the-worlds-most-influential-gay-club.

12. Ibid.

13. Ibid.

14. Thompson, *The Rocky Horror Picture Show FAQ: Everything Left to Know About
the Campy Cult Classic.*

15. Ibid.

16. Max Bell, "The Rise and Fall of Mick Ronson," *Classic Rock,* April 25, 2017.

17. *Classic Albums: Lou Reed: Transformer,* directed by Bob Smeaton (BBC, 2001), DVD.

18. Bullock, *David Bowie Made Me Gay: 100 Years of LGBT Music.*

19. Gill, *Queer Noises: Male and Female Homosexuality in Twentieth Century Music.*

20. Alex Sharpe, "My Favourite Album: David Bowie's Diamond Dogs," *The Conversation,* September 24, 2017, http://theconversation.com/my-favourite-album
-david-bowies-diamond-dogs-84047.

10. AOR, PROG, AND YACHT ROCK

1. "WPLJ: AOR Years (1971–1983)," Wikipedia, https://en.wikipedia.org/wiki/WPLJ#
AOR_years (1971–1983).

2. "Album-Oriented Rock," Wikipedia, https://en.wikipedia.org/wiki/Album-oriented
_rock.

3. Claude Hall, "Scientific Programming Can Represent Clearer Ratings," *Billboard,*
April 7, 1973, 24.

4. Ibid.

5. Ibid.

6. Ibid.

7. Ibid.

8. Ibid.

9. Ibid.

10. "Mike Harrison Biography," *Inside Radio,* https://www.ebay.com/itm/Radio -Show-Rock-Connections-W-Mike-Harrison-7-31-87-Album-Oldies-But-Goodies -/302294259028.

11. Ibid.

12. Ibid.

13. Ibid.

14. "Album-Oriented Rock," Wikipedia.

15. Greg Smith, "Lee Abrams: Rock Radio SuperStar," *Radio Today,* May 20, 2016, https://radiotoday.com.au/lee-abrams-rock-radio-superstar/.

16. Breithaupt and Breithaupt, *Precious and Few: Pop Music of the Early '70s.*

17. "List of *Billboard* Hot 100 Number-One Singles of 1973," Wikipedia, https://en .wikipedia.org/wiki/List_of_Billboard_Hot_100_number-one_singles_of_1973.

18. Tufayel Ahmed, "The Beatles Were Louder than a Jumbo Jet at Shea Stadium, Data Reveals," *Newsweek,* September 14, 2016, https://www.newsweek.com /louder-beatles-fab-four-made-more-noise-jumbo-jet-data-reveals-498285.

19. Jarnow, *Heads: A Biography of Psychedelic America.*

20. Browne, *So Many Roads: The Life and Times of the Grateful Dead.*

21. "45 Years Ago the Grateful Dead Debuted the Wall of Sound and Changed Music Forever," *Live,* March 23, 2019, https://livemusicblog.com/features/grateful-dead -wall-of-sound/.

22. James S. Granelli, "A Concert Tradition in a New Light," *Los Angeles Times,* August 24, 2005, https://www.latimes.com/archives/la-xpm-2005-aug-24-fi-cellphone 24-story.htmlhttps://www.sandiegoreader.com/news/2002/aug/29/what-band -started-tradition-holding-lighters-conce/#.

23. *Prog Rock Britannia: An Observation in Three Movements,* directed by Chris Rodley (BBC, 2009), DVD.

24. Weigel, *The Show That Never Ends: The Rise and Fall of Prog Rock.*

25. Anthony Bozza, "A Boy's Life (in Sex, Drugs and Rock & Roll)," *Rolling Stone,* October 12, 2000, https://www.rollingstone.com/movies/movie-news/a-boys-life -in-sex-drugs-and-rock-roll-163369/.

26. *Genesis: Together and Apart,* directed by John Edginton (BBC, 2014), DVD.

27. Collins, *Not Dead Yet: The Memoir.*

28. "Master of Disguise: Peter Gabriel's Mind-Blowing Make-Up, Masks and Costumes from the 70s," *Genesis Fan,* February 2, 2016, https://www.genesisfan.net /genesis/articles/2016/master-of-disguise-peter-gabriels-mind-blowing-make-up -masks-and-costumes-from-the-70s.

29. "Deacy Amp," Wikiedpia, https://en.wikipedia.org/wiki/Deacy_Amp.

30. *SHOT! The Psycho-Spiritual Mantra of Rock,* directed by Barney Clay (Eagle Rock Entertainment, 2016), DVD.

31. *The Doobie Brothers: Let the Music Play,* directed by Barry Ehrmann (2012), DVD.

32. Spencer Doar, "Q&A with a Doobie Brother," *Minnesota Daily,* April 4, 2013.

33. Cameron Crowe, "Nice Guys Don't Win, but Doobies Do," *Rock Magazine,* March 13, 1973, http://www.theuncool.com/2015/08/31/doobie-brothers-rock -magazine-1973/.

34. Patrick S. Pemberton, "Doobie Brothers Are Still Smokin' After All These Years," *Tribune News,* April 26, 2012, https://www.sanluisobispo.com/entertainment/music -news-reviews/article39201462.html.

35. "China Grove," Wikipedia, https://en.wikipedia.org/wiki/China_Grove (song).

36. Ward Meeker, "Doobie Brothers: A Discussion with Tom Johnston and Patrick Simmons," *Vintage Guitar,* August 5, 2012.

37. "The Doobie Brothers," *Guitar Player,* November 15, 2017 (updated), https:// www.guitarplayer.com/miscellaneous/the-doobie-brothers.

38. "Doobies Are Still Takin' It to the Streets," *Goldmine,* July 6, 2011, https://www .goldminemag.com/articles/backstage-pass-doobies-are-still-takin-it-to-the -streets.

39. *The Doobie Brothers: Let the Music Play,* directed by Barry Ehrmann (2012), DVD.

40. O'Rourke, *The Steely Dan File.*

41. Sweet, *Steely Dan: Reelin' in the Years.*

42. *Captain Midnight Show,* 1977, http://steelydanreader.com/1987/04/01/metal-leg-1/.

43. Rob Brunner, "Back to Annandale," *Entertainment Weekly,* March 17, 2006.

44. Damian Fanelli, "Elliott Randall Nailed Steely Dan's 'Reelin' in the Years' in One Continuous Take," *Guitar World,* December 7, 2016.

45. Cameron Crowe, "The Second Coming of Steely Dan," *Rolling Stone,* December 29, 1977, https://www.rollingstone.com/music/music-news/the-second-coming-of-ste ely-dan-189824/.

46. Brunner, "Back to Annandale."

47. Dave Goldiner, "Meet Springsteen's Rosalita and Rock Muses Rikki and Sharona, Too," *New York Daily News,* April 19, 2008.

48. Sweet, *Steely Dan: Reelin' in the Years.*

49. Ibid.

50. Rachel Corcoran, "The Doobie Brothers Lead Singer Michael McDonald: Where Is He Now?" *Express,* March 10, 2018, https://www.express.co.uk/life-style/life /928440/the-doobie-brothers-lead-signer-michael-mcdonald-tom-johnston.

51. Drew Toal, "Sail Away: The Oral History of 'Yacht Rock,'" *Rolling Stone,* June 26, 2015, https://www.rollingstone.com/tv/tv-news/sail-away-the-oral-history-of-yacht -rock-49343/.

52. Candice Pires, "Daryl Hall and John Oates on 50 Years of Friendship," *Guardian,* June 4, 2014, https://www.theguardian.com/lifeandstyle/2014/jun/15/daryl-hall -john-oates-50-years-friendship-relationships.

53. *Behind the Music: Hall and Oates* (VH1, 2002), DVD.

11. THE HARDER THEY COME

1. Robert Christgau, "Jimmy Cliff et al.: The Harder They Come," *Robert Christgau,* https://www.robertchristgau.com/get_album.php?id=1708.

2. Klive Walker, "How *The Harder They Come* Created Jamaican Cinema," *Tiff,* December 9, 2017, https://www.tiff.net/the-review/how-the-harder-they-come-created -jamaican-cinema.

3. Len Comaratta, "Interview: Jimmy Cliff," *Consequence of Sound,* July 18, 2012, https://consequenceofsound.net/2012/07/interview-jimmy-cliff/.

4. John Doran, "Many Rivers Crossed: Jimmy Cliff Interviewed," *The Quietus,* May 15, 2013, https://thequietus.com/articles/12237-jimmy-cliff-interview.

5. *Hard Road to Travel: The Making of "The Harder They Come"* (2015), DVD.

6. Dave Simpson, "How We Made: Songwriter and Actor Jimmy Cliff and Actor Carl Bradshaw on *The Harder They Come,*" *Guardian,* August 20, 2012, https://www.theguardian.com/film/2012/aug/20/how-made-harder-they-come.

7. Marc Myers, "The Song That Put Reggae on the Map," *Wall Street Journal,* February 14, 2013, https://www.wsj.com/articles/SB10001424127887324196204578300320318244126.

8. Ray Connolly, "Jimmy Cliff," *London Evening Standard,* July 17, 1972, https://www.rayconnolly.co.uk/jimmy-cliff/.

9. Neil McCormick, "Jimmy Cliff Interview: 'I Still Have Many Rivers to Cross,'" *Telegraph,* July 12, 2012, https://www.telegraph.co.uk/culture/music/rockandpopfeatures/9382022/Jimmy-Cliff-interview-I-still-have-many-rivers-to-cross.html.

10. Ibid.

11. "Most Groundbreaking Albums of All Time," *Rolling Stone,* https://www.rollingstone.com/interactive/most-groundbreaking-albums-of-all-time/.

12. *Hard Road to Travel: The Making of "The Harder They Come"* (2015), DVD.

13. "Frederick 'Toots' Hibbert: The Reggae King of Kingston," *Independent,* June 4, 2004, https://www.independent.co.uk/arts-entertainment/music/features/frederick-toots-hibbert-the-reggae-king-of-kingston-41301.html.

14. Dave Simpson, "Toots and the Maytals: How We Made *Pressure Drop,*" *Guardian,* September 6, 2016, https://www.theguardian.com/culture/2016/sep/06/toots-and-the-maytals-how-we-made-pressure-drop.

15. Bill Murphy, "Bass Culture: Dub Reggae's Low-End Legacy," *Bass Player,* November 1996.

16. Christgau, "Jimmy Cliff et al.: The Harder They Come."

17. Bordowitz, *Every Little Thing Gonna Be Alright: The Bob Marley Reader.*

18. *Bob Marley: Freedom Road,* directed by Sonia Anderson (2007), DVD.

19. David W. Stowe, "Babylon Revisited: Psalm 137 as American Protest Song," *Black Music Research Journal,* Spring 2012.

20. *Hard Road to Travel: The Making of "The Harder They Come"* (2015), DVD.

21. Doran, "Many Rivers Crossed: Jimmy Cliff Interviewed."

22. Ibid.

23. Ibid.

12. BALLERINA WOLFMEN

1. McNeil and McCain, *Please Kill Me: The Uncensored Oral History of Punk.*

2. Cameron Crowe, "Candid Conversation," *Playboy,* September 1976.

3. Harry Swift, "Alice Cooper: America's Rock & Roll DeSade," *Rolling Stone,* May 10, 1973, https://www.rollingstone.com/music/music-news/alice-cooper-americas-rock-roll-desade-231958/.

4. "In the Future Everyone Will Be Bisexual," *Dangerous Minds,* https://dangerousminds.net/comments/in_the_future_everyone_will_be_bisexualalice_cooper_1974.

5. Matheu and Bowe, *CREEM: America's Only Rock 'n' Roll Magazine.*

6. "The Queen of Rock and Roll," *Sir!,* May 1973.

7. *Marc Bolan: The Final Word,* directed by Mark Tinkler (2007), DVD.

8. Buckley, *Strange Fascination: David Bowie: The Definitive Story.*

9. David Cavanagh, "Glam Rock Bottom: Why Did It Go So Sour for Sweet?," *Guardian,* September 23, 2010, https://www.theguardian.com/music/2010/sep /23/sweet-strange-history.

10. Reynolds, *Shock and Awe: Glam Rock and Its Legacy, from the Seventies to the Twenty-First Century.*

11. Simon Reynolds, "Roxy Music: The Band That Broke the Sound Barrier," *Guardian,* September 1, 2011, https://www.theguardian.com/music/2012/sep/02/roxy -music-40-years.

12. "Marc Bolan," *David Bowie News,* September 11, 2012, https://davidbowienews .wordpress.com/2012/09/11/marc-bolan-david-bowie/.

13. Goddard, *Ziggyology.*

14. Paul Du Noyer, "Mott The Hoople: Young Dudes and Old Feuds," *Paul Du Noyer,* https://www.pauldunoyer.com/mott-the-hoople-interviews/.

15. "The Story Behind Mott's Classic Hit," *Uncut,* January 2008, https://www.uncut .co.uk/features/the-making-of-all-the-young-dudes-by-mott-the-hoople-72431.

16. Michael Bailey, "Bryan Ferry Talks Roxy Music on the Eve of His 2019 Australian Tour," *Financial Review,* November 16, 2018, https://www.afr.com/lifestyle/arts -and-entertainment/music/bryan-ferry-talks-roxy-music-on-the-eve-of-his-2019 -australian-tour-20181108-h17nhp.

17. Djuna Parnes, "Another Glam World: Brian Eno's Adventures in Roxy Music," *Rock's Backpages,* June 2001, http://www.moredarkthanshark.org/eno_int_rbp -jun01.html.

18. Cavanagh, "Glam Rock Bottom: Why Did It Go So Sour For Sweet?."

19. Kristin Anderson, "The New York Dolls's Sylvain Sylvain on the Band's Ground-breaking Style and His Clothing Line," *Vogue,* November 19, 2015, https://www .vogue.com/article/sylvain-sylvain-new-york-dolls-truth-and-soul-clothing.

20. Blush, *New York Rock: From the Rise of the Velvet Underground to the Fall of CBGB.*

21. McNeil and McCain, *Please Kill Me: The Uncensored Oral History of Punk.*

22. Ramone and Herschlag, *Punk Rock Blitzkrieg: My Life as a Ramone.*

23. McNeil and McCain, *Please Kill Me: The Uncensored Oral History of Punk.*

24. Ibid.

25. Ruskin, *High on Rebellion: Inside the Underground at Max's Kansas City.*

26. Ibid.

27. Ibid.

28. Rosemary Feitelberg, "Bebe Buell Details David Bowie's Early Rock 'n' Roll Days in New York," *Women's Wear Daily,* January 12, 2016, https://wwd.com/fashion -news/fashion-features/david-bowies-beb-buell-early-rock-n-roll-days-in-new -york-city-10312467/.

29. McNeil and McCain, *Please Kill Me: The Uncensored Oral History of Punk.*

30. Jada Yuan, "Bebe Buell on Being a 'Rock Girlfriend,' Moms like Dina Lohan, and

Bikini Waxing," *Vulture*, September 27, 2011, https://www.vulture.com/2011/09/bebe_buell_1.html.

31. Buell and Bockris, *Rebel Heart: An American Rock 'n' Roll Journey*.
32. Lisa Robinson, "Rebel Nights," *Vanity Fair*, February 14, 2002, https://www.vanityfair.com/culture/2002/11/new-york-rock-scene-1970s?verso=true.
33. Mark Arm, "Motor City Motherfuckers: The MC5's Rock 'n' Roll History Lesson," *The Stranger*, July 1, 2004, https://www.thestranger.com/seattle/motor-city-motherfuckers/Content?oid=18674.
34. Johnson Cummins, "Alice Cooper: We Will Take On Any Band of 20-Year-Olds and Blow Them off the Stage," *Montreal Mirror*, October 10, 2008, http://www.blabbermouth.net/news/alice-cooper-we-will-take-on-any-band-of-20-year-olds-and-blow-them-off-the-stage/.
35. Heesch and Scott, *Heavy Metal, Gender and Sexuality: Interdisciplinary Approaches*.
36. Lester Bangs, "The Stooges: The Apotheosis of Every Parental Nightmare," *Stereo Review*, July 1973.
37. Greg Prato, "Stooges Guitarist James Williamson Talks Bowie," *Long Island Pulse*, March 22, 2018, http://lipulse.com/2018/03/22/stooges-guitarist-james-williamson-talks-david-bowie/.
38. Richard Buskin, "New York Dolls 'Personality Crisis,'" *Sound on Sound*, December 2009, https://www.soundonsound.com/people/new-york-dolls-personality-crisis-classic-tracks.
39. Ibid.
40. "Perry King Talks About the Making of Andy Warhol's 'Bad,'" *TV Store Online*, April 17, 2015.

13. HONKY TONK HEROES

1. Bob Dylan, "Read Bob Dylan's Complete, Riveting MusiCares Speech," *Rolling Stone*, February 9, 2015, https://www.rollingstone.com/music/music-news/read-bob-dylans-complete-riveting-musicares-speech-240728/.
2. Ibid.
3. David Bowman, "Kris Kristofferson," *Salon*, September 24, 1999, https://www.salon.com/1999/09/24/kristofferson/.
4. Jennings and Kaye, *Waylon: An Autobiography*.
5. Malone, *Classic Country Music: A Smithsonian Collection*.
6. Andrew Goldman, "Willie Nelson, the Silver-Headed Stranger," *New York Times Magazine*, December 14, 2012, https://www.nytimes.com/2012/12/16/magazine/willie-nelson-the-silver-headed-stranger.html.
7. Chet Flippo, "Willie Nelson: Holy Man of the Honky Tonks," *Rolling Stone*, July 13, 1978, https://www.rollingstone.com/music/music-country/willie-nelson-holy-man-of-the-honky-tonks-118425/.
8. Cheryl McCall, "Willie Nelson: Yesterday's Outlaw," *People*, September 1, 1980, https://people.com/archive/cover-story-willie-nelson-yesterdays-outlaw-vol-14-no-9/.

9. Kelley Shannon, "Austin Music Seeds Sewn at Hall Loved by Cowboys, Hippies and Performers," Associated Press, September 22, 2002, http://www.lawrence .com/news/2002/sep/22/austin_music/?print.

10. Nelson, *The Tao of Willie: A Guide to the Happiness in Your Heart.*

11. Michael Corcoran, "Willie Nelson's Performance at Armadillo World Headquarters (1972) #1 Most Significant in Austin Music History," *Still Is Still Moving,* September 22, 2014, http://stillisstillmoving.com/willienelson/willie-nelsons-performance-at -armadillo-world-headquarters-1972-1-most-significant-in-austin-music-history/.

12. Nelson, *It's a Long Story: My Life.*

13. Ibid.

14. Jennings and Kaye, *Waylon: An Autobiography.*

15. Ibid.

16. Ibid.

17. Ibid.

18. *Lost Highway: Beyond Nashville,* directed by Ben Southwell (BBC, 2003), DVD.

19. Jennings and Kaye, *Waylon: An Autobiography.*

20. Shaver and Reagan, *Honky Tonk Hero.*

21. Jennings and Kaye, *Waylon: An Autobiography.*

22. Shaver and Reagan, *Honky Tonk Hero.*

23. Ibid.

24. Jennings and Kaye, *Waylon: An Autobiography.*

25. Flippo, "Willie Nelson: Holy Man of the Honky Tonks."

26. Jennings and Kaye, *Waylon: An Autobiography.*

27. Streissguth, *Outlaw: Waylon, Willie, Kris, and the Renegades of Nashville.*

28. Jennings and Kaye, *Waylon: An Autobiography.*

29. Stephen L. Betts, "Hazel Smith, 'Outlaw Country'Journalist and Artist Confidante, Dead at 83," *Rolling Stone,* March 19, 2018, https://www.rollingstone.com/music /music-country/hazel-smith-outlaw-country-journalist-and-artist-confidante-dead -at-83-201931/.

30. *Lost Highway: Beyond Nashville,* directed by Ben Southwell (BBC, 2003), DVD.

31. Streissguth, *Outlaw: Waylon, Willie, Kris, and the Renegades of Nashville.*

14. THE ONCE AND CURRENT KINGS

1. Williamson and Shaw, *Elvis Presley: A Southern Life,* 33.

2. Michael Werner and Bianca Weber, "Aloha from Hawaii Via Satellite: Fact & Fancy," *Elvis Australia,* March 11, 2018, https://www.elvis.com.au/presley/aloha -from-hawaii-via-satellite-fact-fancy.shtml.

3. "The Story of the Aloha TV Special," *Elvis in Hawaii,* July 25, 2011, http://www .elvisinhawaii.com/story4.html.

4. Guralnick, *Careless Love: The Unmaking of Elvis Presley.*

5. Ibid.

6. Nash, *Elvis and the Memphis Mafia.*

7. Ibid.

8. "The Immortals: The Fifty Greatest Artists of All Time," *Rolling Stone,* April 15, 2004.

9. Brando, *Brando: Songs My Mother Taught Me.*
10. Dexter Thomas, "Meet the Woman Who Refused Marlon Brando's Oscar and Inspired Jada Pinkett Smith's Boycott," *Los Angeles Times,* February 5, 2016, https://www.latimes.com/entertainment/movies/moviesnow/la-et-mn-sacheen-littlefeather-oscars-20160204-htmlstory.html.
11. Nick Vivarelli, "Bernardo Bertolucci Responds to 'Last Tango in Paris' Backlash over Rape Scene," *Variety,* December 5, 2016, https://variety.com/2016/film/global/bernardo-bertolucci-responds-to-last-tango-in-paris-backlash-1201933605/.
12. "Downhill Ride for Maria After Her Tango with Brando," *Sydney Morning Herald,* June 22, 2006.
13. Elahe Izadi, "Why The 'Last Tango In Paris' Rape Scene Is Generating Such an Outcry Now," *Washington Post,* December 5, 2016, https://www.washingtonpost.com/news/arts-and-entertainment/wp/2016/12/05/why-the-last-tango-in-paris-rape-scene-is-generating-such-an-outcry-now/?noredirect=on&utm_term=.09d33f729f75.
14. Ariston Anderson, "Hollywood Reacts with Disgust, Outrage over 'Last Tango in Paris' Director's Resurfaced Rape Scene Confession," *Hollywood Reporter,* December 3, 2016, https://www.hollywoodreporter.com/news/hollywood-reacts-disgust-outrage-last-tango-paris-directors-resurfaced-rape-scene-confession-95.
15. Manso, *Brando: The Biography.*
16. Brando, *Brando: Songs My Mother Taught Me.*
17. Hofler, *Sexplosion: From Andy Warhol to "A Clockwork Orange": How a Generation of Pop Rebels Broke All the Taboos.*
18. Lina Das, "I Felt Raped by Brando," *Daily Mail,* July 19, 2007, https://www.dailymail.co.uk/tvshowbiz/article-469646/I-felt-raped-Brando.html.
19. *Charles Michener, "Tango: The Hottest Movie," Newsweek,* February 12, 1973.
20. Sandford, *McCartney.*
21. Badman, *The Beatles Diary,* vol. 2, *After the Break-Up, 1970–2001.*
22. Spizer, *The Beatles Solo on Apple Records.*
23. Sheff, *All We Are Saying: The Last Major Interview with John Lennon and Yoko Ono,* 213.
24. Sloman, *Steal This Dream: Abbie Hoffman and the Countercultural Revolution in America.*
25. Jamie Dunn, "Bob Gruen," *Uncut Legends,* issue 7, 117.

15. GOODBYE TO GLITTER

1. Reynolds, *Shock and Awe: Glam Rock and Its Legacy, from the Seventies to the Twenty-First Century.*
2. Ibid.
3. Greco, *David Bowie in Darkness: A Study of "1. Outside" and the Late Career.*
4. Cameron Crowe, "Marc Bolan: The Little Dynamo Spouts Off on the Competition and (Natch) His Own Genius," *Creem,* July 1973.
5. Jones, *David Bowie: The Oral History.*
6. *Ziggy Stardust and the Spiders from Mars,* directed by D. A. Pennebaker (1973), DVD.

7. Griffin, *David Bowie: The Golden Years*.

8. Tony Parsons, "David Bowie Interview," *Arena,* Spring/Summer 1993, https://welcomebackbowie.wordpress.com/articles/david-bowie-interview-in-arena-springsummer-1993/.

9. J. Bryan Lowder, "Was David Bowie Gay?" *Slate,* January 11, 2016, https://slate.com/human-interest/2016/01/was-david-bowie-dead-at-69-gay-the-glam-rocker-had-a-complicated-relationship-with-queerness.html.

10. Egan, *Bowie on Bowie: Interviews and Encounters with David Bowie*.

11. Cameron Crowe, *Playboy,* September 1976.

12. Parsons, "David Bowie Interview."

13. Ibid.

14. DeCurtis, *Lou Reed: A Life Hardcover*.

15. Lester Bangs, "Lou Reed: A Deaf Mute in a Telephone Booth," *Let It Rock,* November 1973, https://www.theguardian.com/music/2011/nov/08/lou-reed-lester-bangs-interview.

16. Bettye Kronstad, "Bettye Kronstad Speaks for the First Time About Her Marriage to Lou Reed: 'Fame Is a Fiend. It Turns People into Monsters,'" *Independent,* April 10, 2015, https://www.independent.co.uk/arts-entertainment/music/features/bettye-kronstad-speaks-for-the-first-time-about-her-marriage-to-lou-reed-fame-is-a-fiend-it-turns-10166659.html.

17. Nick Duerden, "Lou Reed's First Wife on Her Memoir: 'I Hadn't Read a Book That Had Got Him Right,'" *Independent,* October 19, 2016, https://www.independent.co.uk/arts-entertainment/books/features/perfect-day-lou-reed-memoir-bettye-kronstad-interview-david-bowie-a7367991.html.

18. DeCurtis, *Lou Reed: A Life*.

19. Ibid.

20. Sarah Grant, "Iggy Pop on Bob Dylan Wannabes, Ruining Joe Perry's LSD Trip," *Rolling Stone,* November 6, 2016, https://www.rollingstone.com/music/music-news/iggy-pop-remembers-bob-dylan-wannabes.

21. McNeil and McCain, *Please Kill Me: The Uncensored Oral History of Punk*.

22. Ambrose, *Gimme Danger: The Story of Iggy Pop*.

23. Bangs, *Psychotic Reactions and Carburetor Dung,* 206–7.

24. McNeil and McCain, *Please Kill Me: The Uncensored Oral History of Punk*.

25. Sewall-Ruskin, *High on Rebellion: Inside the Underground at Max's Kansas City*.

26. Ambrose, *Gimme Danger: The Story of Iggy Pop*.

27. Ibid.

28. McNeil and McCain, *Please Kill Me: The Uncensored Oral History of Punk*.

29. Tommy Keene, "From the Desk of Tommy Keene: Intimate Rock Concert Moments, Volume 2—Iggy Pop," *Magnet Magazine,* February 22, 2009, http://magnetmagazine.com/2009/02/22/from-the-desk-of-tommy-keene-intimate-rock-concert-moments-volume-2-%E2%80%94-iggy-pop/.

30. *Mike Judge Presents: Tales from the Tour Bus,* directed by Mike Judge (Cinemax, 2017), DVD.

31. *Storytellers: David Bowie* (VH1, 1999), DVD.

32. Rob Hughes, "The Story Behind the Song: 'Roll Away the Stone' by Mott the Hoople," *Classic Rock,* May 13, 2014, https://www.loudersound.com/features/the-story-behind-the-song-roll-away-the-stone-by-mott-the-hoople.

33. "List of Best-Selling Music Artists," Wikipedia, https://en.wikipedia.org/wiki/List_of_best-selling_music_artists.

34. Sharp with Simmons and Stanley, *Nothin' to Lose: The Making of KISS, 1972–1975.*

35. Leaf and Sharp, *Kiss: Behind the Mask—Official Authorized Biography.*

36. *Kiss: Beyond the Makeup* (2001), DVD.

37. Leaf and Sharp, *KISS: Behind the Mask—Official Authorized Biography.*

16. COUNTERCULTURE '73

1. Jason Rodrigues, "40 Year Anniversary: Forgotten US Rock Festival That Was Bigger than Woodstock," *Guardian,* July 26, 2013, https://www.theguardian.com/theguardian/from-the-archive-blog/2013/jul/26/summer-jam-woodstock-music-rock.

2. Browne, *So Many Roads: The Life and Times of the Grateful Dead.*

3. Moore, *Here Comes Trouble: Stories from My Life.*

4. Andrew Radolf, "Haight Street: Six Blocks in Search of a New Identity," *New York Times,* April 22, 1973, https://www.nytimes.com/1973/04/22/archives/haight-street-six-blocks-in-search-of-a-new-identity.

5. McNally, *A Long Strange Trip: The Inside History of the Grateful Dead.*

6. Jarnow, *Heads: A Biography of Psychedelic America.*

7. Jennifer Kane, "Pot Lore: The True Story of 420, a Marijuana Tradition, Told by the Stoners Who Invented It," *Reno Gazette Journal,* April 16, 2018, https://www.rgj.com/story/news/marijuana/2018/04/16/true-story-420-told-stoners-who-invented/464003002/.

8. Zoe Wilder, "The Story of 4/20," *Rolling Stone,* April 20, 2018, https://www.rollingstone.com/culture/culture-news/the-story-of-4-20-627949/.

9. "We Added 420 to the OED," *Oxford Dictionaries,* https://blog.oxforddictionaries.com/2017/04/20/420/.

10. Tuedio and Spector, *The Grateful Dead in Concert: Essays on Live Improvisation.*

11. Will Welch, "The Unified Theory of Ram Dass," *GQ,* November 27, 2018, https://www.gq.com/story/the-unified-theory-of-ram-dass.

12. *Dying to Know: Ram Dass & Timothy Leary,* directed by Gay Dillingham (2014), DVD.

13. Lasch-Quinn, *Race Experts: How Racial Etiquette, Sensitivity Training, and New Age Therapy Hijacked the Civil Rights Revolution.*

14. "Kurt Lewin," Wikipedia, https://en.wikipedia.org/wiki/Kurt_Lewin#cite_note-Lasch-Quinn,_E._2001-8.

15. Sandi Doughton, "Author Richard Bach Injured in Plane Crash," *Seattle Times,* September 1, 2012, https://www.seattletimes.com/seattle-news/author-richard-bach-injured-in-plane-crash/.

16. Timothy Foote, "It's a Bird! It's a Dream! It's Supergull!" *Time,* November 13, 1972.

17. Ibid.

18. Ibid.

19. *Tales from the Jungle: Carlos Castenada,* directed by Naomi Austin and Helen Seaman (2007), DVD.

20. Ian Glendinning, "Biographical Timeline of Robert Pirsig," *Pirsig Pages of Psybertron,* http://www.psybertron.org/timeline.html.

21. Daniel Silliman, "How a Small Occult Publisher Changed America," *Real Clear Religion,* August 30, 2017, https://www.realclearreligion.org/articles/2017/08/30/how_a_small_occult_publisher_changed_america_110176.html.

22. Douglas Martin, "Alex Comfort, 80, Dies; a Multifaceted Man Best Known for Writing 'The Joy of Sex,'" *New York Times,* March 29, 2000.

23. Ibid.

24. Ibid.

25. Boulware, *Sex, American Style: An Illustrated Romp Through the Golden Age of Heterosexuality.*

26. Ibid.

27. Christopher Ryan, "Not All Military Adultery Results in Scandal," *Psychology Today,* November 16, 2012, https://www.psychologytoday.com/us/blog/sex-dawn/201211/not-all-military-adultery-results-in-scandal.

28. Joe Capozzi, "Two New York Yankees Swapped Wives 44 Years Ago. Still Married?" *Palm Beach Post,* March 24, 2017, https://www.palmbeachpost.com/sports/two-new-york-yankees-swapped-wives-years-ago-still-married/H8WVHAing5YWbQ0EXiPxJP/.

29. Gil Troy, "How the Great Yankee Wife Swap Scandalized—and Changed—America," *Daily Beast,* June 24, 2017, https://www.thedailybeast.com/how-the-great-yankee-wife-swap-scandalizedand-changedamerica.

30. Mark Jacobson, "The Big Trade," *New York,* June 17, 2011, http://nymag.com/guides/summer/2011/mike-kekich-fritz-peterson/index1.html.

31. Bart Barnes, "'Joy of Sex' Author Alex Comfort Dies at 80," *Washington Post,* March 29, 2000, https://www.washingtonpost.com/ . . . alex-comfort . . . /f53ca3bc-c84b-4adf-a070-61305dab.

32. Williamson and Bacon, *An Extraordinary Life.*

33. Lisa Robinson, "An Oral History of Laurel Canyon, the 60s And 70s Music Mecca," *Vanity Fair,* March 2015, https://www.vanityfair.com/culture/2015/02/laurel-canyon-music-scene?verso=true.

34. *Newsweek,* March 13, 1974.

35. "Streaking," Wikipedia, https://en.wikipedia.org/wiki/Streaking#cite_note-11.

36. Pete Senoff, "Female Rocker Roundup," *Fusion,* December 26, 1969.

37. Ibid.

38. Boulware, *Sex, American Style: An Illustrated Romp Through the Golden Age of Heterosexuality.*

39. Robert Hofler, "'Genuinely Oversexed': How 'Carnal Knowledge,' 'Deep Throat' and '70s Rebels Led to 'Wolf of Wall Street,'" *Salon,* February 16, 2014, https://www.salon.com/2014/02/15/genuinely_oversexed_how_carnal_knowledge_deep_throat_and_70s_rebels_led_to_wolf_of_wall_street/.

40. Ibid.
41. Vincent Canby, "What Are We to Think of 'Deep Throat'?" *New York Times,* January 21, 1973, https://www.nytimes.com/1973/01/21/archives/what-are-we-to-think-of-deep-throat-what-to-think-of-deep-throat.html?searchResultPosition=1.
42. Richard Corliss, "Porn's Pied Piper: *Deep Throat* Director Dies," *Time,* October 27, 2008, http://content.time.com/time/arts/article/0,8599,1854297,00.html.
43. Biskind, *Easy Riders, Raging Bulls.*
44. Ibid.
45. Ryan Teague Beckwith, "George Lucas Wrote 'Star Wars' as a Liberal Warning. Then Conservatives Struck Back," *Time,* October 10, 2017, http://time.com/4975813/star-wars-politics-watergate-george-lucas/.
46. Stratton, *Jews, Race and Popular Music.*
47. Jarnow, *Heads: A Biography of Psychedelic America.*
48. Stewart Brand, "S P A C E W A R: Fanatic Life and Symbolic Death Among the Computer Bums," *Rolling Stone,* December 7, 1972.
49. Isaacson, *Steve Jobs.*
50. Ibid.
51. Ibid.

17. SOUTHERN ROCK

1. Chet Flippo, "Nashville Skyline: Gregg Allman's Autobiography Tells Almost All," CMT, September 20, 2012, http://www.cmt.com/news/1694200/nashville-skyline-gregg-allmans-autobiography-tells-almost-all/.
2. *American Revolutions: Southern Rock,* directed by Anne Fentress (2005), DVD.
3. *Sweet Home Alabama: The Southern Rock Saga,* directed by James Maycock (2012), DVD.
4. Fetherolf, *The Guitar Story: From Ancient to Modern Times.*
5. Clapton, *The Autobiography,* 128.
6. John J. Moser, "Butch Trucks' Last Interview: The Complete Transcript," *Morning Call,* January 25, 2017, http://www.mcall.com/entertainment/lehigh-valley-music/mc-butch-trucks-last-interview-the-day-he-died-allman-brothers-co-founder-talked-with-lehigh-valley-mus-20170125-story.html.
7. Alan Paul, "The Allman Brothers Band: The Road Goes On Forever," *Guitar World,* July 2009, https://www.duaneallman.info/theroadgoesonforever.htm.
8. Ibid.
9. *Allman Brothers—After the Crash,* directed by Tom O'Dell (2016), DVD.
10. Paul, *One Way Out: The Inside History of the Allman Brothers Band.*
11. Allman and Light, *My Cross to Bear.*
12. Crowe, *The Day the Music Died: A Rock 'n' Roll Tribute.*
13. Thompson, *1000 Songs That Rock Your World: From Rock Classics to One-Hit Wonders, the Music That Lights Your Fire.*
14. Cameron Crowe, "The Allman Brothers Story," *Rolling Stone,* December 6, 1973.
15. Paul, *One Way Out: The Inside History of the Allman Brothers Band.*
16. Marsh, *The Heart of Rock and Soul.*

17. Anthony Bozza, "A Boy's Life (in Sex, Drugs and Rock & Roll)," *Rolling Stone,* October 12, 2000, https://www.rollingstone.com/movies/movie-news/a-boys-life-in-sex-drugs-and-rock-roll-163369/.

18. Crowe, "The Allman Brothers Story."

19. Bozza, "A Boy's Life (in Sex, Drugs and Rock & Roll)."

20. Ibid.

21. Ibid.

22. Ibid.

23. Nicki Gostin, "'Baybrah' Gregg Allman Talks Duane, NYC, 'My Cross to Bear," *Billboard,* June 6, 2012, https://www.billboard.com/articles/news/484311/baybrah-gregg-allman-talks-duane-nyc-my-cross-to-bear.

24. *If I Leave Here Tomorrow: A Film About Lynyrd Skynyrd,* directed by Stephen Kijak (2018), DVD.

25. Gary Graff, "Rickey Medlocke of Lynyrd Skynyrd Remembers Gregg Allman's 'Unmistakable Voice," *Billboard,* May 29, 2017, https://www.billboard.com/articles/columns/rock/7809653/gregg-allman-brothers-rickey-medlocke-lynyrd-skynyrd-remembers.

26. Alan Paul, "Gimme Three Chords—Inside Lynyrd Skynyrd's Greatest Hits," *Alan Paul,* http://alanpaul.net/2014/05/gimme-three-chords-inside-lynyrd-skynyrds-greatest-hits/.

27. "Free Bird," Wikipedia, https://en.wikipedia.org/wiki/Free_Bird#cite_note-14.

28. Paul, "Gimme Three Chords—Inside Lynyrd Skynyrd's Greatest Hits."

29. Ibid.

30. *Guitar World* Staff, "100 Greatest Guitar Solos: No. 3 Free Bird," *Guitar World,* October 14, 2008, https://www.guitarworld.com/lessons/100-greatest-guitar-solos-no-3-free-bird-allen-collins-gary-rossington.

31. *The Old Grey Whistle Test* (Warner Home Video, 2003), DVD.

32. Caren Burmeister, "A Subdivision with Southern Rock Roots," *Jacksonville Daily Record*, August 10, 2017, https://www.jaxdailyrecord.com/article/a-subdivision-with-southern-rock-roots.

33. Durchholz and Graff, *Neil Young: Long May You Run: The Illustrated History.*

34. *Guitar World,* April 2000, via Hyper Rust, https://hyperrust.org/General/Skynerd.html

35. Young, *Waging Heavy Peace: A Hippie Dream.*

36. Ballinger, *Lynyrd Skynyrd: An Oral History.*

37. Ibid.

38. Andy Greene, "Tom Petty on Past Confederate Flag Use: 'It Was Downright Stupid,'" *Rolling Stone,* July 14, 2015, https://www.rollingstone.com/politics/politics-news/tom-petty-on-past-confederate-flag-use-it-was-downright-stupid-177619/.

39. David Browne, "Clydie King, Unsung Backup Singer for Ray Charles and Bob Dylan, Dead at 75," *Rolling Stone,* January 10, 2019, https://www.rollingstone.com/ . . . /clydie-king-ray-charles-bob-dylan-singer-dead-777417.

40. *If I Leave Here Tomorrow: A Film About Lynyrd Skynyrd,* directed by Stephen Kijak (2018), DVD.

41. Flippo, "Nashville Skyline: Gregg Allman's Autobiography Tells Almost All."

42. Jaan Uhelszki, "Gregg Allman Still Dreams," *Relix,* April–May 2009, https://relix
.com/articles/detail/gregg-allman-still-dreams-relix-revisited/.

18. KEEP GETTIN' IT ON

1. Werner, *Higher Ground: Stevie Wonder, Aretha Franklin, Curtis Mayfield, and the
Rise and Fall of American Soul.*
2. Jon Landau, "Innervisions," *Rolling Stone,* June 6, 1974, https://www.rollingstone
.com/music/music-album-reviews/innervisions-246460/.
3. Ribowsky, *Signed, Sealed, and Delivered: The Soulful Journey of Stevie Wonder.*
4. Williams and Brady, *Stevie Wonder.*
5. "Innervisions," Wikipedia, https://en.wikipedia.org/wiki/Innervisions.
6. Ritz, *Divided Soul: The Life of Marvin Gaye.*
7. Gaye and Ritz, *After the Dance: My Life with Marvin Gaye.*
8. "Just to Keep You Satisfied," Wikipedia, https://en.wikipedia.org/wiki/Just_to
_Keep_You_Satisfied.
9. Gaye and Ritz, *After the Dance: My Life with Marvin Gaye.*
10. "ASCAP Legends Elvis Costello, Marvin Gaye, Tom Petty, Chic's Bernard Edwards
to Be Inducted into Songwriters Hall of Fame," *ASCAP,* https://www.ascap.com
/playback/2016/02/action/2016-shof-inductees.
11. Posner, *Motown: Music, Money, Sex, and Power.*
12. George, *Where Did Our Love Go? The Rise and Fall of the Motown Sound.*
13. Jacksons and Bronson, *The Jacksons: Legacy.*
14. Ibid.
15. Jackson, *Moon Walk.*
16. Ibid.
17. Alexis Petridis, "Joe Jackson Was One of the Most Monstrous Fathers in Pop,"
Guardian, June 27, 2018, https://www.theguardian.com/music/2018/jun/27/joe
-jackson-one-of-the-most-monstrous-fathers-in-pop.
18. Taraborrelli, *Michael Jackson: The Magic, The Madness, The Whole Story, 1958–
2009.*
19. Andersen, *Michael Jackson Unauthorized.*

19. STAR-CROSSED IN PLEASURE

1. Richards, *Life.*
2. Wyman, *Rolling with the Stones.*
3. "Goats Head Soup," *Time Is on Our Side,* http://www.timeisonourside.com/lpGoats
.html.
4. Masouri, *Steppin' Razor: The Life of Peter Tosh.*
5. Richards, *Life.*
6. Bill Janovitz, "Angie," *AllMusic,* September 1, 2009, https://www.allmusic.com
/song/angie-mt0007824883.
7. MJD, "CSPC: The Rolling Stones Popularity Analysis," *ChartMasters,* December 3, 2016, https://chartmasters.org/2016/12/cspc-the-rolling-stones-popularity
-analysis/.
8. Faithfull, *Faithfull: An Autobiography.*

9. "Bell, Book, and Candle," *Encyclopaedia Britannica,* https://www.britannica .com/topic/bell-book-and-candle-Roman-Catholicism.

10. Faithfull, *Faithfull: An Autobiography.*

11. Davis, *Old Gods Almost Dead: The 40-Year Odyssey of the Rolling Stones.*

12. Sanchez, *Up and Down with the Rolling Stones.*

13. Richards, *Life.*

14. Andersen, *Jagger Unauthorized.*

15. Christopher Andersen, "Mick Jagger's Affair with David Bowie Revealed in New Book: They 'Were Really Sexually Obsessed with Each Other,'" *New York Daily News,* July 9, 2012, http://www.nydailynews.com/entertainment/gossip/new -book-takes-mick-jagger-affair-david-bowie-article-1.1109887.

16. Ibid.

17. Ibid.

18. Marissa Charles, "I Was the Filling in a 'Cookie' with David Bowie and Mick Jagger," *New York Post,* January 17, 2016, https://nypost.com/2016/01/17/my-love -affair-with-david-bowie-and-mick-jagger/.

19. Jake Malooley, "David Bowie's Ex-Girlfriend Discusses Their Love Affair, Inter-racial Dating, Mick Jagger, and the Infamous Labyrinth Bulge," *Chicago Reader,* January 13, 2016, https://www.chicagoreader.com/chicago/david-bowie-dead-ava -cherry-girlfriend-mick-jagger/Content?oid=20856025.

20. Andersen, "Mick Jagger's Affair with David Bowie Revealed in New Book."

21. "Time Waits for No One," *Time Is on Our Side,* http://www.timeisonourside.com /SOTimeWaits.html.

22. Ibid.

23. *Jump Back* liner notes, 1993.

24. Bockris, *Keith Richards: The Biography.*

25. "It's Only Rock 'n Roll," *Time Is on Our Side,* http://www.timeisonourside.com /SOIt%27sOnlyRock.html.

26. Richards, *Life.*

27. Paytress, *The Rolling Stones—Off the Record.*

28. "It's Only Rock 'n Roll," *Time Is on Our Side.*

29. Jann S. Wenner, "Mick Jagger Remembers," *Rolling Stone,* December 14, 1995, https://www.rollingstone.com/music/music-news/mick-jagger-remembers-92946/.

30. Angie Spray, "1973–74: It's Only Rock 'n Roll," *Rockapedia,* February 15, 2015, http://www.rockapedia.com/biography/mick-taylor/1973%E2%80%9374-its-only -rock-n-roll.

31. *Mojo,* September 2003, via *Steve Hoffman Music Forums,* https://forums.steve hoffman.tv/threads/rolling-stores-mick-taylor-in-a-nick-of-time.855416/page-5.

32. Jann S. Wenner, "Mick Jagger Remembers."

20. THE WORLD IS A GHETTO

1. Smith, *The One: The Life and Music of James Brown.*

2. Ibid.

3. "James Brown Nixon's Clown," *New York Amsterdam News,* May 26, 1973.

4. Al Sharpton, "Sharpton: James Brown Biopic 'Get On Up' Has Uncomfortable Scenes but Speaks the Truth," *New York Daily News,* July 30, 2014, http://www .nydailynews.com/entertainment/movies/sharpton-brown-biopic-puts-pain -display-article-1.1885036.

5. Smith, *The One: The Life and Music of James Brown.*

6. Ibid.

7. Bruns, *Jesse Jackson: A Biography.*

8. Caroline Howe, "Revealed: Dick Clark's Brazen Scheme to Oust Don Cornelius and Replace 'Soul Train' with His Own All-Black Dance Show," *Daily Mail,* March 21, 2014, https://www.dailymail.co.uk/news/article-2585503/Exposed-Dick -Clarks-brazen-scheme-replace-Don-Cornelius-Soul-Train-black-dance-show .html.

9. *Maynard,* directed by Samuel D. Pollard (2017), DVD.

10. George, *Buppies, B-boys, Baps & Bohos: Notes on Post-Soul Black Culture.*

11. *The Black Panthers: Vanguard of the Revolution,* directed by Stanley Nelson (2015), DVD.

12. Ibid.

13. Ibid.

14. Ibid.

15. "Bobby Seale," Wikipedia, https://en.wikipedia.org/wiki/Bobby_Seale.

16. "Black Panther Party," Wikipedia, https://en.wikipedia.org/wiki/Black_Panther _Party.

17. Kramer, *The Hard Stuff: Dope, Crime, the MC5, and My Life of Impossibilities.*

18. "List of Best-Selling Albums by Year in the United States," Wikipedia, https://en .wikipedia.org/wiki/List_of_best-selling_albums_by_year_in_the_United _States#1970s.

19. "Year-End Charts—Year-End Albums—The Billboard 200," *Billboard,* February 14, 2008, https://web.archive.org/web/20080214165824/http://www.billboard .com/bbcom/charts/yearend_chart_display.jsp?f=The+Billboard+200&g=Year -end+Albums&year=1973.

20. Gavin Haynes, "Soundtrack of My Life—50 Cent on Miley, Michael Jackson and Bobby Womack's Power to Move," *New Musical Express,* July 30, 2015, https://www.nme.com/blogs/nme-blogs/soundtrack-of-my-life-50-cent-on-miley -michael-jackson-and-bobby-womacks-power-to-move-16206.

21. Werner, *Higher Ground: Stevie Wonder, Aretha Franklin, Curtis Mayfield, and the Rise and Fall of American Soul.*

22. Bogle, *Toms, Coons, Mulattoes, Mammies, and Bucks: An Interpretive History of Blacks in American Films,* 231–66.

23. "Blaxploitation Cinema," *Oxford African American Studies Center,* http://www .oxfordaasc.com/public/features/archive/0513/photo_essay.jsp?page=9.

24. Maurice Peterson, "Ron Was Too Light for 'Shaft,' but . . . ," *New York Times,* September 17, 1972, https://www.nytimes.com/1972/09/17/archives/ron-was-too-light -for-shaft-but-ron-was-too-light-for-shaft-but.html.

25. Brown and Tucker, *James Brown: The Godfather of Soul.*

26. Smith, *The One: The Life and Music of James Brown*.

27. Ibid.

28. Ibid.

29. Ibid.

30. Clinton and Greenman, *Brothas Be, Yo like George, Ain't That Funkin' Kinda Hard on You? A Memoir*.

31. *Mike Judge Presents: Tales from the Tour Bus*, directed by Mike Judge (Cinemax, 2018), DVD.

32. Corbett, *Extended Play: Sounding Off from John Cage to Dr. Funkenstein*, 149–50.

33. Shelley Salant, "George Clinton Lays It All Down," *Metro Times*, May 4, 2016, https://www.metrotimes.com/detroit/george-clinton-lays-it-all-down/Content?oid =2441830.

34. Clinton and Greenman, *Brothas Be, Yo like George, Ain't That Funkin' Kinda Hard on You? A Memoir*.

35. Ibid.

36. Ibid.

37. Ibid.

38. Ibid.

39. Chang, *Can't Stop Won't Stop: A History of the Hip-Hop Generation*.

40. Maya Rattrey, "Knowledge Session: The Griot Tradition," *I Am Hip Hop*, March 18, 2018, http://www.iamhiphopmagazine.com/thegriottradition/.

41. "Dub Music," Wikipedia, https://en.wikipedia.org/wiki/Dub_music.

42. Ibid.

43. Michael A. Gonzales, "Party over Here: An Oral History of Kool Herc's Historic Back-to-School Jam," *Mass Appeal*, https://massappeal.com/kool-herc-oral -history-party-over-here-birth-of-hip-hop/.

44. *Sample This*, directed by Dan Forrer (2012), DVD.

45. Ibid.

46. Angus Batey, "DJ Kool Herc Djs His First Block Party (His Sister's Birthday) at 1520 Sedgwick Avenue, Bronx, New York," *Guardian*, June 12, 2011, https:// www.theguardian.com/music/2011/jun/13/dj-kool-herc-block-party.

47. Steven Hager, "Afrika Bambaataa's Hip-Hop," *Village Voice*, September 21, 1982.

21. COUNTRY ROCK

1. James Sullivan, "Q & A with Linda Ronstadt," *SFGate*, June 21, 1998, https://www .sfgate.com/music/popquiz/article/Q-A-With-Linda-Ronstadt-3003615.php.

2. Faithfull, *Faithfull: An Autobiography*.

3. Sullivan, "Q & A with Linda Ronstadt."

4. Ronstadt, *Simple Dreams: A Musical Memoir*.

5. Sullivan, "Q & A with Linda Ronstadt."

6. Ben Fong-Torres, "Linda Ronstadt: Heartbreak on Wheels," *Rolling Stone*, March 27, 1975, https://www.rollingstone.com/music/music-news/linda-ronstadt -heartbreak-on-wheels-172427/.

7. Ronstadt, *Simple Dreams: A Musical Memoir*.

8. Ibid.

9. Ibid.

10. Ibid.

11. Ibid.

12. Stephen Deusner, "Linda Ronstadt: 'There Are Always Predators Around, and You Have to Keep an Eye Out for Them," *Salon,* October 7, 2013, https://www .salon.com/2013/10/07/linda_ronstadt_there_are_always_predators_around_and _you_have_to_keep_an_eye_out_for_them/

13. "You're No Good," Wikipedia, https://en.wikipedia.org/wiki/You%27re_No_Good #Linda_Ronstadt_version.

14. Fong-Torres, *Hickory Wind: The Life and Times of Gram Parsons.*

15. *Sisters in Country: Dolly, Linda and Emmylou,* directed by Dione Newton (BBC, 2016).

16. Ben Fong-Torres, "Emmylou Harris: Whole-Wheat Honky-Tonk," *Rolling Stone,* February 23, 1978, https://www.rollingstone.com/music/ . . . /emmylou-harris-whole -wheat-honky-tonk-10663.

17. Fiona Sturges, "Emmylou Harris: 'I Smoked Country Music but I Didn't Inhale'," *Independent,* April 17, 2011, https://www.independent.co.uk/arts-entertainment /music/features/emmylou-harris-i-smoked-country-music-but-i-didnt-inhale -2267867.html.

18. Meyer, *Twenty Thousand Roads: The Ballad of Gram Parsons and His Cosmic American Music.*

19. Fong-Torres, *Hickory Wind: The Life and Times of Gram Parsons.*

20. Meyer, *Twenty Thousand Roads: The Ballad of Gram Parsons and His Cosmic American Music.*

21. Holly George-Warren, "The Long Way Around," *No Depression,* July/August 1999, https://www.nodepression.com/gram-parsons-a-long-lost-soul-for-a-long-long-time/.

22. Meyer, *Twenty Thousand Roads: The Ballad of Gram Parsons and His Cosmic American Music.*

23. Fong-Torres, *Hickory Wind: The Life and Times of Gram Parsons.*

24. Sturges, "Emmylou Harris: 'I Smoked Country Music but I Didn't Inhale.'"

25. Ibid.

26. John Harris, "Tomb Raider," *Guardian,* February 5, 2004, https://www.theguardian .com/music/2004/feb/06/popandrock.gramparsons.

27. Einarson, *Desperados: The Roots of Country Rock.*

28. Ibid.

29. Ronstadt, *Simple Dreams: A Musical Memoir.*

30. "And Then There were Two," *Goldmine,* August 2, 1996, via *The Linda Ronstadt Homepage,* https://www.ronstadt-linda.com/intgm.htm.

31. George-Warren, "The Long Way Around.

32. Sturges, "Emmylou Harris: 'I Smoked Country Music but I Didn't Inhale.'"

33. Cameron Crowe, "Eagles: Chips off the Old Buffalo," *Rolling Stone,* September 25, 1975, https://www.rollingstone.com/music/music . . . /eagles-chips-off-the-old -buffalo-163348/.

34. Cameron Crowe, "Conversations with Don Henley and Glenn Frey," *The Uncool,* August 2003, http://www.theuncool.com/journalism/the-very-best-of-the-eagles/.

35. Jack Tempchin, "Jack Tempchin's Story About Writing 'Peaceful Easy Feeling,'" https://mypeacefuleasyfeeling.com/post/391244337/jack-tempchins-story-about -writing-peaceful-easy.

36. Pierre Perrone, "Glenn Frey: Singer and Songwriter Who Co-founded the Eagles, the Biggest Selling American Rock Band of All Time," *Independent,* January 19, 2016, https://www.independent.co.uk/news/obituaries/glenn-frey-singer-and-songwriter -who-co-founded-the-eagles-the-biggest-selling-american-rock-band-of-a6821876 .html.

37. Crowe, "Conversations with Don Henley and Glenn Frey."

38. Ibid.

39. Ibid.

40. Ibid.

41. Goodman, *The Mansion on the Hill: Dylan, Young, Geffen, Springsteen, and the Head-on Collision of Rock and Commerce.*

42. *History of the Eagles,* directed by Alison Eastwood (2013), DVD.

43. Crowe, "Conversations with Don Henley and Glenn Frey."

22. PAPA, DON'T LAY THAT S**T ON ME

1. Brett Callwood, "Glycerine Queen, Forever!," *Detroit Metro Times,* December 14, 2013.

2. Rachel Martin, "'We Had to Do It Ourselves': Joan Jett Looks Back on Being a Conduit for Women in Rock," NPR, September 28, 2018, https://www.npr.org /templates/transcript/transcript.php?storyId=651438020.

3. Evelyn McDonald, "Joan Jett on 20 Years as Rock's Toughest Woman," *Rolling Stone,* November 13, 1997, https://www.rollingstone.com/ . . . /joan-jett-on-20-years -as-rocks-toughest-woman-89995.

4. Jaan Uhelszki, "Joan Jett: Rebel with a Cause," *Classic Rock,* January 29, 2018, https://www.loudersound.com/features/joan-jett-rebel-with-a-cause.

5. McDonnell, *Queens of Noise: The Real Story of the Runaways.*

6. Ann Powers, "You've Got a Home: June Millington's Lifelong Journey in Rock," NPR, November 19, 2015, https://www.npr.org/sections/therecord/2015/11/19 /456581427/youve-got-a-home-june-millingtons-lifelong-journey-in-rock.

7. Ibid.

8. Ibid.

9. Eric R. Danton, "Fanny Lives: Inside the Return of the Pioneering All-Female Rock Band," *Rolling Stone,* March 16, 2018, https://www.rollingstone.com/music /music-features/fanny-lives-inside-the-return-of-the-pioneering-all-female-rock -band-125635/.

10. Jan Moir, "The Last of the Red-Hot Babes," *Mojo,* June 1994.

11. Steven X. Rea, "Bonnie Raitt Lightens Up," *High Fidelity,* June, 1982.

12. Moir, "The Last of the Red-Hot Babes."

13. Simon Edge, "Battle of the Sexes: When Bobby Riggs Called Out Billie Jean King," *Express,* June 20, 2013, https://www.express.co.uk/sport/tennis/408768 /Battle-of-the-sexes-When-Bobby-Riggs-called-out-Billie-Jean-King.

14. Justin Kroll, "Emma Stone and Steve Carell Face Off in First Trailer for 'Battle of the Sexes,'" *Variety,* May 16, 2017, https://variety.com/2017/film/news/battle -of-the-sexes-trailer-emma-stone-billie-jean-king-video-watch-1202428850/.

15. "Billie Jean King Speaks About Impact of Beating 'One of Her Heroes' in 'Battle of the Sexes,'" *Women in the World,* September 21, 2017, https://womenintheworld .com/2017/09/21/billie-jean-king-speaks-about-impact-of-beating-one-of-her -heroes-in-battle-of-the-sexes/.

16. Larry Schwartz, "Billie Jean Won for All Women," ESPN, https://www.espn.com /sportscentury/features/00016060.html.

17. Britni de la Cretaz, "Maria Pepe: The New Jersey Girl Who Sued to Play Baseball with the Boys," *Guardian,* September 23, 2018, https://www.theguardian.com /sport/2018/sep/23/maria-pepe-bfa-baseball-series-now.

18. Anna Wade, "#Shortstops: Maria Pepe Changes the Face of Little League," *National Baseball Hall of Fame.org,* https://baseballhall.org/discover/short-stops /nothing-little-about-it.

19. de La Cretaz, "Maria Pepe: the New Jersey Girl Who Sued to Play Baseball with the Boys."

20. Ibid.

21. "Little League in Jersey Ordered to Allow Girls to Play on Teams," *New York Times,* November 8, 1973, https://www.nytimes.com/1973/11/08/archives/little -league-in-jersey-ordered-to-allow-girls-to-play-on-teams.html.

22. Eileen Shanahan, "A.T.&T. To Grant 15,000 Back Pay in Job Inequities," *New York Times,* January 19, 1973, https://www.nytimes.com/1973/01/19/archives/att-to-grant -15000-back-pay-in-job-inequities-36000-expected-to.html.

23. Gloria Steinhem, "What Do Women Expect," *The American Association of Advertising Agencies,* https://www.aaa.org/timeline-event/gloria-steinems-impassioned -feminist-speech-4as/.

24. John Updike, "Jong Love," *New Yorker,* December 17, 1973.

25. Matthew Rettenmund, "A Penis on Every Page: The Rise and Fall of *Playgirl,*" *Esquire,* June 24, 2017, https://www.esquire.com/entertainment/a55592/playgirl -magazine-history/.

26. Ibid.

23. TROUBADOUR UNDERDOGS

1. "Roberta Flack Recalls Debuting "Killing Me Softly" at the Greek Theatre with Marvin Gaye," *The WAVE,* April 27, 2011.

2. Hoskyns, *Lowside of the Road: A Life of Tom Waits.*

3. Ibid.

4. Ibid.

5. Cameron Crowe, "Conversations with Don Henley and Glenn Frey," *The Uncool,* http://www.theuncool.com/journalism/the-very-best-of-the-eagles/.

6. Hoskyns, *Lowside of the Road: A Life of Tom Waits.*

7. Ibid.

8. Maher, *Tom Waits on Tom Waits: Interviews and Encounters.*

9. Hoskyns, *Lowside of the Road: A Life of Tom Waits.*
10. Brian McCollum, "Bob Seger on Friend Glenn Frey: 'He Was My Cheerleader,'" *Detroit Free Press,* January 18, 2016, https://www.freep.com/story/entertainment/music/2016/01/18/bob-seger-friend-glenn-frey-he-my-cheerleader/78984718/.
11. David Browne, "Glenn Frey: An Oral History," *Rolling Stone,* January 28, 2016, https://www.rollingstone.com/music/music-news/glenn-frey-an-oral-history-182045/.
12. Stephen Thomas Erlewine, "Back in '72," *AllMusic,* https://www.allmusic.com/album/back-in-72-mw0000838598.
13. Patrick Goldstein, "Bob Seger: A Star in His Own State," *Rolling Stone,* July 29, 1976.
14. McCollum, "Bob Seger on Friend Glenn Frey: 'He Was My Cheerleader.'"
15. Timothy White, "The Fire This Time," *Rolling Stone,* May 1, 1980, https://www.rollingstone.com/music/music-news/the-fire-this-time-37716/.
16. "All Possibilities: The 'Purple Rain' Story," NPR: *All Things Considered,* December 6, 2014, https://www.npr.org/2014/12/06/368508262/all-possibilities-the-purple-rain-story.
17. Schruers, *Billy Joel: The Definitive Biography.*
18. Chris Willman, "The Story of How Billy Joel Became the 'Piano Man,'" *Yahoo Music,* May 8, 2014, https://www.yahoo.com/entertainment/blogs/music-news/the-story-of-how-billy-joel-became-the--piano-man-030544179.html.
19. Schruers, *Billy Joel: The Definitive Biography.*
20. Ibid.
21. Ibid.
22. Willman, "The Story of How Billy Joel Became the 'Piano Man.'"
23. Ibid.
24. Ibid.
25. Schruers, *Billy Joel: The Definitive Biography.*
26. Bego, *Billy Joel: The Biography.*
27. Schruers, *Billy Joel: The Definitive Biography.*
28. *The Helen Reddy Show,* July 19, 1973.
29. Croce and Rock, *I Got a Name: The Jim Croce Story.*
30. Ibid.
31. Ibid.
32. "I'll Have to Say I Love You in a Song," Wikipedia, https://en.wikipedia.org/wiki/I%27ll_Have_to_Say_I_Love_You_in_a_Song.
33. "The Lori Lieberman Team," *Billboard,* December 14, 1974.
34. Croce and Rock, *I Got a Name: The Jim Croce Story.*

24. QUADROPHENIA

1. Townshend, *Who I Am: A Memoir.*
2. Cohn, *Awopbopaloobop Alopbamboom.*
3. Townshend, *Who I Am: A Memoir.*
4. Robert Christgau, "The Who: Quadrophenia," *Robert Christgau,* https://www.robertchristgau.com/get_album.php?id=3912.

5. Charles Perry and Andrew Bailey, "The Who's Spooky Tour: Awe and Hassles," *Rolling Stone,* January 3, 1974.

6. Ken Sharp, "The Quiet One Speaks! A Chat with the Ox, the Who's John Entwistle," *Goldmine,* July 5, 1996, https://www.thewho.net/bibliography/articles/johngold .html.

7. *Quadrophenia: Can You See the Real Me?,* directed by Matt O'Casey (BBC, 2013), DVD.

8. Gary Graff, "Pete Townshend on 'Quadrophenia,' the Who's 'Last Great Album,'" *Billboard,* November 11, 2011, https://www.billboard.com/articles/news/465182 /pete-townshend-on-quadrophenia-the-whos-last-great-album.

9. Groonrikk, "Quadraphonic: 1970s Rock Albums (4.0 Surround)," *Rate Your Music,* https://rateyourmusic.com/list/groonrikk/quadraphonic-1970s-rock-albums-4_0 -surround/.

10. Walker, *What You Want Is in the Limo: On the Road with Led Zeppelin, Alice Cooper, and the Who in 1973, the Year the Sixties Died and the Modern Rock Star Was Born.*

11. Egan, *Who on the Who: Interviews and Encounters.*

12. Ibid.

13. Andy Greene, "Dazed and Confused: 10 Classic Drugged-Out Shows," *Rolling Stone,* June 6, 2013, https://www.rollingstone.com/music/music-lists/dazed-and -confused-10-classic-drugged-out-shows-10948/5-keith-moon-at-the-cow-palace -1973-horse-tranquilizers-and-brandy-16001/.

14. Fletcher, *Moon: The Life and Death of a Rock Legend.*

15. Adrian Deevoy, "The Who's Roger Daltrey and Pete Townshend Give Their First Interview in a Decade . . . and It Just Might Cause a Big Sensation," *Daily Mail,* October 25, 2014, https://www.dailymail.co.uk/home/event/article-2803957/The -s-Pete-Townshend-Roger-Daltrey-Pete-came-knocked-spark-Roger-Daltrey-Pete -Townshend-interview-decade-just-cause-big-sensation.html.

16. Townshend, *Who I Am: A Memoir.*

17. Stephen Lewis, "The Day the Who Were Arrested in Montreal," *Ultimate Classic Rock,* December 2, 2015, https://ultimateclassicrock.com/the-who-arrested-in-montreal/.

18. Glynn, *Quadrophenia.*

19. Graff, "Pete Townshend on 'Quadrophenia,' The Who's 'Last Great Album.'"

25. STANDING ON THE SOUND OF SOME OPEN-HEARTED PEOPLE

1. *VH1 Legends: Neil Young* (VH1, 2000).

2. Ibid.

3. Steve Erickson, "Neil Young on a Good Day," *New York Times Magazine,* July 30, 2000, https://www.nytimes.com/2000/07/30/magazine/neil-young-on-a-good-day .html.

4. McDonough, *Shakey: Neil Young's Biography.*

5. Young, *Waging Heavy Peace (Deluxe).*

6. McDonough, *Shakey: Neil Young's Biography.*

7. Michael Roberts, "Nils Lofgren on Bruce Springsteen, Neil Young and His Stellar Solo Career," *Westword,* March 28, 2016, https://www.westword.com/music/nils -lofgren-on-bruce-springsteen-neil-young-and-his-stellar-solo-career-7666253.

8. McDonough, *Shakey: Neil Young's Biography.*

9. Andrew Wallace Chamings, "Neil Young's 'Tonight's the Night' at Forty," *Drowned in Sound,* August 27, 2013, http://drownedinsound.com/in_depth/4146783-%E2 %80%9Ci-have-no-idea-where-the-fuck-it-came-from%E2%80%9D-neil -young%E2%80%99s-tonight%E2%80%99s-the-night-at-forty.

10. Greg Prato, "Nils Lofgren of the E Street Band," *Song Facts,* https://www.songfacts .com/blog/interviews/nils-lofgren-of-the-e-street-band.

11. McDonough, *Shakey: Neil Young's Biography.*

12. Cameron Crowe, "The Rebellious Neil Young," *Rolling Stone,* August 14, 1975, https://www.rollingstone.com/music/music-news/the-rebellious-neil-young-117887/.

13. McDonough, *Shakey: Neil Young's Biography.*

14. Ibid.

15. Ibid.

16. King, *The Operator: David Geffen Builds, Buys, and Sells the New Hollywood.*

17. McDonough, *Shakey: Neil Young's Biography.*

18. Ibid.

19. Ibid.

20. Ibid.

21. Young, *Waging Heavy Peace (Deluxe).*

22. Clemons and Reo, *Big Man: Real Life and Tall Tales.*

23. Paul Lester, "Clive Davis: 'Janis Joplin Thought Sleeping with Me Would Make Things Seem Less Corporate,'" *Guardian,* November 5, 2014, https://www.theguardian .com/culture/2014/nov/05/30-minutes-with-clive-jones-record-producer.

24. Carlin, *Bruce.*

25. David Remnick, 'We Are Alive: Bruce Springsteen at Sixty-Two," *New Yorker,* July 23, 2012, https://www.newyorker.com/magazine/2012/07/30/we-are-alive.

26. Carlin, *Bruce.*

27. "The Wild, The Innocent & The E Street Shuffle—Studio Sessions," *Brucebase,* http://brucebase.wikidot.com/stats:the-wild-the-innocent-the-e-street-shuffle -studio-sess.

28. Carlin, *Bruce.*

29. Springsteen, *Born to Run.*

30. Carlin, *Bruce.*

31. "The Wild, The Innocent & The E Street Shuffle—Studio Sessions."

32. Bruce Springsteen, "I Sold My Heart to the Junkman" (audio), 1974, https://www .youtube.com/watch?v=M99gSHyVVCE.

33. Carlin, *Bruce.*

34. Sandford, *Springsteen: Point Blank.*

35. Michael Goldberg, "The Second Coming of Robbie Robertson," *Rolling Stone,* November 19, 1987, https://www.rollingstone.com/music/music-features/the-second -coming-of-robbie-robertson-75297/.

36. Doggett, *CSNY: Crosby, Stills, Nash and Young.*

26. TIME TO GET DOWN

1. Robert Christgau, "Jackson 5," *Robert Christgau,* http://robertchristgau.com/get_artist.php?name=Jackson+5.
2. Echols, *Hot Stuff: Disco and the Remaking of American Culture.*
3. Jackson, *A House on Fire: The Rise and Fall of Philadelphia Soul.*
4. Ibid.
5. Dannen, *Hit Men: Power Brokers and Fast Money Inside the Music Business.*
6. Jackson, *A House on Fire: The Rise and Fall of Philadelphia Soul.*
7. "For the Love of Money," Wikipedia, https://en.wikipedia.org/wiki/For_the_Love_of_Money.
8. Jackson, *A House on Fire: The Rise and Fall of Philadelphia Soul.*
9. Ibid.
10. Tom FitzGerald, "A Hall of Fame Hitmaker Finds Happiness and Harmony in Bellingham," *Seattle Times,* February 15, 2018, https://www.seattletimes.com/pacific-nw-magazine/thom-bell-a-hall-of-fame-hitmaker-with-more-than-30-gold-records-has-found-happiness-and-harmony-in-bellingham/.
11. Jackson, *A House on Fire: The Rise and Fall of Philadelphia Soul.*
12. "Earl Young Explains His Revolutionary Disco Drum Beat!" YouTube, https://www.youtube.com/watch?v=gsf51_a1ceI.
13. Jackson, *A House on Fire: The Rise and Fall of Philadelphia Soul.*
14. Mark Skillz, "DJ Hollywood: The Original King of New York," *Medium,* November 19, 2014, https://medium.com/cuepoint/dj-hollywood-the-original-king-of-new-york-41b131b966ee.
15. Echols, *Hot Stuff: Disco and the Remaking of American Culture.*
16. Jarnow, *Heads: A Biography of Psychedelic America.*
17. Brewster and Broughton, *Last Night a DJ Saved My Life.*
18. "David Mancuso & The Loft," *Maestro,* 2003, https://www.youtube.com/watch?v=FftLQPE9TqU.
19. Lawrence, *Love Saves the Day: A History of American Dance Music Culture, 1970–1979.*
20. *Top 40 Weekly,* https://top40weekly.com/1973-all-charts/.
21. Lawrence, *Love Saves the Day: A History of American Dance Music Culture, 1970–1979.*
22. Ibid.
23. "The Hustle," Wikipedia, https://en.wikipedia.org/wiki/Hustle_(dance).
24. Hermes, *Love Goes to Buildings on Fire: Five Years in New York That Changed Music Forever.*
25. "Do the (Salsoul) Hustle: Big Break Celebrates Salsoul Records Legacy with Four Reissues," *The Second Disc,* August 4, 2017, https://theseconddisc.com/2012/10/do-the-salsoul-hustle-big-break-celebrates-salsoul-records-legacy-with-four-reissues/.
26. Hermes, *Love Goes to Buildings on Fire: Five Years in New York That Changed Music Forever.*
27. Will González, "Yankee Stadium Fielded a Memorable Night of Music in 1973,"

ESPN, September 22, 2008, http://www.espn.com/espn/hispanicheritage2008/news/story?id=3596100.

28. "Barry White," Wikipedia, https://en.wikipedia.org/wiki/Barry_White#cite_note-9.

29. "Rock the Boat," Wikipedia, https://en.wikipedia.org/wiki/Rock_the_Boat_(The _Hues_Corporation_song).

30. *George McCrae,* http://www.georgemccrae.com/?p=295.

27. UNDERGROUND VIBRATIONS

1. *Almost Famous,* directed by Cameron Crowe (2000), DVD.

2. Cohn, *Awopbopaloobop Alopbamboom.*

3. Ibid.

4. Reynolds, *Totally Wired: Postpunk Interviews and Overviews.*

5. Lester Bangs, "Of Pop & Pies & Fun: A Program of Mass Liberation in the Form of a Stooges Review, or, Who's the Fool?" *Creem,* November–December 1970.

6. Jon Wilde, "Every Night I Thought I'd Be Killed," *Guardian,* July 31, 2008, https://www.theguardian.com/music/2008/aug/01/popandrock.suicide.

7. Miller, *Detroit Rock City: The Uncensored History of Rock 'n' Roll in America's Loudest City.*

8. Gendron, *Between Montmartre and the Mudd Club: Popular Music and the Avant-Garde.*

9. "Hi, I Am Jac Holzman, Founder of Elektra Records and the Lucky Guy Who Signed the Doors," *Reddit,* https://www.reddit.com/r/IAmA/comments/1gon4r/hi _i_am_jac_holzman_founder_of_elektra_records/.

10. Carl Cafarelli, "Lenny Kaye: The Nuggets Interview," https://carlcafarelli.blogspot .com/2016/03/lenny-kaye-nuggets-interview.html.

11. Ibid.

12. "Punk Rock," Wikipedia, https://en.wikipedia.org/wiki/Punk_rock.

13. Damien Love, "The Making of . . . Richard Hell & the Voidoids' 'Blank Generation,'" *Uncut,* June 7, 2013, https://www.uncut.co.uk/features/the-making-of -richard-hell-the-voidoids-blank-generation-22461.

14. Bangs, *Psychotic Reactions and Carburetor Dung: The Work of a Legendary Critic.*

15. Hell, *I Dreamed I Was a Very Clean Tramp: An Autobiography.*

16. Nate Freeman, "No Fury: The Bowery's Changed, but Richard Hell Doesn't Mind," *Observer,* March 5, 2013, https://observer.com/2013/03/no-fury-the-bowerys -changed-but-richard-hell-doesnt-mind/.

17. Fred Ferretti, "Theater Owner Reports Warning of Hotel Collapse," *New York Times,* August 9, 1973, https://www.nytimes.com/ . . . /theater-owner-reports-warn ing-of-hotel-collapse-council.

18. Wall, *Lou Reed: The Life.*

19. Paul Nelson, "Lou Reed Live," *Rolling Stone,* June 5, 1975, https://www.rolling stone.com/music/music-album-reviews/lou-reed-live-101884/.

20. Joe Tangari, "The Life and Music of Alex Chilton," *Pitchfork,* March 22, 2010, https://pitchfork.com/features/article/7779-the-life-and-music-of-alex-chilton/.

21. *Big Star: Nothing Can Hurt Me,* directed by Drew DeNicola and Olivia Mori (2012), DVD.

22. Eaton, *Big Star's Radio City.*

23. Dave Lifton, "Infinite Play: Big Star, September Gurls," *Popdose,* March 19, 2010, http://popdose.com/infinite-play-big-star-september-gurls/.

24. Douglas Wolk, "September Gurls," *Time,* October 21, 2011, http://entertainment .time.com/2011/10/24/the-all-time-100-songs/slide/september-gurls-big-star/.

25. Sam Sutherland, *Billboard,* December 22, 1973, quoted in "Max's Icon: Big Star," *Max's Kansas City,* http://maxskansascity.com/maxs-icon-big-star/.

26. *Big Star: Nothing Can Hurt Me,* directed by Drew DeNicola and Olivia Mori (2012), DVD.

27. Michael Hann, "Cult Heroes: Raspberries—60s-Loving Progenitors of Powerpop," *Guardian,* July 12, 2016, https://www.theguardian.com/music/musicblog/2016/jul /12/cult-heroes-raspberries-powerpop-big-star.

28. Ibid.

29. Ibid.

30. Richie Unterberger, "Kingdom Come: Journey," *AllMusic,* https://www.allmusic .com/album/journey-mw0000320953.

31. Needs, *Suicide: Dream Baby Dream, a New York City Story.*

32. Heller, *Strange Stars: How Science Fiction and Fantasy Transformed Popular Music.*

28. COURT AND SPARK

1. Yaffe, *Reckless Daughter: A Portrait of Joni Mitchell.*

2. Ibid.

3. Weller, *Girls like Us: Carole King, Joni Mitchell, Carly Simon—and the Journey of a Generation.*

4. Ibid.

5. Lois Alter Mark, "Sheila Weller on Joni Mitchell and the 40th Anniversary of 'Court and Spark'," January 18, 2014, *Joni Mitchell,* https://jonimitchell.com/library /view.cfm?id=2734.

6. Bego, *Joni Mitchell.*

7. Weller, *Girls like Us: Carole King, Joni Mitchell, Carly Simon—and the Journey of a Generation.*

8. Yaffe, *Reckless Daughter: A Portrait of Joni Mitchell.*

9. Weller, *Girls like Us: Carole King, Joni Mitchell, Carly Simon—and the Journey of a Generation.*

10. "Jackson Browne: 25 Great Songs," *Telegraph,* January 19, 2016, https://www .telegraph.co.uk/music/artists/jackson-browne-25-great-songs/jackson-browne -25-great-songs21/.

11. Weller, *Girls like Us: Carole King, Joni Mitchell, Carly Simon—and the Journey of a Generation.*

12. King, *The Operator: David Geffen Builds, Buys, and Sells the New Hollywood.*

13. Yaffe, *Reckless Daughter: A Portrait of Joni Mitchell.*

14. Bill Flanagan, "Joni Mitchell Builds Shelter from the Rainstorm," *Musician Magazine,* May 1988, https://jonimitchell.com/library/view.cfm?id=200.

15. Yaffe, *Reckless Daughter: A Portrait of Joni Mitchell.*

16. Ibid.

17. King, *The Operator: David Geffen Builds, Buys, and Sells the New Hollywood*.

18. Joni Mitchell, "Album Notes: The Lost Years," https://jonimitchell.com/music/album.cfm?id=24.

19. Bego, *Joni Mitchell*.

20. Ibid.

21. Leonard Feather, "Joni Mitchell Has Her Mojo Working," *Los Angeles Times*, June 10, 1979, https://jonimitchell.com/library/view.cfm?id=595.

22. Bill Flanagan, "Joni Mitchell Has the Last Laugh," *Musician Magazine*, December 1985, https://www.jonimitchell.com/library/view.cfm?id=133.

23. Cameron Crowe, "Joni Mitchell—Never Boring," *Rolling Stone*, July 26, 1979, http://www.theuncool.com/2014/10/12/archives-joni-mitchell-never-boring/.

24. Hoskyns, *Joni: The Anthology*.

25. Ibid.

26. Cameron Crowe, "The Durable Led Zeppelin," *Rolling Stone*, March 13, 1975, https://www.rollingstone.com/music/music-news/the-durable-led-zeppelin-2-74034/.

27. Davis, *Hammer of the Gods: The Led Zeppelin Saga*.

28. Weller, *Girls like Us: Carole King, Joni Mitchell, Carly Simon—and the Journey of a Generation*.

29. Ibid.

30. "Joni Mitchell and John Guerin Romance," from *John Guerin Discography* blog, April 13, 2012, *Joni Mitchell*, https://jonimitchell.com/library/print.cfm?id=3000.

31. Whitall, *Joni on Joni: Interviews and Encounters with Joni Mitchell*.

32. Robert Hilburn, "Joni Mitchell: The Mojo Interview," *Mojo*, February 2008, https://jonimitchell.com/library/view.cfm?id=1834.

29. HEADBANGERS APOTHEOSIS

1. Davis, *Walk This Way: The Autobiography of Aerosmith*.

2. Pete Makowski, "How Aerosmith Got Their Wings: A Look Back at Their Classic First Four Albums," November 13, 2008, *Louder: Classic Rock*, https://www.loudersound.com/features/aerosmith-they-re-the-wonder-years-because-we-wonder-what-happened.

3. Tyler, *Does the Noise in My Head Bother You? A Rock 'n' Roll Memoir*.

4. Davis, *Walk This Way: The Autobiography of Aerosmith*.

5. "Aerosmith 1973," *Setlist*, https://www.setlist.fm/search?query=artist:%28Aerosmith%29+date:%5B1973-01-01+TO+1973-12-31%5D.

6. Tyler, *Does the Noise in My Head Bother You? A Rock 'n' Roll Memoir*.

7. Bill DeMain, "Aerosmith: How We Made 'Toys in the Attic,'" *Louder: Classic Rock*, November 6, 2016, https://www.loudersound.com/features/aerosmith-the-making-of-toys-in-the-attic.

8. Tyler, *Does the Noise in My Head Bother You? A Rock 'n' Roll Memoir*.

9. "Headbanging," Wikipedia, https://en.wikipedia.org/wiki/Headbanging.

10. Ibid.

11. A. S. Van Dorston, "The Birth of Metal," *Fast 'n' Bulbous*, September 25, 2015, https://fastnbulbous.com/the-birth-of-metal/.

12. Mike Saunders, "Heavy Metal: A Brief Survey of the State of Metal Music Today," April 1973, *Alice Cooper eChive,* https://www.alicecooperechive.com/articles /feature/prma/730400.
13. Rebecca Woods, "Black Sabbath: 'We Hated Being a Heavy Metal Band,'" *BBC News,* February 4, 2017, https://www.bbc.com/news/uk-england-birmingham -38768573.
14. Ibid.
15. Wall, *Black Sabbath: Symptom of the Universe.*
16. "Tony Iommi: After My Finger Accident, I Used Banjo Strings," *Ultimate Guitar,* December 19, 2017, https://www.ultimateguitar.com/news/general_music_news /tony_iommi_after_my_finger_accident_i_used_banjo_strings.html.
17. Wall, *Black Sabbath: Symptom of the Universe.*
18. Dan Epstein, "Original Members of Black Sabbath Look Back on 30-Plus Years of Demonic Riffing in 2001," *Guitar World,* December 23, 2011.
19. Ghost story from liner notes to *Reunion* (1998); "Satanists" from Wall, *Black Sabbath: Symptom of the Universe.*
20. Ibid.
21. Ibid.
22. *Black Sabbath, Volume 1: 1970–1978* (1991), DVD.
23. Osbourne and Ayres, *I Am Ozzy.*
24. Epstein, "Original Members of Black Sabbath Look Back on 30-Plus Years of Demonic Riffing in 2001."
25. Wall, *Black Sabbath: Symptom of the Universe.*
26. "Sabbath Bloody Sabbath," Wikipedia, https://en.wikipedia.org/wiki/Sabbath _Bloody_Sabbath.
27. Wall, *Black Sabbath: Symptom of the Universe.*
28. Welch, *Peter Grant: The Man Who Led Zeppelin.*
29. Alex Ashlock, "How 'Rock's Greatest Manager' Shaped Led Zeppelin's Success," November 26, 2018, WBUR, https://www.wbur.org/hereandnow/2018/11/26/led -zeppelin-peter-grant-manager.
30. Michael Hann, "Stairway to Heaven: The Story of a Song and Its Legacy," *Guardian,* October 22, 2014, https://www.theguardian.com/music/2014/oct/22/stairway -to-heaven-unreleased-mix-led.
31. Cameron Crowe's liner notes for *Led Zeppelin: The Complete Recordings,* quoted in Akkerman, *Experiencing Led Zeppelin: A Listener's Companion,* 91.
32. Wall, *When Giants Walked the Earth: A Biography of Led Zeppelin.*
33. Lewis, *The Complete Guide to the Music of Led Zeppelin.* London: Omnibus, 1955.
34. Mick Wall, "Kashmir: How Led Zeppelin Made Their Epic *Physical Graffiti* Album Track by Track," *Classic Rock,* January 30, 2019, https://www.loudersound.com /features/the-story-behind-the-song-kashmir-by-led-zeppelin.

30. IF WE MAKE IT THROUGH DECEMBER

1. Sullivan, *Encyclopedia of Great Popular Song Recordings,* vol. 3.
2. Marsh, *The Heart of Rock and Soul: The 1001 Greatest Singles Ever Made.*
3. Haggard and Carter, *My House of Memories: An Autobiography.*

4. Nick Murray, "Merle Haggard: Original Gangster, Country Prankster," *Third Bridge Creative,* April 2016, http://blog.thirdbridgecreative.com/2016/04/rememberingmerle/.

5. Emily Yahr, "Merle Haggard's Too-Good-to-Be-True Story About Johnny Cash? It Really Happened," *Washington Post,* April 8, 2016, https://www.washingtonpost.com /news/arts-and-entertainment/wp/2016/04/08/merle-haggards-too-good-to -be-true-story-about-johnny-cash-it-really-happened/?utm_term= .75fa1c497f39.

6. Jennings and Kaye, *Waylon: An Autobiography.*

7. Cantwell, *Merle Haggard: The Running Kind.*

8. Aljean Harmetz, "Reagan Entertained by Singer He Once Pardoned," *New York Times,* March 8, 1982, https://www.nytimes.com/1982/ . . . /reagan-entertained -by-singer-he-once-pardoned.html.

9. John Berlau, "The Battle over 'Okie from Muskogee,'" *Weekly Standard,* August 18, 1996, https://www.weeklystandard.com/john-berlau/the-battle-over-quotokie -from-muskogee.

10. Aaron Latham, "'There Is Tape in the Oval Office,'" *New York Magazine,* June 17, 1974.

11. Ibid.

12. Yergin, *The Prize: The Epic Quest for Oil, Money, and Power.*

13. Sandbrook, *Mad as Hell: The Crisis of the 1970s and the Rise of the Populist Right.*

14. "King Faisal Warns U.S. of Oil Cutoff," *New York Times,* August 31, 1973, https:// www.nytimes.com/1973/08/31/archives/king-faisal-warns-us-of-oil-cutoff.html.

15. "Historical Crude Oil Prices (Table)," *InflationData,* https://inflationdata.com /articles/inflation-adjusted-prices/historical-crude-oil-prices-table/.

16. Yergin, *The Prize: The Epic Quest for Oil, Money, and Power.*

17. Tim Weiner, "That Time the Middle East Exploded—and Nixon Was Drunk," *Politico,* June 15, 2015, https://www.politico.com/magazine/story/2015/06/richard -nixon-watergate-drunk-yom-kippur-war-119021_Page2.html.

18. Victor Israelian, "Nuclear Showdown as Nixon Slept," *Christian Science Monitor,* November 3, 1993, https://www.csmonitor.com/1993/1103/03191.html.

19. Eric Grundhauser, "How the 'Rose Mary Stretch' Sold Watergate to the People," *Atlas Obscura,* November 7, 2017, https://www.atlasobscura.com/articles/rose -mary-stretch-nixon-scandal.

20. Bennighof, *The Words and Music of Paul Simon.*

21. Jeff McCarty, Interview with the Author for *1973* on Changes in Film Technology.

22. Johnston, *Lesbian Nation: The Feminist Solution.*

23. "The Spook Who Sat by the Door," Wikipedia, https://en.wikipedia.org/wiki/The _Spook_Who_Sat_by_the_Door_(novel)#cite_ref-11.

24. "Lyndon LaRouche," Wikipedia, https://en.wikipedia.org/wiki/Lyndon_LaRouche# 1973:_Political_shift;_%22Operation_Mop-Up%22.

25. Killen, *1973 Nervous Breakdown: Watergate, Warhol, and the Birth of Post-Sixties America.*

26. Ibid.

27. Ibid.

28. "Remembering River Phoenix, 23 Years After His Death," *Vanity Fair,* October 31, 2016.

29. Jonas Schoen-Philbert, "25 Songs with the Tritone," *Uberchord,* February 13, 2015, https://www.uberchord.com/blog/tritone-songs/.

30. Wall, *Black Sabbath: Symptom of the Universe.*

31. Lewis, *Led Zeppelin: A Celebration.*

32. "Aleister Crowley," Wikipedia, https://en.wikipedia.org/wiki/Aleister_Crowley# CITEREFMedway2001.

33. Walker, *What You Want Is in the Limo: On the Road with Led Zeppelin, Alice Cooper, and the Who in 1973, the Year the Sixties Died and the Modern Rock Star Was Born.*

34. Sharp with Simmons and Stanley, *Nothin' to Lose: The Making of KISS, 1972–1975.*

35. Tom Vickers, Interview with the Author for *1973* on Funkdelic.

36. Jake Austen, "If Nobody Else Is Willing to Say This Out Loud, I'll Step up to the Plate. Barack Obama Is Totally Ripping Off Sammy Davis Jr.," *Vice,* May 1, 2008, https://www.vice.com/en_us/article/yvnzey/sammy-devil-jr-v15n5.

37. Killen, *1973 Nervous Breakdown: Watergate, Warhol, and the Birth of Post-Sixties America.*

38. Cameron Crowe, "David Bowie: Ground Control to Davy Jones," *Rolling Stone,* February 12, 1976, https://www.rollingstone.com/music/music-news/david-bowie -ground-control-to-davy-jones-77059/.

39. *The Mayor of Sunset Strip,* directed by George Hickenlooper (2003).

40. Peter S. Greenberg, "Clockwork Rodney's," *Newsweek,* January 7, 1974.

41. Hoskyns, *Waiting for the Sun: A Rock 'n' Roll History of Los Angeles.*

42. Ryan Richardson, https://www.star1973.com/.

43. Lori Mattix [Maddox] (as told to Michael Kaplan), "I Lost My Virginity to David Bowie," *Thrillist,* November 3, 2015, https://www.thrillist.com/entertainment /nation/i-lost-my-virginity-to-david-bowie.

44. Ibid.

45. Ibid.

46. Thea De Gallier, "'I Wouldn't Want This for Anybody's Daughter': Will #MeToo Kill off the Rock'n'Roll Groupie?," *Guardian,* March 15, 2018, https://www .theguardian.com/music/2018/mar/15/i-wouldnt-want-this-for-anybodys-daughter -will-metoo-kill-off-the-rocknroll-groupie.

47. Mattix, "I Lost My Virginity to David Bowie."

48. Davis, *Hammer of the Gods.*

49. Wall, *When Giants Walked the Earth: A Biography of Led Zeppelin.*

50. Mattix, "I Lost My Virginity to David Bowie."

51. Ibid.

52. McNeil and McCain, *Please Kill Me: The Uncensored Oral History of Punk.*

53. "The Runaways' Jackie Fuchs Claims She Was Raped by Manager Kim Fowley in 1975," *Guardian,* July 9, 2015.

54. Biskind, *Easy Riders, Raging Bulls: How the Sex–Drugs–and Rock 'n' Roll Generation Saved Hollywood.*

55. Hearn, *The Cinema of George Lucas.*

56. Baxter, *Mythmaker: The Life and Work of George Lucas.*

57. Biskind, *Easy Riders, Raging Bulls: How the Sex–Drugs–and Rock 'n' Roll Generation Saved Hollywood.*
58. Ibid.
59. "Remarks to Oprah Winfrey," *The Oprah Winfrey Show,* February 26, 2008.
60. "Northern Soul: 40 Years of the Sound of Wigan Casino," September 20, 2013, http://www.bbc.co.uk/arts/0/24164508.
61. Ibid.
62. Chris M. Junior, "Hop Aboard the Midnight Train to Georgia with Gladys Knight & The Pips," *Goldmine,* April 14, 2010.
63. Marc Myers, "Anatomy of a Song: 'Midnight Train to Georgia,'" *Wall Street Journal,* August 8, 2013, https://www.wsj.com/articles/anatomy-of-a-song-midnight-train-to-georgia-1376004450.
64. Marsh, *The Heart of Rock and Soul: The 1001 Greatest Singles Ever Made.*

31. I HOPE YOU'RE HAVING FUN

1. "Paul McCartney: I Was Robbed at Knifepoint," *Metro,* November 5, 2010, http://metro.co.uk/2010/11/05/paul-mccartney-i-was-robbed-at-knifepoint-571696/.
2. Badman, *The Beatles Diary,* vol. 2, *After the Break-Up, 1970–2001.*
3. Ibid.
4. "Picasso's Last Words (Drink to Me)," *Beatles Bible,* https://www.beatlesbible.com/people/paul-mccartney/songs/picassos-last-words-drink-to-me/.
5. Sandford, *McCartney.*
6. Brown, *Tearing Down the Wall of Sound: The Rise and Fall of Phil Spector.*
7. Goldman, *The Lives of John Lennon.*
8. Connolly, *Being John Lennon: A Restless Life.*
9. Evan Petersen, "John Lennon's "A Matter of Pee" Letter to Phil Spector Sells for Over $88,000," *Zumic,* March 30, 2014, https://zumic.com/john-lennons-matter-pee-letter-phil-spector-sells-88000.
10. Shipton, *Nilsson: The Life of a Singer-Songwriter.*
11. Sheff, *All We Are Saying: The Last Major Interview with John Lennon and Yoko Ono.*
12. Goldman, *The Lives of John Lennon.*
13. Ibid.
14. Ibid.
15. Ibid.
16. Badman, *The Beatles Diary,* vol. 2, *After the Break-Up, 1970–2001.*
17. Schaffner, *The Boys from Liverpool: John, Paul, George, Ringo.*
18. Townshend, *Who I Am.*
19. Boyd and Junor, *Wonderful Tonight: George Harrison, Eric Clapton, and Me.*
20. Wood, *Ronnie: The Autobiography.*
21. Boyd and Junor, *Wonderful Tonight: George Harrison, Eric Clapton, and Me.*
22. *News of the World,* 1983, via *Harihead,* https://harihead.livejournal.com/2049.html.
23. Boyd and Junor, *Wonderful Tonight: George Harrison, Eric Clapton, and Me.*
24. *News of the World,* 1983, via *Harihead,* https://harihead.livejournal.com/2049.html.

25. Boyd and Junor, *Wonderful Tonight: George Harrison, Eric Clapton, and Me.*
26. O'Dell, *Miss O'Dell: My Hard Days and Long Nights with the Beatles, the Stones, Bob Dylan, Eric Clapton, and the Women They Loved.*
27. Ibid.
28. Lennon, *John.*
29. Brown and Gaines, *The Love You Make: An Insider's Story of the Beatles.*
30. McGee, *Band on the Run: A History of Paul McCartney and Wings.*
31. Blaney, *Lennon and Mccartney: Together Alone.*
32. "Let Me Roll It," *Beatles Bible,* https://www.beatlesbible.com/people/paul-mccart ney/songs/let-me-roll-it/.
33. Pete Hamill, "Long Night's Journey into Day: A Conversation with John Lennon," *Rolling Stone,* June 5, 1975, http://www.beatlesinterviews.org/db1975.0605 .beatles.html.

32. BOB MARLEY

1. Jonathan Ringen, "The Cosmic Journey of Jimmy Cliff," *Rolling Stone,* July 5, 2012, https://www.rollingstone.com/music/music-news/the-cosmic-journey-of-jimmy-cliff -185437/.
2. Mark Binelli, "Chris Blackwell: The Barefoot Mogul," *Men's Journal,* March 19, 2014.
3. Ringen, "The Cosmic Journey of Jimmy Cliff."
4. *Marley,* directed by Kevin Macdonald, (2012), DVD.
5. Timothy White, "Bob Marley: 1945–1981," *Rolling Stone,* June 25, 1981, https:// www.rollingstone.com/music/music-news/bob-marley-1945-1981-231448/.
6. Lee Jaffe, "Chris Blackwell," *Humanity,* December 9, 2015, https://mag.citizens ofhumanity.com/blog/2015/12/09/chris-blackwell/.
7. Ibid.
8. Ibid.
9. Ibid.
10. Brent Hagerman, "Chris Blackwell: Savvy Svengali," *Exclaim!,* January 1, 2006, http://exclaim.ca/music/article/chris_blackwell-savvy_svengali.
11. "The Story of Wayne Perkins & Concrete Jungle," January 23, 2013, http:// marcoonthebass.blogspot.com/2013/01/the-story-of-wayne-perkins-concrete .html.
12. Maureen Sheridan, *Bob Marley: the Stories Behind Every Song.*
13. "The Story of Wayne Perkins & Concrete Jungle."
14. Salewicz, *Bob Marley: The Untold Story.*
15. Steffens, *So Much Things to Say: The Oral History of Bob Marley.*
16. Ibid.
17. Moskowitz, *The Words and Music of Bob Marley.*
18. Steffens, *So Much Things to Say: The Oral History of Bob Marley.*
19. Ibid.
20. Roger Steffens, "Burnin': Added to the National Registry," 2006, http://www.loc .gov/static/programs/national-recording-preservation-board/documents/Burnin .pdf.

21. Steffens, *So Much Things to Say: The Oral History of Bob Marley.*

22. Sewall-Ruskin, *High on Rebellion: Inside the Underground at Max's Kansas City.*

23. Ibid.

24. Steffens, *So Much Things to Say: The Oral History of Bob Marley.*

25. "At Last, Peter Tosh Gets a Museum of his Own," *Guardian,* November 7, 2016, https://www.theguardian.com/music/musicblog/2016/nov/07/peter-tosh-museum -kingston-jamaica-reggae-legend.

26. Eric Olsen, "Peter Tosh Interview, Los Angeles, CA (August, 1983)," *Midnight Raver,* May 31, 2012, https://marleyarkives.wordpress.com/2012/05/31/peter-tosh -interview-berkeley-ca-august-1983-by-eric-olsen/.

27. *Marley,* directed by Kevin Macdonald, (2012), DVD.

28. Rob Kenner, "Vincent Ford Dies at 68; Inspired Classic Bob Marley Songs," *New York Times,* January 3, 2009, https://www.nytimes.com/2009/01/04/arts/music /04ford.html.

29. Bordowitz, *Every Little Thing Gonna Be Alright: The Bob Marley Reader.*

30. David Fricke, "Chris Blackwell Remembers," *Rolling Stone,* March 10, 2005, https://www.rollingstone.com/music/music-news/chris-blackwell-remembers -232535/.

31. Zack O'Malley Greenburg and Natalie Robehmed, "The Highest-Paid Dead Celebrities Of 2018," *Forbes,* October 31, 2018, https://www.forbes.com/sites /zackomalleygreenburg/2018/10/31/the-highest-paid-dead-celebrities-of-2018 /#23781d5e720c.

32. Ringen, "The Cosmic Journey of Jimmy Cliff."

33. John Doran, "Many Rivers Crossed: Jimmy Cliff Interviewed," *The Quietus,* May 15, 2013, https://thequietus.com/articles/12237-jimmy-cliff-interview.

33. GOODBYE YELLOW BRICK ROAD

1. Doyle, *Captain Fantastic: Elton John's Stellar Trip Through the '70s.*

2. Ibid.

3. Ibid.

4. Joe Bosso, "Davey Johnstone—My Career with Elton John," *Music Radar,* April 4, 2011, https://www.musicradar.com/news/guitars/exclusive-interview-davey-johnsto ne-my-career-with-elton-john-413589.

5. Ibid.

6. Doyle, *Captain Fantastic: Elton John's Stellar Trip Through the '70s.*

7. Bronson, *The Billboard Book of Number One Hits.*

8. "Goodbye Yellow Brick Road," Wikipedia, https://en.wikipedia.org/wiki/Goodbye _Yellow_Brick_Road.

9. Bosso, "Davey Johnstone—My Career with Elton John."

10. Doyle, *Captain Fantastic: Elton John's Stellar Trip Through the '70s.*

11. Ibid.

12. Jason Newman, "Elton John Talks Miguel and Wale's 'Bennie and the Jets' Cover," *Rolling Stone,* March 21, 2014, https://www.rollingstone.com/ . . . /elton-john -talks-miguel-and-wales-bennie-and-the-jets-cover.

13. Buckley, *Elton: The Biography.*

14. "Bennie and the Jets," Wikipedia, https://en.wikipedia.org/wiki/Bennie_and_the _Jets#Song_composition.

15. Karen Bliss, "The Legacy of Rosalie Trombley, Radio Pioneer Immortalized in Bob Seger's 'Rosalie' and Breaker of 'Bennie and the Jets,'" *Billboard,* January 21, 2016, https://www.billboard.com/articles/news/6851506/legacy-rosalie-trombley -radio-pioneer-bob-seger-guess-who-elton-john.

16. Andy Greene, "Elton John and Bernie Taupin Look Back at 'Goodbye Yellow Brick Road,'" *Rolling Stone,* March 14, 2014, https://www.rollingstone.com/music /music-news/elton-john-and-bernie-taupin-look-back-at-goodbye-yellow-brick -road-205112/.

17. Bronson, *The Billboard Book of Number One Hits.*

18. Andy Greene, "Flashback: Elton John Hits Number One with 'Bennie and the Jets,'" *Rolling Stone,* April 11, 2019, https://www.rollingstone.com/music/music -features/elton-john-bennie-jets-number-one-821152/.

19. "Goodbye Yellow Brick Road," Wikipedia.

20. Greene, "Elton John and Bernie Taupin Look Back At 'Goodbye Yellow Brick Road.'"

21. Doyle, *Captain Fantastic: Elton John's Stellar Trip Through the '70s.*

22. Ibid.

23. Robert Christgau, "Elton John: The Little Hooker Who Could," *Village Voice,* November 24, 1975, https://www.villagevoice.com/2019/03/01/elton-john-a-bitch-is -born/.

24. Richard Buskin, "Elton John: Goodbye Yellow Brick Road," *Sound on Sound,* October 2011, https://www.soundonsound.com/people/elton-john-goodbye-yellow -brick-road.

EPILOGUE: KEEP ON TRUCKIN'

1. Andrew H. Malcolm, "Fuel Crisis Dims Holiday Lights," *New York Times,* November 25, 1973, https://www.nytimes.com/1973/11/25/archives/fuel-crisis-dims -holiday-lights-not-an-enthusiast.html.

2. "List of Best-Selling Music Artists: 250 Million Units," Wikipedia, https://en .wikipedia.org/wiki/List_of_best-selling_music_artists.

3. "List of *Billboard* 200 Number-One Albums of 2018," Wikipedia, https://en .wikipedia.org/wiki/List_of_Billboard_200_number-one_albums_of_2018.

4. "Rap's New Generation Took Over, Rock Ruled the Road and Radio Still Mattered," *Rolling Stone,* January 2, 2019, https://www.rollingstone.com/music/music -features/hip-hop-rock-pop-trends-new-generation-771767/.

5. Hugh McIntyre, "Hip-Hop/R&B Is the Dominant Genre in the US for the First Time," *Forbes,* July 17, 2017, https://www.forbes.com/sites/hughmcintyre/2017/07 /17/hip-hoprb-has-now-become-the-dominant-genre-in-the-u-s-for-the-first-time /#cd7f2c553834.

6. "U.S. Sales Database," RIAA, https://www.riaa.com/u-s-sales-database/.

7. Nick Messitte, "Drum Replacement: The Dirty Little Secret That Changed Rock," *Forbes,* April 30, 2014, https://www.forbes.com/sites/nickmessitte/2014/04/30/drum -replacement-the-dirty-little-secret-that-changed-rock/#43ba18bd30a3.

8. Greg Milner, "They Really Don't Make Music like They Used To," *New York Times,* February 7, 2019, https://www.nytimes.com/ . . . /what-these-grammy-songs-tell -us-about-the-loudness-wars.

9. Oliver Burkeman, "Acoustics, They Are A-Changin', Complains Unhappy Dylan," *Guardian,* August 24, 2006, https://www.theguardian.com/uk/2006/aug/24/top stories3.arts.

10. Amy X. Wang, "Inside Garageband, the Little App Ruling the Sound of Modern Music," *Rolling Stone,* March 16, 2019, https://www.rollingstone.com/music/music . . . /apple-garageband-modern-music-784257/.

11. "CMT All-Time Top 40: Eagles," CMT, July 14, 2014, http://www.cmt.com/news /1728330/cmt-all-time-top-40-eagles/.

12. "Vince Gill Talks Eagles' Impact on Country, Joe Walsh Project," *Rolling Stone,* February 16, 2016, https://www.rollingstone.com/music/music-country/vince-gill -talks-eagles-impact-on-country-joe-walsh-project-223554/.

13. Neil Shah, "Hip-Hop Is Huge, but on the Concert Circuit, Rock Is King," *Wall Street Journal,* October 3, 2018, https://www.wsj.com/articles/rap-is-huge-but-on -the-concert-circuit-rock-is-king-1538575751.

14. "Resolution for a New Era," *New York Times,* January 1, 1974, https://www .nytimes.com/1974/01/01/archives/resolution-for-a-new-era.html.

15. Lane Windham, "VW Workers Not First Southern Auto Workers to Face Choice on Union," *Facing South,* February 12, 2014, https://www.facingsouth.org/2014 /02/vw-workers-not-first-southern-auto-workers-to-face.html.

16. Alex Morris, "Why Can't Allyson Get Ahead?," *Rolling Stone,* November 13, 2018, https://www.rollingstone.com/culture/culture-features/american-middle-class -disappearing-754735/.

17. Diana Hembree, "CEO Pay Skyrockets to 361 Times That of the Average Worker," *Forbes,* May 22, 2018, https://www.forbes.com/sites/dianahembree/2018/05/22 /ceo-pay-skyrockets-to-361-times-that-of-the-average-worker/#2374b5a8776d.

18. Jena McGregor, "What's the Right Ratio for CEO-to-Worker Pay?" *Washington Post,* September 19, 2013, https://www.washingtonpost.com/ . . . /2013/ . . . /whats -the-right-ratio-for-ceo-to-worker-pay.

19. "List of Tallest Buildings in the United States," Wikipedia, https://en.wikipedia .org/wiki/List_of_tallest_buildings_in_the_United_States.

20. Weiss, *Encyclopedia of KISS: Music, Personnel, Events and Related Subjects.*

21. Lead and Sharp, *KISS: Behind the Mask.*

22. Ibid.

23. Sharp with Simmons and Stanley, *Nothin' to Lose: The Making of KISS, 1972–1975.*

24. Criss, *Makeup to Breakup: My Life in and out of Kiss.*

25. Sharp with Simmons and Stanley, *Nothin' to Lose: The Making of KISS, 1972–1975.*

26. Ibid.

27. Ibid.

28. Philip Bump, "In 1927, Donald Trump's Father Was Arrested After a Klan Riot in Queens," *Washington Post,* February 29, 2016, https://www.washingtonpost.com / . . . /in-1927-donald-trumps-father-was-arrested-after-a-klan-riot-in-Queens.

29. Kranish and Fisher, *Trump Revealed: The Definitive Biography of the 45th President.*

30. Sandbrook, *Mad as Hell: The Crisis of the 1970s and the Rise of the Populist Right.*

31. Ibid.

32. Edward Alwood, "How Do You Turn Walter Cronkite into a Friend of Gay Rights? Zap Him," *Washington Post,* July 26, 2009, http://www.edwardalwood.com/doc /Cronkite.pdf.

33. Dan Avery, "The Time Gay Activists Interrupted Walter Cronkite on the *CBS Evening News,*" *Queerty,* June 5, 2012, https://www.queerty.com/the-time-gay-activists -interrupted-walter-cronkite-on-the-cbs-evening-news-20120605.

34. Mark Segal, "Walter Cronkite Was My Friend and Mentor," *Philly Ad Club,* July 19, 2009, https://phillyadclub.com/mark-segal-walter-cronkite-was-my-friend-and -mentor/.

35. Segal, *And Then I Danced: Traveling the Road to LGBT Equality.*

36. "David Bowie Wrote 'Rebel Rebel' 'to Piss Mick Jagger Off,'" *Uncut,* February 26, 2014, https://www.uncut.co.uk/news/david-bowie-wrote-rebel-rebel-to-piss-mick -jagger-off-11918.

37. Ibid.

38. Sharon DeLano, "The Torch Singer," *New Yorker,* March 3, 2002, https://www .newyorker.com/magazine/2002/03/11/the-torch-singer.

39. McNeil and McCain, *Please Kill Me: The Uncensored Oral History of Punk.*

40. Smith, *Just Kids.*

41. Ibid.

42. DeLano, "The Torch Singer."

43. McNeil and McCain, *Please Kill Me: The Uncensored Oral History of Punk.*

44. Smith, *Just Kids.*

45. McNeil and McCain, *Please Kill Me: The Uncensored Oral History of Punk.*

Bibliography

✳

BOOKS

Abramowitz, Alan. *The Great Alignment: Race, Party Transformation, and the Rise of Donald Trump*. New Haven, CT: Yale University Press, 2018.

Aerosmith and Stephen Davis. *Walk This Way: The Autobiography of Aerosmith*. New York: Dey Street Books, 2012.

Akkerman, Gregg. *Experiencing Led Zeppelin: A Listener's Companion*. London: Roman & Littlefield, 2014.

Allman, Gregg, and Alan Light. *My Cross to Bear*. New York: William Morrow, 2012.

Ambrose, Joe. *Gimme Danger: The Story of Iggy Pop*. London: Omnibus Press, 2008.

Andersen, Christopher. *Jagger Unauthorized*. New York: Delacorte Press, 1993.

———. *Michael Jackson Unauthorized*. New York: Simon & Schuster, 1994.

Badman, Keith. *The Beatles Diary*, vol. 2, *After the Break-Up, 1970–2001*. London: Omnibus Press, 2001.

———. *The Beatles: Off the Record*. London: Omnibus Press, 2009.

Ballinger, Lee. *Lynyrd Skynyrd: An Oral History*. Los Angeles, CA: Xt377 Publishing, 2002.

Bangs, Lester. *Psychotic Reactions and Carburetor Dung: The Work of a Legendary Critic*. New York: Anchor, 1988.

Baxter, John. *Mythmaker: The Life and Work of George Lucas*. New York: William Morrow, 1999.

Bebergal, Peter. *Season of the Witch: How the Occult Saved Rock and Roll*. New York: Tarcher Perigee, 2015.

Bego, Mark. *Aretha Franklin: The Queen of Soul*. New York: Robert Hale, 1990.

———. *Billy Joel: The Biography*. New York: Thunder's Mouth Press, 2007.

———. *Cher: If You Believe*. New York: Cooper Square Press, 2001.

———. *Joni Mitchell*. New York: Taylor Trade Publishing, 2005.

Bennighof, James. *The Words and Music of Paul Simon*. New York: Praeger, 2007.

Biskind, Peter. *Easy Riders, Raging Bulls*. New York: Simon & Schuster, 1998.

Blake, Mark. *Comfortably Numb: The Inside Story of Pink Floyd*. New York: Thunder's Mouth Press, 2007.

Blaney, John. *Lennon and McCartney: Together Alone*. London: Jawbone, 2007.

Blush, Steven. *New York Rock: From the Rise of the Velvet Underground to the Fall of CBGB*. New York: St. Martin's Griffin, 2016.

Bockris, Victor. *Keith Richards: The Biography*. New York: Da Capo, 2003.

Bogle, Donald. *Toms, Coons, Mulattoes, Mammies, and Bucks: An Interpretive History of Blacks in American Films*. New York: Viking Press, 1973.

Bordowitz, Hank. *Billy Joel: The Life and Times of an Angry Young Man*. Milwaukee, WI: Hal Leonard Corporation, 2011.

———. *Every Little Thing Gonna Be Alright: The Bob Marley Reader*. Boston: Da Capo, 2004.

Boulware, Jack. *Sex, American Style: An Illustrated Romp Through the Golden Age of Heterosexuality*. Port Townsend, WA: Feral House, 1997.

Bowie, Angela, and Patrick Carr. *Backstage Passes: Life on the Wild Side with David Bowie*. New York: Cooper Square Press, 2000.

Boyd, Pattie, and Pen Junor. *Wonderful Tonight: George Harrison, Eric Clapton and Me*. London: Headline Review, 2007.

Brando, Marlon. *Songs My Mother Taught Me*. New York: Random House, 1994.

Bream, Jon. *Whole Lotta Led Zeppelin: The Illustrated History of the Heaviest Band of All Time*. London: Voyageur Press, 2008.

Breithaupt, Don, and Jeff Breithaupt. *Precious and Few: Pop Music of the Early '70s*. New York: St. Martin's Griffin, 1996.

Brewster, Bill, and Frank Broughton. *Last Night a DJ Saved My Life*. New York: Grove Press, 2014.

Bright, Spencer. *Peter Gabriel: An Authorized Biography*. London: Sidgwick & Jackson, 1999.

Bronson, Fred. *The Billboard Book of Number 1 Hits*. New York: Billboard Books, 1992.

Brown, James, with Bruce Tucker. *James Brown: The Godfather of Soul*. London. Fontana/Collins, 1988.

Brown, Mick. *Tearing Down the Wall of Sound: The Rise and Fall of Phil Spector*. New York: Vintage, 2007.

Brown, Peter, and Stephen Gaines. *The Love You Make: An Insider's Story of the Beatles*. New York: McGraw Hill, 1983.

Browne, David. *Fire and Rain: The Beatles, Simon and Garfunkel, James Taylor, CSNY, and the Lost Story of 1970*. Philadelphia: Da Capo, 2011.

———. *So Many Roads: The Life and Times of the Grateful Dead*. Boston: Da Capo, 2016.

Bruns, Roger. *Jesse Jackson: A Biography*. Westport, CT: Greenwood, 2005.

Buckley, David. *Elton: The Biography*. London: Andre Deutsch, 2007.

———. *Strange Fascination: David Bowie: The Definitive Story*. London: Virgin Books, 2005.

Buell, Bebe, and Victor Bockris. *Rebel Heart: An American Rock 'n' Roll Journey*. New York: St. Martin's Press, 2001.

Bullock, Darryl W. *David Bowie Made Me Gay: 100 Years of LGBT Music*. New York: Harry N. Abrams, 2019.

Cantwell, David. *Merle Haggard: The Running Kind*. Austin: University of Texas Press, 2013.

Carlin, Peter Ames. *Bruce*. New York: Atria Books, 2012.

———. *Paul McCartney: A Life*. New York: Touchstone, 2009.

Chang, Jeff. *Can't Stop Won't Stop: A History of the Hip-Hop Generation*. New York: Picador, 2005.

Christgau, Robert. *Is It Still Good to Ya? Fifty Years of Rock Criticism, 1967–2017*. Durham, NC: Duke University Press, 2018.

Clapton, Eric. *Clapton: the Autobiography*. New York: Three Rivers Press, 2008.

Clemons, Clarence and Don Reo. *Big Man: Real Life and Tall Tales*. New York: Grand Central Publishing, 2009.

Clinton, George, and Ben Greenman. *Brothas Be, Yo like George, Ain't That Funkin' Kinda Hard on You? A Memoir*. New York: Atria Books, 2017.

Cohn, Nik, *Awopbopaloobop Alopbamboom: The Golden Age of Rock*. St. Albans: Paladin Press, 1970.

Coleman, Ray. *Lennon*. New York: McGraw-Hill, 1987.

Collins, Phil. *Not Dead Yet: The Memoir*. London: Archetype, 2016.

Connolly, Ray. *Being John Lennon: A Restless Life*. New York: Pegasus Books, 2018.

Corbett, John. *Extended Play: Sounding Off from John Cage to Dr. Funkenstein*. Durham, NC: Duke University Press, 1994.

Criss, Peter, and Larry Sloman. *Makeup to Breakup: My Life in and out of Kiss*. New York: Scribner, 2012.

Croce, Ingrid, and Jimmy Rock. *I Got a Name: The Jim Croce Story*. Boston: Da Capo, 2012.

Crowe, Cameron (contributor). *The Day the Music Died: A Rock 'n Roll Tribute*. New York: Plexus Publishing, 1989.

Dallas, Karl. *Pink Floyd: Bricks in the Wall*. New York: Shapolsky Publishers, 1987.

Dannen, Fredric. *Hit Men: Power Brokers and Fast Money Inside the Music Business*. New York: Vintage, 1991.

Davis, Clive, and Anthony DeCurtis. *The Soundtrack of My Life*. New York: Simon & Schuster, 2013.

Davis, Sammy, Jr., with Jane Boyar and Burt Boyar. *Sammy: An Autobiography*. New York: Farrar, Straus & Giroux, 2000.

Davis, Stephen. *Hammer of the Gods: The Led Zeppelin Saga*. New York: It Books, 2008.

———. *Old Gods Almost Dead: The 40-Year Odyssey of the Rolling Stones*. New York: Crown Archetype, 2001.

DeCurtis, Anthony. *Lou Reed: A Life*. New York: Little, Brown, 2017.

Denisoff, R. Serge. *Waylon: A Biography*. Knoxville: University of Tennessee Press, 1983.

DeRogatis, Jim. *Let It Blurt: The Life and Times of Lester Bangs, America's Greatest Rock Critic*. New York: Broadway Books, 2000.

Des Barres, Pamela. *I'm with the Band: Confessions of a Groupie*. Chicago: Chicago Review Press, 2005.

———. *Let's Spend the Night Together: Backstage Secrets of Rock Muses and Supergroupies*. Chicago: Chicago Review Press, 2008.

Doggett, Peter. *Are You Ready for the Country: Elvis, Dylan, Parsons and the Roots of Country Rock*. New York: Penguin Group, 2001.

———. *CSNY: Crosby, Stills, Nash and Young*. New York: Atria Books, 2019.

————. *Electric Shock: From the Gramophone to the iPhone—125 Years of Pop Music.* London: Random House UK, 2017.

————. *There's a Riot Going On: Revolutionaries, Rock Stars, and the Rise and Fall of the '60s.* New York: Grove, 2009.

————. *You Never Give Me Your Money.* New York: HarperCollins, 2009.

Doyle, Tom. *Captain Fantastic: Elton John's Stellar Trip Through the '70s.* New York: Ballantine Books, 2017.

Durchholz, Daniel, and Gary Graff. *Neil Young: Long You Run: The Illustrated History.* Minneapolis, MN: Voyageur Press, 2010.

Eaton, Bruce. *Big Star's Radio City.* New York: Continuum, 2009.

Echols, Alice. *Hot Stuff: Disco and the Remaking of American Culture.* New York: W. W. Norton, 2010.

Editors of *Guitar World. The Complete History of Guitar World: 30 Years of Music, Magic and Six-string Mayhem.* Milwaukee, WI: Backbeat Books, 2010.

Egan, Sean. *Bowie on Bowie: Interviews and Encounters with David Bowie.* Chicago: Chicago Review Press, 2015.

————. *Who on the Who: Interviews and Encounters.* Chicago: Chicago Review Press, 2017.

Einarson, John. *Desperados: The Roots of Country Rock.* New York: Cooper Square Press, 2001.

Evans, Mike. *Neil Young: The Definitive History.* Toronto, ON: Sterling, 2012.

Faithfull, Marianne. *Faithfull: An Autobiography.* New York: Little, Brown, 1994.

Faludi, Susan. *Backlash: The Undeclared War Against American Women.* New York: Broadway Books, 2006.

Farrell, John. *Richard Nixon: The Life.* New York: Vintage, 2018.

Fetherolf, Bob. *The Guitar Story: From Ancient to Modern Times.* Pennsauken, NJ: BookBaby, 2014.

Fieseler, Robert. *Tinderbox: The Untold Story of the Up Stairs Lounge Fire and the Rise of Gay Liberation.* New York: Liveright, 2018.

Flanagan, Bill. *Written in My Soul: Conversations with Rock's Great Songwriters.* New York: Contemporary Books, 1987.

Fleischman, Mark. *Inside Studio 54.* Los Angeles: Rare Bird Books, 2017.

Fletcher, Tony. *Moon: The Life and Death of a Rock Legend.* New York: It Books, 2014.

Fong-Torres, Ben. *Hickory Wind: The Life and Times of Gram Parsons.* New York: St. Martin's Griffin, 1998.

Foxe-Tyler, Cyrinda, and Dan Fields. *Dream On.* New York: Newstar, 1997.

Frum, David. *How We Got Here: The 70's: The Decade That Brought You Modern Life for Better or Worse.* New York: Basic Books, 2000.

Gambaccini, Paul, ed. *Paul McCartney: In His Own Words.* New York: Music Sales Corp., 1976.

Gaye, Janice, and David Ritz. *After the Dance: My Life with Marvin Gaye.* New York: Amistad, 2017.

Gendron, Bernard. *Between Montmartre and the Mudd Club: Popular Music and the Avant-Garde.* Chicago: University of Chicago Press, 2002.

George, Nelson. *Buppies, B-boys, Baps & Bohos: Notes on Post-Soul Black Culture*. New York: HarperCollins, 1993.

———. *The Death of Rhythm and Blues*. New York: Penguin, 2003.

———. *Where Did Our Love Go? The Rise and Fall of the Motown Sound*. Champaign: University of Illinois Press, 2007.

George, Nelson, and Alan Leeds. *The James Brown Reader: Fifty Years of Writing About the Godfather of Soul*. New York: Plume, 2008.

Gill, John. *Queer Noises: Male and Female Homosexuality in Twentieth-Century Music*. Minneapolis: University of Minnesota Press, 1995.

Gimarc, George. *Punk Diary: The Ultimate Trainspotter's Guide to Underground Rock, 1970–1982*. San Francisco: Backbeat, 2005.

Gitlin, Todd. *The Sixties: Years of Hope, Days of Rage*. New York: Bantam, 1987.

Gleason, Ralph J. *The Rolling Stone Interviews*. New York: St. Martin's Press, 1981.

Glynn, Stephen. *Quadrophenia*. New York: Wallflower Press, 2014.

Goldman, Albert. *The Lives of John Lennon*. London: Bantam, 1988.

Goodman, Fred. *The Mansion on the Hill: Dylan, Young, Geffen, Springsteen, and the Head-On Collision of Rock and Commerce*. New York: Vintage, 1998.

Gordy, Berry. *To Be Loved: The Music, the Magic, and the Memories of Motown: An Autobiography*. New York: Grand Central Publishing, 1994.

Grant, Colin. *Natural Mystics: Marley, Tosh, and Wailer*. New York: W. W. Norton, 2011.

Greco, Nicholas P. *David Bowie in Darkness: A Study of "1. Outside" and the Late Career*. Jefferson, NC: McFarland, 2015.

Greenfield, Robert. *Dark Star: An Oral Biography of Jerry Garcia*. New York: HarperCollins, 2012.

Griffin, Roger. *David Bowie: The Golden Years*. London: Omnibus Press, 2016.

Guralnick, Peter. *Careless Love: The Unmaking of Elvis Presley*. New York: Little, Brown, 1999.

Haggard, Merle, and Tom Carter. *My House of Memories: An Autobiography*. New York: It Books, 2010.

Harrington, Joe. *Sonic Cool: The Life & Death of Rock 'n' Roll*. New York: Hal Leonard, 2002.

Harris, John. *The Dark Side of the Moon: The Making of the Pink Floyd Masterpiece*. Boston: Da Capo, 2005.

Hearn, Marcus. *The Cinema of George Lucas*. New York: Harry N. Abrams, 2005.

Heesch, Florian, and Niall Scott. *Heavy Metal, Gender and Sexuality: Interdisciplinary Approaches*. New York: Routledge, 2016.

Hell, Richard. *I Dreamed I Was a Very Clean Tramp: An Autobiography*. New York: HarperCollins, 2013.

Heller, Jason. *Strange Stars: David Bowie, Pop Music, and the Decade Sci-Fi Exploded*. Brooklyn, NY: Melville House, 2018.

Hermes, Will. *Love Goes to Buildings on Fire: Five Years in New York That Changed Music Forever*. New York: Farrar, Straus & Giroux, 2012.

Hilburn, Robert. *John Cash: The Life*. New York: Little, Brown, 2013.

Hirshey, Gerri. *We Gotta Get out of This Place: The True, Tough Story of Women in Rock*. New York: Grove Press, 2002.

Hofler, Robert. *Sexplosion: From Andy Warhol to "A Clockwork Orange": How a Generation of Pop Rebels Broke All the Taboos*. New York: It Books, 2014.

Hoskyns, Barney. *Joni: The Anthology*. New York: Picador, 2017.

———. *Lowside of the Road: A Life of Tom Waits*. New York: Three Rivers Press, 2009.

———. *Trampled Under Foot: The Power and Excess of Led Zeppelin*. London: Faber & Faber, 2012.

———. *Waiting for the Sun: A Rock 'n' Roll History of Los Angeles*. Milwaukee, WI: Backbeat, 2009.

Hyden, Steven. *Twilight of the Gods: A Journey to the End of Classic Rock*. New York: Dey Street Books, 2018.

Ingham, Chris. *The Rough Guide to the Beatles*. London: Rough Guide Limited, 2009.

Isaacs, Arnold R. *Vietnam Shadows: The War, Its Ghosts, and Its Legacy*. Baltimore, MD: Johns Hopkins University Press, 2000.

Isaacson, Walter. *Steve Jobs*. New York: Simon & Schuster, 2011.

Jackson, John. *A House on Fire: The Rise and Fall of Philadelphia Soul*. New York: Oxford University Press, 2004.

Jackson, Laura. *Paul Simon: The Definitive Biography*. New York: Kensington Publishing, 2002.

Jackson, Michael. *Moon Walk*. New York: Crown Archetype, 2009.

The Jacksons and Fred Bronson. *The Jacksons: Legacy*. New York: Black Dog & Leventhal, 2017.

Jarnow, Jesse. *Heads: A Biography of Psychedelic America*. Boston: Da Capo, 2016.

Jennings, Waylon, and Lenny Kaye. *Waylon: An Autobiography*. New York: Hachette, 1996.

Johnston, Jill. *Lesbian Nation: The Feminist Solution*. New York: Simon & Schuster, 1974.

Jones, Dylan. *David Bowie: The Oral History*. New York: Three Rivers Press, 2018.

Jones, Kenny. *Let the Good Times Roll: My Life in Small Faces, Faces, and the Who*. New York: Thomas Dunne Books, 2018.

Jones, Steve. *Lonely Boy: Tales from a Sex Pistol*. Boston: Da Capo, 2017.

Kaliss, Jeff. *I Want to Take You Higher: The Life and Times of Sly & the Family Stone*. New York: Backbeat, 2009.

Killen, Andreas. *1973 Nervous Breakdown: Watergate, Warhol, and the Birth of Post-Sixties America*. New York: Bloomsbury USA, 2006.

King, Thomas R. *The Operator: David Geffen Builds, Buys, and Sells the New Hollywood*. New York: Broadway Books, 2001.

Kingsbury, Paul, ed. *The Encyclopedia of Country Music: The Ultimate Guide to the Music*. New York: Oxford University Press, 2012.

Kooper, Al. *Backstage Passes & Backstabbing Bastards: Memoirs of a Rock 'n' Roll Survivor*. New York: Backbeat, 2008.

Kramer, Wayne. *The Hard Stuff: Dope, Crime, the MC5, and My Life of Impossibilities*. Boston: Da Capo, 2018.

Kranish, Michael, and Marc Fisher. *Trump Revealed: The Definitive Biography of the 45th President.* New York: Scribner, 2016.

Kubernik, Harvey. *Canyon of Dreams: The Magic and the Music of Laurel Canyon.* New York: Sterling, 2009.

Lasch-Quinn, E. *Race Experts: How Racial Etiquette, Sensitivity Training, and New Age Therapy Hijacked the Civil Rights Revolution.* New York: W. W. Norton, 2001.

Lawrence, Tim. *Love Saves the Day: A History of American Dance Music Culture, 1970–1979.* Durham, NC: Duke University Press Books, 2004.

Leaf, David, and Ken Sharp. *KISS: Behind the Mask.* New York: Grand Central Publishing, 2008.

Lee, Martin A., and Bruce Shlain. *Acid Dreams: The Complete Social History of LSD: The CIA, the Sixties, and Beyond.* New York: Grove Press, 1992.

Leigh, Wendy. *Bowie: The Biography.* New York: Gallery Books, 2014.

Leng, Simon. *The Music of George Harrison: While My Guitar Gently Weeps.* London: Firefly, 2003.

Lennon, Cynthia. *John.* New York: Three Rivers Press, 2005.

Levy, Joe. *Rolling Stone's 500 Greatest Albums of All Time.* New York: Wenner, 2005.

Lewis, Dave. *The Complete Guide to the Music of Led Zeppelin.* London: Omnibus, 1995.

———. *Led Zeppelin: A Celebration.* London: Omnibus, 1991.

Luerssen, John. *Bruce Springsteen FAQ: All That's Left to Know About the Boss.* New York: Backbeat, 2012.

Maher, Paul. *Tom Waits on Tom Waits: Interviews and Encounters.* Chicago. Chicago Review Press, 2011.

Malone, Bill. *Classic Country Music: A Smithsonian Collection.* Washington, DC: Smithsonian, 1990.

Manso, Peter. *Brando: The Biography.* New York: Hyperion, 1994.

Marcus, Greil. *Mystery Train: Images of America in Rock 'n' Roll Music.* New York: Plume, 2015.

Marom, Malka. *Joni Mitchell: In Her Own Words.* Toronto, ON: ECW Press, 2014.

Marsh, Dave. *The Heart of Rock and Soul: The 1001 Greatest Singles Ever Made.* New York: Da Capo, 1989.

Marsh, Dave, with John Swenson. *The Rolling Stone Record Guide.* New York: Random House, 1979.

Masouri, John. *Steppin' Razor: The Life of Peter Tosh.* London: Omnibus Press, 2013.

Matheu, Robert, and Brian J. Bowe. *CREEM: America's Only Rock 'n' Roll Magazine.* New York: Collins Living, 2007.

McCorvey, Norma, and Andy Meisler. *I Am Roe.* New York: HarperCollins, 1994.

McCrohan, Donna. *Archie and Edith, Mike and Gloria: The Tumultuous History of "All in the Family."* New York: Workman, 1988.

McDonnell, Evelyn. *Queens of Noise: The Real Story of the Runaways.* Boston: Da Capo, 2013.

McDonough, Jimmy. *Shakey: Neil Young's Biography.* New York: Anchor Books, 2003.

McGee, Garry. *Band on the Run: A History of Paul McCartney and Wings.* New York: Taylor Trade Publishing, 2003.

McNally, Dennis. *A Long Strange Trip: The Inside History of the Grateful Dead*. New York: Broadway, 2002.

McNeil, Legs, and Gillian McCain. *Please Kill Me: The Uncensored Oral History of Punk*. New York: Grove Press, 2006.

Meyer, David N. *Twenty Thousand Roads: The Ballad of Gram Parsons and His Cosmic American Music*. New York: Villard, 2008.

Miller, Steve. *Detroit Rock City: The Uncensored History of Rock 'n' Roll in America's Loudest City*. Boston: Da Capo, 2013.

Monk, Katherine. *Joni: The Creative Odyssey of Joni Mitchell*. Vancouver, BC: Greystone Books, 2012.

Moore, Michael. *Here Comes Trouble: Stories from My Life*. New York: Grand Central Publishing, 2011.

Moskowitz, David. *The Words and Music of Bob Marley*. Westport, CT: Greenwood, 2007.

Nash, Alanna. *Elvis and the Memphis Mafia*. London: Aurum Press, 2012.

Needs, Kris. *Suicide: Dream Baby Dream, a New York City Story*. London: Omnibus Press, 2015.

Nelson, Willie. *The Tao of Willie: A Guide to the Happiness in Your Heart*. New York: Gotham, 2006.

Nelson, Willie, and David Ritz. *It's a Long Story: My Life*. Boston: Back Bay Books, 2016.

Nelson, Willie, and Bud Shrake. *Willie: An Autobiography*. New York: Cooper Square Press, 1988.

Norman, Philip. *John Lennon: The Life*. New York: Random House, 2009.

———. *Mick Jagger*. New York: Ecco/HarperCollins, 2012.

———. *Symphony for the Devil*. London: Penguin, 1984.

O'Dell, Chris, and Katherine Ketcham. *Miss O'Dell: My Hard Days and Long Nights with The Beatles, The Stones, Bob Dylan, Eric Clapton, and the Women They Loved*. New York: Touchstone, 2009.

O'Rourke, Stephen. *The Steely Dan File*. 2008.

Osbourne, Ozzy, and Chris Ayres. *I Am Ozzy*. New York: Grand Central Publishing, 2010.

Pang, May, and Henry Edwards. *Loving John*. London: Corgi, 1983.

Paul, Alan. *One Way Out: The Inside History of the Allman Brothers Band*. New York: St. Martin's Press, 2014.

Paytress, Mark. *The Rolling Stones—Off the Record*. London: Omnibus Press, 2005.

Pegg, Nicholas. *The Complete David Bowie*. London: Titan Books, 2011.

Perlstein, Rick. *Nixonland: The Rise of a President and the Fracturing of America*. New York: Scribner, 2008.

Perry, Joe, and David Ritz. *Rocks: My Life in and out of Aerosmith*. New York: Simon & Schuster, 2014.

Posner, Gerald. *Motown: Music, Money, Sex, and Power*. New York: Random House, 2002.

Povey, Glenn. *Echoes: The Complete History of Pink Floyd*. Chicago: Chicago Review Press, 2007.

Priore, Domenic. *Riot on Sunset Strip: Rock 'n' Roll's Last Stand in Hollywood*. London: Jawbone Press, 2007.

Quirk, Lawrence J. *Totally Uninhibited: The Life and Wild Times of Cher*. New York: William Morrow, 1991.

Ramone, Marky, and Richard Herschlag. *Punk Rock Blitzkrieg: My Life as a Ramone*. New York: Touchstone, 2016.

Reddy, Helen. *The Woman I Am*. New York: Tarcher Perigee, 2006.

Rees, Paul. *Robert Plant: A Life*. New York: It Books, 2013.

Reynolds, Simon. *Shock and Awe: Glam Rock and Its Legacy, from the Seventies to the Twenty-First Century*. New York: Dey Street Books, 2016.

———. *Totally Wired: Postpunk Interviews and Overviews*. Berkeley, CA: Soft Skull Press, 2010.

Ribowsky, Mark. *Signed, Sealed, and Delivered: The Soulful Journey of Stevie Wonder*. Hoboken, NJ: John Wiley & Sons, 2010.

Richards, Keith, and James Fox. *Life*. New York: Little, Brown, 2010.

Ritz, David. *Divided Soul: The Life of Marvin Gaye*. New York: Da Capo, 1991.

———. *Respect: The Life of Aretha Franklin*. New York: Little, Brown, 2014.

Robenalt, James. *1973: Watergate, Roe v. Wade, Vietnam, and the Month That Changed America Forever*. Chicago: Chicago Review Press, 2017.

Rodriguez, Robert. *Fab Four FAQ 2.0: The Beatles' Solo Years, 1970–1980*. Milwaukee, WI: Backbeat Books, 2010.

Ronstadt, Linda. *Simple Dreams: A Musical Memoir*. New York: Simon & Schuster, 2014.

Rosen, Craig. *The Billboard Book of Number One Albums*. New York: Billboard Books, 1996.

Rosenstiel, Tom, and Amy S. Mitchell, eds. *Thinking Clearly: Cases in Journalistic Decision-Making*. New York: Columbia University Press, 2003.

Ruoff, Jeffrey. *An American Family: A Televised Life*. Minneapolis: University of Minnesota Press, 2001.

Ruskin, Yvonne Sewall. *High on Rebellion; Inside the Underground at Max's Kansas City*. New York: Thunder's Mouth Press, 1998.

Salewicz, Chris. *Bob Marley: The Untold Story*. New York: Farrar, Straus & Giroux, 2014.

Sanchez, Tony. *Up and Down with the Rolling Stones*. New York: Da Capo, 1996.

Sandbrook, Dominic. *Mad as Hell: The Crisis of the 1970s and the Rise of the Populist Right*. New York: Anchor, 2012.

Sandford, Christopher. *McCartney*. Boston: Da Capo, 2007.

———. *Springsteen: Point Blank*. New York: Little, Brown, 1999.

Schaffner, Nicholas. *The Beatles Forever*. New York: McGraw-Hill, 1978.

———. *The British Invasion: From the First Wave to the New Wave*. New York: McGraw-Hill, 1982.

Schmidt, Randy L., ed. *Dolly on Dolly: Interviews and Encounters with Dolly Parton*. Chicago: Chicago Review Press, 2017.

Schruers, Fred. *Billy Joel: The Definitive Biography*. New York: Three Rivers Press, 2014.

Segal, Mark. *And Then I Danced: Traveling the Road to LGBT Equality*. New York: OpenLens, 2015.

Shadwick, Keith. *Led Zeppelin: The Story of a Band and Their Music, 1968–1980*. San Francisco: Backbeat Books, 2005.

Sharp, Ken, with Gene Simmons and Paul Stanley. *Nothin' to Lose: The Making of KISS, 1972–1975*. New York: It Books, 2014.

Shaver, Billy Joe, and Brad Reagan. *Honky Tonk Hero*. Austin: University of Texas Press, 2005.

Sheff, David. *All We Are Saying*. New York: St. Martin's Press, 2000.

Shelton, Robert. *No Direction Home: The Life and Music of Bob Dylan*. Milwaukee: Backbeat Books, 2011.

Sheridan, Maureen. *Bob Marley: The Stories Behind Every Song*. New York: Carlton Books, 2011.

Shipton, Alyn. *Nilsson: The Life of a Singer-Songwriter*. New York: Oxford University Press, 2013.

Simon, Carly. *Boys in the Trees: A Memoir*. New York: Flatiron Books, 2016.

Sloman, Larry. *Steal This Dream: Abbie Hoffman and the Countercultural Revolution in America*. New York: Doubleday, 1998.

Smith, Patti. *Just Kids*. New York: Ecco, 2010.

Smith, R. J. *The One: The Life and Music of James Brown*. New York: Avery, 2012.

Smith, Suzanne E. *Dancing in the Street: Motown and the Cultural Politics of Detroit*. Cambridge, MA: Harvard University Press, 2000.

Somach, Denny. *Get the Led Out: How Led Zeppelin Became the Biggest Band in the World*. Toronto, ON: Sterling, 2012.

Spitz, Bob. *Dylan: A Biography*. New York: W. W. Norton, 1989.

Spitz, Marc. *Jagger: Rebel, Rock Star, Rambler, Rogue*. New York: Avery, 2011.

Spizer, Bruce. *The Beatles Solo on Apple Records*. New Orleans: 498 Productions, 2005.

Springsteen, Bruce. *Born to Run*. New York: Simon & Schuster, 2016.

Steffens, Roger. *So Much Things to Say: The Oral History of Bob Marley*. New York: W. W. Norton, 2017.

Stempel, Tom. *Storytellers to the Nation: A History of American Television Writing*. Syracuse, NY: Syracuse University Press, 1996.

Stevens, Jay. *Storming Heaven: LSD and the American Dream*. New York: Grove Press, 1987.

Stratton, Jon. *Jews, Race and Popular Music*. New York: Routledge, 2016.

Streissguth, Michael. *Johnny Cash: The Biography*. Cambridge, MA: Da Capo, 2006.

———. *Outlaw: Waylon, Willie, Kris and the Renegades of Nashville*. New York: HarperCollins, 2013.

Sugerman, Danny. *Wonderland Avenue: Tales of Glamour & Excess*. London: Abacus, 1993.

Sullivan, Steve. *Encyclopedia of Great Popular Song Recordings*. Vol. 3. Lanham, MD: Scarecrow Press, 2013.

Sweet, Brian. *Steely Dan: Reelin' in the Years*. London: Omnibus Press, 2016.

Taraborrelli, J. Randy. *Call Her Miss Ross: The Unauthorized Biography of Diana Ross*. New York: Carol Publishing Group, 1988.

———. *Michael Jackson: The Magic, the Madness, the Whole Story, 1958–2009*. New York: Grand Central Publishing, 2009.

Thomas, Frank. *What's the Matter with Kansas? How Conservatives Won the Heart of America.* New York: Metropolitan Books, 2007.

Thomas, Pat, and Gary Groth. *Listen, Whitey! The Sights and Sounds of Black Power, 1968–1975.* New York: Fantagraphics Books, 2012.

Thompson, Dave. *1000 Songs That Rock Your World: From Rock Classics to One-Hit Wonders, the Music That Lights Your Fire.* Iola, WI: Krause Publications, 2011.

———. *Hearts of Darkness: James Taylor, Jackson Browne, Cat Stevens, and the Unlikely Rise of the Singer-Songwriter.* New York: Backbeat, 2012.

———. *The Rocky Horror Picture Show FAQ: Everything Left to Know About the Campy Cult Classic.* Milwaukee, WI: Applause, 2016.

———. *Your Pretty Face Is Going to Hell: The Dangerous Glitter of David Bowie, Iggy Pop, and Lou Reed.* New York: Hal Leonard, 2009.

Thompson, Wayne. *To Hanoi and Back: The U.S. Air Force and North Vietnam, 1966–1973.* Washington, DC: Smithsonian Institution Press, 2002.

Tolinski, Brad. *Light and Shade: Conversations with Jimmy Page.* New York: Crown, 2012.

Townshend, Pete. *Who I Am: A Memoir.* New York: HarperCollins, 2013.

Troy, Sandy. *Captain Trips: A Biography of Jerry Garcia.* New York: Thunder's Mouth Press, 1994.

Trudeau, Garry. *40: A Doonesbury Retrospective.* Kansas City, MO: Andrews McMeel Publishing, 2010.

Trynka, Paul. *David Bowie: Starman.* Boston: Little, Brown, 2011.

Tuedi, Jim, and Stan Spector. *The Grateful Dead in Concert: Essays on Live Improvisation.* Jefferson, NC: McFarland, 2010.

Turner, Tony, with Barbara Aria. *Deliver Us from Temptation: The Tragic and Shocking Story of the Temptations and Motown.* New York: Thunder's Mouth Press, 1992.

Tyler, Steven, and David Dalton. *Does the Noise in My Head Bother You? A Rock 'n' Roll Memoir.* New York: HarperCollins, 2011.

Vaughan, Andrew. *The Eagles: An American Band.* Toronto, ON: Sterling, 2010.

Vincent, Rickey. *Funk: The Music, the People, and the Rhythm of the One.* New York: St. Martin's Griffin, 1996.

Walker, Brian. *Doonesbury and the Art of G. B. Trudeau.* New Haven, CT: Yale University Press, 2010.

Walker, Michael. *What You Want Is in the Limo: On the Road with Led Zeppelin, Alice Cooper, and the Who in 1973, the Year the Sixties Died and the Modern Rock Star Was Born.* New York: Spiegel & Grau, 2013.

Wall, Mick. *Black Sabbath: Symptom of the Universe.* New York: St. Martin's Press, 2015.

———. *Lou Reed: The Life.* London: Orion, 2014.

———. *When Giants Walked the Earth: A Biography of Led Zeppelin.* New York: St. Martin's Griffin, 2010.

Ward-Royster, Willa. *How I Got Over: Clara Ward and the World-Famous Ward Singers.* Philadelphia: Temple University Press, 2000.

Weigel, David. *The Show That Never Ends: The Rise and Fall of Prog Rock.* New York: W. W. Norton, 2017.

Weiss, Brett. *Encyclopedia of KISS: Music, Personnel, Events and Related Subjects*. Jefferson, NC: McFarland, 2016.

Welch, Chris. *Peter Grant: The Man Who Led Zeppelin*. London: Omnibus Press, 2003.

Weller, Sheila. *Girls like Us: Carole King, Joni Mitchell, and Carly Simon and the Journey of a Generation*. New York: Atria Books, 2008.

Werner, Craig. *Higher Ground: Stevie Wonder, Aretha Franklin, Curtis Mayfield, and the Rise and Fall of American Soul*. New York: Crown Archetype, 2007.

Whitall, Susan. *Joni on Joni: Interviews and Encounters with Joni Mitchell*. Chicago: Chicago Review Press, 2018.

White, Timothy. *Catch a Fire: The Life of Bob Marley*. New York: Holt, 2006

Whitsett, Josh Sides. *Erotic City: Sexual Revolutions and the Making of Modern San Francisco*. New York: Oxford University Press, 2009.

Williams, Tenley, and James S. Brady. *Stevie Wonder*. Langhorne, PA: Chelsea House, 2001.

Williamson, Barbara, with Nancy Bacon Bloomington. *An Extraordinary Life*. Carlsbad, CA: Balboa Press, 2014.

Williamson, Joel. *Elvis Presley: A Southern Life*. New York: Oxford University Press, 2014.

Williamson, Nigel. *The Rough Guide to Led Zeppelin*. London: Rough Guides, 2007.

Woffinden, Bob. *The Beatles Apart*. London and New York: Proteus Books, 1981.

Wood, Ronnie. *Ronnie: The Autobiography*. London: Palgrave Macmillan, 2007.

Wurtzel, Elizabeth. *More, Now, Again: A Memoir of Addiction*. New York: Simon & Schuster, 2007.

Wyman, Bill. *Rolling with the Stones*. New York: DK, 2002.

Yaffe, David. *Reckless Daughter: A Portrait of Joni Mitchell*. New York: Sarah Crichton Books, 2017.

Yergin, Daniel. *The Prize: The Epic Quest for Oil, Money, and Power*. New York: Simon & Schuster, 1991.

Young, Neil. *Special Deluxe: A Memoir of Life and Cars*. New York: Blue Rider Press, 2014.

———. *Waging Heavy Peace: A Hippie Dream*. New York: Penguin Group, 2013.

Zinn, Howard. *A People's History of the United States*. New York: Harper Perennial Modern Classics, 2015.

WEB PAGES AND WEBSITES

Australian Financial Review
www.afr.com

Alice Cooper eChive
www.alicecooperechive.com

AllMusic
www.allmusic.com

AP News
www.apnews.com

ASCAP
www.ascap.com

Bass Player
www.bassplayer.com

BBC
www.bbc.com

Beatles Bible
www.beatlesbible.com

Beatles Interviews
www.beatlesinterviews.org

Billboard
www.billboard.com

Blabbermouth
www.blabbermouth.net

Bowie Songs
www.bowiesongs.wordpress.com

Brain Damage
www.brain-damage.co.uk

Bruce Base
www.brucebase.wikidot.com

Chicago Reader
www.chicagoreader.com

Classic Bands
www.classicbands.com

CMT
www.cmt.com

Consequence of Sound
www.consequenceofsound.net

Christian Science Monitor
www.csmonitor.com

Daily Beast
www.thedailybeast.com

Daily Mail
www.dailymail.co.uk

Dangerous Minds
www.dangerous minds.net

Detroit Free Press
www.freep.com

Elton John
www.eltonjohn.com

Eloquent Woman
www.theeloquentwoman.com

Encyclopedia.com
www.encyclopedia.com

Encyclopedia Britannica
www.britannica.com

Entertainment Weekly
www.entertainment weekly

ESPN
www.espn.com

Esquire
www.esquire.com

Express
www.express.co.uk

Facing South
www.facingsouth.org

Fast 'n' Bulbous
www.fastnbulbous.com

FiveThirtyEight
www.fivethirtyeight.com

Forbes
www.forbes.com

Genesis Fan
www.genesisfan.net

Goldmine Magazine
www.goldminemag.com

GQ
www.gq.com

Guardian
www.theguardian.com

Guitar Player
www.guitarplayer.com

Guitar World
www.guitarworld.com

History.com
www.history.com

Hollywood Reporter
www.hollywoodreporter.com

Howard Stern
www.howardstern.com

Huffington Post
www.huffpost.com

I Am Hip-Hop Magazine
www.iamhiphopmagazine.com

Independent
www.independent.co.uk

InflationData
www.inflationdata.com

Interesting Engineering
www.interestingengineering.com

It's Only Rock and Roll
www.iorr.org

Joni Mitchell
www.jonimitchell.com

Kiplinger
www.kiplinger.com

Linda Ronstadt
www.ronstadt-linda.com

Live Music
www.livemusicblog.com

Los Angeles Times
www.latimes.com

Magnet Magazine
www.magnetmagazine.com

Mass Appeal
www.massappeal.com

McCall
www.mcall.com

Medium
www.medium.com

Men's Journal
www.mensjournal.com

Metro Times
www.metrotimes.com

Music Radar
www.musicradar.com

Neil Young News
www.neilyoungnews.com

New Musical Express
www.nme.com

Newsweek
www.newsweek.com

New Yorker
www.newyorker.com

Nilsson Schmilsson
www.nilssonschmilsson.com

No Depression
www.nodepression.com

NPR
www.npr.org

New York Daily News
www.nydailynews.com

New York Magazine
www.nymag.com

New York Post
www.nypost.com

New York Times
www.nytimes.com

Observer
www.observer.com

Palm Beach Post
www.palmbeachpost.com

PBS
www.pbs.org

People
www.people.com

Pew Research
www.pewresearch.org

Pitchfork
www.pitchfork.com

Please Kill Me
www.pleasekillme.com

Politico
www.politico.com

Pop Dose
www.popdose.com

Psychology Today
www.psychologytoday.com

Quietus
www.thequietus.com

Real Clear Religion
www.realclearreligion.org

Record Collector
www.recordcollectornews.com

Red Bull Music Academy
www.daily.redbullmusicacademy.com

Reddit
www.reddit.com

Relix
www.relix.com

Recording Industry Association of America
www.riaa.com

Robert Christgau
www.robertchristgau.com

Rockapedia
www.rockapedia.com

Rolling Stone
www.rollingstone.com

Salon
www.salon.com

Seattle Times
www.seattletimes.com

Setlist
www.setlist.fm

SFGate
www.sfgate.com

Slant
www.slantmagazine.com

Slate
www.slate.com

Something Else
www.somethingelsereviews.com

Song Facts
www.songfacts.com

Sound on Sound
www.soundonsound.com

Steely Dan Reader
www.steelydanreader.com

Sun
www.thesun.co.uk

Telegraph
www.telegraph.co.uk

Thrillist
www.thrillist.com

Time
www.time.com

Time Is on Our Side
www.timeisonourside.com

Top 40 Weekly
www.top40weekly.com

Ultimate Classic Rock
www.ultimateclassicrock.com

Ultimate Guitar
www.ultimateguitar.com

The Uncool
www.theuncool.com

Uncut
www.uncut.co.uk

Vanity Fair
www.vanityfair.com

Variety
www.variety.com

Vice
www.vice.com

Village Voice
www.villagevoice.com

Vogue
www.vogue.com

Vulture
www.vulture.com

Washington Post
www.washingtonpost.com

Weekly Standard
www.weeklystandard.com

The Who
www.thewho.net

Wikipedia
www.wikipedia.org

Wall Street Journal
www.wsj.com

Women's Wear Daily
www.wwd.com

Yahoo
www.yahoo.com

YouTube
www.youtube.com

FILMS AND TELEVISION
All the President's Men Revisited. Directed by Peter Schnall. Discovery. 2013.
Allman Brothers: After the Crash. Directed by Tom O'Dell. Sexy Intellectual. 2016.
Almost Famous. Directed by Cameron Crowe. Dreamworks. 2000.
American Graffiti. Directed by George Lucas. Universal Pictures. 1973.
American Revolutions: Southern Rock. Directed by Anne Fentress. CMT. 2005.
Behind the Music: Hall and Oates. VH1. 2002.
Big Star: Nothing Can Hurt Me. Directed by Drew DeNicola and Olivia Mori. Magnolia Pictures. 2012.

The Black Panthers: Vanguard of the Revolution. Directed by Stanley Nelson. Firelight Films. 2015.

Black Sabbath, Volume 1: 1970–1978. Sanctuary. 1991.

Bob Marley: Freedom Road. Directed by Sonia Anderson. Tuff Gong Pictures. 2007.

Classic Albums: Deep Purple: Machine Head. Directed by Matthew Longfellow. ITV. 2002.

Classic Albums: Lou Reed: Transformer. Directed by Bob Smeaton. BBC. 2001.

Crooklyn. Directed by Spike Lee. 40 Acres and a Mule Filmworks. 1994.

The Doobie Brothers: Let the Music Play. Directed by Barry Ehrmann. 2012.

Dying to Know: Ram Dass & Timothy Leary. Directed by Gay Dillingham. CNS Communications. 2014.

The Exorcist. Directed by William Friedkin. Warner Bros. 1973.

Genesis: Together and Apart. Directed by John Edginton. BBC. 2014.

Gimme Danger. Directed by Jim Jarmusch. Magnolia Pictures. 2016.

Gloria: In Her Own Words. Directed by Peter Kunhardt. HBO. 2011.

Hard Road to Travel: The Making of "The Harder They Come." 2015.

Hawkwind: Do Not Panic. Directed by Simon Chu. BBC. 2007.

History of the Eagles. Directed by Alison Eastwood. Showtime. 2013.

Hotel California: LA from the Byrds to the Eagles. Directed by Chris Wilson. BBC. 2007.

If I Leave Here Tomorrow: A Film About Lynyrd Skynyrd. Directed by Stephen Kijak. CMT. 2018.

James Brown: Soul Survivor. Directed by Jeremy Marre. *American Masters,* PBS. 2003.

Kiss: Beyond the Makeup. Directed by Paul La Blanc. VH1. 2001.

The Last Detail. Directed by Hal Ashby. Columbia Pictures. 1973.

Last Tango in Paris. Directed by Bernardo Bertolucci. United Artists. 1972.

Looking for Johnny. Directed by Danny Garcia. Chip Baker Films. 2014.

Lost Highway: Beyond Nashville. Directed by Ben Southwell. BBC. 2003.

Marc Bolan: The Final Word. Directed by Mark Tinkler. BBC. 2007.

Marley. Directed by Kevin Macdonald. Shangri-La Entertainment. 2012.

Maynard. Directed by Samuel D. Pollard. Auburn Avenue Films. 2017.

The Mayor of Sunset Strip. Directed by George Hickenlooper. Lakeshore Entertainment. 2003.

Mike Judge Presents: Tales from the Tour Bus. Directed by Mike Judge. Cinemax. 2017.

More Than This: The Story of Roxy Music. Directed by Bob Smeaton. BBC. 2008.

The 1980 Floor Show. Directed by Stan Harris. *The Midnight Special.* 1973.

The Old Grey Whistle Test: Lynyrd Skynyrd in Concert. BBC. 1975.

The Passing Show: The Life and Music of Ronnie Lane. Directed by Rupert Williams. BBC. 2006.

Prog Rock Britannia: An Observation in Three Movements. Directed by Chris Rodley. BBC. 2009.

Quadrophenia: Can You See the Real Me? Directed by Matt O'Casey. BBC. 2013.

Sample This. Directed by Dan Forrer. Propinquity Films. 2012.

SHOT! The Psycho-Spiritual Mantra of Rock. Directed by Barney Clay. Eagle Rock Entertainment. 2016.

Sisters in Country: Dolly, Linda and Emmylou. Directed by Dione Newton. BBC. 2016.

The Song Remains the Same. Directed by Peter Clifton and Joe Massot. Warner Bros. 1976.

Standing in the Shadows of Motown. Directed by Paul Justman. Lionsgate. 2003.

Storytellers: David Bowie. VH1. 1999.

Sweet Home Alabama: The Southern Rock Saga. Directed by James Maycock. BBC. 2012.

Tales from the Jungle: Carlos Castenada and the Shaman. Directed by Naomi Austin and Helen Seaman. BBC. 2007.

The Way We Were. Directed by Sydney Pollack. Columbia Pictures. 1973.

Velvet Goldmine. Directed by Todd Haynes. Killer Films. 1998.

Vinyl (television series). HBO. 2016.

Ziggy Stardust and the Spiders from Mars. Directed by D. A. Pennebaker. 20th Century Fox. 1973.

Index

✳